CONTEMPORARY FICTION WRITERS OF THE SOUTH

CONTEMPORARY FICTION WRITERS OF THE SOUTH

A BIO-BIBLIOGRAPHICAL SOURCEBOOK

EDITED BY

JOSEPH M. FLORA

AND

ROBERT BAIN

Greenwood Press
WESTPORT, CONNECTICUT • LONDON

Library of Congress Cataloging-in-Publication Data

Contemporary fiction writers of the South : a bio-bibliographical
   sourcebook / edited by Joseph M. Flora and Robert Bain.
      p. cm.
   Includes index.
   ISBN 0–313–28764–3 (alk. paper)
      1. Novelists, American—Southern States—Biography—Dictionaries.
   2. Authors, American—Southern States—Biography—Dictionaries.
   3. Novelists, American—20th century—Biography—Dictionaries.
   4. Authors, American—20th century—Biography—Dictionaries.
   5. American fiction—Southern States—Bio-bibliography. 6. American
   fiction—20th century—Bio-bibliography. 7. American fiction—
   Southern States—Dictionaries. 8. American fiction—20th century—
   Dictionaries. 9. Southern States in literature—Dictionaries.
   I. Flora, Joseph M.   II. Bain, Robert (Robert A.)
   PS261.C565   1993
   813′.5409′03—dc20
   [B]   92–36515

British Library Cataloguing in Publication Data is available.

Library of Congress Catalog Card Number: 92–36515
ISBN: 0–313–28764–3

First published in 1993

Greenwood Press, 88 Post Road West, Westport, CT 06881
An imprint of Greenwood Publishing Group, Inc.

Printed in the United States of America

The paper used in this book complies with the
Permanent Paper Standard issued by the National
Information Standards Organization (Z39.48–1984).

10 9 8 7 6 5 4 3 2 1

For Louis D. Rubin, Jr.

Since the 1950s, Louis D. Rubin, Jr., has championed the study of Southern literature and has taught thousands of students and teachers to read and appreciate it. Author and editor of more than thirty books, mostly about Southern life and literature, he founded in 1968 with his friend C. Hugh Holman the *Southern Literary Journal*. In that journal Rubin published articles about many writers whose works are the subject of this book. As a founder and editor of Algonquin Books of Chapel Hill, North Carolina, Rubin encouraged and published such writers as Clyde Edgerton, Jill McCorkle, and Kaye Gibbons. A proud native of Charleston, South Carolina, he has always remembered in the whirlwind of his work how to be human and generous. He has always set an example of excellence, challenging his students and colleagues to match his energy and intelligence. For the blessings of his work and his person, we dedicate this book to our friend and mentor, Louis D. Rubin, Jr.

Contents

Preface

Contemporary Fiction Writers of the South: A Bio-Bibliographical Sourcebook presents a preliminary report on the flurry of good books Southerners have written in the last two or three decades. Our report doubtless includes some authors whose works will be footnotes a quarter century from now, and we have surely omitted worthy writers. For these sins of commission and omission, the editors take responsibility. But we believe this book accurately describes a "flowering" comparable to the Southern Renascence in the first four decades of this century. None of the writers discussed here has yet earned the reputation of a Faulkner, a Welty, an O'Connor, or a Warren, but many have captivated readers and critics in the United States and abroad. Some have made strong claims on a significant place in American literature, but only time will tell whether or not their fame lasts.

Because the number of worthy contemporary Southern authors exceeds that which can be treated in depth in a single volume, we are completing a companion volume to this one entitled *Contemporary Poets, Dramatists, Essayists, and Novelists of the South: A Bio-Bibliographical Sourcebook*. This companion volume will include essays on some fifty more writers. A Table of Contents of this second volume appears in Appendix B of this book.

In dividing the two volumes, we have separated fiction writers from poets, playwrights, and nonfiction writers. These groupings essentially define the scope of the two books. But this distinction is by no means clear-cut. Many fiction writers included in the present work have written successfully in other literary forms; the same observation holds for the poets and other authors in the companion volume (to the extent that "novelists" appears in its title). We have placed authors in the volume that best describes the primary thrust of their work, but the individual essays about them discuss their work in all genres. Because fiction writers of distinction outnumber other writers, those who have made major contributions in other genres appear in the second volume.

Forty-seven scholars have contributed to *Contemporary Fiction Writers of the South* essays that assess the achievements of forty-nine authors. The essays reveal the range of literary forms and attitudes of Southerners who have stayed at home to write and of those expatriates who live outside the South but still carry the cargo of their heritage. The chief events influencing these writers are not the Civil War, Reconstruction, and World War I, but World War II, the Vietnam War, the civil rights movement, new understandings of race and cultures, new roles for women, and new sexual freedoms afforded by the age of the pill. They record their responses to such radical changes in the South as the decline of rural living and the rise of cities and towns, the influence of television and shopping malls, Southerners' obsessions with sports and cars, the preoccupation with getting rich, and the social mobility that comes with wealth.

Unlike the Renascence authors, most of whom were white males and came from the upper and upper-middle classes, many contemporary writers come from the middling and the rising-middle classes. And the formidable voices and talents of black and women authors play a much more important role in the second Renascence than they did in the first.

But many concerns of earlier Southern writers continue to appear in the work of these contemporary authors. These continuities include the attachments to place, the tangled webs of family relationships, the importance of art, an emphasis upon the grotesque, the self-consciousness of being different from people of other regions, the pervasive influence of religion, and the impact of the past on the present. And these writers, following Faulkner's advice in his Nobel Prize speech, focus attention on those "old verities" of love and honor and courage and sacrifice.

We selected writers for inclusion in this volume on three grounds: (1) Each author needed to have written four books (Alex Haley is one notable exception); (2) each author should have been reviewed widely; and (3) each author should have achieved critical recognition outside the South. With few exceptions, we have followed these guidelines.

The format of *Contemporary Fiction Writers of the South* follows the format of our previous volumes, *Fifty Southern Writers before 1900* and *Fifty Southern Writers after 1900*, both published by Greenwood Press in 1987. Each essay, written by a knowledgeable scholar or critic, contains five parts: a biographical sketch, a discussion of the author's major themes, an assessment of reviews and scholarship, a chronological list of the author's works, and a bibliography of selected criticism. We hope readers working their way through this volume will gain a clearer idea of what is happening in Southern letters.

We have included in this book only one author from *Fifty Southern Writers after 1900*—Anne Tyler. She serves as our "bridge" between the two sets. Studies of John Barth, Doris Betts, Harry Crews, Ernest Gaines, Reynolds Price,

Elizabeth Spencer, William Styron, and Peter Taylor—all of whom we could have grouped with these contemporary writers—appear in *Fifty Southern Writers after 1900*. In Appendix A of *Contemporary Fiction Writers of the South*, we have updated the ''Works by'' and ''Studies of'' sections for all eight of these writers. Likewise, several writers treated in the present volume might have been included in that earlier book. John Ehle and Cormac McCarthy come to mind. *Contemporary Fiction Writers of the South*, with its companion volume, *Contemporary Poets, Dramatists, Essayists, and Novelists of the South*, enables us to acknowledge significant omissions from our earlier book. Now, as then, we know our wisdom cannot equal Solomon's.

We have many people to thank for their help and counsel. Our greatest debt is to our contributors for their willingness to share their knowledge and love of Southern writing. Their work constitutes an act of faith. Like all students of Southern literature, we owe much to Louis D. Rubin, Jr., to whom this book is dedicated. His scholarship and good sense have enlightened thousands of students and teachers. Marilyn Brownstein, Maureen Melino, Penny Sippel, and their colleagues at Greenwood Press, especially Cynthia Garver, have helped us with their editorial counsel and patience in the long and complicated process of editing. Laurence Avery, our department chairman, has supported our work enthusiastically, and Erika Lindemann has lent us her office and computer and has read and criticized our pages. We thank also Frances Coombs, Christine Flora, Charlotte McFall, Susan Marston, and Dorothy Moore for their aid and kindnesses. Special thanks go to Judith K. Logan for her excellent help in compiling the index to this book. Finally, we thank the many teachers who have found our earlier books useful in introducing students to the delights of studying Southern letters. Their enthusiasm has helped sustain us.

CONTEMPORARY FICTION WRITERS OF THE SOUTH

Introduction

Something's happening in the South. Though no one knows just what. Commentators agree that the last three decades have produced a remarkable number of fine Southern fiction writers and books. *Contemporary Fiction Writers of the South* attempts a preliminary report on those happenings. Some South-watchers have compared this fictional flowering with the Southern Renascence between 1920 and 1940. But South-watchers, often a cantankerous and disputatious bunch, have also catalogued dramatic differences between the Renascence and what's happening now. The most obvious difference: More women and black writers have earned recognition than during the Renascence.

Some South-watchers believe that the region no longer exists. The Northern migrations of the last three decades and the homogenizing that has resulted from television and "development" have led some pundits to pronounce the South dead.[1] That view has had formidable opposition. In *The History of Southern Literature* (1985), Louis D. Rubin, Jr., has argued: "The facts are that there existed in the past, and there continues to exist today, an entity within American society known as the South, and that for better or worse the habit of viewing one's experience in terms of one's relationship to that entity is still a meaningful characteristic of both writers and readers who are or have been a part of it" (5). A number of scholars and novelists have affirmed Rubin's view in Dudley Clendinen's *The Prevailing South: Life and Politics in a Changing Culture*

---

1. See Hodding Carter III, "The End of the South," *Time* (August 6, 1990): 82, for this view. Carter argues that the "South as South, a living, ever regenerating mythic land of distinctive personality, is no more. At most, it is an artifact lovingly preserved in museums of culture and the shops of tourist commerce precisely because it is so hard to find in the vital centers of the region's daily life."

(1988)—among them Pat Conroy, James Alan McPherson, Ferrol Sams, and C. Vann Woodward.

The truth is that "the South" (or "the solid South") has existed only in the imaginations of the people using the word. Though Southerners have often subscribed to notions created about "the South," they have never fully believed that fiction. No self-respecting Southerner—in 1860 or in 1990—would ever confuse Appalachia with the Deep South, or the Tidewater with the Upland South. But most Southerners believe they share a common heritage beyond the Lost Cause (the Confederacy), though they have fussed about its particulars. That agreement, most Southerners argue, makes them different from people in other regions.

What *I'll Take My Stand*, the manifesto of the Agrarians, so compellingly invoked when first published in 1930 was a set of common images that separated the South from the rest of the nation. Written by articulate, thoughtful men, that book defined the South as agrarian, religious, individualistic, conservative, idealistic, and committed to community and place. Renascence fiction writers chronicled these values, explored the social changes taking place, and transformed the moonlight-and-magnolia South into one that more truthfully rendered the reality of its past and present.

Those novelists and storytellers also criticized their culture. Had many of William Faulkner's neighbors read what he had to say about race, they would have horsewhipped him and run him out of town. Thomas Wolfe's neighbors did revile him for telling his truth about his South—that "Dark Helen of his soul." The best Renascence stories—archetypal tales about people's confrontations with God, the Fates, society, and themselves—embodied the universal in a specific Southern time and place. These writers often distinguished more precisely among the "Souths" than did the commentaries of scholars and South-watchers. In *Absalom! Absalom!* (1936) and elsewhere, Faulkner distinguished sharply among "Souths" by dramatically delineating differences among the cultures of Thomas Sutpen's Virginia mountain birthplace, the Tidewater, and the Deep South.[2]

The new generation of novelists and story writers has shattered the old paradigms for defining "the South's" geography and culture as it was invented by the Agrarians and other cultural observers. Likewise, they have often come from and portrayed characters from social and economic classes different from those of the Renascence. Most writers of the Renascence were white men from the upper or upper middle classes; writers from the new flowering cut more dramatically across racial, social, and gender lines. Distinguishing among these

---

2. In *A Summons to Memphis* (1986), Peter Taylor distinguishes sharply between "the Upper South" of Nashville and the "river culture of the Deep South" (1–3) that he associates with Memphis. Among the few writers making such distinctions in *I'll Take My Stand*, Robert Penn Warren speaks of the "deep South," the "middle South" (249), and the "border states" (261).

various writers' Souths may clarify our understanding of the recent flowering of prose fiction—and perhaps Renascence writing as well.

Instead of hailing from a single South,[3] then, the writers represented in this book come from eight Souths—(1) the Tidewater, (2) the Piedmont, (3) Appalachia, (4) the Deep South, (5) the Upland South, (6) the Southwest, (7) the Catholic and Cajun country of New Orleans and environs, and (8) central and west Georgia, north Florida, and parts of south Alabama. No sharp boundary lines demarcate these Souths; they always fade into one another. But the distinctions are discernible in the geography and in the fiction that arises from each region.

The Tidewater includes the Atlantic coastal plains from Maryland's eastern shore to below Savannah, Georgia. First settled of the Southern regions, the Tidewater centered its culture in tobacco, cotton, rice, and indigo plantations and in towns that served as the colonies' capitals—Annapolis, Williamsburg, Edenton, Charleston, and Savannah. Ellen Glasgow and James Branch Cabell represented this region during the Renascence. William Styron and John Barth provide a link between the Renascence authors and younger writers such as Pat Conroy, Josephine Humphreys, James Alan McPherson, Bob Shacochis, and Susan Shreve.

The Piedmont—ranging from western Maryland to North Georgia—presents a hilly and timbered landscape suitable for timbering, farming, and growing tobacco and cotton. Though the Piedmont had some plantations, this region was the home of yeoman farmers and small business owners. The number of contemporary fiction writers from this region truly impresses—Alice Adams, Doris Betts, Rita Mae Brown, James Dickey, Clyde Edgerton, Kaye Gibbons, Marianne Gingher, Jill McCorkle, Tim McLaurin, T. R. Pearson, Ferrol Sams, Anne Tyler, Sylvia Wilkinson, and Calder Willingham.

Appalachia, which stretches from West Virginia to north Georgia and Alabama, includes the mountains of Virginia, North Carolina, Kentucky, Tennessee, and South Carolina. Settled mainly by Scots, Irish, Scots-Irish, and some English, this region remained isolated from the rest of the South until the beginning of this century (and perhaps later). An area of small farms and towns, its principal businesses have been timbering, farming, furniture making, and coal mining. During the Renascence, Thomas Wolfe wrote powerfully of this region, and some of the most compelling contemporary voices hail from Appalachia—Lisa Alther, John Ehle, Gail Godwin, William Hoffman, Cormac McCarthy, Jane Anne Phillips, Mary Lee Settle, Lee Smith, and John Yount. If one adds such poets and novelists as Fred Chappell, Robert Morgan, and Miller Williams, the writers rising from this rich cultural heritage astound.

The Deep South (the old Southwest), settled by sons and daughters of the

3. C. Hugh Holman discusses three Souths—the Tidewater, the Piedmont, and the Deep South—in *Three Modes of Modern Southern Fiction* (1966). Other literary commentators have talked about different Souths, but no one has made the distinctions we are making here.

Tidewater and Tennessee, imitated the Tidewater plantation society, but with significant differences. Geographically, Alabama and Mississippi sit at the center of this South. Areas of Louisiana and southwestern Tennessee, especially around Memphis and along the Mississippi River, also belong to this South. With its rich soil and long growing seasons, cotton was and is still king. Timbering was important until the forests disappeared. William Faulkner and Eudora Welty stand at the head of a long list of distinguished Renascence authors, with Shelby Foote and Walker Percy providing links with the younger writers. The Deep South continues to produce distinctive voices—Larry Brown, John W. Corrington, Ellen Douglas, Andre Dubus, Jesse Hill Ford, Ernest Gaines, Ellen Gilchrist, Barry Hannah, Beverly Lowry, Berry Morgan, Helen Norris, Elizabeth Spencer, and James Wilcox.

The Upland South[4]—running along the Ohio, Mississippi, Tennessee, and Kentucky rivers—includes middle Tennessee; most of Kentucky; areas of southern Ohio, Indiana, and Illinois; parts of Missouri extending along the Mississippi River as far north as Hannibal; and the Ozark country of southern Missouri and northern Arkansas. First settled by people from Appalachia, Kentucky, and Tennessee, this South early had some plantations, but mainly small farms and villages populated this region. Most of the Agrarians and Elizabeth Madox Roberts came from this area during the Renascence; Madison Smartt Bell, Alex Haley, Gayl Jones, Madison Jones, and Bobbie Ann Mason number among contemporary authors of the Upland South.

The Southwest includes parts of Arkansas, southwestern Missouri, western Louisiana, and east Texas. Settled by pioneers from the Deep South, from Tennessee and Kentucky, and from other parts of the South, this region was originally made up of small farms and towns. Cattle ranching was a major enterprise. Katherine Anne Porter is the major Renascence writer of this region; William Humphrey and Charles Portis represent the present generation.

Another South, the most cosmopolitan of them all, is New Orleans and environs, with its mixture of Spanish, French, and British cultures. Americans settled late (after 1803) in this Catholic culture. This ''island culture'' in the midst of a largely Protestant South has fascinated Southern novelists and storytellers since the middle of the last century. Mark Twain, George Washington Cable, Grace King, and Kate Chopin wrote of this region in the nineteenth century, but mainly as outsiders. During the Renascence Shirley Ann Grau and Lillian Hellman set much of their work there. Among newer writers, Peter Feibleman and John Kennedy Toole stand at the fore. But Southerners from the Deep South have also written powerfully of this island culture—Faulkner during the Renascence, and Elizabeth Spencer and Ellen Gilchrist among contemporary authors.

Central and west Georgia, north Florida, and parts of southeastern Alabama—

---

4. Rather than use ''Upper South'' or ''Border States,'' we have called this region the ''Upland South,'' a term historians have used.

a South represented by such writers as Flannery O'Connor and Harry Crews—comprise an area markedly different from the Tidewater or the Deep South. That South extends to Gainesville, Florida, or thereabouts; mid- and south-Florida are transplanted versions of the Northeast and Midwest. No one has yet named this South, but most recognize it as different. With its literary roots in Augustus Baldwin Longstreet's *Georgia Scenes* (1835), this region has mainly small farms and towns in its landscape. Often characterized as Crackers (the word *Cracker* dates from eighteenth-century Charleston, South Carolina, newspapers), these Southerners came primarily from Appalachia and the Tidewater to seek land and opportunity. Besides O'Connor, Zora Neale Hurston set much of her fiction there during the Renascence. Crews, Padgett Powell, and Alice Walker, are among this region's contemporary writers.

Geographical and cultural distinctions among the various Souths delineate telling differences between the Renascence and the current flowering, but gender, race, and social class account for greater ones. Women authors such as Ellen Glasgow, Carson McCullers, Katherine Anne Porter, and Eudora Welty contributed to the Renascence, but twenty-three writers—almost half—discussed in this book are women. Black writers, also more numerous than during the Renascence, have captured national and international recognition—Toni Cade Bambara, Alex Haley, James Alan McPherson, Ishmael Reed, Alice Walker, and Margaret Walker, among others.

Writers' social and economic classes differ dramatically, too. Ferrol Sams observed: "I was raised in the middle-class South but taught that it was Upper Class" (in Clendinen 53). Many contemporary Southern writers could echo Sams' observation, or a variation on it. Because many newer writers come from working and middle-class backgrounds, they present perspectives long silent in Southern fiction. Larry Brown's Deep South looks different from Gilchrist's and Spencer's. Alice Adams' fiction about the Piedmont recounts a perspective different from Tim McLaurin's. Lisa Alther's Appalachia has a different ring from John Yount's. Haley and Alice Walker present much different versions of their Souths than do their white contemporaries. Regional similarities exist, but the perspectives change radically with gender, race, and class.

Another major distinction between the Renascence and the present flowering is that most contemporary writers have not allowed Faulkner's ghost to haunt them. Born between 1930 and 1960, most fiction writers discussed in this book revere Faulkner's genius, but have refused to imitate him, a temptation some authors of his generation and the one immediately following could not resist. Recognizing Ralph Waldo Emerson's dictum that imitation is suicide, the new fiction writers have cultivated their own voices and styles. They have learned from Faulkner, but they have sought other mentors, too.

Price has written lovingly about Hemingway; Edgerton has talked in interviews about Emerson's influence. For both men and women writers, the work of O'Connor, Porter, and Welty has loomed large. Along with Betts and Spencer, these three authors have provided examples for and are "foremothers" of such younger writers as Kaye Gibbons, Ellen Gilchrist, and Lee Smith. John Yount perhaps best reflects the younger writers' putting Faulkner in perspective. Yount admires Faulkner's "absolute daring" and "great authority," but he also cites Hemingway, F. Scott Fitzgerald, Joseph Conrad, and Fyodor Dostoyevski among his favorites, though he adds that "none of us is smart enough to isolate influences" (505).

The literary climate for contemporary Southern writers is also more favorable than that of the Renascence. Renascence writers depended on the Northern literary establishment for publication. Though Northern publishers still dominate, Southern commercial presses—such as Peachtree Publishers of Atlanta; Longstreet Press of Marietta, Georgia; and Algonquin Books of Chapel Hill, North Carolina—have introduced readers to numerous authors, including Larry Brown, Edgerton, Gibbons, McCorkle, and Sams. Peachtree has also issued *A Modern Southern Reader* (1986), edited by Ben Forkner and Patrick Samway, an anthology that introduces readers to new fiction writers and poets. Southern university presses have encouraged the region's writers by publishing the fiction of John W. Corrington, William Hoffman, and John Kennedy Toole.

In addition, literary magazines such as the new *Southern Review*, the *Georgia Review*, the *Carolina Quarterly*, the *South Carolina Review*, and the *Sewanee Review* have published the region's fiction writers. Along with these magazines, scholarly journals such as the *Mississippi Quarterly*, the *Virginia Review*, the *Hollins Critic*, and the *Southern Literary Journal* have provided forums for critical discussion of many new authors' work. Equally important has been critical recognition outside the South—especially in the book sections of such papers as the *New York Times*, the *Washington Post*, the *Chicago Tribune*, the *Los Angeles Times*, the *London Times*, and the *Denver Post*.

Though some observers believe that master of fine arts programs do more harm than good, these programs have given young writers the opportunity to study under the critical eyes of fine writers. Programs such as Fred Chappell's at the University of North Carolina at Greensboro, Harry Crews' at the University of Florida in Gainesville, R.W.B. Dillard's at Hollins College, Heather Ross Miller's at the University of Arkansas, George Garrett's at the University of Virginia, and Lee Smith's at North Carolina State University have given young writers a place to develop their talents.

Undergraduate creative writing programs at many Southern colleges, universities, and two-year colleges have also fostered new talents. Anne Tyler has spoken glowingly of her experience in Reynolds Price's undergraduate classes at Duke University, as have many of Price's other students. Tim McLaurin has paid similar tributes to Max Steele and Doris Betts, teachers in the undergraduate writing program at the University of North Carolina at Chapel Hill. Randall Kenan, a young black writer who has just published his first novel, *A Visitation of Spirits* (1992), also studied in Chapel Hill's undergraduate writing program, as did Kaye Gibbons. Throughout the South, these programs have trained young writers and have taught undergraduates to read more critically.

Unlike the Renascence authors who heard Civil War stories from their grand-fathers, contemporary writers have heard and lived different stories. The Lost Cause still figures in some Southern fiction, but mainly as background. For most authors discussed in this book, World War II, the Korean War, the Vietnam War, the Great Depression, the civil rights movement, family roots, and radical social and economic changes provide major backdrops. Gilchrist's *Victory over Japan* (1984), Godwin's *A Southern Family* (1987), Walker's *The Color Purple* (1983) (a pun on "the colored people"), Smith's *Oral History* (1983), and Richard Ford's *The Sportswriter* (1986) reflect the fictional territory of many contemporary novelists and short-story writers.

Many contemporary Southern writers are also less self-conscious about their Southernness than were the Renascence authors. Several—Alice Adams, Lisa Alther, Andre Dubus, Richard Ford, and John Yount—have lived outside the South most of their adult years. Cormac McCarthy, like Ford, has been a va-gabond. McCarthy has lived in Tennessee, Spain, Kentucky, France, Illinois, Italy, and Texas. Ford, whose first novel was set in the South and whose later books have featured non-Southern settings, has declared that "southern region-alism as a factor in the impulse that makes us write novels . . . has had its day. . . . The south is not a place any more: it's a Belt, a business proposition, which is the nearest thing to anonymity the economy recognizes" (290). Dubus has set many of his books in New England, and Alice Adams has written novels and stories that are in many ways un-Southern. Yet critics have detected in the works of all these authors qualities associated with Southern writing. Anne Tyler, who has lived on the South's fringe in Baltimore since 1967 and has set much of her work there, "has stated that whatever remained 'undeniably Southern' in her helped forge her allegiance to Baltimore, a city she has pronounced 'won-derful territory for a writer' " (829).

One point of contention among contemporary writers remains—they react differently to the label "Southern." Following the lead of Flannery O'Connor and Walker Percy, who deplored that label, Harry Crews said recently in an interview with Thomas Harrison: "Ever'body wants to pin a regional tag on me. It's why I've always resisted that 'southern novelist' s—— that only Southerners have to put up with. I don't think of myself as a 'southern' novelist. We don't talk about 'northern' novelists."[5] But Crews has never denied his Southern heritage.

Florence King also resists. When asked, "What distinguishes Southern writing from other subject matter?" she replied: "The typical Southern novel has an oversensitive child protagonist, and it's full of descriptions of smells: the earth smell, the river smell, the man smell, the woman smell, the smell of fear, the

5. Some Southern authors have been particularly defensive about such labels, perhaps because of the stereotyping that journalistic and some academic critics use in book reviewing. Western writers, less sensitive to such labeling, often wear "Western" writer proudly.

smell of defeat, and always, the smell of sex. As much as I love the South, I can't stand most Southern writing, and I don't want to be typed as a Southern writer'' (Nash 51). Acknowledging his Southern and Appalachian heritage, John Yount believes he would be writing about the same things if he had been born an Eskimo, though he would have had ''a lot more to say about snow.'' But many Southerners, among them Elizabeth Spencer and Kaye Gibbons, do not object to the label. Clyde Edgerton tolerates the noun-adjective ''Southern'' so long as the noun ''writer'' follows. Pat Conroy has said, ''the South is an obsessive theme with me,'' and he takes seriously ''the responsibility of being Southern'' (in Clendinen 120, 133).

Commentators describing the recent flowering have not always flattered. Critics have used terms like ''K-Mart'' and ''Mall'' fiction to disparage some novels and stories—especially those written by women. ''Grit Lit'' has also achieved some currency among reviewers. Pat Conroy has said that his mother believed she could sum up much Southern fiction in a single sentence: ''On the night the hogs ate Willie, Mamma died when she heard what Daddy did to Sister.'' In his essay on Calder Willingham in this volume, Donald R. Noble notes that Willingham chose to spoof much Southern Gothic fiction of the earlier period and his own day. Noble cites Willingham's *Eternal Fire* (1963) as a good example of that spoofing.

But, for the most part, journalistic and academic critics have taken seriously the fiction of the last 30 years. Gene Lyons has called the current flowering ''yet another literary uprising, a far better word than 'renaissance,' with its imitations of mugged up classicism'' (71). Lyons has his caveats, however:

It follows that the best Southern fiction today tends to be both comic and nostalgic: written by urban college graduates (often enough, indeed, by faculty members) about unsophisticated country folks. Sooner rather than later, one suspects, it's bound to run thin. But if the region is changing, it's in little danger of disappearing. Tomorrow's tales will be different from today's, but the continuing vitality of the Southern literary tradition ensures that they will get told. (74B)

One of the most astute observers of the current scene, Fred Hobson—in *The Southern Writer in the Postmodern World* (1991) and in a *Southern Review* article entitled ''Surveyors and Boundaries: Southern Literature and Southern Literary Scholarship after Mid-Century'' (Autumn 1991)—argues that remarkable changes have occurred in Southern fiction in the past fifteen or twenty years (''Surveyors'' 754). Hobson believes that the ''South had—so said the self-congratulators—thrown off the old albatross of racism, and with that gone the South was no longer what it had been: defeated, failed, poor, guilt-ridden, tragic.'' That success, says Hobson, ''would require a new voice—and less reliance on models of the past'' (''Surveyors'' 752).

What has resulted from this liberation in the last couple of decades is that Southern fiction writers feel less the ''love-hate'' relationship with their region and "a relative *lack* of southern self-consciousness." Hobson cites Bobbie Ann Mason, Anne Tyler, and Richard Ford as examples of this phenomenon. "That is not to say," continues Hobson, "that the voice isn't southern—with writers such as Clyde Edgerton and Lee Smith it most assuredly is—or that those old preoccupations of the southern writer, the family and the past, are any less in evidence." Though black writers such as Alice Walker and James Alan Mc-Pherson have not forgotten the pains and injustices of the South and though the Southern Gothic lives in novels by Cormac McCarthy, Harry Crews, and Barry Hannah, Hobson argues that many younger white writers are less preoccupied with "regional self-consciousness" ("Surveyors" 753–54). He regards this distinction as major in the fiction of the last fifteen to twenty years.

Still, Southerners have been conscious and self-conscious—sometimes to the point of boredom—about their separate identities. Expatriates such as Cormac McCarthy, Bobbie Ann Mason, and Alice Adams sometimes wear their South-ernerness like a badge of courage or perversity. Because Southerners love sto-rytelling and because many Americans still know nothing but stereotypes about the South, Southerners delight in the great "put-on."

In 1992, Dennis Rogers, a columnist for the Raleigh (North Carolina) *News and Observer*, reported, with tongue in cheek, that the "Washington Post uses 'redneck' in news stories. The New York Times says the South is the 'land of Chevy trucks.' New York newspapers call [Bill] Clinton 'Bubba.' " Then Rogers notes:

According to a Knight-Ridder report, the National Opinion Research Center surveyed 1,372 people about images of five ethnic groups: Jews, blacks, Asians, Hispanics, and white Southerners. (Odd, isn't it, that we are an ethnic group rather than a regional group, like, say, Oregonians.) The respondents compared each group against a standard called, "white Americans," which we were not thought to be. "White Southerners" came off as dumber and lazier than "white Americans." (August 3, 1992, B1)

Rogers is amused, but not much. The headline on his column reads "South-bashing still in vogue."

Acutely aware of such stereotyping, Roy Blount, Jr., says that Northerners don't think they are typical, and Southerners are too polite to tell them otherwise. Blount observes:

Southerners get a charge out of being typical. If a Northern visitor makes it clear to Southerners that he thinks it would be typical of them to rustle up a big, piping hot meal of hushpuppies and blackstrap, Southerners will do that, even if they were planning to have just a little salad that night.

Then the visitor will ask how to eat hushpuppies and blackstrap. If a Southerner were to go up North and ask how, or why, he was supposed to eat sushi, Northerners would snicker. But Southerner's don't even let on to a Northerner that he is being typical when he asks you how to eat hushpuppies and blackstrap.

The strictly accurate answer is that nobody in his or her right mind eats these two things, together, in any way at all. So the Southerner may say, "First you pour your plate full of molasses, then you crumble your hushpuppies up in it, and then you take the *back* of your spoon, and. . . . " Southerners will say things like that just to see whether it is still true that Northerners will believe anything. About the South. (28–29)

The hushpuppie and blackstrap principle may work on ignorant visitors to and writers about the South, and Blount's joke is a good one. But when it comes to serious writing, that principle will work only for a page or two, not for whole books. Roy Blount knows that.

So what this generation of Southern writers is doing with the material at hand makes all the difference. There will probably be no new Faulkners to write universality into a postage stamp called Yoknapatawpha County, but the new writers are discovering ways to write universality into a shopping mall or Black Ankle, North Carolina, or God knows what. Their stories sound different from Faulkner's, and they should. But they are in their own ways addressing the old verities Faulkner so admired. Their success in this awesome pursuit will finally be the test of their generation. At last report, they are doing pretty well.

WORKS CITED

Blount, Roy, Jr. *What Men Don't Tell Women*. Boston: Little, Brown, 1984.

Clendinen, Dudley, ed. *The Prevailing South: Life and Politics in a Changing Culture*. Atlanta: Longstreet, 1988. Essays by 16 Southerners, including Pat Conroy and Ferrol Sams.

Forker, Ben, and Patrick Samway. *A Modern Southern Reader*. Atlanta: Peachtree Publishers, 1986.

Harrison, Thomas B. "Interview with Harry Crews." *St. Petersburg* (Florida) *Times* (May 21, 1989): D7.

Hobson, Fred. *The Southern Writer in the Postmodern World*. Mercer University Lamar Memorial Lectures, No. 33. Athens: University of Georgia Press, 1991.

———. "Surveyors and Boundaries: Southern Literature and Southern Literary Scholarship after Mid-Century." *Southern Review* (Autumn 1991): 739–55.

Holman, C. Hugh. *Three Modes of Modern Southern Fiction*. Mercer University Lamar Memorial Lectures, No. 9. Athens: University of Georgia Press, 1966.

Lyons, Gene. "The South Rises Again." *Newsweek* (September 30, 1985): 71, 73–74, 74B.

Nash, Alanna. "Florence King Confesses." *Writer's Digest* (July 1990): 40–43, 51.

Rubin, Louis D., Jr., gen. ed. *The History of Southern Literature*. Baton Rouge: Louisiana State University Press, 1985.

Rubin, Louis D., Jr., ed. *I'll Take My Stand: The South and the Agrarian Tradition*. Baton Rouge: Louisiana State University Press, 1977. (Originally published in 1930)

BARBARA A. HERMAN

Alice Adams
(1926–   )

Alice Adams' first published short story, "Winter Rain," appeared in *Charm* in July 1959; her first novel, *Careless Love*, was published in 1966 and, according to the author, "really bombed." From this inauspicious beginning emerged a best-selling novelist and a premier short-story writer. Since 1975 Adams has published six novels, including the best-seller *Superior Women* (1984), four collections of short stories, and a nonfiction book about Mexico. In her fiction she depicts with sensitivity and intelligence the contemporary woman's search for self-identity, independence, and stable relationships with her fellow men and women. Her stories appear regularly in such magazines as *Redbook*, *McCall's*, *Mademoiselle*, *Paris Review*, *The Atlantic*, and *The New Yorker*. With the exception of 1983 and 1985, a story of hers has appeared in every annual edition of *Prize Stories: The O. Henry Awards* from 1971 through 1991. In 1982 she received the O. Henry Special Award for Continuing Achievement, and in 1992 she received an award in literature from the American Academy and Institute of Arts and Letters.

BIOGRAPHY

Alice Boyd Adams was born August 14, 1926, in Fredericksburg, Virginia, the only child of Agatha Erskine Boyd Adams and Nicholson Barney Adams. From shortly after her birth until she was 16, she lived in Chapel Hill, North Carolina, where her father taught Spanish at the University of North Carolina. In "My First and Only House" (*Return Trips*) Adams depicts the family as "three difficult, isolated people" who "got along much better when there were others around" (194). Consequently, they entertained a lot. Her unhappiness with her early family life is also reflected in "Roses, Rhododendron" (*Beautiful Girl*), "Child's Play" (*After You've Gone*), and "At First Sight" (*To See You*

Again). "Berkeley House" (*To See You Again*) describes Adams' resentfulness toward her father and her feelings when she was disinherited after he died and left her "first and only house" to her stepmother, who promptly put it up for sale.

In spite of Agatha Adams' lack of closeness to her daughter, she inspired in her child an early interest in literature. She read poetry to her for hours, and Alice became "one of those annoying kids who wrote poetry at four." Adams says: "I came from the kind of intellectual background that made writing seem like the most praiseworthy thing to do, so there was never anything else" (Feineman 33). She notes that her mother believed a writing career was "a wonderful thing" (Rothstein 30) and was "depressed" and "unhappy" about her own failure as a writer (Feineman 33). Adams hoped to win her mother's acceptance by becoming a writer herself. Poetry, however, was not her only youthful literary interest. Adams recalls the family summers in a little town in Maine and her visits to the library. To her mother's horror, she became "addicted to a really trashy series called the Grace Harlow books" (Madrigal 11). At this time the idea for *Superior Women* began to germinate. Fiction rather than poetry became her genre.

When Adams entered Radcliffe at 16, she enrolled in a short-story course under Kenneth Kempton from Harvard. He suggested that she forget about writing and get married. Determined to be a writer, Adams continued to write short stories and collect rejection slips from *The New Yorker*. She also took a summer creative writing course from Phillips Russell at the University of North Carolina. From him she learned the five-act formula for writing stories—ABDCE: action, background, development, climax, ending—a formula she continues to promote.

After Adams received her B.A. from Radcliffe in 1946, she worked for a New York publishing house, which fired her after several months. One problem was all the time off she took to visit Mark Linenthal, Jr., at Harvard. They married in 1947 and spent the following year in Paris, where Linenthal studied at the Sorbonne. Although there were marital difficulties, Adams loved Paris. From that year stems her first published short story.

Upon their return to the United States in 1948, the couple settled in California, where Linenthal studied and taught English. He joined the faculty of San Francisco State University in 1954 and received his Ph.D. from Stanford University in 1957. Meanwhile, the couple had their only child, Peter Adams Linenthal, born in 1951. Adams remembers the 1950s with "sheer horror": "I was writing only in the most spasmodic, desperate way. I was married and I had a very small child. . . . I disliked my husband, and we didn't have any money, et cetera" (Prescott and Ross 11). This troubled period led her to a psychiatrist who told her to "stop writing and stay married" (Ibid.). As she had not followed Kenneth Kempton's advice at Radcliffe, neither did she follow her psychiatrist's advice. Instead, she divorced her husband in 1958 and continued to write.

The years following her divorce were occasionally lonely as Adams supported herself and her son with bookkeeping jobs, engaged in a few love affairs, and wrote. Her affair with a man she describes as "a married, Catholic, Fascist diplomat" (Faber 53) is incorporated into her first novel, *Careless Love* (1966). Although the American edition was not well received, the English edition, published the following year by Constable as *The Fall of Daisy Duke*, did much better. Americans were too inclined to take the tall, voluptuous divorcée seriously, whereas the British were attuned to the satire. Adams was discouraged by the novel's poor reception and returned to writing short stories.

As she struggled to launch her literary career, Adams received important support from two men. One of these was Robert K. McNie, an interior designer with whom she lived in San Francisco for about 20 years. The other was William Abrahams, whom Adams met in 1948 at Stanford and who became a close personal and professional friend.

In November 1969 Adams achieved a literary breakthrough when her short story "Gift of Grass" (*Beautiful Girl*) appeared in *The New Yorker*. It is the story of a troubled teenager whose sudden discovery of her stepfather's own despair elicits the gift of grass. When the stepfather finds the two joints of marijuana secretly laid on his desk in the study, he experiences his own revelation. The publication of "Gift of Grass" is important in three ways. It is the first in a long line of Adams' stories published in *The New Yorker*. It is also her first story to be selected for *Prize Stories: The O. Henry Awards* and is the first of many prize-winning stories. Finally, "Gift of Grass" is one of those subtle, quiet epiphanies that have become a hallmark of Adams' short fiction.

In the 1970s Adams published two novels and a collection of short stories in quick succession—*Families and Survivors* (1975), *Listening to Billie* (1978), and *Beautiful Girl* (1979). Though the reviews for *Families and Survivors* were mixed, it was better received than *Careless Love* had been. The novel chronicles the life of Louisa Calloway, daughter of a "tobacco-rich" Virginian, from 1941 to New Year's Eve 1970–71. Although Adams later revealed that the novel seemed to her "a rather simple-minded piece of social history" (Feineman 32) and expressed impatience with Louisa, who "could have done a lot more with her life" (Prescott and Ross 12), *Families and Survivors* is nevertheless important in her development as a novelist. In it she more firmly stakes her claim to the literary territory loosely mapped out in *Careless Love*—the contemporary woman (usually over 30) coming to terms with herself, her sexuality, her need for independence, and her interpersonal relationships. The novel was nominated for a National Book Critics Circle Award in 1975, and the following year Adams received a fiction grant from the National Endowment for the Arts.

Adams received a John Simon Guggenheim Memorial Fellowship in 1978, the same year she published *Listening to Billie*. She considered this third novel "a better book" than the previous one, as did the majority of reviewers, but "a terribly hard book to write" (Feineman 28). Adams made Eliza Quarles a poet, thus establishing an affinity between her own profession and Eliza's. Over the 25-year span of the novel, Eliza, like Louisa Calloway, strives to put her life in order and come of age.

During the 1970s, Adams established her reputation as a short-story writer by appearing frequently in *The New Yorker* and elsewhere and by being an annual O. Henry prize winner. Reviewers were thus favorably predisposed when her first collection of short stories, *Beautiful Girl*, appeared. Eight of the sixteen stories had been included in *Prize Stories: The O. Henry Awards*. These carefully crafted stories are about relationships between lovers, spouses, friends, siblings, and parents and children involved in love and loss. In style and subject matter, they set the tone for Adams' future short stories. Of special note is "The Swastika on Our Door," the first story that Adams outlined using the ABDCE formula.

With her literary territory claimed, her reputation established, and her success assured, Adams moved through the 1980s at full speed, publishing three novels and three collections of short stories. Although she continued to write about the mature woman's social and personal relationships, each of her new novels is also a departure—whether in style, in subject matter, or in both. She began the decade with the publication of *Rich Rewards* (1980), the only novel she has written in the first person. Adams believes it is also "more directly sexual" than any of her previous novels. She explains that men have been saying what they think about women for some time, yet women have been reluctant to say what they think about men. Therefore, she wanted to show what Daphne thinks about men (Warga 3) and depicts her as talking freely about her sexual inhibitions and her "nutty obsessiveness with love and men" (*Rich Rewards* 57). In *Superior Women* (1984) Adams wrote a novel almost twice as long as any she had written before. It covers the lives of five Radcliffe girls from 1943 to 1983. The idea for the novel had been germinating since her youthful addiction to the Grace Harlow novels and long before Mary McCarthy's *The Group*, with which *Superior Women* is frequently compared. The novel became a best-seller, her first. Like *Superior Women*, her last novel of the decade, *Second Chances* (1988), is long and has several major characters; its departure from the past is mainly in subject, for the characters are mostly in their 60s and 70s. Though their concerns are the same as those of their younger counterparts in the previous novels— lovers, spouses, friends, and work—they view these concerns from a different perspective. Because of their age, they are also aware of sickness and death. These concerns probably reflect Adams' own thoughts as she experienced a brush with cancer while writing the novel. Adams' novels of the 1980s indicate her continuing interest in contemporary woman's search for self-respect and self-fulfillment, but the various departures from the past also emphasize her desire to experiment and to grow.

Adams has said that the short story is "the form I love best" (Feineman 35), and she exemplified her mastery of the form in the three collections of stories published in the 1980s: *To See You Again* (1982), *Return Trips* (1985), and *After You've Gone* (1989). (*Molly's Dog*, a single story, was published in 1983; it also appears in *Return Trips*.) The first collection deals mainly with women making discoveries about themselves, their husbands, their lovers, and their friends, prompted sometimes by events of the present, sometimes by memories of the past. In *Return Trips*, as the title implies, the past plays an even greater role. In *After You've Gone* Adams continues the theme of relationships between spouses, lovers, and friends and considers the latter extremely important, especially to women. In all three books Adams accents her characters' epiphanies, as she did in her first collection, *Beautiful Girl*.

In 1990 Adams published her first nonfiction book, *Mexico: Some Travels and Some Travelers There* (1990); it was followed by her seventh novel, *Caroline's Daughters* (1991). During over twenty trips to Mexico, Adams developed a "love-hate relationship" with that country, a relationship she says "seems mostly love," since she continues to travel there (*Mexico* xvi, xix).

Adams continues to make her home in San Francisco and occasionally shares her expertise by teaching creative writing courses at Stanford University and the University of California at Davis and at Berkeley.

MAJOR THEMES

Two major themes pervade the novels and short stories of Alice Adams: The maturation of women and interpersonal relationships. She depicts middle- or upper-middle-class women, intelligent and well traveled, in the process of maturing and of achieving self-respect, self-identity, and independence through friendship and work. Interwoven with this theme is the theme of women's relationships with their husbands, lovers, friends, and, to a lesser extent, parents and children. For the most part, Adams' women are survivors. They learn and grow in the process of discovering themselves, of understanding their associations with others, and, of finding satisfying employment. The successful Adams heroine knows the value of friendship—whether between women and men or women and women—and the importance of work to self-fulfillment.

The germ of these themes appears in her first novel, *Careless Love*. After an unsuccessful marriage, a debilitating love affair with a married man, and a subsequent abortion, Daisy Duke Fabbri begins to establish her independence. When her new date invites her to bed on their first meeting, she slaps his face, a gesture she sees ever after as a "blow for freedom" (172). She begins to visit with her friends more often; to go to parties with her platonic friend, Jimmy Frankfort; and to work part-time in an art gallery. About her latest lover Daisy says: "We like each other. I'm not sure that Pablo [her married lover] and I did" (179). Although Adams meant this novel to be humorous, she nevertheless depicts Daisy beginning to learn the same lessons her successors do: Good friends and satisfying work are necessary for one's happiness. With variation Adams develops more fully this idea in her following novels.

In *Families and Survivors* Adams traces the 30-year friendship between Kate Flickinger and Louisa Calloway, a friendship that remains constant through husbands, lovers, and children. She also explores the emotional life of Louisa, who finally emerges from a failed marriage and a series of pre-, extra-, and postmarital affairs to establish her career as a painter and to marry a childhood friend. Through her successful career and friendship in marriage, Louisa achieves self-respect and self-fulfillment. Kate, too, saves herself and perhaps her marriage by becoming a social worker in a psychiatric clinic. From this emerges newfound confidence and a stronger self-identity.

In an interview with Patricia Holt, Adams said that in *Listening to Billie* she wanted to write about "the idea of women getting to work" (8). Consequently, she develops in detail Eliza Quarles' relationship with her co-workers at the hospital and depicts her career as a budding poet. Eliza even shares with her creator an interest in refinishing furniture. Her husband having committed suicide, Eliza becomes self-sufficient, supporting herself and her young daughter, Catherine. Surrounded by the suicides of her father, her husband, and a lover, however, she sometimes falls into despair and feels that "blind deathward surge" (194). But unlike these men, she has the will and the strength to survive. Adams enlarges her treatment of familial relationships as she shows Eliza coming to terms with her domineering mother, herself a successful writer, and her hippie daughter, who cheerfully bears children out of wedlock. Eliza's happiness is based finally on her career as a poet and her genuine friendship with Harry Argent, a man as engrossed in his work as she becomes in hers.

Like her predecessor, Daphne Matthiessen in *Rich Rewards* also gains self-respect and independence. She leaves her cruel lover and goes to San Francisco to decorate a house for an old school friend. From this point she gradually emerges as a happy, sensitive, and self-sufficient woman. In a fairy-tale conclusion, Adams "rewards" the now mature Daphne by reuniting her with Jean-Paul, her great love of almost 20 years past. Even then sensible Daphne states: "What with the various uncertainties involved in our plan, including Jean-Paul's health, I had, at last, to concentrate on work" (204).

In *Superior Women*, Adams deals with her major themes in all their ramifications. She depicts the lives of five Radcliffe women over a period of 40 years and shows their relationships with each other, their husbands and lovers, their parents and children, and their work as they strive for self-fulfillment and personal happiness. Some achieve this; some do not. Megan Greene, the central character, remains unmarried and becomes a success in the publishing world. Having come to understand and accept her eccentric mother, the carhop, she finds contentment when the two of them move to Georgia to help run a temporary shelter for homeless women. Here she has her friends and her work. The owner of the shelter is big, jolly, motherly Peg, whose search for happiness leads her through a marriage, four children, and a nervous breakdown to settle in Georgia with her friend and lover, Vera. Janet (on the fringes of the group because she is Jewish), once her husband leaves her, fulfills her ambition of attending medical school. Adams is too realistic a writer, however, to imply that all women—or men, for that matter—achieve happiness. Cathy is jilted by her boyfriend, becomes pregnant by a Catholic priest who leaves his profession but marries someone else, and eventually dies of cancer. Beautiful, intelligent, prejudiced Lavinia with her remarkably inferior values remains unhappily married to Potter Cobb because he is a wealthy and proper husband and to divorce him would be to admit "original error" (178). In Adams' schema, it is noteworthy that Lavinia is unemployed. Through these five women, particularly Megan and Lavinia as opposites, Adams projects the alternatives of life.

In *Second Chances*, Adams concentrates on love and loss and the importance of friendship in recovery from that loss. She writes about six friends (the seventh has just died) living in San Sebastian, California. These friends, in their 60s and 70s, have already passed through many of the experiences of the protagonists in the preceding novels, but theirs is not a placid progress into old age. They worry about the widow, Celeste, and just what her relationship is with the younger Bill, who looks so much like her late husband. The long, stormy yet loving marriage of Sam and Dudley is ended when Sam dies. Edward's longtime but much younger lover, Freddy becomes a gay rights activist and leaves him. These upheavals make friendship among them even more important, but they also initiate in each a small measure of greater independence. Only the eccentric philanthropist Polly, who has never married, experiences a new adventure in love. In this novel in particular, Adams depicts the loss of loved ones through separation or death and the importance of friends and one's own self-reliance in adjusting to that loss.

In *Caroline's Daughters*, Adams continues her analysis of familial and social relationships as she depicts the lives of Caroline and her five daughters, offspring of three marriages. Against a backdrop of picturesque San Francisco and social commentary on the 1980s, Adams depicts a year in the complex lives of these women as they search for self-identity, successful relationships, and satisfying work. They achieve these goals in varying degrees. Perhaps the most successful daughter is Sage, who finally leaves her handsome and adulterous husband, establishes a relationship with a male friend, and has a rewarding career as a ceramicist. Liza, a happily married mother of three, approaches total fulfillment when her writing career begins to blossom. The other daughters are not as fortunate. Wealthy Fiona and Jill, a restaurateur and a lawyer-stockbroker, respectively, founder in their social relationships. Portia, the youngest daughter, is confused about her sexuality, her career, and life in general. As Adams traces the fortunes and misfortunes of these sisters, she emphasizes her major themes: the maturation of women and interpersonal relationships.

Adams continues the major themes in her short fiction. In "The Break-In" (*To See You Again*), "True Colors" (*To See You Again*), and "You Are What You Own: A Notebook" (*Return Trips*), women assert their independence by leaving their lovers or husbands. In "The Girl Across the Room" (*To See You Again*) the woman remains in the relationship but as a stronger person. Not all

Adams' women are strong, however. Some, like Jessica Todd in the Todd stories, remain trapped in unhappy marriages. Constant in the stories is the theme of love—the fear of losing it, the loss of it, the recovery from that loss. In "Ripped Off" (*Beautiful Girl*), a young girl feels "diminished" by a robbery and fears her lover will love her less; in "On the Road" (*After You've Gone*), a woman on a lecture tour worries about whether her husband is having an affair. Some stories depict the grief over the departure ("Ocracoke Island" [*After You've Gone*]) or death ("Verlie I Say Unto You" [*Beautiful Girl*]) of a loved one, whereas others concentrate on the recovery ("Your Doctor Loves You" [*After You've Gone*]). In "A Pale and Perfectly Oval Moon" (*Beautiful Girl*) the extent of the love is not recognized until too late. Many of the stories also concern friendship—friendship between a man and a woman, as in "Time in Santa Fe" (*Return Trips*), and between women, as in "New Best Friends" (*Return Trips*), about a friendship that fails; "Elizabeth" (*Return Trips*), about two friends 30 years apart in age; or "La Señora" (*Return Trips*), about a friendship between a maid in a grand hotel and a very old North American guest.

With a sharp eye and a sympathetic voice, Adams writes about woman's coming of age in contemporary society—discovering her identity, working out her social and personal relationships, and finding a rewarding occupation. For her heroines, especially in the novels, the "they married and lived happily every after" ending will not suffice. Adams believes that the contemporary woman has more or at least different criteria for a meaningful life.

SURVEY OF CRITICISM

Although there are no book-length studies of Alice Adams and few critical articles, several reference works provide broad overviews: *Dictionary of Literary Biography Yearbook: 1986*, *Current Biography Yearbook 1989*, and *Contemporary Authors*, New Revision Series, volume 26 (1989). The latter contains an interview with Adams and a bibliography of biographical and critical sources (mostly book reviews); listing over seventy items, this bibliography is the most extensive one available. For excerpts from the major reviews of Adams' work, *Contemporary Literary Criticism*, volumes 6 (1976), 13 (1980), and 46 (1988) are helpful.

Neil Feineman's excellent interview makes available Adams' views about her life and early writings. In addition, Adams talks about her experiences with specific novels in the following briefer articles: *Listening to Billie* in Patricia Holt's interview for *Publishers Weekly*; *Rich Rewards* in Wayne Warga's article, "A Sophisticated Author Gets By with Help from Her Friends"; *Superior Women* in Alix Madrigal's interview, "The Breaking of a Mold"; and *Second Chances* in both Mervyn Rothstein's "On Death and the Job of Getting There" and Kim Heron's "Horror and Romance." Additional biographical material is included in Nancy Faber's interview, "Out of the Pages," in *People Weekly*.

Only four critical articles have been published on Adams' work. In "Succeeding in Their Times: Alice Adams on Women and Work,'' Cara Chell places Adams in a group of contemporary women writers who are revamping old forms. She sees Adams as rejecting the "passive" and "romantic" heroine of the past for the woman who asserts herself through her work in order to survive and to discover her self-identity. Chell demonstrates her thesis in *Families and Survivors*, *Listening to Billie*, and *Rich Rewards*. In "Order and Chaos in Alice Adams' *Rich Rewards*,'' Larry T. Blades discusses the "odd balance" between order and chaos in the novel. He sees Daphne's positive movement toward order as "temporary and personal" when counterbalanced by the "forces of chaos" (192) and the "craziness threatening the modern world of *Rich Rewards*'' (193). The other two critical articles concern Adams' short fiction. In "Changing the Past: Alice Adams' Revisionary Nostalgia,'' Lee Upton discusses the way in which Adams' "women rechart their lives, actually returning—imaginatively and, more often than not, physically—to past landscapes" (33). And in her book *From the Hearth to the Open Road*, Barbara Frey Waxman includes a section entitled "Alice Adams's Middle-Aged Women-Adventurers.'' She discusses three stories, "A Wonderful Woman,'' "Lost Luggage,'' and "To See You Again,'' as miniature reifungsromane, stories in which middle-aged women discover their self-identities and determine new directions for their lives.

The number of book reviews on Adams indicates not only the quantity of her publications but also their quality. (A selection of these reviews appears in the bibliography. A more complete listing can be found in *Contemporary Authors*, *New Revision Series*.) Although reviews of her works have been mixed, she is generally highly regarded as a short-story writer; John Updike calls her "a natural" at it (160). Her recent novels have brought her popular acclaim (*Superior Women*) and probably her highest critical acclaim to date (*Second Chances*). The field of biographical and critical studies on Alice Adams is open.

BIBLIOGRAPHY

Works by Alice Adams

Careless Love. New York: New American Library, 1966. Republished as *The Fall of Daisy Duke*. London: Constable, 1967.
Families and Survivors. New York: Knopf, 1975.
Listening to Billie. New York: Knopf, 1978.
Beautiful Girl. New York: Knopf, 1979.
Rich Rewards. New York: Knopf, 1980.
To See You Again. New York: Knopf, 1982.
Molly's Dog. Concord, N.H.: Ewert, 1983.
Superior Women. New York: Knopf, 1984.
Return Trips. New York: Knopf, 1985.
Second Chances. New York: Knopf, 1988.
After You've Gone. New York: Knopf, 1989.
Mexico: Some Travels and Some Travelers There. New York: Prentice-Hall, 1990.
Caroline's Daughters. New York: Knopf, 1991.

Studies of Alice Adams

Barnes, Joanna. "The Loneliness of the Later Intimacies." *Los Angeles Times Book Review* (May 8, 1988): 13.

Blades, Larry T. "Order and Chaos in Alice Adams' *Rich Rewards*." *Critique: Studies in Modern Fiction* 27 (Summer 1986): 187–95.

Bryfonski, Dedria, ed. "Adams, Alice." *Contemporary Literary Criticism* 13 (1980): 1–3.

Carlson, Ron. "Clobbering Her Ex." *New York Times Book Review* (October 8, 1989): 27.

Chell, Cara. "Succeeding in Their Times: Alice Adams on Women and Work." *Soundings: An Interdisciplinary Journal* 68 (Spring 1985): 62–71.

DeMott, Benjamin. "Stories of Change." *New York Times Book Review* (April 11, 1982): 7 ff.

Faber, Nancy. "Out of the Pages." *People Weekly* (April 3, 1978): 48 ff.

Feineman, Neil. "An Interview with Alice Adams." *StoryQuarterly* No. 11 (1980): 27–37.

Goodwin, Stephen. "Alice Adams' San Francisco Chronicles." *Washington Post Book World* (May 9, 1982): 4 ff.

Heron, Kim. "Horror and Romance." *New York Times Book Review* (May 1, 1988): 11.

Holt, Patricia. "Alice Adams." *Publishers Weekly* (January 16, 1978): 8–9.

Kakutani, Michiko. "Books of the Times." *New York Times* (August 21, 1985): C17.

Lehmann-Haupt, Christopher. "The Rising and Falling in One Family." *New York Times* (March 21, 1991): C21.

Madrigal, Alix. "The Breaking of a Mold." *San Francisco Chronicle Review* (September 9, 1984): 11.

Marowski, Daniel G., and Roger Matuz, eds. "Alice (Boyd) Adams." *Contemporary Literary Criticism* 46 (1988): 13–23.

Merkin, Daphne. "Tale of a Woman Writer." *New Leader* (March, 27, 1978): 21–23.

Moritz, Charles, ed. "Adams, Alice." *Current Biography Yearbook* (1989): 6–10.

Petroski, Catherine. "Tales of Broken Love." *Tribune Books* (Chicago) (September 3, 1989): 4–5.

Phelps, Teresa. "Alice Adams' Short Stories 'Make Sense.' " *Chicago Tribune Book World* (September 1985): 31.

Pollitt, Katha. "Good Ole Boys and Wistful Hippies." *New York Times Book Review* (January 14, 1979): 14 ff.

Prescott, Jani, and Jean W. Ross. "Adams, Alice (Boyd)." *Contemporary Authors*. New Revision Series 26 (1989): 8–13.

Quart, Barbara Koenig. "A Woman's 'Naked and the Dead.' " *Ms.* (September 1984): 28.

Riley, Carolyn, and Phyllis Carmel Mendelson, eds. "Adams, Alice." *Contemporary Literary Criticism* 6 (1976): 1–2.

Robinson, Jill. "A New Place, a Chillier Season." *Washington Post Book World* (February 23, 1975): 3.

Rothstein, Mervyn. "On Death and the Job of Getting There." *New York Times* (May, 19, 1988): C30.

Schindehette, Susan. "*Return Trips*." *Saturday Review* (December 1985): 73–74.

Stull, William L. "Alice Adams." *Dictionary of Literary Biography Yearbook: 1986* (1986): 271–80.

Updike, John. "No More Mr. Knightlys." *New Yorker* (November 5, 1984): 160 ff.

Upton, Lee. "Changing the Past: Alice Adams' Revisionary Nostalgia." *Studies in Short Fiction* 26 (Winter 1989): 33–41.

Warga, Wayne. "A Sophisticated Author Gets By with Help from Her Friends." *Los Angeles Times Book Review* (November 16, 1980): 3.

Waxman, Barbara Frey. *From the Hearth to the Open Road: A Feminist Study of Aging in Contemporary Literature*. Westport, Conn.: Greenwood, 1990.

Williamson, Barbara. "Aging Without the Rage: Fiction of Old Friends Confronting Change." *Washington Post* (May 6, 1988): B4.

Wood, Susan. "Stories of Love and Loss." *Washington Post Book World* (January 21, 1979): 3.

Yardley, Jonathan. "That Old Gang of Hers." *Washington Post Book World* (September 2, 1984): 3.

Lisa Alther
(1944–   )

A native Southerner who has lived in the North for her entire adult life, Lisa Alther has published four novels, two situated in the South and two in New England. Having grown up in the 1960s, Alther felt that, though there are subtle differences between Northern and Southern perspectives, her shift in locale was not significant in developing her main theme of the ironies involved in the search for meaning by characters trying to avoid stereotypical responses to the hostile forces of twentieth-century life.

BIOGRAPHY

Lisa (Elisabeth) Alther was born on July 23, 1944, in Kingsport, a small city in East Tennessee, and attended public schools there. She was one of five children of John Shelton and Alice Margaret Reed. From her father, a surgeon, she gained an interest in science that has found expression in writing about ecology and in reading works of popular science as a source of metaphors for her fiction. From her mother, who had been an English major in college and an English teacher afterwards, she early acquired an interest in books and reading; she read the older generation of Southern women writers—Eudora Welty, Flannery O'Connor, Katherine Anne Porter, Carson McCullers—long before they became famous. Her long-term interest in cooking and in gardening resulted in some of her earliest publications—recipes and articles on food and the environment in the *Vermont Freeman* in the 1970s. In 1966 she graduated from Wellesley College with a B.A. and on August 26 returned home for a big family wedding to Richard Philip Alther, a painter. Their daughter, Sara Halsey, was born November 15, 1968. Alther is now divorced.

Living in rural Vermont, Alther pursued a career as a writer, but for over a decade she had no success in publishing her chosen genres, the novel and short story. She wrote journalistic pieces while continuing to write fiction; she says she had 250 rejection slips before her first novel, *Kinflicks*, was published in 1976. Following in the vein of sexual frankness made popular by Erica Jong's *Fear of Flying* (1973), *Kinflicks* became a best-seller. Alther has continued to live quietly, occasionally lecturing or teaching, and she has traveled widely. She says she is a slow writer, and writes four or five drafts of each work before submitting it for publication. This has meant that her novels have appeared at long intervals: *Original Sins* in 1981; *Other Women* in 1984; and *Bedrock* not until 1990. Though she has written many short stories, she has been satisfied enough with only four in publication.

When her daughter was an infant, Alther needed to go away to find the time to write, leaving her daughter in her father's care. She wrote half of *Kinflicks* in a white heat of creativity while spending two weeks every two months for two years at a boardinghouse in Montreal. She needed to make few changes in this part of the novel, but felt it lacked the depth to answer the question she was posing for herself and prospective readers: How can a person satisfy needs both for security and for adventure? She wrote an additional half to *Kinflicks*, alternating chapters on the adventurous life of a young Southern woman seeking personal identity and sexual freedom in the 1960s with chapters on her return home at age 27 to the South to care for her dying widowed mother. Alther continued to write regularly, during her daughter's school hours, and more recently since her daughter has been in college, in the early mornings until mid-afternoon, when she breaks for exercise and relaxation. She gains perspective on her writing by letting several months go by between drafts. Thus, though she does not write with any specific audience in mind, she says, she becomes her own first audience. Alther has a circle of friends—writers, painters, sculptors, some academics—whom she trusts as early readers; and for her first three novels she had the same helpful editor at Alfred A. Knopf.

Alther's first three novels have all been great commercial successes; in July 1990, *Kinflicks* was in its twenty-ninth paperback reprinting, the other two novels both in their thirteenth. It may be that each has appealed to specific audiences as well as to the general public. *Kinflicks* certainly appealed to survivors of the 1960s who had themselves been trying to find meaning in the women's movement, the civil rights movement, and the Vietnam era. *Original Sins*, the story of five young Southerners from high school to middle age, probably had a wide audience, both in the South and among the many Southerners, who like Alther and others of her generation and before, had left the South. *Other Women*, which tells the story of a confused client and her woman psychotherapist, has a special appeal for psychotherapy patients. In both of these works Alther, though she continued her verbal wit, did not use the wilder humor of plot and situation that had characterized *Kinflicks*. In *Bedrock* she uses an almost farcical humor to portray the people of a small town in Vermont. She parallels these scenes with another, more serious plot about an older woman photographer in search of a firm foundation for her life. While rebuilding an old house in the town, she reexamines her relationships and finds bedrock within the self she comes to know in the process.

Alther has always felt that she would continue to write fiction, as she did for 12 years, even without an audience. She writes fiction in order to answer questions about life that she herself has puzzled over; thus there is always a serious purpose underlying the comic, often self-ironic, tone of her writing. Alther's works draw on her own life and those of her generation; she says that most characters are at the beginning a conglomerate of four or five people whose experience she knows about; then they become their own people, separate from any initial model. Her novels are not autobiographical in any simplistic sense. Her father did not die in a terrible accident as did Ginny Babcock's in *Kinflicks*; nor did her mother die of a blood disease, her life painfully prolonged by technology. Her parents are alive and well in Tennessee, and she visits them frequently, as well as siblings still in the South, one in Memphis and another in Chapel Hill. She feels that even though she has been transplanted for more than half her life, her roots both as a person and as a writer are in the South. In an article she wrote for the *New York Times* in 1979, "Will the South Rise Again?" she quotes a letter of Flannery O'Connor who describes the South as a "story-telling section." Alther feels that her desire to answer serious existential questions by telling stories is part of her Southern heritage. And her transplantation has been essentially from one small town in the setting of beautiful mountains to another. The brick house she lives in now, just outside a small town in central rural Vermont, set in a wide lawn with a beautiful garden, could be in the South. In her fiction Alther continues to respond to the questions and dilemmas of her age, adapting methods she learned in her youth in the South.

MAJOR THEMES

Though she has responded to the problems common to those who grew up in the 1960s, Alther's themes are timeless; even when she uses a Southern setting, her themes have to do with what is happening in America as a whole. Her characters, especially the young, are looking for meaning but find hypocrisy and greed in those around them, especially the adults. Alther uses wit and humor—as in Voltaire's *Candide*—to expose the particular brands of human failings she has found in religion, sexual mores, race relations, or, in her first novel, especially with regard to the war in Vietnam. Alther's target is stereotypes, primarily sexual ones; she exposes the sanctions of tradition and religion behind twentieth-century emphasis on male sexual conquest. Her focus is not on sexual escapades per se but on the development of warped attitudes toward sex as young people struggle with adult sanctimoniousness. Her frankness about female sexual desires and experience may be titillating because of its originality, but her wit puts the focus on the irony between piety and conduct.

Alther's major technique in all her books is to juxtapose the separate stories of individuals, using both first-person and third-person narration. This allows for irony of situation, especially when characters unknowingly reveal truths about themselves they are hiding from others. Added to this basic structural comedy is a verbal wit that undergirds the satiric message. In some of her books Alther adds characteristics from the picaresque novel as her characters move from place to place in their search for meaning. As did Odysseus in the comic epic, the characters sometimes return home before any self-discovery; at other times they find more modern means of self-discovery, such as psychotherapy. All of Alther's novels end with at least hope of a workable solution to some of the characters' problems: Alther is thus essentially a comic author, in spite of her dark picture of the world.

Kinflicks has a very formal juxtaposition of plots. Seven chapters told in the first person are a flashback to Ginny Babcock's coming-of-age. Six chapters, told in the third person, tell of the thirty days during which she returns home to be at the bedside of her dying mother. Ginny's frantic energy in exploring sex and meaning is all the more hilarious because we first see her at the end of her pursuit—still young, however—facing death vicariously by helping her mother accept the reality of her situation. It is ironic that through her unselfish and successful attempt to come to terms with her mother, Ginny also comes to terms with her doubts about *being* a mother. Her anger during an episode when she attempts to rescue some baby birds abandoned by their parents and her failed attempt at suicide are presented as comic, but they underline the desperation she feels at the prospect of being an orphan. As the birds die one by one, Ginny accepts her own limitations: She cannot expect to "have it all." A major source of irony is Ginny's own awareness of the inconclusiveness of her reactions and thoughts. Alther lets us see Ginny's confusion and at the same time her sincerity and neediness by entering into her consciousness during the flashback to Ginny's past in high school and college, her working life in Cambridge, her abortive attempt at lesbianism in Vermont. The comic tone is maintained by a verbal wit capable of illuminating even Ginny's ruminations about the pessimism of Nietzsche and Schopenhauer. On the other hand, in the humorous chapters, tragedy lurks close at hand: Ginny's possessive lesbian partner dies in a tragic accident and the house in Vermont goes up in flames. In the more serious parts, Alther's comic image of Mrs. Babcock's attempt to find meaning by reading the entire encyclopedia comes through as insight into her self-awareness during her role-playing as a mother; her permitting Ginny to share her awareness frees Ginny from the guilt she has felt about not repeating her mother's role. As Mrs. Babcock prepares for death with dignity, Ginny comes to admire and wants to emulate her courage, both in life and at her death. The story ends inconclusively, but Ginny's willingness to follow in at least some of her mother's footsteps allows the reader to hope that she will find a way to adjust to her own role as mother.

In *Original Sins* Alther juggles the stories of five protagonists, often with an effect of irony but not with the wit of a first-person narrator who sees herself all too clearly. Here Alther is the omniscient author, letting us see all the reasons, conscious and unconscious, why "the five" find their small-town Southern environment pernicious. Alther does not spare the simplistic radicalism and subtle racism that three of the five find when they go North, but the brunt of her anger is on the corruption of family, religion, industry, and education that they find at home in the South. In *Kinflicks* the picaresque form places the emphasis on the journey away from home; *Original Sins* is more static, with the emphasis on home. Alther makes it clear that the myth of the South as having escaped Americanization is false: like the rest of the country, the South, which was once a wilderness whose Indians yielded to the rifle and the plow of her characters' ancestors, is now an industrial area controlled by absentee landlords. It is the South's continuing status as the "Bible belt" that is the target of Alther's most vehment satire. In a chapter entitled "Hollowed Be Thy Name," she castigates the hypocrisy of denominations from upper-class Episcopalians to lower-class Baptists and Methodists; all of them condone the particular sins appropriate to their position. Parents' prohibitions about sex—the "original sin"—cause the children the most grief and also blind the parents to other sins, such as their own greed and selfishness. The book starts with an Edenic scene of the five children seated in a tree looking down on their world; at the end, "the Five" are reunited at the death of one of them at 30, and their children look down from the same tree but with less naiveté than their parents had had. Alther leaves us with some hope that the distance the five have achieved from their origins— and from some of their own and their parents' original sins—will lead their children, at least, to a will to change what they can, whether at home or away. This conclusion seems to pinpoint the "original sins" as those of the parents of the five; the sins the five pass on are less likely to be mortal since they have become aware of them.

Sally and Emily Prince, the two females among the five main characters of *Original Sins*, experience devastating sexual initiations. Sally is forced to marry when she becomes pregnant before graduating from high school, and Emily, like Ginny Babcock in *Kinflicks*, goes North to college and becomes a lesbian in response to the male domination she associates with sexuality. Alther's third novel, *Other Women*, focuses even more closely on female rites of passage. Again two plots intertwine, but this time the parallel between the disillusioning experiences of Caroline Kelly, a nurse, and the abuse and tragedy suffered by Hannah Burke, her therapist, reinforce each other. Instead of irony, the mode of *Other Women* is description of multiple female roles and the struggle of women to avoid the stereotypes imposed on them. After rebelling against parents too busy doing good to strangers to care for their own children and grandchildren, and having failed at both marriage/motherhood and a long-term lesbian affair, Caroline is weary. She is tired of fulfilling the female role of caring for others, which she has experienced in her profession as well as in her personal life. She is tempted to marry again because "life would be easier with a man. The roles were defined." This mood reflects that of many survivors of the 1960s and 1970s; in 1984 many readers could identify with Caroline's turn to psychotherapy. From Hannah she learns how to be alone and how to get past the depression that has made her internalize universal suffering as her own. The relationship between patient and therapist, shown as one of loving nurturance between two women, leads to a cure for Caroline's malaise, one not often achieved so rapidly in conventional therapy.

Other Women returns to the focus of *Kinflicks* on a relationship between an older and a younger woman, but its theme is irrelevant to any specific regional locale; only the small-town ambience is maintained. And in Caroline's self-awareness and reactions to Hannah's therapy, the witty voice of Ginny Babcock is often heard. In *Bedrock* Alther also returns to the juxtaposition of two plots. One focuses on the search for meaning by Clea Shawn, a successful middle-aged photographer, married with two children; the other focuses on a weird assortment of characters in a Vermont town, Roches Ridge—a place not unlike Starks Bog, near which Ginny and her lesbian friends had established a commune but which they had never really lived in. In *Bedrock* Alther's New Yorkers do penetrate the town; Roches Ridge, like Sherwood Anderson's *Winesburg, Ohio*, is fully revealed as Clea remodels a decaying house and tries to find traditional American values among her townspeople. Instead she learns that her preconceptions have, like her own photography, been superficial. The town is full of mean, selfish people. In this book Alther's humor is aimed not at the central character but at the townspeople, who appear less vicious than farcical. Clea, like Alther's other heroines, comes to understand herself. Instead of resorting to psychotherapy or returning to her original home, she abandons her adopted urban home. Her new self-knowledge comes partly from the encounter with her strange neighbors but mostly from the realization that her long friendship with a woman sculptor has really been the great love of her life. Accepting the truth about herself and deciding to live with Elka, she is able to form both a loving relationship with her adolescent children and a new friendship with her promiscuous husband.

Both *Other Women* and *Bedrock* are in one sense less political than Alther's earlier works; in the 1980s her focus shifted to the personal, though not without her earlier feminist identification of the personal with the political. Once straightened out in her relationships, Clea can turn to becoming a good citizen of Roches Ridge, her adopted home, a possibility also for some of Alther's other characters.

SURVEY OF CRITICISM

Alther's books have been widely reviewed; from the beginning high praise has been countered by strongly negative views. One often suspects that the vehemence of some writers stems from a perspective threatened by Alther's own anger against traditions and those powerful enough to inflict them on others. Many reviewers saw *Kinflicks* as a stunning first novel that its author would find hard to follow; many critics have agreed that Alther has not again achieved the high level of wit, insight, and timeliness that made her first novel a best-seller.

Characteristic of the high praise is John Leonard's review of *Kinflicks* in the *New York Times* (March 14, 1976). He first compares Alther to Doris Lessing, seeing them as "sharing an energetic intelligence, an absence of self-pity, an appetite for experience." He finds "Ginny's choosing sides at college" among philosophers "genuinely moving," and the treatment of Mrs. Babcock's preparation for death as "quite simply beyond the power of most novelists, first or otherwise, to evoke." And he relished the "exuberant yawp" of Alther's wit, seeing her narrative voice as one that "has been missing in American fiction for years," like that of "Holden Caulfield, Augie March, and, ultimately, Huck Finn." On the other hand, Walter Clemons in *Newsweek* (March 15, 1976, 91), found her humorous aim "erratic," the book full of "arch jocosity," "sophomoric overwriting" and a failure to live up to its intention of being a " '60s '*Candide.*' " Paul Gray in *Time* (March 22, 1976, 80) saw the book as "an abundantly entertaining progress through the 60s," and admired Alther for demonstrating that "women can write about physical functions just as frankly and, when the genes move them, just as raunchily as men." But he finds Ginny shallow and her attempt to find meaning through her mother abortive. On the other hand, Alice Adams finds Ginny "wholly likable . . . brave and bright and honest and self-doubting. She is a loving person and *funny*, especially about sex" (*Harper's*, May 1976, 94). William C. Woods in the *Washington Post* (March 26, 1976) thinks that most of the characters are "stick figures," but he finds the relationship between Ginny and her mother portrayed with "a caring detachment" that few other novels can rival. Another reviewer found that "Ginny's sexual adventures and misadventures . . . are possibly among the funniest ever recorded" and compares her to Holden Caulfield as "a symbol of everything that is right and wrong about a generation" (*The New Yorker*, March 29, 1976). Reviewers from *Vogue* to *Ms.* and *Cosmopolitan* praised the novel; its continued reprints in the Signet paperback testify to its solid popularity.

Original Sins met with differences of opinion similar to those about *Kinflicks*. Paul Gray found it a worthy successor to her "truly successful first novel"; she paints a "broad social portrait of nearly two decades of American life," he thought, in "an old-fashioned novel in the best sense of the word," full of "page-turning verve and intelligence." Alther does not simplify the "cussed complexities of daily life," but allows her characters to keep searching for meaning (*Time*, April 27, 1981). Other reviewers found the book powerful, wise, brilliant; it was chosen as a Book-of-the-Month Club selection. Against all this glowing praise the negative reviews seem self-indulgent, focusing on specific problems that seem to be more those of the reviewer than of the author. John Alfred Avant (*The Nation*, April 25, 1981) finds the narrative "turgid," full of "easy ironies," the wit limited to the prologue and epilogue; he accuses Alther of "dumping on Southern values," of making being a Southerner the original sin. Mark Schechner agreed that it "was an all-out assault" on the South "for its rigidly maintained double standards on matters of race, sex, and class"; he finds Alther pinpointing men as villains, and sees only Emily and Sally as well-represented characters (*New Republic*, June 13, 1981). Mary Cantwell, a British critic, thought that Alther had missed her aim in writing a serious novel on the same themes as her first one; she "does not doubt either the accuracy of her anecdotes or her knowledge of the terrain," but cannot understand why Alther would choose to "smother" her "true comic genius" (*Times Literary Supplement*, June 26, 1981).

In the first critical article about Alther to appear, Bonnie H. Braendlin discusses *Kinflicks* as a feminist bildungsroman; she sees it as a picaresque comic novel, and identifies the third-person narrator of the alternate chapters as "the Ginny of the later years." Mary Anne Ferguson considers *Kinflicks* as a novel of female development following the general plot of the myth of Psyche. Ginny's journey of self-discovery is a "journey through the kingdom of death," and the book "becomes an artifact of its own theme: to make death comic is a triumph of art equivalent to the feat of making a fallible woman—everywoman—a true hero" (237). In an article in the *Southern Quarterly* reprinted as a chapter for a book, *Women Writers of the Contemporary South*, Ferguson compares Alther's first two books, finding *Original Sins* "not a browntone version of *Kinflicks* but a post-modern novel in the guise of an old-fashioned chronicle." She sees Alther as taking the risk of a style that "spells out infinitely varied perceptions of the same "facts" and refuses to find a unitary view or a final solution. The novel's circular structure is an ironic comment on the easy irony of the epic of comic return. Alther did not have the conventional happy ending of the comic epic; the only hope for a better world she finds in "the irony at its core: the worst may have at least side effects." Alther's purpose in giving such a limited outlook to her chrraracters is to "bring into consciousness the underlying question of the nuclear age: is survival enough?" (114). Some of the negative views of the book as denigrating the South may well stem from readers' reluctance to face this question.

Other Women received criticism much like that of Alther's first two books, but this time negative reviews stem both from those missing the wit of *Kinflicks* and those who find psychotherapy itself an uninteresting topic. Nancy Evans disliked the book for both these reasons (*New York Times*, November 11, 1984, 7:26–27); she thinks the book does not rise above "women's novel slumber party talk" and sees both patient and therapist as sob sisters. Other reviewers used such terms as "sensitive and humorous," "rich, multi-dimensional and thoroughly involving . . . a quantum leap forward," "true food for the soul." More important, the book received some serious criticism. Adrian Oktenberg thinks the book is Alther's most challenging and successful work to date. Its topic is the psychotherapy of one woman undertaken with another, its theme is the achievement of adulthood in this childishly topsy-turvy world, its triumph is in its struggle to come to terms with things as they are and things as we wish them to be" ["Odd Couple," in *New Directions for Women*, 14 (January–February 1985), 17, 20]. Oktenberg continues her high praise for Alther's "outward" emphasis rather than inward self-analysis: "All comedy is tragic; all tragedy is finally comic. That Lisa Alther understands this, and fuses the two, is one of her great gifts as a writer.'' Francis King also found *Other Women* outstanding; he praises it because of its equal focus on patient and therapist and for Alther's perception that neurosis "originates in The Pattern: that is the bad emotional and behavioural habits we pick up in childhood" that must be unlearned. It is through the relationship with Hannah that Caroline relives and outgrows her sense of meaninglessness; in showing both sides of the relationship, Alther reveals the power of feminist therapy. "Love between women has rarely been treated with more sympathy, truth, and tact," King concluded [*Spectator*, 254 (March 9, 1985), 23–24]. In a dissertation on Alther's first three novels, Gwendolyn Hale White focuses on Alther's treatment of the self and the other.

Bedrock has received fewer and even more divided reviews than Alther's earlier books. One of them is perhaps an ominous indication that the book will not find the wide general audience reached by the first three. Instead of a long article near the front page of the Sunday Book Review, the *New York Times* gave *Bedrock* a paragraph in its "In Short" reviews of fiction (June 3, 1990, 23). Terry Cochran found Clea Shawn a "sleek middle-aged heroine" whose successful search for "bedrock" to give her life meaning is not convincing. Cochran finds the rural characters lifeless, as does Jeff Danziger (*Boston Globe*, May 6, 1990, B51–52). In a long review, largely plot summary, Danziger finds that the book "does not equal comedy or drama or anything more than confusion." On the other hand, Barbara Rich in the *Women's Review of Books* (July 1990, 25) considered the book both comic and richly meaningful. She finds the consummation of Clea's lesbian love affair "not as tedious as one might suppose," and praises Alther especially for her "insights into the lives of people who live in the tiny, inbred town" in Vermont. Questioning the relationship of Alther's picture to the real Vermont, as did Danziger, Rich concludes that "this is Alther's Vermont, and ain't it a gas?" Reviewers were responding to Alther's version of her adopted home as some did to her version of the South. Reviewers in as varied sources as *Time* (May 21, 1990), the *Milwaukee Journal* (June 17, 1990), and the *Christian Science Monitor* found little to praise in *Bedrock*; others as varied had at least partially positive views. Susan Dooley in the *Washington Post Book World* (May 21, 1990) said: "Without ever diminishing the humor she has managed the difficult feat of using the nuttiness in our society as a counterpoint to a more serious examination of love in all its varieties," and Bruce Bawer found the book "a wise, highly diverting novel . . . that ponders urban sensibilities with both a compassionate heart and a sardonic eye" (*Wall Street Journal*, June 7, 1990). At least some reviewers perceive the novel's serious purpose. I see it as belonging to a subgenre of fiction only recently defined as the "midlife novel" in which a protagonist moves upward in the journey of self-discovery to a plateau of peace and happiness instead of declining to despair and old age. By ending her furious search among the crazies of a small town, Clea repeats the pastoral conclusion that has been a major American pattern; but she does it as a middle-aged woman instead of as a young man.

Though Alther has never been closely autobiographical, clearly she is following the experience of her generation. In *Bedrock* she finds positive values for her characters and more hope for a better life than she has found before.

BIBLIOGRAPHY

Works by Lisa Alther

"Encounter." *McCall's* (August 1976).
Kinflicks. New York: Knopf, 1976.
"Will the South Rise Again?" *New York Times*, (December 16, 1979) VII: 7, 34.
Original Sins. New York: Knopf, 1981.
Other Women. New York: Knopf, 1984.
"Termites," in *Homewords*, ed. Douglas Paschall and Alice Swanson. Knoxville: University of Tennessee Press, 1986.
"The Writer and Her Critics" (Rev. of two books about Doris Lessing). *Women's Review of Books* (October 1988): 11–12.
"What I Do When I Write." *Women's Review of Books* (July 1989): 24.
"The Politics of Paradise," in *Louder than Words*, ed. William Shore. New York: Random House, 1990.
Bedrock, New York: Knopf, 1990.

Studies of Lisa Alther

Braendlin, Bonnie H. "Alther, Atwood, Ballantyne, and Gray: Secular Salvation in the Contemporary Feminist Bildungsroman." *Frontiers* 4 (1979): 18–21.
———. "New Directions in the Contemporary Bildungsroman: Lisa Alther's *Kinflicks*," 160–71 in *Gender and Literary Voice*, ed. Janet Todd. New York: Holmes and Meier, 1980.
Ferguson, Mary Anne. "The Female Novel of Development and the Myth of Psyche," 228–43 in *The Voyage In: Fictions of Female Development*, ed. Elizabeth Abel, Marianne Hirsch, and Elizabeth Langland. Hanover, N.H.: University Press of New England, 1983. Also published in *Denver Review* 17 (Winter 1983): 58–74.
———. "Lisa Alther: The Irony of Return?" *Southern Quarterly* 21 (Summer 1983): 103–15. Reprinted in *Women Writers of the Contemporary South*, ed. Peggy Prenshaw. Jackson: University Press of Mississippi, 1984.
Hall, Joan Lord. "Symbiosis and Separation in Lisa Alther's *Kinflicks*." *Arizona Quarterly* 38 (Winter 1982): 336–46.
Waage, Frederick G. "Alther and Dillard: The Appalachian Universe," 200–208 in *Appalachia/America*. Proceedings of the Appalachian Studies Association, 1980.
White, Gwendolyn Hale. "Subjugation and Emancipation in the Fiction of Lisa Alther." *Dissertation Abstracts*, 1988, December 49 (6): 1458A.

NANCY D. HARGROVE

Toni Cade Bambara
(1939–   )

Defining herself as "a Pan-Africanist-socialist-feminist in the United States" ("What It Is" 154), Toni Cade Bambara is aggressively committed to the empowerment of the African-American community, and to its women in particular. She sees writing and, more recently, filmmaking as political/social acts, as her way of contributing to the attainment of that goal. Her major themes of resistance to oppression and the quest for meaningful selfhood, as well as her use of black females as her leading characters and her creation of an innovative style based on black language and imagery, are largely determined by these beliefs. Yet, despite her seriousness, an irrepressible comic spirit—now crackling with wit, now sharp with sarcasm, now gentle with compassion—informs the whole of her work.

While she considers herself a Northern urban writer, Bambara can legitimately be included in studies of Southern writers in that she lived in the South for approximately 10 years in addition to making frequent visits both before and after this time. She also employs Southern settings and Southern characters in some of her work, and she has been influenced in style, structure, and imagery by certain aspects of Southern culture, such as gospel and blues ("Interview" 43).

BIOGRAPHY

Toni Cade Bambara was born in New York City on March 25, 1939, to Helen Brent Henderson Cade, whom she has called "my first friend, teacher, map maker, landscape aide" (Dedication, *The Salt Eaters*). Her childhood was spent in various urban neighborhoods from Harlem and Queens to Jersey City; here she first became aware of "the power of the word, the importance of the resistance tradition, and the high standards our community has regarding verbal performance'' (''Salvation'' 46). Her mother took her to Speaker's Corner at Seventh Avenue and 125th Street where she heard ''Garveyites, Father Diviners, Rastafarians, Muslims, trade unionists, communists, Pan-Africanists ('' ''What It Is'' 155), while her father introduced her to the Apollo Theater and to the Peace Barber Shop, where she learned ''what it meant to be a good storyteller'' (''Toni'' 28–29). As a ''nosey kid running up and down the street, getting into everything'' (''Commitment'' 233), she met a great variety of people who would later influence her writing, as would the music she heard in ''bebop heaven,'' her term for New York City (''Toni'' 29).

While the outside world provided her with stimulations of the imagination and models for communicating, her mother gave her the freedom and privacy to develop the inner self: ''In our household, our selves were our turf, and our mental zones were as respected as physical zones are in some others'' (''Thinking'' 156). Indeed, one of Bambara's fondest, and most telling, memories is of her mother's mopping around the 9-year-old daydreaming in the middle of the kitchen floor (Dedication, *The Salt Eaters*). Her mother not only gave her ''permission to wonder, to dawdle, to daydream'' (''Toni'' 28) but also served as a role model both on the literary and political levels—reading books, building bookcases, and taking bold stands against unfair or racist treatment of blacks. In ''Thinking about My Mother,'' Bambara recalls a striking example of the latter, describing her mother's classroom visit to a teacher who had been guilty of ''racist lunacies''; forcing an apology from the terrified teacher, she was seen not just as Bambara's mother, but as ''everybody's champion'' (155).

Bambara began her literary career by ''scribbling tales'' on strips from her father's newspapers and on white cardboard squares from her mother's stocking boxes (''Salvation'' 41) and soon progressed to writing plays on important black figures such as Frederick Douglass and George Washington Carver for elementary school programs. In high school, by her own admission, she ''hogged the lit journal,'' and as an undergraduate at Queens College she was active in theatre and wrote in every genre (even ''unnameables''), winning the John Golden Award for Fiction and graduating with a degree in theater arts and English literature in 1959 (''Salvation'' 41). That year also saw the publication of her first short story, ''Sweet Town,'' in *Vendome*. These stories appear in *Gorilla, My Love* (1972).

During the 1960s, a period during which she has said that she came of age, Bambara began to develop her myriad interests, being involved in literary, cultural, educational, and political activities. She published several more short stories, including ''Mississippi Ham Rider'' (*Massachusetts Review*, 1960), ''The Hammer Man'' (*Negro Digest*, 1966), and ''Maggie of the Green Bottles'' (*Prairie Schooner*, 1967), as well as reviews, although at this stage of her life she considered writing ''rather frivolous,'' an avocation or entertainment set aside from one's ''real work'' (''Commitment'' 232). After her graduation from Queens, she worked for a year at the Harlem Welfare Center and then spent 1961 in Italy and France studying theatre. From 1962 to 1965, she was simultaneously pursuing the M.A. in American literature at City College of New York (1963) and serving as director of recreation in Metropolitan Hospital's psychiatric department (1962–64), as program director at Colony House Community Center (1964–65), and as coordinator of various neighborhood programs. In 1965, her relationship with the educational world shifted from student to teacher when she became an English instructor at the City College of New York, a position she held until 1969. She devoted much of the next 15 years to teaching, lecturing, and giving workshops. She has described herself as "a very seductive teacher, persuasive, infectious, overwhelming, irresistible," who encouraged her students not to succumb to "mere charm and flash" but to challenge and critique her; she first wrote seriously when she began teaching as "a way to keep track of myself, to monitor myself" ("Toni" 18–19).

The decade of the 1970s was Bambara's most prolific in terms of her writing, for she produced two anthologies, two short story collections, a novel, and numerous articles and essays; yet she also continued to teach and made several trips that significantly affected her views and attitudes. From 1969 to 1974 she was an assistant and then associate professor of English at Livingston College of Rutgers University in New Brunswick, New Jersey. In 1970 she edited *The Black Woman*, an important anthology of writings by black women defying both racism and sexism in a search for fulfillment, identity, and power that challenges and rejects the conventional position of the black woman as "de mule uh de world" (Bell 239). In the preface, she describes the book as "a beginning—a collection of poems, stories, essays . . . that seem best to reflect the preoccupations of the contemporary Black woman in this country" (11). As the editor as well as the author of the preface and three articles, Bambara established herself as a leading spokesperson for the black feminist movement. In a 1985 interview, feeling that "by now [*The Black Woman*] should just be considered an interesting historical curiosity," she expressed alarm that it "is still used and is startling in some quarters" ("Not About" 148).

While she wrote and edited as Toni Cade through the publication of *The Black Woman*, in 1970 she added Bambara to her name after finding a book with a similar signature in her great-grandmother's trunk (Deck 13). The name of this tribe in the upper Niger region of the Republic of Mali—known for their indigenous method of writing, their remarkable system of cosmology, and their animistic cults and myths ("Bambara," *Encyclopaedia Britannica*)—no doubt appealed to her in its evocation of her African heritage, her vocation as a writer, and her interests in metaphysics and the language of symbols.

Using this new name, she edited a second anthology entitled *Tales and Stories for Black Folks* in 1971. As Bambara notes in the preface, the intention of the book is to present black youths with the opportunity "to learn how to listen, to be proud of our oral tradition, our elders who tell their tales in the kitchen. For they are truth" (12). The anthology contains stories "I wished I had read growing up" ("Commitment" 240) by established black writers such as Alice Walker, Langston Hughes, Ernest Gaines, and Bambara herself as well as Afro-American fables by lesser-known writers and by students in Bambara's composition course at Livingston College. Many of the tales have political undertones, particularly those written by her students, who altered traditional European stories to "promote critical thinking, critical reading" for the youngsters they were working with in independent community schools ("Commitment" 241); for example, "The Three Little Panthers" by Bambara and Geneva Powell is an allegory asserting that minorities should not adapt to the hostile dominant culture but seek enrichment and selfhood in their own.

In 1972 *Gorilla, My Love*, her first collection of short stories, was published to good reviews. Focusing largely on children and teens in urban environments, the stories won praise for their accurate portrayal of black life, for their reproduction of black dialect, and for their combination of humor and wisdom. Perhaps most striking are the young female protagonists, who are both tough and sensitive, streetwise and naive, aggressive and vulnerable. Bambara has described most of these stories as "on-the-block, in-the-neighborhood, back-glance pieces" ("Toni" 24).

Bambara's trips to Cuba in 1973 and to Vietnam in 1975 enriched and expanded her political views and her concept of writing. In Cuba her experiences with the Federation of Cuban Women in particular made her realize the possibilities for resolving both class and color conflicts inherent in "a mass organization" ("Commitment" 238); in addition, the trip led her to acknowledge for the first time that "writing was my way of doing my work in the world, . . . a legitimate way, an important way, to participate in the empowerment of the community that names me" ("Salvation" 42). From this point on, Bambara combined her two great interests to become a writer with a declared political agenda of advancing the cause of her race and especially of black women. In Vietnam she was again struck by the power generated when women band together ("Commitment" 238) and saw more fully the effectiveness of activism and organization on the community level, with the result that she dedicated herself to forming coalitions of blacks, of women of color, and of writers as a means of achieving support and gaining power.

Along with her four-year-old daughter Karma, Bambara moved to Atlanta, Georgia, in 1974. During the next several years, she held teaching posts in various colleges, universities, and schools: Visiting professor of African American Studies at Duke University (1974); artist-in-residence at Stephens College (1975) and at Spelman College (1974–77); consultant in Women's Studies at Atlanta University and Emory University (1976); and Program Coordinator for the Arts-in-the-Schools Project of the Atlanta Public School System (1976). Concurrently, she was involved in a number of community activities and was a founding member of such cultural/literary organizations as the Southern Collective of African-American Writers and the Conference Committee on Black South Literature and Art.

As Alice A. Deck indicates, the stories in her 1977 collection *The Seabirds Are Still Alive*, most of which were written in the early to mid-1970s, reflect the influences of her foreign travels, her move to Atlanta, and her involvement in community and cultural groups (18). Bambara herself describes them as "on-the-block and larger-world-of-struggle pieces, very contemporary, and much less back-glance" ("Toni" 24). Longer than those in the first collection and more directly political in content, many focus on young women searching for their niche in the world, particularly in terms of their role in the struggle of black people for autonomy ("The Apprentice," "Broken Field Running," "The Organizer's Wife," and "The Long Night," for example). Although the majority take place in urban settings of the North and the South, "The Organizer's Wife" is located in the rural South and the title story in an Asian country.

Although preferring the short story's "form, . . . size, . . . [and] modest appeal for attention" ("Not About" 149), Bambara turned in the late 1970s to the novel because "the major publishing industry, the academic establishment, reviewers, and critics favor the novel. . . . [The] move to the novel was not occasioned by a recognition of having reached the limits of the [short story] genre or the practitioner's disillusion with it, but rather Career, Economics, Critical attention" ("Salvation" 43). The tour de force, *The Salt Eaters* (1980), reflects the new motivation; it is complex and difficult in content and in style. Although centered on the immediate problem of restoring the will to live to a mature black woman who has attempted suicide as a result of her disillusionment with her personal life, her political aspirations, and the world at large, the book projects into the future, raising disturbing questions about much larger issues including the fate of the black race, of black women, of the human race and the planet itself. As Bambara herself defines it: "It's on-the-block, but the borders of the town of Claybourne, Georgia . . . do not contain or hem in the story" ("Toni" 24). It received the American Book Award in 1981.

In the early 1980s, Bambara continued "the stretch out toward the future," considering issues such as effective alliances within the black community (linking "our warriors with our medicine people") and among women of color in the last quarter of the century as well as experimenting with the English language by pressing it "to accommodate flashforwards and potential happenings" ("Toni" 25) and searching for a new vocabulary for the black, particularly female, experience of the future. She began a second novel based on the Atlanta Missing and Murdered Children case, originally entitled *Till Blessing Comes* (see "Not About" 151–53). She has described this work as a "documentary narrative that reads like a novel in which I invite the reader to look at the Missing and Murdered Children case as one in a series of multiple killings that took place . . . in Atlanta, to look at the case in light of what is happening throughout Blackamerica—the escalation of unprovoked attacks on Blacks physically, economically, culturally, politically" ("Interview" 44). However, she withdrew it from publication in the late 1980s and continues work on it under the title *Ground Cover*.

Currently living in Philadelphia, Bambara has turned to film and video as a new means of expression. As she indicated in an interview in the early 1980s:

"I'm much more interested in filmmaking [now]. . . . There's not too much more I want to experiment with in terms of writing" ("Toni" 25). As a media activist working in independent black cinema, she produced the award-winning PBS documentary "The Bombing of Osage Avenue" (1986) and is at work on various other film projects, including one on Senegalese, African-American, and other blacks in the concentration camps during World War II. In the future she plans to continue making films and training community videomakers. She feels that black female filmmakers are part of the significant worldwide breakthrough evident in the chorus of black female writers, artists, scholars, and academics who are now reclaiming their tradition.

MAJOR THEMES

As essayist, short-story writer, novelist, and filmmaker, Bambara takes an adversarial stance. Probing, challenging, defiant, she is often unsettling and disturbing as she forces her audience to rethink well-established conventions, to experience new modes of expression, and to adopt new views of community and the world. She would no doubt respond as has Edward Albee to the comment that his work is disturbing with "I certainly hope so!" Raised "to be a combatant" ("Salvation" 45), she sees writing (and now filmmaking) as a political/ social act, as "a perfectly legitimate way to participate in struggle. I don't have to be out there running in the streets or at the barricades. This counts too" ("Searching" 51). Calling herself "a brazenly 'message' writer" ("What It Is" 161), she has a clearly declared dual political agenda: To encourage the black community in general and its women in particular to seek autonomy, power, and fulfillment and to warn whites, males, and apathetic blacks that a new day is coming. This "message" is essentially positive and optimistic in its implication that such an achievement is possible (Salaam 53) and should be ardently striven for despite obstacles, setbacks, and disappointments. As she herself describes the "givens" that inform her work: "One, we are at war. Two, the natural response to oppression, ignorance, evil, and mystification is wide-awake resistance. Three, the natural response to stress and crisis is not breakdown and capitulation, but transformation and renewal to" ("Salvation" 47).

Her commitment to the empowerment of the black community determines not only content and theme but also style and structure in her work. Her major themes in this arena include the search for black autonomy, the ongoing resistance to the dominant white culture, and the return to the African heritage as a source of strength and wisdom. Her fable "The Three Little Panthers" uses allegory to urge young blacks to reject the dominant alien culture in favor of their own, in which they will "be loved and be for real" (*Tales* 141). In "The Lesson," one of her best-known short stories, Sylvia is forced to confront the harsh reality of being, by virtue of her race, on the short end of the economic stick: After taking her and her friends to F.A.O. Schwartz, their mentor asks them to "imagine for a minute what kind of society it is in which some people can spend on a toy what it would cost to feed a family of six or seven" (*Gorilla* 95). In "The Apprentice" the ardent community activist Naomi asks the young woman whom she is training: "Can you just imagine . . . the energy that would be released if we were working for ourselves, for our neighbors, our children? If we owned the country? The whole damn country, I'm talking about? If it was ours to administer, to develop, ours?" (*Sea Birds* 37).

Her concern with racial identity also leads her to break with the literary conventions of white, European-American culture and instead to "invent . . . new forms, new modes and new idioms," to "create a written language in English that can express the African-American experience" ("Searching" 48). To that end she writes in the black voice, echoing the actual diction, grammar, pronunciation (indicated by spelling words as they would be pronounced), and sayings of the vernacular: "Yawl better tell me what's up . . . 'cause this here getting spoooo-keeee" (*Sea Birds* 177); "[Aunt Gretchen] been screwed into the go-along for so long, it's a blood-deep natural thing with her. Which is how she got saddled with me and Sugar and Junior in the first place while our mothers were in a la-de-la apartment up the block having a good ole time" (*Gorilla* 88). As Hull points out: "No one writing today can beat [Bambara] at capturing the black voice" (223). Further, the essentially black musical forms of jazz, blues, be-bop, gospel, and spiritual are evident not only in her speech rhythms but also in her structures, which sometimes follow improvisational and nonlogical modes in place of traditional linear European ones. Finally, her images and symbols reflect both the contemporary black world and ancient African traditions. Allusions to the Washington movie theatre on Amsterdam Avenue, the Chicken Shack restaurant, soul food, Jiffy Mart, the projects, drug dealers on urban corners, co-op schools, bronze Barbie dolls, and "big fro murder-mouth militant sister[s]" (*Sea Birds* 172) contribute a sense of reality, while those to Kwanza celebrations, voodoo queens, and a Yoruba cultural center convey the strength, richness, and wisdom available in the cultural heritage.

Equally important in Bambara's work is the emphasis on black feminism, which also influences both theme and technique. She is concerned to present the complexities of black female experience, portraying black women who resist oppression both by white society and by black males, who search for and often attain independence, creativity, and power, and who join together in a bond of solidarity. As early as 1970 in *The Black Woman*, she argues that black women must "find out what liberation for ourselves means, what work it entails, what benefits it will yield" (7) and that they must not depend on white feminists but must turn to each other (9); further, she insists that they must share in "policymaking and privileges" and be treated as equals by black males as were their African foremothers (103).

In her short fiction she gives center stage to a gallery of black females memorable for their spunk, their vulnerability, their determination, and their wit. Collectively, they form a broad spectrum of black female experience, from that of young girls through that of old women. Many of her youngsters must confront harsh realities, but they do so with strength, defiance, or simply acceptance: Ollie spends a sad birthday alone in "Happy Birthday" (*Gorilla, My Love*); Sylvia learns the painful truth that she is a member of an economically deprived class in "The Lesson" (*Gorilla, My Love*); and Rae Ann suffers both terror and humiliation when she has her first menstrual period in "A Girl's Story" (*The Seabirds Are Still Alive*), one of Bambara's most moving pieces. A more positive portrait is found in Hazel Elizabeth Deborah Parker in "Raymond's Run" (*Gorilla, My Love*), for she becomes her own person, refusing to be in the Maypole dance and preferring instead to run in the May Day races—and win; even more admirable is Hazel's unselfish love for her retarded brother.

In writing about young black girls Bambara attempts to fill a void. As she puts it: "The initiation or rites of passage of the young girl is not one of the darlings of American literature" ("Commitment" 247). The college girl who narrates "The Johnson Girls" (*Gorilla*) observes with great sensitivity and appreciation the support and advice given by a group of women to Inez when her lover deserts her. Naomi in "The Apprentice" and Lacey in "Broken Field Running" (both in *Seabirds*) are committed workers for the people who refuse to give in to despair. Honey, the leading character in "Witchbird" (*Seabirds*), is a middle-aged blues singer struggling to succeed in her career and to break free of her victimization by a former lover. Miss Hazel, the elderly narrator of "My Man Bovanne" (*Gorilla*), shocks and embarrasses her grown children when she behaves in a manner that they consider unacceptable for a woman her age. Sweet Pea in "Medley" (*Seabirds*), a working woman who excels at her job as manicurist and who finally rejects the weak, unsuccessful man opposing her desire for independence and selfhood, may best represent Bambara's ideal for the contemporary black female. Bambara has created realistic rather than stereotypic images of black women (Bell 242), characters whose power derives, as Mary Helen Washington suggests, from the fact that her attitude toward them is "deeply partisan—she is fully invested in them, likes them, wants them to succeed, refuses to diminish them" ("[Re]Visions" 353).

In writing about the black female experience, Bambara seeks to create a female vocabulary and imagery. As she notes: "We've only just begun, I think, to fashion a woman's vocabulary to deal with the 'silences' of our lives" ("Toni" 20). Although she feels that young black women writers will be the ones to develop this "new vocabulary of images" ("Searching" 51), she clearly has made an impressive start. Perhaps most obvious are her allusions to black female blues singers, early civil rights activists, and African foremothers; however, she also makes inventive use of domestic imagery, such as comparing a perfect man to a "blue-plate special" and symbolizing the ending of a relationship by the water turning cold in the shower.

Her two major themes combine powerfully in her novel *The Salt Eaters*, in that its protagonist Velma Henry has attempted suicide as a result of her disillusionment as a political leader dedicated to the advancement of her race and as a woman in search of identity, fulfillment, and strength in her varied female roles. The book's concerns move out in ever-widening circles, an image noted by Gloria Hull (217), to include larger political, cultural, economic, racial, and feminist issues such as the inferior role accorded to black women in politics, the problem of industrial pollution, and the power to be gained by creating coalitions of women of color.

The Salt Eaters is stunning not only for its powerful themes but also for its innovations in structure, vocabulary, and imagery. Its daring and radical originality in terms of black women's literature of the 1980s might be compared to that of T. S. Eliot's *The Waste Land* in terms of white male European-American literature of the 1920s; indeed, *The Salt Eaters* shares a number of techniques with those of Eliot's great poem. Its fragmented and chaotic structure reflects the fragmentation of Velma's shattered self; its panoramic scope suggests the universality of its concerns; its mood of malaise expands from the individual to the entire civilization; its shuttling back and forth between time periods denotes the simultaneity of time; and its images and allusions draw on archetypal African and female material (the mud mothers and the loas) as well as on contemporary culture. Finally, as in *The Waste Land*, the ending implies a hope, however ambiguous or unclear in specifics, for healing and wholeness, not just for Velma but also for the race and sex for which she is a symbol. The key, as Bernard Bell points out, is found in one's own people and traditions, particularly those that are of a spiritual, nonrational nature (268).

Bambara has called herself an upbeat writer, one who is convinced that "everything will be all right" ("What It Is" 158). Her essentially positive attitude is reflected in the endurance of her characters who survive despite pain and hardship; in her conviction that black people in general and black women in particular will attain power, selfhood, and fulfillment; and in her sense of humor, her comic spirit, which informs her work as a whole with joy, surprise, and delight. Yet she never loses sight of her commitments (1) to attack injustice and oppression, (2) to challenge conventions, both philosophical and technical, and (3) to strike out boldly into new territory.

SURVEY OF CRITICISM

Although Bambara is an important voice in contemporary black literature, she has received a rather modest amount of critical attention; indeed, many of the scholarly books on recent black writers overlook her entirely or accord her only brief mention.

Prior to the early 1980s, criticism was limited entirely to reviews of specific works. Her first two publications, *The Black Woman* and *Tales and Stories for Black Folks*, drew virtually no critical response, with the notable exception of a favorable review of the latter by Toni Morrison. *Gorilla, My Love* fared much better, garnering positive reviews in such publications as the *New York Times Book Review*, *Black World*, and *Saturday Review*. In general it was praised for its accurate portrayal of black life and language and for its humor and wisdom;

Lucille Clifton, for example, noted that Bambara "has captured it all, how we really talk, how we really are" (Book cover, *Gorilla*). Although *The Sea Birds Are Still Alive* was also rather widely reviewed, the judgments were more varied; criticism of "the excessive and heavy-handed effort to reproduce the Black idiom" (Rev. of *Seabirds* 854), weak character development, and the blunt political content was interspersed with admiration for her creation of individual characters such as Honey in "Witchbird" and for her poetic use of words. The most important of these early commentaries is perhaps Mary Helen Washington's essay review of *Sea Birds* entitled "Blues Women of the Seventies," in which she extolled "the contemporaneity of these stories, their variety, and their daring to examine previously unexplored aspects of black women's lives" (37); however, her praise was tempered by her criticism that the characters "slip all too easily . . . into being mouthpieces for the writer's ideology" (38).

Publication of *The Salt Eaters* in 1980 evoked a torrent of reviews in magazines from *The New Yorker* to *Ms.* to *Black Scholar*. Owing to the book's complexity of plot and style, reviewers tended to devote a majority of their comments to summaries of what happens and to descriptions of major characters. Most were largely favorable, recognizing its ambitious scope ("a kind of tribal epic," Susan Lardner 170), crackling energy, and innovative techniques; Lardner perhaps best summed up the general appreciation in calling it "a book full of marvels" (171). Black reviewers in particular saw it as a call to regroup, to become revitalized and rededicated, praising Bambara for her foresight and brilliance: "Read the genius work of our sister, Toni Cade Bambara. Let the healing of Velma Henry, and the people of Clayborne, be a part of your own healing" (Angela Jackson 52). Negative comments focused on the most difficult and perplexing elements of the novel: its abrupt shifts in time, its multiplicity of characters, its political content, and its language. Anne Tyler, for example, objected that "too many people swarm by too quickly. Too much is described elliptically" (2), whereas Rumens complained of its "rather introverted and convoluted performance, [which makes few] concessions to the uninitiated" (676). Ironically, its strengths were often also cited as its weaknesses; its enormous, panoramic scope and the complexity of its vision drew both praise and criticism, often from the same reviewer (see, for example, John Wideman). Especially perceptive were the essay reviews of Lardner, Wideman, Jerry W. Ward, Tyler, Kalamu ya Salaam, and Eleanor W. Traylor, the latter of which has been noted by Bambara herself as her own favorite.

The first critical study to consider Bambara's work ("My Man Bovanne" in *Gorilla*) was Jerilyn Fisher's 1978 article on the fiction of black and Chicano women in the 1970s. Not until 1983 with the publication of two essays did a body of criticism begin to emerge. Nancy D. Hargrove's "Youth in Toni Cade Bambara's *Gorilla, My Love*" presents a study of her innovative treatment of the initiation theme in young black girls, suggesting that Bambara creates a black female version of the white male bildungsroman tradition seen in writers such as Mark Twain, James Joyce, and J. D. Salinger, and Gloria Hull's " 'What It

Is I Think She's Doing Anyhow' " is a sensitive and immensely helpful reading of *The Salt Eaters*. Written from a teacher's point of view and aimed specifically at black students who may find the novel difficult, Hull's article argues that there are "compelling reasons for studying [the novel]," the most important of which is that it "fixes our present and challenges the way to the future" (216). Covering plot, theme, characters, language, and symbols, Hull's analysis remains the single best study of the novel to date.

In 1984, two critical essays appeared in Mari Evans' anthology *Black Women Writers*. Ruth Elizabeth Burks explores the inadequacy of language to "provoke positive action" as demonstrated in Bambara's two collections of short stories and her novel, arguing that, "in the final analysis, *The Salt Eaters* does not work" (56). Eleanor W. Traylor, in a revised and expanded version of her earlier review, analyzes the use in *The Salt Eaters* of the jazz mode as a modern stylistic and structural device working in harmony with the ancient lore of African tradition: "The improvising, stylizing, vamping, recreative method of the jazz composer is the formal method by which the narrative genius of Toni Cade Bambara evokes a usable past testing its values within an examined present moment while simultaneously exploring the re-creative and transformative possibilities of experience" (65).

The year 1985 saw the publication of three more essays, as well as a chapter in a book on recent black literature. Alice Deck's informative and comprehensive article in the *Dictionary of Literary Biography* offers the first overall view of Bambara's life and literary career. Proceeding chronologically, she presents biographical material, discusses her work from *The Black Woman* through *The Salt Eaters*, and summarizes the critical response to each. In "The Comic Sense in the Short Stories of Toni Cade Bambara," Nancy D. Hargrove focuses on Bambara's skillful use of the elements of comedy in *Gorilla, My Love*, concluding that through humor she not only provides enjoyment but also makes serious comments about the human experience. Ruth Rosenberg, although writing in an elementary style, does an intriguing study of the names of the major characters in the novel. Finally, Keith E. Byerman's *Fingering the Jagged Grain: Tradition and Form in Recent Black Fiction* contains a chapter on Bambara and Alice Walker (a pairing questioned by Washington, "[Re]Visions" 393), in which he argues that both writers present folk wisdom as the principal source of strength for black women in their struggle to survive the bleak, often painful circumstances of their lives. Although he traces this theory through the short stories and the novel, Byerman dilutes his argument by dealing with various other issues (gender, male-female conflict, ideology, race). Furthermore, his suggestion that *The Salt Eaters* calls for an abandonment of feminism, capitalism, ecology, and other ideological systems in favor of a return to the folk wisdom of ancient beliefs (125) is debatable.

In 1987 and 1988, Bambara received substantial treatment in three more important books on contemporary black literature and in a scholarly article. In "Problematizing the Individual" (1987) Susan Willis considers Bambara's fiction from a political/historical perspective, focusing on the role of the individual revolutionary leader. Her reading of *The Salt Eaters* is particularly provocative. Bernard Bell's comprehensive study, *The Afro-American Novel and Its Tradition* (1987), offers brief but perceptive comments on Bambara as a champion of black women who presents realistic rather than stereotypical images of them; classifying *The Salt Eaters* as a novel of critical realism that explores the theme of black feminism, he praises its "extraordinarily insightful synthesis of traditional and modern conventions" (277). In *Being and Race: Black Writing since 1970* (1988) Charles Johnson devotes several pages to a discussion of Bambara as a "truly comic writer... [whose] strength is snappy, hip dialogue and an ever-crackling narrative style" (103–4). Byerman's essay "Healing Arts" in *Postscript*'s 1988 issue is a further consideration of the relationship of folklore to the development of the female self in *The Salt Eaters*.

Most recently, Martha M. Vertreace explores the relationship between the individual and the community in Bambara's short stories in an essay in *American Women Writing Fiction* (1989). Although she contributes little original discussion, the extensive bibliography is valuable even though marred by errors. Another helpful bibliography is found in Rhonda Glikin's *Black American Women in Literature: A Bibliography, 1976–1987* (1989). Washington's *Black-Eyed Susans/Midnight Birds* (1990), a combination and revision of her two earlier anthologies of stories by and about black women, contains an excellent introduction with specific references to Bambara in addition to a short essay on her female characters and a brief annotated bibliography.

Given the relative paucity of scholarship on Bambara's work, her comment that the critical world insists on a writer's producing novels in order to win its attention ("Salvation" 43) seems, unfortunately, to be all too true. Although publication of her second novel, *Ground Cover*, on which she is still working, would certainly inspire further commentary, it is to be hoped that, as the body of scholarship on contemporary black women writers continues to grow, Bambara's fiction will be given the more extensive treatment that it deserves, with or without the appearance of additional novels.

BIBLIOGRAPHY

Works by Toni Cade Bambara

The Black Woman: An Anthology, ed. Toni Cade. New York: Signet, 1970.
Tales and Stories for Black Folks, ed. Toni Cade Bambara. Garden City, N.Y.: Zenith, 1971.
Gorilla, My Love. New York: Random House, 1972.
"Thinking about My Mother." *Redbook* (September 1973): 73, 155–56.
Southern Exposure: Southern Black Utterances Today, ed. Toni Cade Bambara and Leah Wise. Atlanta: Institute for Southern Studies, 1975.
The Sea Birds Are Still Alive. New York: Random House, 1977.
The Salt Eaters. New York: Random House, 1980.

"What It Is I Think I'm Doing Anyhow," in *The Writer on Her Work*, ed. Janet Sternburg.
    New York: Norton, 1980.
"Salvation Is the Issue," in *Black Women Writers (1950–1980): A Critical Evaluation*,
    ed. Mari Evans. Garden City, New York: Doubleday, 1984.

Interviews

"Commitment: Toni Cade Bambara Speaks." Interview by Beverly Guy-Sheftall, in
    Sturdy Black Bridges: Visions of Black Women in Literature, ed. Roseann Bell,
    Bettye S. Parker, and Beverly Guy-Sheftall. Garden City, N.Y.: Doubleday, 1979.
"Searching for the Mother Tongue." Interview by Kalamu ya Salaam, *First World* 2
    (1980): 48–52.
"Interview with Toni Cade Bambara." Interview by Deborah Jackson, *Drum Magazine*
    (Spring 1982): 43–44.
" 'The Organizer's Wife': A Reading By and Interview with Toni Cade Bambara."
    Interview by Kay Bonetti, in Columbia, Mo.: American Audio Prose Library,
    1982.
"Toni Cade Bambara." Interview by Claudia Tate, in *Black Women Writers at Work*,
    ed. Claudia Tate. New York: Continuum, 1983.
"Not About to Play It Safe: An Interview with Toni Cade Bambara." Interview by Justine
    Tally, *Revista Canaria de Estudios Ingleses* 11 (November 1985): 141–53.
"Voices Beyond the Veil: An Interview of Toni Cade Bambara and Sonia Sanchez."
    Interview by Zala Chandler, in *Wild Women in the Whirlwind: Afro-American
    Culture and the Contemporary Literary Renaissance*, ed. Joanne M. Braxton and
    Andrea Nicola McLaughlin. New Brunswick, N.J.: Rutgers University Press,
    1990.

Television and Film Scripts and Productions

"Zora." WGBN, 1971.
"The Johnson Girls." WNET, 1972.
"The Long Night." ABC, 1981.
"Epitaph for Willie." K. Herman Productions, 1982.
"Tar Baby." Adaptation of Toni Morrison's novel. Sanger, Brooks Film Productions,
    1984.
"Raymond's Run." American Short Story Series, PBS, 1985.
"The Bombing of Osage Avenue." WHYY, 1986.
"Cecil B. Moore: Master Technician of Direct Action." WHYY, 1987.

Studies of Toni Cade Bambara

Bell, Bernard. *The Afro-American Novel and Its Tradition*. Amherst: University of Mas-
    sachusetts Press, 1987.
Burks, Ruth Elizabeth. "From Baptism to Resurrection: Toni Cade Bambara and the
    Incongruity of Language," in *Black Women Writers (1950–1980): A Critical
    Evaluation*, ed. Mari Evans. Garden City, N.Y.: Doubleday, 1984.
Byerman, Keith E. *Fingering the Jagged Grain: Tradition and Form in Recent Black
    Fiction*. Athens: University of Georgia Press, 1985.
———. "Healing Arts: Folklore and the Female Self in Toni Cade Bambara's *The Salt
    Eaters*." *Postscript* 5 (1988): 37–43.

Clifton, Lucille. Book cover. *Gorilla, My Love*. New York: Random House, 1972.

Deck, Alice A. "Toni Cade Bambara," in *Dictionary of Literary Biography: Afro-American Writers after 1955*. Detroit: Gale Research, 1985.

Fisher, Jerilyn. "From Under the Yoke of Race and Sex: Black and Chicano Women's Fiction of the Seventies." *Minority Voices: An Interdisciplinary Journal of Literature and the Arts* 2 (1978): 1–14.

Glikin, Ronda. *Black American Women in Literature: A Bibliography, 1976–1987*. Jefferson, N.C.: McFarland, 1989.

Hargrove, Nancy D. "The Comic Sense in the Short Stories of Toni Cade Bambara." *Revista Canaria de Estudios Ingleses* 11 (November 1985): 133–40.

———. "Youth in Toni Cade Bambara's *Gorilla, My Love*." *Southern Quarterly* 22 (1983): 81–99. Reprinted in *Women Writers of the Contemporary South*, ed. Peggy Whitman Prenshaw. Jackson: University Press of Mississippi, 1984.

Hull, Gloria. " 'What It Is I Think She's Doing Anyhow': A Reading of Toni Cade Bambara's *The Salt Eaters*," in *Home Girls: A Black Feminist Anthology*, ed. Barbara Smith. New York: Women of Color Press, 1983. Reprinted in a slightly different version in *Conjuring: Black Women, Fiction, and Literary Tradition*, ed. Marjorie Pryse and Hortense J. Spillers. Bloomington: Indiana University Press, 1985.

Jackson, Angela. Rev. of *The Salt Eaters*. *The Black Scholar* 13 (Fall 1982): 52.

Johnson, Charles. *Being and Race: Black Writing since 1970*. Bloomington: Indiana University Press, 1988.

Lardner, Susan. "Books: Third Eye Open." *The New Yorker* (5 May 1980): 169–73.

Rev. of *The Seabirds Are Still Alive*. *Choice* 14 (September 1977): 854.

Rosenberg, Ruth. " 'You Took a Name that Made You Amiable to the Music': Toni Cade Bambara's *The Salt Eaters*." *Literary Omnastics Studies* 12 (1985): 165–94.

Rumens, Carol. "Heirs to the Dream." *Times Literary Supplement* (18 June 1982): 676.

Salaam, Kalamu ya. "Commentary." *First World* 2 (1980): 52–53.

Traylor, Eleanor W. "*The Salt Eaters*: My Soul Looks Back in Wonder." *First World* 2 (Summer 1981): 44–47, 64. Reprinted in revised form as "Music as Theme: The Jazz Mode in the Works of Toni Cade Bambara," in *Black Women Writers (1950–1980): A Critical Evaluation*, ed. Mari Evans. Garden City, N.Y.: Doubleday, 1984.

Tyler, Anne. "At the Still Center of a Dream." *Washington Post* (30 March 1980): 1–2.

Vertreace, Martha M. "Toni Cade Bambara: The Dance of Character and Community," in *American Women Writing Fiction*, ed. Mickey Pearlman. Lexington: University Press of Kentucky, 1989.

Ward, Jerry W. Rev. of *The Salt Eaters*. *New Orleans Review* 18 (Summer 1981): 207–8.

Washington, Mary Helen. "Blues Women of the Seventies." *Ms.* (July 1977): 36–38.

———. "(Re)Visions: Black Women Writers—Their Texts, Their Readers, Their Critics" and "Toni Cade Bambara," in *Black-Eyed Susans/Midnight Birds*, ed. Mary Helen Washington. New York: Anchor, 1990.

Wideman, John. "The Healing of Velma Henry." *New York Times Book Review* 1 (June 1980): 14.

Willis, Susan. "Problematizing the Individual: Toni Cade Bambara's Stories for the Revolution," in *Specifying: Black Women Writing the American Experience*. Madison: University of Wisconsin Press, 1987.

R. REED SANDERLIN

Madison Smartt Bell
(1957–   )

Even though he is relatively young, Madison Smartt Bell is making a name for himself as one of the brightest and best of the new generation of Southern writers. His publication record to date includes six novels and two collections of short stories; a novel about the Haitian slave revolt is under way. In some respects his work is a blend of traditional narrative techniques and some of the features characteristic of work designated by the term postmodern, though his style and approach come nowhere near the excesses of those writers preceding his generation or of his generation who wanted to expose the "fictionality" of fictions. In fact, in most ways his narratives are traditional in form; it's the tone, the voice, the framing imagination lying behind the narrative that strike one as contemporary and fresh. His viewpoint is both Southern rural and big city urban, and at his best he is adept at switching from one setting to another and being perceptive and convincing in both. Certainly he is among those Southern fictionalists most capable, since William Styron, of incorporating that rural-urban, innocent-corrupt, naive-sophisticated diversity of what can be termed "modern consciousness."

BIOGRAPHY

Madison Smartt Bell was born on August 1, 1957, in Franklin, Tennessee, a small rural town in Williamson County, not far from Nashville. His mother, whose maiden name was Georgia Allen Wiggington, and his father, Henry Denmark Bell, still live in Franklin. His father is a lawyer who became circuit court judge for four rural counties, including Williamson. With the growth of Nashville and the development of the interstate highway system, Franklin and similar towns outlying Nashville have almost become like suburbs of the growing metropolis, so that Bell, like many of his generation, grew up in a farming area while having easy access to the life of a larger city close by. In fact, as a teenager he attended the Montgomery Bell Academy, a prestigious private boys' school in Nashville, from which he graduated in 1975.

From 1975 to 1979 he attended Princeton University and distinguished himself there with a major in English literature, graduating *summa cum laude* and being selected for Phi Beta Kappa. While attending Princeton he took courses from or worked with a number of outstanding teachers of fiction and fiction writing, and he cites several of these as having been important in his development as a writer. His writing received early honors during these undergraduate days, and in 1977 he won the Ward Mathis Prize for his short story "Triptych" and the following year the Francis Lemoyne Page Award for fiction.

Following his graduation from Princeton, he took a year off from his studies and lived in New York, where he worked at a variety of jobs, including security guard, production assistant, and sound man. He was also a picture research assistant and writer of readers' guides for the Franklin Library, and he worked as a manuscript reader and copy writer for Berkeley Publishing Corporation. In 1979 he cofounded a filmmakers' group called "185" and was a director of this commercial venture until 1984. In the group, his role included various kinds of technical work, and one of his film jobs was as a sound man for a movie about drug rehabilitation done for an Italian project. His work with movies and his experience as a sound technician are reflected in the thriller novel *Straight Cut* (1986).

In 1980 he enrolled in Hollins College to pursue a master's degree in English and creative wrting; during this year the outstanding quality of his work was once again acknowledged when he received the Andrew James Purdy Award. Finishing at Hollins in 1981, he moved back to New York, where he lived for the next four years. His first novel, *The Washington Square Ensemble*, was published by Ticknor and Fields in 1983.

He moved to Baltimore in 1985, where he married his wife, the poet Elizabeth Spires, on June 15, 1985. This was the same year his second novel, *Waiting for the End of the World*, was published. He became writer-in-residence in the English department of Goucher College, where he taught until 1986. In 1986, his third novel, *Straight Cut*, appeared. Following his teaching at Goucher, he taught at the University of South Maine and was a fellow of the McDowell Artist's Colony.

From 1984 on he has published, along with his novels, a significant number of short stories in such magazines as *Hudson Review*, *Harper's*, and *Cosmopolitan*, and his 1984 story "The Naked Lady" was collected in *The Best American Short Stories 1984*, as was the story "The Lie Detector," for *The Best American Short Stories 1987*. For two years, from 1984–86, at the beginning of this productive short-story period, he was lecturing and running fiction workshops at the Poetry Center of the 92nd Street Young Men and Young Women's Hebrew Association in New York City. More recently, he has had stories published in the *New Writers from the South*, a series now issued annually by

Algonquin Books. His first full collection of short stories was published in 1987 under the title *Zero db*, and his most recent collection, *Barking Man*, appeared in early 1990. Some of his most impressive work is with the short story, and "Barking Man," the title story of the recent collection, is a modernized version of the metamorphosis theme and a story likely to end up in fiction anthologies for years to come.

For a brief period Bell was involved with the Iowa Writer's Workshop at the University of Iowa, serving as visiting lecturer during 1987–88. He ran graduate-level fiction workshops and taught graduate seminars in the contemporary short story and the contemporary political novel. While he was at Iowa, *The Year of Silence*, his fourth novel, was published. In 1988 Bell returned to Goucher in Baltimore, the city where he currently resides. He has also served as an adjunct faculty member at Johns Hopkins University where he taught an advanced fiction workshop. His novel *Soldier's Joy* won the Southern Regional Council's Lillian Smith Award for fiction when it was published in 1989. This novel has for its setting a rural area just outside Nashville and is in some respects a work very different from his previous four novels, which were all either set in New York or had portions set in some other large urban areas.

Besides his fiction writing and teaching, Bell has also become in recent years a frequent reviewer of books for such publications as the *New York Times Book Review*, and the *Village Voice*, the *Philadelphia Inquirer*, the *London Standard*, the *North American Review*, *Southern Magazine*, the *Boston Globe*, and others. He has also written two screenplays, one for his novel *Waiting for the End of the World*, commissioned by Cine Paris, and another entitled *The Safety Net*, commissioned by Roger Corman. One of his early forays into the marketplace for academic writing between 1979 and 1983 resulted in several reader's guides for the Franklin Library. He has also contributed literary essays on the short story to various magazines or journals, one of the more interesting being "Less Is Less: The Dwindling American Short Story," which appeared in the April 1986 issue of *Harper's*. To date, his novels and the story collections have all been printed in one or more German, Danish, Dutch, Spanish, or Japanese translations.

MAJOR THEMES

Though he grew up in a rural area south of Nashville, Bell's earliest works display a recurring fascination with urban life, especially for those *isolato* types who frequent the modern streets. One of his most outstanding talents as a writer is the ability to create very different character types and to fashion voices distinctly their own. But up until *Soldier's Joy* the preponderance of his characters have been urban ones, usually disturbed and obsessive, at times tending to violence, dealing in drugs, and roaming the streets or the subterranean caverns beneath them.

As David Montrose said of Bell's first novel, *The Washington Square Ensemble*, Bell's purpose is to "anatomize the circumstances that create violent deeds instead of simply providing details of those deeds." This novel resembles a jazz composition in that its basic narrative technique is the use of five alternating voices that chronicle twenty-four hours in the life of heroin dealer Johnny B. Goode and four of his companions. By alternating the narrative perspectives, Bell establishes each character's background and emotional condition as they tread through the seedy underworld of New York City.

Johnny B. Goode, the central character, is a streetwise and charismatic heroin dealer whose consciousness forms the center of the novel and whose dominant will energizes his troop of pushers. The other members of this modern "jazz" group are Jusuf Ali, a seven-foot black muslim; Holy Mother, a veteran of the Attica uprising and a pusher-user; Santa Barbara, a voodoo cultist who is both crazy and reliable; and Porco Miserio, a burned-out saxophonist. This collection of misfits turns out to be not so much a chorus of voices as a series of solo performances used by Bell to depict the complexity and inner reality of those marginal to societal life.

The world of the deviant continues in Bell's next novel, *Waiting for the End of the World*. The central character is Clarence Larkin, who is a drunk, a failed pianist, and an epileptic mystic type who photographs the sick and maimed at Bellevue Hospital. Clarence is involved in a revolutionary plot with four others to blow up New York with a bomb device made from a stolen shipment of atomic materials. Each member of the group has been drawn to the radical group for various motives, and the novel's most interesting feature is the depiction of these characters. Other key figures are Simon Rohnstock, a rich ex-Harvard student turned radical; David Hutton, a Vietnam veteran; Charles Mercer, a graduate of the University of Chicago; and Ruben Carrera, a Puerto Rican youth who knows explosive devices. The shifting omniscient point of view permits Bell to construct the inner worlds of his strange characters that he so much likes to develop.

In *The Year of Silence* Bell again employs the narrative technique of multiple voices and shifting points of view. This novel also focuses on a set of characters alienated from each other, from life around them, and even from themselves. Thomas Larkin has returned from Europe following the disappearance of his brother, Clarence (the character from the previous novel, who apparently died from radiation sickness). In memory of his brother, Thomas has vowed to practice the piano for a year only on a wooden fingering board, even though he is a concert pianist. He has resumed his acquaintance with Weber, a friend from college. The novel is essentially about reactions to the death of Marian, Weber's girlfriend, from a drug overdose. This book also told from multiple perspectives, seems the weakest of Bell's novels, though even here there are some brilliant sections, especially the "Hour of Lead" chapter, which describes Marian's death.

One of Bell's concerns as a writer is the split he sees having occurred between the types of fiction read by the larger public and provided by publishing houses, and the types of fiction being written by serious writers. In the important essay on literature as a form of pleasure, published in *Antaeus*, Bell sees traditional realistic fiction more or less trapped in a kind of fictional ghetto. Today fictional realism is frequently identified with the genre books being produced by hack writers for a mass market, while more serious writers have become caught up in "postmodern" or "superfiction" techniques that have essentially cut off all but an "unspecified elite" of intellectuals and academics. The split occurs even in the use of such terms as *genre* and *literary*: for one group genre writing means second-rate, pulp realism; for the other, literary means cryptic, obscurantist, self-referential word games.

In his defense of literary realism, Bell says that recognition on the part of the reader is one of the joys of the literary experience: "Recognition, the reprise of the reader's prior knowledge in some form on which another imagination has worked, is not the only literary pleasure which exists, but is an important one" (133). This kind of recognition is more likely to occur, he says, "from literature which sincerely attempts to maintain some rapport, however tenuous, with a real world outside its own text."

From this reasoning, Bell concludes that to enlarge its readership serious fiction must recover something of its realistic traditions and must even be willing to tap the popular genre forms such as science fiction, the mystery story, the historical novel, the romance, and so forth. This was certainly part of his intent in his novel *Straight Cut*, a somewhat elevated and certainly stylistically sophisticated mystery story about a drug-trafficking scheme told by a first-person narrator who becomes innocently implicated.

Soldier's Joy is in many respects a very different novel from Bell's previous ones. For one thing, the setting is the rural South, just outside Nashville, and the narrative focus remains centered on the principal character, Thomas Laidlaw. Laidlaw, a returned Vietnam veteran, has settled on the homeplace where he grew up, living alone in a tenant house that remained after the main house owned by his father burned. Almost compulsively Laidlaw practices the banjo, eventually learning the drop-thumb style proficiently enough to become a regular performer on the Nashville nightclub scene.

The other main character is Rodney Redman, also a returned veteran whom Laidlaw has known for years. In fact, Redman is the son of the black man who once lived in the tenant house and worked for Laidlaw's father. Much of the novel treats the reconciliation of friendship between Laidlaw and Redman, the attempts to thwart a Ku Klux Klan plot to burn out Laidlaw, and Laidlaw's rescue of Brother Jacob, an evangelistic preacher who advocates the virtues of brotherly love and racial harmony, from an assassination attempt. This is the most typically "Southern" novel of any of Bell's longer fiction, and certainly the character types are a bit more traditional and conventional than those in his other works, though still eccentric.

Doctor Sleep (1991), Bell's sixth novel, has proven problematic for readers.

Adrian Strother, a former drug addict, is an American hypnotherapist now practicing in the London of Elizabeth II. He suffers from insomnia as intense as that of any of his patients. Jerry Leath Mills perceives that Strothers' condition is mirrored in the elliptical, disjunctive nature of the narrative he relates. Mills recognizes that the same angst with a disjointed world that disturbed the Italian scholar, scientist, philosopher, and declared heretic Giordano Bruno also disturbs Strother. But Mills is puzzled to find a reason why a writer as accomplished as Bell "decided to invest his talents in so blurred and unsinewed a tale."

The best answer probably comes from Bell himself. In "An Essay Introducing His Work in a Rather Lunatic Fashion," Bell gives an account of his Southern heritage and reflects on the condition of the contemporary world and the impending destruction of all life. He pays special attention to the issues that Bruno confronted and to issues that, in our time, Walker Percy has raised best. Bell ends by making an apologia for *Doctor Sleep*. Strother, he says, makes "the attempt in our age that Giordano Bruno did in his—to revive the ancient mythology and make it meet the new conditions, which perhaps are not so new after all. He often suspects he is losing his mind, and indeed he really is a maniac of sorts, but he is also a visionary."

Bell's two collections of short stories are a mixture of laconic humor, sensitive portraits of lonely and isolated people, and startling violence. In the first collection, *Zero db*, "Today Is a Good Day to Die," the story of the Battle of Little Bighorn from the point of view of one of the calvary officers, and the title story, "Zero db," are two of the most striking. "Barking Man," the title story in the second collection, *Barking Man*, equals the best of Kafka, and the stories "Witness" and "Black and Tan" are simple yet stunning accounts of physical violence on the one hand and emotional violence on the other.

SURVEY OF CRITICISM

There has been since the publication of his first novel in 1983 wide critical acclaim for Bell's work by reviewers, both as a novelist and as a short-story writer. Reviewers agree that Bell's key strengths are his keen eye for detail, an imagination that responds powerfully to city life, a lyrical sensitivity to the nuances of words, and his ability to create a wide range of unusual character types with distinctive voices. There were numerous plaudits for his first novel. Thomas Ruffan, in a review for the *Los Angeles Times*, praised it as "a flawed yet brilliant first book." He went on to say: "Bell has that rarest of literary gifts: the ability to make word into flesh, to delineate compelling vivid characters who bring to life the stark, harrowing world of tenements, derelict bars, shadowy alleyways and inner-city parks where deviant behavior is the norm." Ken Kalfus, writing in *The Nation*, qualified his praise by saying that the craziness of Bell's characters "tells us little that is important or true" (407). Mary Furness, in the *Times Literary Supplement*, called Bell "a master of demotic stream-of-consciousness and the descriptive commentary" (915).

Enthusiasm for *Waiting for the End of the World* was more subdued, though Bell was still widely praised for his writing skills and talent. *Kirkus Reviews* complained that the novel was "fashionably apocalyptic" and that the suspense was "woodenly inevitable and gothic and cliched." Meg Wolitzer praised the book in the *New York Times Book Review* but noted that the lyricism and terrorism of the novel did not quite mesh. David Remnick noted in his review for the *Washington Post* that there were problems with the plan of the novel itself though it contained "passages of real brilliance."

The widely held opinion seems to be that Bell is at times a brilliant writer, adept at developing rich and complicated characters and extremely good at discovering and presenting expressive details, as well as at powerful passages full of lyrical intensity.

But Bell seems to have some trouble working out plot structures, and at times the novels struggle to reach adequate closure. In some respects the endings of almost all of the novels seem forced, even the highly praised *Soldier's Joy*. David Bradley in a review for the *New York Times Book Review*, after heaping a great deal of praise, laments at the close of his review that the novel "loses its way at the end, degenerating into a gun-and-chase sequence a la 'Miami Vice.' " To a significant degree, the plot of *Straight Cut*, the mystery novel that in most ways is the least ambitious of his works and the most traditional in technique, works well, and the demands of the genre itself may have helped Bell with his structuring of plot events.

So far there are no book-length studies of Bell's fiction, though it probably will not be long before masters' theses and doctoral dissertations begin to appear. Currently the most important critical work is comprised of reviews and review essays in major newspapers. There is no doubt that Bell's work will receive a great deal of attention in the future, and from all indications his career as a novelist, short-story writer, and essayist will be a distinguished one.

BIBLIOGRAPHY

Works by Madison Smartt Bell

The Washington Square Ensemble. New York: Viking, 1983; Penguin, 1984.
Waiting for the End of the World. New York: Ticknor and Fields, 1985; Penguin, 1986.
Straight Cut. New York: Ticknor and Fields, 1986; Penguin, 1987.
Zero db. New York: Ticknor & Fields, 1987. Penguin, 1988.
The History of the Owen Graduate School of Management. New York: Vanderbilt University, 1988.
The Year of Silence. New York: Ticknor and Fields, 1987; Penguin, 1989.
Soldier's Joy. New York: Ticknor and Fields, 1989; Penguin, 1990.
Barking Man. New York: Ticknor and Fields, 1990; Penguin, 1991.
Doctor Sleep. New York: Harcourt Brace Jovanovich, 1991.
"An Essay Introducing His Work in a Rather Lunatic Fashion," *Chattahoochee Review* 12 (Fall 1991): 1–13.

Interviews

Interview by Bob Summer, *Publishers Weekly* (December 11, 1987).
Interview by Ann Kolson, *Philadelphia Inquirer* (March 1988).
Interview by John X. Kim and Yong Lee, *Zeniada* (Johns Hopkins University) 11, No. 1 (Fall 1988).
Interview by Robert Bradley, *AWP Newsletter* (May 1989).

Studies of Madison Smartt Bell

Bradley, David. "The Battles Didn't End with the War." *New York Times Book Review* (July 2, 1989): 3–23.
Furness, Mary. "Do-be-do-be-do," *Times Literary Supplement*, 4195 (August 26, 1983): 915.
Garret, George. "A Singular View of New York." *Washington Times* (January 1988).
Kalfus, Ken. "Tough It Out," *The Nation*, 236, 13 (April 1, 1983): 406–8.
"Madison Smartt Bell," 53–54 in *Contemporary Authors*, New Revision Series, ed. Hal May and James G. Lesnick. Detroit: Gale Research, 1990.
"Madison Smartt Bell," 51–54 in *Contemporary Literary Criticism*, Vol. 41, ed. Daniel G. Marowski and Roger Matuz. Detroit: Gale Research, 1987.
Mills, Jerry Leath. "A Snoozer from Madison Smartt Bell." Raleigh (N.C.) *News and Observer* (February 24, 1991): 4J.
Ruffan, Thomas. "A Crowd of Toughs in the Underbelly," *Los Angeles Times Book Review* (February 27, 1983): 3.

THOMAS J. RICHARDSON

Larry Brown
(1951–   )

In his appearance on NBC's *Today* in October 1989, Larry Brown told host Jane Pauley that he writes about "survival." His own survival as a self-taught writer, detailed in his autobiographical essay *A Late Start* (1989), is mirrored in the long odds battled by his characters from the poor side of town in *Facing the Music* (1988), *Dirty Work* (1989), *Big Bad Love* (1990), and *Joe* (1991). In *Facing the Music*, his first collection of stories, his working-class characters attempt to hold life together as they confront such problems as the disfigurement of a wife following breast cancer, alcoholism, extreme poverty, rape, murder, suicide, and the general meaninglessness of modern existence. In *Dirty Work*, Brown's first published novel, his two narrators, one black and one white, both from Mississippi, share memories and talk as severely wounded patients in a VA hospital, "shot all to pieces" in Vietnam.

Life in the collection *Big Bad Love* seems lighter in comparison, but characters are desperate here, too—failed in love, lonely, bored, traveling the backroads with nowhere to go but a bad drunk. Brown's most recent novel, *Joe*, may be his best work thus far, as his blue-collar hard-living good man, now close to 50, crosses paths with a boy from a family whose poverty and meanness are beyond description. These books have been tremendously well received. In all his work, Larry Brown's strengths are his genuine, honest, unflinching vision in the face of the human predicament, his tough realism in defining contemporary life, and his ear for authentic vernacular dialogue. He has also completed work on a play adaptation of *Dirty Work* for American Playhouse and PBS.

BIOGRAPHY

William Larry Brown was born July 9, 1951, in the farming community of Potlockney, near Oxford in Lafayette County, Mississippi, and not far from

Yocona (Yocknee) where he lives today. His father, a sharecropper, moved the family to Memphis when Larry was 3, then back to Oxford when he was 13. In Memphis, life was a series of rented houses; Brown says in his autobiographical essay *A Late Start*: "It was like trouble followed us from place to place." His father worked at a trailer company, his mother at an electric company. The family's hard times came in large part from his father's alcoholism. *Dirty Work* is dedicated to his father, "who knew what war does to men," for his father's drinking followed from nightmarish experiences in the Battle of the Bulge. Brown knew firsthand his father's reaction to the war, as he came to know hard times. He recalls his father spending the last dollar of grocery money for a bottle, yet he also remembers his father's warmth when sober, as well as his mother's resourcefulness in times of trouble.

After his father's death in 1968, Brown's family continued to live outside Oxford. Brown graduated from Oxford High School in 1969 and was a member of the Marine Corps from 1970 to 1972. He remembers doing so poorly in English in high school that he had to repeat it in order to graduate. In the Marine Corps, he served in North Carolina and Philadelphia, where, he says, he spent significant time in a bar frequented by wounded veterans who were patients in an adjunct VA hospital. His ear for those conversations would later pay dividents in the subject matter for *Dirty Work*.

When Brown returned to Oxford in 1972, he married (1973), and he and his wife, Mary Annie, settled down in the Yocona community and raised a family. They now have three children—two boys, Billy Ray and Shane, and a girl, Le Anne. He began work for the Oxford Fire Department in 1972 and also, as he tells us in *A Late Start*, supported his family by working a variety of extra jobs—"on my days off I had set out pine trees, done carpentry work, cleaned carpets, cut pulpwood, deadened timber, you name it. I'd built those chain-link fences from Sears . . . and painted houses, and I'd hauled hay." He became captain of the fire department, and he worked there until January 1990, after the success of *Dirty Work*, when he resigned to have more time to write. He told Peter Applebome in the *New York Times*: "I don't want to be known as . . . the fireman-writer. I wanted to be known as Larry Brown, writer."

Brown built the brick home he and his family live in today on about sixty acres next to the house where Mary Annie grew up. His mother has been the postmaster of Tula, a community just down the road, and she has owned a country store, which Larry and his family have managed. It is in this context that Larry Brown has emerged as a writer of serious and successful fiction. The story of how he became a writer, detailed in *A Late Start*, is compelling. When he graduated from high school, more education was not on his mind: "All I wanted to do was get me a job and buy me a car." He says: "I always wanted to be a fireman. It never occurred to me that I would become a writer." Yet, when he was 29, he stopped and looked at life and wondered if he was ever going to do anything with it. He says he was always fascinated by writing, but the idea of actually putting words on paper seemed out of reach. At the fire station, he had read a great deal—Stephen King, Harold Robbins, and Louis L'Amour, among others. He wondered, he says, if "writing might be like learning how to build houses, or lay brick or even fight fires." And "I had absolutely no idea of the odds against me when I decided to try it."

At any rate, he sat down with his wife's portable typewriter and wrote a novel about a man-eating bear in Yellowstone Park, "a place I'd never been to," a novel that "had a lot of sex in it." He says, "I thought sex sold, because of the Harold Robbins novels I'd read. I was wrong. Nobody in New York wanted it." He wrote five more novels and over 100 short stories during what he calls his apprenticeship, almost all not published, and the rejection slips piled up. An editor at *Outdoor Life* sent him helpful advice: "Write the way you'd write a letter to a friend." In addition, Brown realized that he needed to read books about the craft of writing as well as better literature. With the encouragement of Willie Morris and Barry Hannah, both writers-in-residence at the University of Mississippi, Brown audited a writing workshop with Ellen Douglas.

In 1982 he had published his first story, one he "wouldn't want to see reprinted now," in *Easy Rider*, a motorcycle magazine, and another in *Twilight Zone*. In 1984 he sold a story to *Fiction International*, but it was his story "Facing the Music," published in 1986 in the *Mississippi Review*, that attracted attention. Frederic Barthelme, editor of the *Mississippi Review* and director of the Center for Writers at the University of Southern Mississippi, remembers his first reading of this story told by a man dealing with his wife's mastectomy: "My hair just stood up on end," Barthelme recalls. (Interview with Thomas J. Richardson, June 1990.) The story also attracted the attention of Shannon Ravenel, senior editor at Algonquin Books, who remembers reading the story on a flight to the 1987 American Booksellers' Convention and her impressions of its honesty and tenderness. Ravenel was also series editor for *Best American Short Stories*, and when Richard Howorth recommended "Facing the Music" for her consideration, she got Brown's address and began the process that resulted in the selection and publication in 1988 of the ten stories in *Facing the Music*.

Brown gives much of the credit for his success to the encouragement and editorial work of Ravenel, especially on *Dirty Work*, a novel he had begun in 1986 when he moved into his new house. The novel went through five drafts before publication in 1989, and Brown told Sid Scott, "there were times I thought I would never deliver what she wanted." *Dirty Work* has been both successful in the marketplace and among the critics. It was named by *USA Today* as one of the best fiction books of 1989, and the paperback edition appeared in 1990. It has been translated into several foreign editions; at the same time, *Facing the Music* won the 1989 Mississippi Institute of Arts and Letters Award for Literature.

Success has not changed Larry Brown's genuine, friendly, down-home personality, though he's had significant public demands on his time. His reading of *A Late Start* in Chattanooga in April 1989 brought many in the audience to tears. He recently bought a new home in Tula to secure a private place to write; as noted earlier, he resigned from the Oxford Fire Department in January 1990.

His biography tells a remarkable story of a self-taught writer whose early family experiences, work at other jobs, and wonderful honesty in language and subject matter have come together to give us a significant new voice in contemporary literature. He has his wish: he's not the fireman-writer anymore. He's Larry Brown, writer. A very good writer.

MAJOR THEMES

In his essay *A Late Start*, Brown says that he may "make readers know more than they want to about the poor, or the unfortunate, or the alcoholic, but a sensible writer writes what he or she knows best, and draws on the material that's closest, and the lives that are observed." Brown's characters live in a violent world, sometimes "on the edge of desperation," as Don O'Briant suggests ("Fireman"), and he writes about "broken marriages and alcoholism, battered women and desperate lovers, mastectomies and murder." The titles of his first two books of fiction are telling:—*Facing the Music* and *Dirty Work*— and one of Brown's gifts is that he handles his subjects with what his editor Shannon Ravenel describes as "incredible directness and courage."

Brown says further in *A Late Start*: "I try to write as close as I can to the heart of the matter. I write out of experience and imagination, toward blind faith and hope." Rick Bass suggests that his voice is also compassionate, and while it is right to say, as Peter Applebome does in the *New York Times*, that Brown "has created a dark painful world of gritty Southern voices, usually those of ordinary people coping with extraordinary pain," we are not finally overcome with pessimism and despair.

But we do come close. In the *Village Voice* Barry Walters notes, quite rightly, that Brown "does not ask for sympathy for his hopeless characters." At the same time, Walters says that Brown's "voice is an ironic deadpan . . . bored and uneasy and snickering under his breath all at the same time." We come dangerously close to viewing characters as dead animals in the road, but Brown gives us much more than that. He makes us care about the desperate people he creates, and our estimates of his fiction must include his broad themes of survival and compassion. Life is complex and hard, and there is often no resolution to the problems his people face, but they manage to go on.

Facing the Music is a collection of ten stories, some earlier published in magazines. The title story, one of Brown's best, is told by a man torn between his love for his wife and responsibility toward their marriage, on the one hand, and his lack of desire for her sexually because of her disfigurement from a mastectomy, on the other. He attempts to escape from her sexual advances by staying up and watching all-night movies on stations from Memphis and Tupelo. On this night, he is drinking and watching Ray Milland in *The Lost Weekend*. Milland plays an alcoholic who eventually must "face the music," and the narrator knows he must also when his wife starts to make love. He recently had a one-night stand with a woman with wonderful breasts, and he is caught by the

memory of that as he tries to evade his wife and avoid a scene of her crying in
the bathroom. Over 40 now, married 23 years with children gone, he remembers,
too, the physical sensation of his honeymoon in Hattiesburg those years ago.
Like Ray Milland in the movie, he tries "to do what he knows he should. He
has responsibilities to people who love him and need him . . . but he's scared to
death." As she turns the light off, they "reach to find each other in the darkness
like people who are blind." There is no resolution to the complex problem of
love and sex in this situation. In *A Late Start*, Brown says: "It took a long time
to understand what literature was, and why it was so hard to write, and what it
could do to you once you understand it. Very simply, it meant that I could meet
people on the page who were as real as the people I knew in my own life. They
were real people, as far as I was concerned, not just characters. And when I
saw that, it was like a curtain fell away from my eyes." The strength of this
superb story is in its reality, both in its situation and in its approach to the human
predicament.

The second story in the collection has also attracted attention and awards,
both from the *Greensboro Review* where it was first published and in *Best
American Short Stories* (1989). "Kubuku Rides (This Is It)" is the relentless
picture of a young wife and mother trapped in alcoholism, and it shows the
tremendous tension in her life between addiction and denial. Told from her
viewpoint in her dialect, the story speaks of her love for her husband and little
boy as she destroys her life by drinking: "Angel hear the back door slam. It
Alan, in from work. She start to hide the glass and then she don't hide the glass,
he got a nose like a bloodhound and gonna smell it anyway, so she just keep
sitting on the couch. She gonna act like nothing happening, like everything cool.
Little boy in the yard playing, he don't know nothing. He think Mama in here
watching Andy Griffith." Her husband cuts his hand badly taking a bottle away
from her (the emergency room will cost more than he makes unloading lumber),
and she remembers her recent barhopping and wreck in the car: "Beer sack
down in the floor. Have to lean over and take her eyes off the road just a second
to get that beer, no problem." Her continued denial of her problem brings us
to the conclusion where she tries to sneak out of the house for another drink:
"She turn the wipers on to see better. The porch light shining out there. . . .
This light show her home, this warm place she own that mean everything to
her. This light, it always on for her. That what she thinking when it go out."
Brown's creation of this woman, who loves her husband like "God love Jesus"
but can't stop drinking, is both powerful and honest.

"The Rich," like "Facing the Music," was first published in the *Mississippi
Review*. It tells of a man who works at a travel agency and deals with the rich
as they plan their vacations, but it exposes the tremendous difference between
the world and values of the rich and those who serve them, like Mr. Pellisher.
Since Mr. Pellisher is poor, he yearns to be one of the rich, but he also hates
them: "What he'd really like to do is machine-gun the rich. . . . He'd like to see
the rich suffer everything he ever suffered that all their money could heal."

"Old Frank and Jesus" offers a picture of a burned-out farmer and sometime barber so overcome by his debts, loneliness, and other problems of a changed society that he is planning to commit suicide. He has recently shot his old squirrel dog, Frank, as prevention for a rabies epidemic, and now, at age 58, he lies on his couch and stares at the picture of Jesus on the wall of his living room.

"Boy and Dog," incongruously told in verse, is the violent account of a little boy throwing a brick at a car that has run down his dog in the road. He knocks the driver unconscious, the car hits a tree, the gas tank explodes, the car and driver burn to a crisp, the fireman lose their truck in a pond, and so on. There is an ironic distance in the narrator's voice in the face of violence and death as life goes on for the little boy. "Julie: A Memory" is challenging, but interesting technically because it juxtaposes in alternate sentences the narrator's memory of an attack and rape of his pregnant girlfriend with his account of his revenge and murder of her attackers. He had planned to marry Julie so that she would not have an abortion; his revenge is for the lost, unborn child as well.

"Samaritans" is a hard-nosed account of the plight of "poor white trash" and the ambivalence between judgment and sympathy in dealing with them. The first-person narrator inadvertently gets involved with a "trash" family—a dirty, ratty woman; her ancient mother; and the woman's four children in the "burning-hot" parking lot of a roadside bar. They are in "a junky-ass old Rambler, wrecked on the right front end, with the paint almost faded off, and slick tires, and a rag hanging out of the grill." One of the kids, a minor, tries to buy cigarettes; then the woman pushes the narrator for a cold beer: " 'It's some people in this world has got thangs and some that ain't,' she said. 'My daddy used to have money . . . you ought to see him now. We cain't even afford to put him in a rest home.' " Refusing her offer to get a room in a motel, he gives the family thirty dollars to get them to "Loozeanner," but the two women go back in the bar to get drunk. The little boy tells the narrator: " 'Boy you a dumb sumbitch.' And in a way I had to agree with him."

"Night Life," set in Jackson, tells a direct story of blue-collar bar life and the narrator's involvement with a woman recently separated from her husband. His discovery that she locks her children, ages 2 and 4, in the house while she is out on the town arouses his anger, and he hits her. His compassion for the children is set against the lonely, desperate world of barhopping and looking for women. "Leaving Town" employs two narrators who alternately tell the story of themselves and their relationship: Richard, a carpenter who works extra fix-it jobs at night, and Myra, a woman recently divorced, who drinks alone in her house. In Richard, we see the hard knocks of the workingman's life and the loneliness of his live-in relationship with Betty, a woman who cares for nothing except grocery store magazines, and her little girl; in Myra, we see the desperation of life after divorce and the fright of loneliness. At the conclusion of the story, Richard leaves town to find better work in Florida, taking only the little girl with him, but he "might call" Myra later to follow up on their brief but passionate encounter when he did some fix-it work at her house. The last story, "The End of Romance,'' brings together the end of a romantic relationship—''We both had the creep of something bad coming up on us''—with the shotgun attack of one black man on another at a convenience store. The cynicism in the voice of the narrator is reminiscent of Barry Hannah and is somewhat different from the dominant Larry Brown in *Facing the Music*: The good-hearted workingman who is down and out, blasted by loneliness, hard times, and the absurdity of modern life. We are in the world of contemporary country music here, and Brown understands it very well. Small wonder that Tom T. Hall said to him: ''Next time one of your characters plays a song on the jukebox, it had better be mine'' (interview with Thomas Richardson, July 1990).

The power evident in *Facing the Music* is more visible in *Dirty Work*, Brown's first published novel. If *Facing the Music* was widely praised, the applause for *Dirty Work* has been thunderous. Such praise is well deserved. To some extent, Braiden Chaney and Walter James, the two narrators who alternate in telling the story in *Dirty Work*, extend the definition of Brown's narrators in his earlier collection, just as they are representative of the American soldiers who fought the Vietnam war: they come from poor backgrounds; they are not highly educated; as John Justice notes, they have ''patriotism that outstripped their knowledge of the war's purpose.''

This is a Vietnam novel, and it is also a Southern novel. Braiden Chaney is black, and he's been a quadraplegic for 22 years, ''shot all to pieces'' in Vietnam when he was 18. His new companion in the VA hospital, Walter James, is white, and he's shot in the head and face, severely disfigured and subject to intermittent seizures and blackouts. Both are from Mississippi, and their talk to themselves and to each other over a day and night in the hospital draws on their memories of place, family, and community in the deep South as well as on the horrors of Vietnam they share.

Both characters escape a great deal to television movies, and they remember and talk over *The Young Lions*, *One Flew over the Cuckoo's Nest*, and *Johnny Got His Gun*, Dalton Trumbo's antiwar novel first published in 1939. *Dirty Work* is compared in a number of reviews to *Johnny Got His Gun*, especially since it makes a direct allusion to it. Some have complained that the ending of *Dirty Work* is not only melodramatic but overtly similar to *One Flew over the Cuckoo's Nest*. Along with his sister, a nurse on the ward who takes care of the two men, Braiden pushes Walter toward a mercy killing to take him out of his misery. When Walter asks, ''Do you wish you were dead?'' Braiden's answer is ''Not a minute don't go by.''

The strength of the novel builds on the strengths of Brown's short fiction. Peter Prescott, writing in *Newsweek*, notes that this is ''a spare piece, set out in real time, that could have been a one-act play like Sartre's *No Exit*. We may not be in hell, but we're surely in hell's anteroom.'' As Rick Bass has pointed out, however, the characters in *Dirty Work* ''manage to stay ahead of their many horrors, never yielding to them, and so the grisliness of the novel is kept at bay.

There are no willing victims here, not even the limbless Braiden.'' There is both "vitality and humor" in the novel as well as "existential courage."

The novel opens with Braiden's "talk," as he watches Walter pretend to be asleep in the next bed. As Herbert Mitgang has noted, these are "short, stacatto characters with indisputably authentic language" that demonstrate Brown's remarkable ear for dialect, both black and white. In addition to his memories of being shot in Vietnam and growing up as a poor black in Mississippi, Braiden dreams a great deal. He dreams of being an African king, and in the opening chapters he imagines a dialogue between the African boy and his father about killing lions. Later he has "lions to kill, and tribes to fight off. Got maidens. Many of them." He is sometimes on a safari, a tracker who knows much more than "Bwana." He mixes these dreams in with memories of his mother's peas and biscuits, with reactions to the inane television commercials, soaps, and game shows providing background in his ward, and with what Susan Wood calls "the great unanswerable questions." "Whole world's a puzzle to me, though. Why it's got to be the way it is. I don't think the Lord meant for it to be like this originally. I think things just got out of hand."

His nurse keeps him supplied with beer, which he keeps hidden in a cooler under his bed, and he offers Walter cold beer, conversation, and a sometimes willing ear. It becomes apparent that Braiden sees Walter as "being sent," a common spirit who will take him out of this life. In one of his dreams, Braiden visits with Jesus and an angel child and discusses his wish to die. As Prescott says, this is "an immensely difficult business for an author to bring off without falling into sentimentality," but Brown succeeds, because "this Jesus is Braiden's invention, no more of a divinity than this dreaming man can grasp."

In comparison to Braiden, Walter is a newcomer to the hospital. Indeed, he has been most recently living at home with his mother and brother, though he has had long stints in hospitals to deal with his severe head wounds and seriously disfigured face. A big man at 250 pounds, Walter had grown up poor white in rural Mississippi, and he remembers considerable violence in his childhood. He stabbed the neighborhood bully for calling his father a jailbird. His father had been in the penitentiary, and he remembers his father killing a mule with his bare hands, after the mule had kicked a black neighbor to death. Walter's head injuries are such that he escapes to home movies and an isolated life, since no one could stand to look at him, not even his family. Recently he had met Beth at a convenience store, a young woman similarly scarred from a childhood attack by a dog. While parked with Beth in a creekbed, however, Walter has one of his blackouts, apparently pinning Beth in the car, and she drowns in a flash flood. Walter was just high enough in the car to escape being drowned himself, and now he is in the hospital with Braiden, where he learns of Beth's death. These sensational events don't control the novel, however, and neither does the controversial ending. The power of *Dirty Work* is in the talk itself, and in these two characters who deal with life, and death, and life-in-death, together.

Big Bad Love continues to give readers the material and the people that Brown knows best. Part I includes eight stories, beginning with "Falling out of Love." There's some of Barry Hannah's bored, sardonic humor here, as there was in "The End of Romance," the last story in *Facing the Music.* In "Falling out of Love," love with Sheena-Baby has come to two flat tires on an empty road. The narrator says: "I didn't know why something that started off feeling so good had to wind up feeling so bad. Love was a big word, and it covered a lot of territory. You could spend your whole life chasing after it and wind up with nothing, be an old bitter guy with long nose and ear hair and no teeth, hanging out in bars looking for somebody your age, but the chances of success went down then. After a while you got too many strikes against you." "The Apprentice" offers a reversal of Brown's own long apprenticeship as a writer. The husband of the would-be writer tells the story here, tongue-in-cheek, about the perils of living with someone whose life is "writewritewritewritewrite." Her story, "The Hunchwoman of Cincinnati," makes the rounds, as does her first novel about a man-eating grizzly in Yellowstone.

The next four stories, "Wild Thing," "Big Bad Love," "Gold Nuggets," and "Waiting for the Ladies," although different, offer Brown's typical narrator: a lonesome, vulnerable working man out on the road, six-pack at hand, trying to deal with the absurdity of life and the depth of his loneliness. His affair with a "wild thing" he meets in a bar is always interrupted—by the police on a drug bust, by her boyfriend, or by his own guilt. In "Big Bad Love," he not only can't go home to a wife he can't satisfy sexually, he has to face the fact that his dog has just died. When his wife leaves him, he can't quite get around to burying the dog, and "the loneliness I have been speaking of really started to set in." "Gold Nuggets" is set on the gulf coast, where a man from north Mississippi loses his shrimp money, his control, maybe his identity, in heavy drinking and tawdry bar life. In "Waiting for the Ladies," the narrator travels the rural roads looking for an exhibitionist who has exposed himself to the narrator's wife.

"Old Soldiers" and "Sleep" seem more like the stories in *Facing the Music.* "Old Soldiers" tells of the affection of the narrator for Mr. Aaron, a veteran who runs the local country store, and the connection of Mr. Aaron to his father and others in the community who were deeply affected by war. "Sleep" may be the best story in *Big Bad Love.* Tightly constructed, it offers the perception of an elderly man whose wife insists that he get up in the night and check on an imaginary noise in the house. The house is cold, and he thinks about places where he has been cold, and of growing old.

Parts II and III of *Big Bad Love* are longish stories, "Discipline" and "92 Days." Like "The Apprentice," they are both about writing, but they are quite different from each other. "Discipline" is a burlesque, somewhat surreal; it describes a parole hearing of a man in prison for plagiarism. Told like a court proceeding, it describes life in prison for writers like Mr. Lawrence [Larry? Narrators in other stories are named Leo, Lonnie, Leroy, Louis, and Leon], where they are punished by forced sex with obese women who are members of book clubs. In the final scene Mr. Lawrence is forced to read a hilarious manuscript that shows that he continues to imitate Faulkner. The original title of this collection, "92 Days," brings together in one character the apprentice writer struggling to publish with the lonesome beer-drinking man looking for love in all the wrong places. Perhaps because many of the short stories also focus on the good old boy in the pick-up truck, "92 Days" seems a few days too long. The dirt-road sport, always out of money, often drunk and desperate, wears a little thin, even if he does want to write. Yet Brown knows how to save a story with his endings, and the conclusion to "92 Days" is first-rate. Through a story he is writing about a little girl and her parents running from "something beyond bad," Leon is able to articulate something of his own desperation as well as that power that compels a writer to create: "They were running, running, the cars going by, and I could see the slippery sidewalks, and the lights in the stores, and I could see my mother and my father looking back over their shoulders at whatever was chasing us, and I ran as fast as I could, terrified, not knowing how it would end, knowing I had to know."

Joe, Brown's most recent novel, is his best work thus far. In *Joe*, Brown brings his work to a new level, both in the power of his language and the dimensions of his characters and ideas. *Joe* is the well-known Larry Brown character now nearing 50: divorced, he drinks and gambles too much; alone, he rides the backroads in an old truck (he does get a new one); hardworking in the Mississippi heat, he supervises a crew of blacks who poison the hardwood forest for Weyerhauser so that profitable pines can be planted, and looks for a fight, even with the police. Joe is more than a hell-raiser, though, and he understands not only the environmental implications of his work, but also the consequences of his failed relationships with his wife, daughter, and new grandchild.

Joe's character is further revealed in his relationship with Gary Jones, a 15-year-old whose family is the lowest level of white trash: Ignorant, abused, without money, job, food, or hope. Gary's father, Wade Jones, is filthy and vile, an alcoholic who steals and murders for his next drink. He has sold one of his children, an act that sends Gary's mother into helpless insanity, and he sells his youngest daughter, a mute from earlier abuse, into prostitution. In the Jones family, we see the depths of degradation in contemporary rural America, beyond Faulkner's Snopes clan, beyond Erskine Caldwell, beyond John Steinbeck's tramps and migrants, equal to Flannery O'Connor's world of violence and the grotesque.

SURVEY OF CRITICISM

The published criticism of Larry Brown's work has been in newspaper and magazine reviews of *Facing the Music*, *Dirty Work*, *Big Bad Love*, and *Joe*. These reviews are numerous, however, and many are quite good. My count during the early summer of 1990 yielded almost 100 reviews of the first two books, and I have listed the most substantial reviews of all four in the bibliography. Many of these reviews have been collected by Algonquin Books.

Brown's role as the "fireman-writer" has been left behind since his resignation from the Oxford Fire Department in January 1990, but a number of the reviews make a great deal of the unusual nature of Brown's background as a writer who served a long apprenticeship and essentially taught himself to write. A number of the reviews include brief interviews with Larry Brown, and they are helpful and revealing about biographical details. Among the best of these are Peter Applebome's essay in the *New York Times*, Berkley Hudson's comments in the *Los Angeles Times*, and Don O'Briant's two reviews in the *Atlanta Journal/ Constitution*. Sid Scott's biographical sketch and interview in the Tupelo, Mississippi, *Daily Journal View Magazine* is helpful, as is Lisa Ross' essay in the Memphis Commercial Appeal. For straight reviews of *Dirty Work*, look especially to Rick Bass's essay in the *New York Times Book Review*, Herbert Mitgang's review in the *New York Times*, and Peter Prescott's "Pillow Talk" in *Newsweek*.

The reviews on Brown's books have been phenomenally good, and critics have been quick to note Brown's strengths. As Shannon Ravenel noticed early about Brown's work, it "pulls no punches," but "confronts head-on the dark side of the human condition." Michael Dean of the University of Mississippi has argued in an excellent paper read at the Mississippi Philological Association in February 1990 that Larry Brown is a Southern novelist as well as a novelist about Vietnam. He points out that Brown's sense of place, community, religion, character, and racial relations is unerring, as is his ear for Southern language.

Inevitably, Brown will be compared to Faulkner, since he is from Oxford, but Brown is influenced by other writers as well, including Raymond Carver, Cormac McCarthy, and Flannery O'Connor. A number of contemporary writers have estimated his work highly—Harry Crews, Barry Hannah, Willie Morris, and Richard Ford, among others. But the single most helpful comment on Larry Brown is by Brown himself in his essay *A Late Start*, first read at the Fifth Biennial Conference on Southern Literature in Chattanooga in April 1989, where he describes his beginnings as a writer. Readers anticipate his continued success.

BIBLIOGRAPHY

Works by Larry Brown

Facing the Music. Chapel Hill, N.C.: Algonquin, 1988. New York: Harper and Row, 1989.
Dirty Work. Chapel Hill, N.C.: Algonquin, 1989. New York: Random House, 1990.
A Late Start. Chapel Hill, N.C.: Algonquin, 1989.
Big Bad Love. Chapel Hill, N.C.: Algonquin, 1990. New York: Random House, 1991.
Joe. Chapel Hill, N.C.: Algonquin, 1991.

Studies of Larry Brown

Allen, Bruce. "Vietnam Aftershocks: 2 Novel Views." *USA Today* (September 8, 1989): D4.

Applebome, Peter. "Larry Brown's Long, Hard Journey on the Road to Acclaim as a Writer." *New York Times* (March 5, 1990): C11.

Bass, Rick. "In the Hospital, Waiting for a Savior." *New York Times Book Review* (October 1989): 15.

Cryer, Dan. "The Soldiers' Story." *Newsday* (August 20, 1989): 12–13.

Goodrich, Chris. "Books from Oxford and Algonquin Question Idea of a 'Good' War." *Publisher's Weekly* (June 23, 1989): 31–32.

Hobson, Linda. "Ongoing Battles with Vietnam." *New Orleans Times-Picayune* (December 10, 1989): E6–7.

Holland, Gina. "Oxford Firefighter Writes Stories with Southern Flavor." *Commercial Appeal* (Memphis) (October 30, 1989): B3.

Hudson, Berkley. "Country Boy Hits Big Time." *Los Angeles Times* (September 17, 1989): VI1, 7.

Johnson, Greg. "Stirring Story of Veterans' Painful Lives." *Atlanta Journal/Constitution* (September 3, 1989): L10.

Justice, John. "Rough Moral Fiction." *Communicant* (October 4, 1989): 4.

Koeppel, Fred. "Mississippian's First Novel Intense, Awkward." *Commercial Appeal* (Memphis) (August 20, 1989): G4.

Leepson, Marc. "Suffering the Scars of War." *Washington Post* (August 14, 1989): B3.

Mabe, Chauncey. "After Years of Rejection, Publishers Woo 'Dirty Work' Author." *Tallahassee Democrat* (January 14, 1990): 61, 62.

———. "Author's Post-Vietnam Novel Reflects Short-Story Style." *Fort Lauderdale Sun-Sentinel* (December 24, 1989): 61, 63.

———. "A Mississippi Firefighter Becomes Hot Novelist." *Philadelphia Inquirer* (January 9, 1990).

Mitgang, Herbert. "2 Strangers Telling Each Other Their War Stories." *New York Times*, Late Ed. (September 23, 1989): A13.

O'Briant, Don. "Apprenticeship Is over, and Powerful Stories Are Result." *Atlanta Journal/Constitution* (December 4, 1988): K10.

———. "Fireman Brown a Blazing New Southern Voice." *Atlanta Journal/Constitution* (August 20, 1989): L1, 10.

Pate, Nancy. "An Echo in Faulknerland," *The Orlando Sentinel*, 17 Dec. 1989: D1, 6.

Prescott, Peter S. "Pillow Talk." *Newsweek* (November 20, 1989): 80.

Raksin, Alex. "Facing the Music: Stories." *Los Angeles Times Book Review* (September 4, 1988): 4.

Reed, Fred. "Vietnam Veterans Live in a World Where 'Things Just Got out of Hand,' " *Washington Times* (July 31, 1989): E8.

Ross, Lisa M. "Brown Stirs Literary Fire." *Commercial Appeal* (Memphis) (November 24, 1989): B1–2.

Scott, Sid. "Special Delivery: Book Begins New Chapter in Life of Larry Brown." *Daily Journal View Magazine* (Tupelo) (November 12, 1989): F6–7.

Slater, Joyce. " 'Facing the Music' Has a Firefighter's Searing Perceptions." *Atlanta Journal/Constitution* (December 4, 1988): K10.

Streitfeld, David. "Crackerjacks: A New Generation of Southern Writers Finds Refuge at Algonquin Books." *Fame* (October 1989): 30.

Walters, Barry. "Down on the Farm," *Village Voice*. (November 22, 1988): 56.

Wood, Susan. "Trying to Answer the Great Unanswerable Questions." *Houston Post* (August 27, 1989): C6.

BARBARA LADD

Rita Mae Brown
(1944–   )

With the publication in 1973 of her first novel, *Rubyfruit Jungle*, Rita Mae Brown established herself as one of the most promising writers of the women's movement. Since that time, she has continued to publish novels of strong women who best the odds with their courage and humor. Her work, with one or two exceptions, is essentially comic, its humor often resting on surprising role reversals and the burlesquing of social and literary conventions.

BIOGRAPHY

"Writers will happen in the best of families" (*Starting from Scratch* 3). Rita Mae Brown was born in Hanover, Pennsylvania, on November 28, 1944, the daughter of unknown parents. All we know is what Brown tells us—that her father was reputed to be a Virginia Venable and her mother a Pennsylvania Young. She was adopted by Ralph and Julia Brown. Julia Brown, nee Buckingham, was originally from Maryland, Ralph Brown from Pennsylvania. Until Rita Mae was 11, the family lived in Pennsylvania, very close to the Mason-Dixon line.

Throughout her early childhood Brown toured the battlefields of the Confederacy, with her father's encouragement, and spent long Saturday afternoons in the library reading about the Civil War. She said: "I have always had the strangest sensation that I was not really learning anything but rather I was being reminded of something I already knew." Brown had indeed heard about the Civil War much earlier. In the introduction to her Civil War novel, *High Hearts*, she recalls listening to her great-grandfather Huff, when she was 3 or 4 and he 100, tell her the story of his experiences as a soldier in the "War of Northern Aggression" (her grandmother's term). Although she was too young at the time of the telling to remember the details of his stories, they did ignite her curiosity about the

Civil War, as well as an awareness of her great-grandfather's "passionate need to tell her about the central event of his life." Later, when she was doing the research for *High Hearts* in an attempt to be faithful to the language of the slaves, she came to understand that language "is a means of maintaining power; it is also a means of resistance to power."

Brown's parents were working-class people—Ralph a butcher; Julia an employee in a bakery and sometimes mill worker—and the author became aware early in life of the differences between working-class and middle-class life. When, in the fourth grade, Rita Mae was transferred to a school that served the children of professionals, she soon discovered that middle-class kids did not always adhere to the working-class dictum that you stick up for your friends no matter what. In the autobiographical essay with which she begins her writers' manual, *Starting from Scratch* (1988), she reports that her new friends would buckle easily under pressure from authorities—teachers and parents. This perception that people from the middle class are not always to be trusted persists. During the late 1960s and 1970s, Brown's relationship with the middle-class women who led the women's movement was often stormy. In particular she objected to Roxanne Dunbar's dismissal of lesbianism as removed from the class struggle, to the bias among many feminists against leadership and individualism, and to the assumption among some radical feminists that downward mobility was essential for the politically active. On the contrary, she charges that downward mobility is no more than "a mockery of working class life . . . poverty made fashionable."

Another point of conflict is her portrayal of women. Some reviewers have criticized her for creating women who are unrealistic—too strong, too resourceful, too tough, too funny, and much too free for their era and their class. In an interview with Leonore Fleischer of the *Washington Post Book World*, Brown responds that "literature is predominantly written by middle-class people for middle-class people and their lives were real different. But those of us who were the underclass will tell vastly different stories." Her women characters are strong, like the women she grew up with: "The men weren't weak, but somehow the women . . . were the ones you paid attention to."

When Brown's family moved to Fort Lauderdale, Rita Mae at 11 felt liberated from what she calls "the bonds of her illegitimacy," the label "bastard" with which she had sometimes been taunted. She describes Fort Lauderdale as a tropical paradise where she spent long days outside or in the library close to her home. She played tennis with friends, some of whom were retirees who brought books to the courts for her; and she recalls being followed around by a very young Christine Evert. By the time she reached high school, Rita Mae was studying Latin—becoming fascinated by the stylistic consequences of inflections and reading Horace, Plautus, and Terence. There remains a strong classical influence in her writing.

In 1962 the University of Florida offered her a scholarship, and she began college, where she did well both academically and socially. But when she became involved in the civil rights movement in 1964, she began to lose her white friends; soon she lost her university scholarship as well. After an angry exchange with one of these friends who warned Brown about mixing with "those people," she was abruptly called into the office of the dean of women where she was accused of seducing the president of the Tri Delts and numerous other female students, as well as sleeping with black men *and* with black women. Like Molly Bolt, the protagonist of the autobiographical *Rubyfruit Jungle*, Rita Mae Brown fled to New York, where she became a student at New York University, receiving in 1968 a B.A. from that institution, as well as a cinematography certificate from the New York School of Visual Arts. She then did graduate work at the Institute for Policy Studies in Washington, D.C., and received her Ph.D. in 1973, the year *Rubyfruit Jungle* was published.

This first novel, published by the feminist press Daughters, Inc., earned her only $1,000 during this period, and she supported herself by fixing up old cars and selling antiques until the Massachusetts Council of the Arts awarded her a stipend. Not long afterward the National Endowment for the Arts awarded her a fiction grant. In the meantime, her second novel, *In Her Day*, had appeared to bad reviews and few sales. The funds she received enabled her to complete her third novel, *Six of One*, which did much better. Since that time, Brown has published six more novels, a book of essays, a writers' manual, and a number of screenplays and teleplays. She lives with her cats in Charlottesville, Virginia— "a very civilized little place." She is "aspiring to be silly," like one of her favorite playwrights, Aristophanes.

MAJOR THEMES

Brown, who objects to being labeled a "lesbian writer," insists upon her identity as a Southerner and, according to one critic, her early work, primarily autobiographical, is a series of attempts to return to Southern roots. *Rubyfruit Jungle* is about a working-class Southerner who travels north and then south again to find her own history in filming a documentary about her mother's life. It is also the story of that young woman's failure to make it in New York and her longing to return for good to the South of her childhood. After her stunning film, Molly Bolt graduates to no prospects at all: "What the hell. I wished I could be that frog back at Ep's old pond. I wished I could get up in the morning and look at the day the way I used to when I was a child."

Brown's second novel, *In Her Day* (1976), is also set in New York, and the protagonist is once again a Southerner. Art professor Carole Hanratty, a Virginian with working-class origins, begins seeing a radical feminist from the upper class. Inevitably Ilse's ideological fervor begins to get on each one of Carole's individual nerves; and Carole persists in her individualism despite Ilse's efforts to reform her. The break comes, although both women move the slightest bit in the direction of the other side. This novel, which begins as "mother possums and the Virginia summers of childhood" recede from Carole's memory, ends like *Rubyfruit Jungle*, with the protagonist "longing for . . . childhood . . . that time when things were pure." Unlike the young Molly Bolt, who resolves to stay in New York until she makes it, Carole Hanratty, a much older woman, decides to return to Richmond.

In *Six of One* (1978), the author herself did indeed return to the South, albeit just barely, setting the story in a town that straddles the Pennsylvania-Maryland state line. Her characters are once again the small-town, working-class people of Brown's own childhood; they are once again bound by shared history, family loyalties, and sibling rivalries. The three generations of women who constitute the focus for the events of the novel are once again blessed with incredible energy and resilience, not to mention a healthy portion of egotism.

It is no coincidence that Brown's most successful novels since *Six of One* have all been set in the South, where the author can explore the characters and themes she understands best. They are full of colorful, idiosyncratic characters who defy any convention that threatens to interfere with their happiness. But in *Southern Discomfort*, *High Hearts*, and *Bingo*, Brown has replaced her typical protagonist, the larger-than-life ego who can defeat all comers, with characters who are more human in their inability to cross all boundaries. As a result, she has produced much richer work. Despite their humor and instinct for spiritual survival, Banana Mae Parker and Blue Rhonda Latrec, the two prostitutes who appear in *Southern Discomfort* (1982), are people whose lives are twisted by the roles they play in order to survive. Such is also the case for the wealthy Hortensia Reedmuller Banastre whose momentarily liberating relationship with a black adolescent by the name of Hercules Jinks can be nothing but brief, largely because Hortensia does not possess the innocence that would allow her to run away to Chicago as her naive young lover longs to do. The one female character who reminds us of Molly Bolt in her innocence, who escapes unscathed by history or passion, is Hortensia's and Hercules's mulatto daughter, Catherine, still a child.

High Hearts (1986) is the story of a young bride's decision to disguise herself as a man and follow her husband onto the battlefields of the Confederacy, where she out-soldiers him to win the respect of her colleagues and commanding officer. In this novel, which Brown wrote as a celebration of the contribution of women in the Civil War, the action moves from the front lines, where Geneva Chatfield is fighting with the cavalry, to the plantations and the hospitals, where the horrors of war press just as hard upon Geneva's female relatives and neighbors. Brown's control of her material, always a problem in her earlier work, is impressive here. She is equally adept whether describing surgical practices or military maneuvers. The end of the novel is something of a disappointment, however, as the aging Geneva—who returned from battle to marry her commanding officer after her first husband had conveniently died in battle—tells a granddaughter the story of her experiences in the war. Here the author exhibits once again the old problem of attempting to tie up loose ends with exposition. Nevertheless, Brown shows herself to be capable, as she was in *Southern Discomfort* and will be once again in *Bingo*, of treating her characters with greater fidelity to the very real tragedies that even the most courageous can suffer.

In *Bingo* (1988), Brown returns to the Runnymede of *Six of One* and to the characters of the earlier novel: Nickel, a young lesbian; "Juts," a strong and matter-of-fact matriarch patterned after the author's own mother, Julia Ellen Brown; and Louise, Juts's crazy sister, who is said to be based loosely on Julia Ellen Brown's sister Mary. As Nickel struggles to save the Runnymede news-paper, the *Clarion*, from corporate ownership, she grows impatient with the shenanigans of her mother and her aunt, both in their 90s, who are competing for the romantic attentions of the new man in town, Ed Tutweiler Walters. About her own childhood with Julia and Mary, Brown writes that she saw them as "almost mythical," two women who "didn't give a rat's a—— what anybody thought. They'd say anything to anybody, and they did as they damn well pleased." She continues to find in them rich material for her comedy.

Brown's subject has always been, as Annie Gottlieb points out, "the misfit between human passions and societal conventions," and she continues to believe in "the fundamental innocence of passion," but between the writing of *Rubyfruit Jungle* and *Bingo*, Brown has become more willing to write about characters whose innocence is less impenetrable and about men and women whose courage doesn't always see them through. As a result, her work seems richer and more controlled.

SURVEY OF CRITICISM

Brown's work has been praised for its energy—for the warmth and humor with which she characterizes her women characters and for her willingness to defy any convention that would stifle her or her characters. Annie Gottlieb, one of Brown's most perceptive reviewers, writes that for Brown "duplicity is the stuff of human comedy" and "sexuality is a first cousin of imagination, involving an irrepressible urge to honor and rival the crazy abundance of life." At the same time, readers have been disturbed by what appears to be a lack of direction in much of her early fiction, by a lack of careful craftsmanship, and by her tendency to sidestep, sometimes through humor and at other times through the shameless manipulation of plot, certain issues that demand to be worked out with greater fidelity to the premises of her fiction.

Writing in *Ms.*, Marilyn Webb describes *Rubyfruit Jungle* as "an inspiring, bravado adventure story of a female Huck Finn named Molly Bolt." Although the book was rejected by the mainstream press and eventually brought out by a small feminist publishing firm, feminist readers have often agreed with Shelly Temchin Henze of the *New Boston Review* that the novel is a "classic American success story . . . not about revolution, nor even particularly about feminism. It is about standing on your own two feet, creaming the competition, looking out for Number One." The surprising sales of this "underground" novel, over 70,000 copies, attest to its wide appeal. Terry Curtis Fox of *Village Voice* attributes its success to the fact that "you don't have to be gay or female to identify with Molly Bolt—she is one of the outsiders many of us believe ourselves to be."

While acknowledging that *Rubyfruit Jungle* breaks with convention by refusing to portray lesbianism as a parody of heterosexuality and by celebrating "the joys of lesbian life" rather than its tragedies as had earlier authors like Radclyffe Hall, Leslie Fishbein charges Brown with depicting "lesbianism as too exclusively sexual" and with lacking any "genuine affection for women." She concludes that "the novel is completely narcissistic and selfish. It is an utterly individualistic tale that has no social consciousness or sense of commitment to a lesbian community." Of course, as we have seen, Brown has a different attitude toward individualism than many of those with whom she lived and worked during the early and mid-1970s when she was so heavily involved in the struggle for civil rights for gays and women. During these years, at about the same time that she was composing the essays that appeared in *A Plain Brown Rapper* (1976) and which were so critical of some of the leaders of the women's movement for their middle class standards and antilesbian stance, she was also writing *In Her Day*, her second novel, a work reviewers hated for its clumsy, didactic style, but one in which she takes on the class conflict within the women's movement. This novel sold only enough copies to cover printing costs. In her introduction to *Starting from Scratch*, Brown claims that she wanted to make the jump from the first- to the third-person point of view—a difficult jump for a young writer—and that she succeeded. "After *In Her Day*, I knew I would gradually grow in strength until I could handle a main plot and as many subplots as my powers could carry. In fact, each novel I have written has been more complicated than the last, although on the surface the language is fairly simple. You'd be surprised how hard it is to be simple." (14)

In her next novel, *Six of One*, Brown reclaimed her market popularity, and her tenuous hold on the reviewers. John Fludas of the *Saturday Review* praises the novel for its warmth and color, likening Brown to an American Evelyn Waugh. Others criticized it for what was becoming the author's chief problem—lack of direction and control. *Southern Discomfort*, which appeared 4 years later, was also popular although readers sometimes find that it moves too quickly, resorts too often to authorial intrusions, and ignores too deliberately the consequences of miscegenation in a small Southern community in the 1920s.

Sudden Death (1983), written at the request of Judy Lacy, a sports columnist for the *Boston Herald American*, was not the success that *Rubyfruit Jungle* and *Six of One* had been. It treats corruption on the women's professional tennis circuit, where everyone's Big Secret (lesbianism) has to remain a secret and where almost everyone will do almost anything to ensure that it does remain under wraps. The results are a hurried marriage, which is designed to rescue Carmen Semana, a young Argentine tennis star, from allegations of lesbianism brought by a competitor and the professional ruin of the only sympathetic character in the novel, a teacher who has been Semana's lover. Despite Brown's disclaimer, Amy Wilentz and others have insisted that the novel is based on the author's own relationship with Martina Navratilova: "It would spare readers of romans à clef so much time and worry if the authors who insisted on writing them could call a spade a spade, or, in this case, a Martina a Martina." Most agree that Brown seems less involved with the material than she needs to be. Elisabeth Jakab writes that "the novel tends to read like the casebook of an anthropologist stranded in the midst of a disappointingly boring tribe. . . . We can almost hear the pieces of the plot clanking into their proper slots."

High Hearts, according to Mark Childress, "contains what must surely be the first in-saddle marital squabble between two members of a Virginia cavalry regiment," and it may be Brown's most successful work to date. Childress praises it for its depiction of the Civil War as a war that happened both on and off the battlefield. Brown's stated purpose is to recreate the contribution of women to the Civil War, and she does so in a manner that pleases most reviewers. In fact, her descriptions of the makeshift hospitals, with the stench of burning flesh coming from the piles of amputated limbs, are enough to make any would-be nurse long for a battlefield instead. Reviews of *Bingo* have been brief but fairly positive. Her return to Runnymede and to Juts and Wheezie has pleased her readers.

Wish You Were Here (1990), promoted as a "Mrs. Murphy Mystery," may be one result of Brown's aspiration to be "silly" (like Aristophanes). Mrs. Murphy is a cat who, along with a house dog called Tee Tucker, assists the postmistress of a small Virginia town not far from Charlottesville in solving a spate of murders. These "household gods" have noses for evidence that escapes the human sleuths. Opinion on the novel is divided, it appears, between those reviewers who love cats and those who do not, but even cat lovers agree that attributing coauthorship to Sneaky Pie Brown, a cat, is silly.

Only a few articles have appeared on the work of Rita Mae Brown. The most complete is Martha Chew's "Rita Mae Brown: Feminist Theorist and Southern Novelist." Chew provides an excellent overview of Brown's early political activities and attempts to show that the author's interest in issues of class influenced her first four novels. She also makes a case for understanding Brown's work as Southern and explores Brown's use of doubles as a technique for bridging the social boundaries between classes. James Mandrell, in "Questions of Genre and Gender: Contemporary American Versions of the Feminine Picaresque," claims that Chew's is too sympathetic a reading and suggests that Molly's final reconciliation with her mother in *Rubyfruit Jungle* is less a class issue than an acknowledgment of the similarities of their positions as women alienated by a male culture. He charges that Molly, like her mother, "acquiesces to the authority of that alienation." Leslie Fishbein's "*Rubyfruit Jungle*: Lesbianism, Feminism, and Narcissism" offers a harsh evaluation of *Rubyfruit Jungle* as a work that is amoral and hedonistic, "unfit . . . to be a celebration of lesbian feminism." Fishbein concludes that the novel is "the perfect document of the ME generation:

it takes the new selfishness and makes it both gay and good.'' Brown's most recent work has yet to be studied in any depth.

BIBLIOGRAPHY

Works by Rita Mae Brown

The Hand That Cradles the Rock. New York: New York University Press, 1971.
Hrotsvitra: Six Medieval Latin Plays. (translation) New York: New York University Press, 1971.
Rubyfruit Jungle. N.p.: Daughters, Inc., 1973.
Songs to a Handsome Woman. (poems) N.p.: Diana Press, 1973.
In Her Day. N.p.: Daughters, Inc., 1976.
A Plain Brown Rapper. (essays) N.p.: Diana Press, 1976.
Six of One. New York: Harper, 1978.
Southern Discomfort. New York: Harper, 1982.
Sudden Death. New York: Bantam, 1983.
High Hearts. New York: Bantam, 1986.
The Poems of Rita Mae Brown. Marshall, Minn.: Crossing Press, 1987.
Bingo. New York: Bantam, 1988.
Starting from Scratch: A Different Kind of Writers' Manual. (essays) New York: Bantam: 1988.
Wish You Were Here (A Mrs. Murphy Mystery). New York: Bantam, 1990.

Interviews

Alexander, Delores. ''People: Rita Mae Brown—The Issue for the Future Is Power.'' *Ms.* 3, No. 3 (September 1974): 110–13.
Fleischer, Leonore. ''Leonore Fleischer Talks with Rita Mae Brown.'' *Washington Post Book World* (October 15, 1978): 16.
Holt, Patricia. ''PW Interviews: Rita Mae Brown.'' *Publishers' Weekly* 214, No. 14 (October 2, 1978): 16–17.
Horn, Carole. ''Rita Mae Brown: For Her, Being Different Isn't So Different Anymore.'' *Washington Post* (October 24, 1977): C1, 13.
Klemesrud, Judy. ''Underground Book Brings Fame to Lesbian Author.'' *New York Times* (September 26, 1977): 38.
Ross, Jean W. ''Rita Mae Brown: CA Interview.'' *Contemporary Authors.* New Revision Series 11: 99–100.
Shister, Gail. ''Rita Mae Brown: A Nice Southern Girl Makes Good as a Chronicler of Unconventional Love.'' *Philadelphia Inquirer* (May 12, 1983): D 12.
Turner, Alice K. ''Fall Preview: Rita Mae Brown.'' *New York* 11, No. 38 (September 18, 1978): 60.
Uehling, Mark D., and Nikki Finke Greenberg. ''Update: Life without Martina.'' *Newsweek* 106, No. 8 (August 19, 1985): 9.
White, Diane. ''At Large: Brown Denies Categorization.'' *Boston Globe* (November 21, 1978).

Studies of Rita Mae Brown

Chew, Martha. ''Rita Mae Brown: Feminist Theorist and Southern Novelist.'' *Southern Quarterly* 22, No. 1 (Fall 1983): 61–80.

Childress, Mark. Rev. of *High Hearts. New York Times Book Review* (April 20, 1986): 22.

Davenport, Gary. ''The Fugitive Hero in New Southern Fiction'' (Rev. of *Southern Discomfort*). *Sewanee Review* 91, No. 3 (Summer 1983): 439–45.

Fishbein, Leslie. ''*Rubyfruit Jungle*: Lesbianism, Feminism, and Narcissism.'' *International Journal of Women's Studies* 7, No. 2 (March/April 1984): 155–59.

Fludas, John. Rev. of *Six of One. Saturday Review* (September 12, 1977): 4.

Fox, Terry Curtis. Rev. of *Rubyfruit Jungle* and *In Her Day. Village Voice* (September 12, 1977): 4.

Garrett, George. ''American Publishing Now'' (Rev. of *Starting from Scratch*). *Sewanee Review* 96 (July 1988): 516–25.

Gottlieb, Annie. ''Passion and Punishment'' (Rev. of *Southern Discomfort*). *New York Times Book Review* (March 21, 1982): 10.

Henze, Shelly Temchin. Rev. of *Rubyfruit Jungle. New Boston Review*, April–May, 1979. Excerpted in *Contemporary Authors*. New Revision Series 11. Edited by Ann Evory and Linda Metzger. Detroit: Gale Research Company, 1984, p. 97.

Horn, Carole. Rev. of *Rubyfruit Jungle. Washington Post* (February 14, 1974): D6.

Irwin, Edward E. ''Freedoms as Value in Three Popular Southern Novels.'' *Proteus: A Journal of Ideas* 6 (Spring 1969): 37–41.

Jakab, Elisabeth. ''Tennis and Diplomacy'' (Rev. of *Sudden Death*). *New York Times Book Review* (June 19, 1983): 12.

King, Florence. ''Rita Mae Brown's Tomboy Scarlett O'Hara.'' *Washington Post Book World* (May 4, 1986): 3, 8.

Levine, Daniel B. ''Uses of Classical Mythology in Rita Mae Brown's *Southern Discomfort*.'' *Classical and Modern Literature* 10, No. 1 (Fall 1989): 51, 63–70.

Macdonald, Cynthia. Rev. of *Six of One. Washington Post Book World* (October 15, 1978): E1.

Mandrell, James. ''Questions of Genre and Gender: Contemporary American Versions of the Feminine Picaresque.'' *Novel* 29, No. 2 (Winter 1987): 149–66.

Meyer, Charlotte M. Rev. of *Southern Discomfort. American Book Review* 5, No. 2 (January–February 1983): 22.

Webb, Marilyn. Rev. of *Rubyfruit Jungle* in ''Daughters, Inc.: A Publishing House Is Born.'' *Ms.* 11.2 (June, 1974): 37.

Wilentz, Amy. Rev. of *Sudden Death. Village Voice* 28, No. 29 (July 19, 1983): 35.

LAMAR YORK

Pat Conroy
(1945–   )

Though born in Atlanta and reared on the "necklace of Marine bases strung through the swampland of the Carolinas and Virginia" (*The Great Santini* 49), Pat Conroy's territory is the South Carolina Lowcountry, specifically the estuaries that host the cities of Beaufort and Charleston. Despite a famous conjecture that the coastal South produces no literature, and the inclination of criticism to sustain that conjecture, Conroy writes passionately about a Lowcountry as palpable as any place in Southern fiction. So impressed was the novelist by the land of his youth that there is no struggle, no attempt to search for that most compelling ingredient in Southern fiction—the right place. From the beginning of his writing, he has known what his place is, that his place is his weakness. "I am a patriot of a singular geography on the planet" (*The Prince of Tides* 5), he has declared with finality. Concerning his life there, Conroy is among the most relentlessly, authentically autobiographical of novelists. In five books between 1970 and 1986, he has told his story in detail from childhood through early adulthood. If his books continue to be utterly autobiographical, his readers might expect that his themes will now shift from the problems of growing up, of dealing with siblings and parents, and of life in college, to the problems of adulthood touched on only as narrative structure in his most recent novel. Early indications about his next novel suggest that the transition to adult themes will occur there: It reportedly deals extensively with one of Conroy's most serious concerns, dealt with only circumspectly before, the problem of racism, especially the problems faced by Jews in the South. If, on the other hand, Conroy does not continue to write his own story, he has already painted a picture of his times so bleak as to suggest that his observations of modern life will result in a powerful story, whatever the setting or the age of the characters he writes about.

BIOGRAPHY

Donald Patrick Conroy was born in Atlanta on October 26, 1946. His father, known to readers as the Great Santini, is Marine Colonel Donald Conroy, a native of Chicago; his mother was Peggy Egan Peek of Rome, Georgia, and Beaufort, South Carolina. She died in 1984. He is the oldest of seven children, most of whom still live in South Carolina, especially around Columbia. He began his education at Sacred Heart School on Courtland Street in Atlanta. In and out of many primary and secondary parochial schools as his father's Marine career advanced, Conroy spent his last two years of high school in Beaufort, South Carolina, and was graduated from there in 1963. It was his only exposure to public school before going away to college. He was president of his senior class and a star athlete. Though he preferred Duke University or the University of North Carolina at Chapel Hill or Newberry College, Conroy enrolled, at his father's urging, at The Citadel. He played varsity basketball and wrote for the college newspaper, the *Brigadier*. His first publication was a poem entitled "Poem to Thomas Wolfe" in the college literary magazine, the *Shako*, in the fall of 1963. As a freshman at The Citadel he won the Charleston *Post-Courier* award presented annually to the three best writers in the student newspaper. He was graduated in 1967 with a B.A. in English. He returned to Beaufort to teach English and coach basketball from 1967 to 1969 in the high school he had himself attended. The third year after college, 1969–70, he taught on Daufuskie Island, commuting by boat from Beaufort, but was fired from that job, a dismissal he fought through litigation, though he has not returned to teaching. During that year (1969), he married Barbara Bolling Jones of Beaufort, a recent Vietnam widow then pregnant with her second child. They were divorced in 1977. There is a daughter, Megan, from that marriage.

Conroy published his first book in 1970, *The Boo*, a defense of Lt. Colonel Thomas Nugent Courvoisie, the assistant commandant of cadets at The Citadel, who had been demoted within months of Conroy's graduation. With the vanity press publication of *The Boo*, Conroy moved to Atlanta and became the leading figure in a growing literary community there. Almost immediately the Atlanta press was calling him an "Atlanta writer," despite the consistency with which he uses the South Carolina Lowcountry as his setting. Two years later he began his association with Houghton Mifflin when they published his second book, *The Water Is Wide* (1972), completed with the help of a Ford Foundation grant. It sold only 3,000 copies. It is the story of his year on Daufuskie Island and became the movie "Conrack," starring Jon Voigt in the role of Conroy himself. It was also adapted for the theatre by Granville Burgess, Anne Crosswell, and Lee Pockriss, and directed by Stuart Ross. It opened in New York off-Broadway at the AMAS Repertory Theater, 13 East 104th Street, on November 4, 1987. In reviewing it in the *New York Times*, Stephen Holden wrote that though it is "too small in scale and intimate in tone" for Broadway, it is nevertheless "a well-made family show that has something to say" (*New York Times*, November 5, 1987).

In 1976 Conroy published his first novel, *The Great Santini*, based on his years at John C. Calhoun High School in Beaufort. Conroy's brother has said of *The Great Santini* that it is an even better picture of his sister Carol Conroy, author of *The Jewish Furrier* (1980, Old New York Book Shop Press, Atlanta, and *The Beauty Wars*, published in 1991 by W. W. Norton), than of Pat Conroy. It sold 18,000 copies, to become his first real success in the literary marketplace. It, too, has been made into a movie, starring Robert Duvall as Conroy's father and Michael O'Keefe as Conroy. While working on his next book he married Lenore Gurewitz Fleischer of Atlanta, with whom he has another daughter, Susannah. In 1980 Conroy published *The Lords of Discipline*, a novel of his years at The Citadel. It sold 40,000 copies and further cemented his claim to the attention of the book-buying public. It became a movie starring David Keith in the role of Conroy. Keith had earlier played the role of the murdering redneck, Red Pettus, in *The Great Santini*.

From 1981 to 1983 Conroy lived in Rome, Italy, partly because of a custody fight with the father of Lenore's children. After he moved back to Atlanta, Conroy published his fifth and most recent book, *The Prince of Tides* (1986) with a first printing of 250,000 copies. It remained on the *New York Times* best-seller list for over a year. It returned to Conroy's adolescent years in Beaufort for its setting and again owes much to the family role of his sister Carol, an accomplished poet. It has been filmed, once again on location in South Carolina, starring Barbra Streisand and Nick Nolte. It is the first film from a novel of his own for which Conroy has written the screenplay. He wrote an earlier screenplay for a television film called *Invictus*, which premiered in January 1989 under its English title, *Unconquered*. Conroy is currently at work on one screenplay with Doug Marlette called *The Ex*, concerning child abuse, and on another based on the dismissal of Bill Kovach as editor of the Atlanta *Journal-Constitution*, tentatively entitled ''The Editor'' or ''Above the Fold.'' Conroy and his family lived in Italy again from 1986 to 1988, then returned to Atlanta. In 1990, following the active role he took in a management dispute with the Atlanta newspapers, Conroy moved to San Francisco. As of this writing, his sixth book is in progress.

MAJOR THEMES

For his themes, Pat Conroy has relied largely on sources familiar in Southern fiction in general, and he has treated them all with humor: A sense of place, ties to family, the spiritual dimension of life, antiracism and antisemitism and, most important, the rite of passage from adolescence. ''My wound is geography'' (*Prince of Tides* 1), he wrote in opening his most recent novel. In five books he has delineated the features of the Lowcountry with an exactitude of detail worthy of Chinese landscape painting. Accepting college dormitory life as a version of family life, Conroy never reaches outside family for plot, setting, or character: All of his material is drawn from the events of family life. There are none of the events that isolate one from the family, no boy-girl romances, no sex life, no heroic frontiersman, no captains of industry or statecraft—only the ordinary people who make up families. He writes about brothers and sisters, mothers and fathers, grandparents, and fraternal roommates. The absence of a family member is used to show how the family responds to a member's absence rather than how the one family member isolated from others gets along. When the father is called to battle in *The Great Santini*, his absence serves only to heighten the dynamics of relationships among those members of the family left behind. Only family relationships count in these books.

Conroy's adolescent Catholic protagonists constantly battle the spiritual isolation brought on by a Catholic upbringing in the decidedly Protestant rural South, the "land of the hardshell, the barren hardscrabble of the spirit where the sign of the cross conjured up rich images in lands that had been totally immersed in the waters of a hard-assed Christ" (*Great Santini* 308). Yet, Conroy is never interested in theology or ritual, only with the socially isolating effect of Catholicism on the individual in much of the South.

The problems of blacks and Jews in the South melded into one argument for Conroy in his first novel. Sammy Wertzberger, the son of a merchant in Beaufort and the protagonist, Ben Meecham's best friend, says to Ben: "Thank God for the schwartze. If it wasn't for the schwartze, they'd be screwing the Jews. If it wasn't for the niggers, my father wouldn't stay in Ravenel for five minutes" (*Great Santini* 336). Antisemitism is a theme that has continued to interest Conroy, with at least one representative character in each book. The next book is promised as a more definitive statement on the isolation faced by Jews in the South.

All of Conroy's protagonists, regardless of their age, tell the story of their emergence from adolescence. Book reviewers sometimes cite initiation as an overworked theme peculiar to Southern fiction, but Conroy gives voice to a motif legitimatized repeatedly in art. Willa Cather asserted that art is possible only when one stops inventing and begins remembering. Picasso observed that when he was young he could paint like Rembrandt, but only later was able to paint like a child. Like them, Conroy relies exclusively on how one's own past influences the shape that life takes. But for Conroy the rite of passage is a dark time, coming to an end symbolically for him with a vicious sodomy scene, after which the young protagonist-victim declares the rapist had "mortgaged a portion of my boyhood, had stole my pure sanction of a world administered by a God who loved me and who had created heaven and earth as an act of dividing and scrupulous joy. Randy Thompson had defiled my image of the universe, had instructed me exceedingly well in the vanity of holding fast to faith in Eden" (*Prince of Tides* 416).

If the rite of passage is Conroy's most pervasive theme, his most powerful is his discontent with the unhappy century we have fashioned. As winning at basketball is his symbol of the best moment in adolescence, the symbol of the worst moment comes in *The Prince of Tides* in the destruction of a town in the Lowcountry to make way for a nuclear plant. Because of his use of heavy-handed humor, it is sometimes easy to forget why, other than having to grow up, Conroy finds it so painful to live in the twentieth century. The reason is inherent in all his other themes—the destruction of place, the rape of innocence, the loss of the functional family. The end of innocence occurs simultaneously for the protagonist and for the century he inherits: "It has always been difficult for me to face the truth about my childhood because it requires a commitment to explore the lineaments and features of a history I would prefer to forget" (*Prince of Tides* 134). In his use of place, his fervent love of the Lowcountry, there is the theme of the destructiveness of this century: "In Charleston [because it still feels like the Old World] you get the feeling that the twentieth century is a vast, unconscionable mistake" (17). Yet for Conroy, his own time is the inescapable beginning point for the writer. Addressing the Lillian Smith Award luncheon in Atlanta in 1982, in an address read for him in absentia by his friend Bernie Schein, Conroy cited "the transcendence of the artist over the unspeakable atrocities of her time." He has transcended the prevailing South in order to write about it. Despite Pat Conroy's irrepressible humor, these are dark, elegiac books.

SURVEY OF CRITICISM

As to their ultimate worth, Conroy seems to give grudging attention to his literary reputation, apparently aiming only for an appreciative readership. He demeans himself as a writer. In a letter to a friend he wrote: "The Citadel as a school and Conroy as a writer are both terrified that it will be discovered that we are mediocre and second-rate." Although those sentiments about himself were expressed privately, Conroy has expressed the same opinion in public. To an Atlanta *Journal-Constitution* interviewer he complained that "in so many things [writing a novel, an opera, a symphony, a book review, a play, an essay] Atlanta is in a holding pattern over a country known as 'Second-Ranked.' I'm a novelist who holds a passport in the same country" (Atlanta *Journal-Constitution*, October 6, 1987). Conroy has offered part of the reason for his self-analysis. He recently found himself in the thick of a controversy involving the resignation of Bill Kovach as editor of the Atlanta *Journal-Constitution*. Writers and editors took sides with Kovach or with the newspaper's management. Conroy sided with Kovach and carried on a protracted verbal battle with Lewis Grizzard, a *Journal-Constitution* columnist. In a letter to the *Journal-Constitution*, not published there but in another Atlanta paper, *Creative Loafing*, Conroy wrote to Grizzard: "We are now inextricably bound in the history of Southern literature. I don't think either one of us is going to be rated very highly. There was too much deprivation, sorrow and pure burlesque in our pinched and narrow childhoods. We carry the scars and griefs too heavily" (*Creative Loafing*, November 26, 1988).

After five books in 20 years, Pat Conroy has been the subject of only two critical articles, one in *Critique* and one in the *Southern Literary Journal*. The University of South Carolina Press recently judged him not yet ready for inclusion in the series of critical and biographical works called *Understanding Contemporary American Literature*. Similarly, Twayne Publishers does not rate him qualified for one of its *Twayne United States Authors Series*. He has no Pulitzer, no National Book Award, not even Atlanta's own Jimmy Townsend Award for Fiction, in effect only since his last book, *The Prince of Tides*, was published. In 1988 he was inducted into the South Carolina Academy of Authors Hall of Fame, which also honors DuBose Heyward, Julia Peterkin, William Gilmore Simms, Mary Boykin Chesnut, James Dickey, and Josephine Pickney, who was inducted simultaneously with Conroy. Ironically, the induction took place soon after the most recent round of anticensorship battles Conroy has had to contend with in the state he has honored with all his written work.

If not widely read by critics, Conroy's rhetoric has come to the attention of a large number of readers and reviewers. He has also attracted the attention of Hollywood's filmmakers, which might help explain his failure to appeal to larger numbers of scholarly and academic essayists. It is axiomatic in American letters that popular attention and scholarly attention are not mutual attractions. Atlanta writers in particular refer to this as the "Gone with the Wind" syndrome. Atlanta itself as a choice of places to write from, or about, does not lend much help to professional readers of Southern literature. Southern writers are assumed by definition to be from, and interested in writing about, less cosmopolitan venues of the South.

The serious reader of Southern literature might well ask what Goethe, Defoe, Chekhov, Chaucer, Cervantes, Caesar, St. Augustine, Hesiod, Magellan, Ovid, Plutarch, Pizzaro, Plato, Voltaire, Thucydides, Turgenev, Tacitus, and Marlon Brando have in common. Among other things they doubtless share is a place in *The History of Southern Literature* (1985). But like all compendiums, this book is as well defined by what it doesn't include as by what it does. It does not include Pat Conroy. Granted, Conroy has done very little to attract the attention of scholars by writing novels needing analysis. He should, however, appeal strongly to any reader interested in the modern South. The purpose in his books is to tell a rousing good story. They will likely be among the most readable metaphors from which the history of the later twentieth-century South comes. If Conroy does not share with Plato and Chaucer some brief mention in *The History of Southern Literature*, which was published after the appearance of four of his five books thus far, he does share with Betty Adcock, Michael Bishop, Lonnie Coleman, Rosemary Daniel, Ann Deagon, Paul Hemphill, Keith Maillard, Richard Marius, Peter Meinke, Marion Montgomery, Larry Rubin, Bettie Sellers, Anne Rivers Siddons, R. T. Smith, Mark Steadman, John Stone, Ellen Voigt, and Vinnie Williams the fate of not having been included in that volume. Though few critics are among them yet, his readers are sufficient in number to guarantee that he will stay in print until critics read him too, that his career as a novelist will not finally be summed up as "the night the hogs ate Willie" (*Southern Living*, June 1981, 104).

BIBLIOGRAPHY

Works by Pat Conroy

The Boo. Verona, Va.: McClure Books, 1970.
The Water Is Wide. Boston: Houghton Mifflin, 1972.
The Great Santini. Boston: Houghton Mifflin, 1976.
The Lords of Discipline. Boston: Houghton Mifflin, 1980.
The Prince of Tides. Boston: Houghton Mifflin, 1986.

Studies of Pat Conroy

Burkholder, Robert E. "The Uses of Myth in Pat Conroy's *The Great Santini*." *Critique: Studies in Modern Fiction* 21 (1979): 31–37.
Holden, Stephen. "The Stage: 'Conrack,' Musical Based on Novel." *New York Times* November 5, 1987, natl. ed., sec. 2:4.
York, Lamar. "Pat Conroy," 43–46 in *Biographical Dictionary of Contemporary Catholic American Writing*, ed. Daniel J. Tynan. New York: Greenwood, 1989.
———. "Pat Conroy's Portrait of the Artist as a Young Southerner." *Southern Literary Journal* 19 (1987): 34–46.

TERRY ROBERTS

John William Corrington
(1932–1988)

In a 1981 interview for the *Contemporary Authors* series, John William Corrington spoke bluntly about his regional identity.

If someone said, "Are you an American writer or a Southern writer?" I'd say very clearly, "I'm a Southern writer." I have no desire to represent or even fiddle around with New York and California or the rest of it. They appear in my work simply because I've been there . . . and the experience is useful. But I would maintain I am a Southern writer, and if nobody else wants to be, that's fine; then we would have only one: me. (Walters and Ross 115)

Partly in response to an introduction to *Southern Writers in the Sixties* written by Corrington and Miller Williams, critics have found four key elements in Corrington's Southernness: "a strong concern with religion of the Calvinist variety; a deep awareness of the past; a pervasive feeling for the land; a powerful sense of responsibility, not only to others but also for the self" (Granville Hicks, *Saturday Review*, December 24, 1966, 43). Indeed, the lack of serious scholarly reply to Corrington's fiction may be partly the result of his having remained so traditionally *Southern* when many of his contemporaries have either fled the South or denied the importance of regionalism altogether.

Though a number of critics have dismissed Corrington's work as Faulknerian, he created a body of fiction that explores, and in a sense attempts a reply to, a frightening postmodernist world. In addition to the qualities listed by Granville Hicks, Corrington was also deeply concerned with human suffering and sought in his fiction to define an appropriate response to the pain he saw around him. His protagonists often attempt to apply a systematic moral structure—either philosophical, religious, or legal—to their lives in an effort to place them in a larger, more meaningful context. Significantly, they are actively rather than passively sensitive to moral complexity. They are never victims.

A retrospective reading of Corrington's work reveals that he sought to define a metaphysics of action appropriate to the twentieth century.

BIOGRAPHY

John William Corrington was born October 28, 1932, in Memphis, Tennessee, to John Wesley and Viva Shelley Corrington. Raised in a Catholic household, he was educated both in public and Catholic private schools, which may have sparked his long-running debate with Catholic doctrine. (He was expelled from a Jesuit high school for "having the wrong attitude.") His early interest in literature was nurtured at Centenary College. He not only finished a B.A. there in 1956, he also learned his way around the Shreveport area, the Northern Louisiana town that would become the Yoknapatawpha of his fiction. He married Joyce Elaine Hooper (a chemistry professor and writer) in 1960 just prior to earning an M.A. at Rice University. Unable to finish a planned Ph.D. at Rice because of a dispute with a professor, Corrington moved to England to study with David Daiches at the University of Sussex, where he earned his D.Phil. in 1964. During and after his work in England, Corrington served on the faculty at Louisiana State University (LSU) despite growing dissatisfaction with the politics and overspecialization of American academics.

While on the faculty at LSU, Corrington was asked by the university press to read a manuscript by historian Eric Voegelin. Already interested in Southern history, particularly the history of the Civil War, Corrington was mesmerized by Voegelin's theories on biblical history:

When I finished Israel and Revelation, I had the distinct feeling that Professor Voegelin had shown me how God did it—. . . that the world looked different, less arbitrary and more intelligible. . . . All the things that interested me: theology, literary criticism, symbolic studies, even psychology . . . [were] made coherent by Voegelin's work. (Walters and Ross 115)

Inspired by Voegelin, Corrington sought in his early fiction—particularly the Civil War novel *And Wait for the Night* (1964)—to "transfigure the past in such a way as to resist historicism, . . . particularly a secularism devoid of purpose" (Mills 588). He hoped to dramatize the significant patterns in human experience revealed by an inspired historical overview. This early fascination with the past as the key to the present led many critics to make the inevitable but misleading comparison to Faulkner, a comparison that continues to haunt his reputation.

Corrington's life as a scholar was intense if relatively short-lived. After publishing a number of essays on modern writers (notably James Joyce) and serving as department chair at LSU, he left academia in 1973 for law school. This career change reflected a change in direction in Corrington's fiction as well. From the mid-1970s on, Corrington exhibited a growing interest in ideas of justice, whether personal, legal, or metaphysical. He often portrayed the extremes of human suffering juxtaposed against the sincere efforts of good people to understand and perhaps even to relieve it. Although Corrington only practiced law in New Orleans from 1975 to 1979, its effect is obvious throughout his work, even in the two novellas (*Decoration Day* and *The Risi's Wife*) collected under the title *All My Trials* (1987) a year before his death. The central figure of these two long stories, retired Judge Albert Sidney Finch, is in many ways the most typical of Corrington heroes. He is old enough to exhibit wisdom and yet young enough and involved enough to pursue justice.

While still involved in private legal practice, Corrington began co-writing with his wife both screenplays and television scripts. While most of their screenplays were not transformed into memorable films (they include *Battle of the Planet of the Apes* and *Killer Bees*), the pair were head writers for a number of successful daytime television shows (including "General Hospital"). Their partnership culminated in the coauthorship of the four "New Orleans Mysteries" (*So Small a Carnival*, *A Civil Death*, *A Project Named Desire*, and *The White Zone*) published for a mass-market audience during the 1980s (the last, published posthumously in 1990). Corrington was careful to distinguish between screen-writing (which he admitted they did strictly for the income it provided) and fiction. The mysteries, however, do reflect clearly the husband and wife's shared background in screenwriting; they are dramatic and almost hectically fast-paced. Although Corrington once argued that no good novel could be effectively dramatized, the mysteries seem tailor-made for television. However these books are to be addressed critically, Corrington continued to write "serious" fiction during their creation.

The novels and short stories written during the 1970s and 1980s reflect Corrington's continued interest in the problems of human violence and suffering, as well as his search for a theological answer. His interest in the structure and values of Catholicism remained evident; in fact, all of his books contain the dedication "A.M.D.G." an abbreviation of the Latin motto of the Jesuits, *ad maiorem Dei gloriam*. While he remained a practicing Catholic, his theological interests grew in scope to include the study of Eastern religions. Two of his last stories were about Buddhism ("Heroic Measures/Vital Signs" 1986) and Hinduism ("The Risi's Wife"). In his 1989 memoir of Corrington, William Mills quoted the last letter Corrington wrote to a friend:

I see you haven't lost your faith in God, or your love of His Word. Neither have I. I've spent all the time since I saw you watching for His utterances in Louisiana swamps. I can't say for certain, but it seems as I get older, I begin to see Him everywhere. I am persuaded that the Vedantists and the masters of Kabbalah are right. He did not create the world—He expressed the world within Himself. (594)

Though he came far theologically from the high school boy arguing with his Jesuit teachers, John William Corrington's life still seems prematurely cut off. His death on November 24, 1988, from a sudden heart attack, quieted a mature but still restless intellect, a questing spirit. He had worked his way through a number of literary genres, always seeking theological as well as technical solutions. His style, influenced by his legal as well as his screenwriting career, matured into a concise, sensuous prose that served his metaphysical pursuits well. For in retrospepct, Corrington's constant challenging of himself with new careers and new modes of expression seems to have been only one facet of his constant theological self-challenge.

Although Corrington's poetry was primarily the product of his student days, he continued to work in the genre throughout his life. As Mills points out, his poetry from the early 1960s introduces many of his themes: The effect of violence on both individual and community, the complex influence of the past, and the search for transcendence. The influence of Auden and of Cummings, references to Joyce and Lorca suggest Corrington's extensive and sensitive reading in modern literature. If anything, Corrington's early poems too much reflect a life of scholarship, a weakness that he eventually overcame in his fiction.

Corrington's first novel, *And Wait for the Night* (1964), was set during and just after the Civil War, principally in Shreveport. His depiction of the horrors of postwar occupation caused many critics to label him a Southern apologist. Granville Hicks wrote that "Corrington is still trying to demonstrate that the Confederacy should have won the War" (*Saturday Review*, May 23, 1964, 40). In retrospect, however, the novel's regionalism seems less significant than its exploration of history and violence. What seemed at the time a narrow-minded apology now reads as a first effort by a novelist of ideas. *The Upper Hand* (1967), a more self-consciously literary novel, is in part allegorical. Set in Shreveport and New Orleans, it examines the conflicts experienced by a spiritual man adrift in a secular society. Corrington's third novel (the last he was to publish for 14 years) was *The Bombardier* (1970). Corrington called it "a philosophical meditation" that attempted "to explain the present [the rootless 1960s] as it rose from the past" (Walters and Ross 115).

Corrington's early novels were widely reviewed and generally well accepted, but critics agree that he wrote most effectively in the short story. Between 1968 and 1981 he published three significant collections of short fiction. These stories are tightly constructed, tautly written (reflecting his apprenticeship in poetry), and often experimental in the modernist tradition. They focus on serious and sensitive protagonists faced with difficult problems, dilemmas that often have grave theological implications and whose solution requires delving into the past. Influenced by Voegelin, Corrington's treatment of time is tied to his treatment of spirituality. One of the main characters of "If Time Were Not/A Moving Thing" is a devout nineteenth-century Creole woman who decides mystically that time "is surely the fool of love" (*Lonesome Traveler* 23). Her opposite, the protagonist of the alternate narrative, is a twentieth-century soul who studies the nightly TV news for the scientific truths to be found there. The spiritual and temporal worlds are joined, Corrington seems to be saying in all these stories, but not in the way we suspect.

This connection is also suggested in what is probably Corrington's best novel, *Shad Sentell* (1984). The narrator, scion of a wealthy Louisiana oil family, is forced to choose emotionally between his cold, business-obsessed father and his rowdy, womanizing uncle. The reader realizes early on that Uncle Shad, the title character, is the boy's biological father and his mother the only woman Shad ever truly loved. (The theme of the search for the father, suggested perhaps by Joyce, is common in Corrington's work, as it illustrates dramatically the influence of the past on the present.) At first glance the novel seems to validate a stereotyped redneck violence and indiscriminate lust for female flesh that, while comic, is not at all vintage Corrington. Behind the comic, even slapstick, facade, however, lurks a deeper point, one that may have been the result of Corrington's studies in Eastern religions. The protagonist of the novel, Shad Sentell, is a famous fighter of oil rig fires in the mold of Red Adair. He is also blessed with extraordinary sexual prowess. (The working title of the novel was "The Man Who Slept with Women.") His crudeness and violence mask a deeper nature, however. And in the context of the rest of Corrington's fiction, Sentell is clearly a sort of redneck avatar, exhibiting a God-like power for both destruction and creation. Seen in this light, it is easier to accept his lust for his own biological daughter and his miraculous survival of an oil platform explosion near the end of the novel. As a character, Sentell carries a heavy figurative burden of mythological power, but he does so successfully because of the breezy light-heartedness of much of the book. In 1980, when he had just finished a draft of the book, Corrington told an interviewer that "it was the best novel . . . [he] ever wrote," a judgment that time has validated (Walters and Ross 115).

The theological weight of Corrington's fiction does not at first seem to mesh with his career in screen and mystery writing. The four New Orleans mysteries, however, should not be dismissed as mere money-makers. They suggest important insights into serious fiction. The three "detectives"—a sophisticated black policeman, a cynical reporter, and a debutante turned D.A.—face lonely decisions that first isolate and then lead them back into the community of men and women. The seamy New Orleans atmosphere is classic to the genre, and the plots (unlike those of some Corrington novels) are suspensefully tight. In fact, the genre itself fits the Corrington pattern nicely: A morally sensitive individual must delve into his own and his culture's past to unravel the modern dilemma.

MAJOR THEMES

Corrington's first concern is almost always with the past and its mysterious influence on the present. For Corrington's characters, wisdom is most often to be found in the study of their culture's past or in honest acceptance of their own. In the title story of the 1978 collection, *The Actes and Monuments* (the title is taken from John Foxe's 1563 *The Actes and Monuments of These Latter and Perilous Days* or *Foxe's Book of Martyrs*), a semi-retired New York lawyer takes up residence in Vicksburg, where he meets and befriends the mysterious older attorney, W. C. Grierson. Grierson lives in an old, ramshackle office whose walls hide an amazing legal library. Although Grierson's services are not often required in the present, he is slowly working his way through the documented legal cases of Western history, secular as well as religious, sorting out facts and righting wrongs by writing appeals and briefs. Taken out of the context of the story, the activity seems at best escapist fantasy on Grierson's part, but for the physically and emotionally drained New York lawyer, Grierson's legal knowledge and human wisdom become an oasis in a modern desert. His study of the past has justified, insofar as it is possible to do so, the present. In *Shad Sentell*, the narrator believes he is Shad's nephew until the end of the novel. When his true father's identity is revealed to him, that single piece of the puzzle causes his entire life to leap into focus. His personal past suddenly makes sense, and his personality is genetically and emotionally validated. This belief in the primary significance of the past is such a hallmark of Southern writing that it has in a sense damaged Corrington's reputation. He has occasionally been dismissed as yet one more haunted Southerner.

This simple-minded criticism has also been fed by Corrington's determination to remain primarily a realistic writer, whose experiments in technique and point of view are not very different from those of William Faulkner and Thomas Wolfe in the 1930s and 1940s. What critics have largely failed to understand, however, is that Corrington's theological themes (Eastern as well as Western) in many ways necessitated a realistic format. In fact, one of his consistent concerns is what correct action may be taken in a world gone starkly secular. His detailed evocation of the Louisiana landscape—and his constant attention to the pleasures and pains afforded by food, alcohol, sex, violence, music, and fishing—is a technical counterpoint to those passages dedicated to the inner realities of thought, intuition, and mediation. His subtextual message throughout is that either the spiritual or physical alone is incomplete, sterile. Even when conscious of a higher reality, a Corrington character must act in the fallen world—act and take responsibility for those actions.

The theme of responsibility is tied directly to his constant concern with man as a moral agent. He considered his own Southern, Catholic traditions a vital foundation for life in a less than certain modern world. And while he expanded on those traditions in his own thinking, he returned again and again in his fiction to the need for individuals to accept their own moral responsibility for past action, to accept loss and failure as a prelude to a wiser, more humane existence. In Corrington's universe, a human being possesses a conscience and a soul.

In recognizing their own spiritual nature, Corrington's characters are often able to build hope for the future out of a mean past. One of the reasons they are able to do so is their reference to, if not outright dependence on, a systemized code of behavior. Whether it be the church, the legal system, or cultural tradition, Corrington's characters strive to unite a larger vision with the ability to act. Technically, he characteristically portrays the struggle for synthesis with a first-person narrative that blends retrospection with concise description of environment and action. The speculative voice and active character being one and the same achieves in many instances the powerful sense of wholeness too often missing from modern life.

SURVEY OF CRITICISM

Other than reviews of separate works and some few interviews, there has been little written about Corrington's work. Although his early fiction was published by Putnam and widely reviewed, after 1970 his serious work was published by various university presses to smaller audiences. Ironically, his style became sharper and more evocative, and his character-narrators more engaging and complex as he matured as a writer. The one readily available, good article on Corrington is poet William Mills' 1989 memoir.

The lack of serious attention is undeserved. Corrington's short fiction in particular establishes him as a serious and important Southern voice. There are a number of elements in his work—the relationship of time and spirituality, the conflict between secular law and abstract justice, the influence of history on cultural and personal identity—that deserve close examination. Ultimately, all his fiction and much of his poetry are about the efforts of an individual to act morally and constructively in a corrupt world. And although it is easy for many critics to dismiss his work because of its very Southernness, his best stories address timeless issues with a depth and power that transcend regionalism.

BIBLIOGRAPHY

Works by John William Corrington

Poetry

Where We Are. Washington, D.C.: Charioteer Press, 1962.
The Anatomy of Love and Other Poems. Ft. Lauderdale: Roman Books, 1964.
Mr. Clean and Other Poems. San Francisco: Amber House, 1964.
Lines to the South and Other Poems. Baton Rouge: Louisiana State University Press, 1965.

Criticism

Southern Writing in the Sixties: Fiction, ed. and intro. with Miller Williams. Baton Rouge: Louisiana State University Press, 1966.
Southern Writing in the Sixties: Poetry, ed. and intro. with Miller Williams. Baton Rouge: Louisiana State University Press, 1967.

Fiction

And Wait for the Night. New York: Putnam, 1964.
The Upper Hand. New York: Putnam, 1967.
The Lonesome Traveler and Other Stories. New York: Putnam, 1968.

The Bombardier. New York: Putnam, 1970.
The Actes and Monuments. Urbana: University of Illinois Press, 1978.
The Southern Reporter. Baton Rouge: Louisiana State University Press, 1981.
Shad Sentell. New York: Congdon and Weed, 1984.
"Heroic Measures/Vital Signs." *Southern Review* 22 (1986): 804–27.
All My Trials: Two Novellas. Fayetteville: University of Arkansas Press, 1987.
The Collected Stories of John William Corrington. Baton Rouge: Louisiana State University Press, 1991.

With Joyce H. Corrington

So Small a Carnival. New York: Viking, 1986.
A Civil Death. New York: Viking, 1987.
A Project Named Desire. New York: Viking, 1987.
The White Zone. New York: Viking, 1990.

Studies of John William Corrington

This selective bibliography omits many scholarly articles on modern literature and the philosophy of history. Although there is no definitive bibliography available on Corrington, *Contemporary Authors* (New Revision Series, vol. 8) offers a starting point through 1980.

Hicks, Granville. "The Continuing War." *Saturday Review* 23 (May 1964): 39–40.
———. "Something of Value from the South." *Saturday Review* 24 (December 1966): 43–44.
Mills, William. "Risking the Bait: John William Corrington, 1932–1988." *Southern Review* 25 (1989): 586–94.
Walters, Marian, and Jean W. Ross. "John William Corrington." *Contemporary Authors*, New Revision Series, ed. Ann Evory and Linda Metzger. Detroit: Gale Research 8 (1983):113–17.

Ellen Douglas
[Josephine Ayres Haxton]
(1921–   )

A traditionalist in her attention to the craft of storytelling and her incisive portrayal of Southern families going about their ordinary lives, Ellen Douglas is also an unconventional writer who dares to choose such unlikely heroines as aging and elderly women and to place at center stage such treacherous subjects as day-to-day relationships between black and white women. In her treatment of the latter, only Peter Taylor is her rival.

BIOGRAPHY

Josephine Ayres Haxton—who publishes under the pseudonym Ellen Douglas—was born July 12, 1921, in Natchez, Mississippi, home of her grandparents. The child of Laura Davis Ayres and Richardson Ayres, she grew up with two sisters and a brother in Hope, Arkansas, and Alexandria, Louisiana. Her father, a civil engineer, worked for the Arkansas highway department before moving his family to Louisiana, where he built roads and bridges as an independent contractor.

Both sides of the family were "old Mississippi." Haxton has said that her ancestors moved into Adams County near the end of the eighteenth century. As a child, she loved visiting relatives in Natchez every summer. As an adult, she has lived almost exclusively in Mississippi. Following two years at Randolph-Macon Woman's College in Virginia, she graduated from the University of Mississippi in 1942 with majors in English and sociology. In 1944 she married Kenneth Haxton, whom she had met at Ole Miss, and in 1945 they moved to Greenville, where he entered his parents' clothing business and she began raising a family. Haxton lived in Greenville until 1983, when she and her husband divorced and she moved to Jackson.

Although as a child she had dreamed of being a writer, Haxton did not turn seriously to writing until she was 34 years old, and she did not publish her first book until she was 40. As she explained in an interview with John Griffin Jones, she grew up in a time and a place in which "men were expected to enter professions or to be successful in business, and women were expected to be homemakers." Thus, though she worked briefly after college—at a radio station and a U.S. Army induction center near Alexandria and at Gotham Book Mart in New York City, where she had gone "to see the world"—once she married, she devoted full-time to homemaking. After the last of her three sons entered nursery school, she began to find time for writing. She told Laurie L. Brown in an interview that having servants—as was possible in the South at that time—helped free her to write: "I was a Southern woman in a particular period in history when it was possible to have servants; and that's probably why it was possible for me to do the work I did. If I had had the care of a house, and the raising of children entirely on me, I probably wouldn't have had the time to do it."

Haxton has frequently said that much of her writing is inspired by memories of family storytelling and family experiences but that she transforms these extensively and imaginatively as she writes. She began her writing career by drafting several separate stories based on such transformed memories and experiences, but along the way she realized (as Eudora Welty had in writing *The Golden Apples*) that a number of the stories were actually about the same characters at different points in their lives. She then revised and combined these to produce her first novel, *A Family's Affairs* (1962).

Her 6-year struggle to write this novel and several additional short stories was rewarded with unusually easy and quick transition to publication and acclaim. In several interviews Haxton has recounted how *A Family's Affairs* came to be published. She had given the manuscript to a friend to read, and he, without telling her, had passed it on to an editor at Houghton Mifflin. When the editor called Haxton out of the blue to ask that she enter the manuscript in the press's 1961 fellowship competition, she resisted, saying she did not feel the manuscript was yet ready for publication. He replied that if she would consent to enter it, he could tell her that *A Family's Affairs* had already won the competition.

It was at this time that Josephine Haxton became Ellen Douglas: "Maybe I wanted to separate my private life and my family from my public life. Maybe I was shy" (interview with Sylvia Campbell). In a recent interview, the author explained that she chose her grandmother's name, Ellen, because her grandmother had been an inspiration to her: "My grandmother wrote stories with her children and grandchildren as heroines. She made me see writing as something I might do too." Looking for a Scottish surname to parallel her own Scottish maiden name (Ayres), she chose "Douglas" at the suggestion of her publisher (telephone interview, July 26, 1990).

At the same time that Houghton Mifflin was preparing Douglas's first book for publication, *The New Yorker* was bringing out her first story, "On the Lake" (August 29, 1961). It was included in the O. Henry collection of best stories in

1962. In 1963, Houghton Mifflin published Douglas's second book and only collection of short fiction, *Black Cloud, White Cloud*, which included a revised version of "On the Lake" under the new title of "Hold On." These first two books are connected through the character Anna McGovern. In her afterword to a new edition of *Black Cloud, White Cloud* (1989), Douglas describes the two books this way: "The novel explores the lives of the grown people by whom Anna is surrounded and formed—her family's lives. More central to the stories are the moral dilemmas posed for the child and young woman [Anna] living among black people in the South." *A Family's Affairs* and *Black Cloud, White Cloud* were each named by the *New York Times* as among the five best works of fiction for the respective years of their publication.

Following this auspicious and prolific beginning, Douglas has steadily turned out a new book at roughly five-year intervals. *Where the Dreams Cross* (1968), *Apostles of Light* (1973), and *The Rock Cried Out* (1979) all deal with topical issues—prejudice and corruption; the treatment (or mistreatment) of the elderly in nursing homes; and the racial tensions of the late 1960s and early 1970s. *Apostles of Light* was nominated for a National Book Award, and *The Rock Cried Out* was written with the help of a grant from the National Endowment for the Arts. *A Lifetime Burning* (1982) and *Can't Quit You Baby* (1988) are focused more on realism of character than on issue. *A Lifetime Burning* is narrated in diary form by a 62-year-old woman who wants to get at the truth of her past but who has trouble telling the truth because the past is painful. *Can't Quit You Baby* portrays the work relationship and uneasy friendship of a white home owner and her black maid, while also revealing the two women's separate histories. Douglas has also published a children's book, *The Magic Carpet and Other Tales* (1987), in which she retells some favorite fairy tales.

For several years, Douglas has taught creative writing at the University of Mississippi during the fall semester. Prior to her association with that school, she taught one semester a year for four years at Northeast Louisiana University. She was visiting writer at the University of Virginia in the spring semester of 1984, and she held the Eudora Welty chair at Millsaps College in the spring of 1985 and again in the fall of 1992. She is currently at work on a new novel. Her son Brooks Haxton is also a published writer, author of four books of poetry.

In 1989, Douglas received the fiction award from the Southern Fellowship of Writers in recognition of her overall repertoire.

MAJOR THEMES

Like many other Southern writers, Ellen Douglas writes about families and individuals molded by the values and conditions common in the South of the early and mid-twentieth century. But she resists suggestions that the Southern literary tradition in general or the "Greenville literary tradition" in particular may have influenced her. When she was very young, she did, she admits, unwisely attempt to imitate William Faulkner; and living in Greenville she enjoyed friendships with Shelby Foote and Walker Percy while they too were living there—friendships that fed, she says, her reading but not her writing. She names Fyodor Dostoyevski, Thomas Mann, Joseph Conrad, and Henry James as more likely influences, for she was reading them while thinking about writing, and she found their visions of the world intriguing (Jones interview).

Douglas perceptively suggests that the greatest influences on her writing have not been certain writers but certain elements in her background and in the South: (1) her strict Presbyterian upbringing and the King James version of the Bible; (2) the extended family in which she grew up, composed of people forever interested in one another's character and personality and forever telling tales and listening to tales; and (3) the South's racial situation, which from childhood she found puzzling and burdensome (Brown interview). These three influences are indeed reflected in her fiction.

The first and second come together in her first novel to create and introduce one of her general themes: responsibility. The extended Anderson family of *A Family's Affairs* resembles in many ways Douglas's own extended family, the young character Anna McGovern possibly being a fictional version of the young Josephine Haxton. The setting of the novel is Homochitto, Mississippi, home of Anna's grandmothers and aunts, whom Anna and her family visit regularly on holidays and summer vacations, traveling across the Mississippi River from Louisiana to get there—just as young Josephine and her family regularly crossed the river from Arkansas and Louisiana to visit relatives in Natchez. Anna's mother's side of the family is a close-knit group who spend much time telling tales about their pasts, analyzing happenings, and minding one another's business. The women of the family especially feel that any family member's problem is the whole family's affair; they consider it their responsibility to help resolve that problem. Here, the theme of responsibility appears as the responsibility of the individual to the family unit. The Andersons abide by an unstated but clearly felt code that an individual should not operate in isolation but owes allegiance first and always to the family, and they are always acting for, even sacrificing for, one another.

This attitude is apparent from the comic first chapter, "A Courtship," in which the matriarch of the clan, Kate Anderson, undertakes to promote the slow-moving courtship between her daughter Charlotte and Ralph McGovern; to the last chapter, "Death and Homecoming," in which the always-wayward Anderson son, Will, finally comes into the fold and assumes his responsibility to the family as his mother, Kate, is dying.

The intensity of the family's feelings for each other, their sense of responsibility to and for one another, can be explained not just by the central role of family to the Southerner but also by the family's upbringing in the Presbyterian church. For though the McGovern side of the family is more seriously and rigidly religious, the church is as much a part of all their lives as is Sunday dinner. Their church stresses that an individual must assume responsibility to the church, family, and mankind, as we see in the second chapter when the Presbyterian pastor pressures Ralph McGovern to fulfill his responsibilities to all three by becoming an elder in the church. The hymn referred to early and late in the novel—"Bles't be the tie that binds"—applies to the tie that binds the family together in love and responsibility, as well as to the tie of Christian love and responsibility.

Anna McGovern, like Ellen Douglas, is aware that her family's bind can be stifling and harmful at times, yet she appreciates the moral consciousness that this family heritage imparts. During her grandmother's funeral at the end of the book, Anna thinks:

Whatever you say about them . . . however far you may go away, your reasons for going would never include that . . . they were ignoble. They live by their own lights, and they blame their failures on themselves. And what could they have given me—what could anyone give a child—more precious than the habit of moral consciousness, the conviction that one must be a man, must look after his own, must undertake, must dare, and always every man in the shadow of death? [italics in original]

The theme of responsibility appears, under various guises, repeatedly in Douglas's fiction. In *Apostles of Light*, where Douglas's concern is the care of the aged, Aunt Martha's relatives are happy to assign responsibility for her care to others—unlike the Anderson daughters of *A Family's Affairs*, who care for Kate until her death at age 85. Despite their good intentions, Martha's relatives even fail to visit her consistently in the nursing home. In her interview with Jones, Douglas said that this novel was inspired by her own visits to relatives in nursing homes, though she never encountered such extremes of neglect and corruption as she associates with the nursing home depicted in *Apostles*.

The theme of responsibility appears most frequently in conjunction with the third influence on Douglas's fiction, the South's racial situation. Douglas has written one novel to reflect the tensions and horrors of the racial conflicts that erupted during the civil rights movement of the 1960s and 1970s. In *The Rock Cried Out*, her narrator seeks to understand a particular tragedy from that period. In discussing how she came to write this novel, Douglas herself expresses the sensitive white Southerner's burden of guilt and sense of responsibility for not trying to promote change during that period: "One always had a gnawing guilt, or I did, because I wasn't particularly an activist of any kind. I didn't do any of a number of things I might have done to influence events. . . . That was a source of guilt to a great number of people all over the state, and certainly it was to me, too" (Jones interview). This book became her way of now assuming responsibility, of trying to do something, if no more than to tell the truth about the past.

Douglas may not have been sufficiently detached from her material with *The Rock Cried Out*, but in two other works—*Black Cloud, White Cloud* and *Can't Quit You Baby*—her treatment of relations between black and white individuals and of the theme of the white society's burden of responsibility for the racial past is generally masterful. In the afterword to the 1989 edition of *Black Cloud, White Cloud*, Douglas indicates that she felt a moral responsibility to write about the coming together of black and white lives: "For how could I, living in this time and place, fail to write about these lives—about the corrosive hatreds, the crippled loves, the confusions, the flashes of nobility and heroism, the ways of making do, making room?"

In one story in the collection, "I Just Love Carrie Lee," the unnamed white narrator pats herself on the back for the responsibility she has assumed for Carrie Lee, the family's longtime maid. Douglas makes the reader realize, however, just how shallow and self-serving the narrator's remarks are. In "Jessie" and "Hold On," a sensitive white woman—this time she is Anna McGovern Glover—takes actions toward individual blacks predicated on her sense of guilt and responsibility for the South's racial past. The actions have unfortunate consequences, suggesting that guilt and a sense of obligation are not sound grounds for employing someone or for attempts at friendship. The theme of *Black Cloud, White Cloud* might be that the white Southerner's sense of guilt, together with the long history of inequality, makes comfortable relations between blacks and whites difficult, despite efforts on either side.

Can't Quit You Baby is one of the few novels ever to take as its essential subject the everyday lives of Southern white and black women in that space where such lives have historically most often come together: in the white woman's kitchen. In her portrayal of Cornelia O'Kelly and Julia "Tweet" Carrier, Douglas creates the everyday world of mistress and servant so convincingly that we wonder why more authors have not turned to this subject. The novel's omniscient narrator comments on this choice of setting: "There would have been no way in that time and place—the nineteen-sixties and seventies in Mississippi—for them to get acquainted, except across the kitchen table from each other, shelling peas, peeling apples, polishing silver. . . . In this house the white woman had to choose to sit down to set the tone of their connection." The novel is about more than the relation between the two women. Through Tweet's storytelling across the kitchen table and through the narrator's reflections on Cornelia's family, we see the separate—and contrasting—pasts that have made the two women who they are. We also see events occur that cause the two women eventually to remove their masks, Cornelia to stop turning a deaf ear to Tweet's stories and to move out of her sheltered Southern lady's world, their roles to reverse (the scene shifts from Cornelia's kitchen to Tweet's living room), and the possibility of a more honest bonding between them to emerge.

A related but underlying motif connects many of Douglas's works. From young Anna of *A Family's Affairs* to Corrine of *A Lifetime Burning* and the awakened Cornelia of the last section of *Can't Quit You Baby*, there are characters who feel compelled to figure out, to understand—to know—the meaning of events in their lives and their pasts. They feel a moral responsibility not to float along on the surface of life but to recognize and to report the truth. Moreover, Douglas's own concern with knowing, with telling, with recognizing the slipperiness of truth, frequently shapes the form of her narration. This motif moves to the surface of her fiction in *Can't Quit You Baby*, in which she speaks as author/narrator and comments directly not only on the action but also on the author's role in shaping the story that gets told. In *A Lifetime Burning*, the main character, Corrine, is the narrator, and her sense of moral obligation to tell the truth—and her conflicting difficulty in facing the truth—comprises the novel's action and determines the shape the novel takes as well. The novel is in the form of a diary the 62-year-old Corrine is writing to her children and grand-children. Corrine wants to leave them a record of the truth of her life; she doesn't want to hide anything, from them or from herself. But the truth that she must tell about herself and her husband is not something she finds easy to tell, so she repeatedly creates more acceptable fictions about the past, only then to admit the falsity and to try one more time to be honest. Her diversions are comic, her attempts at honesty noble, and the novel that results is original in both form and content.

Corrine's attempt to tell the truth is a positive thing, an implicit expression of faith in the future. That belief is Douglas's too; she expresses it over and over in her fiction through characters who, as she has said, "move out and affirm, in some way, a humanity larger than they thought themselves capable of." In an interview with Jerry Speir, Douglas commented on this philosophy that underlies her fiction:

I suppose I'm just not temperamentally able to believe that the world will die. I have to assume that there is a past which I in the present can attempt to give to a future that will exist. And I think I've said that over and over again in my stories. The narrator in [*A Lifetime Burning*] says it, too, because what she's doing, of course, is attempting to give her life as if it were a gift, however explosive and unwelcome a gift it might be, to her children, to make whatever use they can of it. It's an active act of communication, whatever the cost.

Corrine at age 62 is an angry and passionate woman, more sexually passionate, in fact, than she was as a young woman. And therein lies a universal theme of writers, an interest in the human passions. Douglas's distinction in this regard is in so often choosing middle-aged and older women as her heroines. Through Corrine, Kate Anderson of *A Family's Affairs*, Aunt Martha of *Apostles of Light*, the middle-aged Cornelia and Tweet of *Can't Quit You, Baby*, and other "older" characters, Douglas shows us that middle age and old age are as interesting as youth. "It's my profound conviction," she said in the interview with Speir, "that people of fifty or sixty or seventy or eighty feel very deeply the human passions that they felt at fifteen, twenty-five, and thirty-five. The human passion is there until you die."

SURVEY OF CRITICISM

No books have as yet been written about Douglas, but in recent years she has been the subject of several articles. In "Ellen Douglas's Small Towns: Fictional

Anchors," Michael P. Dean discusses the importance of place to her fiction, his thesis being that Douglas "uses small town settings to provide, paradoxically, both restriction and freedom, order and image, to her work." Other articles have been designed (like this one) as general introductions to the author and her fiction. In an essay in *Women Writers of the Contemporary South*, Carol S. Manning discusses Douglas as a moralist and realist. In an article in *Southern Women Writers: The New Generation*, Panthea Reid Broughton and Susan Millar Williams offer a biographical sketch of the author and a brief study of each of her works.

Whereas major scholarly studies of Douglas are yet to come, her works have, since the beginning of her career, attracted the notice of reviewers for major publications. Four of her books—*A Family's Affairs*; *Black Cloud, White Cloud*; *A Lifetime Burning*; and *Can't Quit You Baby*—received almost universally positive reviews. Writing for the *Saturday Review*, Walter Spearman said of *Black Cloud, White Cloud*: "Not since Eudora Welty's early stories in the 1940s or perhaps Katherine Anne Porter's stories in the Thirties has the Southern scene produced [a new woman writer] of the perception and talent of Ellen Douglas." Other reviewers have called Douglas "a fine and feeling writer" and a "highly gifted writer" and her works "sad and deeply felt" and "beautifully constructed." Response to Douglas's other books has been mixed, though more favorable than negative. Doris Grumbach found that *Apostles of Light* exhibits the excesses of gothic fiction yet also the virtues of concern for the helpless old. Jonathan Yardley described *The Rock Cried Out* as "powerful and disturbing," whereas Walter Sullivan judged it anachronistic and its characters puppets to the novelist's design.

Ellen Douglas has established herself as a serious artist who is not afraid to take chances and who makes us recognize things about human nature and life in the South that we had never quite grasped before. Her reputation is sure to grow.

BIBLIOGRAPHY

Works by Ellen Douglas

A Family's Affairs. Boston: Houghton Mifflin, 1962.
Black Cloud, White Cloud. Boston: Houghton Mifflin, 1963; 2nd ed., 1989.
Where the Dreams Cross. Boston: Houghton Mifflin, 1968.
Commentary on Walker Percy's The Last Gentleman. New York: Seabury, 1969.
Apostles of Light. Boston: Houghton Mifflin, 1973.
The Rock Cried Out. New York: Harcourt Brace Jovanovich, 1979.
"Faulkner in Time," 284–301 in *"A Cosmos of My Own": Faulkner and Yoknapatawpha, 1980*, ed. Doreen Fowler and Ann J. Abadie. Jackson: University Press of Mississippi, 1981.
"Faulkner's Women," 149–67 in *"A Cosmos of My Own": Faulkner and Yoknapataw-*

pha, 1980, ed. Doreen Fowler and Ann J. Abadie. Jackson: University Press of
	Mississippi, 1981.
A Lifetime Burning. New York: Random House, 1982.
The Magic Carpet and Other Tales. Illus. Walter Anderson. Jackson: University Press
	of Mississippi, 1987.
Can't Quit You Baby. New York: Macmillan, 1988.

Interviews

Brown, Laurie L. "Interviews with Seven Contemporary Writers." *Southern Quarterly*
	21 (Summer 1983): 3–22. Reprinted in *Women Writers of the Contemporary South*,
	ed. Peggy Whitman Prenshaw. Jackson: University Press of Mississippi, 1984.
Campbell, Sylvia. "Haxton as Elusive as Character She Portrays." *Jackson Clarion
	Ledger/Daily News* (October 17, 1982).
Jones, John Griffin. "Ellen Douglas," 47–73 in *Mississippi Writers Talking II*, ed. John
	Griffin Jones. Jackson: University Press of Mississippi, 1983.
Speir, Jerry. "Of Novels and the Novelist: An Interview with Ellen Douglas." *University
	of Mississippi Studies in English*, New Series 5 (1984–1987): 231–48.

Studies of Ellen Douglas

Broughton, Panthea Reid, and Susan Millar Williams. "Ellen Douglas," 46–69 in *South-
	ern Women Writers: The New Generation*, ed. Tonette Bond Inge. Tuscaloosa:
	University of Alabama Press, 1990.
Dean, Michael P. "Ellen Douglas's Small Towns: Fictional Anchors." *Southern Quar-
	terly* 19 (Fall 1980): 161–71.
Manning, Carol S. "Ellen Douglas: Moralist and Realist." *Southern Quarterly* 21 (Sum-
	mer 1983): 117–34. Reprinted in *Women Writers of the Contemporary South*, ed.
	Peggy Whitman Prenshaw. Jackson: University Press of Mississippi, 1984.
Tate, Linda Kay. "Southern Women's Fiction, 1980–1990: Traditions and Revisions."
	Ph.D. Dissertation. Madison: University of Wisconsin, 1991.
Wilson, Deborah. "Patterning the Past: History as Ideology in Modern Southern Fiction."
	Ph.D. Dissertation. Baton Rouge: Louisiana State University and Agricultural and
	Mechanical College, 1991.

Reviews

Bellows, Silence Buck. "One Step toward Finding Answers." *Christian Science Monitor*
	(October 31, 1963): 7.
Broughton, Panthea Reid. "Scarlet Rage." *Times Literary Supplement* No. 4, 190 (July
	22, 1983): 791.
Buckmaster, Henrietta. "Fiction: Families and Individuals." *Christian Science Monitor*
	(June 14, 1962): 7.
Davenport, Gary. "The Two Worlds of Contemporary American Fiction." *Sewanee
	Review* 92 (Winter 1984): 128–36.
Grumbach, Doris. "Questioning the Human: In Church, Fable, and Fiction." *America*
	128 (April 14, 1973): 338.
Isaacs, Susan. "Not Going Gentle at All." *New York Times Book Review* (October 31,
	1982): 11.

Lyell, Frank H. "Time Marches on in Homochitto." *New York Times Book Review* (July 8, 1962): 18.

Maloff, Saul. "To Be Southern Is to Be Obsessed." *New York Times Book Review* (October 6, 1963): 5.

Prescott, Peter S. "Evil in the Golden Age." *Newsweek* 81 (March 5, 1973): 84.

Rosenthal, L. Rev. of *Where the Dreams Cross. Washington Post Book World* (September 29, 1968): 20.

Spearman, Walter. "Light on a Southern Exposure." *Saturday Review* 46 (November 16, 1963): 42.

Sullivan, Walter. "The Feckless Present, the Unredeemed Past: Some Recent Novels." *Sewanee Review* 88 (July 1980): 432.

Uhry, Alfred. "Where There's Water, There Are Snakes." *New York Times Book Review* (July 10, 1988): 13.

Yardley, Jonathan. "The Fabric of a Marriage, the Fabrications We Live By." *Washington Post Book World* (October 31, 1982): 3.

———. "Old Southern Themes." *New York Times Book Review* (September 23, 1979): 13.

ANNE E. ROWE

Andre Dubus
(1936–   )

Although Andre Dubus's fictional landscape is generally considered to be working-class New England, a strong case can be made for his inclusion in a study of Southern writers. A native of Louisiana, Dubus spent his childhood in the South and was educated there. Much of his fiction is set outside the South, but some of his best writing, including his stories of childhood and growing up, have Southern settings. Although Southern settings are more prominent in his early work, they occasionally are found in his later writing.

BIOGRAPHY

Dubus has spent much of his life away from the South, but his roots are indubitably Southern. Born August 11, 1936, in Lake Charles, Louisiana, to Andre Jules and Katherine Burke Dubus, he was the youngest of three children, including Kathryn Claire, born in 1930, and Elizabeth Nell, born in 1933.

In 1944 the Dubus family moved from Baton Rouge to Lafayette, Louisiana, where he enrolled in the Christian Brothers School from which he graduated in 1954. Following his graduation Dubus entered McNeese State College in Lake Charles, Louisiana, where he studied English and journalism, earning a B.A. in 1958. In the same year he married Patricia Lowe and was commissioned as a lieutenant in the U.S. Marine Corps. Four children were born to this marriage: Suzanne (1958), Andre III (1959), Jeb (1960), and Nicole (1963).

In 1963, Dubus's father died at the age of 59. Subsequently Dubus resigned his commission in the Marine Corps where he had achieved the rank of captain. He has commented on the relationship between these two events in his life: "Only later did I realize it was my father's death that gave me the freedom to resign. . . . I do not think I would have had the courage . . . to explain to him that I was leaving a good and secure and honorable, in those days, profession and was going to take a family of one wife and four children to Iowa City for an assistantship of $2,400 a year.'' This same year his first story, ''The Intruder,'' was published in the *Sewanee Review*.

In January 1964, Dubus entered the M.F.A. program at the University of Iowa. After attaining his degree in 1965 he accepted a position as lecturer in English at Nichols State College in Thibodaux, Louisiana.

The year 1966 marks what may be considered Dubus's apparently permanent departure from the South. He accepted a teaching position at Bradford College, Bradford, Massachusetts, in modern fiction and creative writing—an association that lasted until his retirement in 1984.

Dubus's first novel, *The Lieutenant*, was published in 1967, followed by a number of short stories. ''If They Knew Yvonne,'' for example, was published in 1969 and selected for inclusion in *Best American Short Stories*, 1970.

During the 1970s Dubus's two short-story collections, *Separate Flights* (1975) and *Adultery and Other Choices* (1977), appeared. Dubus was divorced from Patricia Lowe in 1970 and was married briefly to Tommie Gale Cotter (1975–1978). In 1976 Dubus received a Guggenheim Fellowship and in 1978 he was awarded a grant from the National Endowment for the Arts. In 1979 he married Peggy Rambach. Two daughters were born in this marriage: Candace (1982) and Madeline Elise (1987).

In the 1980s Dubus published three collections—*Finding a Girl in America* (1980), *The Times Are Never So Bad* (1983), *The Last Worthless Evening* (1986)—and a novella, *Voices from the Moon* (1984). He has continued to receive fellowships and grants, and his stories frequently have been selected for inclusion in anthologies. Most recently Dubus has overcome the tragedy of losing a leg in a highway accident in which he was giving aid to an accident victim (1986). He has continued to receive critical acclaim for his work, including a special issue of *Delta* (1987) treating his fiction.

Not only does Dubus continue to write excellent fiction, he has also fostered a writer in his own family. In 1989 a fine collection of stories, *The Cage Keeper and Other Stories*, by his son Andre Dubus III was published.

MAJOR THEMES

Andre Dubus's primary literary genre is fiction, and although he has published two novels, the short story and novella are his most characteristic forms.

Dubus's fiction treats a variety of subjects, but almost all of his work portrays what may be summed up as failed relationships. This is not to say that his fiction is necessarily hopeless or dark, for in spite of the human frailties he describes, his works generally bear testimony to the power of his characters to endure in spite of their losses.

It is difficult, if not impossible, to impose an organizational pattern on Dubus's work that would reflect a chronological treatment of subjects. Dubus often returns to subjects (and characters) that he has treated in earlier fiction. Nor is it possible to divide his work to reflect his movement from the South to the North, as these two settings occur and recur.

One of the predominant themes in Dubus's work is the difficulty of the passage from childhood to the adult world. His story "If They Knew Yvonne," which was included in his first short-story collection, *Separate Flights* (1975), is one of the best examples of Dubus's stories that deal with a youth's initiation into maturity along with the discovery of the flawed character of human nature. The narrator, Harry, tells us: "I grew up in Louisiana, and for twelve years I went to a boys' school taught by Christian Brothers, a Catholic religious order," a place where he learned about the nature of sin, especially sexual.

"If They Knew Yvonne" deals with Harry's coming to terms with the fallibilities of his parents and sister. Harry's sexual experiences with Yvonne also lead him into knowledge of his own failings: "[Yvonne] was a Catholic, and had been taught by nuns for twelve years, but she wasn't bothered as much as I was." Harry discovers: "The Brothers hadn't prepared me for this. If my first time had been with a whore, their training probably would have worked, for that was the sort of lust they focused on. But they were no match for Yvonne, and next morning I woke happier than I had ever been." Harry must come to terms with his sin or his perception of his act as sin, but the story does achieve resolution, as Harry thinks of his nephews, conceived also out of sin, and muses: "I hoped they would grow well, those strong little bodies, those kind hearts."

Dubus continues to explore the initiation into knowledge in the stories of Paul Clement, from his boyhood until entering into the Marines, including "An Afternoon with the Old Man," "Contrition," "The Bully," and "Cadence," collected in *Adultery and Other Choices*. Paul is described as believing he and a friend "could endure grammar school bullies together and by the time they reached high school they would change or the world would change. He did not know precisely how." It is the not knowing precisely how that Paul must come to terms with, and, like Harry of "If They Knew Yvonne," he learns that no one, not even adults, ever has the final, and precise answer to the mysteries of life.

If childhood is a period of coming to terms with limitations, adult life is portrayed by Dubus as the continued working out of the same problems. Failed friendships, in and out of marriage, is a subject in many of Dubus's stories. Representative of these marriages are those of Jack and Terry Linhart and Hank and Edith Allison in "We Don't Live Here Anymore" (*Separate Flights*), "Adultery" (*Adultery and Other Choices*), and "Finding a Girl in America" (*Finding a Girl in America*).

One of the most striking aspects of the failed marriages is the way in which husbands and wives are unable to perceive the needs of their mates. Jack Linhart, as he leaves home to be with his lover, thinks of his wife: "I wished she were the one going off to wickedness; I would stay home and make cookies from a recipe book." And Edith Allison realizes in "Adultery" that her husband has this limitation: "Hank needed and loved men, and when he loved them it was because of what they thought and how they lived. He did not measure women that way; he measured them by their sexuality and good sense.''

In ''We Don't Live Here Anymore,'' Jack thinks: ''I am surrounded by painful marriages that no one understands.'' What is apparent in these and Dubus's other stories of marriage is that the failed marriages are a symptom of a graver disease: men and women in his fiction cannot understand one another.

In many ways Dubus's fiction seems to reflect a point of view that shows insight into men more than women; there emerges from his fiction an explanation of why men and women often cannot communicate. Dubus suggests in a number of his stories that his male characters have a sense of purpose that the women characters lack. In ''Adultery,'' for example, Edith is described this way: ''She was pretending to be in her first year of graduate school, in American history, so she could be near Hank; she attended class, even read the books and wrote the papers, even did rather well; but she was pretending.'' In contrast, Edith knew Hank ''had found his center,'' in this case, in his work.

It is this search for center, so to speak, or the realization of a lack of it, that characterizes many of the women in Dubus's fiction. And although readers may despair of the emptiness of the women's lives in Dubus's work, it must be conceded that his portraits of women in such stories as ''The Fat Girl'' (*Adultery and Other Choices*), reflect some of his best writing. ''The Fat Girl'' tells the story of Louise, the only unattractive member of a family driven by appearances: ''[Her father] was thin and kind and she could see in his eyes when he looked at her the lights of love and pity. . . . Her mother was slim and pretty, carried herself erectly, and ate very little. The two of them would eat bare lunches, while her older brother ate sandwiches and potato chips, and then her mother would sit smoking while Louise eyed the bread box, the pantry, the refrigerator.'' Louise's friends, she thought, would always remember her as ''a girl whose hapless body was destined to be fat. No one saw the sandwiches she made and took to her room when she came home from school.'' For Louise, ''eating lightly in public had become as habitual as good manners.''

Louise goes away to college where her roommate helps her start a rigid diet that eventually transforms her into the slender, pretty girl her parents always wanted. She is rewarded with the family's approval and the ultimate prize, marriage to Richard, a young lawyer in her father's firm. But this story does not end with the fairy-tale transformation of the frump into the princess. Dubus writes of Louise: ''She thought of the accumulated warmth and pelf of her marriage, and how by slimming her body she had bought into the pleasures of the nation. . . . But these moments of triumph were sparse. On most days she went about her routine of leisure with a sense of certainty about herself that came merely from not thinking. . . . There were times . . . when she was suddenly assaulted by the feeling that she had taken the wrong train and arrived at a place where no one knew her, and where she ought not to be.'' Louise begins to gain weight again: ''Returning from work in the evenings Richard looked at a soiled plate and glass on the table beside her chair as if detecting traces of her infidelity.''

The reader, however, realizes that Louise knows that she must come to terms with who she is, not what others want her to be, and for this reason her character, rather than pathetic, is complex and strong.

The book that best encompasses all of Dubus's themes is *Voices from the Moon*, a novella treating the Stowe family in which the parents, Greg and Joan, have divorced, and, incredibly, Greg has fallen in love with and will marry Brenda, the ex-wife of his son Larry. The story is told from the points of view of the family members including the younger brother, Richie, and sister, Carol. The novella opens with Richie thinking: "Today is the math test; Howie is going to get you after school. . . . It's divorce that did it . . . he was twelve and too young for it and had done nothing at all to cause it." A complicated tale that does not summarize well, it expresses many of Dubus's concerns: the painful process of growing up, and, as adults, the pain and frustration within marriage.

In *Voices from the Moon*, as in many of Dubus's stories, a female character has perhaps the most profound insight. Here, Joan concludes: "We don't have to live great lives, we just have to understand and survive the ones we've got." And that is, finally, what Dubus seems to express in all of his fiction—the importance of the struggle to survive and understand.

At the conclusion of the novella, Richie is lying "on the grass and the soft summer earth, holding [his friend] Melissa's hand, and talking to the stars." Like his father, mother, and brother, Richie will suffer, but those who can look up at the stars will perhaps not be great people, but they will transcend, spiritually at least, their everydayness, and in Dubus's fiction that is the most that anyone can hope to achieve.

SURVEY OF CRITICISM

As with most contemporary writers, the bulk of the critical treatment of Andre Dubus's work is made up of book reviews. There are also a number of perceptive articles (including an entire issue of *Delta*) treating his work. In addition, there is a very useful book-length study of his work, *Andre Dubus: A Study of the Short Fiction* by Thomas E. Kennedy, which provides an excellent overview of Dubus's shorter fiction. Since this is the most comprehensive treatment of Dubus's fiction to date, its major features should be noted.

In his introduction Kennedy states: "The world of Dubus's fiction is one in which the word *sin* again becomes valid, for it is a world in which men and women are responsible for their actions. . . . This 'rediscovery' of sin and, perhaps more important, the identification of sin as an affront against the human beings for whom we are responsible [is] a vital part of Dubus's fiction." Kennedy argues that the fifty or so stories Dubus has published all contain elements of his vision of "moral blindness, isolation, the lack of self-knowledge, the confusion between hunger and love."

Kennedy divides his study into three parts: An analysis of the short fiction, two interviews with Dubus, and a survey of the critical reception of Dubus's work. In the first section Kennedy divides Dubus's work into categories: childhood, girls (or women), military life, violence, marriage and divorce, fathers. Although some of these categories seem arbitrary and overlapping, Kennedy's synthesis of common themes is excellent. Dubus's vision, he concludes, is one "of human beings in isolation and ignorance seeking contact with one another, seeking to transcend the limitations of self-concern in order to achieve a higher level of humanity. The way for Dubus's characters to find this community is awareness, knowledge of self." Kennedy also notes that "blindness, actual and metaphorical, is a recurrent indicator for lack of awareness in Dubus's fiction as surely as it was for Sophocles."

Kennedy includes two interviews with Dubus, one he conducted in 1987 by sending questions to Dubus, which he responded to in a number of cassette recordings, and a second by Patrick Samway in 1986 that originally appeared in *America* (1987). Both contain Dubus's comments on other writers, on his work, and on his views of the uses of fiction. In the Kennedy interview Dubus acknowledges the influence of Anton Chekov and Ernest Hemingway on his work. Another statement he makes is reminiscent of Carson McCullers: "I believe there is an essential and ultimate loneliness which one experiences within love, that there are parts of the lover and beloved which can never meet."

On the purposes of fiction, Dubus comments that "the first objective of fiction is to give pleasure. . . . I think the next objective is through the pleasure to draw the reader out of himself or herself and take that reader into a search where both of you go in without knowing the answer. . . . We confront mortality, we try to live other lives, to leap into the heart of another and understand."

In the Samway interview Dubus speaks specifically of Southern writers, noting especially the influence of Faulkner. Of Flannery O'Connor he comments: "She frightens me. I don't read her much." But of his Catholicism, an aspect of his work that has certainly evoked comparison with O'Connor, he notes: "I think my Catholicism has increased my sense of fascination and my compassion. . . . I still think the main problem with the United States is that we lost God and we lost religion and we didn't replace God or religion with anything of value."

The third section of Kennedy's study contains excerpts from reviews and articles treating each of Dubus's story collections. Kennedy's selection is useful because it provides representative responses and includes both positive and negative critiques. Typical of the response to his first collection, *Separate Flights*, is an excerpt from Joyce Carol Oates's review that first appeared in the *Ontario Review*: "All of his people are ordinary, though some have pretensions to being intellectual; many are trapped in stultifying marriages, though Dubus never suggests that they might have been capable of arranging other fates. . . . Their defenses against the panic of dissolution are commonplace: drinking and adultery."

Edith Milton's review of *Adultery and Other Choices* sums up the relationships of Dubus's characters this way: "Ambivalence is the pivot of Dubus's world, which is a world in splinters, where men and women face in opposite directions.

. . . A man, to feel himself a man, must sacrifice himself on the altar of masculine ritual, and even adultery stems from routine and a sense of what one owes oneself more than it does from real feeling.''

Kennedy also includes one of the most negative treatments of Dubus's work in which Julian Moynahan summarizes Dubus's work:

The typical Dubus male grows up in a decaying, contracting small industrial city like Haverhill, or a bypassed port such as Newburyport, has boyish adventures at the seaside and develops a lifelong passion for the Red Sox—those heartbreakers!—sees something of the world during a peacetime stint in the Marines during the mid-1950s, then settles back into the home region where he may develop problems with drink, job, or with the drive for liberation and autonomy of his womenfolk. A variant of this type is the writer figure . . . whose social origins are the same but who tries to live the freer life of the artist without betraying or denying his class and regional roots. Yet this longer narrative is a failure precisely because Mr. Dubus and his hero, Hank Allison, hold such a self-centered, self-indulgent view of the artist and his responsibilities.

A representative treatment of *The Times Are Never So Bad* is Brian Stonehill's essay, in which he notes that Dubus's fiction "resembles O'Connor, too, in his concern with matters spiritual. Even more explicitly than she, he focuses on the place of faith and grace in a Catholic heart. He hunts for purity's place in all of this, and is too clever and clear-sighted to settle for an easy answer."

Harriet Gilbert's review of *We Don't Live Here Anymore: The Novellas of Andre Dubus* describes Dubus's fiction as in the school of Dirty Realism: "Its deft, economical, concentrated prose exposes an introverted USA of six-packs, all-day television, fishing-and-shooting trips for the men, bourbon numbness for the women. But it's also often something different. Almost alone among books by men, from *any* literary school, it's questioning what being 'male' really means."

John Updike's review of *Voices from the Moon* is a perceptive analysis of Dubus's work: "As a writer Andre Dubus has come up the hard way, with a resolutely unflashy style and doggedly unglamorous, unironical character." Comparing Dubus with Kerouac, Updike concludes: "For Jack Kerouac, another Franco-American from the Merrimac Valley, Roman Catholicism had dwindled to a manic spark, a frenetic mission to find the sacred everywhere; for Mr. Dubus, amid the self-seeking tangle of secular America, the Church still functions as a standard of measure, a repository of mysteries that can give scale and structure to our social lives."

Kennedy's inclusion of James Yaffe's comments on *The Last Worthless Evening* is important because Yaffe effectively sums up Dubus's place in contemporary fiction: "Andre Dubus writes novellas—long stories that run about a fifth to a third the length of ordinary novels—and this probably accounts for the fact that, after seven distinguished books, he hasn't achieved a large readership of widespread critical recognition. This is a pity, because on the strength of his eighth book, *The Last Worthless Evening*, I have no hesitation in calling him one of the best writers of fiction in America today.''

Although Kennedy includes a sampling of many perceptive commentaries on Dubus's work, there are others that are equally of value. Walter Sullivan's review of *Separate Flights* is a balanced assessment of the stories in this collection. In his comments on ''Miranda over the Valley'' Sullivan notes: ''To get inside the mind of a woman and to portray her joy and her agony as Dubus has done here is accomplishment indeed. We have no right to ask him to do better.''

Steve Yarbrough's ''Andre Dubus: From Detached Incident to Compressed Novel'' is a structural analysis of Dubus's fiction that he divides into three categories: detached incident with straightforward narrative; stories with circular narrators; and stories he terms compressed novels. Although those categories at times seem forced, Yarbrough's approach is important for its extended analysis of Dubus's technique.

Lisa Zeidner's review of *Voices from the Moon* notes that Dubus ''beat the new Realists to New Realism by over two decades'' and concludes: ''As in much of Mr. Dubus's work, the pleasure comes less from the resolution of the plots than the insights.''

The publication of *Selected Stories of Andre Dubus* (1988) has elicited a generally positive critical response. John B. Breslin's ''Playing Out the Patterns of Sin and Grace'' surveys Dubus's fiction and concludes: ''Dubus accepts our flawed condition as a given, but he manages to view his characters' failings with a compassion that bespeaks an equal condition that grace is powerfully at work in the world.'' Bruce Weber's ''Andre Dubus's Hard Luck Stories'' includes a detailed account of Dubus's accident in 1986. Weber chronicles Dubus's dogged and heroic response to overcoming this tragedy. He summarizes Dubus's fiction:

For years now, Dubus has been building a fictional population in the real-life landscape around his home, towns like Bradford, Amesbury, and Haverhill, in the stubbornly pretty but economically troubled Merrimack Valley. Bartenders, teachers, salesgirls, small-business men, mothers and fathers and kids, theirs is a full but circumscribed and isolated world. When things go wrong, when disaster inevitably strikes, the conflict that most frequently entangles his characters is about loyalty and love. Do we owe ourselves or owe one another?

Two recent studies of Dubus compare him with other contemporary writers. Greg Johnson's ''Three Contemporary Masters: Brodkey, Carver, Dubus'' treats collections of selected stories by these writers, each appearing in 1988. Johnson notes: ''They differ markedly in subject matter, prose style, and aesthetic program, but each has developed a distinct, immediately recognizable narrative voice, and each has explored the possibilities of the form with the relentless and often ideosyncratic authority of a master.'' Of Dubus, he comments: He ''seems less interested in fictional technique than in the hearts of his people, whose stories he develops with an intuitive, relatively plotless method that seldom fails to illuminate the essence of a beleaguered but dignified human being.''

Vivian Gornick's "Tenderhearted Men: Lonesone, Sad, and Blue" compares and contrasts Hemingway's fiction with that of Raymond Carver, Richard Ford, and Andre Dubus: "Hemingway held an allegorical view of life in which women were idealized as the means of spiritual salvation, then condemned as agents of subversion." The three contemporary writers "are neither sexists nor misanthropes. On the contrary: tenderness of heart is their signature trait. These men share an acute sense of the compatriot nature of human suffering. Their women are fellow victims." What these writers do share with Hemingway, however, is that "the narrator [of their fiction] invariably subscribes to an idea of manhood that hasn't changed in half a century, and the women he knows seem to subscribe to similar notions." She describes Dubus's "Adultery" as "not a plea for the return of old-fashioned monogamous marriage; it is only the description of one kind of spiritual hell. Because marriage means so much to Mr. Dubus, he is able to use its corrupted form to describe the dictates of the human heart under the vile circumstances in perilous times." Gornick describes this work as Dubus's "blueprint for his fundamental text on men and women together." Gornick's review pays tribute to the strength of Dubus's writing while also expressing a wish that Dubus and the others not "have a keen regret that things are no longer as they once were between men and women, a regret so strong that it amounts to longing."

This very contemporary assessment of his fiction in many ways reflects the critical response to Dubus over the past two decades: A wish that things were not the way they are in his fiction, but a strong admiration for the strength and endurance of his characters and for Dubus's mastery of his craft.

BIBLIOGRAPHY

Works by Andre Dubus

The Lieutenant. New York: Dial, 1967.
Separate Flights. Boston: David R. Godine, 1975.
Adultery and Other Choices. Boston: David R. Godine, 1977.
Finding a Girl in America: A Novella and Seven Short Stories. Boston: David R. Godine, 1980.
The Times Are Never So Bad: A Novella and Eight Short Stories. Boston: David R. Godine, 1983.
Land Where My Fathers Died. Winston-Salem, N.C.: Palaemon, 1984.
Voices from the Moon. Boston: David R. Godine, 1984.
We Don't Live Here Anymore: The Novellas of Andre Dubus. New York: Crown, 1984.
The Last Worthless Evening: Four Novellas and Two Stories. Boston: David R. Godine, 1986.
Selected Stories of Andre Dubus. Boston: David R. Godine, 1988.

Studies of Andre Dubus

Breslin, John B. "Playing out the Patterns of Sin and Grace." *Commonweal* (December 2, 1988): 652–56.

Escuret, Annie. "Une nouvelle d'Andre Dubus: 'The Doctor' ou le pont, le flot et l'enfant." *Delta* 24 (February 1987): 109–26.

Feeney, Joseph J. "Poised for Fame: Andre Dubus at Fifty." *America* (November 15, 1986): 269–99.

Gilbert, Harriet. "States of Desire." *New Statesman* 108, no. 2799 (November 9, 1984): 32.

Gornick, Vivian. "Tenderhearted Men: Lonesome, Sad, and Blue." *New York Times Book Review* (September 16, 1990) 1, 32–35.

Hathaway, Dev. "A Conversation with Andre Dubus." *Black Warrior Review* 9 (Spring 1983): 86–103.

Hubert, Thomas. "The Louisiana Connection in the Fiction of Andre Dubus." *McNeese Review* 26 (1979–80): 74–81.

Johnson, Greg. "Three Contemporary Masters: Brodkey, Carver, Dubus." *Georgia Review* (Winter 1989): 785–94.

Kennedy, Thomas E. *Andre Dubus: A Study of the Short Fiction*. Boston: Twayne, 1988.
———. "The Existential Christian Vision in the Fiction of Andre Dubus." *Delta* 24 (February 1987): 91–102.
———. "A Fiction of People and Events." *Sewanee Review* 95 (Spring 1987): xxxix–xli.
———. "The Progress from Hunger to Love: Three Novellas by Andre Dubus." *Hollins Critic* 24 (February 1987): 1–6.
———. "Raw Oysters, Fried Brain, the Leap of the Heart: An Interview with Andre Dubus." *Delta* 24 (February 1987): 21–77.

Milton, Edith. *"Adultery and Other Choices."* *New Republic* 178 (February 4, 1978): 33–35.

Moynahan, Julian. "Hard Lives." *New York Times Book Review* (June 22, 1980): 12.

Nathan, Robert. "Interview with Andre Dubus." *Bookletter* (Harper's Magazine Co.) 3 (February 14, 1987): 14–15.

Oates, Joyce Carol. "People to Whom Things Happen." *New York Times Book Review* (June 26, 1983): 12, 18.
———. "Separate Flights." *Ontario Review* (Fall-Winter 1976–77).

Read, Mimi. "Interview with Andre Dubus." *Sunday Times-Picayune, Dixie Roto Magazine* (New Orleans) (Summer 1984).

Samway, Patrick J. "Dubus's *Voices from the Moon*: More Mystery and Manners." *Delta* 24 (February 1987): 78–90.
———. "An Interview with Andre Dubus." 1985, in ms.

Schildhouse, Amy. "Our Dinners with Andre." *Indiana Review* 10 (1987): 9–20.

Stonehill, Brian. "Memory, the Lens to Look at Life." *Los Angeles Times Book Review* (August 14, 1983): 5.

Sullivan, Walter J. "Separate Flights." *Sewanee Review* (Summer 1975): 544–46.

Updike, John. "Ungreat Lives." *New Yorker* (February 4, 1985): 94, 97–98.

Vauthier, S. "Au-dela du realisme: 'Sorrowful Mysteries.' " *Delta* 24 (February 1987): 127–50.

Weber, Bruce. "Andre Dubus's Hard Luck Stories." *New York Times Magazine* (November 20, 1988): 48 ff.

Whittaker, S. "Andre Dubus's 'His Lover' and the Classical Temper." *Delta* 24 (February 1987): 103–8.

Yaffe, James. *"The Last Worthless Evening."* *Denver Post Books* 7 (December 1986).

Yarbrough, Steve. "From Detached Incident to Compressed Novel." *Critique* (Fall 1986):
    19–27.
Zeidner, Lisa. "Surviving Life." *New York Times Book Review* (November 18, 1984):
    26.

R. STERLING HENNIS, JR.

Clyde Edgerton
(1944–   )

"I can't believe it!" exclaimed a woman after reading *Raney*. "I know all of these people. They are all of my family. Even the names are the same." Such reactions are not uncommon for readers of Clyde Edgerton's fiction, for he has created an authentic fictional world, neither epic nor earthshaking, to which many can readily relate. His characters—often innocent and trusting, with a devout faith—are caught up in real, everyday preoccupations that define activities in the lives of everyone. Even though the setting of his writing is the South and his people are drawn primarily from one segment of society, his insight into the human spirit makes his work universal.

As with many Southern writers, Edgerton's stories have a strong sense of place, but it is the family that is central to his fiction. It is through the relationships nurtured in the family that his characters gain their strength and identity. He also sometimes shows the clash between the past and present, between institutions and the family, that can create problems in ongoing relationships.

One of Edgerton's greatest skills is his complete mastery of detail. The vivid and rich descriptions of the physical appearance of characters, the authentic dialect and speech patterns of the region, and the portrayal of mundane activities give him an uncanny power to evoke humor and richness from minutae.

BIOGRAPHY

Few who knew Clyde Edgerton during his childhood would have predicted that he would grow up to be a writer. Odds would have been placed on his being either a professional baseball player or a rock musician, or, if his parents' wishes had been fulfilled, a missionary or a concert pianist. He loved to hunt and fish and hang out with his "good buddies." There was little indication that he had the slightest literary leanings.

Edgerton was born May 20, 1944, in Durham, North Carolina, and then lived in a small community, Bethesda, on the outskirts of the city. He was the only child of Truma and Ernest Edgerton. Even though his immediate family was small, he lived near a total of twenty-three aunts and uncles and many cousins. Most of these relatives from both sides of his family lived within a radius of fifteen miles in Wake and Durham counties. He visited in their homes and saw them at reunions, at grave cleanings, and on other special occasions. His mother's family were primarily cotton farmers, and his father's family grew tobacco. His parents were among the first of the family members to leave the farm.

It is not unusual for writers to draw heavily on their own families for inspiration in their fiction. Edgerton, too, created many of his characters and events out of his experiences with relatives and his family's traditions. But most of his knowledge of family came from the many stories and tales he heard from his mother and two of her sisters, Oma and Lila. Both of these aunts were married, but childless. They were very close to Truma and visited often with each other. Since Edgerton's mother was 40 years old when he was born, he probably received more adult attention than a child with several brothers and sisters. Through the many conversations he heard from his aunts and mother, characters and family events became very real to him. This oral tradition continued in his family, accompanied with a rich and descriptive dialect, became a part of his everyday life, giving him a valuable source to draw on later.

In addition to his mother, father, and two aunts, Edgerton had another relative with whom he had much contact. Before he was born, Uncle Clem, Truma's brother, moved in with the Edgertons. Clem lost an arm while on active duty during World War I. After that he was never able to function well on his own. His depression and alcoholism led to his suicide in 1978.

Growing up in a rural area, Edgerton had a happy childhood. His outgoing personality and keen sense of humor contributed to his popularity in the community. He easily fit in with the "good ole boys." "Drama during this period," Edgerton recalled, "came from baseball, hunting, and playing Robin Hood with my friends in the woods." He was particularly proficient in baseball. His interest in this sport was encouraged by his father who, it was said, had had a chance to play professional baseball in 1925. For nine summers, including his freshman year in college, Edgerton played on some type of baseball team. Even though he spent more time with his mother, he was very devoted to his father, who taught him to hunt in the wooded areas near his home. His interest in fishing was due to his Uncle Bob, his mother's brother, who lived in Ocala, Florida.

Perhaps Edgerton's interest in music was due to his mother's insistence on his taking piano lessons when he was 7. "I was brought to the piano the same way I was brought to eggs and bacon," he said. "Mother used to put a bite of eggs on a fork and say, 'You'd better hurry and eat this egg before some little piggy gets it.' She did the same thing with the piano. By the time I was ready to begin lessons, she had made the whole idea of playing the piano so exciting that I couldn't resist.'' He continued to take piano lessons for 5 years. In the seventh grade he began to play the trombone. Throughout high school he played in Dixieland bands; during college, he played in rock-and-roll bands.

Although a very good student in high school, he had not given much thought to higher education. Fortunately, he was selected to attend a summer session of Boys' State held on the campus of the University of North Carolina at Chapel Hill. Even though Chapel Hill is approximately fifteen miles from his home, Edgerton's arrival at Boys' State was his first visit to the university town. As a consequence of his attendance at this session, he was sent an application for entrance to the university. He remembers that he loved the school colors of Carolina blue and white on the application form. He decided then that he wanted to be a student at a school with those colors. The reputation and the programs offered were not as important as the colors. ''In fact,'' he said, ''I didn't know anything at all about the programs offered.'' Following graduation from Southern High School in Durham County in June 1962, he entered the university that September.

Even though the town of Chapel Hill was close in miles to his home, in terms of attitudes the distance was very great. Edgerton came to the small university community a staunch conservative who supported Barry Goldwater in the 1964 presidential campaign. He even wrote a right-wing poem that was published in the *Daily Tar Heel*, the student newspaper. When he returned for graduate work in 1972, however, he worked for George McGovern for president. He attributes his move from a conservative political attitude to a more liberal one to his experiences during his active duty in Vietnam, as well as to the atmosphere he encountered while a student at Chapel Hill. Even in high school, however, he had been fascinated with issues of conformity and nonconformity.

Edgerton's choice of English as a major in college evolved slowly. Though he was a good student who enjoyed literature, his reading had been somewhat sporadic. During high school he remembers being impressed by the essays of Ralph Waldo Emerson, Henry David Thoreau's ''Civil Disobedience,'' and the works of Mark Twain. After reading Ernest Hemingway's *A Farewell to Arms* as a college sophomore, he decided to be an English teacher. He wanted to share his excitement for such literature with others. While a graduate student, he discovered the stories of Eudora Welty. He particularly loved ''Why I Live at the P.O.''

During his undergraduate years, Edgerton was a student in the Air Force ROTC program, where he learned to fly a small plane. Upon graduation from the university in 1966, he received a commission and entered the U.S. Air Force. For the next 4 years he served on active duty as a fighter pilot based in the United States, Korea, and Japan. In 1970–71 as a forward air controller flying reconnaissance and strike contact missions over the Ho Chi Minh Trail in Laos, he flew 187 combat missions. During his time in the military, he read in more depth some of his favorite authors, as well as Stephen Crane and others.

After his return from the Air Force, Edgerton decided to complete a master's degree before starting a teaching career. With the Master of Arts in Teaching from the University of North Carolina in hand, he accepted a faculty position as an English teacher at Southern High School, his alma mater. He was an outstanding teacher, willing to try innovative and creative strategies in his classroom. His wit and enthusiasm contributed to his popularity with both his students and his colleagues.

Because of his success as a teacher, Edgerton was encouraged to return once again to the university to begin a doctoral program. In 1973 he entered the Ph.D. program in English Education. As a graduate student he worked as a teaching assistant in the program designed for prospective teachers of English. He became interested in the langue of film as a subject for serious study and focused his doctoral research on that topic.

In graduate school, Edgerton met another graduate student in English Education, Susan Ketchin, who was to have a major influence on his life. Born and raised in Atlanta, Susan played the guitar and sang, in addition to her interest in writing and literature. Like Edgerton, she loved teaching, literature, and music. They mutually admired Eudora Welty, often quoting lines from her stories to each other. Susan also liked the stories of Flannery O'Connor and shared her enthusiasm with Edgerton. They were married in his home church, Bethesda Baptist, in 1975.

After completing the requirements for the doctorate, Edgerton accepted a faculty position at Campbell University located in Buies Creek, North Carolina. He taught English Education and writing at this conservative Baptist school from 1977 until 1985. Instead of moving to Buies Creek, the newlyweds bought an old, rambling house in Apex, a community located approximately halfway between Raleigh and Buies Creek. This location enabled Susan to teach classes in writing and literature in Raleigh at North Carolina State University. While they lived in Apex, their only child, Catherine, was born in 1982.

Edgerton continued to write, even though his teaching schedule was demanding. The influence of Welty's writing began to bear fruit. "While reading Eudora Welty," he said, "I finally realized that I, too, would write about people and things I know best. I did not have to write about exotic subjects nor create fantastic, complicated plots." In addition to writing a few songs, he sent some of his stories to publishers. After receiving hundreds of rejection slips, he finally had one accepted for publication in a small, obscure periodical, *Just Pulp*. It told the story of a young boy, named Meredith, who fell through a kitchen floor into an abandoned well under the house. The inspiration for this story came from Edgerton's noticing a weak spot in the kitchen floor of their old house in Apex. When he found that a weak floor covered an old well under the house, the story of a boy's falling into it began to take shape. For some time Edgerton had been working on a longer piece of fiction concerning a Southern family involved with the Vietnam War, but he was having difficulty finding the structure or focus that he wanted. He abandoned this project for a time and concentrated on a story that was later expanded into his first published novel, *Raney*.

Edgerton's decision to be a serious writer was a very deliberate one, but somewhat of a surprise even to him. He had been keeping a journal, jotting down ideas, feelings, characters, and events on paper. He planned to use this resource in case he continued to write. In May 1978, the Edgertons watched Welty read one of her stories on public television. That night he wrote in his journal: "May 14, 1978—Tomorrow, May 15, 1978—I would like to start being a writer and I can enter Meredith somewhere. The first task is to get it typed. The next task is to learn to type." A few months later, another journal entry was made concerning his intent to be a writer: "September 17, 1978—I'm finally sure that what I always wanted to do (since college)—be a writer—is still what I want to do. But I don't have the right habits—the guts to stick to it for long hours alone."

He finally completed the rather lengthy short story that he had been working on. This story described the relationship between a young woman from a rural background and a young man from cosmopolitan Atlanta. He shared his story with his friend Sylvia Wilkinson, novelist from Durham, who encouraged him to continue writing and suggested that he take a course with Louis Rubin, an English professor at Chapel Hill who was a well-known scholar of Southern literature and founder of a new, small publishing company. Impressed with Rubin's critical judgment through having taken a seminar in Southern fiction, Susan suggested that he show his work to Rubin. Following her advice, Edgerton sent Rubin parts of the story he had just written. Rubin liked what he read and told Edgerton to send the entire manuscript to Shannon Ravenel, his fiction editor. Thus began a writer-editor relationship that launched Edgerton on a productive career as a writer.

Published in 1985, *Raney* received excellent reviews in newspapers and periodicals from all over the country. Edgerton was excited about his novel's success and thought that the administration at Campbell, where he was still teaching on a year-to-year contract, would be pleased. He was regarded as an outstanding teacher, and everyone seemed to be pleased with his work. Asked to meet with the provost shsortly after the book was published, he was stunned to learn that his contract was in jeopardy. The administration suggested that *Raney* did not further the goals and purposes of Campbell University. In the administration's view certain scenes did not depict the kinds of wholesome relationships that the college wanted to project.

Greatly disappointed, Edgerton did not want to create trouble for the school or himself, but he did want his contract renewed or to be shown that he had not performed his teaching duties adequately. While he was in the process of requesting that a faculty committee review his grievances, the press became aware of the controversy and asked questions about the differences between Edgerton and the administration. The issues were widely reported and discussed in the newspapers and on television. Because academic freedom became the focus of the controversy, many faculty members at Campbell and other colleges and universities supported Edgerton and expressed serious concern about the position taken by Campbell's administration. Finally, after his contract was renewed but without a raise, Edgerton resigned and accepted a teaching position at St. Andrews Presbyterian College in Laurinburg, North Carolina, for the next academic year, 1985–86.

This episode was difficult for Edgerton, for his family's livelihood was threatened. He had hoped *Raney* would be received on its own merits, not because of some "controversy" surrounding it. He became more aware of the time he required for writing. His contract with St. Andrews included provisions that allowed more time for writing.

While teaching at St. Andrews he completed two more novels, *Walking across Egypt* (1987) and *The Floatplane Notebooks* (1988). The success of *Walking across Egypt* was particularly rewarding to Edgerton because it rested on the writing and was not clouded by controversy. Originally he planned his second novel to be the story with the Vietnam setting that he had started several years before, but he continued to have problems with that novel's structure.

One day in a conversation, his mother told him how she had recently fallen through the seat of a chair she had planned to send off for repairs. She was stuck in the chair for about fifteen minutes. Edgerton thought this was one of the funniest things he had ever heard, quickly realizing that it would make a great scene in a story. In a short time he completed several pages describing the incident and shared it with his wife and with Ravenel. They both agreed it had possibilities for a much longer work. Since the setting and characters were similar to those in *Raney*, it seemed to be a logical place for his labors. He quickly completed *Walking across Egypt* and turned his attention once again to the problematical novel in progress.

The Floatplane Notebooks, more serious in tone than the first two novels, began to take form when he decided to give each of the major characters a voice and to include a wisteria vine—which he remembered in the woods near the family cemetery—as a narrator. A scene he saw on Lake Wheeler in Wake County also provided additional structure for the book. One day across the lake he saw a man wearing a football helmet and waders trying to launch a homemade floatplane that looked like a Rube Goldberg invention. He also was able to incorporate his first short story about Meredith falling into the well into the new book.

This third novel, too, was well received by reviewers and established him as a major new Southern writer. *The Floatplane Notebooks* was cited as one of the best novels of 1988 by *Publishers Weekly*. Edgerton books created a devoted following, and he became much in demand for speaking engagements and readings. He reads his own material with great feeling and wit, often assuming the dialect and mannerisms of his characters. He is also an excellent musician, who performs and sings his own songs. With the sale of his books and the money generated by his speaking engagements, he was able to devote more of his time to writing.

After receiving a Guggenheim Fellowship for 1989–90, Edgerton took a leave of absence from St. Andrews to complete his fourth novel, *Killer Diller* (1991), much earlier than would have been possible with some teaching responsibilities. This novel continued the story of Wesley from *Walking across Egypt* as he becomes interested in theology and preaching. *In Memory of Junior* (1992), Edgerton's fifth novel, is a humorous, but serious book about mixed-up grave plots and tombstones and divided family loyalties. A Lyndhurst Fellowship awarded in 1991 enabled him to devote most of his time to this novel.

Two of his books have been dramatized. *Walking across Egypt* and *Raney* have been performed in several cities and have received excellent reviews. The scripts for both plays were written by John Justice.

Controversy, however, continues to plague Edgerton. In June 1992 the school board in Carroll County, Virginia, responding to complaints from parents, ruled that *The Floatplane Notebooks* would be removed from the schools because of its profanity and sexual theme.

MAJOR THEMES

Love—love for one another, for family, for neighbors; love for the old and young, for churchgoers and nonchurchgoers; love for the educated and the misinformed, for the poor and the affluent—runs like a winding road through Edgerton's fiction. But the family is often the unit through which love best functions, binding people together to give purpose and direction to their lives. The family, in turn, derives its strength and power from its heritage, its traditions, its roots. The continuity of the family is assured through the tradition of storytelling, the recounting of tales and events from family life from one generation to the next. This progression from love to family to heritage to history provides a framework, it seems, for Edgerton's whole body of literature.

In Edgerton's fictional world the family is where caring and meaningful relationships are formed and nurtured. The outward manifestations of such love are depicted in vignettes of everyday living. The importance of such loving and supportive family relationships seems second nature to most of his characters. It is difficult for Raney, for example, to comprehend a life without strong family ties. She feels that Charles "just don't have a single sense about family, about having family" (53). She is sorry that he had to grow up as an only child with little family around. Witnessing the nurturing qualities of Flossie, Charles wished "he had had an Aunt Flossie in his family. His aunts are all out West or in Connecticut" (33).

Those who have few family ties emphasize the need for such a unit most poignantly. Both Mark, who had no father, and Wesley, who is an orphan, have more trouble with relationships than most others in his fiction who have stronger family ties. Sometimes the reverse can be true. The family can become so isolated, even within its own confines, that certain subjects are never discussed. In *The Floatplane Notebooks*, Bliss noted, for example, that the Copelands could not talk about war.

Even though the family presented in his novels has, most often, a very positive

influence on its members, Edgerton is concerned about the potential clash between the past and present values, as well as that between the family and other
social institutions such as the church, schools, or governmental agencies. Elaine
and Robert, for example, do not necessarily reflect all the traditional family
values held by their mother. Whether or not this difference is the result of Mattie's
overprotective mothering or of the influence of change in society is not stated,
but the problems are evident.

The continuity of the family, its heritage and its traditions, gives substance
and meaning. Raney is concerned that, with the exception of his parents and
aunts and uncles, Charles did not even know the names of his relatives. "I
couldn't imagine aunts and uncles not sitting around telling about *their* aunts
and uncles" (54). In *Walking across Egypt* Mattie, too, understood her connectedness with the past and with the future. She did not want to die before she
had grandchildren:

She often thought of the links that extended back to Adam, a direct line, like a little dirt
road that extended back through forests of time, through a little town that was her mother
and father, on back through her grandparents, a little road that went back and back and
back across lands and woods and back across to England and back to deserts and the
flood and Noah and on back to Adam and Eve. A chain, thousands and thousands of
years long, starting way back with Adam and Eve, heading this way, reaching the last
link with Robert and Elaine Rigsbee, her own two children, two thousand years after
Jesus. (52)

In *The Floatplane Notebooks*, the vine provides much of the history of the
Copelands from the mid-1800s to Meredith. It documents the roughness, hard-
headedness, toughness, and durability of a family struggling to endure. It also
reveals the sense of a loving response to stories and language that plays a vital
part in the continuity of the family.

But family is more, in Edgerton's fiction, than simple bloodlines. A family
is a relationship, a unit in which individuals can love and support one another.
Even with her concern for "that stream of blood flowing unbroken since Adam
and Eve," Mattie understands the broader concept of family. She tries to justify
Wesley as a member, even though he is not related through genes: "There must
be some other way to think about it, Mattie thought. Here's a young man I can
do something for if not in blood, in spirit" (144). So Mattie sets out to create
her own grandson by bringing Wesley into her extended family. Building on his
experiences with Mattie, Wesley, in turn, moves toward creating *his* own family
in *Killer Diller*. Cooking for Vernon and his dad, as Mattie did for him; supporting Phoebe when she felt alone; sacrificing for his roommate, Ben, in times
of trouble—through these means, Wesley slowly forms a caring family.

In *The Floatplane Notebooks*, Edgerton broadens the concept of connectedness
beyond the extended family. He sees a relationship with all peoples, suggesting
that the human race is family. While flying a mission over the Ho Chi Minh

Trail during the Vietnam War, Mark looks down from his plane and sees a man walking down a country road. "It is a man . . . shaped like a human being. . . . He is alive. . . . The road another road, a country road in North Carolina and the man is someone I know; the road is a dirt road that I know with a man I know walking on it, walking on the dirt road along which he lives somewhere and the person is Meredith, Uncle Albert, Tyree, Ross, an American man from *The Grapes of Wrath*" (185).

Even Wesley in *Killer Diller* begins to see the connectedness of all: "I got to thinking about the whole part of people that's below the surface," he said to Ben at the Columbia Grill. "I even got to thinking about the communists—I mean, you know, they're people. They understand about being in love just as good a people in America—or they could if they was taught. They got potential. Chinese, too" (126).

The development of themes in his work is not, Edgerton says, deliberate or conscious. He starts with a character and lets it develop, listening to what it says. The story evolves from the characters' interactions with each other. His stories do not, he contends, start with plot: "I hesitate to analyze what guides me because it's a consequence of all my experience, and everything I've ever seen, everything I've ever thought, somehow come together and help me to formulate the character" ("A Southern Voice" 21). But his editor Shannon Ravenel differs with Edgerton's own perception. She thinks that his work is theme driven, even though he may begin writing with interactions between characters. She finds that Edgerton's focus throughout all his novels is on the struggle to live the good life—a Christian life in which the family and church play an integral part. For this reason Ravenel told me that she would classify Edgerton as a Christian writer, who explores and ultimately affirms the message of hope and renewal of life that is to be found in the mysteries of love. Whether or not his thematic development is conscious or not, Edgerton's work is alive with characters and situations that result in a strong thematic focus.

SURVEY OF CRITICISM

Hundreds of reviewers have greeted Edgerton's novels enthusiastically, often comparing his work favorably to such authors as Twain, Hemingway, Welty, and Faulkner. Calling attention to his humor and his ability to capture exquisite nuances of character, Andrew Rosenehim, in his discussion of *Walking across Egypt*, believes that Edgerton's gentle comedy is grounded in an essentially realistic world," far removed from the kind of strange humour we have come to associate with the South: the grotesque moral comedies of Flannery O'Connor." In her review of *The Floatplane Notebooks*, Barbara Kingsolver said: "So perfect is the author's control that each voice, like an individual bell in a handbell choir, rings true. Edgerton's gift is for dialect that places its speaker squarely—not on a geographical map, but a psychological one." Some reviewers comment that the strength of Edgerton's books lies less in plot than in characters, but even so, most agree, they teem with emotion and drama. Critics seem to agree that the appeal of his work is based on the development of his characters, their innocence and trust, their unaffected goodness and sincerity. Even though they find his approach appealing, some reviewers consider his novels slow and predictable.

The comments about Edgerton's work have primarily been made in reviews of his books, but more detailed assessment of his fiction will surely be forthcoming. One of the first articles to consider three of his novels is Michael Pearson's "Stories to Ease the Tension: Clyde Edgerton's Fiction." He believes that the importance of family, race, and the idioms of tradition are central to Edgerton's world. He finds that his novels are not historical romances, but, rather, "social satires, not nostalgic but comic structures braced with an often poignant and graphic realism. Edgerton's South is in the midst of change. It's the country turning into the suburbs. He captures the chameleon as it's changing colors, the old South becoming the Sunbelt." He cites *Raney* as an example of such change, stating that the story, both literally and figuratively, is about the marriage of cultures. With Edgerton's keen understanding of the South and its mores, a gentle humor, and a rural boy's sense of ironic understatement, Pearson believes that Edgerton is "a comic writer of enormous gifts."

BIBLIOGRAPHY

Works by Clyde Edgerton

"Natural Suspension," *Just Pulp* 3, No. 2 (Spring/Summer 1980): 70–76. (First story accepted for publication.)
Raney. Chapel Hill, N.C.: Algonquin, 1985.
Walking across Egypt. Chapel Hill, N.C.: Algonquin, 1987.
The Floatplane Notebooks. Chapel Hill, N.C.: Algonquin, 1988.
"Changing Names," *Southern Review* 25, No. 1 (January 1989): 230–34.
Killer Diller. Chapel Hill, N.C.: Algonquin, 1991.
In Memory of Junior. Chapel Hill, N.C.: Algonquin Books, 1992.

Interviews

"Four Blades," 79–92 in *Family Portraits: A Remembrance by 20 Distinguished Writers*, ed. Carolyn Anthony. New York: Doubleday, 1989.
McGlinn, Jeanne M. "To Make a Good Story: An Interview with Clyde Edgerton." *Arts Journal* 14, No. 2 (November 1988): 36–37.
"A Southern Voice: Clyde Edgerton on Religion, Fiction and Academia." *Excursus: A Review of Religious Studies* 2, No. 1 (March 1988): 18–23.
Summer, Bob. "Clyde Edgerton." *Publishers Weekly* 234, No. 12 (September 16, 1988): 58–60.
Walsh, William J. "Clyde Edgerton," 115–24 in *Speak, So I Will Know Thee: Interviews with Southern Writers* (Jefferson, N.C.: McFarland, 1990).

Sound Recordings

Clyde Edgerton Reads the Floatplane Notebooks. Two cassettes. Random House Audio-
      books, 1989.
Killer Diller Tapes. Chapel Hill, N.C.: Algonquin Books, 1991.
Walking across Egypt: Songs and Readings from the Books *Raney* and *Walking across
      Egypt*. Sung and played by the Tarwater Band: Clyde Edgerton, Susan Edgerton,
      and Jim Watson. Chicago: Flying Fish Records, 1987.

Studies of Clyde Edgerton

Clark, Miriam Marty. Rev. of *Walking across Egypt*. *National Forum* (Winter 1988):
      47.
Coleman, Julie. Rev. of *Walking across Egypt*. *North Carolina Books* (Winter 1987):
      222.
"Edgerton, Clyde (Carlyle)," 147–55 in *Contemporary Authors*, Vol. 134, ed. Susan
      M. Trosky. Detroit: Gale Research, 1992.
"Clyde Edgerton," 52–54 in *Contemporary Literary Criticism Yearbook 1985*, Vol. 39,
      ed. Sharen Hall. Detroit: Gale Research, 1986.
Kingsolver, Barbara. "Albert Uplifts Anything." *New York Times Book Review* (October
      9, 1988): 10.
Pearson, Michael. "Stories to Ease the Tension: Clyde Edgerton's Fiction." *Hollins
      Critic* (October 1990).
Rosenheim, Andrew. "Voices of the New South." *Times Literary Supplement* (Novem-
      ber 25–December 1, 1988): 1306.

John [Marsden] Ehle, Jr.
(1925–   )

Although the body of his work includes a significant achievement in nonfiction, John Ehle is best known for his series of novels set in the mountains of western North Carolina. Consistently praised by reviewers for his meticulous representations of Appalachian culture from the eighteenth century to the present day, for his vivid sense of place, and for a surprisingly lyrical style marked by simplicity and humor, Ehle uses his dramatic setting to highlight themes of justice and individual conscience versus the traditional rights of the family and the good of the community.

BIOGRAPHY

John Ehle was born on December 13, 1925, in Asheville, North Carolina, the eldest of five children born to Gladys Starnes and John Marsden Ehle. John Ehle, Sr., became successful in the insurance business, eventually owning his own agency, and was a respected and active participant in the public life of the town. Gladys Starnes came from a family that had settled in the North Carolina mountains just after the Revolutionary War, and her son has attributed his choice of literary subject matter to the influence of his mother's family who were distinctly Appalachian people. "I'm writing," he said, "about the people who make up the story of my own background." Another early influence was the Bible, which the author recalls he read through so many times that his grandmother was sure he would become a preacher.

After serving with the U.S. Army infantry in World War II, Ehle attended the University of North Carolina at Chapel Hill, where he entered the department of radio, television, and motion pictures (RTVMP), earning a B.A. in 1949 and then, in 1953, an M.A. in drama. Ehle recalls that playwriting courses were required for the RTVMP major, and he quickly discovered he was rather good at it—good enough, in fact, to be hired as a writer by the university's Communications Center before he graduated. From 1954 to 1956, he achieved national recognition with his American Adventure series of radio plays, produced in the studios at the university and broadcast by NBC. These twenty-six half-hour dramas, all written by Ehle himself, presage the author's later work. Most required historical research; the plays' themes are centered on human dignity, justice, and personal courage; and several focus on slavery and on the American Negro. Two of the plays specifically suggest Ehle's later books, *The Free Men* (1965) and *The Journey of August King* (1971): Episode twenty, "The Free Man," is the story of "a citizen who stands against social pressures," and episode twenty-one, "Runaway Justice," tells of a man who "aids two runaway slaves."

Ehle was also trying his hand at short stories; episode ten of American Adventure, "Dial Emergency," was rewritten and eventually published as "Emergency Call" in the January 21, 1957, *Woman's Day* magazine. Another short story was sent to Rogers Terrill, a literary agent in New York, who suggested it could be the basis of a novel. Ehle showed the story to his friend Paul Green, the playwright, who encouraged him to write *Move Over, Mountain*, his first novel, published in 1957 by William Morrow. Four more books followed in quick succession. With the publication of *Lion on the Hearth* in 1961 Ehle made a generally happy marriage with Harper and Row and editor M. S. Wyeth, whom Ehle credits as a third important critic, alongside Terrill and Green, in his development as a novelist.

By 1961 Ehle was an associate professor on the verge of a break with the university at Chapel Hill. Frustrated by the university's lack of support for artists, especially the lack of scholarships in the creative arts and the negligible number of artists on the faculty, he wrote a highly critical letter to the administration that was shown to the poet Robert Frost when he arrived on campus for his annual spring lecture. On the evening of March 3, 1961, Frost used Ehle's letter to scold the educators assembled to hear him in Memorial Hall. The aging poet delivered a moving plea that the faculty find some way to accommodate the young artist, the "problem child in the middle of all this learning." Encouraged by Frost, Ehle published his concerns in an article that appeared in the May 14, 1961, *Raleigh News and Observer*, "What's the Matter with Chapel Hill?" Ehle's ideas about education impressed North Carolina Governor Terry Sanford, who asked Ehle to join his staff as a special assistant.

In 1962 Ehle went to work for Sanford, raising money to fund educational experiments brainstormed by Ehle himself. Among the author's enduring achievements from that era are the establishment of the state's Governor's School (the first in the country) and the founding of the North Carolina School of the Arts. Ehle also played a strong role in the creation of the North Carolina Fund, which served as the model for the community action plan in President Lyndon Johnson's antipoverty program. Ehle's high visibility with the Sanford administration as an "idea man" led to appointments to the White House Group for Domestic Affairs (1964–66) and the first National Council on the Humanities

(1966–70). Ehle left Sanford's staff in April 1964 and served for one year as a program officer for the Ford Foundation. Although he published two books during this period—*The Land Breakers* (1964) and *The Free Men* (1965)—he felt that he was "designed to be a writer" full-time, not a fund-raiser, program consultant, or educator. Nevertheless, Ehle has continued an active life of public service. Among his many projects have been the North Carolina School of Science and Mathematics (which he helped a later North Carolina governor create) and two foundations established with his guidance to identify and help gifted black and Native American students within the state.

In 1967 John Ehle married his second wife, the British actress Rosemary Harris, and his travels with her are reflected in *The Cheeses and Wines of England and France, with Notes on Irish Whiskey* (1972) and *The Changing of the Guard* (1974). The Ehles have a daughter, Jennifer, and reside variously in Winston-Salem and Penland, North Carolina; New York City; London; and wherever Harris' roles chance to take them.

MAJOR THEMES

John Ehle's apprenticeship years at the University of North Carolina Communications Center allowed experimentation and practice with playwriting, the short story, and documentary film scripts, but it was in the longer forms of the novel and the nonfiction book that Ehle found his strength. His first major publication, *Move Over, Mountain*, a novel about a black man determined to support his family without leaving their small North Carolina town, demonstrated the young author's originality, his imaginative and narrative promise, and his interest in place, culture, and the plight of those who have been in some way disfranchised—themes that became the hallmarks of both his mature work and his life. His second book, *The Survivor* (1958), a biography, confirmed these patterns and, with the single exception of *The Cheeses and Wines of England and France, with Notes on Irish Whiskey* (the author at play in a witty culinary dissertation that won encomiums from even the redoubtable James Beard), Ehle's nonfiction has been consistently woven from the strands of social conscience and human drama.

The Survivor is the story of a young German soldier left without family or country following World War II. Based on a series of letters Ehle received from Eddy Hukov, formerly a Polish citizen and a survivor of the French Foreign Legion as well as Hitler's army, the account vividly suggests the universality of human suffering brought about by war, be the sufferer enemy or friend. In *Shepherd of the Streets* (1960), Ehle recounts in a straightforward and, by reviewers' consensus, frequently moving narrative, the battles of a New York City Episcopal priest against the slumlords and for the bodies and souls of the children of his Puerto Rican parishioners.

But it was with *The Free Men* that Ehle achieved his most powerful social commentary, focusing national attention on what had been the strictly local story of the civil rights movement in Chapel Hill. Critics were virtually unanimous in their expressions of surprise at the conflict in this supposedly liberal university community, and in their praise of the book as a piece of extraordinary reporting using novelistic techniques, "an eloquent account . . . full of perceptive insights and human interest" (*Saturday Review*). The *New York Times* underlined the significance of the book as a "calm yet dramatic analysis of the oppressive use of the law to stifle protest," a judgment seconded by the *Pittsburgh Post-Gazette*'s salute to Ehle for his "penetrating analysis of today's civil rights 'revolution' as seen through the eyes of some of its most impassioned leaders."

A generation later, similar cries of critical approval greeted Ehle's 1988 return to the passionate nonfiction of human cruelty and injustice with the publication of *Trail of Tears: The Rise and Fall of the Cherokee Nation*. The book, suggested to Ehle by an editor at Doubleday, met with immediate popular success. Ehle's presentation of the infamous forced march of the Cherokee people from their homes in the southeastern United States to Oklahoma is but the culmination of a detailed and sometimes lyrically written "dramatic history" that Dee Brown likens to "Shakespeare's bloody chronicles." Most reviewers cited Ehle's meticulous research (including much primary material as well as sources not used in previous histories of the Cherokee Nation), deft characterizations, and a lively and poignant narrative style as the ingredients of new and unexpected emotional impact from an oft-told tragic tale of American history.

Ehle's second novel, *Kingstree Island* (1959), takes place on North Carolina's Outer Banks and represents a false start in the author's search for a confining but rich geographical setting where the confluence of history, terrain, and human nature could be imaginatively played out with suitable dramatic intensity. With *Lion on the Hearth*, he found that setting in his home region of western North Carolina and the Great Smoky Mountains which he himself has said are the "main character" in his mountain novels: "I was born under them, they cupped me as a boy, have shaded my own life, they've lorded it over me, and in my novels they lord it over my people." If, given the complexity of his literary achievement to date, Ehle appears to overstate the case for a simple fact of geography, it must be remembered that in Southern literature everything grows out of the simple facts of place and history, and Ehle's abiding concerns have proven to be profoundly Southern: the demands of family and of community, of religion and tradition, in a particular culture, place, and time.

Through eight novels set in and around Asheville, North Carolina, he has explored his themes from 1779 to the present day. A consummate storyteller, Ehle's rich characterizations of the Wright, King, and Plover families depend on the author's ear for authentic dialogue, his mastery of dramatic technique in creating pivotal scenes, and an ironic sense of humor that flows naturally from his mountain people's acceptance of life and God's great joke on us all. Both realistic and romantic in his approach to literature, Ehle combines research that yields a sense of everyday life with a gift for the poetic line and cadence that suggest something of the mysterious tie between these people's lives and the land that shapes them.

In *Lion on the Hearth*, Ehle's concern is with the psychological story of the family, the intricate relationships of its members, the power struggle among siblings, the sons' challenge of the father, and the coming of age of the young protagonist. To some extent this story of the King family in the Asheville of the 1920s and 1930s—Caleb King, his wife Lottie, their niece and sons—could take place anywhere, but enriching the novel is Ehle's continuing reference to the importance of place and community. Caleb's commercial success with his general store despite the Depression is presented as an outgrowth of his refusal to forget his identity as a mountain man and his responsibilities to the community of mountain people. Ehle provides a point of view on the 1929 stock market crash in Asheville somewhat different from that of Thomas Wolfe, who concentrated on the catastrophe to those who had been corrupted by newfangled ways of making money. On King Street, mountaineer Caleb King ponders the spectacle of Asheville's fall: "This, as he analyzed it, was the return on the lazy notion that a man can work only with paper and be productive. He had never believed it." Caleb King remains aloof from the Asheville wheelers and dealers, preferring to invest in his store as a thriving marketplace for the mountain people of the surrounding coves. And in spite of their residence in town, Cal sees to it that his sons know who the Kings really are: "Let the city people . . . look down on King Street if they wanted to. . . . He was one of the mountain people and proud of it. . . . He was of the blue peaks and ridges. . . . He was of their hard ground."

Three years later, in *The Land Breakers*, Ehle explored the origins of this fierce connection to the Appalachian land and the imperatives of community there by depicting the struggles of the late eighteenth-century pioneers who settled western North Carolina. Ehle's unobtrusive use of research into the details of everyday living on the Carolina frontier fascinated critics and readers alike. The book's success undoubtedly influenced him to write more fiction based on extensive research. Both *The Road* (1967) and *Time of Drums* (1970) follow the descendants of the Wright and Plover families introduced in *The Land Breakers*.

In *The Road*, Ehle tells the gripping and violent story of how the Western North Carolina Railroad Company blasted out a roadbed and laid tracks from Old Fort to the Swannanoa Gap in the late 1870s. Ehle's themes of place and community are chiefly developed through the character of Weatherby Wright, the master roadbuilder, whose effort to open his home region to increased trade and the tourist industry proves to be a personal disaster. Tormented by his own moral sense that with machinery and the forced labor of black convicts he has violated something greater and more important than the road can bring, Wright comes to fear the mountain, believing it to be a living enemy that means deliberately to destroy him—as it does.

In *Time of Drums*, Ehle emphasizes the tensions among individual, family, and community as Colonel Owen Wright struggles with his duty to conscript soldiers for the Confederacy, while remaining loyal to his bitterly divided family and their hard-won civilization. *Time of Drums* is unusual among Civil War novels. Its canvas is small; scenes of the conflict are neither romantic nor glorious, with the domestic details of camp life receiving more attention than the fighting; there is a good deal of unexpected humor; and the Southern homefront contains no plantations. Instead, a rural community figures how to survive in the midst of a wilderness with so many of its best craftsmen and farmers killed or crippled by war. *Time of Drums*, with its somewhat shorter length, its concern with complexities of family life, and character development similar to Ehle's work in *Lion on the Hearth*, signaled a development away from extensively researched historical fiction (though Ehle has never abandoned his careful attention to cultural details and folkways). Indeed, the novel had been preceded by a much longer Civil War manuscript that the author discarded entirely.

Only a year after the publication of *Time of Drums*, the long dwelling on a cruel war about slavery, the emotional turmoil surrounding Ehle's writing of *The Free Men* and its aftermath (an involvement not long behind him), and his own maturing talents were distilled into a short novel of artistic distinction. *The Journey of August King* is the compactly written account (only 218 pages) of an ordinary farmer's heroic rescue of a black slave girl. Returning home after a successful trade of the year's crops in Morganton, North Carolina, August King learns that a reward is being offered for two escaped slaves. When he stumbles across one of them, a 15-year-old girl, August wishes only to be relieved of this inconvenient responsibility. Nevertheless, he grumbles his way through a harrowing two-day journey of real danger, to set the girl Annalees on the trail north to freedom. At the core of this remarkable book are August's conversations with the girl, who is hidden in his cart, and his own internal monologues, during which he reflects on the meaning of his predicament: "I was selected to take care of her, he told himself, say what you will. I was singled out. Whether by God or some other mystery I don't know, and whether for God's pleasure or by reason of his displeasure I don't know. Do I amuse him with my bungling? I wonder."

Many reviewers were powerfully moved by the novel, which is distinguished by its simplicity of style, an engaging humor, and the echoes of biblical themes of sacrifice, as August sustains increasingly serious losses in the course of his journey. Comparisons with the recent civil rights movement were inevitable, given the questions this nation had faced about its own predicament and the kind of people who risked everything to join the movement. Although the novel is set in 1810 and the civil rights movement is now itself a subject for both fictional and historical analysis, the issues of justice, compassion, self-sacrifice, and individual conscience versus community mores that Ehle addresses through August King are universal and timeless.

Ehle's next novel was such a startling departure from his accustomed venue that the manuscript went to Random House rather than the author's usual publishers, Harper and Row. *The Changing of the Guard* is the contemporary tale of the making of a movie about the French Revolution on location in Paris, and it examines the change in the movie industry from old-style, romantic, star-centered Hollywood filmmaking to the realism and abrasive creativity of the "New Wave" directors. Embedded in Ehle's accurate depiction of the craft of the film and his account of the interrelationships of this particular film's makers, is the drama of Louis XVI and Marie Antoinette. Ehle's play-within-a-play is an engrossing and pathetic story, presumably the basis for the script that gradually affects the emotional lives of the film's actors. Most major reviewers were impressed with Ehle's tour de force, and at least one academic film critic finds the novel an accurate reflection of the "ferment in the film industry" in the 1960s and 1970s, classing it with the "relatively small number of important Hollywood novels" such as West's *The Day of the Locust* and Fitzgerald's *The Last Tycoon* (Parrill).

Despite its favorable reception, *The Changing of the Guard* was not sufficiently popular at the bookstores to persuade Ehle he should change his pattern and fictional territory. The uncharacteristic lapse of 8 years before the publication of his next novel suggests some sort of upheaval or unrest in the author's life; at least one completed manuscript was shelved during this period—like *The Changing of the Guard*, a contemporary novel about life among the offbeat and wealthy. In 1982 Ehle returned to his regular schedule of creative productivity and the Smoky Mountain country that has inspired his best work.

In *The Winter People* (1982)—by many critical estimates Ehle's masterpiece—the author once again addresses the question of responsibility to family and community in conflict with individual will and desire, and, as in *The Journey of August King*, he finds his answers in biblical wisdom. The story tells of Collie Wright, her bastard infant son, two feuding mountain families, and a gentle clockmaker from Pennsylvania who finds himself trapped in a timeless, isolated, violent frontier landscape unrelated to the Depression-wracked civilization that lies outside this mountain fastness. In Ehle's masterful hands the cultural details of time and region—Collie's public laying out of the body of her dead lover, Cole Campbell, and the bear hunt to test the outsider Waylon's manhood—become compelling revelations of character. Descriptions of the harshness of season and place suggest the universal cruelty of life itself; only Solomon and Jesus Christ can find the way out of the mess Collie's unrestrained passion has caused. In the great bargaining scene that is the novel's brilliant denouement, Collie faces Cole's father, the Campbell patriarch, who seeks revenge: "An eye for an eye, a son for a son. That's Biblical." "A life for a life, Mr. Campbell," Collie replies, "does that have to be a life lost?" With the giving up of her child to his grandfather, Collie finds the solution that will satisfy Old Testament justice, while preventing further loss of life within the community through Christian self-sacrifice.

This remarkable, tightly plotted book was followed two years later by a more rambling, "old-fashioned" novel that surprised those readers who had only just met Ehle through the pages of *The Winter People*. *Last One Home* (1984) follows the fortunes of a mountain family that moves to town. A companion piece to *Lion on the Hearth*, it provides another look at Asheville in the 1920s and 1930s, this time as a growing center for tourism. Ehle's use of humor is more pervasive and more sophisticated in this novel, as his parody of the rapacious American entrepreneur E. W. Grove illustrates: "Dr. Clove," owner of the famous "Clove Park Inn," the former quinine king, proposes to give Asheville a new reputation by burning all the tuberculosis sanitoriums. In a cooperative spirit, Pinkney Wright, Ehle's protagonist, inquires "with a friendly nod," whether Clove would "burn the patients as well?" Of special interest in this book is Ehle's portrayal of the American businessman as no respecter of community: "I think of this as being a town for mountain people to trade in," Pink says to Dr. Clove, "while I suppose you see it for tourists to use." Ehle's consideration of the moral imperatives of doing business 50 years ago has a painful contemporary relevance.

Even more painfully contemporary is *The Widow's Trial* (1989), Ehle's first mountain novel with a present-day setting and no explicit presence for the mountains themselves, only the indirect result of that presence, the culture of the region. This short novel is a bold foray into the subject of wife abuse, exploring through a series of narrators and a murder trial the question of why a reasonably intelligent, physically healthy, attractive young woman with sympathetic family living nearby would continue to live with a consistently violent, drug-dealing husband. The answer Ehle suggests is no plot gimmick, but, rather, the deepest, darkest well of old sexual mystery and the merciless maternal drive that goes with it. The native voices are straight out of contemporary Appalachia, and the humor is vintage Ehle: "Winnette had always been attracted to danger," the novel begins, "not finding much danger even so. Except as a baby she kept pulling her own diapers off." The author's concerns with justice are played out this time literally in a courtroom, and the jury's confusion, misogny, "rancor and personality quirks" raise troubling questions about the community's ability to judge fairly. The lone juror who holds out for a verdict of self-defense, Miss Rachel Famous Turner, here joins Collie Wright, August King, and the young students of *The Free Men* in Ehle's literary gallery of courageous heroes of conscience.

SURVEY OF CRITICISM

Widely and favorably reviewed from the publication of his first book in 1957 to his most recent, John Ehle has, since the late 1960s, regularly inspired reviewers to ask where he has been all their lives, as each new book is published and admired, enjoys respectable sales in this country, and then disappears over the bookstore horizon (frequently to Europe, where Ehle's sales have usually been much better than in the United States). Writing for the *American Scholar* in 1972, Saunders Redding was moved to observe that one of America's most talented "regional novelists . . . has been shamefully and inexcusably neglected.'' Many writers believe that the tag ''regional'' automatically diminishes their work somehow in the estimate of the critical establishment; certainly *The Changing of the Guard*, with its contemporary, international setting, received lengthy approvals from both the *New York Times* and the *Washington Post* critics, with the latter ''surprised to see that it's John Ehle's eighth novel.'' *The Winter People* received almost universal praise, with some reviewers who knew Ehle's previous work calling for him to find the larger national audience he deserved. All liked the fast-moving, dramatic story, but some pointed out that with this novel Ehle had achieved more than a good read. Representative of these critical estimates was the comment in *Kirkus Reviews* that *The Winter People* ''partakes of the territory of myth and racial memory. Indeed, Ehle . . . provides scenes . . . which have the sort of out-of-time tribalness that you find in the late works of Eudora Welty. . . . These people, seemingly beyond place, could be Celts or Mongols or Greeks.'' *Last One Home* suffered somewhat by comparison with its more violent predecessor, many reviewers commenting on the novel's leisurely pace. Chicago critic James Idema praised Ehle's use of language, the ''variable poetic voice'' that ''gives ordinary people and events the quality of myth.'' For inscrutable reasons of its own, the *New York Times Book Review* classified *The Widow's Trial* as ''Crime/Mystery,'' leaving the reviewer to wonder over this ''unusual,'' ''Rashomon-like,'' ''splendidly inventive'' so-called mystery. *Kirkus Reviews*, recognizing a novel when it sees one, found *The Widow's Trial* a ''work of real power and distinction,'' with its ''kaleidoscopic, oral history format'' and clash of drug culture with ''conservative mountain culture, protective of male dominance.''

Given the length and productivity of John Ehle's literary career, the fact that his work is published by major houses both here and abroad, and the consistently favorable and serious notice given his books by reviewers in the national press, the lack of substantive literary criticism is surprising and disappointing. Omitted from most standard literary reference guides—and most notably from those that specifically examine twentieth-century Southern literature—John Ehle has been so completely ignored by academic critics that the question of why has to be raised. Ehle himself has admitted that after the publication of *The Free Men* he was for quite a few years persona non grata in Chapel Hill, where the University of North Carolina has been an influential center for the study of Southern literature. William Parrill, in a 1987 essay, argues that the post–World War II ''new criticism'' favored writers who taught at colleges and universities and who themselves also wrote criticism, those who belonged to an approved school or tradition, and those who wrote symbolic or absurdist fiction. Further, he contends that Ehle has been neglected because the author writes out of a dramatic rather than a Faulknerian tradition, and because he uses the past as a clarifying vehicle for his themes, thus opening himself to the charge of ''historical novelist,'' a term, Parrill notes, that ranks in the academic lexicon ''somewhere between child rapist and mass murderer.'' In a recent symposium paper (1990) Terry Roberts suggests that John Ehle's novels and Appalachian literature itself may have been the victims of a subtle "cultural prejudice," and that, as the literary canon undergoes revision, the time has come to look again "not only at writers that may have been excluded by racial or sexual boundaries but also at writers who may have been excluded by simple geographical ones." Whether condemned for being "historical" or tarred with the "regional" brush, John Ehle sees the question as moot, as he told *Publisher's Weekly* in 1982: "The novelist's part of the world," he said, "is another country."

BIBLIOGRAPHY

Works by John Ehle

Move Over, Mountain. New York: William Morrow, 1957.
The Survivor. (Biography). New York: Holt, 1958.
Kingstree Island. New York: William Morrow, 1959.
Shepherd of the Streets. New York: Sloane, 1960.
Lion on the Hearth. New York: Harper and Brothers, 1961.
The Land Breakers. New York: Harper and Row, 1964.
The Free Men. New York: Harper and Row, 1965.
The Road. New York: Harper and Row, 1967.
Time of Drums. New York: Harper and Row, 1970.
The Journey of August King. New York: Harper and Row, 1971.
The Cheeses and Wines of England and France, with Notes on Irish Whiskey. New York: Harper and Row, 1972.
The Changing of the Guard. New York: Random House, 1974.
"PW Interviews: John Ehle." *Publisher's Weekly* (5 March 1982): 6–7.
The Winter People. New York: Harper and Row, 1982.
Last One Home. New York: Harper and Row, 1984.
"A Conversation: John Ehle and Wilma Dykeman." *Iron Mountain Review* 3 (Spring 1987): 6–11.
Trail of Tears: The Rise and Fall of the Cherokee Nation. New York: Anchor/Doubleday, 1988.
The Widow's Trial. New York: Harper and Row, 1989.

Studies of John Ehle

Banner, Leslie. "The North Carolina Mountaineer in Native Fiction." Ph.D. Dissertation. Chapel Hill: University of North Carolina, 1984.
———. *A Passionate Preference: The Story of the North Carolina School of the Arts*. Winston-Salem, N.C.: North Carolina School of the Arts Foundation, 1987.
———. "John Ehle and Appalachian Fiction." *Iron Mountain Review* 3 (Spring 1987): 12–19.
Brown, Dee. "The End of the Cherokee Trail" (Rev. of *Trail of Tears*). *Los Angeles Times* (September 11, 1988).
Broyard, Anatole. "Books of the Times: Double Feature" (Rev. of *The Changing of the Guard*). *New York Times* (January 7, 1975).

"The 'Free Generation' " (Rev. of *The Free Men*). *Pittsburgh Post-Gazette* (May 29, 1965): 6.

Fuller, Richard. "In Short" (Rev. of *The Widow's Trial*). *New York Times Book Review* (October 15, 1989): 50.

Gold, Ivan. "Mountain People" (Rev. of *The Winter People*). *New York Times Book Review* (May 9, 1982): 13.

Guy, David. "A Novelist's Tale of Family Intrigue Set in the N. Carolina Mountains" (Rev. of *Last One Home*). *Philadelphia Inquirer* (October 21, 1984).

Handlin, Oscar. "A Conflict as Fateful as the Civil War" (Rev. of *The Free Men*). *New York Times Book Review* (July 4, 1965): 3.

Idema, James. "All Roads Lead to Home in Ehle's Warm New Novel" (Rev. of *Last One Home*). *Chicago Tribune* (September 30, 1984): A10.

"John (Marsden) Ehle (Jr.)," 101–07 in *Contemporary Literary Criticism*, Vol. 27, ed. Jean C. Stine. Detroit: Gale Research, 1984.

Lang, John. "A Matter of Craft and Value." *Iron Mountain Review* 3 (Spring 1987): 2.

Leary, Lewis. "A Spirited Tale of the Appalachians" (Rev. of *The Winter People*). *Carolina Lifestyle* (June 1982): 36, 38.

Parrill, William. " 'No Whales in Asheville': The Fictional World of John Ehle." *Iron Mountain Review* 3 (Spring 1987): 20–24.

Prescott, Orville. "Books of the Times: The Violent Life of Carolina Pioneers" (Rev. of *The Land Breakers*). *New York Times* (February 12, 1964).

Rackham, Jeff. "A Real and Mythical Appalachian World: John Ehle's New Novel" (Rev. of *Last One Home*). *Arts Journal* (October 1984): 10.

Redding, Saunders. "The Revolving Bookstand." *American Scholar* (Summer 1972): 486–87.

Roberts, Terry. "The Affirmation of John Ehle." *Arts Journal* 6 (August 1981): 9–11.

———. "Within the Green Bowl: Community in the Mountain Fiction of John Ehle." Paper presented at the Southern Writers' Symposium, Methodist College, Fayetteville, N.C., March 24, 1990.

Schott, Webster. "A Cream Puff Movie" (Rev. of *The Changing of the Guard*). *Washington Post Book World* (January 19, 1975): 3.

See, Carolyn. "A Novel That Asks to Be Loved" (Rev. of *The Winter People*). *Los Angeles Times* Part V (March 16, 1982): 6.

Spearman, Walter. "A Town's Reputation and Reality" (Rev. of *The Free Men*). *Saturday Review* (May 1, 1965): 38.

"The Widow's Trial." *Kirkus Reviews* 57 (August 1, 1989): 1093.

"The Winter People." *Kirkus Reviews* 50 (January 1, 1982): 22.

Yardley, Jonathan. "Love Affairs and Family Feuds in the Smoky Mountains" (Rev. of *The Winter People*). *Washington Post Book World* (March 7, 1982): 3, 14.

CHARMAINE ALLMON MOSBY

Jesse Hill Ford
(1928–   )

Best known for novels about violence associated with racial conflict, Jesse Hill Ford has written most effectively about ordinary people of rural west Tennessee. His unsentimental treatment of these characters and their dilemma is reinforced by his precise ear for Tennessee speech and his lean, almost spare, style.

BIOGRAPHY

Born December 28, 1928, in Troy, Alabama, Jesse Hill Ford grew up in Nashville, Tennessee, attending Parmer School, Montgomery Bell Academy, and Vanderbilt University. He also was a reporter for *The Tennesseean* (1950–51). Ford was strongly influenced by two leading Nashville Agrarians, studying with Donald Davidson at Vanderbilt (B.A., 1951) and Andrew Lytle at the University of Florida (M.A., 1955). In Gainesville, Ford also continued his journalistic career, working as an editorial newswriter (1953–55). He was public relations director for the Tennessee Medical Association (1955–56) and the American Medical Association (1956–57). Since 1957 he has been a free-lance writer and a columnist for *USA Today*. Most recently he wrote the script for a television movie dealing with Nashville minister David Terry's murder of the church handyman (at Emmanuel Church of Christ Pentecostal Oneness), also the subject of ''Murder in the Chapel''—Ford's article in the July 1988 issue of *Southern* magazine (vol. 2, no. 10, pp. 44–47, 65–66, 68–69).

Ford has been a Fulbright Scholar at the University of Oslo (1961), recipient of a Guggenheim Fellowship (1966), visiting fellow at Wesleyan University's Center for Advanced Study (Middletown, Connecticut (1965), writer-in-residence at Memphis State University (1969–71), a visiting professor at the University of Rochester (1975), and writer-in-residence at Vanderbilt University (1987). He received an *Atlantic Monthly* Award (1959) for ''The Surest Thing in Show Business''; an *Atlantic Monthly* Grant (1959) for *Mountains of Gilead*; honorable mention in the competition for a Columbia Broadcasting System Grant-in-Aid (1960); O. Henry awards for "How the Mountains Are" (1961), "To the Open Water" (1966), and "The Bitter Bread" (1967); and an Edgar Award from the Mystery Writers of America for "The Jail" (1975). In 1968 Lambuth College (Jackson, Tennessee) awarded Ford an honorary D. Litt.

MAJOR THEMES

Caught between conflicting values, Ford's characters must choose those to which they will be committed; although some people are obsessive, others must learn the importance of commitment itself. The appropriate decisions—made sometimes at great personal cost—enable individuals to develop a realistic view of themselves, to achieve maturity, to accept responsibility for their actions, and, ultimately, to gain triumph and peace, even in defeat. The ideally balanced identity is most fully realized in the nineteenth-century frontiersman/planter Elias McCutcheon in *The Raider* (1975).

In *Mountains of Gilead* (1961), Ford's central theme is the quest for identity. The principal characters are in different ways incomplete, searching for an object or idea to give life structure and significance. Each must find the internalized idea that constitutes identity. The most profoundly lost character, Gratt Shafer, in each experience looks for something that will matter to him, but he finds nothing important enough to merit commitment and concern. After a long-term relationship with Patsy Jo McCutcheon, he marries Eleanor Fite because he realizes she will demand nothing from him. Eventually, though, deaths and a birth shift Gratt's focus beyond himself. In Tom McCutcheon he sees someone whose commitment to a code makes him willing to kill and to die for it. Gratt also comes to acknowledge his responsibility in Eleanor's death and to recognize its essentially sacrificial nature. His marriage to Patsy Jo and the birth of their son draw him out of his isolation, and the death of Bojack Markam severs Gratt's last bond to his past.

Patsy Jo McCutcheon has always waited for marriage to Gratt to give her life meaning. When she reads of his engagement, Patsy Jo goads her father to kill him and so free her of her obsession. For Patsy Jo, her father's death is sacrificial, forcing her finally to establish an identity. She now can be honest with Gratt because she can survive without him. Her beauty "went deeper now, and the old brittleness was gone, scoured away, leaving great strength in its place and a sort of fierce majesty" (340).

Tom McCutcheon has never really established his own identity. Forced to confront Gratt's insult to Patsy Jo, he assumes the role of avenger, hoping at last to become like his Grandpa Tommy, who "killed a man once for insulting him and never lost a night's sleep over it afterwards" (175). Studying a picture of St. George and the dragon, Tom wonders whether the dragon's claw is pushing away the lance or forcing it deeper, but he fails to grasp the picture's implication:

actions defensive in intent may be self-destructive, and one usually bears some responsibility for one's own annihilation. Defending family honor, Tom becomes the dragon who destroys himself. Although his will is strong enough to overcome his physical weakness, poor judgment and poor aim cause Tom to miss Gratt and instead kill Eleanor. Nevertheless, Tom finally seizes control of his life when he turns his gun on himself.

The television version of *The Conversion of Buster Drumwright* (1964) develops the themes of vengeance, honor, and repentance. The stage version adds the theme of religious fakery in the essentially choric character of Ralph Swiggert, the banjo-playing gospel singer who has deserted his wife, Kathleen Hedgepath, to become Minnie Mayfair Mundine's partner in an evangelism scam. The hypocritical Swiggert serves as a foil for Ocie Hedgepath, whose pose as a preacher also initially is false, but becomes genuine as he is himself converted. The weakness of conventional religion is further seen in the unnamed preacher, who makes only a perfunctory effort to convert Drumwright and then mouths the platitudes about justice, quickly acceding to the Hedgepaths' demands for revenge.

Buster Drumwright, a convicted murderer being held in the Trammel County (Tennessee) jail, is guarded by Deputy Sheriff Fate Stanhope. In the stage version, the locale is specified as east Tennessee, though in fact the characters seem closely akin to Ford's rural west Tennesseans. This later version also emphasizes the theme of personal values by making Stanhope a relatively complex character to whom guarding Drumwright is a source of inconvenience but also a duty and a matter of honor. Likewise, Ford expands the role of the bystander; no longer merely a vehicle for exposition, he becomes the embodiment of mindless mob violence.

The theme of vengeance is personified in Dan, Rance, and Ocie Hedgepath, whose sister Kathleen and her baby were killed by Buster. In Dan, the most impetuous of the brothers, obsession with revenge has unleashed a fury that causes him to reject—and, in the theatrical version, insult and physically abuse—his wife, who urges the brothers to leave Buster to the punishment of the law and the vengeance of God. The central character, however, is Ocie, the eldest brother, who ran away years ago and so considers killing Buster a debt he owes his family.

According to Ford, the stage version of the play was strongly influenced by his study of "the saga tales of Iceland, in which nothing figures more positively than an overweening hunger for blood vengeance" (ix). As Donald Davidson observes in his foreword to the published plays, Ocie, much like Hamlet, is duty-bound to avenge his sister's murder (xvi). Noting Ford's immersion in Southern-style Christianity, Davidson also points out parallels between Ocie and St. Paul, the subject of Ocie's conversations with Buster. Just as Saul, persecutor of Christians, was miraculously converted to become Paul, preacher of the Christian gospel, Ocie enters the jail a would-be avenger but becomes the instrument of salvation for both Buster (xxi–xxii) and himself. With his conversion, Ocie becomes—at least in the stage version—a martyr like St. Paul.

The Liberation of Lord Byron Jones (1965) depicts the corrupting effect of racial bigotry. For the individual, the results are unacknowledged guilt and loss of integrity; human relationships are damaged and eventually destroyed, and the person becomes isolated, unable to sustain human ties. Brutality can lead to change, however, by forcing one to question tradition and standards, to define personal beliefs and ethics, and, ultimately, to take a stand or capitulate. In this novel, Ford again portrays the individual struggle to overcome the stifling effects of the past, to establish ethical values, and so to develop a sense of identity.

Descended from slaveholders, Oman Hedgepath represents the past, repeatedly contrasting the present with his father's and grandfather's times. A 52-year-old bachelor, Oman has cut himself off from intimacy; the person closest to him is his black servant, Henry, but since the age of 13, Oman has made Henry call him Mr. Hedgepath. To fill the void in his personal life, Oman has brought his nephew, Steve Mundine, to Somerton as his law partner and surrogate son. Nella, Steve's wife, describes Oman as "the unloved, the bitter. . . . so God-damned miserable and so God-damned lost . . . Oman wants to be human, but his dead fathers and his dead grandfathers own him" (41).

Responsible for the deaths of Lord Byron Jones, Stanley Bumpas, and Willie Joe Worth, Oman believes that his mistake is taking Jones' divorce case. Actually, his is a moral error: to save a white man's job, Oman violates the code of legal ethics, fails to serve his client's interests and even becomes an accessory in the client's murder. As Steve tells him, Oman is worse than the actual murderers because he fully comprehends the implications and the outcome of his actions.

Emma Jones resembles Oman, although she is a young black woman and he is a middle-aged white man. Both act deceitfully, with full recognition of the results, to achieve their own ends. Just as Oman was warped by the influence of his ancestors, Emma is the flawed product of attempts to save her from her background. Taken from her family at age 5 and raised in an almost cloistered environment, Emma was a romantic when she married Jones, but when she suggested having sex in their hayfield, Jones equated her with promiscuous field hands, slapping her and calling her a whore. Emma's revenge is to take Willie Joe as her lover, taunt Jones about his inadequacies, and eventually provoke Willie Joe to kill him.

Lord Byron Jones embodies the theme of liberation. A wealthy middle-aged black man, he has profited by observing Somerton's degrading traditions. Not only has he never risked his position by speaking out, but he has accepted the white society's values, coming to despise his people's ways. He married Emma because she had been raised essentially by white standards. Her rejection of those standards angers him, but also forces him finally to choose whether to continue following Somerton's rules or to insist on his rights as a citizen and a man. By naming a white man publicly as correspondent in a divorce, Jones knows he is guaranteeing his own death, but he concludes: "Finally it is a decision inside man himself, what he will do in any given situation, how he will choose to live or to die. . . . Someday, somebody must make a stand" (287). Corresponding to Oman in age and social position, Jones differs in choosing principle over expediency, and his commitment makes Oman's actions seem even more heinous. Jones ultimately confronts his murderers, accepting death as a liberation.

Jones' death also helps liberate Steve Mundine, the voice of Oman's conscience and the man his uncle might have become, given different circumstances. A Southern moderate who believes he can change Somerton society from within, Steve grows to despise himself for his failure to take a stand, and Nella worries that he is being emasculated, as Oman already has been. Although initially vacillating, Steve decides that legal ethics and humane behavior are absolutes that must not be sacrificed, and the realization that his efforts are futile drives him away from Oman and from Somerton. Like the double ledgers of the police, entirely different sets of rules apply to white and black citizens, and vicious mistreatment takes place beneath a veneer of benevolent paternalism.

Like Steve, William (Sonny Boy) Mosby, another surrogate son, finds his identity through Jones' death. When Bumpas and Willie Joe murder Jones, Mosby considers himself a failure. He has promised to protect Jones, but he simply stands and watches, powerless to change the situation and afraid to try. Deciding that he must act, Mosby pushes Bumpas into a hay baler, thus dismembering the man who castrated Jones. At Jones' funeral, Mosby accepts the Nation of Islam, and he leaves Somerton as Mosby X.

Death is emphasized from the first chapter, when Oman Hedgepath hopes to read his ex-fiancée's obituary, until the final pages, when he contemplates his own death. As Lavorn Smith knows, she soon will die of cancer. Other deaths are violent, however, reflecting unacknowledged and untreated social ills: Storekeeper Jimmy Bivens is killed when he refuses to return Mosby's gun; frustrated by his own powerlessness, Henry Parsons beats his young son to death; Lord Byron Jones is shot in the head, then castrated; Stanley Bumpas is dismembered; John F. Kennedy is assassinated in Dallas; and Willie Joe Worth finally slams his patrol car into a bridge. Of these, only Jones and Willie Joe decide when and why they will die.

Of the nineteen stories in *Fishes, Birds and Sons of Men* (1967), six involve initiation. "The Savage Sound" is the account of Bud Morgan's instilling blood lust in his two young whippets. An aging family servant and an old dog teach young Coy Rickman Turner of "The Cow" that all living things die. In "The Trout" an older Coy learns the value of patience when he losses a rare trout because he tries to land it too soon. On his 13th birthday, George of "The Cave" experiences his first infatuation; however, an Indian skull his elderly cousin gives him is—like the aged relative himself—a reminder of mortality. Doug, who casually borrows snakes and lizards from Mitch, the narrator of "The

Surest Thing in Show Business," successfully performs extremely dangerous stunts because he does not know enough about reptiles to realize that these acts are impossible. In "How the Mountains Are" Mary, the black nursemaid, finally sees the Smoky Mountains and also realizes the dangers that confront her young charges.

Two stories deal with misfits who achieve some degree of acceptance. In "Wild Honey" a widow—originally from Aurora, Illinois—remains apart from, and critical of, Tennessee ways until George and a swarm of wild bees change her mind. Clarence Perks of "Beyond the Sunset" has been sent to Somerton to manage the People's Dandy Store, replacing a deceased local hero. Perks is an outsider until he demonstrates that not only is he the best pool player in West Tennessee but also he can defend himself in a fight. He does not feel really "safe," however, until he realizes that the town's hostility has turned from him to the hero's widow, who is dating again.

Relationships between men and women are also central to several stories. After years of anticipating death from his weak heart, Tommy Hassell, of "Fishes, Birds and Sons of Men" marries and decides to confront death by living. In "The Messenger," as the postmaster deplores the destruction of Gabe French's mansion, he wonders why the most enthusiastic member of the wrecking crew is Henty, whose previous job as the Frenches' butler required him to repeat messages among three generations of this family who occupied the same rooms but loathed each other and communicated only through Henty. "The Britches Thief" treats lightly the theme of marital jealousy; when Buddy Potter steals expensive moleskin britches from their store, the Frenches make him serve his jail sentence in another town and so wonder about his bride's faithfulness.

Infidelity figures also in "A Strange Sky," an early version of *Mountains of Gilead*. A friend tells Patsy Jo McCutcheon that Gratt Shafer is dating a girl in Memphis, but he pretends their relationship is unchanged. Unlike the character in the novel, Gratt seems deliberately exploitive, but Patsy Jo lacks the will to break with him. Arthur of "Winterkill" likewise cannot leave his unfaithful wife, and his older brother John, who generally is content with only the barest essentials in life, is involved in a convenient, but meaningless, sexual relationship. John decides life is a wait for autumn's killing frost.

Death is the dominant theme in six stories. Robert, of "The Bitter Bread," is devoted to his young wife, but the hospital allows her to die before he can raise the fifty dollars cash required for her to be treated. In "The Rabbit," Enoch Patterson has tried for years to kill his wife's pet rabbit. While Enoch is with his mistress, his wife dies, and Enoch tries to assuage his guilt by cuddling the rabbit and talking baby talk to it. Little Frank, in "The Highwayman," discovers that a simple robbery can lead to murder and betrayal. In "Acts of Self Defense," two lifelong friends feud over the location of a new barn until one is dead and the other wounded. The unnamed narrator of "To the Open Water" dies because of a similar stubborn pride—going hunting on a day too cold, and attempting to reach the incomparable spot to shoot, the unfrozen center of the river. In

"Look Down, Look Down," Mrs. Gannaway idealizes her son, Arthur, whose plane crashed into the Mediterranean in 1943. Choosing not to investigate fully the possibility that he may actually be alive, she prefers to preserve her image of a pure, heroic son. While supervising the making of an equally artificial rose garden, she dies, much as she has imagined Arthur did.

The Feast of Saint Barnabas (1969) describes a day of racial violence in black sections of Ormund City, Florida. Ford's primary interest is the way the riot reveals his characters' true natures and changes their lives. Using multiple narrators, Ford focuses on a series of episodes that directly affect specific characters. Together, the individual accounts create a mosaic of the events of June 11, the feast day of St. Barnabas. Just as no one in Ormund City knows precisely what happened, the reader's sense of the facts remains ambiguous, shifting with each new perspective. Thus, Ford also demonstrates the oversimplifications in accepted historical fact.

The person most responsible for the riot is Purchase Walker, the black vice lord. Approached by Father Ned about defusing the racial tension, he makes the negative choice described in Father Ned's sermon; Walker, more than any other single character, determines the course of events, deliberately provoking the riot for business advantage. The riot changes Walker, however. He maintains a Christian facade, but reportedly he "drinks chicken blood," goes out on his roof "alone and in darkness and seems either to pray for forgiveness or to converse with someone," and, when drunk, "howls like a murdered dog" (307). He remains the leader of his people, but—no longer convinced that he loves them—they now fear him. Thus, Walker—who could have been a St. Barnabas figure, if not St. Paul—fails himself and everyone else.

Miss Ton-Ton, Walker's mistress, also fails as a St. Barnabas figure; she sees Walker's responsibility for the deaths and destruction that occur, but, like him, she has chosen material instead of moral values, and, having participated in his schemes, she has lost both the right to condemn him and the power to influence him positively. More quickly than Walker, she recognizes the evil in their schemes, but she also is quickly resigned to it.

Father Ned Matthews, a black Episcopal priest, is closely identified with St. Barnabas, whose name means the son of consolation. Father Ned preaches about choice, telling his parishioners that the lesson of St. Barnabas is the importance of Christian love and, in their case, forgiveness. The sermon fails to persuade them, but Father emulates St. Barnabas as he walks through the streets, cares for the wounded and dying, and generally attempts to supply people's needs, physical and psychological as well as spiritual. Until the riot, Father Ned has given his community only limited service; his preoccupation with his personal tragedies is, however, subsumed in the riot's tragedies, and the fiery violence purges him of cynicism and fatalism. When the riot has run its course, Father Ned pronounces a kind of benediction, speaking of "the peace that passes all understanding" and "the love that is living in our hearts" (305).

Another narrator in the "Son of Consolation" chapter, Boston Humes, cultivates the image of the cynic and the tightwad, but secretly he believes being a man requires one to "take on and worry about everybody in the whole world" (137); so he supplies food and advice to young men like Leroy and Hatcher, and he tolerates pool hustlers like Huey Bolls. Eventually, profoundly changed by the riot, Boston serves the community as a member of the Biracial Committee, though he is too wise to believe the discussions really change Ormund City.

An incomplete St. Barnabas figure is Louise Hollan, known on the street as Gyp. A go-go dancer and prostitute, she initiates Hatcher sexually, and they, like Cutler and Cynthia, plan to marry. Hatcher's effect on Gyp is as positive as Cynthia's on Cutler; this young innocent calls her Louise, and she seems destined to abandon her identity as Gyp. Her presence in the "Son of Consolation" chapter suggests that, with the influence of Hatcher, another avatar of St. Barnabas, Gyp too could have made the right choice; after Hatcher's death, however, she instead joins the clapping mob, rationalizing that "if you can't shut 'em up you better join 'em" (303).

Minor characters also display St. Barnabas' concern for others' well-being. Allen Sappington, who has the meaningless title of consul for Norway, eventually is given the dangerous task of driving the "crowd control vehicle" through the riot area. Several times the police sergeant calls him "the consoler" instead of the consul (235–36), and, in fact, that is Sappington's function; but though to the sergeant Sappington is "the Norwegian consoler," the term more accurately describes the Norse sailor, Gudliev Lid, who is primarily responsible for saving Cutler and Cynthia. Unable to speak the language or comprehend the underlying issues, he hears their cries and charges into the mob, inspiring others to help.

Assisting others is not always enough to qualify one as a St. Barnabas figure. The black doctor in the riot area struggles to save the wounded and dying who overflow his clinic, but being called "Uncle Tom" forces him to acknowledge his alienation from other black people. He has struggled to build security for his family and himself; yet as his army experiences proved, he is completely isolated, respected by neither race. The riot only increases his emotional distance from the community; he senses later that his clinic has been tainted, but he fails to see that the source is his own pride and self-absorption.

Rann Cutler, too, is isolated, trusting no one. He says his family's decline cut him off from his only satisfactory identity. A 35-year-old misfit, Cutler describes himself as a classy "judas goat willing to lead another man to the slaughter . . . to abuse and ultimately to betray a friendship built entirely upon false pretenses" (92). Walker calls him a "catch dog," who earns his living by finding the hog and catching it for his master (158).

Originally the antithesis of the St. Barnabas figure, Cutler is changed by his relationship with Cynthia, a young woman he intends merely to use; her love and acceptance help him realize the mess he has made of his life. For Cutler, who has spent most of his life avoiding commitment or closeness, the riot reinforces a rather halfhearted commitment and confirms his decision to marry Cynthia, reconcile with his family, and become a responsible husband and father—to create an identity.

Attracted to Cutler because of his patience and independence, Cynthia is the most successful avatar of St. Barnabas. Her virginity prior to her relationship with Cutler indicates her essential innocence. Cynthia has already rejected the materialistic values that enslave Cutler. Early in her life, she chose a simple life with her father in Ormund City over wealth with her mother's relatives in the northeast. Dreading loss of her freedom, Cynthia, too, has always avoided commitment, but her experiences during the riot teach her the necessity of emotional bonds, and she chooses to marry Cutler. Her role in his life parallels that of St. Barnabas in the life of St. Paul.

The Raider (1975) encompasses the lifetime of Elias McCutcheon, Ford's version of the fully developed identity. His story is that of West Tennessee in microcosm. In the 1830s he enters the wilderness, builds a cabin, and carves out a farm. He trades first with an Indian and later at nearby Fort Hill, which grows from a trading post to the town of Somerton. Attacked by a band of robbers resembling the outlaw confederation of John Murrell, Elias leads a raid much like the one that wiped out Murrell's gang. Like many antebellum West Tennesseeans, Elias does not believe in slavery, but as his holdings expand and he turns from hunting and trapping to growing cotton, he acquires slaves. As might be expected in a region that rejected secession in the first statewide referendum, he is a Unionist, but he eventually accepts a command in the Confederate army because he believes he owes his neighbors this obligation. In the war he again becomes a successful raider, whose tactics and achievements resemble those of Bedford Forrest. The war costs him dearly, however. His wife, Jane, and his son Willy are killed; his home is destroyed; and Isaac, his other son, moves east to become a scholar. At the war's end, Elias—like many other West Tennessee Confederates—returns to live in his original cabin.

An epic figure, Elias McCutcheon is the archetypal Southern frontiersman turned planter. His prosperity is built on hard work and careful management. He shows forethought in constructing his first cabin of square timbers; using round logs would be easier, but these timbers make his house warm and bulletproof. Even after becoming a planter with many slaves, Elias works with his hands. He is also a generous friend, but his willingness to help others leads to anguish when he ignores the warnings of Jane and the Indian Leola, opening the door to supposed itinerant preachers who are, in fact, outlaws.

Elias is a brilliant military leader because he is brave, practical, and somewhat ruthless. He rides near Yankee camps, strikes suddenly, and knows almost instinctively when to press his advantage and when to retreat. His tactics are more practical than the theories in military textbooks. Elias also acts decisively, attacking Yankee-occupied Somerton and burning anything useful to the Union army.

The two women in Elias' life parallel his roles as frontiersman and planter.

Jane Nail McCutcheon is a suitable mate for the frontiersman. Slender, strong, and attractive, she is not conventionally pretty, but she is as unspoiled as the wilderness itself. Ellen Ashe reflects the elegance of plantation life. Her beauty and sophistication appeal to Elias, but their affair is Ellen's choice, not his. As exploitive as the plantation system itself, the self-centered Ellen takes Elias as her lover and continues the relationship until she decides to end it. Attracted to power, Ellen—like the Southern Bourbons—allies herself with the occupying Yankees.

Elias' sons inherit the two sides of his identity. The child of his frontier period, Isaac shares his father's love for the land, his distaste for slavery, and also his sense of duty. Thorough and hardworking like his father, Isaac learns everything books can teach him about artillery and military strategy. Isaac has no romantic illusions about fighting, but reluctantly he kills a man in a duel to defend his honor. Caught up in the romanticism of the cavalier code, Willy, the younger son, also possesses his father's courage and determination, but he is easily swayed by the war fever in Somerton.

Gabriel French and Dutt Callister are essentially typical planters. Sophisticated and apparently prosperous, French, too, is generous and practical, but his speculative dealings with the occupying Yankees eventually cause him to be imprisoned. Callister has been ruined by his image of himself as a cavalier; he is poor because he is too genteel to work. He longs for the adventure of war and considers the war years the only happy period of his life. As Elias' lieutenant, he finally establishes an identity and earns the respect he has always so badly wanted.

Loyalty is another major theme. Elias joins the Confederate army only out of loyalty to the neighbors who fought with him against the outlaws. He convinces Jasper Coon, a Free Soiler, to come along because Elias and Isaac need him; and, unlike many West Tennessee Confederates, Jasper does not desert when the fighting at Shiloh gives him the opportunity. Willy's loyalty to a friend causes him to disregard the law and cultural taboos to help Edward Ashe flee to Canada with the slave Betsy and their child. Friendship is also the basis of Jake's loyalty to Elias, who treats him more as a partner than as a slave. Jake—who devotes his life to serving Elias—has only contempt for the slaves who leave their masters. Perhaps the most loyal character is Jane McCutcheon, who refuses to question Elias about the old love letters she finds, repeatedly rejects Leola's suggestions that she burn them, and eventually dies trying to save them from a looting Yankee soldier.

SURVEY OF CRITICISM

Ford's work has received little scholarly attention. Donald Davidson has pointed out the influence of the Bible and *Hamlet* on *The Conversion of Buster Drumwright*. Edith Schimmel Irwin has examined Ford's use of the classical conventions of the revenge motif in *Mountains of Gilead, The Liberation of Lord*

Byron Jones, The Feast of Saint Barnabas, "A Strange Sky," "To the Open Water," and *The Conversion of Buster Drumwright.* Most critical consideration of Ford's work, however, has appeared in book reviews.

Robert Scholes (*New York Times Book Review,* July 2, 1961) praises *Mountains of Gilead* as "a work of considerable promise . . . [and] a strong and satisfying performance in its own right." The strengths Scholes identifies have been consistently pointed out: An "acute sense of time and place"; a "crisp, clear prose style"; a "strong feeling for action" that makes the novel "move with the fast pace of an adventure story"; "solidly realized characters [who] behave in a manner at once convincing and dramatic, in an authoritatively rendered social scene"; and a "bittersweet conclusion" that is "a satisfying resolution of the action" (6).

Roderick Cook (*Harper's* 231:14D, Sept. 1965) commends Ford's "good ear for dialogue and dialect" (140). Analyzing *The Feast of Saint Barnabas,* Granville Hicks (*Saturday Review* 52:22, Feb. 8, 1969) notes "abundance of action," "sharply drawn and memorable" principal characters, and "powerful" descriptions of the riot and its consequences (22). R. J. Redden (*Library Journal* 100:1844, Oct. 1, 1975) describes *The Raider* as "a good historical novel" with "well-drawn" characters and "rich and colorful" descriptions (1844). Likewise *Virginia Quarterly Review* (52:130, Autumn 1976) praises Ford's "faithfulness to detail," "believability of characterization," and ability to "write in sentences which emphasize nuance and emotion, though not at the expense of action and excitement"—concluding that it is "in every sense an epic novel" (120).

Reactions to Ford's novels have consistently been mixed, however. Dorothy Leer (*Library Journal* 86:2816, Sept. 1, 1961) says about *Mountains of Gilead:* "The characters, the setting, the plot are all believable, but their combination fails to produce a novel with any literary appeal" (2816). Likewise, the generally favorable *Booklist* (58:21, Sept. 1, 1961) review speaks of "some undiluted melodrama and patches of overwritten prose" (21). Ford's multiple narrators are confusing for C. M. Weisenberg (*Library Journal* 94:778, Feb. 15, 1964), Roderick Cook (*Harper's,* 66:85, July 5, 1965), and the *Newsweek* reviewer of *The Liberation of Lord Byron Jones* (231:140, Sept. 1961). Granville Hicks (*Saturday Review* 52:22, Feb. 8, 1969) praises *The Feast of Saint Barnabas,* but observes that "the elaboration of subsidiary plots and the introduction of superfluous characters have, it seems to me, weakened the effect" (22). The *Choice* (6:642, July 1969) review also mentions "weaknesses in structure and tone" but asserts that *The Feast of Saint Barnabas* still is "an absolute must for contemporary fiction collections" (642).

BIBLIOGRAPHY

Works by Jesse Hill Ford

"The Thundering Tide." M.A. Thesis. Gainesville: University of Florida, 1955.
Mountains of Gilead. Boston: Little, Brown, 1961.

The Conversion of Buster Drumwright: The Television and Stage Scripts. Nashville: Vanderbilt University Press, 1964.

The Liberation of Lord Byron Jones. Boston: Little, Brown, 1965.

Fishes, Birds and Sons of Men. Boston: Little, Brown, 1967.

Fiction Writing: Random Comments on the Business and the Art. New York: J. Norton, 1968.

The Feast of Saint Barnabas. Boston: Little, Brown, 1969.

Learning to Write the Short Story. New York: Writer's Voice, 1972.

The Liberation of L. B. Jones: The Screenplay. With Stirling Silliphant. Columbia Pictures, 1969; RCA/Columbia Pictures Home Video, 1984.

The Raider. Boston: Little, Brown, 1975.

Mr. Potter and His Bank: A Life of Edward Potter, Jr. Nashville: Commerce Union Bank, 1977.

Fiction Writing: The Business and the Art. New York: J. Norton, 1980.

Drumwright: The Musical. (1982).

"Happy Birthday, Stevie Wonder," *Chattahoochee Review* 12, (Fall 1991): 18–34.

Among the Ford papers deposited in the Mississippi Valley Collection at the John Willard Brister Library, Memphis State University, are copies of thirty short stories (six of which are not collected elsewhere), two poems, and twenty-three articles or reviews. The collection also contains typescript fragments of five novels ("Nickajack: A Romantic Novel," "The Sons-in-Law: A Novel," "Let Us Honor Our Fathers," "The Second Sunday after Trinity," and "The Night That Paddy Murphy Died") and several stories.

Studies of Jesse Hill Ford

Alvis, John. "Jesse Hill Ford," 100–104 in *Dictionary of Literary Biography, Vol. 6: American Novelists since World War II,* 2nd series, ed. James E. Kibler, Jr. Detroit: Bruccoli, Clark, 1980.

Berryhill, Kenneth. "Jesse Hill Ford: His Motif of Death." *Tennessee Philological Bulletin* 10, No. 1 (July 1973): 31.

Burke, W. J. and Will D. Howe, revised by Irving Weiss and Anne Weiss, eds. "Ford, Jesse Hill," in *American Authors and Books,* 3rd rev. ed. New York: Crown, 1972.

Clark, Anderson. "Violence in the Fiction of Jesse Hill Ford." *Tennessee Philological Bulletin* 10, No. 1 (July 1973): 30–31. Also unpublished M.A. thesis, Nashville: Vanderbilt University, 1970.

Cook, Martha E.. "Jesse Hill Ford," 163–64 in *Southern Writers: A Biographical Dictionary,* ed. Robert Bain et al. Baton Rouge: Louisiana State University Press, 1979.

Davidson, Donald. "Foreword," xv–xxiv in *The Conversion of Buster Drumwright.* Nashville: Vanderbilt University Press, 1964.

Evory, Ann. ed. "Ford, Jesse Hill (Jr.)," 198 in *Contemporary Authors,* New Revised Series, Vol. 1. Detroit: Gale Research, 1981.

"Ford, Jesse Hill," 319 in *The Writers Directory 1988–90,* 8th ed. Chicago and London: St. James Press, 1988.

Irwin, Edith Schimmel. "The Revenge Motif in the Fiction of Jesse Hill Ford." Ph.D. Dissertation. Tuscaloosa: University of Alabama, 1974. (*DAI.* 35, xiA, 7308A)

Jones, Madison. Rev. of *The Liberation of Lord Byron Jones. Mississippi Quarterly* 20 (Winter 1967–68): 61–64.

Landess, Thomas H. "The Present Course of Southern Fiction: Everynegro and Other Alternatives." *Arlington Quarterly* 1 (Winter 1967–68): 61–69.

Loyd, Dennis. "Contemporary Writers," 183–202 in *Literature of Tennessee,* ed. Ray Willbanks. Macon: Mercer University Press, 1985.

McKinley, James. "An Interview with Jesse Hill Ford." *Contempora* (Atlanta) 2, 1: 1–7.

Seay, James. "The Making of Fables: Jesse Hill Ford," 199–212 in *Kite-Flying and Other Irrational Acts: Conversations with Twelve Southern Writers,* ed. John Carr. Baton Rouge: Louisiana State University Press, 1972.

Sexton, Franklin D. "Jesse Hill Ford: A Biographical and Critical Study." Ph.D. Dissertation. Hattiesburg: University of Southern Mississippi, 1973. (*DAI.* 34, 4285A)

Thomas, William. "The Liberation of Jesse Hill Ford." *Mid-South, The Commercial Appeal Magazine* (April 24, 1966): 4–7.

Weeks, Edward. *Breaking into Print: An Editor's Advice on Writing.* Boston: The Writer, 1962.

————. *In Friendly Candor.* Boston: Little, Brown, 1959.

White, Helen. "Jesse Hill Ford: An Annotated Check List of His Published Works and of His Papers." *Mississippi Valley Conference Bulletin* No. 7. Memphis: John Willard Brister Library, Memphis State University, 1974.

FRANK W. SHELTON

Richard Ford
(1944–   )

None of his work after his first novel is set in the South, but in the last two decades Richard Ford has written significant fiction exploring the nature of the American experience. With the publication of *The Sportswriter* in 1986 and *Rock Springs* in 1987, he has been recognized as one of the finest "new realists" writing in America today.

BIOGRAPHY

Richard Ford was born on February 16, 1944, in Jackson, Mississippi, an only child who came relatively late in his parents' marriage (when they were in their 30s). His father was a traveling starch salesman who spent only the weekends home with his family. Although Ford was raised in Jackson, during summers he and his mother traveled with his father. He also spent time during summers and school holidays with his grandfather, who ran a hotel in Little Rock, Arkansas. Thus early in his life he was exposed to itinerant people, the effect of which can be seen in his own later life and in his fictional characters. In 1960, when he was 16, Ford witnessed the death from a heart attack of his father. He and his mother continued to live in Jackson, but their relationship and situation changed. Not only did she have to get a job, but she sat him down and told him she could no longer look after him, that he had to assume more responsibility, and that they would be partners in life.

In 1962 Ford left the South to attend Michigan State University. Initially he planned to study hotel management and emulate his grandfather, but he eventually majored in literature. After graduation he taught school for a year and then spent one semester attending law school at Washington University in St. Louis. In 1968 he married his wife, Kristina, to whom all his books are dedicated, and they moved to California for two years where he studied writing at the University of California at Irvine with Oakley Hall and E. L. Doctorow.

During the next two years he wrote and tried unsuccessfully to publish short stories, but finally decided to try to write a novel instead. He received a fellowship in 1972 at the University of Michigan where he stayed for three years, taught writing, and wrote *A Piece of My Heart*. In 1976 he published that novel, which received generally respectful reviews and was runner-up for the Ernest Hemingway Award for the best first novel of the year. His next novel was *The Ultimate Good Luck* (1981). His career definitely advanced in 1986 with the publication of *The Sportswriter* as a paperback original in the Vintage Contemporaries series. The novel was widely and positively reviewed and was followed the next year with *Rock Springs,* a collection of stories that had previously appeared in such publications as *The New Yorker, Esquire,* and *Harper's. Rock Springs* was generally hailed as an excellent volume. His most recent novel, *Wildlife* (1990), was based on a situation explored in some of the stories in *Rock Springs*. In addition, over the past several years Ford has published numerous essays, primarily in *Harper's* and *Esquire,* that provide revealing insights into his own life and his perspective on literary life. Ford titled his 1992 Hopwood Lecture at the University of Michigan, "What We Write, Why We Write It, and Who Cares."

Ford and his wife lead itinerant lives. They choose not to have children and have moved frequently, often in connection with Kristina Ford's career (she has a Ph.D. in urban and regional planning). They have lived in a variety of locations, including Michigan, Vermont, New Jersey, Montana, Mississippi, and Mexico. Ford has taught at numerous colleges and universities, but has now given up teaching to devote full time to writing. Although he owns some property in Mississippi, he appears not to have any close ties to the South. In fact, he needs to move frequently to stimulate his imagination.

MAJOR THEMES

As the above biographical sketch indicates, Ford feels no special allegiance to the South, and his fiction reflects that fact. His first novel, *A Piece of My Heart,* set primarily in Arkansas, is recognizably Southern, but his later works are set in such locales as Mexico, New Jersey, and Montana, places where he has lived during his adult life. As he had commented in connection with Walker Percy: "Southern regionalism as a factor in the impulse that makes us write novels . . . has had its day. . . . The South is not a place any more: it's a Belt, a business proposition, which is the nearest thing to anonymity the economy recognizes." Although his characters, like Frank Bascombe of *The Sportswriter,* at times have vaguely Southern roots, that fact plays no significant role in their lives. In fact, Ford has declared that his ambition is the same as that of William Dean Howells: to "create a literature worthy of America." His interest then is not in a particular region but in the country as a whole. Place is important to

Ford's fiction, but, referring to Eudora Welty, he observes that place "is wherever we do good work. It is wherever we can gain dominion over our subject (whether we find it there or not) and make it convincing." Ford finds the way people accommodate themselves to a place inherently dramatic, remarking: "I try to exhaust my own interest in a place. Then I'll just move on, write about some-place else where I kind of notice again how people accommodate themselves to where they live. That accounts for the kinds of things I write."

In discussions of his place in contemporary American fiction, Ford is not linked with Southerners but with such short-story writers as Raymond Carver (at least his late work) and Tobias Wolff under the rubric "new realism" or "dirty realism." Like most writers, Ford has little use for such labels, but these do seem accurate in that they place him with those who reacted against the minimalism and metafiction prevalent in the 1960s and 1970s. While Ford's style can be almost Hemingwayesque in its understatement, he does not exper-iment with the form of fiction and sees social factors as important elements in his characters' lives. Additionally, his ambition to write about the American character and American experience links him with such writers as Carver and Wolff.

His characters generally lack a past or roots. Often they are divorced or otherwise cut off from others. They are wanderers, which gives Ford the op-portunity to write of the highways, motels, and hotels of America. His often lower or lower-middle-class characters typically lack a great deal of education and self-consciousness, but they do struggle in their own ways for meaning and for transcendence of their seemingly meaningless lives. Although Ford does not envision a permanent value system governing human life, he and his characters resist succumbing to an easy nihilism. His central characters are male, but almost all his plots revolve around the relationship of men and women. Though his characters often live lives on the edge, they can be redeemed by affection. Ford believes that "it's just those little moments of time, those little, almost invisible, certainly omittable, connections between people which save your life or don't, and that if your life has a habit of seizing those little moments, then, I think, life can go on for you, have the possibility of being better." In his article on Ernest Hemingway, F. Scott Fitzgerald, and William Faulkner, Ford makes an observation applicable to his own fiction: "What they wrote about was people living ordinary lives for which history had not quite readied them. And it is, I think, a large part of why we like them so much when we read them. They were like us. And what they wrote about reminded us of ourselves and sanctioned our lives." Thus, Ford seeks to give voice to the voiceless in fiction through which human lives can be made meaningful.

Ford's first novel, *A Piece of My Heart,* is set in the legendary, mythical South and is his one attempt at a Southern novel. It takes place primarily on an island in the river between Arkansas and Mississippi, a seeming oasis away from the modern world but an oasis in decay, an island that symbolically does not appear on any of the charts of the region. The novel tells the story of two men drawn home to the South. Robard Hewes leaves his wife and home in California to return to Arkansas, drawn by sexual attraction for his cousin Buena. Sam Newell, a deracinated intellectual from Mississippi who is about to receive a law degree in Chicago, returns South to try to find the missing part of himself in his past and the Southern land and people. The characters are mirror images of one another, with Hewes driven by blood and passion, Newell by a sense of intellectual emptiness. They experience fates that are intertwined. The novel is in the Southern tradition in its inclusion of grotesque, maimed characters. Curiously enough, Mr. and Mrs. Lamb—the elderly proprietors of the island, one hard of hearing and the other with a glass eye—have a stability lacking in the young men. Neither of the men finds in the South what he needs or seeks. Hewes is killed in a mindless, absurd act of violence. Newell at the end of the novel returns to Chicago, really no closer to any solution to his problems. Perhaps the central insight of the novel is contained in Hewes' comment to Newell: "Just cause you think up some question don't mean there's an answer." Without self-consciousness or self-understanding, Hewes is doomed to failure; Newell, on the other hand, because he recognizes the futility of searching for meaning in the South and his Southern past, may be freed to make a life for himself. *A Piece of My Heart,* focusing on typically alienated characters, represents Ford's homage and farewell to the Southern literary tradition. He has not set another work of fiction in the region.

The Ultimate Good Luck, Ford's next novel, is a thriller in the mode of Graham Greene. Set in Mexico during a time of chaos and threatened revolution, the novel focuses on Quinn, an American Vietnam veteran attempting to free his former girlfriend's brother Sonny, who has been arrested for drug running. Marginal and rootless, Quinn is a typical Ford character, whose lack of commitment has driven away his girlfriend, Rae. Partly because of his experience in Vietnam, he takes a "wary" view of everything in an attempt to maintain self-control. He is determined to live only in the present, avoiding attachments and ignoring the past and future. His credo is: "The best thing you could do was to take events one at a time, in order, and hope one event by itself wouldn't cut you up too bad." Typically of the genre, the plot is murky and involves conspiracies and counterconspiracies. The uncertainty of events creates a doubtful, threatening, and incomprehensible world. Although Quinn is not successful in getting Sonny freed, he is skillful in negotiating such a world. More important, he comes to realize that his unattached, rootless life is empty. Rae's question of him at the end of the novel is crucial: "Do you think you're old enough to live your life unprotected, Harry?" His implicit answer is yes. In an attempt to protect himself from danger and hurt, he has avoided commitment to others. By the conclusion of the novel, he realizes that, although the world is a dangerous place, meaning can be gained through accepting the vulnerability that comes from close relations with others.

In *The Sportswriter* the context of Ford's fiction is different. Gentle and meditative, the novel does not include the episodes of random violence characteristic of his first two novels. Frank Bascombe, the narrator, is a philosophical sort who devotes much of the novel to musings about human life. He early declares that "for your life to be worth anything you must sooner or later face the possibility of terrible, searing regret. Though you must also manage to avoid it or your life will be ruined. I believe I have done these two things. Faced down regret. Avoided ruin." Though with a Southern background, Bascombe declares that the past is really irrelevant to his life. One discovers, however, that two events from his past are crucial: the death of his son from Reye's syndrome and his subsequent divorce from his wife. He has taken up sportswriting because it enables him to glide on the surface of life. Sportswriting has taught him that "there are no transcendent themes in life. In all cases things are here and they're over, and that has to be enough." He lives in a New Jersey suburb because its ordinariness and his anonymity there enable him to lead such a life.

Bascombe thus seems to have a pleasant existence, but gradually the reader discovers that, in his determination to avoid regret and ruin, he is estranged not only from others but from his own feelings as well. He is occasionally subject to feelings of bereavement, regret, and dread, but he always fights them down. Bascombe is a decent man, trying to do as little harm as possible, but though more self-conscious and philosophical than other Ford protagonists, he is typical in his alienation and isolation. Covering the three days of Easter weekend, the novel is episodic and comes to no real conclusion. Several events are revealing, however. His girlfriend, Vicki, whom Frank says he wants to marry, rejects him and the superficiality of their relationship. An acquaintance, Walter Luckett, reaches out to Bascombe in personal anguish. Though Bascombe does not reject him, he yet does not respond in a forthcoming way. Luckett then commits suicide. These events do temporarily upset Bascombe's equilibrium, but by the end of the novel he is back on an even keel. He states that he has come to terms with his son's death, but it is not at all clear that he is any less a loner or outsider, or that he has fully faced his tendency to avoid problems and engagement with life. Thus he remains as alienated from himself and others as he was at the beginning of the novel. He is a Binx Bolling lacking an awareness of the dangers of sinking into life's "everydayness."

Rock Springs contains stories previously published in national magazines. The collection possesses a remarkable homogeneity; all stories focus on males who lead unstable lives. They are generally unemployed or divorced or in other ways unattached drifters. Failure is usually the norm of their lives, but even though they tend to be passive and unambitious, they also yearn for solace and meaning to their lives. Almost all the stories are set in or near Montana; as one character says: "We're out on a frontier here, aren't we, sweetheart? It feels like that." The frontier is not only geographic but emotional, as characters try to make some sense out of seemingly senseless and random events. More directly than anything else he has written, the stories illustrate Ford's description, in an article on Bruce Springsteen, of what a poet sometimes does: "He dignifies small feelings with the gravity of real emotion, defines innocence in terms new to it, makes rote gestures seem heartbreaking, and gives a voice of consequence to the unlistened to.''

The title story is illustrative. The narrator, a petty criminal, is fleeing to Florida with his daughter, for whom he has assumed responsibility, and a woman, Edna, in a stolen automobile. The car breaks down near Rock Springs, Wyoming, and, as Earl plans to steal another car, Edna tells him she wants to leave him so she will not get caught. He has no choice but to let her go. Feeling abandoned, he wanders the motel parking lot as the story closes searching for another car to steal and examining the evidence of human lives in the automobiles. He speculates that the difference between successful and unsuccessful people is the number of troubles, through luck or design, people have had to face and how well they are able to put them out of their minds. He ends the story by addressing the reader directly:

And I wondered, because it seemed funny, what would you think a man was doing if you saw him in the middle of the night looking in the windows of cars in the parking lot of the Ramada Inn? Would you think he was trying to get his head cleared? Would you think he was trying to get ready for a day when trouble would come down on him? Would you think his girlfriend was leaving him? Would you think he had a daughter? Would you think he was anybody like you?

Thus the narrator gropes for some connection with others and some understanding that will enable him to cope with his problems.

Though in some ways morally superficial, Earl is philosophically inclined and seeks understanding of his life and what happens to him. All the stories in *Rock Springs* suggest that man has a moral dimension, which indicates his humanity. The struggle for that humanity and for some understanding of life's meaning, most often incompletely resolved in the stories, defines Ford's fiction.

Wildlife, his most recent novel, is loosely based on the situation of "Great Falls," one of the stories in *Rock Springs*. A 16-year-old boy witnesses and narrates the breakup of his family as his parents separate. This situation has autobiographical resonance for Ford, for he was 16 when his father died. Perhaps Ford is interested in such situations because they are the moments when characters seem to lose control of their lives—when connections fall apart and chaos threatens. Unlike some of Ford's other characters, the mother and father do not act blindly. They are aware of the choices they make and accept responsibility. The son, Joe, is the witness who does not judge but tries to understand the meaning of the breakup of everything that had provided stability to his life. He wonders ''if there was some pattern or an order to things in your life—not one you knew but that worked on you and made events when they happened seem correct, or made you confident about them or willing to accept them even if they seemed like wrong things. Or was everything just happening all the time, in a whirl without anything to stop it or cause it.'' Joe comes to no conclusion about such matters, but a comment by his father suggests the most that man can know:

"People think they live in eternity, don't they?...Everything just goes on forever. Nothing's final.... Wouldn't that be gratifying." Things change, often without warning and in wounding ways. The novel seems to end disappointingly. After it focuses throughout its length on the breakup of the family, a brief coda reveals that a year later the mother returns and they all resume their lives almost as before. Ford means to imply that such a conclusion is really no conclusion at all, because Joe has been exposed to the impermanence of life. He may continue to look back nostalgically on the seeming perfection of the past and his childhood, but he now knows that change can occur at any moment and that insecurity is man's natural state.

Ford's fiction manifests great variety in setting and plot. In all his work, however, he portrays humans trying to find their way in an uncertain world. This search for meaning, rarely fulfilled, provides their lives and Ford's fiction a central moral dimension.

SURVEY OF CRITICISM

A review of materials that shed light on Richard Ford's fiction should begin with his own nonfiction. He would not claim or aspire to be a professional literary critic, but he has written two essays that help us understand both their subjects and Ford's attitudes. "Walker Percy: Not Just Whistling Dixie," written on the occasion of the appearance of *Lancelot,* reveals Ford's perspectives on Percy, the South, and fiction. "The Three Kings: Hemingway, Faulkner, and Fitzgerald" concerns Ford's reactions to these writers and an assessment of their significance to him and to modern Americans. Another essay, "Country Matters," begins as a discussion of why so many writers move to the country but expands to consider the role of place in fiction. Additionally, Ford has published a number of autobiographical essays that touch in various ways on his writing life. The most substantial are "First Things First: One More Writer's Beginnings" and "My Mother, in Memory." Since Ford's ambition is to write about America, he has written essays examining different aspects of American culture, essays that reflect his general attitudes. Particularly interesting are "Accommodations" and "Heartbreak Motels," meditations on the anonymity and standardization of American life, and "The Boss Observed," a consideration of Bruce Springsteen and his capturing of American culture in his music.

Only one interview with Ford has appeared to date—in the *Missouri Review.* It is, however, wide-ranging. Since it was conducted at about the time of the appearance of *The Sportswriter,* it concentrates on the fiction up to that time, especially that most recent novel. Ford also addresses his writing method and his career. Two essays on Ford are notable. "Richard Ford's Uncommon Characters" by Bruce Weber is an extensive *New York Times Magazine* profile. Based on a long interview with Ford, it is the most comprehensive survey of his life and career published at the time of this writing. Raymond A. Schroth's "America's Moral Landscape in the Fiction of Richard Ford" concentrates on

The Sportswriter but also covers briefly Ford's other works. Schroth believes Ford's works, in a way more revealing than the works of any other contemporary writer, "help illuminate the moral consciousness of America in the '80s."

Ford's fiction has been always relatively widely, if not uniformly favorably, reviewed. Reviewers generally recognized the evidence of Ford's writing talent in *A Piece of My Heart*, but some, Larry McMurtry for example, criticized its derivative Southern gothic nature and excessive symbolism. *The Ultimate Good Luck* received mixed reviews. Those who praised the style of the first novel generally did so again, but a number of reviewers considered the thriller aspect of the novel derivative and not well controlled. *The Sportswriter* was Ford's watershed book, both in terms of sales and critical reputation. It was widely and generally favorably reviewed (see, for example, reviews by Alice Hoffman and Robert Towers), though there is some disagreement among reviewers as to how "decent" and admirable Frank Bascombe is. *Rock Springs* was also frequently and positively reviewed (see reviews by Alfred Kazin and John Wideman). In fact, a number of reviewers judged that Ford's greatest strength is in the short-story form rather than the novel, that in fact he is one of the finest short-story writers working today. *Wildlife* has been received in a generally favorable manner, but not with quite the enthusiasm that greeted the two previous works.

Since the publication of *The Sportswriter* in 1986, Richard Ford has become a highly regarded writer, whose every new work will be read with interest by those concerned about the direction of contemporary American fiction. Still needed are general critical assessments of his career and his place in contemporary American fiction, as well as close consideration of his individual works. That process takes an important stride with Edward Dupuy's "The Confessions of an Ex-Suicide: Relenting and Recovery in Richard Ford's *The Sportswriter*" and with Fred Hobson's overview of postmodern writing in the South.

BIBLIOGRAPHY

Works by Richard Ford

A Piece of My Heart. New York: Harper and Row, 1976.
"Walker Percy: Not Just Whistling Dixie." *National Review* 29 (May 13, 1977): 558–64.
"Country Matters." *Harper's* 263 (July 1981): 81–84.
The Ultimate Good Luck. New York: Houghton Mifflin, 1981.
"The Three Kings: Hemingway, Faulkner, and Fitzgerald." *Esquire* 100 (December 1983): 577–84.
"The Boss Observed." *Esquire* 104 (December 1985): 326–29.
The Sportswriter. New York: Vintage, 1986.
"An Interview with Richard Ford," ed. Kay Bonetti. *Missouri Review* 10 (1987): 71–96.
"My Mother, in Memory." *Harper's* 275 (August 1987): 44–57.
Rock Springs. New York: Atlantic Monthly Press, 1987.

"Accommodations." *Harper's* 276 (June 1988): 38–40.
"First Things First: One More Writer's Beginnings." *Harper's* 277 (August 1988): 72–76.
"Heartbreak Motels." *Harper's* 279 (August 1989): 12–15.
Wildlife. New York: Atlantic Monthly Press, 1990.
"An Urge for Going: Why I Don't Live Where I Used to Live." *Harper's* 284 (February 1992): 60–68.
"What We Write, Why We Write It, and Who Cares." *Michigan Quarterly Review* 31 (Summer 1992): 373–89.

Studies of Richard Ford

Dupuy, Edward. "The Confessions of an Ex-Suicide: Relenting and Recovering in Richard Ford's *The Sportswriter*." *Southern Literary Journal* 23 (1990): 93–103.
Hobson, Fred. "Richard Ford and Josephine Humphreys: Walker Percy in New Jersey and Charleston." *The Southern Writer in the Postmodern World*. Athens: University of Georgia Press, 1991.
Hoffman, Alice. "A Wife Named X, a Poodle Named Elvis." *New York Times Book Review* (March 23, 1986): 14.
Kazin, Alfred. "Fallen Creatures." *New York Review of Books* 34 (November 5, 1987): 12.
McMurtry, Larry. Review of *A Piece of My Heart*. *New York Times Book Review* (October 24, 1976): 16.
Schroth, Raymond A. "America's Moral Landscape in the Fiction of Richard Ford." *Christian Century* 106 (March 1, 1989): 227–30.
Towers, Robert. "Screams and Whispers." *New York Review of Books* 33 (April 24, 1986): 38–39.
Weber, Bruce. "Richard Ford's Uncommon Characters." *New York Times Magazine* (April 10, 1988): 50–51, 59, 63–65.
Wideman, John. "Love and Truth: Use with Caution." *New York Times Book Review* (September 20, 1987): 1, 35.

JULIAN MASON

Kaye Gibbons
(1960–   )

Kaye Gibbons has now published two more novels since she burst upon the public's awareness with her 1987 novel, *Ellen Foster,* to acclaim and awards. She has shown herself to be a skillful, imaginative, sensitive, and interesting novelist, who has taken the perseverance of the human spirit and Nash County, North Carolina, where she grew up, for her continuing literary domain, as she explores its people, ways, and past. Her work is bold and experimental, but easily accessible, winning for her a large body of readers. She is young, but already established, and not breaking stride as she continues to produce challenging and satisfying fiction at a steady pace.

BIOGRAPHY

The daughter of a tobacco farmer, Charles Batts, and his wife, Alice, who lived in the rural Nash County community of Bend of the River (near the Tar River), about seven miles south of Rocky Mount, North Carolina, Kaye Batts was born on May 5, 1960, in a hospital in Wilson, North Carolina. She has a brother 13 years older than she, and a sister 9 years older. They are related to Nathaniel Batts, the first-known permanent white settler in North Carolina, who built a home in coastal North Carolina in 1655. She grew up on the family's farm in Nash County, which is in the upper center of the coastal plain of eastern North Carolina, experiencing the agricultural seasons and hot summers and being relatively poor.

Gibbons greatly admired her mother, who was called Shine and who provided order and stability through perseverance and hard work. After her mother killed herself at age 47 with an overdose of pills in March 1970, Gibbons stayed on with her father until she went to live with her mother's sister near Bailey, North Carolina, in 1971. This was not a satisfactory arrangement, and after Gibbons' alcoholic father died in May 1972 she moved to a foster home, also near Bailey, which she had chosen partly on the basis of observing at church the woman whose home it was. During 1972–73 she also had extended visits with various other relatives. In June 1973 her brother married, and she moved into his home in Rocky Mount and benefited from the interest in her shown by his wife. She lived there until she entered North Carolina State University, in Raleigh, in fall 1978, having graduated from Rocky Mount High School.

   While growing up, Gibbons had watched television and read as much as possible, early becoming fascinated with both oral and written language and what could be done with it. In the fourth grade she discovered both the fiction and poetry of Poe, and later Shakespeare's sonnets and the works of numerous other writers. At one stage she wanted to be a lab technician, then later a lawyer; and she became more and more interested in the world beyond her immediate environs, and in reading. She also began writing and publishing poetry. She loved school and the discipline, order, stimulation, and opportunities for learning that it provided. In the rather chaotic year after her mother's death, school kept her going. In high school she was somewhat bookish and an outsider, though she also participated in some extracurricular activities. She went to North Carolina State University with a scholarship from the Veterans Administration, and she also worked at the university library. At the university she decided to major in political science, then switched to history, and finally to English, because in it more writing and analyzing of writing were required.

   In the summer before she transferred to the University of North Carolina at Chapel Hill in fall 1980, Gibbons had manic-depressive problems, and in August 1981 she entered a hospital in Raleigh, staying there till March 1982, meanwhile again attending classes at North Carolina State. In 1983 she had another attack and remained out of school for some time. During this period she worked at various jobs, including as a waitress and in a bookstore. In 1984 she met Michael Gibbons, 12 years her senior, originally from Queens, New York, then a graduate student in landscape architecture at North Carolina State; and on May 12, 1984, they were married. They have three daughters—Mary (1984), Leslie (1987), and Louise (1989).

   In summer 1985 she returned to classes at Chapel Hill, and in the fall she enrolled in Louis Rubin's course in Southern literature. During the course, in Rubin's lectures and in the writings of James Weldon Johnson, Mark Twain, and others, she encountered various emphases on the use of and validity for everyday speech in literature and on the relationships of language and place. Also, a voice came to her which led to her writing the poem ''June Bug,'' which was eventually published in the *Carolina Quarterly,* but more immediately was the stimulus for the thirty pages of fiction she began in November 1985 and showed to Rubin. He recognized her talent and at the end of November encouraged her to finish the work. In early January, Rubin had her first novel, *Ellen Foster* (1987). With little revision, it was published by Algonquin Books of Chapel Hill. Then, in 1986, while Gibbons was taking a seminar in the

Southern novel with Rubin, she wrote an essay on the Miranda stories of Katherine Anne Porter; it was soon published in the *Kenyon Review*.

Her second novel went through four drafts, the first of which was poor, but which yielded the principal male character for the final version, published by Algonquin as *A Virtuous Woman* (1989). For each of the first two novels her imagination had depended primarily on her memories and experiences and on those of her family. The third novel, *A Cure for Dreams*, which went through four drafts before being published by Algonquin (1991), required a good bit of research, the results of which were blended with memories or what Gibbons had heard from relatives and others, as the novel deals with decades before she was born.

In the early stages of work on it she had read *Such as Us: Southern Voices of the Thirties* (edited by Tom Terrill and Jerrold Hirsch, University of North Carolina Press, 1978), based on oral histories collected by the Federal Writers' Project under the direction of W. T. Couch. This led her to the hundreds of such personal histories transcribed by the project from interviews and available at the university library in Chapel Hill. Gibbons read these extensively, gathering not so much characters or actions but mostly metaphors, terms, language patterns, customs, and general ambience. She was impressed with the respect that the project's interviewers had for their subjects, how they helped the person's own voice come through. She also read printed collections of North Carolina folklore. However, while she used in the novel much that she found in her reading, if she needed a term that she did not have, she sometimes made up one of the same type as those she had encountered.

Gibbons' first two novels had been composed on a typewriter. For the third she used a computer. Although she had a study at the North Carolina State University library during 1989 and 1990, as its first (and then reappointed) Writer of the Year, most of her writing is done at home, often at night, sometimes in the wee hours of the morning. This schedule helps keep her close to her children, who also are a high priority for her. The obligation has become more important following her recent divorce.

Although she does not plan to read, Gibbons has been a success on the reading circuit, and she makes appearances on radio and television. In October 1989 she shared the platform with Eudora Welty as the two invited speakers to inaugurate the annual Eudora Welty Writers' Symposium as part of the activities for the inauguration of the first woman president of Welty's alma mater, Mississippi University for Women. Gibbons spoke on the influence of Welty in her finding her own self as a writer. Gibbons also occasionally writes book reviews for the *New York Times Book Review* and other periodicals.

Gibbons cherishes the order and stability that her children and her writing provide. She has said that only after writing *Ellen Foster* could she really be herself and feel good about that. In *How I Became a Writer* she wrote:

My mother's death both freed me and marked me. . . . If she was still living, I would still be bound to my old home, and I know I would not have turned to literature and used it as I have. (5)

I write novels to set order to what memories my mind has allowed me and to create something of lasting value in all those gaps I seem to have. (4)

My life changed with the marriage and the birth [of my daughter], and the memory of my mother escorted me through the transition from a girl who loved literature better than her life to a woman who overcame her past and got at the business of living. (5)

As she said to one interviewer: "Between good genes and a harsh environment, I think I turned out OK"; and so have her books, the first two already having sold over 25,000 copies each in hardback and over 40,000 each in paperback.

MAJOR THEMES

Most of the themes that one finds in Gibbons' works fit well what in other contexts she has said are her primary beliefs and concerns as a writer and as a person. She has definite ideas about what she believes she should try to do as a writer, what her concerns are, and how she hopes to present them to the reader. She writes about the "commonplace" things of the everyday lives of her characters in order to show the tensions, passions, opportunities, and effects on the human spirit of this aspect of living (as opposed to, but related to, the larger, more dramatic occurrences), both on the surface and below it. This larger aspect of the experiences of most people also has important value for understanding a character and what that character is, thinks, and does. One reviewer wrote that Gibbons "recounts mundane details of everyday life in such a compelling and innovative way that we are left both stunned and wiser." She wants the reader to listen to and look at closely this particular richness and how it can lead to art and to fulfilling life, even in its many disguises.

Gibbons emphasizes the quiet, strong heroism of survivors, especially women, who persevere to bring order and peace out of chaos, good and joy out of difficulty, getting through the day, the years, a life, and making the best one can of it all, in spite of mistakes, catastrophes, misunderstandings, threats, injury, inadequate resources, sorrow, grief, disappointment, pain, death, disillusionment, and weariness. She finds hope in the strong, self-reliant individual coping with the quiet dramas and firm challenges of every day's journey and what that requires not only to survive but also to triumph, at least to the point of having inner peace, or even joy in the soul, from taking hold and doing what needs to be done, from bouncing back and going on. In this hope she reflects various aspects of her own experience and the admiration she has for her mother, and the epigraphs for her novels come from Emerson, the Bible, and a statement of belief in the validity of each person's own experience and voice.

She wants her characters to speak to us directly, for themselves, in truth and honesty, about life without illusions. Not only are her principal characters well drawn and memorable, but many of her lesser ones are vividly and well drawn, too, though they tend to pale in the shadows of her dominant first-person central characters. She explores experience in relation to family, in relation to interactions between people who should be close because of birth or because of choice, as through such relationships they try to effect order, stability, happiness, love, and validity for themselves and their existence. Gibbons explores the difficulty of knowing and shaping the self, particularly in relation to others and to one's past, both personal and collective. In doing this, she helps us see the universal in the particular and the magic amidst the mundane.

Gibbons finds it most pertinent to focus her concerns and interests through women characters and to explore the "phenomenon of being female" and the burdens of women, particularly as wives and mothers, and especially among less affluent women in the South. In doing this she has made good use of her memories of her own experiences and those of her family, as she attempts to give them order and meaning, to understand, control, shape, and accept. She has written in How I Became a Writer: "So I believe that it is under the incredible burden of memory that I write, and I cannot trade my memory, as much as I've often wanted to do so. My past is what it is. All that memory will allow me or any other writer to do is order it through language" (5).

With each of her three novels she has gone further back in time for settings, characters, and other material—into her own past and into the past that impinges on her past. Though the format differs, each book quickly establishes a chronological and developmental position at which the central characters have arrived and then, retrospectively and with a first-person point of view, explores how they arrived at that point, with almost no concern in the particular novel for what might come later than, or because of, its beginning point. It is likely that through research and her imagination she will continue to explore further and further back. In this regard, her fourth novel will really be part two of A Cure for Dreams, bringing that focus even further toward our time. One result of this movement back into the past is a lessening of intensity with each novel, resulting in more clarity and in changes of format and tone as she is forced into even more distance from her material than she has cultivated in her earlier work. Also, with each book she covers more time, as she continues to develop her portrayal of interactions between the old South and the more modern South and their ways and traditions.

Students of Southern writing often point to concerns with place (and land), family (and history), and religion (and sin and guilt) as primary themes or concerns in the body of Southern literature. Gibbons does little with the last, but she certainly emphasizes the other two. With each novel she has become more specific about both time and place as her literary imagination has been accepted and praised and as she has become more comfortable with being a writer and with using material from the locale she came from. Also, books that cover more time require more specificity, for both writer and reader. Most reviewers understood her first two novels to be set in the South, and North Carolina reviewers understood them to be in set in North Carolina; but others mistakenly have written of her settings as "deep South," "backwoods," or even Georgia, which is not as likely to happen again.

She has pointed out that all three novels are set in the same "landscape," and some readers have noticed that some of the characters and places in one novel appear also elsewhere in her fiction, though we see them somewhat differently in each novel or story because of time differences, narrator differences, familial and geographical angle differences in focusing and vantage points, and different emphases—as in the works of William Faulkner, Wendell Berry, and others who write extensively about one particular locale.

One reviewer has suggested that Gibbons intends a series of interlocking novels. Certainly she is mining the rich artistic possibilities of human experience (history, mores, and language) in the rural Nash County, North Carolina, area in which she was raised and near which she lived even after moving into town; and she has found it a fertile and worthy locale for her explorations, which helps with the reality of her details (that ring true to one who knows that area). However, in much less-effective, less-important, and less-developed uses, she does deal briefly with western and coastal North Carolina in *A Virtuous Woman*, and with Kentucky and Ireland in *A Cure for Dreams*. She has said that in each of her novels she hopes to convey an accurate impression of a place and time and a respect for their traditions.

Language and voice are important components of Gibbons' art—important to her realistic intentions and her faithfulness to time and place, and important to the effectiveness and success of what she is trying to accomplish in the reader's experience. She wants the reader to sense the worth and uniqueness of the character through that person's distinctive voice, usually as she or he speaks directly to the reader, thus better enabling sharing of feeling. Like James Weldon Johnson, she has chosen to avoid dialect, but to strive for an awareness of idiom characteristic of and appropriate for that particular individual and time and place. This depends more on metaphors, word choice, and syntax than on pronunciation and grammar.

Some of her characters are not formally well educated, but are intelligent, highly aware of their world, and often wise; they are not caricatures, nor condescended to, but are presented with respect. She begins her conceptualization of a work with character and voice, not with plot or abstract ideas. She strives for a direct, concrete experience—not of exaggerated local color, but of regional realism and the universal therein. Through a focus on the area she knows best, she wants to emphasize for the reader not oddities or pecularities or differences, but universal and eternal verities and some sense of their flavor in that time and place. She uses rural anecdotes and sayings because her characters would use them, to help them understand, control, and go on as these are adapted and applied to current circumstances. They are not clichés, but pregnant and versatile significations from a body of wise tradition and custom, which she respects, parts of a commonly held and available rich treasure trove of shared community experience. One reviewer wrote that she "makes the colloquial compelling." In her writing, interior experience is more important than surface experience, and language is the important interpretive mechanism for bringing that to the reader, even concerning memories of surface experience.

Gibbons has shown herself to be unafraid of writing from inside characters of various ages, complexities, and backgrounds, male or female, and in varied circumstances and times, many of which she herself has not experienced—and in doing so well and interestingly, and with verisimilitude, insight, and understanding. She is good at using contrast, humor (which she feels is essential), and folk and popular culture, without their being inappropriately intrusive. Each of her novels has been less directly autobiographical than the one before it, and structurally more complex (though quite different in tone) as she has continued to adapt and experiment with a first-person point of view and layerings of structure in her attempt for directness of experience for the reader and the fullness of awareness that comes from multiple focuses and the depth, irony, perspective, counterpoint, and understanding made possible therein—which is how we know and experience life ourselves, not primarily in a linear way.

In *Ellen Foster* she shifts back and forth between past and present as Ellen speaks to us, using her good present to intersperse assurance, and also to provide relief from her persistently bad past, for author, character, and reader. In *A Virtuous Woman* she uses disjointed time as Jack speaks to us of his wife, Ruby, who is already dead, and in alternating chapters, as she approaches death, Ruby speaks to us of Jack. In *A Cure for Dreams* the layering is more complex but not more difficult, even if one does experience less directness of speech because of the form and tone of the book. In it Gibbons has a contemporary (1989) woman briefly introduce and close the book, in between letting that woman's recently dead mother (1920–89) speak to us directly about her own self and even more so about her own mother (who in italics occasionally speaks for herself) and about her own grandmother and the impact of both of them on her, up to the 1942 birth of the introducer. (*Ellen Foster* had covered only a little over a year, focusing primarily on one character, and *A Virtuous Woman* over two and one-half decades, focusing primarily on two characters.)

Such forms require an alert and attentive reader, whose experience is enriched by them. Gibbons has not found the short story to be her genre, saying that she has good ideas for short stories but doesn't find it easy to develop them for that form. The short stories she has published are clearly inferior to her novels and were produced under pressure to do so, the one in *The Quarterly* a rearranged extracting from *Ellen Foster* and the other, "The Headache," a more interesting but flat and somewhat inept story also set in Nash County.

Gibbons is serious about both the art and the craft of writing, though in *How I Became a Writer* she wrote: "I've never believed anyone can will the mind to create a thing of beauty. I like to think artistic creation starts in a more mysterious place, somewhere deep within, probably somewhere way far back in one's past" (5). In addition to writing fiction, she enjoys reading widely and analyzing and writing about literature. This is evident in her book reviews and in her essay on Katherine Anne Porter's Miranda stories (where she finds purpose in fiction in some ways not unlike her own purpose). She respects and enjoys, and has been influenced by, a variety of literature from across the ages, from Geoffrey Chaucer to Flannery O'Connor, William Faulkner, and Eudora Welty. Clearly, as a writer she also has been influenced by the teaching and editorial advice and encouragement of Louis Rubin; and she plans to follow Welty's example and remain with the South as both residence and primary subject.

She is not a writer who writes according to a rigid daily schedule; she does not force her writing. She writes first for herself and is not very self-conscious or audience-conscious while doing so. She writes with great economy and efficiency of style and with control of her material and no wasting of words, which results in novels that are not long, but are compact, yet fully realized; as one reviewer said, they are "all a novel should be and more than most ever are," and as another put it, they are "stunning in their power and grace." This economy of literary means is not a result of her having little to say, but of her having so much to say and with such belief and purpose that she does not wish to lead herself or the reader away from the book's main thrust in any way, resulting in significant accomplishment and no wasted effort for writer or reader, which is but one sign of her well-focused skill.

SURVEY OF CRITICISM

One of the obvious indications of how Gibbons' novels have been received is the awards and editions they have produced. For *Ellen Foster* she received the Sue Kaufman Prize for First Fiction from the American Academy and Institute of Arts and Letters. (The Academy's literary awards committee included Irving Howe, Donald Barthelme, James Dickey, Allen Ginsberg, Anthony Hecht, Elizabeth Spencer, and Anne Tyler.) *Ellen Foster* also received a special citation from the Ernest Hemingway Foundation, and was chosen by the American Library Association as one of the Best Books for Young Adults in 1987. In 1988 *Ellen Foster* was fifth on France's best-seller list, and in 1989 *A Virtuous Woman* led the *Atlanta Journal and Constitution*'s list of best-sellers in the Southeast. That same year Gibbons received from the National Endowment for the Arts a fellowship to aid her in writing a third novel, and for that work-in-progress she received in 1990 the first PEN/Revson Foundation Fiction Fellowship for a writer 35 years old or younger.

The paperback editions of the first two novels are in Random House's Vintage Contemporaries series (for *Ellen Foster* Random House outbid Dell, Viking Penguin, and Washington Square), and Paramount optioned the movie rights for *Ellen Foster*. Editions of both of the first two novels appeared in England, France, Germany, Italy, Spain, and Sweden. *A Virtuous Woman* also was published in Denmark. Both of them were both reviewed and discussed with her widely in the United States and abroad, mostly enthusiastically and favorably, in newspapers and magazines and on radio and television, and led to various interviews in both print and nonprint media. (Anyone using the interviews should consult a chronological spread of them because of how her responses to some things changed over time.)

Many reviewers immediately compared 11-year-old Ellen Foster with some other child of fiction, usually also an orphan, created by a well-known writer— for example, Twain's Huck Finn, Cinderella, Charles Dickens' Oliver Twist or David Copperfield, or J. D. Salinger's Holden Caulfield. That this occurred so often might be seen as demeaning; but upon reading the full reviews, one realizes that this impulse was the result not of a sense of imitation on her part nor even of influence on her, but rather a recognition of Ellen's uniqueness and the book's quality, which let Gibbons seem deserving of consideration alongside such literary predecessors. Most reviewers emphasized Ellen's pluck, perseverance in the face of great and various difficulties, endearing straightforwardness, boldness, wit, spontaneity, resilience, practicality, wisdom, and tough stoicism, along with her coming to grips with friendship with her young black friend, Starletta, and the search for love and familial stability. Generally they found Ellen's voice (the matrix of this first-person narrative) to be matter-of-fact, detached, clear, simple, honest, controlled by the author, convincingly that of a child (even when talking of death, murder, eternity, race, etc.), and, while of course limited in its information, reliable. Unfortunately, several reviewers misinterpreted Ellen's use of "old" when speaking of herself and thought it referred to either or both chronological or experiential age instead of understanding Gibbons' intended use of it as a Southern term of acceptance and endearment (as in: "I like old John there").

A number of reviewers mentioned how close *Ellen Foster* comes to melodrama, yet avoids it by focusing not so much on Ellen's multitude of difficulties themselves, but on her resourcefulness and her belief in herself as she deals with these difficulties. They found the result of Ellen's voice and its speaking directly to us, and of Gibbons' focusing, to be a book not sentimental, but human, humorous, and compassionate, with a believable survivor as its heroine. A number mentioned not only the skill of the characterization in the book, but also how this is enhanced by the book's moving back and forth between Ellen's past and present experience, giving the reader a meaningful counterpoint of awareness and perspective, and greatly assisting the possibility for humor even when things are quite grim and desperate—which is often. A few reviewers who also interviewed Gibbons began to see some parallel between her book and her own life, but they did not explore it very far and usually did not deal with it in their reviews, leaving it to comments within the published interviews.

Even before *Ellen Foster* was published, there was remarkable praise for it, which Algonquin understandably used in its publicity, advertising, and dust jacket for the book. Eudora Welty wrote: "What a marvelous writer she seems to be on almost every page. . . . A stunning new writer. . . . The life in it, the honesty of thought and eye and feeling and word!" Walker Percy wrote: "It's the real thing. Which is to say: a lovely, breathtaking, sometimes heart-wrenching first novel." Alfred Kazin wrote: "A captivating, often hilarious mix of Victorian fairy tale and fresh American lingo . . . [with] the wickedest relatives in literature since *King Lear* . . . in a style primitive, saucy, and exhilarating." Elizabeth

Spencer wrote: "Original, compelling, and frighteningly real, the voice of Ellen Foster makes the reader know her story in her own terms. I was absorbed and moved. Kaye Gibbons is a new writer of great force. She knows how to speak to our hearts." Most reviewers agreed that the author of *Ellen Foster* was one to watch, and in his review Jonathan Yardley wrote: "a work of considerable subtlety and intellectual sophistication. . . . a sly, funny book about a sly, funny girl. . . . Yet it is a mark of Kaye Gibbons' accomplishment that in no way is Ellen a moral or intellectual prodigy; she is simply a good little girl who makes her way out of trouble through the stubborn belief that life can be better than what it's been for her thus far. She is a terrific kid, and 'Ellen Foster' is a terrific book."

When Gibbons' second novel appeared, readers and reviewers were wondering if she had been able to sustain the level of accomplishment that had been so widely praised for *Ellen Foster*. Though *A Virtuous Woman* is in a number of ways quite different from *Ellen Foster,* most who reviewed it believed that she had produced another successful work and a worthy follower of her first book. The approaches of the reviewers of this second novel seem, however, more varied. Padgett Powell wrote of it in comparison and contrast with Faulkner's *As I Lay Dying* and *The Wild Palms,* emphasizing how "banged up" its characters are, calling it a complex novel, and emphasizing its structure and "balances and counterbalances, symmetries and their neat absence that shore up the book, creating a sturdier vessel. . . . there is also some 'moral structure.' " He concluded that the novel is worthy of its interesting characters and its dangerous but somewhat ingenious alternation of first-person point of view chapters, with Ruby talking to us as she approaches death and Jack talking to us after she has died, and together giving us their past, while at first apart and then together. A French reviewer emphasized the book's honesty and integrity, dignity and humility, its themes both simple and deep, its treatment of the daily emotions of the heart. Marilyn Chandler approached the novel in response to its impressive explorations of what love and marriage are and can be, what the relations can be between good and well-intentioned man and woman, which she finds expressed in "a simplicity of language and childlike emotional honesty touching and even gripping" to the readers of today's world. She found a skillful sustaining of tension between the language of the characters and "the depth and magnitude of the feelings and questions they manage to evoke."

Various reviewers praised the language of *A Virtuous Woman,* including its images and metaphors, its rural Southern cadences, and the matter-of-fact power in its storytelling, as its two principal characters speak directly to the reader. Several wrote of it as a deceptively simple and quiet book without much action, yet a deep book as it unsentimentally explores how love comes to be and grows, even with pain. An English reviewer said the book has the simplicity of good country music's focusing on the bare bones of life and traditional values, while a Kansas reviewer compared it to "good fiddle music," and one in Florida wrote of Gibbons' lines as having "the tensile strength of wire; pluck one and it snaps right back.'' Some reviewers found the ending of the book, with its noticeable change to omniscient point of view, flawed or weak; others found it strong, necessary, or helpful. Most found the novel's two major characters admirable and very real, persons who learn a lot about life, love, and sorrow, and whom the reader is glad to have met and to have learned from. One said that Gibbons clearly loves her characters for who they are. Often there was an emphasis on the compelling aspect of the narrative and a declaration that this novel, with its wisdom and art, is far above much of what now passes ''as fine literature.'' Various reviews spoke of grace, joy, decency, gentleness. A North Carolina reviewer called Gibbons an ''exceptional writer who relies on the simplest words to convey the deepest emotions and conditions of the human spirit,'' and Fredric Koeppel wrote: ''The human spirit is a wonderful thing, and it's a rare author who can believably depict its simple grandeur and dignity. That ability is the chief attribute of Kaye Gibbons.''

The reviews of *A Cure for Dreams* appeared widely and were generally praising, but were not as many or usually as long as those for her first two novels, and as a whole they were more muted. Often reviewers tried to focus on this book in relation to her other two and to try to discern themes, concerns, and intentions in all three together, both comparing and contrasting, and making attempts to deal with what was now clearly a writer with a developing career, no longer just a talented beginner. Of course they focused on plot and characterization, and they also usually particularly noticed form and ambience and how these, in their estimations, were or were not more effective than those in her first two books. Although there were emphases on the three novels together, this book also was allowed integrity of its own. Lee Smith called it ''lyrical and lovely, shot through with moments of recognition.'' Valerie Sayers compared its structure to easygoing, meandering Sunday rides in the country, ''willing to take detours if the landscape looks promising, willing to sit awhile if the vista is curious, willing to backtrack'' if something had been missed. She also called attention to ''a highly stylized and charming narrative voice, one that mixes 19th-century formality (and chapter headings) with 20th-century directness.'' Josephine Humphreys wrote of Gibbons' ''delicate hand,'' which keeps the distinctive characteristics of her characters from seeming exaggerated. She said that the story's telling is ''economical and quick,'' with scenes and characters ''drawn surely and sharply,'' and it ''sounds spoken, its language often stranger and stronger than literary language . . . [its] style both simple and baroque.'' For her, ''this is a novel of vision and grace. It shines.'' Stacey D'Erasmo also called attention to a nineteenth-century aspect in Gibbons' novels, and found the three of them together to be ''like a feminist *Spoon River Anthology* for mothers and daughters, full of methods for surviving, escaping, and outliving brutality.'' Most reviewers called attention to the strong, dominant female central characters in this book and in its two predecessors, a focus on the ''eternal feminine,'' and some to the corresponding weakness of the male characters; but Jerry Mills also stated that it is a book for anyone who ''values subtlety and craft and the nuances of feeling that language in skillful hands can evoke. And it is a book for anyone who wants to know what makes the South such fertile literary ground.'' Sayers called attention to the language of the book also: ''What a good ear Kaye Gibbons has . . . [taking us] down the back roads . . . [pointing] out what incredible lives are lived in those ordinary places.'' Dannye Romine's *Charlotte Observer* review concluded: ''Four years ago, we knew nothing of Kaye Gibbons. Then boom! This Nash County native swooped down upon us with fearsome talent . . . giving us music that, in Flaubert's words, will melt the stars.''

BIBLIOGRAPHY

Works by Kaye Gibbons

''June Bug.'' *Carolina Quarterly* 38 (Winter 1986): 55.

Ellen Foster. Chapel Hill, N.C.: Algonquin, 1987.

''The Headache.'' *St. Andrews Review* 32 (Spring/Summer 1987): 3–8.

''The Proof.'' *Quarterly* 1 (Spring 1987): 60–72.

How I Became a Writer. My Mother, Literature, and a Life Split Neatly into Two Halves. Chapel Hill, N.C.: Algonquin, 1988. Without the first five words of this title, the contents of this pamphlet also has appeared in the *Leader* (November 10, 1988): 22–27; and in *The Writer on Her Work, Volume II: New Essays in New Territory,* ed. Janet Sternburg, New York: W. W. Norton, 1991.

''Planes of Language and Time: The Surface of the Miranda Stories.'' *Kenyon Review* n.s. 10 (Winter 1988): 74–79.

''A Nash County Girl's Tribute.'' *News and Observer* (Raleigh, N.C.) (November 5, 1989): 5D.

A Virtuous Woman. Chapel Hill, N.C.: Algonquin, 1989.

Family Life. Rocky Mount, N.C.: North Carolina Wesleyan College Press, 1990. Three chapters from *A Cure for Dreams.* ''To Be Published by Algonquin Books.'' Limited to 500 numbered and signed copies.

A Cure for Dreams. Chapel Hill, N.C.: Algonquin, 1991.

Studies of Kaye Gibbons

Bell, Mae Woods. Writing Is Part of Life for Kaye Gibbons.'' *Rocky Mount* (N.C.) *Telegram* (April 26, 1987): 41.

Brinson, Linda. ''It's OK: Novelist Writes on after a Difficult Revelation.'' *Winston-Salem Journal* (June 18, 1989): H10.

Chandler, Marilyn. ''Limited Partnership'' (Rev. of *A Virtuous Woman*). *Women's Review of Books* 6 (July 1989): 21.

D'Erasmo, Stacey. Rev. of *A Cure for Dreams. Voice Literary Supplement* (April 1991): 5.

Earle, Ralph. ''Vices and Virtues'' (Rev. of *A Virtuous Woman*). *Spectator* (Raleigh, N.C.) (April 27, 1989): 25.

Fleischer, Leonore. ''Is It Art Yet?'' *Publishers Weekly* (May 8, 1987): 34.

Hoffman, Alice. "Shopping for a New Family" (Rev. of *Ellen Foster*). *New York Times Book Review* (May 31, 1987): 13.

Humphreys, Josephine. "Within Marriage, A Secret Life," (Rev. of *A Cure for Dreams*. *Los Angeles Times Book Review* (May 19,1991): 13.

Johnson, Maria C. "Speaking from Experience: At 29, Writer Has Lived Many of Life's Stories." *Greensboro News and Record* (August 31, 1989): B1–B2.

"Kaye Gibbons," 46–50 in *Contemporary Literary Yearbook, 1987* vol. 50. Detroit: Gale Research, 1988.

"Kaye Gibbons." Television interview by William Friday on *North Carolina People*, University of North Carolina Center for Public Television (July 24, 1989).

Koeppel, Fredric. "Household Labels Rile New Novelist Gibbons." *Commercial Appeal* (Memphis) (July 8, 1990): G1–G2.

———. "Novels Feature Southern Setting, Characters without Caricatures" (Rev. of *Ellen Foster* and *A Virtuous Woman*). *Commercial Appeal* (Memphis) (July 8, 1990): G4.

Manuel, John. "Clear Vision: Raleigh Novelist Discusses Fame, Fortune and Her Forthcoming Book." *Spectator* (Raleigh, N.C.) (July 19, 1990): 5–6.

Mills, Jerry Leath. "Kaye Gibbons: 'The Eternal Feminine' in Fiction" (Rev. of *A Cure for Dreams*). *News and Observer* (Raleigh, N.C.) (March 10, 1991): 5J.

Powell, Padgett. "As Ruby Lay Dying" (Rev. of *A Virtuous Woman*). *New York Times Book Review* (April 30, 1989): 12–13.

Romine, Dannye. "Literature Liberates: Raleigh's Kaye Gibbons Finds Freedom, Affirmation in 1st Novel." *Charlotte Observer* (April 26, 1987): 1F, 13F.

Rosenheim, Andrew. "Voices of the New South" (Rev. of *Ellen Foster*). *Times Literary Supplement* (London) (November 25, 1988): 1306.

Sayers, Valerie. "Back Roads, Strong Women" (Rev. of *A Cure for Dreams*). *Washington Post* (April 8, 1991): C3.

Sill, Melanie. "This Perfect Story Has a Happy Ending." *News and Observer* (Raleigh, N.C.) (April 27, 1987): 8A–9A.

Slater, Joyce. " 'A Virtuous Woman' Grabs Reader from Start" (Rev. of *A Virtuous Women*). *Atlanta Journal-Constitution* (May 28, 1989): N8.

Tyler, Phyllis. "Kaye Gibbons: 'To Be a Writer You Have to Eat Literature'." *Independent* (Durham, N.C.) (April 23, 1987): 24–25.

Yardley, Jonathan. "Child of Adversity: A Young Heroine Finds Happiness Overcoming Prejudice" (Rev. of *Ellen Foster*). *Washington Post* (April 22, 1987): C2.

ROBERT BAIN

Ellen Gilchrist
(1935–   )

Ellen Gilchrist has earned in the last decade a reputation for her lively female characters, for her incisive humor and wit, and for a style that startles with its clarity and grace. Since 1979, Gilchrist has published four books of short stories, three novels, two volumes of poetry, a ''journal,'' and a collection of three novellas. *Victory Over Japan,* her second collection of stories, won the American Book Award in 1984. Family relationships, the human penchant for perversity and possibility, the problem of free will and fate, and the permutations of love preoccupy her pages. She sets much of her fiction in Mississippi, North Carolina, and New Orleans, but often sends her characters—conscious of their Southern heritage—over the rooftops of the world on journeys that demand them to confront themselves and others. Much of Gilchrist's fiction deals with characters from the McCamey, the Hand, and the Manning families. Though critics have compared her work with that of Flannery O'Connor, Eudora Welty, Ernest Hemingway, and F. Scott Fitzgerald, Gilchrist's voice is distinctly her own.

BIOGRAPHY

Ellen Louise Gilchrist was born on February 20, 1935, in Vicksburg, Mississippi, the only daughter and the second of three children of William Garth and Aurora Alford Gilchrist. She spent her early years in Mississippi, but her father, an engineer and before his marriage a minor league baseball player, moved his family frequently from the late 1930s to the early 1950s as he pursued his career. During these years, the Gilchrists lived in Mound City and Harrisburg, Illinois, in Seymour, Indiana, and in Kentucky. But Gilchrist and her brother Dooley, 3½ years older than she, spent much time as children at Hopedale Plantation in Issaquena County, Mississippi, the home of her maternal grandparents, Stewart Floyd Alford and Nell Biggs Alford. In *Falling Through Space:*

The Journals of Ellen Gilchrist (1987), she recollects her childhood on Hopedale Plantation and presents from those years photographs of family and friends.

Gilchrist devotes much of "Origins," the first section of *Falling Through Space,* to describing the sights, sounds, places, and people of those Mississippi childhood years at "my home," the place "where I spent endless summer hours alone or with my cousins" and "where the mud first oozed up between my toes" (11). She mines these years to create her characters Rhoda and Dudley Manning, whom she describes as "poorly disguised versions of my brother Dooley and myself" (152).

"I began my roaming years," Gilchrist writes, "during the Second World War—every five or six months I moved to a new town and went to a new school" (31). Though she exaggerates, the family moved often, and as a child away from the freedom of Hopedale Plantation, Gilchrist wrote letters to her grandmother. At Harrisburg (Illinois) High School in the early 1950s, she was feature editor of the *Purple Clarion,* the school newspaper. Throughout her early years, Gilchrist preferred reading to going to school.

In interviews Gilchrist talks generally about her marriages, but has been reticent about specific details. She has been married four times, husbands one and three being the same man (Lyons 83). With her first husband, she had three sons: Marshall Peteet Walker, Garth Gilchrist Walker, and Pierre Gautier Walker. She has four grandchildren. During her first marriage, Gilchrist was often "separated" from her husband; she writes of these child-rearing years briefly in *Falling Through Space* (20–23).

She believes that the "boring little domestic details of my life don't seem to have anything to do with the mental life that makes my stories" (33). After finishing high school, Gilchrist attended Vanderbilt University. As a young woman of 19, she "ran away to the hills of north Georgia to be married by a justice of the peace with a sheriff in attendance" (37). Answering Gene Lyons' question about why she waited until she was 40 to begin writing seriously, Gilchrist replied: "I did what every healthy human being does—I married the first good-looking man who wanted to marry me back and had three beautiful children. I thought I didn't want to be pregnant, but I did. I think every pregnancy is partly willed—an absolute act that defies death. Don't you?" (Lyons 81).

For a while, Gilchrist lived in Jackson, Mississippi, and New Orleans. In New Orleans she became a "tennis machine" (Lyons 83) and lived among that city's rich. She earned a B.A. in philosophy at Millsaps College in Jackson, Mississippi, in 1967; there she also studied creative writing with Eudora Welty, who told her: "I would never encourage anyone to be a writer. It's too hard. It's just too hard to do" (*Falling* 135).

But Gilchrist wouldn't listen. In 1975, while living in New Orleans, she "pulled my old portable typewriter out of a closet and went off to the Caicos Islands to write poetry, I've been writing or wishing I was writing every single day from dawn to noon" (41). In New Orleans, she also edited poetry for the *Vieux Carré Courier,* run by Philip Carter of the Carter family of Greenville,

Mississippi (Lyons 83). Poet and novelist James Whitehead, then teaching at the University of Arkansas, read Gilchrist's poems and invited her to study in Fayetteville. She took postgraduate work in creative writing there in 1976 and began publishing poems and stories in magazines.

A remarkable decade of productivity opened with *The Land Surveyor's Daughter* (1979), a book of poems. Gilchrist followed that volume with her first collection of stories, *In the Land of Dreamy Dreams* (1981). First published by the University of Arkansas Press, this book achieved immediate popularity from newspaper reviews, especially in New Orleans where many stories are set. Little, Brown, publisher of Gilchrist's succeeding fiction, offered her a contract and reissued the book for a national audience in 1985 (Thompson and Garner 233). Gilchrist has published nine books with Little, Brown and has become one of its most popular authors.

The Annunciation (1983), a novel, received mixed reviews, but with *Victory Over Japan* (1984), her second book of stories, Gilchrist won the American Book Award. *Victory Over Japan* follows the adventures of characters Gilchrist had introduced in *In the Land of Dreamy Dreams*—especially Rhoda Manning and Nora Jane Whittington. Excellent reviews sent many readers to her earlier books.

Gilchrist collected her verse in *Riding out the Tropical Depression: Selected Poems, 1975–1985* (1986). She dedicated this book to her father, "the finest man I have ever known. If there are any words he doesn't like he can mark them out as usual." From the poem "Marshall" in this collection, Gilchrist also took the title for *Drunk with Love* (1986), her third book of stories. Though *Drunk with Love* received a biting review in the *New York Times Book Review* (Lesser 18), novelist Lee Smith praised Gilchrist for creating characters "in a way that resembles life, oddly, more than it resembles fiction" (5). For National Public Radio, Gilchrist had broadcast in 1985 and 1986 short journal commentaries on herself and the times; she collected these entries along with speeches, magazine essays, and journal entries in *Falling Through Space*.

Gilchrist had introduced Anna Hand, a woman writer in love with a married physician, in the last story in *Drunk with Love*. For her second novel, *The Anna Papers* (1988), she focused her story on Anna's life, suicide, and the Hand family of North Carolina. *Light Can Be Both Wave and Particle* (1989), her fourth collection of stories, includes two stories revising the ending of *The Annunciation* ("Song of Songs" and "Life on the Earth") and rounds out Gilchrist's productive first decade of published work.

I Cannot Get You Close Enough: Three Novellas (1990) launched Gilchrist's second decade as a writer. These novellas—*Winter, De Havilland Hand,* and *A Summer in Maine*—follow the lives of characters from her earlier stories and novels. The novella, a new form for Gilchrist, demonstrates her talent in all the forms of prose fiction. Her third novel, *Net of Jewels* (1992), traces Rhoda Manning's life from her nineteenth year to her marriage to Malcolm Martin, and beyond. She told Gene Lyons that she has " 'drawers and drawers' full of short stories," a "play making the rounds in New York," and plans to "write and direct a film of her own" (83). Gilchrist's energy and intelligence promise readers another decade of delight.

MAJOR THEMES

Gilchrist told an interviewer that her "avocational interests" were "love affairs (mine or anyone else's), all sports, children, inventions, music, rivers, forts and tents, trees" (Clemens 167). Her avocational interests parallel those of her vocation.

Gilchrist arranges the fourteen stories in *In the Land of Dreamy Dreams* in three sections—"There's a Garden of Eden," "Things Like the Truth," and "Perils of the Nile." Several themes link these stories: Dream, fantasy, or nightmare pervade all the stories; all but two tales ("Rich" and "Suicides") feature female protagonists struggling for self-knowledge or recognition; the theme of death ties together several stories; the pangs of childhood and adolescence appear in many.

In the five stories of "There's a Garden of Eden," all set in New Orleans, Gilchrist explores the dark side of her seemingly Edenic setting. She satirizes sympathetically her wealthy New Orleans characters in "Rich," "The President of the Louisiana Live Oak Society," "There's a Garden of Eden," and "In the Land of Dreamy Dreams." The first two stories end in nightmares of suicide; Alisha Terrebonne, a once famous Southern beauty, temporarily escapes the terrors of aging in "There's a Garden of Eden" by taking a young lover and inventing a dream-like "script." With her portrait of LeGrande McGruder—a self-centered, racist, tennis-playing cheat–Gilchrist presents her most biting satire of the old rich in "In the Land of Dreamy Dreams." "The Famous Poll at Jody's Bar" introduces Nora Jane Whittington, who is "nineteen years old, a self-taught anarchist, and a quick-change artist" (49). Nora Jane, a mixture of innocence and canniness, dreams of her California lover, robs Jody's Bar to get money to join him, and empowers herself through action in a comic story reminiscent of the tall tale.

The theme of death—literal and metaphorical—ties together the stories in the second section, "Things Like the Truth." Gilchrist grimly portrays the madness and self-destruction of Philip Treadway in "Suicides." The story "1957, a Romance" introduces Rhoda Manning, who fears another caesarean birth and convinces her father to help her abort a pregnancy. With irony and understatement, Gilchrist deals poignantly with Rhoda's ambiguous feelings of joy and sorrow about aborting the child. "Generous Pieces" powerfully portrays a child's awareness of her own and her parents' sexuality and her fear that her father's real or imagined love affair with a married neighbor signals the death of her security. "Indignities" recounts the first-person narrator's attempts to deal with her nonexistent relationship with her flamboyant mother, who dies of breast cancer.

The rambunctious Rhoda Manning occupies center stage in three of the five stories in "Perils of the Nile." All focus on children or adolescents. Gilchrist makes Rhoda the narrator of "Revenge," a delightful comic tale of sibling rivalry, perfect vengeance, and self-assertion. Excluded by her brother and male cousins from their training for sports events, 10-year-old Rhoda shouts obscenities at them from her "exile atop the chicken house" (111). During a wedding celebration at which she is maid of honor, Rhoda invades the boys' world, strips down to her cotton underpants, and pole-vaults over the bar as the wedding guests search for her. Before a shocked, admiring crowd, Rhoda has proved to herself, her brother, and the world that she can function well on the athletic field and at weddings.

In "1944" Gilchrist wittily puts 8-year-old Rhoda in a bar where she plays sophisticated adult by drinking Shirley Temples, learning to play water-filled glasses, and singing the "Air Corps Hymn" and "Begin the Beguine." A sixth grader in "Perils of the Nile," Rhoda befriends a motherless boy named Bebber Dyson, who longs for her mother's love. Gilchrist portrays richly the adolescent fantasies of both Rhoda and Bebber.

The last two stories—"Traveler" and "Summer, an Elegy"—contrast the fantasies and nightmares of adolescence and childhood. In the comic "Traveler," Gilchrist creates LeLe Arnold, who lives a fantasy of romance and self-discovery during a Mississippi Delta summer. With irony and understatement, Gilchrist evokes both the self-deception and self-assertion of her adolescent heroine's romantic creation of herself. "Summer, an Elegy," a story of two children named Shelby and Matille, has a more ominous tone. Gilchrist portrays their first sexual fumblings and suggests that Matille was sexually abused by her uncle. Although Matille believes her secret is safe after Shelby's death, Gilchrist implies that these experiences will haunt the child.

Though later works will introduce new themes and characters, the patterns and structures that Gilchrist introduces in *In the Land of Dreamy Dreams* appear in her other books of stories. She also structures her novels around titled sections. In her story collections, she creates story cycles in the manner of Sherwood Anderson's *Winesburg, Ohio* and Ernest Hemingway's *In Our Time*. Rhoda Manning resembles Hemingway's Nick Adams because Gilchrist portrays Rhoda's adventures and growth in several books.

In *The Annunciation,* her first novel, Gilchrist sets an ambitious goal: demythologizing the New Testament annunciation and re-mythologizing the story in a modern Southern context. Dividing her novel into sections titled "Cargo," "Exile," and "The Annunciation," Gilchrist introduces her Mary figure, Amanda McCamey, an adolescent who gives up a daughter fathered by her cousin Guy. Carrying a "cargo" of guilt for giving up the child and for being unable to have more children because she can no longer conceive, Amanda marries the wealthy Malcolm Ashe of New Orleans, but soon discovers the hypocrisy of that life deadening.

With the help of her black maid Lavertis (the truth teller), Amanda recovers from an alcoholism that almost destroys her and discovers meaningful work translating the poems of an eighteenth-century French nun named Helene Renoir. Moving from New Orleans to Fayetteville, Arkansas, to pursue her translations, Amanda finds a new lover, Will Lyons, and new meaning in her art. At age 44, Amanda becomes pregnant with Will's child, and the novel ends with the birth of a son, the death of her lover, and the prospect of being reunited with her first child. Gilchrist closes the novel with Amanda falling ''asleep dreaming of herself in a white silk suit holding her beautiful daughter in her arms. My will be done, she said as she moved in her sleep. My life on my terms, my daughter, my son. My life leading to my lands forever and ever and ever, hallowed be my name, goddammit, my kingdom come, my will be done, so be it, Amanda'' (352–53). Gilchrist's irony asserts both Amanda's power to shape her own life and the limitations of that power. Her new Mary figure, re-mythologized in the form of Amanda McCamey, possesses more than a room of one's own; Amanda has earned her sense of selfhood and has asserted her identity as a woman and an artist.

Gilchrist risks audaciously in *The Annunciation*. Though several critics have dismissed this novel, Gilchrist layers her story's meaning by suggesting parallels with and contrasts between Amanda's story and those of the Virgin Mary and the French poet Helene Renoir, whose works Amanda translates. Allusions to Narcissus (11), Aphrodite (201), Medea (281), and especially Diana (126, 171, 221) also suggest comparisons between Amanda and heroines of classical literature. Dr. Luke Haverty (Gilchrist uses Luke 1:29 as an epigraph) delivers Amanda's son, whom she names Noel because it ''means good news'' (349). The three wise men attending the child's birth are Luke, Garth, and Clinton (346).

Gilchrist's telling criticism of conventional religion and Southern attitudes resonate throughout *The Annunciation*. But she seems to have had second thoughts about the novel's ending, for two stories in *Light Can Be Both Wave and Particle* (''The Song of Songs'' and ''Life on the Earth'') revise the conclusion: The first tells of Amanda's reunion with her daughter, and the second resuscitates Amanda's lover, Will Lyons. The new chapters end the novel on an even more hopeful note.

Though Gilchrist begins and ends *Victory Over Japan* with references to World War II, the themes that unify her book are not the global conflicts of the war, but the battles on the home front. Among the themes unifying her book are conflicts between parents and children, the nature of madness and sanity, the search for love, and the weird warring of family members. Her protagonists again are female, and she tells more tales about Rhoda Manning and Nora Jane Whittington. She introduces two new major characters—Miss Crystal Manning Weiss and her black maid, Traceleen. Gilchrist groups the fourteen stories in four sections titled ''Rhoda,'' ''Crazy, Crazy, Now Showing Everywhere,'' ''Nora Jane,'' and ''Crystal.''

The three stories of ''Rhoda''—''Victory Over Japan,'' ''Music,'' and ''The

Lower Garden District Free Gravity Mule Blight or Rhoda, a Fable''—portray this character as a third grader, as a 14-year-old, and as a 34-year-old woman. In all three stories, Rhoda defies authority to assert her rebellious self. ''Victory Over Japan'' depicts Rhoda's war with her parents against the background of World War II; in ''Music'' Rhoda's father hauls her off to Christian friends in Kentucky ''to make her stop smoking and acting like a movie star'' (17). Rhoda slips away, buys cigarettes, and loses her virginity to the boy from whom she buys the smokes. In the last story, Rhoda cheats a black insurance adjustor named Earl Treadway to get money so that she can divorce her wealthy husband. Then she seduces Earl. The strong-willed, mule-headed Rhoda gets what Rhoda wants.

The four stories in the second section deal with characters and events that seem off center. ''Looking Over Jordan'' features Lady Margaret Sarpie, a writer obsessed with her work, with growing old, and with the need for love. In ''The Gauzy Edge of Paradise,'' three characters in a comic ménage à trois wind up being robbed; ''Defender of the Little Falaya'' brings characters from two generations in conflict with almost disastrous results. ''Crazy, Crazy, Now Showing Everywhere'' examines the nature of madness, sanity, and forms of confinement—external and internal.

Gilchrist follows Nora Jane Whittington's California adventures in ''Jade Buddas, Red Bridges, Fruits of Love'' and ''The Double Happiness Bun.'' Nora Jane's lover, Sandy Halter, does not meet her when she arrives in San Jose, but she soon takes another named Freddy Harwood. Sandy reappears, and Nora Jane returns to him. When she discovers in ''The Double Happiness Bun'' that she is pregnant, Nora Jane says of the father's identity: ''I don't know. It's just a baby. I don't know whose it is'' (194). The gritty Nora Jane, stranded on a bridge during an earthquake, helps a woman with children before all are rescued. At the story's end, Nora Jane has not made up her mind about which lover she loves.

The five tales in ''Crystal'' deal with Crystal Manning Weiss, a rich, spoiled, headstrong woman who is eccentric and ''wild.'' Traceleen, Miss Crystal's black maid, narrates four stories about Crystal's marriage, family, lovers, and eccentricities. Similar to Faulkner's Dilsey, Traceleen tells of Miss Crystal's shenanigans with wonder and sympathy for the plight of this rich white woman. But Traceleen also judges Crystal and her family for their foolishness. In ''Traceleen, She's Still Talking,'' the black maid observes: ''They're rich people, all the ones I'm talking about. Not that it does them much good that I can see. Miss Crystal's married to this man she can't stand. All the money in the world will not make up for that'' (249). Gilchrist artfully satirizes the outlandish doings of the rich in the bemused and compassionate voice of Traceleen.

Gilchrist uses as her epigraph for *Drunk with Love* an Einstein quotation that captures the essence of all her books: ''What has been overlooked is the irrational, the inconsistent, the droll, even the insane, which nature, inexhaustibly operative, implants in an individual, seemingly for her own amusement.'' In this book, she puts her subject—love and its opposite, hate—at the center and dances around it trying to discover its many permutations. Her dance succeeds admirably. Gilchrist again divides the book's thirteen stories into sections: "Drunk with Love," "Bad Times in a Good Land," "The Islands," and "The Dishes Can Wait."

The first story, "Drunk with Love," picks up the adventures of Nora Jane Whittington; three others in the first section feature Rhoda Manning as protagonist. Still torn between two lovers, Freddy Harwood and Sandy George Wade (not Halter in this book), Nora Jane discovers she is pregnant with twin girls. Nora Jane chooses to stay with Sandy, and the story ends with an imagined conversation between the twin girls, Tammill and Lydia, in Nora Jane's womb. In "Nineteen Forty-one," Rhoda Manning escapes serious injury in a fall from a horse; she vents her anger over her brush with death on her father and the horse, which she wants killed. "The Expansion of the Universe" treats Rhoda's adolescent love for Bob Rosen and her rage at her parents for moving to another town. In "Adoration," Gilchrist tells of Rhoda's young married life and love—and the conception and birth of her children.

The most controversial and powerful stories in *Drunk with Love* are the first two in "Bad Times in a Good Land"—"The Emancipator" and "Memphis." Both tales treat interracial marriages, the conflicts of cultures, and the ambiguity of love and hate; both end in murders. In "The Emancipator," Mae Lauer-Cheene, an ex–Peace Corps worker bent on doing good, marries Hadi Karami Deeb, a Lebanese student threatened with deportation. Because both partners enter marriage with different expectations, the two quarrel; Hadi abuses Mae physically and finally strangles her with the cord of her bathrobe.

Aunt Allie Wheeler, the first-person narrator of "Memphis," tells how her white niece, Baby Kate Wheeler, falls in love with and marries a black man named Franke Brown. At first, things go well, but Franke beats his wife and finally snaps her neck. Aunt Allie Wheeler tries to make sense of events by seeing the cause-effect as racial. But the story's implied author sees other implications. In both "Memphis" and "The Emancipator," Gilchrist focuses her attention on the psychosymbiotic relationships of her characters and of the way the irrational functions in all human beings. The irrational is more important than the racial in these two stories. Explorations of the irrational also underlie "The Young Man," "First Manhattans," and "The Last Diet," the other three stories in this section. Ironic comedy propels the last three stories; the tone of "The Emancipator" and "Memphis" is grotesquely tragic.

The two stories in "The Islands" section—"The Blue-Eyed Buddist" and "Belize"—satirize rich characters seeking meaning or escape in the Edenic settings of the Caribbean. Mainly, they find neither. Gilchrist turns in "The Dishes Can Wait" to a story about Crystal Manning. In "Traceleen at Dawn," Traceleen tells "the story of how Miss Crystal stopped drinking" (203). In this story and others narrated by Traceleen, Gilchrist develops Traceleen as her most admirable character, a woman with wit, sense, and insight. The final story,

"Anna, Part I," introduces Anna Hand, the writer who will become the central character in *The Anna Papers*. Anna struggles to tell herself the truth about her love affair with a married man; the story ends with Anna at her typewriter beginning to put on paper "how the unconscious calls the shots" (229).

When Gilchrist finished *Drunk with Love,* her editor asked her what was next. "I think I'll go fall in love," she replied. Her editor advised: "Why don't you just go home and stick your finger in an electric wall socket instead. It would save you the trouble of getting dressed up." More important is what Gilchrist believes she did: "So I have written a book of stories called *Drunk with Love* in which I set out to explore what I know about the subject. I have failed. Not failed as a writer. But I have learned nothing about love and added nothing to our store of understanding. . . . All I did was wade deeper and deeper into the mystery" (*Falling* 106).

Though Gilchrist's stories often seem autobiographical, *Falling through Space* projects a public portrait, not a real autobiography. Dividing her book into sections titled "Origins," "Influences," "Work," and "Provenance," Gilchrist reviews her past and talks intensely about her own spiritual journeys that carried her to writing. On psychoanalysis, she says: "Anyway, I think I'm funnier and wiser and more balanced because of it" (90). She suspects "there may be a limited number of characters any one writer can create and perhaps a limited number of stories any writer can tell" (126). She notes that "the dour old Scot who rules the roost in my subconscious is very suspicious when I tell him that seeing the world is part of a writer's work" (130).

She denies that she is a "feminist": "I have two brothers and nine male first cousins and three sons and four uncles and a grandson and three ex-husbands. All of them are good-looking and all of them like themselves." She adds: "Surrounded by men like that I would be crazy not to love men. Women who really love men may have to spend a certain amount of time running their hands up and down someone's arms, but they are almost never crazy" (152, 156). Gilchrist always asserts that she is a woman and artist, and *Falling through Space* presents a treasure trove of her impressions and beliefs.

Gilchrist uses as epigraph for *The Anna Papers,* her second novel, a quotation from a Hemingway letter to Fitzgerald: "Love is also a good subject, as you might be said to have discovered." Anna Hand, a writer and Southerner who has exiled herself from her roots, discovers she has breast cancer and comes home to Charlotte, North Carolina, to set her affairs in order and to make peace with her large family before she commits suicide. Gilchrist explores the love between men and women, between children and parents, between siblings, and among kinfolk in her book. The themes of free will and fate, death, and the uses of power in human relationships also figure prominently in this novel. Gilchrist again structures her novel in parts: "Prelude," "Anna," "Elegy and Psalm," "The Anna Papers," "Helen," and "The Gods."

Anna's suicide ends both the "Prelude" and the "Anna" sections. Between these frames, Gilchrist plays out the conflicts of Anna's love for a married man named Philip and her lust for a young man named Adam Halliday. She finds her brother Daniel's child by his first wife, resolves her lifelong fusses with her father, and decides to take her life rather than suffer with cancer. Anna also writes furiously.

Against this background, Anna writes herself notes: "Write to Adam. Call Adam. Introduce Adam to a woman he can breed with. Stop wanting to control Adam or anyone" (38). She says of her father: "That glorious old man, she thought. My God, I love him. Every man I ever loved is just a replay of those emotions" (136). Anna also struggles with her feelings about dying: "The alternative [to suicide] was a bed in a hospital and knives and terror. One big terror or a lot of little terrors. Death was going to win, either way" (149). Anna asserts her power by "adopting" her brother's daughter Olivia and by appointing her sister Helen co-literary executor with a poet named Mike Carmichael. She imagines the consequences of these acts after her death.

In "Elegy and Psalm," Gilchrist brings together at Anna's wake three generations of Hands and Mannings to explore their griefs and to dramatize their dealing with death. Gilchrist—in the novel's last three sections—focuses her attention on Anna's sister Helen, a staid, respectable wife and mother. As Helen sifts through her sister's unpublished writing in "The Anna Papers" section, she becomes narrator and author. The more Helen learns about Anna, the more she gains power and authority over her own life. Awakened to these possibilities, Helen takes Mike Carmichael as her lover in the "Helen" section and leaves her family. As narrator of the last section ("The Gods"), Helen sees Anna's ghost twice; the second time, Anna's ghost says: "Helen, I want you to be happy. I want you to have anything you need of mine" (277). Gilchrist's ending suggests that Helen springs almost phoenixlike from Anna's ashes.

The eleven stories of *Light Can Be Both Wave and Particle* follow the further doings of Rhoda Manning, Nora Jane Whittington, Traceleen, and Crystal Manning Weiss, and introduce a Chinese character named Lin Tang Sing. Though Gilchrist does not supply headings for clusters of stories, she separates them into three groups of three and one group of two.

The search for love and the experiences of childhood and adolescence provide themes for many stories. Rhoda discovers in "Some Blue Hills at Sundown" that her romance with Bob Rosen was more prosaic than poetic. Nora Jane decides she loves Freddy Harwood in "The Starlight Express" and returns to him for the harrowing birth of her twins. Lin Tang Sing, a Chinese geneticist who reads and translates poetry, falls in love with Margaret McElvoy in "Light Can Be Both Wave and Particle"; Gilchrist handles delicately the cultural differences of her two lovers in this story. "Mexico," the last and longest story, recounts Rhoda Manning's holiday south of the boarder with her brother Dudley and cousin Saint John. In this story, Rhoda is "fifty-three years old and bored to death" (133). In a story that echoes Hemingway's *The Sun Also Rises,* the aging Rhoda tries to seduce a bullfighter and gets drunk before she can keep her rendezvous with him. The themes of death, aging, growing up, and violence underlie this comic tale of errors.

With *I Cannot Get You Close Enough,* Gilchrist writes in a new form—the novella—and focuses on new themes, as well as old ones. As in all her work, vital and lively characters drive her fiction toward theme, which evolves from the conflicts she invents for her characters. This pattern controls her three novellas—*Winter, De Havilland Hand,* and *A Summer in Maine.*

As epigraphs for her book, Gilchrist quotes from Carl Gustav Jung and Philip Larkin. From Jung she cites the following: "Generally speaking, all the life which the parents could have lived, but of which they thwarted themselves for artificial motives, is passed on to the children in substitute form. That is to say, the children are driven unconsciously in a direction that is intended to compensate for everything that was left unfulfilled in the lives of their parents." Two lines from Larkin's "This Be the Verse" supply the second: "They fuck you up, your mum and dad, / They may not mean to but they do."

Gilchrist assigns authorship of *Winter* to Anna Hand, who "was so vain she couldn't bear for anyone to watch her die" (3). In this heart of darkness story, Anna explores the nature of what she regards as raw evil. Attempting to keep her sister-in-law Sheila MacNiece Hand from gaining custody of her daughter Jessie, Anna characterizes Sheila as "mean, destructive, spoiled, dangerous, unprincipled, remorseless, the worst bitch I have ever known" (3). To keep Sheila from ruining her niece, Anna sets out to gather evidence that Sheila is an unfit mother.

Anna's journey carries her to England and Turkey where she discovers Sheila's connections with drugs and with terrorists. In the filthy back streets of Istanbul, Anna finds Sheila's abandoned and "perhaps hydrocephalic" (66) child by Zeno Makarios, the "Castro of the Mediterranean" (55). Horrified, Anna returns to confront Sheila's wealthy father about Jessie's custody. As she watches Sheila's father, she thinks: "It was Sheila standing in my living room in her black suit, raging and threatening and pretending to have power. This wasn't power, it wasn't even evil. It was the old reptilian brain, old reptile dumbness. Evil is always dumb. How had I forgotten that?" (84). But Anna Hand also knows she shares responsibility for the part she has played in the drama: "Now I had helped steal her [Jessie] from her mother. Any act creates both good and evil and comes from both" (85).

Gilchrist narrates omnisciently *De Havilland Hand,* the story of Anna Hand's finding and bringing her brother Daniel's daughter by his first wife into the Hand family of Charlotte, North Carolina. This novella has as its principal themes the family relationships of three generations of Hands and the conflict of American Indian and white cultures. Gilchrist's story traces Oliva de Havilland Hand's coping with her new sister Jessie and with a way of life that is alien to Olivia's upbringing in Indian Country in Oklahoma.

Gilchrist gathers her gallery of lovable grotesques and eccentrics from the

Manning and Hand families in *A Summer in Maine*. She uses thirteen different narrators to deliver forty-five speeches about loves, lusts, and dreams. Her major theme in this novella is the quirks and twists of family relationships. A letter written by Anna Hand summarizes this theme:

The mystery of children . . . Helen [Anna's sister] gives her life to her children and they pay her back by making her a slave. The Oedipus Complex, the Electra. In our family power is handed down in a strange and complex way. The most powerful older person keeps it all. To access love you must give your power to that figure. To get love you must steal power from your children. This is achieved by giving and receiving money. The Greeks knew everything. A king sacrifices his daughter to fill the sails of the ships bound for Troy. A boy kills his father and marries his mother. A plague comes. (378–79)

In this novella, as in her other works, Gilchrist explores archetypal relationships among family members.

Using multiple narrators in a fashion similar to Faulkner's in *As I Lay Dying*, Gilchrist presents several versions of her characters and events. The narrators include Crystal Manning Weiss, her friend Lydia, Traceleen, and other members of the Hand and Manning families. Traceleen narrates twelve of the forty-five segments. Miss Crystal, Miss Lydia, Olivia, and Jessie Manning, and Traceleen's niece Andria are principal tellers. In one section, the one containing the title of Gilchrist's trilogy (387), Anna Hand speaks from beyond the grave. Miss Lydia, a painter, has ''a vision of Crystal as the prototype of all the southern women I had ever known, worn out from dreaming of perfect worlds, perfect lives, perfect lovers, husbands, children, friends. While the life of the world went on she stopped a moment to look down and gather strength before she went back to motion and to dreaming'' (250). By presenting multiple versions of her main characters, Gilchrist shows their complexity and their ability to surprise readers.

Net of Jewels (1992), Gilchrist's third novel, centers on Rhoda Manning's life during her college years. She falls in love with and marries Malcolm Martin. She gives birth to his children, but finds her marriage in trouble. Using Rhoda as a first-person narrator, Gilchrist develops her heroine in greater detail, and presents further insights into the Manning family and the South.

Gilchrist tells all her stories in prose that is paratactic and powerful. Her dialogue has an authentic ring, and she often writes startling opening sentences and paragraphs. ''This is a story about an old lady who ordered a young man from an L. L. Bean catalog'' (''The Young Man,'' *Drunk* 107). ''Her horror and fascination with his size. His power, his hands, feet, mouth, dick, all that stuff that carried her across the door of that little frame house on T Street and kept her there until her neck snapped'' (''Memphis,'' *Drunk* 90). ''On the twenty-fourth day of August, nineteen hundred and eighty-five, JeanAnne Lori Mayfield, third child and only daughter of Mr. and Mrs. Johnny Wayne Mayfield of Fayetteville, Arkansas, ended her last and final diet by running her navy blue

Toyota into a doughnut shop'' ("The Last Diet," *Drunk* 146). Such sentences propel readers forward, and Gilchrist's paratactic style leads them always in that direction.

Gilchrist has created a remarkable gallery of characters and has forged a style and voice distinctly her own. It remains to see what creatures her imagination will give the world.

SURVEY OF CRITICISM

Though one critic said Gilchrist sometimes sounds like a "foulmouthed Flannery O'Connor" (Allen 486), that epithet falls three counties shy of describing the feisty characters Gilchrist creates, the narrative voices telling many of her stories, and the clear, clean style of her prose. Her narrators and characters sometimes speak in four-letter words, but that language arises naturally from the character and situation rather than from Gilchrist's attempt at sensationalism.

Several commentators have remarked on Gilchrist's "phenomenal success" (Peden 269) as a writer. Coming mostly from working reviewers harried by deadlines, the criticism has mainly praised her work, but has not always been kind. Jeanie Thompson and Anita Miller Garner have written the only extended study, "The Miracle of Realism: The Bid for Self-Knowledge in the Fiction of Ellen Gilchrist."

With few exceptions, critics have consistently praised Gilchrist's female characters. They are "mostly affluent girls and women from families well-rooted in Southern traditions (collapsing, of course)" and are "credible and sympathetic" (Flower 313). Her characters—often "quirky" (Wolitzer 2) and "spoiled Southern belles" (Allen 486)—are women, who "in contrast to their community, are unconventional, nervy, outspoken" (Hoffman). Joan Eades describes Gilchrist's characters as refreshing in their "brazenness," adding; "You have to be fascinated by these characters, but you don't always have to like them. They are often greedy, obsessed with money. They can be amoral to the point of cruelty" (183–84). In a review of *Drunk with Love*, novelist Lee Smith writes: "It is even hard to use the term *characters* in discussing Gilchrist's fiction—you want to say *people* instead." Reviewers agree that she "is self-consciously a Southern writer" (Melmoth).

Several reviewers—even sympathetic ones—have faulted Gilchrist for portraying two-dimensional men characters (Thompson and Garner 235), but Wendy Lesser has delivered the harshest judgment in her comments on *Drunk with Love*. Speaking of the interracial stories there, Lesser said: "This is a touchy business for a white Southern writer to deal with, and Ms. Gilchrist does not handle it well" and "seems implicated in her own characters' attitudes." Charging Gilchrist with stereotyping, Lesser continued: "You notice that there is only a small number of people at the party after all: a weary, neurotic Southern wife, her overworked, insensitive Jewish husband; a cynical female artist or two (one of them a red-haired writer); some faithful black servants; an irresponsible, charming lover; and a few others. . . . Next time Ms. Gilchrist should invite some new guests.''

But Lesser's is a minority report; it fails to take into account the narrative voices of ''Emancipator'' and ''Memphis,'' and it does not acknowledge the judgments of Traceleen, the black maid, on Crystal Manning Weiss, the''neurotic Southern wife.'' Reviewing the same stories in *Drunk with Love,* D. D. Guttenplan said: ''I don't believe you are a racist,'' but the stories ''made me uncomfortable. Which may well have been your intention.''

Meg Wolitzer especially praises Gilchrist for being ''sensitive to the alienation that children and adolescents feel'' (2), and Jim Crace describes the landscape of *In the Land of Dreamy Dreams* as ''adolescence.'' Crace calls ''Revenge'' that volume's ''masterpiece.''

Critics also admire Gilchrist's handling of voice. They have praised her ''unique'' and ''skillful handling of voice,'' noting that the ''author remains detached, paring her fingernails'' (Flower 313). Her voice is ''Startling in its originality yet rich with the echoes of the Southern tradition of Faulkner, Welty, and O'Connor'' (Eades 182). The ''amused ironic distance'' (Allen 486) in her stories often provides the punch. Another describes her as ''a kind of Mississippi magical realist,'' who ''can get away with almost anything'' (Guttenplan).

Even sympathetic reviewers have pointed out flaws in Gilchrist's stories. Lee Smith notes that stories in *Drunk with Love* ''often lack plot.'' In her review of *Victory Over Japan,* Beverly Lowry admires Gilchrist for being a ''very nervy writer'' and ''willing to take risks,'' but believes that sometimes final paragraphs seem ''tacked on'' and that ''her point of view within a story sometimes conveniently wanders.'' But Smith calls the Diet Diary in ''The Last Diet'' a ''minor masterpiece,'' and Lowry says that ''Crystal Manning may be the queen creation of *Victory Over Japan.*''

Reviewers have failed to explore one important quality of Gilchrist's stories—the unity of stories within a book. Meg Wolitzer found missing in *Drunk with Love* ''a thread of commonality running through the stories'' (2) and ''little cohesion'' (12). Dean Flower saw in *Victory Over Japan* a ''strong impulse to tie her stories together . . . with very non-chronological loops'' (314), but did not elaborate. Likewise, Judy Cooke praised *Drunk with Love* as ''stories satisfyingly crafted and complete'' (27), but pursued the idea no further. Reviewing *Victory Over Japan,* Jonathan Yardley noted: ''But because many of the stories are connected in ways both obvious and subtle, you feel as though you are reading a novel'' (B10).

It remains for commentators with more space than working reviewers to explore the ''story cycles'' that Gilchrist has developed within and between her collections. Like Sherwood Anderson and hundreds of story writers after him, Gilchrist consciously writes books that are ''story cycles'' connected by themes, characters, and images.

In the most extended criticism of Gilchrist's work, Thompson and Garner focused their attention on *In the Land of Dreamy Dreams* and *The Annunciation.*

Frances Taliaferro called *The Annunciation* "a cheerful hodgepodge of the social and psychological fashions of the past three decades." Rosellen Brown believed that the novel fell apart: "In the second half of the book, the author has put aside all the things that work wonders for her voice: her nervy vigilance, bracing skepticism, and ferocity of judgment" (54). And Yardley dismissed *The Annunciation* as "flabby, narcissistic, sophomoric" (B1).

But Thompson and Garner argue otherwise. "The view that Gilchrist gives us of the world," they argue, "is a very straight and narrow path of realism, traditional fiction peopled with characters whom life doesn't pass by, characters who lust and kill and manipulate, and most importantly, dream" (233). Evidencing a "type of Romantic Calvinism in her view of women," Gilchrist creates her "young protagonists as simultaneously wonderful and horrible" (235). But in *The Annunciation,* Gilchrist has created Amanda McCamey, her "first female protagonist who may be elevated to the class of hero" (238).

Amanda's "bid for freedom through self-knowledge" (238) and "her life-long search for love and acceptance and peace" (245) culminate in a quest that hints her "heroism" (246). Examining the complexity and ambiguity of allusion, structure, plot, and the "female psyche" (247), Thompson and Garner argue that Gilchrist "is working with amazing confidence" (247). Their essay serves as a model for the kind of criticism Gilchrist's books deserve.

Future commentators on Gilchrist's work might profitably study her prose style, her use of the story cycle as a structuring device, and the way she artfully "gets away with" changing perspectives and viewpoints within her stories and novels.

BIBLIOGRAPHY

Works by Ellen Gilchrist

The Land Surveyor's Daughter (Poems). Fayetteville, Ark.: Lost Roads, 1979.
In the Land of Dreamy Dreams. Fayetteville, Ark.: University of Arkansas Press, 1981.
        Boston: Little, Brown, 1985.
The Annunciation. Boston: Little, Brown, 1983.
Victory Over Japan. Boston: Little, Brown, 1984.
Drunk with Love. Boston: Little, Brown, 1986.
Riding out the Tropical Depression: Selected Poems, 1975–1985. New Orleans: Faust, 1986.
Falling through Space: The Journals of Ellen Gilchrist. Boston: Little, Brown, 1987.
The Anna Papers. Boston: Little, Brown, 1988.
Light Can Be Both Wave and Particle. Boston: Little, Brown, 1989.
I Cannot Get You Close Enough: Three Novellas. Boston: Little, Brown, 1990. [Includes *Winter, De Havilland Hand,* and *A Summer in Maine.*]
Net of Jewels. Boston: Little, Brown, 1992.

Studies of Ellen Gilchrist

Allen, Bruce. "American Short Fiction Today" (Rev. of *In the Land of Dreamy Dreams*). *New England Review* 4 (Spring 1982): 478–88.

Brown, Rosellen. "Coming up Short" (Rev. of *The Annunciation*). *Saturday Review* (August 1983): 53–54.

Clemens, Lori R. "Ellen Gilchrist," 165–68 in *Contemporary Authors*, Vol. 116, ed. Hal May. Detroit: Gale Research, 1986.

Cooke, Judy. "Intimate Voices" (Rev. of *Drunk with Love*). *Listener* (March 19, 1987): 26–27.

Crace, Jim. "The Cold-Eyed Terrors" (Rev. of *In the Land of Dreamy Dreams*). *Times Literary Supplement* (October 15, 1982): 1142.

Eades, Joan. Rev. of *Victory over Japan*. *North Dakota Quarterly* 53 (Summer 1985): 182–84.

Flower, Dean. "Fiction Chronicle" (Rev. of *Victory Over Japan*). *Hudson Review* 38 (Summer 1985): 313–14.

Guttenplan, D. D. "Lie down in Darkness" (Rev. of *Drunk with Love*). *Village Voice* (January 27, 1987): 54.

Hall, Sharon K., ed. "Ellen Gilchrist: *Victory over Japan*," 164–66 in *Contemporary Literary Criticism*, Vol. 34. Detroit: Gale Research, 1985.

Hoffman, Roy. "Smart Enough for Their Own Good" (Rev. of *Light Can Be Both Wave and Particle*). *New York Times Book Review* (October 22, 1989): 12.

Lesser, Wendy. "Home Movies" (Rev. of *Drunk with Love*). *New York Times Book Review* (October 5, 1986): 18.

Lowry, Beverly. "Redheaded Hellions in the Crepe Myrtle" (Rev. of *Victory over Japan*). *New York Times Book Review* (September 23, 1984): 18.

Lyons, Gene. "First Person Singular." *Newsweek* (February 18, 1985): 81, 83.

Marowski, Daniel and Roger Matuz, eds. "Ellen Gilchrist," 114–22 in *Contemporary Literary Criticism*, Vol. 48. Detroit: Gale Research, 1988.

Melmoth, John. "Poor Little Rich Belles" (Rev. of *Drunk with Love*). *Times Literary Supplement* (March 6, 1987): 246.

Morton, Brian. "Southern Death" (Rev. of *The Annunciation*). *Times Literary Supplement* (April 6, 1984): 368.

Peden, William. "Recent Fiction" (Rev. of *Victory Over Japan*). *Western Humanities Review* 39 (Autumn 1985): 269–70.

Smith, Lee. "Loose Characters" (Rev. of *Drunk with Love*). *Spectator* (November 6–12, 1986): 5.

Taliaferro, Frances. Rev. of *The Annunciation*. *Harper's* 266 (June 1983): 76.

Thompson, Jeanie and Anita Miller Garner. "The Miracle of Realism: The Bid for Self-Knowledge in the Fiction of Ellen Gilchrist," 233–47 in *Women Writers of the Contemporary South*, ed. Peggy Whitman Prenshaw. Jackson: University Press of Mississippi, 1984. Reprinted from *Southern Quarterly* 32 (Fall 1983): 101–14.

Wolitzer, Meg. Rev. of *Drunk with Love*. *Los Angeles Times Book Review* (September 14, 1986): 2, 12.

Yardley, Jonathan. "Knockout 'Victory': The Best Stories Yet from Ellen Gilchrist" (Rev. of *Victory over Japan*). *Washington Post* (September 12, 1984): B1, B10.

Marianne Gingher
(1947–   )

In her first novel, *Bobby Rex's Greatest Hit* (1986), and in her short stories, some collected in *Teen Angel and Other Stories of Young Love* (1988), Marianne Gingher writes in a distinctively original voice about the small-town South, about people navigating awkward experiences of change, and about modern, broken families trying to heal. While her settings and situations evoke the soft mood of nostalgia that characterizes many portrayals of the Elvis era, Gingher renders her world in prose that can be sharp and satiric as well as lyrical and meditative. What is most recognizably Southern about her fiction is its energetic style, elements of the tall tale in the storytelling, and fresh, often startling versions of familiar images. She celebrates a transforming sense of mystery that can inject itself into ordinary lives at any moment. Her work has been viewed as reminiscent of both Flannery O'Connor and Larry McMurtry, but she has created her own territory by combining a happy relish for the ridiculous in life with great sympathy for her characters' quests for excitement and dignity.

BIOGRAPHY

Unlike most of her characters, Marianne Gingher has never lived in a small southern town. She was born on February 10, 1947, in Guam to Rod and Betty Buie during her father's tour of duty as a doctor in the U.S. Navy. When she was 3 years old her family returned to Greensboro, North Carolina, the piedmont city that has been home for most of her life. Gingher attended Grimsley High School in Greensboro and Salem College in nearby Winston-Salem. During her college sophomore year, she married Robert Gingher, also from Greensboro and also a future writer and teacher.

After graduation in 1969, Gingher taught art in the Winston-Salem/Forsyth County public schools before returning to Greensboro, where she studied with

Fred Chappell in the graduate creative writing program at the University of North Carolina. She received her M.F.A. from UNC-Greensboro in 1974 and then moved to Chapel Hill where her husband worked on his Ph.D. By 1976 she had published several stories in the *Carolina Quarterly,* including one, "Gift," which received second place in the journal's fiction contest in 1973. This recognition led to a position as instructor of creative writing at UNC-Chapel Hill, and Gingher taught courses on fiction writing, children's literature, and modern British and American literature.

In 1982 the Ginghers had returned to Greensboro, and two children, both boys, born in 1981 and 1983, caused her to put her teaching career on hold. The writing, however, continued in expanded markets; Gingher's stories appeared in *Redbook, Seventeen, Ladies Home Journal,* and the *Village Advocate.* A story about a young boy whose older brother leaves home to become a rock star ("No News"), published in the *North American Review* in 1974, became the basis for a novel that Gingher began around 1984. *Bobby Rex's Greatest Hit,* published by Atheneum Books in 1986, was immediately successful. A collection of short fiction, *Teen Angel and Other Stories of Young Love* (Atheneum, 1988), also received enthusiastic praise. Gingher returned to teaching at UNC-Chapel Hill in 1987. In 1988 she began teaching at Hollins College in Roanoke, Virginia. Robert and Marianne Gingher divorced in 1989. In addition to stories, Gingher regularly publishes fiction reviews for the *Washington Post,* the *Washington Times,* the *Greensboro News and Record,* and the *New York Times Book Review.*

When she was in fifth grade, Gingher wrote an essay on the theme of "What I Want to Be When I Grow Up." Her goals, she said, were marriage, a peaceful country home, and a career as a writer of "many wonderful stories . . . each of them to be a success." Life in a large city and combining marriage, career, and two little boys have made the peaceful country home impossible, but the success of the "wonderful stories" is well-documented by reviews and awards. Two stories have earned Best American Short Stories citations, and Gingher received North Carolina Literary Fellowships in 1985 and 1990. To these honors she has added a PEN Syndicated Fiction Award in 1986, a Bread Loaf Fellowship in 1987, and the Sir Walter Raleigh Award for Fiction in 1987. *Bobby Rex's Greatest Hit* was universally hailed as a stunning first novel and received an American Library Association Best Book Citation in 1986.

Gingher's works draw on some of her own background and experiences: visiting her father's relatives in the tiny town of Potecasi in eastern North Carolina; attending and teaching in a large public high school; marrying young and having two children close together in age. Gingher's training in the visual arts, as well as problems with eyesight, have had an effect on her style. As she puts it: "I first see the world and observe it. . . . Not being able to see very well has always made me get right up on top of things to try to see them." Although Gingher started out as an art teacher, there was never much question that she would always be a writer. From an early age, she says, "I was a strange kid.

Instead of asking for toys, I asked for writing pads.'' Now, as a reviewer, a teacher of writing and literature, and an acclaimed Southern fiction writer, she is seeing and living the results of that choice.

MAJOR THEMES

The titles of Gingher's two books have probably led to more misinterpretation of their substance than anything else about them. One book announces that it is about a recording star named Bobby Rex, conjuring up images of the hip-gyrating Elvis or the moody James Dean. The other names two schmaltzy rock-and-roll songs, ''Teen Angel'' and ''Young Love.'' It is possible to wonder, at first, if Gingher is going to feed her readers sentimental, Sandra Dee slices of life aimed at adolescents or lifetime members of Pat Boone fan clubs. However, her stories' associations with the glow of 1950s- and 1960s-style wonder years help her to create the rich surprises that await those who get beyond, or more deeply into, what the titles infer. Gingher's works are not primarily for, or even about, young people, although the majority of her characters are between ages 12 and 20, and young readers can certainly enjoy her stories. The titles function to recall a mood that becomes the source of the fiction's complex irony. Everyone who dreams, and Gingher's characters are dreamers with a vengeance, has been caught up in the aura that rock-and-roll celebrates—themes that tend to mix the tragic and the trivial. When Gingher was asked to describe what *Bobby Rex's Greatest Hit* is about, she answered: ''Love and death and innocence and separation and longing and ambition and the powerful lure of the heart and the hearth . . . and [in other words, we might add] rock and roll.'' Her fiction is thus about dreamers handling the hard circumstances of their lives through illusions which, like rock-and-roll, can make one laugh or cry, or both.

The characters who dominate Gingher's fiction are people in families, people for whom family constitutes identity. The breaking of family circles is a common theme. In *Bobby Rex's Greatest Hit* Pally Thompson lives with her mother, who was widowed when Pally was ''real little.'' Parallels and contrasts develop between Pally and her friend Shilda, whose mother abandoned her and her father, Eddy Hawk, when she was 3 years old. Pally's father, Speedy, and Shilda's mother, Gloria, were wild, restless, free spirits. The little town of Orfax, North Carolina, population 3,127, with its smell of meat loaf always in the air, could hardly satisfy their longings, and so they escaped, Speedy through death in a motorcycle accident and Gloria by running away with a preacher.

Shilda's response to her situation is a calculated, bitter wildness. Her father, who had never accepted his wife's desertion, finally commits suicide, an act that returns Shilda to reality and provides her an escape to a new home with her grandmother. Pally, watching her mother happily involved in a new romance, responds to her situation in a way that is common to the young ladies of Orfax— she pines after the unattainable, mysterious, sexy Bobby Rex, a man ''with stars for eyeballs.'' Bobby Rex represents not just escape but change, difference, and freedom, all the things that Orfax, North Carolina, seems to have been created just to stifle. Gingher's novel traces Pally's and Shilda's growth into an understanding of their parents' and their own incomplete, ever-changing relationships. In this context, Bobby Rex represents not only the unattainable but also the mystery that can intrude into even the most settled, resolute life.

Pally gives up her dream only to have it come back to haunt her when Bobby Rex writes a song explicitly linking him with her in a fictitious hot summer night's encounter. As she traces the past for clues to explain Bobby Rex's late intrusion into her life, Pally tells a story that uncovers the mystery of her own changing self. In this story, the lure of romance, excitement, and fame is balanced by love for family, loyalty to friends, the security of being needed, so that Bobby Rex becomes, at last, no more for Pally than "my one small and harmless way to leave Orfax while standing at the kitchen sink."

How families function is the question that Gingher's fiction asks repeatedly. *Bobby Rex's Greatest Hit* ends with Pally's family—her husband, stepchildren, mother, and stepfather—marching in to affirm her importance to them. She explains: "I feel them drawing their wagons in a circle around me." The idea of family as protective circle, and the damage that occurs when that circle is broken, forms the thematic center of the stories that make up *Teen Angel and Other Stories of Young Love*. Many stories balance the ideal of "young love" that adolescent protagonists are experiencing for the first time with the failed love of parents. The story entitled "The Magic Circle" strikes a note that dominates the collection; in it, a teenager embarking on his own first love adventure discovers that his father is having an affair, and it makes him think that when he had been younger, his parents had stood in what he calls a "magic circle" that had an "inviolable aura." The parents' love represents the illusion of security and permanence, but also an inpenetrable mystery. When the love fails and the circle breaks, often only the mystery remains. Many of Gingher's stories build on the mystery of failed relationships, with a young person at the center learning not to count on love's permanence—but not to reject its possibilities either.

In a revealing essay that Gingher wrote reviewing three first novels for *Book World,* (July 2, 1989, 8), she says that "first novels are rarely dispiriting" and that, in them, "characters tend to be innovative and resilient rather than downtrodden and cynical." This observation holds not only for her own first novel but also for many of her stories. Although there is little reason for faith, given the messes that most of her couples make of their relationships, her young characters seeking love are never given over to despair, and resilience describes the perspective that most of them reach at last. Gingher explains that "I'm very form-conscious, perhaps too form-conscious . . . I like order."

In her novel and stories, this predilection for order contributes to endings in which characters might not solve all their problems, but do commit themselves to positive courses of action. In her collection's title story, "Teen Angel," we are given the portrait of a family in chaos, with a violent, frustrated father, a mother who retreats into nostalgic escapades that she calls "thinking back-wards," and a daughter who channels her curiosity and rebellion into a reckless promiscuity. The girl narrator who bore witness to this family's painful rages looks back to "honor and cherish" her own part in their wildness and to affirm the "unhindered delusion" even though it was doomed to "looming disappoint-ments." The mother returns meekly to her uncontrollable husband, the pregnant daughter marries, and the narrator affirms the illusions that allow briefly heroic adventures to transform the general messy ugliness of family life. In two other stories of the collection, "Aurora Island" and "Wearing Glasses," the girl narrators also reconcile themselves to disjunctions in their families through a kind of resolute acceptance of diminished hopes still fed by dreams of the transforming power of love.

Gingher constructs her families to give mother-daughter relationships critical weight. Often their bond is strengthened through the mother's memories, like those that Betty Thompson shares with Pally in *Bobby Rex's Greatest Hit*. Their close relationship highlights the tragedy of Shilda's abandonment and the urgency of her determination to keep searching for her mother. In several stories of *Teen Angel*, mothers share not simply their own failed dreams but also their wry faith that love continues to matter nonetheless. Although much of Gingher's work has been targeted for teens and uses first-person, teen voices, it is her mothers who stand out most often as the critical agents of change and survival, passing along the past in key memories as well as protecting and preparing children for the unexplainable future. In an autobiographical essay, "A Hard Place to Get to," Gingher applies some of her most compelling prose to date to the theme of love coming full circle in flawed families where mothers sustain their children's sense of magic while also dealing with bitter memories from the past and the routine drudgery of the present. "Putting the Babies to Bed," which won a 1986 PEN Syndicated Fiction Award, speaks with humor as well as sympathy to the mother's awareness of providing her children with a "fathomless sense of shelter."

In some of Gingher's darker stories, a sense of women's community mitigates the threat of sexual violence. Sexual violation is a lurking danger in many stories, sometimes handled whimsically, as in "Kiss," sometimes balanced against a girl's yearning for sexual initiation as in "Aurora Beach" and "Teen Angel." One of Gingher's most finely wrought stories, "Variation on a Scream," begins with a fairy tale that sets the theme of sexual threat within a universal, mythic context. Then the story swings through several vignettes during which a young woman blends a disturbing memory with several current experiences that define her dread of men's violent, unpredictable aggression.

Gingher's story, "Gift," which brought her early critical attention when it received second prize in the *Carolina Quarterly* Fiction Contest (1973), contains an element that has marked much of her best work in the following years. In the story a young wife, pregnant with her first child, seethes with anger against her great-grandmother, an old country woman who insists that her deceased husband's gift of prophesying has been passed on to her, so that she can foretell that the baby will be a girl. Matched against the girl's very real situation and her bitter, stolid hatred of the heritage the old woman presses upon her is a touch of mystery, a surreal light just potent enough to charge the setting and events with tension and wonderment. Gingher's language helps augment these effects.

In all of her work, images from plain places—a front yard, a kitchen, a local grocery store—are heightened just slightly in crucial scenes to hint at the grotesque, the ridiculous, or even the tragic that lies innocent and dangerous beneath everyday surfaces. From *Bobby Rex's Greatest Hit* to her story "Plutonium Pie" (1991) Gingher starts with characters seemingly trapped in ordinary identities, "so unremorsefully who they are," as she puts it in "Plutonium Pie." In this example, a husband brings surprise to a dull afternoon by insisting on taking over the task of making a pie to take to a party. The failed pie crust becomes a revelation, a wonderfully appropriate symbol of a contaminated marriage about to explode: "Goody and Jack just stand there watching the pie the way Goody suspects you'd watch the sky if the H-bomb were finally dropping." Gingher's fiction seizes upon the mysterious process that allows the ordinary to become the context for explosions of change, life deepening into inexplicable transformations like Bobby Rex's renewing version of Pally Thompson in his song.

SURVEY OF CRITICISM

Critical responses to Marianne Gingher's work have been limited to reviews of her two books. The novel and stories have been widely and appreciatively reviewed, with critics unanimously impressed with the freshness of imagery, the originality of the angle she brings to memories of childhood, and the humor that lightens traditional themes of growing up and failing in love. Fred Chappell, writing one of the most sensitive reviews of *Bobby Rex's Greatest Hit,* notes that it is "a mysterious, even a mystic book," one which renders "ordinary emotions . . . in an extraordinary way." His praise that the novel is "exquisitely rendered" is seconded by *New York Times* book reviewer Ellen Pall, who comments that it is "spangled with brilliant, exact images." In the most extended review that the book has received, Michael McFee stresses the theme of change within the context of "familiarity." He points to a key source of the novel's success; of many recent works about growing up, McFee finds *Bobby Rex's Greatest Hit* "the least mannered," the most natural in style. Alan Gurganus writes too of the language, praising its "hard-earned springiness." The main area of criticism, represented by Nancy Pate, concerns how the novel "trails off a bit at the end as Gingher neatly ties up loose ends." Gingher has acknowledged a need that she felt to have her material "make sense in the end," and perhaps *Bobby Rex,* as well as some of the stories of *Teen Angel,* are finished off too neatly as a result. However, W. L. Taitte, reviewing *Teen Angel* for the *New York Times,* feels that the collection represents an advance over the novel in offering a more natural, less contrived narrative. Pall makes an interesting point that in *Bobby Rex* Gingher seems to celebrate "pre-feminist aspirations and the joys of accepting limits." More recent stories sometimes paint less hopeful portraits of women who have no options beyond marriage and babies. Although Taitte says that the "few stylistic lapses" in *Teen Angel* come from the "sometimes unrestrained optimisim," he and other reviewers of the collection note that Gingher's fictional world is powerfully real when she displays "broken relationships shored up by hard-won insight and emotional courage." As Cathie Pelletier says, "these are painful stories," and Diana O'Hehir stresses that while the young people display a "cheerful stoicism," they "speak in marvelously real, colloquial, raucous voices." The handling of detail, the humor that redeems pain, the authenticity that captures ordinary, yet heartwrenching experiences, the mysteries that lend surprise to simple lives make Gingher a writer who is capturing her own place and time with great skill.

BIBLIOGRAPHY

Works by Marianne Gingher

Bobby Rex's Greatest Hit. New York: Atheneum, 1986; Ballantine, 1987.
Teen Angel and Other Stories of Young Love. New York: Atheneum, 1988; Ballantine, 1989.

Uncollected Stories

"Gift," *Carolina Quarterly,* Spring 1973.
"Plutonium Pie." *Southern Review* 27 (Winter 1991): 93–100.

Stories in Anthologies

"A Hard Place to Get to." *Summer,* eds. Alice Gordon and Vincent Verga. Reading, Mass.: Addison-Wesley, 1990, 81–91.

Studies of Marianne Gingher

Chappell, Fred. " 'Bobby Rex' a Vibrant, Stellar Debut." *Roanoke Times* (November 23, 1986): B6.

Gurganus, Allan. "A Hot Summer Night's Long Sigh" (Rev. of *Bobby Rex*). *Greensboro News and Record* (October 19, 1986): C5.
McFee, Michael. "Permanent Waves" (Rev. of *Bobby Rex*). *Spectator* (October 23, 1986): 27.
O'Hehir, Diana. "Songs of Innocence and Adolescence" (Rev. of *Teen Angel*). *Book World* (June 26, 1988): 3, 7.
Pall, Ellen. "Pally, the Talk of Orfax." *New York Review of Books* (December 12, 1986): 27.

Pate, Nancy. " 'Bobby Rex' a Sweet Breath of Memory." *Orlando Sentinel* (November 23, 1986): C3.

Pelletier, Cathie. "Gingher's *'Teen Angel'* Soars Winningly through the Waters of In-Between Years." *Atlanta Journal and Constitution* (July 17, 1988): 13G.

Taitte, W. L. *"Teen Angel." New York Review of Books* (September 1988): 19.

MARY ANN WIMSATT

Gail Godwin
(1937–   )

An accomplished, a prolific, and a popular writer, Gail Godwin in numerous novels and short stories explores the difficulties that beset talented, ambitious women in the last half of the twentieth century. Godwin's typical protagonist, a young woman in search of herself, confronts obstacles caused by her family, her lovers, her husband, or her own inanition as she struggles to establish her independence and secure her identity through her work. The contemporary sun-belt South is the setting for most of Godwin's fiction. In her recent novels she examines the problems originating in divisions of race and social class that historically have characterized the South.

BIOGRAPHY

Gail Godwin was born in Birmingham, Alabama, on June 18, 1937, to Kathleen Krahenbuhl and Mose Winston Godwin. Her parents were divorced shortly after her birth, and her mother moved to Asheville, North Carolina, where Godwin grew up in a household consisting of her mother and her widowed grandmother. She attended Peace Junior College in Raleigh, North Carolina, from 1955 to 1957 and the University of North Carolina from 1957 to 1959, graduating with a B.A. in journalism.

Godwin was then employed for a year as a reporter for the *Miami Herald,* during which time she was married briefly to a fellow *Herald* reporter, Douglas Kennedy. After her divorce, she worked from 1962 to 1965 for the U.S. Travel Service at the American Embassy in London. In London, she enrolled in a creative writing course at the City Literary Institute, where she met the man who would become her second husband, psychotherapist Ian Marshall. Though their union was short-lived, she has said it helped her confront and overcome certain obstacles, chiefly her fear of failure, that were hindering her from trying to write ("Becoming a Writer" 252).

When she decided to separate from Marshall, Godwin returned to the United States and university life. From 1967 to 1971 she attended the University of Iowa, where she taught English while completing her M.A. and Ph.D. degrees. In the 1970s, she also taught at the University of Iowa, the University of Illinois, Vassar College, and Columbia University. She had meanwhile, between 1970 and 1978, published four novels and a collection of short fiction, her work supported in part by grants from the National Endowment for the Arts (1974–75) and the John Simon Guggenheim Memorial Foundation (1975–76). Between 1982 and 1991, she produced another collection of short fiction and four highly successful novels. She currently lives in Woodstock, New York.

On more than one occasion, Godwin has described how her family background and her upbringing influenced her to become an author. In her autobiographical essay, "Becoming a Writer" (1979), she remarks that in the "manless little family" her widowed grandmother "played mother," cooking, sewing, and cleaning, while my mother "played father; she was the provider" (232). Between 1941 and 1945, Kathleen Godwin, who had received her B.A. and M.A. degrees from the University of North Carolina at Chapel Hill, taught English at an Asheville college in the mornings; in the afternoons and evenings she worked as a newspaper reporter on the Asheville *Citizen*. On weekends, she sat at a typewriter in "a sunny breakfast nook" composing love stories for New York magazines ("Becoming a Writer" 231). Young Gail Godwin's observation of the contrast between her mother's and grandmother's occupations had a lasting effect on her. By age 5, she remarks, "I had allied myself with the typewriter rather than the stove"; by age 9, she had written her first story ("Becoming a Writer" 231, 236–37). After World War II, Godwin's mother married a veteran, Frank Cole, and the family moved to Virginia. Despite the birth of a child and pressing family duties, Kathleen Godwin Cole kept on writing, her efforts serving as inspiration for her daughter.

While a teenager, Godwin had produced a short novel; during college she rewrote and updated "The Otherwise Virgins," a novel her mother had written but, having failed to find a publisher, abandoned (neither work has been published). In London, while working for the U.S. Travel Service, Godwin completed a novel titled "Gull Key," the heroine of which—like heroines in Godwin's later writing—wonders if marriage and motherhood will suit her. Godwin sent the only copy of "Gull Key" to an agency that went out of business without returning the manuscript ("Becoming a Writer" 245).

Even a brief survey of Godwin's fiction against the background of her life reveals that her writing is, broadly speaking, autobiographical: Most of her novels and several of her short stories are grounded in elements of her own experience. From *The Perfectionists* (1970) through *Father Melancholy's Daughter* (1991), her long fiction centers on heroines who experience several of the situations she herself has experienced: difficult family relationships, failed marriages, life in foreign countries, graduate school and university teaching, successful careers (usually in writing or the arts). As she has remarked, the "figurative truths" of her second marriage, "if not the literal ones," lie behind *The Perfectionists*—a tale, set in London and Majorca, of young Dane Empson, whose brief, unhappy union with her psychotherapist husband inhibits her personal development ("Becoming a Writer" 251). In her second novel, *Glass People* (1972), Godwin explores the various ways in which marriage constrains the personal freedom of heroine Francesca Bolt. And in her third book, *The Odd Woman* (1974), she skillfully portrays the dilemma of university professor Jane Clifford—a single woman torn between the demands of her work and her commitment to her lover, who wonders if "there has ever existed in this world a lasting, lively love in which a man and woman exist, for years and years and years, . . . being able to do things better *because* of this love rather than in spite of it" (ch. 8).

Godwin's volumes of short fiction—*Dream Children* (1976) and *Mr. Bedford and the Muses* (1983)—are perhaps less patently autobiographical than her novels; *Dream Children* in particular, however, resembles the long fiction in developing feminist themes through such stories as "A Sorrowful Woman," a widely reprinted narrative containing elements of allegory that portrays the psychological deterioration of a wife and mother who feels trapped, restricted, and despairing. Godwin has also published numerous uncollected essays and short stories in magazines such as *Esquire, Harper's,* and *Ms.,* but her eight substantial novels constitute her major literary achievement.

If these novels up through *The Odd Woman* center on the complexities of a heroine's personal life, particularly those deriving from love or marriage, Godwin's later books explore, with considerable variety of treatment, an increasingly independent heroine's commitment to her work. In *Violet Clay* (1978), Godwin depicts a young artist who after a brief marriage leaves the South for New York City, where she supports herself for 9 years by doing illustrations for "Harrow House" romances. Violet's uncle, novelist Ambrose Clay, influences her profoundly; but the most important difficulties Violet confronts arise from her struggles to become a serious painter rather than from her relationship with a man. In *A Mother and Two Daughters* (1982), men play subordinate roles to the three women of the title—Nell Strickland and her daughters, Cate Galitsky and Lydia Mansfield. Twice married and divorced, Cate is a university professor living out the ideals of the Vietnam era and struggling to hold on to a college teaching post while resisting the temptation to remarry for security in case she does not succeed in retaining a job. Lydia, in youth a quintessential Southern belle and later an apparently happy socialite married to a successful physician, suddenly astounds her friends and family: She leaves her husband, takes a lover, enrolls in university classes, and eventually becomes the hostess of a highly successful television program, like her sister resisting the impulse to remarry. Nell, however, who has been widowed after an extremely satisfying marriage of 40 years, late in the novel marries the widower of one of her college friends and reexperiences the kind of passionate love she had thought was over.

The Finishing School (1985) represents a new direction in Godwin's fiction, one adumbrated by sequences near the end of *Violet Clay*. Late in that novel there emerges a thoroughly self-sufficient woman, Samantha or "Sam" De Vere, who functions as a model for Violet by demonstrating how a woman can attain success without dependence on a man. In *The Finishing School*, Godwin takes the situation of a young woman aided by a female guide and mentor much further, meanwhile fashioning an intriguing book into which she introduces elements of myth hitherto apparent chiefly in such short pieces as "Dream Children." For *The Finishing School*, as for *A Mother and Two Daughters*, Godwin develops more than one central female figure, the mysterious and alluring middle-aged Ursula De Vane and her young protégée, Justin Stokes, who eventually breaks with Ursula but, largely because of what she has learned from her mentor, in maturity becomes a successful actress.

In *A Southern Family* (1987), a long and intricate novel, Godwin traces and contrasts the lives and careers of Clare Campion and Julia Richardson Lowndes while constructing a complex story of the tragic relationships within the Ralph Quick family. As a vibrant, rebellious young widow, Clare's mother, Lily Campion, had shocked Mountain City, Godwin's fictionalized version of Asheville, and had fired the feminist ambitions of the youthful Clare and Julia. By marrying Ralph Quick, Lily has, however, sacrificed independence for security in a union that has become increasingly unhappy, a fact affecting Clare as well as her half-brothers, Theo and Rafe. Theo, a man in his late 20s with a small son, has recently separated from his wife, Snow, a shrewd, attractive young woman from Granny Squirrel Hollow in the Appalachian mountains.

Much of the book centers on the efforts of Clare, Julia, Lily, and Ralph to understand the reasons for Theo's sudden murder of his friend Jeanette and his subsequent suicide. Other sections of the novel depict Julia's ties to her widowed father; Clare's life as a successful writer; her happy relationship with her lover, composer Felix Rohr; Snow's surprisingly sensitive analyses of Theo; and Ralph Quick's satisfying friendship with elegant old Alicia Gallant. To a greater degree than in her earlier fiction, Godwin experiments with shifts among several points of view while weaving the narrative back and forth in time. The result is a long and complex book that is one of her most impressive works to date.

Narrated in the first person, *Father Melancholy's Daughter*, like other Godwin novels, explores the subject of a young woman's relationship with her parents as it influences her quest for individuality and independence. Affecting the situation of protagonist Margaret Gower is the mysterious conduct of her mother, who left the family in the company of another woman when Margaret was 6 and shortly afterward was killed. Further affecting Margaret are the problems of her father, Walter, the rector of St. Cuthbert's Episcopal Church, who suffers from bouts of depression. Set in North Carolina and Virginia, the novel alternates between flashbacks into Margaret's past and scenes of her relationships with her friend Harriet MacGruder and her mother's friend Madelyn Farley. *Father Melancholy's Daughter* is a long, ambitious novel that like *A Southern Family* explores the lasting effects that the personalities and behavior of parents have on the lives of their children.

MAJOR THEMES

Godwin's writing contains several recurring themes that derive, for the most part, from her situation as woman, author, and Southerner. As already indicated, she weaves transmuted versions of personal experience into increasingly sophisticated novels that portray the dilemmas of ambitious and talented women in late twentieth-century America, sometimes contrasting these problems with those faced by women of earlier generations. Her novels explore a series of concerns, notably the problem of the "unclear, undefined, unresolved self" of a woman needing the support and companionship of other people, particularly men, and the relationship among independence, love, marriage, and freedom (*The Odd Woman,* ch. 1). Inevitably, of course, these concerns intersect: Dane Empson and Francesca Bolt, the heroines of Godwin's first two novels, are married, but unhappily so. Jane Clifford of *The Odd Woman* has ostensibly come further than these women because she is single, highly educated, and self-supporting; but she veers between establishing herself in a career and subordinating her work to that of her lover, Gabriel Weeks. In Godwin's later novels, Cate Galitsky, Lydia Mansfield, and Julia Lowndes have each been married, but in the present time of a given book each woman is currently single, having abandoned the security of marriage to embark on a quest for herself that centers on finding a rewarding type of work. Analyzed as a group, Godwin's novels tell a single story, that of a heroine's ultimately successful quest for self-definition and a satisfying career with or without—and occasionally in spite of—the influence of husbands or lovers.

Particularly worthy of comment in a discussion of Godwin's major themes is the role of the South in her novels, whether it appears only briefly as a region from which the main characters flee and to which they occasionally return or whether it functions as a fully portrayed culture influencing the behavior and destinies of her most important figures. In her early novels, Godwin is more intent on exploring the problems faced by her protagonists than she is in elaborating upon Southern settings. The relative emphases she gives to her portrayal of her typical protagonist's dilemma and to the role of the South are apparently connected. As she moves in her later novels toward resolving the problem of her heroine's search for herself through her quest for a satisfactory career, she also moves from Southern settings that are only lightly or briefly sketched to fairly full examinations of Southern culture and its apparently perennial issues of family, race, and social class.

The South figures as a setting in each of Godwin's novels after *The Perfectionists,* which as noted takes place in London and Majorca. But in *Glass People, The Odd Woman, Violet Clay,* and *The Finishing School,* the region is presented chiefly in sections of the novels that are set in the past, and it therefore serves as a backdrop for the main action rather than as a significant influence on it. The protagonist in each of these novels lives outside the South, either because her family has moved or because work or marriage has taken her away. As a partial consequence, perhaps, the pictures of the South that appear in these books tend to be brief and lightly parodic. Justin Stokes's widowed mother in *The Finishing School* eventually weds an old suitor from South Carolina, who bears an honored surname in the state, that of Ravenel. And Violet Clay in the novel of the same title spends a summer in Charleston, a fact that enables Godwin to have some fun with old Charleston pedigrees, evoke the charm of historic St. Michael's Church and the St. Cecilia Ball, and invent supposedly distinctive regional names like that of the old "Fortescue-Clay House."

But in *A Mother and Two Daughters* and *A Southern Family,* the two books in which her protagonists exhibit perhaps the highest degree of satisfaction in their professional and personal lives, Godwin gives the South extended and thoughtful treatment. As a postmodern Southern author, she is not engaged in the kind of searching inquiry into the historical conditions of Southern civilization that precipitated the writing of the Renascence, and she has at best scant sympathy with the excesses of aristocratic customs; but she is undeniably concerned with the problems of the contemporary sunbelt South and with the effects wrought upon the region by time, change, industrialization, and supposed progress. With telling satire, she comments through Julia Lowndes on the triumph of democratic over patrician traditions in the South. On her way to see Clare on Quick's Hill, Julia reflects that the Castleberry estate, where as a child she had eaten "cold oatmeal out of a silver bowl . . . had been torn down, and its rolling pastures leveled and divided into one-acre housing tracts. Farther out, the Van Camps' vast meadowland, where their show horses used to romp and graze, had become a private golf course for a community of mansard-roofed dwellings called 'Townhouse Acres.' '' Observing the changes, her father tartly observes that "death would suit me better than living as a prisoner in one of those Shangri-las of tasteless uniformity'' (ch. 1).

One of the most interesting features of Godwin's fiction is her emphasis on the changes in several generations of Southern families—particularly as these changes bear upon the traditional separation between Southern social classes, as well as between Southerners of different races. Her novels portray the entire spectrum of social classes, represented by the aristocrats Neville Richardson, Anthony Gallant, and Alicia Gallant in *A Southern Family*; by members of the middle or upper-middle class such as Sonia Marks and Jane Clifford in *The Odd Woman*; and by women from the lower classes such as Wickie Lee Blount of *A Mother and Two Daughters* and Snow Mullins Quick, together with her mountain relatives, in *A Southern Family*. Increasingly in her fiction, Godwin is intent on showing the rejection or partial rejection of older aristocratic traditions by contemporary Southern women and men and their efforts, which meet with uneven success, to bridge the gap between the upper or middle and the lower classes.

In *A Mother and Two Daughters,* for example, Theodora Blount, the grande dame of the novel, befriends the pregnant mountain girl Wickie Lee, who turns out to be a distant relative of the Blount family and who eventually establishes herself financially by making exquisite little dolls, meanwhile contracting a successful marriage. In *A Southern Family,* patrician Alicia Gallant consoles and befriends Ralph Quick, a man with a trace of Cherokee Indian blood who is descended from a mountain family. The relationships between the middle-class South and Appalachia are explored at great length in the novel through Theo Quick's marriage to Snow and the tragedy of his subsequent suicide, which brings the Quick and Mullins families into contact. This fact enables Godwin, through Clare and Julia, to describe the ravages in the mountain landscape caused by deforestation and incessant mining and the even worse condition of the people, whose dwellings have piles of debris rising higher than the houses—"visible and tangible evidence," Julia thinks, "of a cluster of attitudes that, if shared by enough people, could bring down civilization: apathy, blindness to beauty, a refusal to be responsible even for your immediate surroundings" (ch. 9).

Particularly noteworthy in Godwin's fiction of the 1980s is her description of racial tensions and interracial friendships in the contemporary South, especially North Carolina. Near the end of *A Mother and Two Daughters,* the Ku Klux Klan appears in Greensboro, and the life of black television producer Calvin Edwards is threatened by the Klan in Winston-Salem. These and other incidents prompt one of the most interesting characters in the novel, Lydia's friend and professor Renee Peverell-Watson—who is descended from a slaveholder and a slave—to enroll in law school in order to train herself to combat the growth of racial injustice and prejudice in the state. In an attempt to show that younger Southerners are cutting through traditional racial boundaries, Godwin emphasizes the close bond between Lydia and Renee and the even closer ties between Lydia's son Leo and Renee's daughter Camille, an accomplished young woman educated in England. By the end of the novel, Godwin has Leo and Camille marry in an action that is obviously designed to symbolize the rapprochement of enlightened people of each race.

Whether South Carolina, North Carolina, Virginia, Georgia, or Maryland, the South that Godwin depicts in her fiction is still a recognizable and distinctive American region, a mixture of rural areas and medium-sized cities flavored with an Appalachian as well as an agrarian heritage. But it is also a part of mainstream American culture, and its inhabitants, like other Americans, must struggle with the problems that historically have been caused by the divisions of race and social class.

SURVEY OF CRITICISM

Gail Godwin's books have been widely and favorably reviewed since her first novel, *The Perfectionists.* During the 1970s, the main commentaries on her writing appeared in magazines such as the *Saturday Review* or in such newspapers as the *Chicago Daily News* and the *Philadelphia Inquirer,* with reviewers typically praising her wit and compassion, the intelligence of her character studies, and her narrative skill. By 1980, her writing had begun to attract the attention of academic critics, and from that time forward it has been the subject of critical essays, essay-reviews, and chapters in books.

Much of the scholarship on Godwin explores feminist concerns or, more broadly, the particular problems faced by women in her fiction—a fact that is not surprising, given her tendency to center on the situation of women in contemporary life. Among important studies of individual Godwin novels are Susan E. Lorsch, "Gail Godwin's *The Odd Woman*: Literature and the Retreat from Life," which holds that protagonist Jane Clifford inhibits her own development through her habit of viewing life through the lenses of literature, and Joanne S. Frye, "Narrating the Self: The Autonomous Heroine in Gail Godwin's *Violet Clay*," which examines the function of narrative design as Violet creates and establishes herself through her increasingly independent actions.

Recent studies that treat several novels include John Alexander Allen, "Researching Her Salvation: The Fiction of Gail Godwin"—which, though centering on *A Southern Family*, devotes some time to *The Finishing School* and *The Odd Woman*—and Mary Ann Wimsatt, "Gail Godwin's Evolving Heroine: The Search for Self," which traces the development of the protagonists in Godwin's long fiction from dependence to autonomy and self-esteem. The role of the South in Godwin's work is the subject of "Gail Godwin and the Ideal of Southern Womanhood," in which Carolyn Rhodes explores the influence of the region on Godwin's characters, and of Joyce Dyer's review-essay of *A Southern Family*, which stresses Godwin's treatment of Appalachian mountain characters. A useful biographical and critical survey, now somewhat out of date, is Carl Solana Week's essay on Godwin for *American Novelists since World War II* in the *Dictionary of Literary Biography* series. Godwin herself has written perceptively about her own writing and her creative processes in "Towards a Fully Human Heroine: Some Worknotes," "Becoming a Writer," and "Keeping Track."

BIBLIOGRAPHY

Works by Gail Godwin

The Perfectionists. New York: Harper and Row, 1970.

Glass People. New York: Knopf, 1972.

"Towards a Fully Human Heroine: Some Worknotes." *Harvard Advocate* 106 (Winter 1973): 26–28.

The Odd Woman. New York: Knopf, 1974.

Dream Children. New York: Knopf, 1976.

Violet Clay. New York: Knopf, 1978.

"Becoming a Writer." 231–55 in *The Writer on Her Work*, ed. Janet Sternburg. New York: W. W. Norton, 1980. (An expanded version of the essay "A Writing Woman," *Atlantic Monthly* 244 [October 1979]: 84–92.)

"Keeping Track," 75–85 in *Ariadne's Thread: A Collection of Contemporary Women's Journals,* ed. Lyn Lifshin. New York: Harper and Row, 1982.
A Mother and Two Daughters. New York: Viking, 1982.
Mr. Bedford and the Muses. New York: Viking, 1983.
The Finishing School. New York: Viking, 1985.
A Southern Family. New York: William Morrow, 1987.
Father Melancholy's Daughter. New York: William Morrow, 1991.

Studies of Gail Godwin

Allen, John Alexander. "Researching Her Salvation: The Fiction of Gail Godwin." *Hollins Critic* 25 (April 1988): 1–9.
Cheney, Anne. "A Hut and Three Houses: Gail Godwin, Carl Jung, and *The Finishing School.*" *Southern Literary Journal* 22 (Spring 1989): 64–71.
Dyer, Joyce. Review-essay of *A Southern Family. Appalachian Journal* 15 (Summer 1988): 382–86.
Frye, Joanne S. "Narrating the Self: The Autonomous Heroine in Gail Godwin's *Violet Clay.*" *Contemporary Literature* 24 (Spring 1983): 66–85.
Gaston, Karen C. " 'Beauty and the Beast' in Gail Godwin's *Glass People.*" *Critique: Studies in Modern Fiction* 21 (1980): 94–102.
[Henderson, Katherine Usher]. "Gail Godwin," in *Inter/View: Talks with America's Writing Women.* Lexington: University Press of Kentucky, 1990.
Lorsch, Susan E. "Gail Godwin's *The Odd Woman*: Literature and the Retreat from Life." *Critique: Studies in Modern Fiction* 20 (1978): 21–32.
Mickelson, Anne Z. "Gail Godwin: Order and Accommodation," ch. 4 in *Reaching Out: Sensitivity and Order in Recent American Fiction by Women.* Metuchen, N.J.: Scarecrow Press, 1979.
Rhodes, Carolyn. "Gail Godwin and the Ideal of Southern Womanhood," in *Women Writers of the Contemporary South,* ed. Peggy Whitman Prenshaw. Jackson: University Press of Mississippi, 1984.
Rogers, Kim Lacy. "A Mother's Story in a Daughter's Life: Gail Godwin's *A Southern Family,*" in *Mother Puzzles: Daughters and Mothers in Contemporary American Literature,* ed. Mickey Pearlman. New York and Westport, Conn.: Greenwood Press, 1989.
Seidel, Kathryn Lee, "Ellen Glasgow and Gail Godwin: Southern Mothers and Daughters," *Tulsa Studies in Woman's Literature* 10 (Fall 1991): 287–94.
Smith, Marilynn J. "The Role of the South in the Novels of Gail Godwin." *Critique: Studies in Modern Fiction* 21 (1980): 103–10.
Weeks, Carl Solana. "Gail Godwin (18 June 1937–)," 105–9 in *American Novelists since World War II,* Second Series, ed. James E. Kibler, Jr., *Dictionary of Literary Biography,* Vol. 6. Detroit: Gale Research, 1980.
Welch, Kathleen. "An Interview with Gail Godwin." *Iowa Journal of Literary Studies* 3 (1981): 77–86.
Wimsatt, Mary Ann. "Gail Godwin's Evolving Heroine: The Search for Self." *Mississippi Quarterly* 42 (Winter 1988–89): 27–45.

MARY KEMP DAVIS

Alex [Murray Palmer] Haley
(1921–1992)

After a long, arduous evolution from "the cook who writes" to a best-selling, Pulitzer prize-winning author, Alex Haley became a literary and cultural phenomenon. His first best-seller captured the simmering discontent of oppressed and marginalized African-Americans; his second tapped the yearning for personal and cultural identity in people of all races and ethnicities. Despite his staggering success, Alex Haley is also somewhat of a conundrum, viewed by turns as a keeper of the dream and its prisoner.

BIOGRAPHY

Called "Palmer" by his family and associates in Henning, Tennessee, where he spent much of his childhood and youth, Alex Murray Palmer Haley was born August 11, 1921, in Ithaca, New York. At his birth, his father, Simon Alexander Haley, and his mother, Bertha George Palmer Haley, were attending graduate school at Cornell University and the Ithaca Conservatory of Music, respectively. Six weeks after his birth, Haley's parents transported him to his maternal grandmother's home in Henning, Tennessee, where he and his mother remained for a time while his father finished his master's degree in agriculture at Cornell. Haley grew up enveloped in the love of a large family. His maternal grandfather, Will E. Palmer, doted on him as the son he never had until he died when Haley was nearly five. Thereafter, his maternal grandmother, Cynthia Murray Palmer, cemented the bonds between himself and his aunts and cousins by inviting them to spend summers at her home.

Although Haley briefly attended two colleges, Alcorn A. and M. College in Mississippi (1937) and Elizabeth City State Teachers College in North Carolina (1937–39), neither of these institutions contributed to his development as a writer as much as his exposure to family storytellers and his stint in the U.S. Coast

Guard (1939–59). As a child, Haley listened to women storytellers reminiscent of Zora Neale Hurston's porch-sitters: his maternal grandmother, his aunts, and other female relatives. Decades later, their stories about their ancestors would spark his desire to search for his "furthest-back person, the African," culminating in *Roots* (1976). On the surface, Haley's early years as a messboy in the Coast Guard would not seem to be the proper preparation for a career as a writer, but soon after his enlistment in 1939, he found himself frantically writing letters to stave off boredom. His shipmates were so envious of the stacks of replies that he received that they soon hired him to write letters for them, especially love letters. At this point, another childhood influence merged with his new role as ghost-writer. Throughout elementary and high school, Haley had been addicted to reading, made all the easier because his maternal grandmother had a well-stocked library in her home. His favorite books were adventure stories; and since being at sea was filled with wonder, he eventually began writing sea adventure stories. His earliest forays into creative writing were doubly adventuresome, for, initially, he tried his hand at writing women's confession stories in a female persona.

During his eight-year apprenticeship as a writer, Haley submitted work to such magazines as *Modern Romances* and *True Confessions* before he sold his first story (circa. 1948–49) to *This Week* magazine, a Sunday newspaper supplement. This piece about the Coast Guard was severely edited, even to the assigned title it bore: "They Drive You Crazy." Several years later while he was working in public relations for the Coast Guard, he met a writer named Glenn Kittler who subsequently referred him to the editor of *Coronet*, Bernie Glaser. After he learned that Glaser was interested in 600-word historical vignettes, Haley submitted four and was shocked when Glaser accepted three. Over the next three years, he wrote thirty or more of these, usually under other names. By the time he retired from the Coast Guard in 1959, having become its chief journalist in charge of public relations, he had published perhaps one hundred sea stories and research-based articles. He published primarily in men's adventure magazines and in *Coronet*, although some of his work appeared in *Reader's Digest*, *Harper's*, the *Atlantic Monthly*, and several other major magazines.

After his retirement from the Coast Guard in 1959, Haley eventually migrated to Greenwich Village in New York, simply because that was what he thought writers did. He promptly became a "starving artist" until in 1962 the editors of *Playboy* magazine launched an interview series for which Haley introduced the basic format. His first assignment was to interview the jazz trumpeter Miles Davis. In the ensuing years, Haley would interview several famous people, including Phyllis Diller, Johnny Carson, George Lincoln Rockwell (the American Nazi Party Leader), Malcolm X, and Dr. Martin Luther King, Jr.

Haley would again interview Malcolm X after the latter asked him to collaborate with him on a book about his life. Haley spent most of 1963 interviewing Malcolm X and finished the work some time in 1964, a mere two weeks before he was assassinated. *The Autobiography of Malcolm X* (1965) traces the personal and political evolution of Malcolm Little to Malcolm X, spokesman and then penetrating critic of the Nation of Islam. The book would sell tens of thousands of copies in hardcover and about six million copies in paperback in a little over a decade; Haley has said that he thinks that the writing in *The Autobiography* is superior to that in his blockbuster *Roots*. Clearly, this early book brought him instant fame. Besieged with more freelance offers than he could accept, Haley estimated that his lectures and articles would have brought him at least $100,000 a year if he had not become so absorbed with a new project.

Two months after he completed *The Autobiography of Malcolm X* in 1964, Haley decided to try to retrieve some of his own family's history after he saw a reference to his great-grandfather, the North Carolinian Tom Murray, in the genealogical records of the National Archives in Washington, D.C. Seeing the mysterious Rosetta Stone in the British Museum later that year steeled his resolve.

In a 1977 article in *Ebony*, Hans J. Massaquoi has vividly characterized the progress and outcome of Haley's heroic quest:

Haley permitted himself to be gripped by an obsession to trace his ancestral roots from his grandmother's front porch along the bloody trail of slavery across the Atlantic Ocean to their African origins. It was an obsession that would not let go of him for 12 years until it had driven him more than a half-million miles across land and sea, frequently to the very limits of his physical and mental endurance; until it had dragged him to the lowest depth of despair, indeed, to the very brink of suicide. (38)

With the publication of *Roots: The Saga of an American Family* (1976), Haley reached the zenith of his writing career. Doubleday published a record 200,000 hardcover copies of the book, only to have them sold out in a matter of weeks. By 1987, the book had sold at least seven million copies in hardcover alone, and it had been translated into upwards of thirty languages. Book sales were only the beginning of the *Roots* phenomenon. In the next two years, Haley reportedly won 217 prizes, the Pulitzer among them. Moreover, in a departure from network tradition, ABC-television began filming a seven-part miniseries based on *Roots* even before the book's publication date (October 1, 1976). Beginning on January 23, 1977 and ending on January 31, the series attracted an estimated 130 million viewers, with an estimated 85 percent of people owning televisions watching at least some of the episodes. Two years later, a seven-part sequel entitled *Roots: The Next Generation* aired on February 18, 1979 and ended on February 25. Two hours longer than *Roots I* and costing almost three times as much to produce, the sequel brought the story forward, from 1882 to 1967. The book and the films were problematic for some, but they were widely used as pedagogical tools. There are also the less quantifiable results. *Roots* intensified family pride and spurred Americans of all races and ethnic groups to search for their own family origins. In the months after *Roots I* aired, Americans jammed archives and genealogical libraries. In fact, at least one viewer, Dorothy

Spruill Redford, a descendant of a North Carolina slave family, was inspired to research her family history and, like Haley, record it in book form (*Somerset Homecoming: Recovering a Lost Heritage*, 1988).

Despite its enviable sales, *Roots* was not without its problems. First was the question of its genre. Just what was *Roots*? The Library of Congress classified it as Afro-American genealogy; Haley called it "faction" (a combination of documented fact and fiction); and still others have called it a "historical romance" or "historical novel," a "slave novel," a "modern epic," a "family chronicle," and simply a "best-selling novel." Its quasi-historical status caused the National Book Awards judges to balk when Doubleday offered it for competition in the history category. The committee eventually gave it a special nonclassified citation, as did the Pulitzer Prize committee. In retrospect, however, these proved minor problems. In March 1977, for instance, Haley had been made an honorary Gambian, but in April, the British journalist, Mark Ottoway, in a highly publicized article in the London *Sunday Times* (April 10, 1977), endeavored to prove "that the factual core of the Kunta Kinte story" was "more tenuous than anyone had thought." He insisted that "British colonial records" and "Lloyd's shipping records" failed to corroborate Haley's assertion that he had found his African ancestor, Kunta Kinte. In fact, he asserted, Haley's principal African informant, the *griot* Kebba Fofana, was "a man of notorious unreliability" and "not a griot at all" (17).

Moreover, two well-known writers sued Haley for plagiarism in the two years after *Roots'* publication. First, Margaret Walker Alexander claimed that Haley had plagiarized her 1966 novel, *Jubilee*, in a case that was dismissed but that reportedly cost Haley $100,000 in legal fees. Then, the noted folklorist Harold Courlander charged that Haley had plagiarized his third novel, *The African* (1967), as well. In a lengthy article in the *Village Voice*, Courlander maintained that "More than 80 passages in *Roots*" came from his novel, "often verbatim or nearly verbatim" (34). After a five-week trial that began on November 6, 1978, Haley settled out of court, reportedly for a half-million dollars.

Negative publicity did not derail Haley's career. In 1979, Haley collaborated with Norman Lear on a television miniseries called *Palmertown, USA*, based on Haley's memories of his childhood in the segregated South. Focusing on the experiences of two nine-year-old boys, one white and the other black, this series began on March 20, 1980 and ran for seven weeks. In 1988, Haley published a ninety-six-page novella, or what he calls a "tale," entitled *A Different Kind of Christmas*. Set in 1855, the book concerns the North Carolinian Fletcher Randall who enrolls at the College of New Jersey, converts to abolitionism, becomes an agent of the Underground Railroad, and helps a group of slaves (some are his own father's) to escape on Christmas Eve. Haley has also published two excerpts from *Henning*, a book forthcoming for some time, entitled "Home to Henning" (1983) and "Easter in Henning" (1985).

Married twice, estranged from his third wife, and the father of three children, Haley has seen his personal life take some bizarre twists. His relationship with

Juffure (his ancestral home in West Africa) soured somewhat during the 1980s—
long after this village, basking in his fame, had been declared a national mon-
ument in the 1970s. Nevertheless, Haley has proved that he *can* go home again,
at least to his *Southern* home. The state of Tennessee purchased his grandparents'
home in Henning for a nominal one dollar and made it into the Alex Haley
House Museum. In addition, he sent down new roots when he bought and restored
a 120-acre, antebellum farm in Norris, Tennessee. He lived on this site until he
died of a heart attack on February 10, 1992, in Seattle, Washington, while on
a speaking tour. He was 70 years old.

MAJOR THEMES

Roots—Alex Haley's story of his family's African origins, descent into slavery
and ascent into freedom and prosperity—can here be described only in its broad
outlines. Two comments on *Roots* are worth quoting in detail because they
underscore what *Roots* is not. Michael Arlen posits in "The Prisoner of the
Golden Dream" that the power of *Roots* comes from fantasy, "family fantasies,
those 'remembrances' of a golden past or golden youth that most of us have
dreamed . . . and still dream . . . when we feel too naked or alone in the world
to deal with cold reality" (119). In this fantasy, we retreat to "the golden summer
of long ago in which everyone's ancestors were, at least briefly, wise, noble,
and benign." He calls it "the fantasy or dream of Going Home" (119–20), and
he chides Haley for "his apparent willingness to leave the fantasies intact and
unchallenged" (124). Taking another tack, David Herbert Donald argues that
Haley was "uncomfortable" writing about a family of "mixed blood who accepted, emulated, and excelled in the white American world." Rather, Haley
"prefer[red] the story of his legendary, almost mythical African ancestors to the
fully documented history of his family since the Civil War." The "real story,"
the one Haley did not tell, is "a typically American success story" (74).

Both of these are alluring interpretations; however, they not only oversimplify
the book, but they ignore Haley's expressed aims and the internal evidence of
the book itself. *Roots* is many texts to many readers, but the best way to understand why the book is not an archetypal American success story, much less
a mere fantasy of a golden dream, is to unravel the mystery of Haley's abrupt
shift from third-person omniscient to first-person point of view in the final two
chapters of the book, a shift that reminds us that the story that he has been telling
us all along is *his* story, that he is one page in a "book" that each member of
his family has been writing generation after generation.

Yet this is only a part of it. *Roots* is not, as Haley once told his publishers,
"the story of a family" in the first place; it is the "saga of a people" "passed
down in this oral history way" ("Black History" 20). The tellers, the telling,
and the tale are one in *Roots*; hence Haley's obsession with the Rosetta Stone
whose three sides (or "mouths") tell one tale. Given the personal and the
collective, the literal and the symbolic "history" that he seeks to convey, Haley

did not and could not rest with a tale of the expulsion from Eden or with an archetypal success story. Haley says that he wept when he heard an African *griot* recount Kunta Kinte's disappearance. In his moment of supreme triumph he wept because he remembered from whence he came and under what tragic circumstances all the Kunta Kintes came to America. Joy would come in the morning, but "first you had to weep," he observes ("Black History" 19). *Roots* begins and ends in the sunlight, but there is a long shadow on his lawn.

Haley's *A Different Kind of Christmas* is a didactic bildungsroman, ostensibly for all ages but seemingly more appropriate for young readers. In it, the North Carolinian Fletcher Randall, age 19 at the outset and reaching his twentieth birthday during the nine-month (gestational) period which the tale covers, matures morally and makes "an irrevocable break with his past" (101). Notwithstanding its narrative simplicity, the plot is quintessentially American in its reinscription of the optimistic Adamic myth so clearly defined by R.W.B. Lewis in his classic study *The American Adam*. Thematically, this tale can also be contrasted with William Faulkner's "Barn Burning," a story that endorses American individualism but in a most conservative way. In betraying his father, ten-year-old Colonel Sartoris Snopes, a member of the poor-white class, aligns himself with the morality of the dominant class. Conversely, the aristocratic Fletcher Randall, son of a senator and sole heir to his father's vast slave plantation, comes to see the utter moral bankruptcy of the Southern slavocracy. He makes war upon the society by helping several slaves (including six of his father's) to escape and then flees to Philadelphia, the City of Brotherly Love, a place that was pivotal in his moral conversion to abolitionism. Having rejected his family, his society, and his past, Fletcher begins anew, perfectly illustrating Lewis' "party of Hope."

More important, the tale fits squarely into the abolitionist, protest, and the trickster traditions in African-American literature. Fletcher Randall's moral conversion, though more extreme, is like Listwell's in Frederick Douglass's "The Heroic Slave." In fact, a letter written by Douglass helps to convert Fletcher. Furthermore, the novella uses a satiric plot device that allows Haley to "signify upon" antebellum Christmas rituals. Fletcher Randall plans "a different kind of Christmas," a huge Southern barbecue, as a cover for the slaves' escape attempt on Christmas Eve. Traditionally, of course, many slaveholders gave the slaves gifts of food, clothing, and money when they assembled on Christmas Day and shouted, "Christmas gift!" Haley constructs his plot so that even as the whites force the slaves to provide food and entertainment for their party, several wily slaves are preparing to give themselves an ever greater gift, the gift of freedom.

SURVEY OF CRITICISM

The bulk of the criticism of Haley's work has been devoted to *Roots*. Haley's most recent book, *A Different Kind of Christmas*, attracted only a few brief notices, and some of these were unkind. One reviewer called it a "transparent" and "heavy-handed story," which, though "[s]implistic and baldly didactic," was still "a painless, sometimes colorful history lesson for the kids" (*Kirkus* 1423). A sampling of the more positive reviews and criticism of *The Autobiography* can be found in *Contemporary Literary Criticism* (12:243–46).

Roots was widely reviewed and was the subject of numerous critical essays. Many reviewers tried to place the book in a broad context so that readers could properly appreciate Haley's signal achievement—or lack of it. For example, David Herbert Donald linked *Roots* to Herbert G. Gutman's revisionist history *The Black Family in Slavery and Freedom*, also published in 1976. He said that *Roots*, like Gutman's book, "reminds us how even in appallingly adverse circumstances blacks often maintained, through oral traditions, a full account of their lineage and proper sense of their individual identities" (70). Carole Meritt and Adam David Miller saw an ideological significance in the book akin to Haley's own. Meritt noted that *Roots* "may be regarded as the first serious challenge to existing popular mythology on the black man's past—that blacks are without a past, without a culture of their own and therefore, an inferior and unworthy people" (211).

It was clear from *Newsweek*'s cover story on July 4, 1977 ("Everybody's Search for *Roots*") that a primary source of *Roots*' astounding popularity was its concern with identity and ancestral origins. This view was implicit in the assertion by Donald MacRae, a British reviewer, that the book gave blacks what all Americans yearn for, "a pedigree" (39). However, the Nigerian Dallible Onyeama attacked the book on just this score, saying that "black Africans . . . [would] question the sanity of any man who feels that his ancestral origins [were] of such significance as to warrant a twelve-year and half-a-million mile search. The inevitable reaction of any such African (I am one) to the resulting book would be . . . *so* what?" (23).

Reviewers held widely different opinions about the value of particular sections of the book. The African section received high praise from James Baldwin, Carole Meritt, Larry King, and R. Z. Sheppard, whereas Russell Warren Howe felt the American sections were "by far the best and the most convincing" (23). Adam David Miller and Carole Meritt were diametrically opposed in their assessment of Haley's treatment of African survivals. Miller praised Haley for challenging the view that Africans "brought nothing of cultural value with them" and "created nothing" after they arrived, and Meritt criticized Haley for making *his* family alone the bearers of the "weightier matters of culture" (212).

From a technical standpoint few reviewers were as extravagant as L. D. Reddick, who called Haley "a superb storyteller" and the book "a literary masterpiece" (253). Most were quite aware of the book's flaws, whether these were its "workmanlike prose" (Donald MacRae, 39), its shift in point of view in the last two chapters (Chester J. Fontenot, 99), its hackneyed treatment of slavery (Larry L. King, 20), or—rarely mentioned in these reviews—its sexiest de-centering of women (Dale Norton, xliv–vi). On the other hand, few panned the book as unequivocally as the Nigerian Dallible Onyeama, who called it "the worst slave novel" he had ever read and who poked fun at its style. Arnold Rampersad's review was also generally negative. He said that the book was "so innocent of fictive ingenuity that it seldom surpasse[d] the standards of the most popular historical romances" (24). Neither David Herbert Donald (73) nor R. Z. Sheppard (109+) felt that Haley had mastered the art of historical fiction, and Jervis Anderson found it jarring to be bounced back and forth between history and fiction (121).

The review-essays and critical essays on *Roots* extend some of the approaches above, add new ones, and subject the book to closer scrutiny. For example, whereas Micheal G. Cooke had explored briefly the four types of "magic" underlying *Roots'* astounding popularity (i.e., "the magic of placebo," "approximation," "sentimentality," and "the misplaced genre"), the historian David A. Gerber dissected *Roots'* appeal in its daunting complexity. And whereas Russell Warren Howe and David Herbert Donald had mentioned briefly the numerous factual errors in Haley's West African and American history, respectively, Elizabeth Shown Mills, Gary B. Mills, Donald Wright, and Harold Courlander challenged *Roots'* historicity in excruciating detail. Indeed, as Richard N. Current has so dryly observed, "Little seems to be left of Haley's family history after these critics [not including Howe and Courlander, who are not covered in Current's article] have disposed of it" (85).

In his brief review mentioned earlier, Howe argued that *Roots'* "central flaw" was that Kunta Kinte's rage was quite uncharacteristic of Africans of his time (24). Harold Courlander pushed this argument even further, saying that Kunta was "un-African . . . most of the time," but especially in Haley's depiction of him as "a primitive being" (295). Consistent with these attacks was Donald R. Wright's effort to "uproot" Kunta Kinte by giving "a critique of Haley's field-work" and "methodology" and by exploring the "problems associated with so-called encyclopedic informants" (206). In effect, Wright tried to "demolish" Haley's claim that he had "identified a specific African ancestor" (214). It was left to Gary B. Mills and Elizabeth Shown Mills, the former a historian and the latter a certified genealogist, to "pick poor Robin clean" (to adapt a phrase from Ralph Ellison). Of the two articles the two published in 1981 and 1984, the earlier one is more valuable because it relies heavily on documentary evidence (plantation and census records, wills, and assorted "county, state, and federal records" [5–6, 15]) to contradict many of Haley's lineage statements and other details in his family history. Most provocative is their contention that it is not possible to connect an African slave arriving on the *Lord Ligonier* in 1767 to a Waller slave named Toby because Toby had been in the Waller family for several years previous (9).

A less-formalized interest in history appears in the essays by Ali R. Mazrui, Sanford Pinsker, and Jane Campbell. Mazri contrasted the "enforced amnesia" of African-Americans with the "political amnesia" of whites who partially severed their connection to the past in becoming denizens of the "*New* World"

(9–10). He also discussed the symbolism of the amputation of Kunta Kinte's foot and showed how the book develops the theme of escape on several levels. Pinsker and Campbell had different perceptions of Haley's stance toward history. Pinsker noted that Haley, restricted by a "hackneyed vision" and "wooden style," felt compelled to authenticate "his spiritual kinship with Kunta Kinte." He contrasted Haley with Toni Morrison, who in *The Song of Solomon* (1977) transcended verifiable truths, gave flight to her own creative imagination, and validated this impulse in her characters. Campbell, on the other hand, contended that far from being tied to the facts of history, Haley "successfully fuse[d] the real and the romantic" in his portraits of his ancestors (122).

Except for the essays by Judith Mudd and Michael Steward Blayney, the remaining authors subject *Roots* to a close textual analysis. Whereas Mudd related her own reactions to the book and those of two East Indians whom she interviewed, Blayney saw the book as a reconfiguration of the "noble savage" myth prevalent in American literature and popular culture. The last three essays overlap. Helen Chavis Othow showed the similarities between *Roots*, "a modern epic" (312), and several classical and modern representatives of the genre. Essays by R. Baxter Miller and Carol Marsh especially complement each other. Miller showed the numerous ways in which Haley appropriated the Graeco-Roman, Haphaetus-Vulcan myth. Marsh revealed that Haley, like the ancient Hebrews and Greeks, not only used such plastic arts as carving, weaving, and blacksmithing to develop the "theme of returning," but that he also equated these arts with "the essence of life itself" (325).

BIBLIOGRAPHY

Works by Alex [Murray Palmer] Haley

The Autobiography of Malcolm X. New York: Grove, 1965.
"My Furthest-Back Person—'The African.' " *New York Times Magazine* (July 16, 1972): 12–16.
"Black History, Oral History, and Genealogy." *Oral History Review*. New York: Oral History Association, 1973, pp. 1–25.
"My Search for Roots: A Black Man's Story." *Reader's Digest* (May 1974): 73–78.
Roots. Reader's Digest (May 1974): 79–84; 227–62; (June 1974): 233–63. [Condensed version].
Roots: The Saga of an American Family. Garden City, N.Y.: Doubleday, 1976.
"*The Black Scholar* Interviews: Alex Haley." With Robert L. Allen. *Black Scholar* 8, 1 (1976): 33–40.
"A Talk with Alex Haley." With Mel Watkins. *New York Times Book Review*. (September 26, 1976): 2, 10, 12.
"Foreword." *From Freedom to Freedom: African Roots in American Soil; Selected Readings Based on Roots: The Saga of an American Family*. Ed. Mildred Bain and Ervin Lewis. Milwaukee, Wisc.: Purnell Reference Books, 1977, pp. xiii–xvii.

"What Roots Mean to Me." *Reader's Digest* 110 (May 1977): 73–76.
"An Interview with Alex Haley." With Willard S. McGuire and Marian S. Clayton. *Today's Education* 66 (Sept.–Oct. 1977): 46–47.
"Alex Haley Talks to Jeffrey Elliot." With Jeffrey Elliot. *Negro History Bulletin* 41 (1978): 782–85.
"The Roots of Alex Haley's Writing Career." With Jeffrey Elliot. *Writer's Digest* 60 (1980): 20–27; 47, 53.
"Home to Henning." *Reader's Digest* (May 1983): 81–90.
"Easter in Henning." *Reader's Digest* (April 1985): 194–98, 202–3, 206–18.
Introduction. *Somerset Homecoming: Recovering a Lost Heritage.* By Dorothy Spruill Redford, with Michael D'Orso. New York: Doubleday, 1988, pp. xiii–xviii.
A Different Kind of Christmas. New York: Doubleday, 1988.

Studies of Alex [Murray Palmer] Haley

"Alex Haley." *Contemporary Literary Criticism.* Ed. Derdria Bryfonski and Gerald J. Senick. Detroit: Gale Research Co., 12: 243–56.
Anderson, Jervis. Rev. of *Roots*, by Alex Haley. *New Yorker* (February 14, 1977): 112–22.
Arlen, Michael J. "The Prisoner of the Golden Dream." *New Yorker* (March 26, 1979): 115–20, 123–25.
Baldwin, James. "How One Black Man Came to Be an American." Rev. of *Roots*, by Alex Haley. *New York Times Book Review* (September 26, 1976): 1–2.
Blayney, Michael Steward. "*Roots* and the Noble Savage." *North Dakota Quarterly* 54 (1986): 1–17.
Campbell, Jane. "The Passage Back." *Mythic Black Fiction: The Transformation of History.* Knoxville: University of Tennessee Press, 1986, pp. 120–35.
Cooke, Michael G. "*Roots* as Placebo." Rev. of *Roots*, by Alex Haley. *Yale Review* 67 (1977): 144–46.
Courlander, Harold. " 'Roots,' 'The African,' and the Whiskey Jug Case." *Village Voice* (April 9, 1979): 33–35; 84–86.
———. "Kunta Kinte's Struggle to Be African." *Phylon* 47 (1986): 294–302.
Current, Richard N. "Fiction as History: A Review Essay." *Journal of Southern History* 52 (1986): 77–90.
Donald, David Herbert. "Family Chronicle." Rev. of *Roots*, by Alex Haley. *Commentary* 62 (1976): 70–74.
"Everybody's Search for Roots." *Newsweek* (July 4, 1977): 26–38.
Fontenot, Chester J. "Radical Upbringing." Rev. of *Roots*, by Alex Haley. *Prairie Schooner* 51 (1977): 98–99.
Gerber, David. "Haley's *Roots* and Our Own: An Inquiry into the Nature of Popular Phenomenon." Rev. of *Roots* by Alex Haley. *Journal of Ethnic Studies* 5 (1977): 87–111.
"Haley Looks to Appalachia." *News and Observer* [Raleigh, N.C.] (April 20, 1990): 2D.
Howe, Russell Warren. "An Elusive Past." Rev. of *Roots*, by Alex Haley. *New Leader* (January 3, 1977): 23–24.
Johnson, Abby Arthur. "The Big Old World of Harold Courlander." *Midwest Quarterly* 25 (1984): 450–70.

Kern-Foxworth, Marilyn. "Alex Haley." *Dictionary of Biography*. Ed. Thadious M. Davis and Trudier Harris. Detroit: Gale Research Co., 1985, 115–19.

King, Larry L. "From the Seed of Kunta Kinte." Rev. of *Roots*, by Alex Haley. *Saturday Review* (September 18, 1976): 20–22.

MacRae, Donald. "Quest for an African Genesis." Rev. of *Roots*, by Alex Haley. *The Sunday Times* [London] (April 17, 1977): 39.

Marsh, Carol P. "The Plastic Arts Motif in *Roots*." *CLA Journal* 26 (March 1983): 325–33.

Massaquoi, Hans J. "Alex Haley in Juffure." *Ebony* (July 1977): 31 + .

———. "Alex Haley: The Man Behind *Roots*." *Ebony* (April 1977): 33–41.

Mazrui, Ali R. "*Roots*: The End of America's Amnesia?" *Africa Report* 22 (May–June 1977): 6–11.

Meritt, Carole. "Looking at Afro-American Roots." Rev. of *Roots*, by Alex Haley. *Phylon* 38 (1977): 211–12.

Miller, Adam David. Rev. of *Roots*, by Alex Haley. *Black Scholar* 8 (1977): 50–51.

Miller, R. Baxter. "Kneeling at the Fireplace: Black Vulcan *Roots* and the Double Artificer." *MELUS* 9 (Spring 1982): 73–84.

Mills, Elizabeth Shown, and Gary B. Mills. "The Genealogist's Assessment of Alex Haley's *Roots*." *National Genealogical Society Quarterly* 72 (1984): 34–49.

Mills, Gary B., and Elizabeth Shown. "*Roots* and the New 'Faction': A Legitimate Tool for Clio?" *Virginia Magazine of History and Biography* 89 (1981): 3–26.

Mudd, Judith. "Returning a Theft of Identity: This Is Also Me; Two Indian Views of *Roots*." *Indian Journal of American Studies* 10 (July 1980): 50–57.

Norton, Dale. "A Usable Past." Rev. of *Roots*, by Alex Haley. *Sewanee Review* 85 (1977): xliii–xlvi.

Onyeama, Dillibe. "Wrong Roots." Rev. of *Roots*, by Alex Haley. *Books and Bookman* (June 1978): 23.

Othow, Helen Chavis. "*Roots* and the Heroic Search for Identity." *CLA Journal* 26 (March 1983): 311–24.

Ottoway, Mark. "Tangled Roots." *The Sunday Times* [London] (April 10, 1977): 17, 21.

Pinsker, Sanford. "Magic Realism, Historical Truth, and the Quest for a Liberating Identity: Reflections on Alex Haley's *Roots* and Toni Morrison's *Song of Solomon*." *Studies in Black American Literature*. Ed. Joe Weixlmann and Chester J. Fontenot (2 vols.). Greenwood, Fla.: Penkevill Publishing Co., 1984, 1: 183–97.

Rampersad, Arnold. Rev. of *Roots*, by Alex Haley. *New Republic* (December 4, 1976): 23–26.

Raspberry, William. "Family History Helps Instill Values." *Tallahassee Democrat* [Fla.] (July 31, 1990): 10A.

Reddick, L. D. "Our Own Story—at Last!" Rev. of *Roots*, by Alex Haley. *Freedomways* 16 (1976): 253–55.

Rev. of *A Different Kind of Christmas*. *Booklist* (December 15, 1988): 682.

Rev. of *A Different Kind of Christmas*. *Kirkus Reviews* 1 (October 1988): 1423.

Rev. of *A Different Kind of Christmas*. *Publisher's Weekly* (October 7, 1988): 116.

Rev. of *A Different Kind of Christmas*. *Southern Living* (December 23, 1988): 128.

Sheppard, R. Z. "African Genesis." Rev. of *Roots*, by Alex Haley. *Time* (October 18, 1976): 109 + .

Wright, Donald R. "Uprooting Kunta Kinte: On the Perils of Relying on Encyclopedic Informants." *History in Africa* 8 (1981): 205–17.

OWEN W. GILMAN, JR.

Barry Hannah
(1942–   )

For the past 20 years, Barry Hannah has been regular in dredging his emotional life to make fictions—some long but mostly short—and the turbulence that has come from this process makes for provocative reading. Hannah's imagined world is one of desperate energy, characters living on the cusp of apocalypse. Many suffer, some die in ways heretofore unimagined, and some live to marry again. The best ones have a zest for music and even play an instrument. Men are drawn to trumpet and sax; women typically play the flute. Hannah's way with language teaches possibility at every turn. And always there are surprises, an abundance of dazzling surprises that serve to mitigate the fragmentation so evident in the lives of his characters. Those surprises are likely to secure Hannah's perch on the cutting edge of American fiction for a good while.

BIOGRAPHY

Mississippi has not been celebrated for very much in the twentieth century, but it can claim title to more than its share of good writers, one of whom is Barry Hannah, who took his first breath in Meridian on April 23, 1942, and who has invariably returned to his home state following any of his forays into other parts of the South or into other regions. Hannah's home town—the place where he had the childhood experiences that appear in various fictions ranging from *Geronimo Rex* (1972), through *Airships* (1978), and then on into the autobiographical spirit of *Boomerang* (1989)—is Clinton, Mississippi, a town of about 10,000 people five miles west of Jackson. His father, William, a graduate of Ole Miss (where he happened to room with James Eastland), was an insurance agent; his mother was Elizabeth King, about whom Hannah has betrayed almost nothing in his writing.

The public school system in Clinton apparently helped point Hannah in the direction of writing, beginning with Mrs. Bunyard in the third grade, who as Hannah says in *Boomerang*, "let me write my stories and draw all over my tablet" (92), thus opening the door to a taste of freedom not always associated with elementary school teachers but one clearly linked to Hannah's lifelong impulse to experiment with literary forms. Years later, mainly in Hannah's high school experience, there was an outlet for his passion for music. Hannah played the trumpet in a school band that became highly reputed. Hannah's identification with the possibilities in life that open up through musical notes informs almost everything he has ever written.

Clinton is also the site of Mississippi College, from which Hannah graduated with a B.S. in 1964. Although for a time Hannah had been intrigued with the idea of a career in medicine, he chose graduate study in English, taking an M.A. in 1966 and then an M.F.A. in 1967, both from the University of Arkansas in Fayetteville. By that point he was married to his first wife, Meridith Johnson, and with family obligations, he began to teach literature and writing at Clemson University. Hannah's first creative impulse, like William Faulkner's, was toward poetry, and he occasionally drops a bit of good "bad" poetry into a narrative as an index of character disposition, but during the Clemson years (1967–73), he settled in as a writer of fiction. When he left Clemson for Middlebury College in Vermont for a year as writer-in-residence, he had three children—Barry, Jr., Ted, and Lee (a daughter); he had received a Bellaman Foundation Award in Fiction (1970) and a Bread Loaf Fellowship (1971); and he had finished two novels, *Geronimo Rex* (published in 1972, but begun during the creative writing program at Arkansas) and *Nightwatchmen* (1973). *Geronimo Rex*, an initiation story that feeds rather directly off Hannah's first 25 years, met critical acclaim, won the William Faulkner Prize, and was nominated for a National Book Award; *Nightwatchmen*, a murder mystery, satisfied almost no one, and of Hannah's nine books, it is the only one no longer in print.

When Hannah left Middlebury in 1975, he went back to the South, this time to the University of Alabama in Tuscaloosa, where he became a teacher of literature and fiction writing. During his 5-year stint in Alabama, he mostly wrote short stories, many of which appeared in *Esquire*, for by this time, Hannah's work had caught the fancy of Gordon Lish, its editor. Lish subsequently moved on to Knopf, and shortly thereafter, Hannah had a new publisher. Knopf published the next four books: *Airships* (a collection of short stories, 1978), *Ray* (a novel, 1980), *The Tennis Handsome* (a novel built from two stories in *Airships*, 1983), and *Captain Maximus* (another collection of stories, 1985). Of these works, *Airships*, which received the Arnold Gingrich Short Fiction Award, and *Ray* (American Book Award nomination) are major achievements, and they came out of the most severely trying years of Hannah's life. By the time he left Alabama, his first marriage had ended, his second marriage—to Patricia Busch ("blue-eyed Nebraska lady" in the *Airships* dedication)—had collapsed in divorce, and he was hard-pressed by the demon booze.

Hannah put himself on the road to recovery in a most improbable place— Hollywood, California, to which he ventured in 1980. He dried out in a hospital, worked sporadically on a project to develop a movie for Robert Altman, and got back in touch with his children. Then came the peripatetic years, with frequent moves from location to location, always as writer-in-residence: University of Iowa (1981), University of Mississippi (1982), University of Montana (1982–83). Regarding the experience of writing in residency, which inevitably carries the responsibility of guiding others in their writing, Hannah has taken a realistic stance, noting in a 1982 interview that "it pays the house rent" ("Spirits" 325). Through all of those programs, including the nine years as writer-in-residence back at the University of Mississippi, Hannah has managed to keep some time free for his own writing projects, the most recent having been *Hey Jack!* (1987), a novel dedicated to Susan Varas Hannah (his third wife); *Boomerang* (1989), a book that announces itself on the cover as a novel but which swells with very real persons and incidents; and *Never Die* (1991), in which "time and distance" (151) are postulated at the story's end as cues to recovery from the sometimes intense pain of being human (experienced in typically Hannahesque extravagance by a turn-of-the-century Texas gunfighter named Fernando Muré), leading to the prospect of a celebratory "dance of history" (152), which reflects Hannah's Southernness perfectly.

Throughout his nearly 20 years as a published author, Hannah has steadfastly maintained his own standard of the creative impulse: "You don't want to be a critic when you write. That's death. You want to be a fool every time you write. You have to be, and to take a lot of risk" ("Spirits" 326). Though short in physical stature (never growing over five feet nine), Hannah has compensated for his self-acknowledged tininess with aggressive risk taking in his fictive texts. Although his life has taken him sometimes to the edge of the precipice, he has been a survivor. His achievements in fiction have been honored by the American Academy of Arts and Letters and a Guggenheim Fellowship. With his fifth decade nearing, surely there will be more occasions for the backward looks that have already secured his own personal past and that of his place. As the narrator of "Water Liars" in *Airships* notes: "My sense of the past is vivid and slow" (4), a point seconded vigorously by Ray in the novel of that name: "I roam in the past for my best mind" (95). Such is the guiding spirit of Hannah's career—past, present, and future.

MAJOR THEMES

Barry Hannah's work has sometimes been likened to that of William Faulkner, but despite the obvious parallel involving evocation of the life of Mississippi people—some of whom are comic exaggerations and some of whom are driven to commit violence—Ernest Hemingway must be recognized as having much greater influence, a point Hannah himself made in a 1982 interview. The driving motifs of Hannah's fiction are derived from his life experience. As he observed in 1982: "It just takes me a hell of a lot of living to write, mainly because I work so close to my own life" ("Spirits" 329); sometimes the transmutations of the life-into-fiction process are not large. Where Hannah has gone, there goes his fiction. Only in *Airships* does he come close to the inventiveness of Faulkner, and even there, many Hannah surrogates appear.

The title of Hannah's eighth book, *Boomerang*, provides a wonderfully suitable pattern for most of the writing in his career. When the boomerang is sent out on its flight pattern, it is meant to return to its source. The return motion is built into its composition. So it is with the Barry Hannah fiction world: It always comes back home. And home, in this case, is intensely masculine, in the old form, unliberated. Men are in action. They tilt after windmills. They get hurt. They need women to nurse them back to strength. They often become sexually overcharged. They pursue women madly. This process frequently leads to violence of one kind or another. Marriages fall apart, and other institutions seem not to be more durable or more helpful. About the only available antidotes to the crushing chaos of life are music and storytelling and sex.

But while Hannah may work with a palette of basic, bold colors, his fiction swirls with incidental mania. Things happen, lots of them, and the incidents pile up. Although Hannah's works never seem as cluttered with piles of wild moments as those that have come from John Irving, they still sometimes suffer from a sense of indirection, a point that serves to differentiate Hannah's fiction from that of Flannery O'Connor, another Southern writer against whom Hannah's work is often measured. O'Connor's fiction, with all of its grotesque characters and scenes, always had an overreaching purpose—illuminating certain principles of faith—and there is no such motive behind anything produced by Barry Hannah. The closest thing to faith in Hannah's world is the process of storytelling. His narratives are more about storytelling than anything else, usually with a first-person narrative voice holding forth in the midst of wild doings. In this regard, Hannah is a happy combination of Mark Twain and Eudora Welty, each of whom created magically voiced texts.

The first sentence/paragraph of *Ray* nicely illustrates this first-person technique: "Ray is thirty-three and he was born of decent religious parents, I say" (3). Here Hannah rings a change on the opening of the *Adventures of Huckleberry Finn*, for the trick or surprise of the book is that "I" actually is Ray, a bit of stylistic schizophrenia that seems purely modern. Most of Hannah's successful books depend on the slipperiness of voice. *Hey Jack!* begins similarly: "I go back to Korea. Do I ever. . . . You will find me changing voices as I slip into the—let us say—*mode* of the closer participant. Otherwise I am sane, except for once in my life, and do not speak in tongues or hear voices as they do in certain churches" (1–2). The specific identity of the telling voice in *Hey Jack!* is not named until the final page of the narrative, where we learn that it is Homer, clearly homage to the genius of epic storytelling, but the function of the voice is not impeded by the absence of a name; the voice has been caught in the midst of human suffering, serving mostly to weave together a set of incidents that all turn on the final words of the story—" 'No mercy,' he said" (133)—words that effectively judge the passage of pain and error from one generation to the next.

The gathering process of *Hey Jack!* is akin to that found in Welty's *The Golden Apples*, but Hannah's book stops short of acknowledging the redemptive value of capturing magic in stories. Anything redemptive in Hannah's work is implicit at best.

Hannah's South is a hard place, visited by painful and shocking twists that come upon its people as fast as the pages of a Hannah story can be turned. As Hannah creates this world, the roughness and danger of which he relishes, always worrying that "the South is turning chicken" ("Spirits" 321), the continuity of past into present is often registered. For a variety of reasons, the South has had an unusual concern for the past. Where the rest of America wants to shunt the past into obscurity so as to dwell happily in the present, the South refuses to let go of history. Hannah's most provocative and rewarding contribution to the Southern sense of the past occurs in *Ray*. Ray is a doctor, so Hannah's personal past interests are revisited, but Ray also has a war in his past, the Vietnam war, and through Ray, America's most extended recent experience of national blood-letting is joined to history.

Just a few pages into the novel, we are informed by "I" (Ray), "I did my part in hurting the gooks back for you, Sister. I flew support missions for B-52 bombers in Vietnam" (10). In fact, Ray flew "an F-4, called the Phantom. It's a jet airplane" (10). Thus Ray is lodged quickly, reminiscently in a moment of historical time. The in-text gloss about the F-4 (it's a jet airplane) is noteworthy on several levels. First, the remark by Ray shows his estimation of Sister Hooch, a sexually responsive figure always sympathetic to Ray's ongoing maladies; she is clueless about the world beyond the bedroom. Second, it reveals that Hannah himself is working airspace beyond his own experience; he has credited his lifelong friend, John Quisenberry (Quadberry in "Testimony of Pilot" in *Airships*), with having supplied his understanding of Vietnam jet jockeys, for Quisenberry went off to the war in such a role. And third, Hannah speaks to an American audience prone to forgetfulness. At some point, perhaps not far into the future, general readers everywhere will need the gloss that Hannah has supplied. He wisely takes nothing for granted, certainly not the past.

But there is a past behind Vietnam—far far back—and Hannah makes that point repeatedly. Ray has a friend, Charlie DeSoto, born of the town of Tuscaloosa. The narrative draws attention to the fact that DeSoto was "of course the namesake of Hernando de Soto, the discoverer of the Mississippi River who perished in 1542, probably of greed and arrogance" (12). Charlie is so intrigued with his ancestor that he reads a diarist's account of de Soto's expedition inland from Florida. The novel includes an interpolated account involving the massacre of thousands of Indians as part of de Soto's mission into the wilderness, all of which serves as an apt paradigm for the American presence in Vietnam, and, in this light, the fact that "Charlie DeSoto read that passage [the massacre scene] to renew himself with his own perhaps ancestor" (15) suggests that the past can become the future. The conservativism of this situation strikes close to the heart of Hannah's position on many matters.

There are many more surprises in *Ray* regarding history and time. Section IV of the novel (the text is broken often by sections, sixty-two in all, spread over just 111 pages) involves a sudden shift to the Civil War, a feature that Hannah had previously used in a few stories in *Airships*, and Ray is there, too, one of the riders in Jeb Stuart's cavalry, up in the Maryland hills. A combat scene ensues, from which there were "too many dead" (41), and "I fell asleep with the banjo music in my head and I dreamed of two whores sucking me" (41). These last details typify the enduring themes of Hannah's career. There is music, but also aberrant, hyperactive sexuality, something that dominates all of the various historical times known to the experience of Ray. Not only is sex timeless for Hannah, it is also a locus of regenerative strangeness. The further one reads in the Hannah corpus, the clearer it becomes that sex is one possible center that can hold, though never for long, requiring nearly incessant repetitions. After the youthful frustrations of Harry Monroe in *Geronimo Rex* are superceded by sexual initiation, no character is ever more than four pages from an act of fornication in any of Hannah's narratives. Call it the impulse to life—"Homo erectus" on the move through time.

Section V contains just two sentences: "I live in so many centuries. Everybody is still alive" (41). This declaration pinpoints the main conclusion being drawn about time: it is all the same. As it was in the campaign of de Soto, so it was in the missions of Jeb Stuart, who is more interesting for Hannah than Robert E. Lee because "he liked music and was capable of being a fool" ("Spirits" 330), and so it was in the B-52 support flights of Ray in his F-4 Phantom over Vietnam.

As a physician, Ray is committed to curing disease, and yet through a couple of centuries, he has been equally a destroyer, one strangely content with the state of war, whether realized in mortal combat or in the equally brutal battles between the sexes. Ray is a living contradiction, testament to the stresses and strains in American life that proceed from radical ambivalence about many things. The themes of *Ray*—men battling with themselves, with other men, with women, with disease (chiefly cancer, which appears as a threat in most of Hannah's long stories and which visited his own father late in life)—are representative of Hannah's whole career.

In *Geronimo Rex*, Hannah explored the rigors of a man's search for an identity. Harry Monroe went off to Hedermansever College—the first of several college environments developed by Hannah, always with wickedly discerning insights about the predilections of "pee aich dees"—and there he eventually found an identity in some dusty volumes obtained from the library. He became fascinated with the stature of the Indian chief Geronimo: "What I especially liked about Geronimo then was that he had cheated, lied, stolen, mutinied, usurped, killed, burned, raped, pillaged, razed, trapped, ripped, mashed, bowshot, stomped, herded, exploded, cut, stoned, revenged, prevenged, avenged, and was his own man" (231). As Harry takes on the aura of Geronimo, there ensues some violence, the strains of which run strong thereafter throughout Hannah's work. Guns and knives are ready by, and they are used frequently. If a gun isn't right for justice (as it is to effect resolution of a string of murders in *Nightwatchmen*), then characters find innovative alternatives. For example, when French Edward, the protagonist of *The Tennis Handsome*, wants to avenge himself on Dr. James Word, who has committed adultery with French's mother, he plays tennis with the old man until he collapses from a crippling stroke. Hannah's fascination with the spirit of Geronimo has not diminished in two decades.

Given the intense maleness of the central figures in each Hannah story, it is not surprising that feminist readers find little solace in the way women are represented. There are just too many former wives who didn't work out, too many women ready to take a submissive role in a male pleasure game. Hannah himself has declared that "I know nothing about women" ("Spirits" 319), and he seems to have kept his innocence well. But the limitations, misunderstandings, and occasionally bizarre permutations in the sexual lives of his characters, who in the aggregate could form a large chapter of "sex and love addicts anonymous," are unquestionably derived from a real world where the ideal relationship is rarely realized. Whether in the sad confusion of Thorpe Trove's love for Didi (he wanted a baby, she didn't) in *Nightwatchmen*; or in the death-as-sex demise of Donna (she dies at climax . . . by tombstone to the head) in "Coming Close to Donna" from the *Airships* collection; or in the scrambled sexuality of Baby Levaster of *The Tennis Handsome*; or in the rampant destructiveness of lovers in *Hey Jack!*, where the love woes of a rock musician eventually surpass the cliché heartbreaks warbled in Nashville's music—everywhere love is rendered as hard—and true. As the narrator of "Water Liars" concludes after hearing an old man's horror story of discovering his daughter making love to a stranger: "We were both crucified by the truth" (7). Hannah chases the truth vigorously, and it often proves hurtful.

Of all Hannah's enduring interests, perhaps music means the most, because it touches the soul so quickly. For example, the deliciously coordinated movement of a marching band under the direction of Harley Butte is evoked lovingly in *Geronimo Rex*, and it lingers in memory: "We left for the car. The band had quit but was still in our ears. Lariat put a hand on my shoulder. 'That was it. Good, good heavens. We're in the wrong field. Music!' " (381). The stories of *Captain Maximus* were conceived during a period when Hannah was intrigued with the life of Jimi Hendrix. In *Boomerang*, Hannah pays tribute to his friend Jimmy Buffett, and he reports proudly of his son's achievements with the guitar. *Hey Jack!* is centered on "Ronnie Foot, the rock star" (27), which allows Hannah an opportunity to explore the stormy romanticism that is axiomatic in contemporary music and that is a close parallel to Hannah's own creative process.

Boomerang contains the report that "Capote when he was really drunk" called Hannah "the maddest writer in the U.S.A." (114), and such an appraisal may well best fit the achievement of Barry Hannah. Invention for Hannah comes out of anger. In "Even Greenland," a story from *Captain Maximus*, two pilots try to outdo each other in inventing a metaphor for freshness, and one of them,

John, buries the plane in the ground in order to claim ownership of "that snow in Mississippi" (33) as a unique concretion for the idea of "fresh." Hannah's fiction reflects the same compulsive ambition to go beyond the limits, and in this regard, he works out on the fringes of the South's great tradition of rhetorical extravagance. As Maximum Ned observes in "Ride, Fly, Penetrate, Loiter," another story from the *Captain Maximum* collection, "The Deep South might be wretched, but it can howl!" (39).

SURVEY OF CRITICISM

The critical response to Barry Hannah has not yet moved far beyond the reviews that have accompanied each of his books. Although sometimes reviewers have labored overmuch trying to understand Hannah in terms of his Southern predecessors, the reviews have been mostly appreciative, and they show that his appeal reaches far beyond his native region. Up to this point, there has been only one dissertation devoted to his fiction, by Andrew Curtis Jackson at the University of North Carolina at Chapel Hill (1990), but Hannah has been the subject of several M.A. theses since 1982. Fred Hobson's latest book, *The Southern Writer in the Postmodern World* (1991), finds Hannah in company with Bobbie Ann Mason and Lee Smith as a writer fundamentally concerned with history and class issues. Given the staying power of *Airships* and *Ray*, it is not surprising that in 1991 Hannah joined the Twayne's United States Authors series, thanks to a serviceable study by Mark Charney.

Two journal articles have served well to point the way to the heart of Hannah's work. Donald R. Noble's " 'Tragic and Meaningful to an Insane Degree': Barry Hannah" provides illuminating commentary on *Geronimo Rex*, *Nightwatchmen*, *Airships*, and *Ray*. Noble's observation that "Hannah's violence is a subject sure to get much attention in the future" (40) is a prophecy just begging to be fulfilled; Allen Shepherd's " 'Firing Two Carbines, One in Each Hand': Barry Hannah's *Hey Jack!*" recently initiated the study of Hannah's violence in the context of Southern American culture. Noble also draws attention to Hannah's brilliance with language, citing a number of typically inventive phrases that show how "Hannah's voice *bends* language; the meanings of words are stretched so that one has never seen the words used in quite that way before" (39). David Madden's essay "Barry Hannah's *Geronimo Rex* in Retrospect," which preceded R. Vanarsdall's "The Spirits Will Win Through: An Interview with Barry Hannah" in a 1983 issue of the *Southern Review*, helpfully evaluates Hannah's talent for creating vivid characters, particularly Peter Lepoyster, called Whitfield because he had spent time in Whitfield, an asylum for the insane. Whitfield Peter is a raging racist, and with his portrayal—violent bigotry linked to dementia—Hannah seems to have taken a progressive stand on the race issue. Madden's conclusion turns on the brilliance of Hannah's style, noting that his "use of language is better *within* each line than *from* line to line" (316). As the journal entry form of *Boomerang* proves, Hannah is still best at the small unit of composition, the sentence. He is our Emerson in fiction, and future scholarship will be obliged to assess Barry Hannah's supercharged style as a mode of being.

BIBLIOGRAPHY

Works by Barry Hannah

Geronimo Rex. New York: Viking, 1972.
Nightwatchmen. New York: Viking, 1973.
Airships. New York: Knopf, 1978.
Ray. New York: Knopf, 1980.
"The Spirits Will Win Through: An Interview with Barry Hannah." With R. Vanarsdall. *Southern Review* 19 (1983): 317–43.
The Tennis Handsome. New York: Knopf, 1983.
Captain Maximus. New York: Knopf, 1985.
Hey Jack! New York: E. P. Dutton/Seymour Lawrence, 1987.
Boomerang. Boston: Houghton Mifflin/Seymour Lawrence, 1989.
Never Die. Boston: Houghton Mifflin/Seymour Lawrence, 1991.

Studies of Barry Hannah

Betts, Doris. "Barry Hannah: Where Energy Is All" (Rev. of *Captain Maximus*). *Washington Post Book World*, (June 23, 1985): 11.
Charney, Mark. *Barry Hannah*. New York: Twayne, 1991.
DeMott, Benjamin. "Rudeness Is Our Only Hope" (Rev. of *Ray*). *New York Times Book Review* (November 16, 1980): 7, 26.
Gold, Ivan. "Yoknapatawpha County of the Mind." *New York Times Book Review* (May 1, 1983): 11, 19.
Hobson, Fred. *The Southern Writer in the Postmodern World*. Athens: University of Georgia Press, 1991.
Jackson, Andrew Curtis. "The Fiction of Barry Hannah." Ph.D. Dissertation. University of North Carolina, 1990.
Madden, David. "Barry Hannah's *Geronimo Rex* in Retrospect." *Southern Review* 19 (1983): 309–16.
Malone, Michael. "Everything that Rises" (Rev. of *Airships*). *Nation* (June 10, 1978): 705–08.
Noble, Donald R. " 'Tragic and Meaningful to an Insane Degree': Barry Hannah." *Southern Literary Journal* 15 (1982): 37–44.
Rafferty, Terrence. "Gunsmoke and Voodoo" (Rev. of *Captain Maximus*). *Nation* (June 1, 1985): 677–79.
Shepherd, Allen. " 'Firing Two Carbines, One in Each Hand': Barry Hannah's *Hey Jack*." *Notes on Mississippi Writers* 21 (1989): 37–40.
Spikes, Michael P. "What's in a Name? A Reading of Barry Hannah's *Ray*." *Mississippi Quarterly* 42 (1989): 69–82.
Updike, John. "From Dyna Domes to Turkey-Pressing" (Rev. of *Geronimo Rex*). *New Yorker* (September 9, 1972): 121–24.

JEANNE R. NOSTRANDT

[Henry] William Hoffman
(1925–   )

A three-evening symposium honoring William Hoffman was not his first recognition for fiction, but it was the first conference devoted entirely to his work. Entitled "The Fictional World of William Hoffman," the meetings were held September 12–14, 1988, at both Longwood College and Hampden-Sydney College in Virginia. The Virginia Council for the Humanities funded and supported the symposium, as did both colleges. That the conference took place in Virginia's farm country is appropriate. William Hoffman writes fiction about Virginia (including West Virginia) and Virginians—the coal mining mountain country, the red-clay tobacco country, and the shell-encrusted Chesapeake Bay country. His war stories show transformations in the lives and values of characters who come from those Virginia and West Virginia locales.

BIOGRAPHY

Born in Charleston, West Virginia, on May 16, 1925, William Hoffman was reared by his maternal grandmother in the Charleston home of her father, James Kay. His mother (Julia, born a Beckley and whose own great-grandfather founded Beckley, West Virginia) died when William was a small child, and his father (Henry William Hoffman divorced from his mother soon after William was born) was working away from the area for many years. The great-grandfather, who would later serve as a model for Hoffman's protagonist in *The Dark Mountains* (1963), was an immigrant from Scotland and a stern Presbyterian. He was responsible for the strict but loving discipline of Hoffman's early years. His religious beliefs, however, did not keep him from his evening drink of Scotch and his recitation of Burns' poems, or from taking the young William to silent movies. (He did not care for the "new" talkies.) With many cousins and relatives in the area, the young Hoffman was often the recipient of the shiny fifty-cent pieces given by Kay to the children on Sunday after they came home from church. With the Depression of the 1930s, though, the Sunday coins became dimes. That immigrant forebear lived by Presbyterian tenets as he rose through his own labors and intelligence to become a mine owner and successful businessman. The strict Presbyterian upbringing and ideas instilled in Hoffman stayed with him; he is a former deacon and head of the board of deacons in his local church. Loyal and faithful to that church, its works, and its principles, Hoffman's deeply embedded belief and Presbyterian layman's experience are evident in his fiction.

Growing up, Hoffman had no idea that he would be a writer. He had a privileged childhood (attending the best summer camps and having everything he needed), was graduated from Kentucky Military Institute in 1943, and went into the army immediately. He was with the medical corps in the early days of the Normandy invasion of June 1944 and at the "Battle of the Bulge" before the end of the year. The war experience would later provide raw material for several of his novels. Having grown up in a strict environment, he loved the discipline of military life, and he always believed he would be a fighter pilot (he flew a plane at age 14), but he found the realities of war not to his liking. As much as he hated war, when the Korean conflict came, he almost signed up again. Hoffman knows and writes about the horrors of war, but he believes, nonetheless, that any young man should want to go to war, should feel it his duty to do so. He is surprised, but adamant, at his own ambivalence.

Two days after leaving the army on September 23, 1946, he began his formal education at Hampden-Sydney College, receiving a B.A. in 1949. Hampden-Sydney was then more a Presbyterian-dominated school than it now is, with many orthodox Presbyterian professors whose method of pedagogy was to "give you a bad time under the theory that suffering was good for you." Hoffman remembers them as strict but caring and sincere; "they were wonderful men," he says. He attended law school at Washington and Lee University for one year– 1949–50; during that year he took a creative writing course "as a lark" and found his natural vocation. *Shenandoah* published his first story in 1950, and Hoffman went off to the Writers' Workshop at the University of Iowa for one year (1950–51). He worked briefly for the *Washington Evening Star* and the Chase National Bank in New York before becoming an instructor in English at Hampden-Sydney College from 1952 to 1959. In New York he had learned something about the publishing circuit and had acquired an agent. His first two novels were published during this tenure teaching, published in reverse order of their writing. Hoffman first wrote *Days in the Yellow Leaf* (1958) from his war experience, which, he says, set the pattern for all the rest of his life. This novel is still his favorite, partly because it gave him so much trouble in the writing and partly because it was his first. His agent had trouble placing the manuscript and sold the second novel first, *The Trumpet Unblown* (1955).

During this instructorship he met and married Alice Sue Richardson of Blue-field, West Virginia. She was visiting relatives in Farmville and was dating his dean, but Hoffman had a blind date with her, "late dated" her after the dean brought her home, and married her on April 17, 1957. They have two grown daughters: Ruth Beckley Hoffman, who lives in Richmond, and Margaret Kay [Hoffman] Huffman, who lives in Albany, Georgia. Rearing children is an education in itself, he says, and he uses much of that "education" in his fiction. After he resigned from Hampden-Sydney in 1959, the Hoffmans moved in 1964 from Farmville to Charlotte Court House where they bought a farm with a pre–Civil War house. Because the house was in such disrepair, the Hoffmans renovated both the outside and the inside. William Hoffman published three more novels before funds became so depleted he needed to go back to teaching: *A Place for My Head* (1960), *The Dark Mountains* (1963), and *Yancey's War* (1966). He returned to Hampden-Sydney College as writer-in-residence, moving from instructor to professor before he again resigned in the early 1970s. In addition to teaching writing, he taught the regular English curriculum during those years. In summer 1967 he was playwright-in-residence at the Barter Theatre in Abingdon, Virginia, when he produced his only play, *The Love Touch*. He returned to teaching only once, teaching a single writing course in fall 1978, as a gift to Hampden-Sydney. He wrote two more novels during that second tenure at Hampden-Sydney: *A Walk to the River* (1970) and *A Death of Dreams* (1973).

The Hoffmans continue to live on the fifty-acre, Charlotte Court House farm, Wynyard, in a beautifully renovated home, with horses and dogs to care for and exceptional gardens to keep. In a large, dark-paneled office with built-in bookshelves and two large windows for fragrant, summer breezes, William Hoffman writes his fiction. Photographs of himself with his wife and daughters, honors he has received, the playbill for his single produced play, and other memorabilia line the walls. For years he wrote on two Royal manual typewriters (one in this office and an identical one at his cottage on the Chesapeake Bay), but he purchased a computer from Sears and learned the joys of faster writing and revising. When he first began using the computer, however, his wife once passed the door to find him staring at the monitor mumbling, "I think I'm going absolutely insane." Though he is now more comfortable with the computer, he keeps the Royal close at hand.

A prolific writer, William Hoffman rises early (about 5:30 or 6:00 a.m.) and goes to his office in his home. He works on novels for several hours in the mornings, a schedule broken only once for breakfast. Then he finishes the morning with "chores." After lunch he returns to the office for several more hours of writing short stories. He does not work long hours, but when he is working, he works "very intensely," he says, not hearing the phone or any other distractions. He always has manuscripts in files or in his bank safety-deposit box waiting to be sent to his agent, and he always keeps something "in the pipeline." Even though his newest novel, *Furors Die* (1990), is recent, another is with his agent and another is in the bank box. He sometimes forgets specifics about his work after it is finished, he says, but he never confuses the novels or the stories on which he is writing.

In addition to the most recent novel, Hoffman has published four other books since he left teaching. Two are short story collections, *Virginia Reels* (1978) and *By Land, By Sea* (1988); two are novels, *The Land That Drank the Rain* (1982) and *Godfires* (1985). Also, he has published a number of short stories in such periodicals as *McCall's, Playboy, Cosmopolitan, Scholastic, Gentleman's Quarterly, Virginia Quarterly Review, Sewanee Review, Transatlantic Review, Carleton Miscellany, Saturday Evening Post,* and *Shenandoah.* Some of these stories appear in the two published collections. He is currently at work on another novel involving four men with four different personality types. He is matching their language to each personality type so that readers will be able to identify each personality and to distinguish each character by his language alone. This is a new style for him. Writing is hard, Hoffman says, but it is "good" work; it does not drain him as it does so many writers. Rather, it exhilarates him even when it tires him.

William Hoffman's manner is warm, sincere, and generous; his style is intelligent, relaxed, and honest. Though he admits to a "tragic" view of life, he has a ready wit and a hearty laugh—as often as not, a laugh on himself. He reveres his God, his church, his family, his country, and his home; he shows a real talent for that quality Southerners traditionally consider an indispensable part of life—hospitality. He makes all guests, even interviewers, feel comfortable and "at home" in his presence. He presents his fiction as honestly and as realistically as he can, and he humorously suggests that his tombstone might read, "He didn't cheat!"

MAJOR THEMES

Hoffman's fiction is rooted in Virginia's piedmont clay, its coal-mined mountains, and its bay-washed beaches. His themes delve into the complexities of the human condition and the plight of the human spirit in any place and at any time. His characters and scenes are distinctly Southern, depicting a strong sense of family and community; deep religious values; and effective, often colorful, language. These characteristics, when they come into conflict with lesser qualities, make up the plots and psychological intricacies of Hoffman's fiction. His "war stories" depict their Southern characters' lifestyles and values as they clash with the horrors and inhumanities of war.

Three novels are war stories in the sense that they are reflections of Hoffman's own experience with the Army Medical Corps during World War II. That experience is something he thinks invaluable; in fact, he sees it almost "like the B.C. and A.D." of his life. It taught him to see things differently, to look more deeply into characters. *Days in the Yellow Leaf* was written "somewhat out of [his] war experiences," he says. It went through six publishers' rejections and many reworkings before being published as his second novel, following the successful reception of his "first" novel. Hoffman used this as his apprentice work, though he had written and been unsuccessful at placing some stories earlier.

Tod Young is the sensitive protagonist of the novel who finds that the demands of life and those of his family and friends bring an ironic twist into his world. Hate, deceit, violence, and death are life's inevitabilities, like those of war, that change and destroy the love, sympathy, and gentleness of the protagonist. *The Trumpet Unblown* is a more direct reflection of Hoffman's war experience. With its strong antiwar themes, the reader follows the youthful Tyree Shelby's story. Shelby encounters not only the enemy but also the primitive, often evil, actions of his fellow soldiers. His Virginia upbringing had not prepared him for the realities he found among his fellow man. He physically survives, but without personality or spirit; he is an early representative in fiction of what medicine has named from the Vietnam "non-war," post-traumatic stress disorder. Hoffman plays out the theme of survival and its costs throughout his fiction.

Finally, *Yancey's War*, published two decades after Hoffman's war years, looks at war's dehumanizing aspect realistically, but also colors it with humor. Marvin Yancey, a veteran of World War I, and Charles Elgar are the central characters. Yancey's failure to survive is a result of his own ineptitude as an officer; Elgar, whose life is intricately entwined with Yancey's, is left in confusion after his well-bred Southern values fail him in the face of war and the unpleasant, uncouth Yancey. The relationship between these two characters provides the conflict and the humor in the story, though the plot reveals as much war horror and psychological dehumanization as do the previous war stories.

The three novels show that the concept of war has as its basic supposition the meaninglessness of man's rites and structures of civilization; the name of the game is to survive, even at the cost of dehumanization and disintegration of character. Hoffman's themes were ahead of their time. Most of the reading public in the early years following the war wanted stories of heroics and victories of World War II, not disparaging accounts of America's role in it. Three decades later the country would focus on these themes as they defined the Vietnam war, only subliminally recognizing them as part and parcel of all wars.

Life itself becomes a kind of war in most of Hoffman's fiction; at least it has its battles to be won or lost. What these battles do to intelligent, hardworking, and civilized men is what interests him. Hoffman reveals his central characters through their interior thoughts, sometimes with humor and sometimes with despair, but always with genuine concern for their confusions and efforts. He has a talent for making the unbelievable believable, according to some critics. James MacGlauglin, the protagonist of *The Dark Mountains*, is one of his best creations. Loosely based on Hoffman's great-grandfather, James Kay, MacGlauglin is the Scotland immigrant who comes to America as a young boy and lives the American dream. He successfully builds his dynasty (unlike William Faulkner's Sutpen of *Absalom!, Absalom!*) because he has an honorable character, a deep-rooted Presbyterian faith, and an industriousness; he is willing to labor and to sacrifice. Believing in the dream, he carves his mining business out of the West Virginia mountains *because* he believes; when the American dream changes during World

War II, MacGlauglin dies without understanding the change. Man's dreams and the values he lives by in conflict with the world hold an almost religious interest for Hoffman. How can man survive if his dreams do not, he seems to ask. Confusion is the mental state of Guy Dion in *A Death of Dreams*. He speaks to the reader out of that confusion from a mental hospital in which he is confined— mistakenly, he believes. As he watches the mountain outside his window appear or disappear, he demonstrates the losses men suffer as they decline in life. "The greatest pain," he says, "is the death of dreams." That same theme appears again with Claytor Lewis Carson, who moves from the dreamland of California to the Cumberland Mountains of eastern Kentucky (near West Virginia) in *The Land That Drank the Rain*. Carson's life, like sun-parched earth, suffers a drought of spirit. His life in California with its sham and dishonesty depleted him of character and meaning, and he seeks renewal in a self-sufficient but hermit's life in the mountains. Only the replenishing "rain" of his concern for a lost and unloved youth draws him back into society; his reborn life is one of self-sacrifice and courage. Love's redeeming quality is the theme.

Three novels concern men who are descendants of "old families" of the small, red-clay Virginia communities in which they live: Angus McCloud of *A Place for My Head*, Jackson LeJohn of *A Walk to the River*, and Billy Payne of *Godfires*. All three men are "dead men" in their own lives; two are lawyers (McCloud and Payne) with no recent cases either won or of any merit; one is the owner of the town's hardware store and chairman of the board of officers in his church (LeJohn). Each comes out of his respective lethargy, mediocrity, and often the bottle at the behest of someone who appeals to his duty or noblesse oblige. As each is revived from this "dead" state, Hoffman reveals the story through his interior viewpoint.

McCloud's inbred values left him vulnerable to the machinations of a new social structure, finally leaving him in a world of situation ethics with no place for his head. LeJohn believes that serving in World War II "killed" him, that his marriage to Kitt brought him to life, and that her death "killed" him again. In his layman position for the church, LeJohn must take up a burden he does not want—to judge the minister accused of "lechering." Theological and psychological questions embroider the plot, and LeJohn, pulled many ways by the dilemma, learns that survival without meaningful activity has no value: "I bit down on my sadness. I thought that even pain had goodness. A dead man couldn't suffer. To grieve, a man had to be alive and to care about something" (336). Payne, a lawyer, is also a detective looking for the murderer of the town's leading citizen. He sees the search as a chance to redeem himself in the eyes of the community, to gain respect, and to win the dead man's widow, whom he has always loved. Hoffman's fictional structure for this story opens with Payne's monologue revealing his imprisonment, his main thoughts focused on a means of escape—to survive. The story alternates between that monologue and an active story of the town (Tobaccoton), the crime (Vin Farr's murder), and the citizens.

Psychotic zeal—religious and criminal—thread the story, and values that mark civilized man again come in conflict with the "relevant" values of a contemporary world.

Hoffman's long study of the changing social milieu of his Virginias moves back to West Virginia. *Furors Die* is the story of two boys, the privileged Wylie Duval and the redneck Amos Cody, as they grow up, get an education, and move into their respective professions. With lives that interconnect throughout the story, Duval and Cody suffer a complete reversal of their moral positions and sense of values. The reversal, however, is not only a result of the modern world impinging on their lives but also the interaction of each life with the other one. Religion shows itself in the early Cody as puritanical and sanctimonious, Duval taking his moral clues from the example of his position and class. Hoffman's plot, however, is more complex than this. He focuses on interrelationships of people on the human level, and while he does not see values as needing relevancy, he does see morality and values as necessary for civilization. These characters' survival depends on the values by which they live and how they handle the complexities of value adjustments.

The themes of human survival and its costs; appropriate standards for living in a world of situation ethics; and rising from impoverishment to success, the American dream, in a modern world permeate Hoffman's fiction, including stories in the two collections. His characters live close to the land and its elements. The nine stories of *Virginia Reels* originally appeared in magazines and periodicals between 1966 and 1978. As the name suggests, the stories take place in both Virginias. Because Hoffman's focus is sharper and more immediate in the stories than in the novels, the reader more readily moves into the narrator's viewpoint and place. For instance, the idea of the river as a place for renewal— baptizing, self-searching, relationship mending—is more obvious in the shorter fiction, though it is as applicable to the novels. The fundamentalism and even religious fanaticism of narrators and plots of "The Spirit in Me," "Amazing Grace," and "A Darkness on the Mountain" reveal the multidimensions of characters as they act within the confines of their communities.

The reader understands, while not accepting, the fanatic's snake handling; senses both humor and pathos of the woman who insists her son "go to the river" before she dies; and laughs with courting antics while cheering the outwitting of rivals in the effort. The other six stories arouse feelings of anger, frustration, loneliness, lust, indignation, respect, and humor as each presents its central figure through his interior feelings and thoughts. Hoffman uses characters from the West Virginia hills, from cities such as Richmond, and from the coastal areas for these stories, showing them in their essential humanness, as not very different from the readers.

The dozen stories in *By Land, By Sea* were written between 1978 and 1988, with some of them having appeared in periodicals, also. If the stories of the first collection narrow their focus on the psychological viewpoints of their main characters, then a broader perspective of these stories considers the environment through the viewpoints; the tone seems more mature. "Fathers and Daughters" (loosely autobiographical), speaks to the actions, attitudes, and doubts of most parents, while it shows the daughter's feelings as she changes from child to young woman. "Landfall" is the single story taking place outside Virginia, in "no man's land"—on water. It is the story of a last voyage, the final cruise for an aging couple on the wooden sloop they have loved and enjoyed for 17 years. Though control, love, and fear characterize this story, a more desperate feeling grips the aging rapist of "Lover" as he cunningly seduces a young girl in a last hope of recapturing his lost life. Similarly, Jess, in "Moorings," ignores his age and his condition to a dire consequence as he is seduced by the youth and wealth of newcomers to his bayside town.

An awareness of aging leads the protagonists of "Cuttings" and "Moon Lady" to take a risk, tackle a difficult chore, or "go home again." Each learns something about himself in the accomplishment. Two Virginia farm stories concern the labor and sacrifice of simple folk who want only self-respect and more in life for their children. In "Smoke," the adolescent narrator learns the real meaning of honor, survival, and self-respect from his reprobate uncle when that uncle is accused of lying: "Sure I'm lying, yet not for money or to damage anybody. Good lies are what we do to get by day to day. Think about it" (59). "Indian Gift" tells of country people who send their son to the University of Virginia at such a sacrifice that they lose everything. The pathos is relieved by humor, however, as a reference to the church organist who comes to practice "cross-eyed" illustrates.

Religion plays a part in most of these stories, but three depict different viewpoints about churches and their purpose. In "Altarpiece," the main character moves to a cottage on the Chesapeake Bay after his wife's death; faces the church women who bombard him with "kindness" and invitations to church; and finally joins, through kinship in grief, the aging woman whom the church shunned. "Faces at the Window" and "The Question of Rain" concern ministers who are the focus of their communities' attention; in each, the church is the center of both social and religious activities in small Virginia towns. Each minister struggles with his place and with his idea of his purpose: One succumbs to sins of the flesh; the other learns that the people, not the building, make the church. The central figure of "Patriot" is reminiscent of James MacGlauglin in *The Dark Mountains*. He, like MacGlauglin, believes in hard work, honesty, duty and simple justice, but finds that such things as war cause values to shift and often leave no place for people who live by them.

Hoffman's people cover the social spectrum at all levels—simple country folk, miners and hill people, successful business executives, military people, coastal inhabitants, professional people, and ministers among them. The common denominator is their humanity, their struggles to survive in an increasingly complex and changing world. Writing of people who live close to the land with a religious perspective and a sense of place, Hoffman examines life and values that do not go out of fashion. He sees the need for a belief in what Faulkner called "the old verities" so that man's spirit, as well as his civilization, will survive the battles of life. Fighting the battles with that belief is what characterizes his fiction. His relaxed manner of storytelling belies his sharp eye for detail, his polished craftsmanship, and his keen ear for language. His power of creating atmosphere is so penetrating that the reader seems to enter into the place of his stories and to recognize its people. When asked what he would like readers to see about his themes, he said: "I think I would like for them to see that life is both tragic and courageous." His fictional themes demonstrate this vision.

SURVEY OF CRITICISM

The most apt recognition of William Hoffman's talent is in the honors he has received. In addition to the symposium at Longwood and Hampden-Sydney Colleges in 1988, Hoffman received an honorary D.Litt. from Hampden-Sydney in 1980. He received the Emily Clark Balch prize for fiction from the *Virginia Quarterly Review* for his story "Sweet Armageddon," judged by the advisory board to be "the best published work of short fiction to appear in the journal in 1988." His story "Dancer" received the Andrew Lytle prize from the *Sewanee Review* in 1989, and that same year he earned the Jeanne Charplot Goodheart prize for fiction from *Shenandoah*. He has had a National Endowment for the Arts Creative Writing Fellowship, was included in *Best American Short Stories*, and was the Virginia Cultural Laureate.

Scholarship in journals and magazines has been slow in coming, but a new interest in his work seems imminent. Early critics of his works often misunderstood the novels, especially the mining stories, and they sometimes categorized him in negative ways. It took the Vietnam conflict to awaken much of society to the long-term effects of war about which Hoffman wrote, and it took time for a fuel-conscious society to balance its sympathies between the owners and the workers of mines. So great was the influence of labor unions in those years that many readers saw *The Dark Mountains* as extolling the virtues of a mine owner, as they failed to see that the novel praised the man who happened to own a mine because he was the laborer who built it. "Patriot" later characterized the virtues and honorable qualities of the laborer, a miner. "Many doors were closed" to him, he says, and "many of those doors are still closed."

A few reviewers dismiss his work as "regional" with "old-fashioned" values, failing to see the regional characteristics of his fiction as vehicles by which Hoffman reaches the larger, human condition. In discussing the 1988 symposium in Virginia, William Frank referred to Hoffman's stories as dealing with "age-old questions of faith and belief, doubt and certainty, relationships and commitment, and some of them can only be called good, old-fashioned love stories." Even so, most evaluations have been reviews of his books rather than in-depth scholarly treatments in such periodicals as the *New York Times Book Review*, the *Washington Post*, *Best Sellers*, *Chicago Sunday Tribune*, *The Nation*, *Saturday Review*, and local newspapers.

As early as 1969, however, Floyd C. Watkins considered two of Hoffman's novels in his Lamar lectures. After publication of Hoffman's first novel in 1955, Judith Margoshes featured him as one of twenty-six "worthy" new novelists in *Library Journal*. In 1979, Sylvia Shorris included Hoffman as one of three writers in an essay review entitled "Literature's Stepchild." Christine Neuberger quotes Hoffman as saying "when there are signs that what I write isn't wanted, I'll just quit. But I don't think I'll ever quit because I've run out of ideas. I've never been to a point where I can't write about something." In 1983 Gary Davenport called Hoffman's fiction "mythic," and in 1988 Michele Wolf saw his protagonists as having a "quiet grandeur" and his fictional endings as "lyrical, with their haunting imagery."

Hoffman's novels are the subject of one doctoral dissertation (Ewell) from the University of South Carolina and one masters' thesis (Davis) from Longwood College. Though no biography or extended critical evaluation exists of William Hoffman or his work, William L. Frank of Longwood College is currently at work on a critical biography. After ten novels and two collections of stories in publication over 35 years (1955–90), any scholarship of Hoffman must consider the entire canon of his work for continuity of meaning and appreciation of themes. He holds most of his manuscripts and all of his correspondence, but some manuscripts are at Hampden-Sydney College; a few are in a museum in Richwood, West Virginia; and one, *The Land That Drank the Rain*, was a gift to the person of dedication. "I think I would like for [readers] to say 'he wrote honestly and well,' " he says. Scholarship will note that William Hoffman continues to write honestly and well.

BIBLIOGRAPHY

Works by William Hoffman

The Trumpet Unblown. Garden City, N.Y.: Doubleday, 1955. Greenwich, Conn.: Fawcett, 1957 (paperback).

Days in the Yellow Leaf. Garden City, N.Y.: Doubleday, 1958. Greenwich, Conn.: Fawcett, 1959 (paperback).

A Place for My Head. Garden City, N.Y.: Doubleday, 1960. Greenwich, Conn.: Fawcett, 1962 (paperback).

The Dark Mountains. Garden City, N.Y.: Doubleday, 1963. New York: Modern Literary Editions, 1969 (paperback).

Yancey's War. Garden City, N.Y.: Doubleday, 1966. Greenwich, Conn.: Fawcett, 1967 (paperback).

The Love Touch (unpublished, produced play). Abingdon, Va.: The Barter Theatre, August 22–27, 1967.

A Walk to the River. Garden City, N.Y.: Doubleday, 1970. London: Robert Hale, 1972. Greenwich, Conn.: Fawcett, 1972 (paperback).

A Death of Dreams. Garden City, N.Y.: Doubleday, 1973. London: Robert Hale, 1975.

Virginia Reels. Urbana: University of Illinois Press, 1978 (simultaneous publication in
    paperback).
The Land That Drank the Rain. Baton Rouge: Louisiana State University Press, 1982.
Godfires. New York: Viking, 1985. New York: Penguin Books, 1986 (paperback).
By Land, By Sea. Baton Rouge: Louisiana State University Press, 1988.
Furors Die. Baton Rouge: Louisiana State University Press, 1990.

Studies of William Hoffman

Buffington, Robert. "The Intolerable Wrestle." *Modern Age* 16 (Winter 1972): 109–11.
Capers, Charlotte. "The Comeuppance of a Gentleman." (Rev. of *A Place for My Head*).
    New York Times Book Review (April 17, 1960): 24.
Coleman, Dero. "Compelling Novel" (Rev. of *A Walk to the River*). *Dallas Times
    Herald* (September 13, 1970): E-7.
Cooperman, Stanley. "Recent Fiction" (Rev. of *The Trumpet Unblown*). *Nation* 182
    (February 11, 1956): 123.
Corwin, Philip. "Hitting the Target More Often than Not" (Rev. of *A Death of Dreams*).
    Washington Post Book World (July 6, 1973): B-4.
Daniels, Lucy. "After the Past, the Present." *Saturday Review* 43 (June 18, 1960): 19–
    20.
Davenport, Gary. "The Fugitive Hero in New Southern Fiction." *Sewanee Review* 91
    (Summer 1983): 439–45.
———. "Good People in Trouble." *National Review* 22 (October 20, 1970): 1113,
    1115.
Davis, Mary H. "Introduction to the Novels of William Hoffman." M.A. Thesis. Farm-
    ville, Va.: Longwood College, 1980.
Davis, Paxton. " 'Furors Die' Author Is Making Mark." *Roanoke Times and World-
    News* (June 10, 1990): F-4.
Ewell, Nathaniel MacGregor, III. "The Novels of William Hoffman." Ph.D. Disser-
    tation. Columbia: University of South Carolina, 1975.
Frank, William."The Fiction of William Hoffman: An Introduction." *Hollins Critic* 28
    (February 1991): 1-10.
——— "Hoffman Doesn't Dodge Life" (Rev. of *Furors Die*). *Farmville Herald* (March
    21, 1990): 1–3A.
———. "Reviewer Finds Novel 'First Rate, Engrossing, and Soul Searching' " (Rev.
    of *A Walk to the River*). *Farmville Herald* (October 2, 1970): n.p.
Friddell, Guy. "A Good One for Sam" (Rev. of *A Death of Dreams*). *(Norfolk) Virginian
    Pilot* (May 27, 1973): n.p.
Hass, V. P. "Weak Stomachs Warned: Here Is War's Horror" (Rev. of *The Trumpet
    Unblown*). *Chicago Sunday Tribune* (January 1, 1956): part 4, 5.
Johnson, Greg. "Wonderful Geographies." *Georgia Review* 43 (Summer 1989): 406–
    16.
Kaufman, Lenard. "Tod Young of the Bleeding Heart" (Rev. of *Days in the Yellow
    Leaf*). *New York Times Book Review* (January 26, 1958): 5.
Kiely, Robert. "Tales and Stories" (Rev. of *Virginia Reels*). *New York Times Book
    Review* (February 25, 1979): 26.
Magill, Frank N., ed. *"Days in the Yellow Leaf,"* 1780–82 in *Survey of Contemporary
    Literature*. Englewood Cliffs, N.J.: Salem, 1977.

Manuel, Diane. "Short Stories" (Rev. of *By Land, By Sea*). *Christian Science Monitor* (March 16, 1988): 20.

Margoshes, Judith. "New Creative Writers." *Library Journal* 80 (October 1, 1955): 2146–47.

Merritt, Robert. "Spirit Prevails in Well-Crafted Tales" (Rev. of *By Land, By Sea*). *Richmond Times-Dispatch* (April 3, 1988): F–5.

Merritt, Robert. "Old-Fashioned Values" (Rev. of *Furors Die*). *Richmond Times-Dispatch* (May 20, 1990): G–5.

Mitgang, Herbert. "War from the Hospital-Unit Level" (Rev. of *The Trumpet Unblown*). *New York Times Book Review* (January 8, 1956): 26.

Neuberger, Christine. "Southside Life Inspires Author." *Richmond Times-Dispatch* (May 15, 1988): C–1.

"Notes on Current Books" (Rev. of *By Land, By Sea*). *Virginia Quarterly Review* 65 (Winter 1989): 19.

Shorris, Sylvia. "Literature's Stepchild" (Rev. of *Virginia Reels*). *Nation* 228 (February 10, 1979): 153–54.

Stone, Jerome. "War's Torture Chamber" (Rev. of *The Trumpet Unblown*). *Saturday Review* 39 (January 14, 1956): 41.

Stuart, Dabney. "Engrossing Novel Tale of Two Men" (Rev. of *Furors Die*). *Roanoke Times and World-News* (June 10, 1990): F–4.

Sullivan, Brad. " 'Godfires' Is about Value Struggles in Virginia." *Richmond Times-Dispatch* (July 28, 1985): F–5.

Sullivan, Walter. "About Any Kind of Meanness You Can Name." *Sewanee Review* 93 (Fall 1985): 649–56.

Taylor, Welford D., ed. "William Hoffman" 63 in *Virginia Authors*. Richmond: Virginia Association of Teachers of English, 1972.

Theroux, Paul. "Saint or Preacher?" (Rev. of *A Walk to the River*). *Washington Post Book World* (October 25, 1970): 6, 13.

Treadwell, T. O. "Being a Man" (Rev. of *The Land That Drank the Rain*). *Times Literary Supplement* (August 13, 1982): 888.

"The Trumpet Unblown." (Rev.) *New Yorker* 31 (December 31, 1955): 55.

"The Trumpet Unblown." (Rev.) *Time* 67 (January 9, 1956): 92.

Waterhouse, Carole. "In Short" (Rev. of *Godfires*). *New York Times Book Review* (July 28, 1985): 18.

Watkins, Floyd C. *The Death of Art*. Athens: University of Georgia Press, 1970.

Wolf, Michele. "In Short" (Rev. of *By Land, By Sea*). *New York Times Book Review* (May 15, 1988): 26.

STEPHEN COOPER

William Humphrey
(1924–   )

In many ways the fiction and nonfiction of William Humphrey have more in common with the works of William Faulkner and Ernest Hemingway than with the works of his own generation, writers who came to prominence after World War II. Like those earlier writers, he takes seriously concepts such as honor, courage, and family responsibility that are often treated ironically or mockingly by contemporary authors. He also has remained firmly in the realist camp, eschewing the self-conscious and self-reflexive experimentation of so many writers of the last three decades. This is not to say that Humphrey's works lack variety or humor. In fact, his novels reveal an impressive variety of subjects and moods. But that variety grows out of the traditional forms and techniques of the realists and focuses on themes that would have been familiar to an earlier generation of writers.

BIOGRAPHY

William Humphrey was born in Clarksville, Texas, on June 18, 1924. He drew heavily on his early experiences in this small Texas town for the setting and themes of his novels and short stories. Clarksville is located in the northeast corner of Texas, near the borders of Oklahoma, Arkansas, and Louisiana. Settled by immigrants from the Old South and with an economy based on cotton, Humphrey has described the Clarksville of his boyhood in his novel *The Ordways* (1965) and his memoir *Farther Off from Heaven* (1977) as a Southern town located close to where the West begins. Because his family moved frequently, he saw all sides of this small Southern town.

Humphrey's father, Clarence, was an automobile mechanic and the son of poor sharecroppers. He used his talent for fixing cars to escape the hardscrabble life of his parents. His wife, Nell, came from a farm family that was a step up on the social ladder—they rented rather than farmed on shares. Nell's family never approved of Clarence, and his continuing love of fast cars and alcohol confirmed their social prejudices. William, an only child, became aware early of the social conflicts and differences in the family.

In *Farther Off from Heaven*, Humphrey has described his relationship with both parents. From his father he learned an appreciation for nature and the value of testing yourself against the natural world. Clarence was a prolific and legendary hunter who initiated his son into the ways of the wild. Nature as a refuge and a test is a recurrent theme in Humphrey's fiction. From his mother Humphrey learned a love of music and order. He also became the focus of her ambitions for a better life and became the best student in his class. Nell instilled in him the beginnings of the aesthetic sense and discipline necessary for a writer.

As he grew older, he saw the relationship between his parents deteriorate as Clarence drank more heavily and perhaps began to see other women, while his mother wanted a more settled family life. The conflict ended when Clarence was killed in a late night car crash in July 1937 when Humphrey was 13. Humphrey and his mother moved to Dallas, where he spent the rest of his adolescence. At 14, he discovered a secondhand bookstore where he bought a copy of *Don Quixote* for a nickel and began his serious interest in literature. After brief stints at Southern Methodist University and the University of Texas, he went to New York City taking a play about Ben Franklin that he had written and that he hoped would make his literary fortune.

In New York he met Dorothy Feinman, a painter, with whom he eloped on his 21st birthday and to whom he is still married. In an effort to launch his writing career he approached such established writers as W. H. Auden and Randall Jarrell. He was impressed with Auden's kindness, but Jarrell gave him good practical advice by suggesting he read the work of his fellow Texan Katherine Anne Porter. Humphrey immediately acquired a copy of *Flowering Judas* and has said: "That good simple direct prose opened up a whole world to me." Soon he was writing his first short stories. In 1953 his first book was published, *The Last Husband and Other Stories.*

During most of the 1950s Humphrey taught at Bard College. His first novel, *Home from the Hill* (1958), a best-seller later made into a movie, brought him national attention and critical acclaim. He and his wife began to travel and lived in Italy for several years. His next novel, *The Ordways* (1965), was also a big seller, though reviews of it were mixed. None of his subsequent novels—*Proud Flesh* (1973); *Hostages to Fortune* (1984); and *No Resting Place* (1989)—has received the attention or had the sales of his first two novels, although his collection of stories—*A Time and a Place* (1968)—and *Farther Off from Heaven* have received critical praise. He has published a brief critical study focusing on the relation of man to nature in American literature, *Ah, Wilderness! The Frontier in American Literature* (1977). In recent years he has collected his writings about the outdoors in *Open Season: Sporting Adventures* (1986) and brought together his short fiction in *The Collected Stories of William Humphrey* (1985).

For the last quarter century Humphrey and his wife have lived in Hudson, New York. He has taught briefly at various colleges, but has mainly devoted himself to writing. He has largely avoided the New York literary scene and gone his own way. His quiet life and low profile may account in part for the lack of attention his later books have received. Humphrey has been content to let his writings speak for themselves.

MAJOR THEMES

Many of the characteristics that link Humphrey to an earlier generation appear in his first novel, the best-seller *Home from the Hill*. The opening description of the central square of a small Southern town in east Texas replete with whittling idlers and a Confederate war memorial reminds us of similar settings in Faulkner's works. Humphrey also echoes Faulkner's style in this novel, as the following sentence illustrates:

One Saturday afternoon that summer he rounded the northeast corner into the square, when a boy his age named Dale Latham, whose hatred he had unconsciously earned by his odd combination of innocence and manliness—innocence which the manliness had already given him so many fine opportunities to lose (Dale had seen them; Theron himself had not)—was suddenly provoked by the sight of him to violate the respect which even he and his gang, the smart ones, the ones with their own notion of manhood, who loitered outside the drugstore on Saturday afternoons, affecting to despise the boys who hung on the edge of the circle of hunting men, had so far kept towards Theron Hunnicutt.

The length and complexity of this sentence, particularly its piling up of qualifying phrases, are reminiscent of Faulkner. Although the average sentence in *Home from the Hill* is not as long or complex as this one, it is by no means unusual in the novel.

The plot and theme of the novel also contain Faulknerian elements. The story centers on Captain Wade Hunnicutt, his wife, Hannah, and their son, Theron. Wade is a legendary hunter and womanizer and his town's wealthiest, most respected, and most feared citizen. A man's man, he seems a throwback to an earlier era when honor and the code of the hunter ruled. Hannah is deeply offended by his womanizing but never mentions it and raises their son to respect his father. Theron becomes a renowned hunter in his own right when he kills a huge wild boar, nearly identical to one his father had killed years before. Theron idolizes his father and lives by what he believes is his father's code. Eventually, Theron's ideals collide with reality, and in the ensuing disillusionment and misunderstanding, the family is destroyed.

In *Home from the Hill* most of Humphrey's characteristic concerns emerge. The novel is a family tragedy, and every one of his novels centers on family life. For Humphrey, understanding who you are means knowing who your people were. It also means knowing where your people came from, and so he is always concerned to explain the social milieu of his characters. In *Home from the Hill* the story begins with all the main characters dead or missing, and we have only the collective memory of the townspeople to take us back to the beginning of the tragedy. Throughout the novel, the Hunnicutts are shown in the context of their small-town world. Within the social scene he creates, Humphrey focuses on the exceptional individual, the person who either through extraordinary courage or extraordinary bad luck is faced with a challenge. His protagonists are almost always tested, and he seems to value what Hemingway called "grace under pressure." Having that grace does not guarantee success or happiness, but it is essential for maintaining personal dignity. Thus even though the Hunnicutt family is destroyed by jealousy, pride, and misunderstanding, the courage and persistence they show in the face of disaster makes their fall tragic.

If Humphrey returns to these themes throughout his work, he does not do so monotonously. His first collection of short stories, *The Last Husband and Other Stories*, which preceded his first novel by 5 years, demonstrates this variety at the beginning of his career. The collection includes several stories that utilize the east Texas setting of his novel and that deal with such themes as a boy's initiation into manhood, the burden of the past, and the primacy of family ties. But *The Last Husband* also contains stories set outside of Texas that deal with very different character types, even if they explore similar themes. The title story concerns commercial artists who live in the suburbs of New York City and again focuses on family relationships and betrayals. "The Fauve" also focuses on artists and failed relationships. The story exposes the self-centeredness and self-deception of James Finley Ruggles, a failed artist and verbally abusive husband. Both "The Fauve" and "The Last Husband" show Humphrey able to deal with the issues of family and personal dignity in settings outside the east Texas landscapes.

But Texas has been the primary setting for his fiction. Humphrey's second novel, *The Ordways*, is in many ways an exploration of the variety of Texas. It opens with a description of Clarksville, Texas, which the narrator describes as one of those places where "the South draws up to a stop." Later, Sam Ordway, the novel's main character, travels the length and breadth of Texas looking for his lost son. In doing this he sees the great variety of Texas. Though rooted in the very Southern town of Clarksville, this novel expands to provide a panoramic view of Texas.

As its title suggests, *The Ordways* is a family chronicle, but of a very different sort from *Home from the Hill*. It focuses on ordinary farmers rather than the aristocratic first family of the town. After the opening section that describes the harrowing journey of the blinded Confederate soldier Thomas Ordway from Tennessee to Texas, the bulk of the novel is comic, focusing on Sam Ordway's quixotic pursuit of his lost son across Texas. Among other things, he works for a circus, speaks at a political rally, and is falsely accused of murder and then exonerated in an absurd trial. Sam's quest fails, but years later the missing son returns. Many of these stories have the tone and substance of tall tales. Since the reader hears the stories from a grandson of Sam, it seems safe to assume that Sam has embellished and polished his adventures over the years.

In this novel family heritage is important to all involved, but it is not as burdensome as it is in other Humphrey novels. There is tragedy and suffering in the Ordway chronicle, but there is also humor and a common stock of stories that knits the family's identity. Sam Ordway is tested by his picaresque journey in search of his son, and he does gain some self-knowledge and dignity from his extraordinary ordeal. But he remains an ordinary man, a man the reader can like and sympathize with, yet far from a tragic hero.

After *The Ordways* Humphrey returned to the short story, and the focus of the collection of stories he published in 1968 is indicated by its title, *A Time and a Place*. The time is the 1930s and the place is the dust bowl in Oklahoma and Texas. Individuals and families are tested by the terrible poverty of this time and place and by sudden wealth when oil is discovered. In these stories, poverty seems to pull families together, but easy money destroys relationships. Humphrey clearly describes the hard lives of the local farmers. But for those who strike oil, the wealth they so desire breeds greed and cares, disrupting their happiness and their family relations as much as poverty did.

Humphrey is sympathetic to the ordinary poor white farmer who struggled to make it in the dust bowl. He also has an interest in the travails of the outsiders in this society. In "A Good Indian," he portrays the growth of bigotry in an ordinary white businessman. Humphrey allows a bigoted car salesman to narrate the story and lets him unknowingly condemn himself. The more the narrator tries to justify himself, the more the reader is disgusted with this white salesman, who has come to accept General Sherman's famous dictum: "The only good Indian is a dead Indian." Humphrey explores a variation on this theme in "Mouth of Brass." In this story, the narrator is a white, middle-class boy who befriends Finus, a black man who sells delicious hot tamales. When a violent, ignorant white man kills Finus over a misunderstanding about a dozen tamales, no one will testify against the white man. The narrator learns that even though his parents condemn what has happened, they feel powerless to intervene, and in a sense acquiesce in the town's bigotry.

A Time and a Place is a stronger, more unified collection than *The Last Husband*. Throughout this collection characters are challenged by hard times, and Humphrey's sympathies are clearly with the outsiders and the marginal characters in the world he creates. He shows the difficult lives of the poor white farmers, but he is also aware of the victims of white bigotry and fascinated by those who operate on the margins of society.

In his third novel, *Proud Flesh*, Humphrey wrote another work about a proud Texas family. The clannish Renshaw family gathers at their homestead as Ma, the family matriarch, mother of ten children, is dying. The members of the family derive their individual identities in large part from being Renshaws—proverbial for their pride, their loyalty to each other, and their violence. Humphrey explores the tormented psychology of this family, which feels bound to each other through their relationship to Ma. On the other hand, the divergent personalities of Ma's children put tremendous strains on those ties. The oldest child, Amy, seems to devote herself fully to her mother, but Ma is repulsed by her suffocating attentions. Clyde, who runs the farm on the family homestead, leads a secret life with a black lover, Shug. Kyle, the youngest and Ma's favorite, left home after a quarrel and has never returned.

Although Humphrey takes the pain and suffering of these characters seriously, through the use of irony and humor he suggests that their pride is excessive, even ridiculous. For example, Clyde is tormented by conflicting feelings about his black lover. But he is also tormented with untimely erections, which Humphrey treats humorously. Amy's tortured relationship with her mother is explored sensitively. But after Ma dies, Amy locks herself in the family's storm cellar and vows never to come out. The cellar becomes a media and a tourist attraction, and finally a kind of shrine as people come to confess their sins to the unresponsive Amy by talking into the ventilator pipe. Through these characters, Humphrey shows the real pain of family ties and the absurdity of carrying family pride to an extreme.

In 1977 Humphrey published a memoir, *Farther Off from Heaven*, which focuses on his childhood in Clarksville. He opens his story with his mother waking him at three o'clock in the morning to go to his badly injured father who would die three days later. Humphrey describes his childhood by means of flashbacks and orders his book associatively. His skillful construction of the book builds suspense by mentioning important childhood events but only telling the full story later in the book. This memoir reads like a carefully crafted novel.

In the story of his childhood we see many of the main themes of his fiction. Family ties and history are important. An only child, Humphrey paints detailed portraits of both his parents, their relationship, and their family backgrounds. He describes clearly the social distinctions of a small Southern town and the flavor of life in the 1920s and 1930s. His father's need to test himself—to prove his manhood and his courage using guns, cars, and women—reminds us of other Humphrey heroes trying to prove or define their manhood. The love of nature that Humphrey learned from his father would inform much of his later writing. The tragedy that ended his childhood and the many ironies it revealed in his own life find their reflection in his concern with the sufferings of his fictional characters and the ironic twists of fate that bedevil them.

After *Farther Off from Heaven* Humphrey turned away from his Texas roots for his next novel, *Hostages to Fortune*. The novel's protagonist, Ben Curtis, is a Princeton-educated writer who has returned to his fishing club in upstate New York after a two-year absence. Since his club mates saw him last, he has lost 35 pounds and his hair has turned white. During those two years, his son, his goddaughter, and his best friend have all committed suicide, and his marriage has broken apart under the strain. After this string of disasters, Ben takes sleeping pills in an unsuccessful suicide attempt.

Ben's meditations on suicide are a major portion of the novel. At first he tries to understand why his intense, intelligent son, a freshman at Princeton, killed himself. He soon turns to what he has to live for now that he has lost his son, his wife, and his best friend. Ben is intensely introspective, but the results of his search for meaning are highly uncertain and tentative. He lacks a belief in an afterlife or in conventional religion. His fly-fishing trip, which frames the novel, seems an attempt to find peace and order in nature and in the rituals of trout fishing. This part of the novel is reminiscent of Hemingway's "Big Two-Hearted River." Like Hemingway's Nick Adams, Ben seeks to heal his psychic wounds and come to terms with himself while fishing.

In its tone, subject matter, and setting, *Hostages to Fortune* marked a departure from Humphrey's previous work. In his most recent novel, *No Resting Place*, he makes another new departure by attempting a historical novel. His subject is the Trail of Tears, the forced removal of the so-called five civilized tribes of Indians from the Southeastern United States to the Oklahoma territory in the 1830s. Like so many other Humphrey works, this novel is a family chronicle. The narrator tells the story, handed down from father to son, of his great-grandfather, Noquisi, who was part Cherokee and walked the Trail of Tears.

In *No Resting Place*, Humphrey shows how America was built on the dispossession of its native inhabitants. What makes the Trail of Tears particularly poignant is that the five tribes rounded up and driven West had made every effort to fit in with white society. Most of them were farmers, many were Christian converts, and a significant number were educated. Noquisi's father was a doctor and lived a fairly conventional middle-class life. Through intermarriage, many of the Indians could pass for white, including Noquisi and his family. Caught between two cultures, Noquisi becomes more and more Cherokee as the persecution escalates, yet he also uses the white man's medical skills that he had picked up from his father to minister to his people on the trail. The ironies of "civilization" are further emphasized by a Scottish missionary to the Indians who accompanies Noquisi and the Cherokees on their journey. An honest and devout man, Reverend Mackenzie comes to doubt most of the Christian precepts he is supposed to preach as he witnesses the brutality of the whites and the courage and endurance of the "savages."

Although Humphrey adopts in *No Resting Place* a form and subject matter that are new to him, his abiding themes remain—the importance of family and the past, sympathy for the dispossessed and persecuted, admiration for courage under pressure, and a sense that an individual's dignity is his or her most important possession.

SURVEY OF CRITICISM

From the beginning of Humphrey's career, reviewers and critics have compared his work to Faulkner's. In a review of Humphrey's first novel, *Home from the Hill*, Walter Havighurst said: "The title is from Robert Louis Stevenson, but the tale is from William Faulkner." He compared the novel to one of

Faulkner's Yoknapatawpha sagas and compared Theron Hunnicutt to Ike McCaslin. Although flattering to Humphrey, constant comparisons to Faulkner are also unfortunate because they set up an impossible standard and mask the originality of Humphrey's best work. For example, Louis Rubin, Jr., in *The Curious Death of the Novel*, uses Humphrey as an example of the dangers of imitating Faulkner's style and themes. He asserts that Humphrey in *Home from the Hill* used a Faulknerian approach "in order to describe an experience that was not really Faulknerian at all. And it fails to convince us." Rubin sees *The Ordways* as a failure because the early journey of Thomas Ordway is almost Faulknerian tragedy and the later journey of Sam Ordway is nearly slapstick. For Rubin, Humphrey uses some of Faulkner's techniques without Faulkner's vision of the world.

Writing two decades later in the *Sewanee Review*, Mark Royden Winchell begins a survey of Humphrey's career by addressing Rubin's charges against Humphrey. Winchell generally accepts Rubin's view of Humphrey's early work, but argues that in his more recent work Humphrey has developed a voice of his own and escaped the shadow of Faulkner. He praises the strong voice and clear focus of *Farther Off from Heaven*. Winchell sees *Hostages to Fortune* as Humphrey's most impressive work and a real advance because in it "he has finally earned his vision and found a voice distinctively his own." For Winchell, an important element in this advance was Humphrey's decision to break away from the Texas setting of his early works and get away from that postage stamp of land that was his Yoknapatawpha. Gary Davenport has also seen Humphrey's later work as his strongest work, but for different reasons. He sees the earlier fiction, particularly *Home from the Hill*, as too devoted to the "conventional version of his regional mythology," whereas the later works take less for granted and earn their emotional depths rather than assuming them.

Contemporary reviewers generally saw Humphrey's early work as stronger than these critics allow. They pointed out his vivid evocation of place and social setting and his sensitive portrayal of family relationships. Reviewers of *The Ordways* pointed out its skillful use of the tall-tale tradition of the Old West. Elizabeth Janeway compared the novel favorably to *Adventures of Huckleberry Finn* in its use of farce and episodic structure. His powerful descriptions, sense of place and family, and original characters have continued to receive praise throughout his career.

The one aspect of Humphrey's work that has received the most negative criticism is his sense of structure. He has often been accused of slipping into melodrama, particularly in *Home from the Hill* and *Proud Flesh*. Although Janeway has praised the episodic structure of *The Ordways*, a number of critics see the book falling into discrete parts with little in common. In both Humphrey's short fiction and his novels, critics have complained of plots that seem farfetched or out of proportion. His memoir *Farther Off from Heaven* is his only work to receive consistent praise for its structure.

Humphrey's work has not received much attention from academic critics. In

1967 James W. Lee published a monograph on Humphrey as part of the Southwest Writers Series. In a survey of all Humphrey's work up to that time, Lee emphasizes his strong sense of place and his stylistic skill, but points out the weakness of many of his plots. In his study of the graveyard motif in Southern fiction, John T. Hiers has examined the graveyard scenes in *Home from the Hill* and *The Ordways* as emblems of character relations and opportunities for self-realization. Sylvia Grider and Elizabeth Tebeaux have published a detailed study of Humphrey's short story "A Job of the Plains." They see this ironic retelling of the Job story as central to *A Time and a Place*, which in their view embodies a bleak vision of a world of suffering without meaning. In a later study, Tebeaux has interpreted Humphrey's entire short-story output in terms of this "cynical philosophy" and the ironies it entails. In an impressive reconsideration of Humphrey's entire career, John M. Grammer has seen him as having more in common with his contemporaries Walker Percy and Flannery O'Connor than with his predecessor Faulkner. Grammer reads Humphrey's works in terms of a confrontation between memory, represented by the South, and modernity, represented by the West. In this conflict, memory is invoked as a stay against the rootlessness of modernity, but with each passing generation remembering becomes more and more an act of will and thus memory becomes increasingly artificial.

Perhaps the dearth of academic criticism of Humphrey can be explained by his old-fashioned approach to fiction and his lack of post modern pyrotechnics. But there is much in his work deserving of attention, and some areas, such as his treatment of minorities and those on the margins of society, have gone largely unexplored.

BIBLIOGRAPHY

Works by William Humphrey

The Last Husband and Other Stories. New York: Morrow, 1953.
Home from the Hill. New York: Knopf, 1958.
The Ordways. New York: Knopf, 1965.
A Time and a Place. New York: Knopf, 1968.
Proud Flesh. New York: Knopf, 1973.
Ah, Wilderness! The Frontier in American Literature. El Paso: Texas Western Press, 1977.
Farther Off from Heaven. New York: Knopf, 1977.
Hostages to Fortune. New York: Delacorte Press/Seymour Lawrence, 1984.
The Collected Stories of William Humphrey. New York: Delacorte Press/Seymour Lawrence, 1985.
Open Season: Sporting Adventures. New York: Delacorte Press/Seymour Lawrence, 1986.
No Resting Place. New York: Delacorte Press/Seymour Lawrence, 1989.

Interviews

Crowder, Ashley Bland. "History, Family, and William Humphrey." *Southern Review* 24 (Autumn 1988): 825–39.
————. "William Humphrey: Defining Southern Literature." *Mississippi Quarterly* 41 (Fall 1988): 529–40.

Studies of William Humphrey

Bowden, Larry R. "A Lament for the Vanishing" (Rev. of *No Resting Place*). *Cross Currents* 41 (Spring 1991): 107–15.
Davenport, Gary. "The Desertion of William Humphrey's Circus Animals." *Southern Review* 23 (April 1987): 494–503.
Grammer, John M. "Where the South Draws Up to a Stop: The Fiction of William Humphrey." *Mississippi Quarterly* 44 (Winter 1990–91): 5–21.
Grider, Sylvia, and Elizabeth Tebeaux. "Blessings into Curses: Sardonic Humor and Irony in 'A Job of the Plains.' " *Studies in Short Fiction* 23 (Summer 1986): 297–306.
Havighurst, Walter. "Prelude to Violence." *Saturday Review* (January 11, 1958): 15.
Hiers, John T. "The Graveyard Epiphany in Modern Southern Fiction: Transcendence of Selfhood." *Southern Humanities Review* 9 (Fall 1975): 389–403.
Hoffman, Frederick J. *The Art of Southern Fiction: A Study of Some Modern Novelists.* Carbondale and Edwardsville: Southern Illinois University Press, 1967.
Janeway, Elizabeth. "Journey through Time." *New York Times Book Review* (January 31, 1965): 1, 40.
Kakutani, Michiko. "Tales of Lost Ways." *New York Times Book Review* (June 22, 1985): 16.
Lee, James W. *William Humphrey.* Southwest Writers Series, Vol. 7. Austin: Steck-Vaughn, 1967.
Price, Reynolds. "Homecountry, East Texas." *New York Times Book Review* (May 22, 1977): 7, 31.
Rubin, Louis, Jr. *The Curious Death of the Novel: Essays in American Literature.* Baton Rouge: Louisiana State University Press, 1967.
Tebeaux, Elizabeth. "Irony as Art: The Short Fiction of William Humphrey." *Studies in Short Fiction* 26 (Summer 1989): 323–34.
Winchell, Mark Royden. "Beyond Regionalism: The Growth of William Humphrey." *Sewanee Review* 96 (Spring 1988): 287–92.
Yardley, Jonathan. "William Humphrey's Hardscrabble Stories." *Washington Post Book World* (July 14, 1985): 3, 7.
Yglesias, Jose. "William Humphrey." *Publishers Weekly* (June 2, 1989): 64–65.

Josephine Humphreys
(1945–   )

Josephine Humphreys is widely recognized and respected as a contemporary writer, highly and justly praised for her three best-selling novels: *Dreams of Sleep* (1984), *Rich in Love* (1987), and *The Fireman's Fair* (1991). All three of her books share the setting of contemporary Charleston, South Carolina. Her themes also prove contemporary—the disillusions of history and the disintegration of the family—though her method—the adept handling of traditional character, plot, setting, and style—creates interesting implications of renewal and reintegration. Her accomplishments unite the romantic and feminine traditions of Southern letters with the minimalist and feminist interests of her contemporaries. Readers of serious fiction by Southern women writers will continue to anticipate her new books.

BIOGRAPHY

Josephine Humphreys was born on February 2, 1945, in Charleston, South Carolina, her home for most of her life and the setting for all three of her published novels. Her family was socially prominent and financially comfortable, with long-time Carolina connections, including an ancestor who served as the Confederate secretary of the treasury. In a reminiscent essay, "My Real Invisible Self," Humphreys recalls family Christmas cards adorned with photographs of well-brushed blonde girls—of whom she was the oldest; these almost angelic portraits contrast with her memories of her own "ornery" nature and her "grouchy and impatient" family. Her eccentric grandmother tried to interest her in the arts, and finally uncovered young Josephine's talent for stories.

Humphreys' love of writing provided the spark for her education in suburban schools and at Duke University (A.B., 1967), Yale University (M.A., 1968), and the University of Texas (doctoral work, 1968–70). At Duke she studied creative writing with William Blackburn and Reynolds Price. She returned to Charleston in 1970 with her husband, Thomas Hutcheson, an attorney; they have two sons, Allen and William. From 1970 to 1977, she was an assistant professor of English at Baptist College of Charleston.

In 1977, when Humphreys suffered health problems under the stress of parenting, teaching, and writing, she turned her energies to fiction. Her first novel took almost 5 years to complete and she mailed the manuscript to Price 20 years after she had taken his creative writing class. With Price's help she secured an agent, Harriet Wasserman, and then with Wasserman's help a publisher, Viking. *Dreams of Sleep* appeared in 1984 to unanimous accolades. In the *New York Times*, novelist Ellen Douglas called it "an extraordinarily accomplished first novel. . . . the best first novel I've read in years." In the *Washington Post*, the sometimes acerbic Jonathan Yardley praised it as an "exceptional performance . . . sturdy, intelligent, and appealing." Ruth MacDougall in the *Christian Science Monitor* said that "*Dreams of Sleep* is beautifully written, intelligent, and evocative." In 1985 the book won the PEN/Ernest Hemingway Prize for the best American first novel.

The success of her first book also helped Humphreys secure a Guggenheim Fellowship in 1985 and a Lyndhurst Fellowship in 1986; with these awards, she was able to finish her second novel, *Rich in Love*, in 1987. Again Humphreys received a chorus of praise. Many reviewers noted that the author had averted the notorious "second-novel slump" by changing her approach in point of view, style, and tone. Fellow Southern author Fred Chappell wrote in the *New York Times*: "Even if *Rich in Love* did not possess its strong characters, entrancing story line and vigorous outlook, it would still be interesting because its author is a dazzling stylist." A dozen other reviewers echoed this praise. The book's best-selling popularity led to a movie version, recently filmed in Charleston by director Bruce Beresford (whose credits include *Driving Miss Daisy*). Although Humphreys did not write the screenplay, she has expressed favorable reaction to the film version.

Humphreys' third novel, *The Fireman's Fair*, was begun immediately after her second was finished, and she completed a draft before Hurricane Hugo struck Charleston in September 1989. In an interview, Humphreys described how her personal epiphany in the midst of the destruction compelled her to include the cataclysm in the novel, both for the sense of contemporary Charleston and as an objective correlative for the chaos of her protagonist's personal life. Humphreys took a year to rewrite the book; it was published to positive response in 1991.

In some ways, the novel returns to the literary achievements of her first book, both in its central male figure and in its neorealistic vision of contemporary Southern culture; again like her first book, possibilities of hope and happiness exist in the very moment of disintegration and disillusionment. If anything, her writing is perhaps stronger and more thoughtful. As the anonymous reviewer for *Publisher's Weekly* says: "Humphreys relates her story in graceful, pithy prose, unerring in tone and emphasis, full of wise and surprising insights.'' Most reviews were just as enthusiastic, repaying her publisher's confident first printing of 50,000 copies.

Humphreys has begun another novel, as yet unfinished. She also has published a number of interesting articles in journals and collections that provide considerable insight into her fiction. It seems clear she is fast becoming a best-selling, important novelist who demonstrates a unique combination of feminine literary traditions and contemporary feminist issues in a symbolic Southern setting.

MAJOR THEMES

Josephine Humphreys is well regarded among readers of serious fiction by Southern women precisely for her unique balance of traditional methods and contemporary interests. Though contrasting in many ways, all her novels combine her major themes—the dislocations of history, particularly Southern history, and the disintegration of the family, particularly the traditional Southern family. Perhaps her most intriguing contribution is the persistent suggestion of renewal and reintegration that pervades her fictions. In an interview she said: ''I write mostly about families, in long-term relationships. . . . We see them as static, but they always change.''

In response to an interviewer's question about writers who inspired her fiction, Humphreys mentioned only two: Louisa May Alcott, a childhood favorite, and Reynolds Price, her mentor at Duke. From Alcott she learned that fiction is a gift of pleasure; from Price that it is a mystery as well. She added: ''Also, I was not only a writer but an English major, so I am steeped in the traditions of fiction.'' The careful reader discerns many influences and parallels, particularly in terms of her Southern literary heritage. From earlier Southern fiction, Humphreys' innocent adolescents confronted by the corruptions of history recall Huck Finn (in another article, Humphreys calls Samuel Clemens ''the greatest American novelist''), while her bewildered young couples mirror Kate Chopin's incisive analyses of Southern domestic entanglements. From the earlier generations of the Southern Renascence, comparisons with Eudora Welty are appropriate. Both writers create ironic yet affectionate and hopeful portraits of eccentric Southern families. Humphreys may also be likened to Carson McCullers because of her tomboy adolescents and complex probings of love and alienation. Like almost all Southern women writing since 1939, Humphreys stands in some relationship to the long shadow cast by Margaret Mitchell, though hers is probably at the opposite pole from her Charleston contemporary, Alexandra Ripley. Reviewers have often grouped Humphreys with contemporary Southern women such as Rob Dew, Gail Godwin, Bobbie Ann Mason, Lee Smith, and Anne Tyler; and, for all their differences, all of these writers do combine contemporary themes in changing Southern settings with more or less traditional methods of fictional presentation in which traditional realism shades to minimalism.

Humphreys begins an essay on Southern literature stating: "To tell the truth the South is once again in ruins." This short article encapsulates the observations of Southern cultural critics as disparate as W. J. Cash, C. Vann Woodward, and Robert Penn Warren in picturing the successive ruins of the Southern frontier, Reconstruction, and Sun Belt development. In fact, "development" becomes a pejorative term for Humphreys in her essay and a negative image in her fiction. Inevitably the ongoing force of history pulls apart the fragile orders of the past. In this respect, her Charleston setting seems made to order; The intellectual capital of the Old South, it is now a bastion of the new, mortgaging its heritage to developers and tourists. As one of her characters muses in the first novel: "Nothing sticks together very long without immense effort." Although he is consciously discussing his antebellum home, this speaker is imaging his family, his city, and his culture.

The failure of marriage and the disintegration of the family prove the central themes of all those writers generally grouped together as contemporary, Southern, and female. Certainly these traditional institutions are changing in American society, and probably the impacts of these changes are more dramatic in the South with its historical emphasis on both relationships. It also seems natural that women writers would be most sensitive to these permutations in social structure, as well as to those in housing patterns. All of Humphreys' novels focus on these moments of personal reformation—of disintegration and reconciliation—in traditional marital and familial settings.

Even more than is the case with her contemporaries, Humphreys' sure handling of traditional aspects of fiction seems to imply possibilities of renewal and reintegration. Reviewers have consistently praised her strong characterizations, particularly of innocent but tough-minded adolescent females who promise love and order for the future. Likewise, her emphasis on traditional plotting, complete with rounded conclusions, implies development and closure, as does the realism of her Charleston settings. In fact, the only major recurring criticism of Humphreys' work is precisely in terms of the hopeful outlook created in her books; some critics complain that her conclusions posit artificial orders that do not proceed from their fictional development. A closer look at her novels demonstrates that her ordering of reality in fiction may occasionally falter, but it never fails; it never prevents the reader from perceiving the complexity and clarity of her vision.

Dreams of Sleep is an amazing first effort. The novel presents a portrait gallery of well-rounded characters who are expertly choreographed through a complex interlocking of plots. The setting of Charleston is well realized, on both literal and symbolic levels. Most successful, perhaps, is the mastery of style and tone in the writing itself. Humphreys' 5 years of effort on seven or eight drafts is evident in the brilliant prose and imagery that illuminate the work. As Michael Malone put it, the novel is not so much narrative as "a beautifully written tone poem, a subtle counterpoint of moods."

Appropriately the book begins with dreams and sleep, controlling metaphors throughout, and with its central couple, Alice and Will Reese. Surely this opening is one of the best written in contemporary fiction:

Before they wake, sunlight is on the house, moving on the high east wall and windows through old glass wavy as broken water, onto the hard bright floor of waxed pine. When Alice opens her eyes she sees its cool path stamped by the shadow of mullions, squares stretching to rhomboids of clear fall sun. Will sleeps behind her, his breath wisping her back. She loves the quiet of light and its mutable geometry, as those wizards did who chinked and slit their stones to let in messages from sun gods. The message to Alice is, Don't move. Not till that first stamp of light touches the wide crack in the floorboards. Till then she is frozen. The room is frozen. Only two things may move—the slow light, and his feathery perfect breath between her shoulder blades.

The next paragraph starts with the abrupt sentence, "But he turns." The plot is in motion, for Will, a "thirty-something" gynecologist, has turned away from Alice, who sacrificed her career as a mathematician to raise their two little girls, Beth and Marcy. He is engaged in a complicated affair with Claire Thibault, the nurse who runs his office. The opening paragraph suggests Alice's response, a sort of hysterical and frigid inertia. Tradition, represented by the Reeses' restored Charleston mansion, is likewise symbolized; of course, their careful restoration has not made it a true home for the Reese family, and already the new materials are decaying, like the social orders around it.

These failures of effort and will multiply in the complications of plot. Recently Claire has become the apex of an interlocking triangle, as she turns from her stalled relationship with Will Reese to his friend and colleague, Danny Cardozo, who was divorced by his wife. Reminiscence and flashback bring in the difficult marriages of both Alice's and Will's parents. His widowed mother, Marcella, has recently remarried a Yankee developer named Duncan, creating another stressful situation for her jealous son.

Most important, this whole section of the novel set in upper middle-class Charleston is mirrored by parallel relationships set in the sad, seedy world of the local housing projects. Central to these parallel relationships is the wonderfully named Iris Moon, Humphreys' tough, but loving, teenaged heroine. She cares for her somewhat adolescent mother, Fay, and her younger brother, Randall, the only white family in a public housing project. Her father, Owen, decamped some years earlier, though he surfaces occasionally to pester Fay or threaten to take the children off to his new home and family in Florida. Iris has a young black admirer, Emory, and through him a surrogate mother, Queen, Emory's putative grandmother. These poor white and black families are splintered even more than the well-off white ones in the novel's other skein of plot.

The connection between the two groups develops when Queen, also Marcella's maid, suggests Iris as a babysitter for the Reese children. The lifeless Alice has to be pushed into the relationship, but she soon comes to view Iris with the same awe as the others in her world. Beth and Marcy fall in love with their new surrogate mother, while Iris plans to take them away from their unhappy home and the hapless Alice to form her own new family. Before Iris can effect her plans, Claire decides to break off her affair with Will and marry Danny, a move that precipitates a crisis for the romantic Will, who battles with almost everyone, finally causing Alice to flee with her children and Iris. The younger woman demonstrates a precocious wisdom, however, and returns Alice and the girls for a reconciliation, while she follows Emory and his real mother, Patrice, to Atlanta. So the very closure of plot implies renewal in a new disposition of relationships, marriages, and families.

In fact, this kaleidoscopic patterning of relations among these many-faceted characters proves at once both the novel's greatest strength and weakness. Although it obviously realizes the major themes—the failure of tradition and disintegration of the traditional family—it also loses focus on any single character. Alice seems intended to be sort of central consciousness, and she is incisively portrayed with the insights of both close experience and careful observation. At the same time, Alice seems too passive throughout to have earned her renewal at the conclusion. This passivity seems especially odd in terms of the action initiated by her husband, Will, the most interesting character in the novel. Yet Will, too, is fragmented—in his devotion to poetry and medicine, as well as to his multiple loves—to center the book. So, in a sense, this task falls to Iris, who proves just a bit too symbolic a figure to provide verity to the conclusions.

Before she came to mother the Reese children, Iris played Snow White to several gnomish old men in a rooming house near the housing project. The association with the fairy tale is Alice's, appropriate enough as she herself wanders the world of Charleston as if it lay beyond a strange looking glass. Iris does exist like a fairy-tale heroine, an ideal of a strong adolescent girl rather than the real thing. Indeed, the whole lower-class section of the plot lacks the immediacy and reality of the upper-class settings. In particular, the black characters seem obscure figures, shadowy reflections of the whites more than real people in their own right. This is not to say that the novel fails in these terms, though it does fall off a bit, as social realism. Finally, this fiction works best at the level of the title, of sleep and dreams, of hidden needs and fears, of unfulfilled fantasies and hungers. When these elements do balance—as in the opening chapter, or in the scene of Will stalking through Claire's darkened apartment, or in Alice's long dreams of symbolic houses—then Humphreys' fiction ranks among the most successful and arresting on the contemporary scene.

In certain respects, Humphreys' second book, *Rich in Love*, demonstrates fictional development beyond the first; it presents a broader, more detailed view of the Charleston setting, a more structured pattern of character and plot, and an interesting variation on style and point of view. The second book is perhaps best read as a complement to the first. Like *Dreams of Sleep*, *Rich in Love* is focused by changing traditions and fragmenting families, but here the emphasis seems more comic than tragic, more "funny" than "gloomy," in Humphreys' own words.

Probably the major element in these changes of tone and emphasis is the use of the first-person point of view, in the past tense, of Lucille Odum, the second of Humphreys' phenomenally precocious adolescents. In fact, the author has commented that she was so taken with Iris Moon while writing the first book that she decided to center her second novel on a variation of the type. Humphreys' choice has both positive and negative effects on her overall narrative. Lucille becomes much better rounded than Iris because she is more carefully conceived but also more fully developed. The youngest child of an eccentric upper-middle-class family, Lucille harks back to the adolescents of J. D. Salinger rather than those of Carson McCullers. Indeed, as a variant on the innocent American child coming of age, Lucille can be traced to Huck Finn. Lucille herself suggests this lineage, stating that Huck's growing-up saga would be darker and more difficult for a female protagonist. The problem with this novel is that it is not darker; rather, it proves a good deal brighter. Lucille is just "too good at her adolescence," as Richard Eder puts it—so spunky and dependable that she becomes something of an author surrogate, incisively skewering the foibles of her place and time.

Lucille's place is Mt. Pleasant, an ocean-side suburb of Charleston, in the early 1980s. Until her story opens, Lucille's life had been, in general, pleasant, though she is concerned about the contemporary problems of the environment, especially in the trashing of her suburban home:

On an afternoon two years ago my life veered from its day-in-day-out course and became for a short while the kind of life that can be told as a story—that is, one in which events appear to have meaning. Before, there had been nothing worth telling the world. We had our irregularities; but every family has something or other out of whack. We had my mother's absent-mindedness, my sister's abnormal beauty, my father's innocence; and I was not without oddities of my own. We were characters, my friend Wayne said. But nothing about us was story material.

Until the day, May 10, when one of us betrayed the rest and set off a series of events worth telling.

The key event of the plot is the departure of her mother, Helen, who has grown bored with her retired husband, Warren, and the ongoing search for her. For the most part directed by Lucille, the search also involves her older sister, Rae, and Rae's new husband, Billy McQueen. Conventional symbolism would play this new marriage off the old, but it is disintegrating quickly because Rae can handle neither the idea of marriage nor that of motherhood. Since Rae is several months pregnant, and Billy is preoccupied with his doctoral dissertation in history, they are not much help in the search for Helen. Nor are the equally eccentric black retainer family, the Pooles, who provide the background shadowing in this novel.

As the weeks and months pass, the familial and romantic relationships slowly shift. Lucille becomes the surrogate mother of the Odum clan, and she is the one who tracks her mother down, through the help of her parallel female figure, Rhody Poole. In the meantime, Warren has an affair with his hair stylist, Vera

Oxendine, and Lucille moves from an abortive affair with her Huck-like boy-friend, Wayne Frobisher, to a tryst with her sister's husband. The story is resolved on Halloween, when Rae delivers her baby prematurely, and Helen returns to help. Although it seems they all have grown together once again, the last chapter shows a reshuffled picture puzzle—Warren with Vera, and Helen with an old love; Billy and Rae and Wayne and Lucille involved once again; and everyone taken with the beautiful baby girl, Phoebe.

Some reviewers found the conclusion perhaps too rounded, but it does seem to develop naturally enough from the motivations of Humphreys' characters. Certainly, it seems to demonstrate Humphreys' major strength—her ability to realize the contemporary themes of historical discontinuity and marital/familial dislocation while suggesting the possibilities of renewal and reconciliation. Lucille recognizes these possibilities in the title phrase itself: "Many things happen invisibly and mysteriously. Creatures have links with their own kind. I knew what love was without the aid of empirical evidence, and furthermore, I believed that I did have it. It was in me. It had been accumulating silently over the years like equity in a house. I was rich in love, even though no one could see it." It is in exactly this poetic, yet precise, use of language, here filtered through the consciousness of her intriguing narrator, that Humphreys' fiction succeeds so well.

As with her first two novels, the title of her third, *The Fireman's Fair*, provides a key to the book's themes and meanings. On a realistic level the fair is the annual fund-raiser for the Volunteer Fire Department of an island community near Charleston, featuring a fish fry, carnival rides, and a "Battle of the Bands." Humphreys' protagonist, Rob Wyatt, is one of the firemen and, like his father before him, one of the fair's organizers. In fact, the fire company has provided a point of stability in Rob's rapidly changing life, and the fair itself becomes a point of focus and reunion after the disintegration engendered by Hurricane Hugo. The hurricane provides the final impetus to change, for Rob, for the characters patterned about him, and for the entire community. In this sense, the fireman's fair becomes the center of the novel, both the symbol of social solidarity and a sort of Vanity Fair demonstrating the chaotic state of contemporary affairs.

The book builds inexorably from the immediate aftermath of the hurricane to the fair and its aftermath in the changed relationships of the central characters. As in the earlier novels, these relationships form a pattern of interlocking triangles that involve several levels and aspects of the Charleston community. The central figure is Rob Wyatt, the poetically named social drop-out, a lawyer who quits his practice, deserts his fashionable apartment, leaves his yuppie friends, and moves back to the island suburb of his youth as he tries to discover his real identity in some elemental connection to the wilderness of the beaches and the swamps. Living alone in a run-down beach house with his Irish setter, Speedo, he begins to find himself in the working world of the island and its volunteer firemen, especially his longtime black friend, Albert, and his new Vietnamese friend, Huang.

Typical of Humphreys' protagonists, Rob's major crisis proves to be his romantic relationship, here with Louise, a former love, who married his friend and former law partner, Hank Camden. An attractive Junior Leaguer, Louise needs Hank for his upward mobility and Rob for his romantic attachment to their mutual past. They remain friends, often meeting socially for golf, which as Humphreys remarked in a interview, seemed a handy combination of the natural and social worlds. Of course, both Rob and Louise need to leave their dead relationship, just as Rob's parents, Jack and Maude, must rediscover the vitality of their relationship instead of moving to a sterile retirement community.

In some neat bits of intertwined plotting and flashback, Louise introduces Rob to Billie Poe, one of Humphreys' adolescent heroines, who is escaping her decidedly odd sailor husband and who provides Rob with a new way of looking at his world. Maude takes a lover, after years of putting up with her husband's philandering, forcing Jack to recognize the cost of his affairs. The two levels or strands of plotting are connected by both the father's and the son's recognition of their betrayal of Maude two decades earlier when she was committed to a rest home for a year. By confronting the past, Jack and Maude reunite after the husband's incoherent but emotional speech about the individual and the collective past to the assembled fairgoers. At the same time, Rob chooses Billie instead of Louise, who, in turn, is reconciled with Hank. Although this conclusion may seem pat in outline, Humphreys handles it with great insight and subtlety, and with no sense of finality or "they lived happily ever after," which they probably don't.

All three of Humphreys' novels are important, if imperfect works, engaging contemporary themes through traditional methods to teach readers something new about the craft of fiction and about life at the close of this century. Humphreys proves especially interesting in her extension of the romantic and feminine traditions of Southern fiction into the feminist and minimalist world of contemporary Southern letters. Serious readers of Southern fiction will await her further developments with justified anticipation.

SURVEY OF CRITICISM

Because Humphreys' first novel was published in 1984, criticism of her work is not extensive. At present no major critical studies specifically concerned with her fiction are in print. The best criticism is found in the standard reference sources and in the major reviews of her two novels. *Contemporary Authors*, Volume 127, provides the fullest biographical information available, as well as a sensible introduction, and an extensive interview. Another important interview was presented in *Publishers Weekly*, September 4, 1987. Humphreys' own article of biographical reminiscence, "My Real Invisible Self," appears in *A World Unsuspected: Portraits of Southern Childhood*.

Perhaps the most important critical piece in terms of Humphreys' fiction is her own essay, "A Disappearing Subject Called the South," collected in *The*

Prevailing South: Life and Politics in a Changing Culture. Although she does not comment specifically on her books, she provides a succinct survey of their background in Southern history and literature. Particularly good reviews of the individual novels include those mentioned in the biographical sketch above. The best of these and several other good ones on *Dreams of Sleep* are excerpted in *Contemporary Literary Criticism,* Volume 34. Insightful reviews of *Rich in Love* include Michael Malone in the *Nation,* October 10, 1987; Susan Rowan in *Commonwealth,* March 25, 1988; and Dorothy Wickenden in *New Republic,* October 19, 1987. A couple of interesting reviews of *The Fireman's Fair* are R. Z. Sheppard's "Imagining Men" in *Time,* May 27, 1991, and the anonymous review in *Publishers Weekly,* March 1, 1991. Certainly, Josephine Humphreys' developing literary reputation will elicit more extensive critical response in the years to come.

BIBLIOGRAPHY

Works by Josephine Humphreys

Dreams of Sleep. New York: Viking, 1984.
Rich in Love. New York: Viking, 1987.
The Fireman's Fair. New York: Viking, 1991.
"My Invisible Self." *A World Unsuspected: Portraits of Southern Childhood.* Chapel
    Hill: University of North Carolina Press, 1987.
"A Disappearing Subject Called the South." *The Prevailing South: Life and Politics in
    a Changing Culture.* Atlanta: Longstreet Press, 1988.

Interviews

Anon. *Publishers Weekly* (September 4, 1987).
Ross, Jean. *Contemporary Authors,* Vol. 127.

Studies of Josephine Humphreys

Chappell, Fred. *"Rich in Love." New York Times Book Review* (September 13, 1987):
    9.
Compagnone, Emily J. "Humphreys, Josephine," 204–8 in *Contemporary Authors,* Vol.
    127. Detroit: Gale Research, 1989.
Douglas, Ellen. "Charleston without Tears." *New York Times Book Review* (May 13,
    1984): 15.
Drzal, Dawn Ann. "Casualties of the Feminine Mystique." *Antioch Review* 46 (Fall
    1988): 450–61.
Eder, Richard. *"Rich in Love." Los Angeles Times* (September 13, 1987): 9.
Rev. of *Dreams of Sleep. Publisher's Weekly* (March 16, 1984): 69.
Rev. of *The Fireman's Fair. Publisher's Weekly* (March 1, 1991): 61.
"Josephine Humphreys," 63–66 in *Contemporary Literary Criticism,* Vol. 34, Detroit:
    Gale Research, 1985.

MacDougall, Ruth Doan. Rev. of *Dreams of Sleep*. *Christian Science Monitor* (May 9, 1984): 15.

Malone, Michael. "Rich in Words." *Nation* (October 19, 1987): 388–89.

Rowen, Suzanne. "The South Rises and Falls." *Commonwealth* (March 25, 1988): 187–89.

Sheppard, R. Z. "Imagining Men." *Time* (May 27, 1991): 68–69.

Wickenden, Dorothy. "What Lucille Knew." *New Republic* (October 9, 1987): 45–46.

Yardley, Jonathan. "Desire under the Magnolias." *Washington Post Book World* (May 6, 1984): 3.

BARBARA PATRICK

Gayl Jones
(1949–   )

Gayl Jones's extreme and complex fiction records accumulated social and sexual ills. Many of her stories reflect an interest in madness and obsession; others explore the limitations of gender and the possibilities and contrariness of language. Known for her inventiveness in using black speech, Jones is primarily a storyteller, using blues rhythms and the ''I'' voice of the torch song to speak of loss, neglect, abandonment, and psychological and physical abuse. Adept in her use of the first-person point of view, Jones prizes what she calls ''the orality of the tale''—its dependence on the hearer even in interior monologues in which the storyteller becomes her own hearer. Jones's emphasis on storytelling and the extended monologue closely link her to the African-American oral tradition.

BIOGRAPHY

Born in Lexington, Kentucky, on November 23, 1949, Jones learned her love of language early from her mother and grandmother, who were also writers. Jones began writing at the age of 7. She attended segregated schools until tenth grade. After earning her B.A. in English from Connecticut College (1971), Jones then went on to Brown University where she earned her M.A. (1973) and D.A. (1975) in creative writing. She now teaches literature and creative writing at the University of Michigan. Author of novels, short stories, poems, and plays, she has received numerous awards, including fellowships to the Breadloaf and Yaddo Artists' Conferences, a grant from the National Endowment for the Arts, an American College Theatre Award, and a Shubert Foundation grant for playwriting.

MAJOR THEMES

Much of Jones's work concerns violence and abusive sexual encounters. In her first novel, *Corregidora* (1975), the protagonist, Ursa Corregidora, struggles to escape the legacy of abuse handed down to her from her grandmother and great-grandmother, both of whom were raped by a Portuguese slaveholder and whoremonger. The women in her family have kept the name Corregidora as a reminder to future generations of the horrors of enslavement. Mother and grandmother repeatedly urge upon Ursa her duty to "make generations" to preserve the family and ensure that the memory of their exploitation not be lost. Ursa is, however, incapable of fulfilling this duty; her own husband, Mutt, by knocking her down a flight of steps, has caused her to lose her unborn child and her ability to bear children.

Corregidore in Portuguese means "judicial magistrate." Jones makes Ursa Corregidora a female judge, a woman whose duty it is to "correct" (from the Portuguese *corrigir*) past abuses. And, like her foremothers, she becomes involved with an angry, violently jealous, abusive man. Ironically, Mutt's violence forces Ursa to reassess her identity and to break the stranglehold of the past. She returns to him—after a 22-year estrangement—with a new sense of her own power, as represented in her role in the sexual encounter that effects the novel's resolution.

In all her work, Jones's primary interest is in her characters—the way they order their experience and make sense of their stories in the retelling. In *Eva's Man* (1976), Eva Medina Canada reviews her own history of sexual exploitation. Imprisoned in a psychiatric institution for having killed her lover and castrating him with her teeth, Eva recalls her crime and remembers fragments of her life—being raped by a playmate with a popsicle stick; being forced by the neighborhood deviate to watch him masturbate; witnessing her father's rape of her mother. Jones structures Eva's account in increasingly narrow and fragmented circles, coming back to Eva's confinement to the psychiatric institution and her imprisonment within the confusion of her own memories and imagination. Eva's story reflects Jones's preoccupation with psychological obsessions and oppressions and documents the dilemma of a woman cast against her will in the role of the femme fatale—Eve and Medusa at once.

Jones's short stories, twelve of which are collected in *White Rat* (1977), display her willingness to invest her characters with "ambivalences and contradictions without making easy judgments," an element of characterization that she identifies as particularly Southern (Rowell 38). The protagonist of "White Rat" is a light-skinned black man from Jones's native Kentucky caught between his hatred of his own race, of "hoogies" (whites), and of himself; "The Return: A Fantasy," written when Jones was 17, concerns a prophetic schizophrenic; "Persona" tells of a female teacher attracted to a female student. In these and all her short stories Jones refrains from passing political or moral judgment on her characters' actions, allowing each protagonist to develop his or her own tale.

Though violence and images of mutilation punctuate her work, Jones writes too of the strength and hope that emerge from oppression and the fight for autonomy. *Song for Anninho* (1981), a book-length narrative poem, excavates from historical invisibility the story of Palmares, a settlement of Africans who escaped from slavery in Brazil in the late seventeenth century. Combining personal and communal history, Jones tells the story of the Palmares community through the story of two lovers—Almeyda, whose narrative voice we hear, and her husband, Anninho. When Portuguese slavemaster Jorge Velho attacked and destroyed the community, Almeyda and Anninho were separated. Though the Portuguese soldiers have cut off her breasts, Almeyda courageously looks to the time when she will reunite with Anninho. Sustained by memories of him and by her friendship with her mystical woman friend, Zibatra, Almeyda grows stronger, and with her physical strength grows hope for the possibility of future happiness. Almeyda's courage springs not only from her love for Anninho and her friendship with Zibatra, but also from her ties to the women who came before her and her belief in the possibility of transformation. Almeyda recalls her grandmother's instruction: "You are the granddaughter of an African, and you have inherited a way of being. And her eyes stayed on mine, Anninho, until all her words and memory and fears and tenderness ran through me like blood. . . . That was the moment when I became my grandmother and she became me" (32–33). A strong woman, Almeyda transcends the abuse heaped upon her. Through her narrative she "shapes for herself an understanding of her past with Anninho and a vision of the future" (Harris 111).

SURVEY OF CRITICISM

Like many black writers writing naturalistic or psychologically realistic fiction, Jones has received criticism for her graphic treatment of sex. Particularly following her second novel, *Eva's Man*, critics objected to Jones's relentless depictions of exploitative relationships within the black community and accused her of furthering the stereotype of the abusive black male. Jones responds, calling this controversy the "dilemma of subject matter in Afro-American literature." She notes that the erotic imagination is problematic for African-American writers, especially women, because "when you write about anything dealing with sexuality it appears as if you're supporting the sexual stereotypes about blacks" (Rowell 46).

Reviewers have evaluated Jones's novels highly. Ivan Webster wrote of her first novel that "no black American novel since Richard Wright's *Native Son* (1940) has so skillfully traced psychic wounds to a sexual source." John Updike commented that Jones's work shows how "our sexual and emotional behavior is warped within the matrix of family and race." Updike noted that Jones's second, more controversial novel, *Eva's Man*, possesses "a sharpened starkness, a power of ellipsis that leaves ever darker gaps between its flashes of rhythmic, sensuously exact dialogue and visible symbol."

Among those critics celebrating Jones's work is John Wideman, whose articles "Defining the Black Voice in Fiction" and "Frame and Dialect: The Evolution of the Black Voice in American Literature" explore Jones's use of both literate and oral traditions as part of a continuum in Afro-American and Euro-American literary traditions. Especially useful to readers interested in Jones's fictional technique is the special issue of *Callaloo: A Black South Journal of Arts and Letters* (October 1982) devoted to Jones. Here the reader will find Charles Rowell's revealing interview with Jones, as well as perceptive discussions of Jones's thematic and technical concerns by Jerry W. Ward, Jr., and Trudier Harris. Ward's analysis focuses on Jones's use of the physical abuse of women "to magnify the absurdity and the obscenity of racism and sexism in everyday life" (95). Harris's commentary deftly traces the political, aesthetic, and spiritual dimensions of *Song for Anninho*.

Interested readers should contrast Ward's interpretation of *Corregidora* with that of Melvin Dixon in "Singing a Deep Song: Language as Evidence in the Novels of Gayl Jones." Whereas Ward finds that Ursa's personality is "arrested" and that her return to her husband is regressive—representing the "slavery of consciousness," Dixon views *Corregidora*'s conclusion in a much more positive light, focusing on the importance of her newfound sexual power over her former abuser. Wideman, Harris, Dixon, and Ward, like so many Jones scholars, hail Jones's use of rhythmic, spoken, and explicitly sexual language as innovative, daring, and essential developments in the African American literary tradition.

BIBLIOGRAPHY

Works by Gayl Jones

Drama

Chile Woman. New York: Shubert Foundation (Shubert Playbook Series, Vol. 2, No. 5), 1974.

Fiction

Corregidora. New York: Random House, 1975.
Eva's Man. New York: Random House, 1976.
White Rat: Short Stories. New York: Random House, 1977.

Poetry

Song for Anninho. Detroit: Lotus Press, 1981.
The Hermit-Woman: Poems. Detroit: Lotus Press, 1983.
Xarque and Other Poems. Detroit: Lotus Press, 1985.

Interviews

Bell, Roseann P. "Gayl Jones Takes a Look at *Corregidora*: An Interview," 282–87 in *Sturdy Black Bridges: Visions of Black Women in Literature*, ed. Roseann P. Bell,

Bettye J. Parker, and Beverly Guy-Sheftall. Garden City, N.Y.: Anchor Books, 1979.

Harper, Michael S. "Gayl Jones: An Interview." *Massachusetts Review* 18 (1977): 692–715. Rpt. 352–75 in *Chant of Saints: A Gathering of Afro-American Literature, Art, and Scholarship*, ed. Michael S. Harper and Robert B. Stepto. Urbana: University of Illinois Press, 1979.

Lake, Ed, and Darryl Alladice. "From a Whisper to a Scream: An Interview with Gayl Jones." *Easy: The Black Arts Magazine* 1 (January 1978): 8–12.

Rowell, Charles H. "An Interview with Gayl Jones." *Callaloo* 16 (October 1982): 32–53.

Tate, Claudia C. "An Interview with Gayl Jones." *Black American Literature Forum* 13 (1979): 142–48. Abridged version rpt. 89–99 in *Black Women Writers at Work*. New York: Continuum, 1983.

Studies of Gayl Jones

Barksdale, Richard K. "Castration Symbolism in Recent Black American Fiction." *CLA Journal* 29 (June 1986): 400–413.

Bell, Roseann Pope. "Gayl Jones: A Voice in the Whirlwind." *Studia Africana* 1 (1977): 99–106.

Byerman, Keith. "Black Vortex: The Gothic Structure of *Eva's Man*." *MELUS* 7 (1980): 93–101.

———. "Gayl Jones," 128–35 in *Dictionary of Literary Biography*, Vol. 33. Detroit: Gale Research, 1984.

———. "Intense Behaviors: The Use of the Grotesque in *The Bluest Eye* and *Eva's Man*." *CLA Journal* 25 (1982): 447–57.

Contemporary Authors New Revision Series, Vol. 27, eds. Hay May and James G. Lesniak. Detroit: Gale Research, 1989, 250–52.

Dandridge, Rita B. "Male Critics/Black Women's Novels." *CLA Journal* 23 (1979): 1–11.

Dixon, Melvin. "Singing a Deep Song: Language as Evidence in the Novels of Gayl Jones," 236–48 in *Black Women Writers: Arguments and Interviews*, ed. Mari Evans. London: Pluto Press, 1985.

Harris, Janice. "Gayl Jones' *Corregidora*." *Frontiers* 5 (1980): 1–5.

Harris, Trudier. "A Spiritual Journey: Gayl Jones's *Song for Anninho*." *Callaloo* 16 (October 1982): 105–11.

Johnson, Herschel. "The New Generation and the Arts." *Ebony* (August 1978): 148–51.

Lee, A. Robert. "Making New: Styles of Innovation in the Contemporary Black American Novel," 222–50 in *Black Fiction: New Studies in the Afro-American Novel since 1945*, ed. A. Robert Lee. London: Vision Press, 1980.

Lee, Valerie Gray. "The Use of Folktalk in Novels by Black Women Writers." *CLA Journal* 23 (1980): 266–72.

Morrison, Toni. "Reading." *Mademoiselle* 81 (May 1975): 14.

Shockley, Ann Allen. "The Black Lesbian in Literature: An Overview." *Conditions* 5 (1979): 133–42.

Tate, Claudia C. "*Corregidora*: Ursa's Blues Medley." *Black American Literature Forum* 13 (1979): 139–41.

Updike, John. "Eva and Eleanor and Everyone." *New Yorker* 52 (August 9, 1976): 74–77.

Ward, Jerry W., Jr. "Escape from Trublem: The Fiction of Gayl Jones." *Callaloo* 16 (October 1982): 95–104. Rpt. 249–58 in *Black Women Writers: Arguments and Interviews*, ed. Mari Evans. London: Pluto Press, 1985.

Washington, Mary Helen. "Gayl Jones," 123–27 in *Midnight Birds: Stories of Contemporary Black Women Writers*, ed. Mary Helen Washington. Garden City, N.Y.: Anchor Books, 1980.

———. "Teaching *Black-Eyed Susans*: An Approach to the Study of Black Women Writers." *Black American Literature Forum* 11 (1977): 20–24. Rpt. 209–17 in *But Some of Us Are Brave: Black Women's Studies*, ed. Gloria T. Hull, Patricia Bell Scott, and Barbara Smith. Old Westbury, N.Y.: Feminist Press, 1982.

Webster, Ivan. "Really the Blues." *Time* 105 (June 16, 1975): 79.

Weixlmann, Joe. "A Gayl Jones Bibliography." *Callaloo* 20 (Winter 1984): 119–31.

Wideman, John. "Defining the Black Voice in Fiction." *Black American Literature Forum* 11 (1977): 79–82.

———. "Frame and Dialect: The Evolution of the Black Voice in American Literature." *American Poetry Review* 5 (September–October 1976): 34–37.

DAVID K. JEFFREY

Madison [Percy] Jones
(1925–   )

In the past 35 years, Madison Jones has published seven novels and one book of interconnected short stories. Each of these works has earned positive reviews, and each has received high praise from such writers as Flannery O'Connor, Allen Tate, James Dickey, and Harry Crews; yet despite this praise and despite the brief attention of Hollywood, Jones's works have gained neither a wide, popular readership nor scholarly attention. Perhaps one reason for this neglect is that all of Jones's works reflect their author's traditional social values and stern Puritanism. In each work he traces the tragic consequences of man's violation of traditional ethical, moral, and legal codes, man's loss of religious faith, and man's adherence to romantic, rationalistic, and modern values.

BIOGRAPHY

Madison Jones was born in Nashville, Tennessee, on March 21, 1925. His father, a businessman, bought a farm north of Nashville in Cheatham County when his son was 13, and the boy spent a good part of his teenage years farming and raising horses. Jones was educated in a public grammar school in Nashville and attended two private high schools there; he completed the seventh through eleventh grades at Wallace School, where his course work included French and Latin, and graduated from Montgomery Bell Academy. Jones attended Vanderbilt University for three semesters, dropped out to work on the family farm for 18 months, returned to Vanderbilt for another three semesters, and was then drafted. He served in Korea as a military policeman in 1945 and 1946, then returned to Vanderbilt, earning his B.A. in 1949. He studied writing there with Donald Davidson and was greatly influenced by Davidson's cultural ideas. To continue his study of writing (under Andrew Lytle), Jones next went to the University of Florida, where he earned an M.A. in 1951. That same year he married Shailah

McEvilley; they have had five children—Carroll, Madison III, Ellen, Michael, and Andrew. Jones did Ph.D. work at Florida from 1951 through 1953, completing his course work and passing his comprehensive examination; he did not write a dissertation but instead began writing his first novel.

Jones began his teaching career at Miami University (Ohio) in 1953–54. He held a *Sewanee Review* Fellowship in 1954–55 and taught at the University of Tennessee in 1955–56. He began teaching at Auburn University in 1956, became their writer-in-residence in 1967 and a full professor in 1968. He was awarded a chaired professorship in 1982 and retired in 1987. Jones held a Rockefeller Foundation Fellowship in 1968 and a Guggenheim Fellowship in 1974.

Besides his eight novels, Jones has published literary criticism in such journals as *Studies in Short Fiction*, *Mississippi Quarterly*, and *South Atlantic Quarterly*. Early in his career, he published short stories in *Arlington Quarterly*, *Perspective*, *Delta Review*, and *Sewanee Review*. "Dog Days," a short story first published in *Perspective*, was reprinted in Martha Foley's *Best American Short Stories* in 1953. Columbia Pictures made Jones's fourth novel, *An Exile*, into the film *I Walk the Line* (1970), starring Gregory Peck and Tuesday Weld. Jones himself wrote a screenplay for his fifth novel, *A Cry of Absence*, but no film of that work has ever been made.

MAJOR WORKS

The moral values and social views that inform all of Jones's work are clearly stated from the first. *The Innocent* (1957) is the story of Duncan Welsh's return to his father's rural Southern farm after 7 years of wandering in the urban North. Disillusioned by his experience there, Duncan believes the modern world is near collapse and modern man lacks identity, is dislocated, and is disloyal. He therefore attempts to reestablish what he takes to be the values of Edenic frontier individualism: Breeding a horse from old mountain stock; loudly opposing the doctrines of his brother-in-law, a Methodist minister; eventually alienating his black farm workers; and finally allying himself with a moonshiner, his doppelgänger, Aaron McCool. Duncan's realization that McCool is no noble savage but a Satanic outcast and misfit occurs too late to save Duncan from murder, exposure, and his own death. The novel establishes the structural pattern of all Jones's plots: The protagonist's innocence of his own moral frailty leads to tragic error, to self-recognition, public confession, and expiation. The novels reflect Jones's grounding in Puritan theology and classical tragedy and his admiration of both Nathaniel Hawthorne and Fyodor Dostoyevski.

Forest of the Night (1960) is a historical novel set in Tennessee during the early nineteenth century. New to the virgin forests outside of Knoxville, Jonathan Cannon fancies himself a free-thinking intellectual and hopes to establish a frontier school modeled after the ideas of his favorite author, Jean-Jacques Rousseau. As the novel opens, Jonathan discovers an Indian, scalped and disemboweled, and offers in a spasm of sentimental pity to help him, but the Indian nearly

kills him. The incident is the first of many in which Jonathan's youthful idealism—his belief that in the New World men can be free of the old "tyrannies"
of thought, custom, religion, and hierarchies—is tested against the savage realities of the wilderness: Is tested and is found wanting. Isolate, withdrawn, and
increasingly corrupted, Jonathan is eventually mistaken for one of the notorious
(and historical) outlaw brothers, the Harpes, and nearly hanged as a result; at
the novel's close, he returns to his settlement school chastened and wiser. The
novel contains some of Jones's most lyrical descriptions of nature and several
powerful scenes of hallucinatory fantasy; its perfunctory conclusion is a flaw
Jones has himself acknowledged ("Madison Jones" 16).

The complex plot of *A Buried Land* (1963), set in a rural Tennessee town
before and after World War II, concerns the moral education of a young lawyer,
Percy Youngblood. Adhering to "progressive" social ideas, Percy encourages
the sale of family land to the Tennessee Valley Authority, denies his complicity
in the death of a girl he has impregnated and for whom he has arranged the
abortion that kills her (burying her body in his own family's plot, soon to be
inundated by a TVA project), arranges to become legal counsel for a patricide,
and eventually murders the dead girl's father. Throughout the novel, Percy is
also tormented by his conscience and excoriated by characters who speak for
traditional religious and social doctrines. Near the conclusion of the novel, driven
nearly mad by the tension between his own ideas and their evil issue, Percy
finds a measure of peace in confession. For some critics, M. E. Bradford, for
example, the novel is Jones's best.

An Exile (1967) is a short, nearly allegorical novel concerning the corruption
of Sheriff Hank Tawes by a Satanic moonshiner, Flint McCain, and his daughter,
Alma, for whom Hank lusts. His sexual involvement with her leads to his
complicity in Flint's moonshining, to the breakup of Hank's marriage, and to
Flint's murders of Hank's deputy, Alma's husband, and finally Hank himself.
Jones's stern belief in the usually unhappy result of sexual desire is particularly
pointed here.

His next novel, *A Cry of Absence* (1971), is an immensely impressive work
that studies the effects of integration and racial conflict in a small Southern town
and on one of its leading citizens, Hester Glenn. Her son, Cam, precipitates that
conflict by murdering a black man, chaining him to a tree and stoning him to
death, an act a second son, Ames, discovers and discloses to Hester, destroying
at once her sense of well-bred class superiority to and her isolation from that
conflict. Her growing sense of responsibility for her son's act leads her nearly
to murder Cam and finally to both his and her own suicides. Within this tragic
pattern, Jones recognizes contributory social factors—the conflict between blacks
and whites, of course; between Southern "aristocracy" and "poor white trash";
and between Northern and Southern ideals. In this work Jones evenhandedly
portrays abstract Northern social ideas based on materialism and glorified Southern notions of a past golden age, seeing both as corrupt and corrupting.

Passage Through Gehenna (1978) represents something of a departure from his previous novels in being, as M. E. Bradford first recognized and as Sandy Cohen has argued convincingly and at length, a romance, a work in which Jones is less concerned with cultural or social matters than with what he has called the "bare confrontation of good and evil, of innocence and guilt" ("Madison Jones" 15). The book details its protagonist's, Jud Rivers's, passage from innocence through hell, his recognition and expiation of guilt through confession and the punishment of a jail term. Among Jud's sins are his pride and self-righteousness, his lust for the witch-like Lily Nunn and the innocent Hannah (whom he impregnates and who dies after an abortion), and his betrayal of a preacher who had saved his life and whose disciple Jud had been. The devastating consequences of moral innocence are clearly stated here.

Season of the Strangler (1982) also represents a departure from Jones's other works; the book is a series of twelve short stories, each focusing on a different citizen in Okaloosa, Alabama, during the summer of 1969, a time of racial change and unrest, when five women are found strangled in their beds. The communal tension generated by the murders illuminates all the characters' lives and precipitates changes in many of their circumstances. All of the characters are lonely and isolated, unable to connect with a society in which suspicion and fear predominate. Jones wrote the book during the year a series of stranglings occurred in Columbus, Georgia (thirty miles from his home), and after reading Sherwood Anderson's *Winesburg, Ohio*, to which Jones's work owes at least its organizational pattern, if not its thematic concerns as well.

Last Things (1989) begins, surprisingly, as an academic satire, with its protagonist, Wendell Corbin, sneering at the intellectual pretensions of a Romantics professor and his feminist lover. Jones's main concern, one to which he quickly turns, is Wendell's own intellectual pretension. His academic gifts lead him to isolate himself from his family and from his community. Believing himself superior to the law and to moral tradition, he enmeshes himself in an adulterous affair that leads to his lover's murder of her mother-in-law and to her own suicide; at the same time, he becomes involved in a drug operation run by a mysterious and Satanic local businessman. He is able to extricate himself, after a descent into near madness, not by confessing his involvement to the legal authorities but to an itinerant preacher, Sears, and by working as his disciple.

Jones's vision throughout his works has been consistent and consistently dark. He views modern man as naive and self-isolating, devoid of moral vision and redeeming religious faith, cut off from family and community (traditional venues of solace) by intellectual pretension and deleterious social change. In his view modern man can seldom escape his tragic fate, can hope at best to live to expiate his guilt.

SURVEY OF CRITICISM

There are very few full-length critical studies of Madison Jones's works. The essays by Bradford and Jan Norby Gretlund present intelligent, general overviews of the works through *Season of the Strangler*. Four essays deal with individual novels: Cohen reads *Passage Through Gehenna* as a romance; John T. Hiers compares *A Buried Land* with Robert Penn Warren's *Flood*; Walter Sullivan concentrates his attention on *An Exile*, and Simone Vauthier concentrates hers on *The Innocent*. The two interviews—in *Southern Quarterly* and *Southern Humanities Review*—reveal Jones as a fine critical reader of his own work and suggest several possibilities for future study.

BIBLIOGRAPHY

Works by Madison Jones

"Dog Days," 189–206 in *The Best American Short Stories 1953*, ed. Martha Foley. Boston: Houghton Mifflin, 1953.

"The Fugitives." *Sewanee Review* 62 (1954): 271–91.

"Prologue." *Sewanee Review* 64 (1956): 615–31.

The Innocent. New York: Harcourt, 1957.

Forest of the Night. New York: Harcourt, 1960.

A Buried Land. New York: Viking, 1963.

An Exile. Sewanee Review 75 (1967): 25–158. Rpt. as *I Walk the Line*. New York: Viking Press, 1967.

"A Look at 'Mr. McGregor.' " *Mississippi Quarterly: Special Issue on Andrew Lytle* 23, No. 4 (1970): 363–70.

A Cry of Absence. New York: Crown, 1971.

"Craft as Mirror." *Sewanee Review* 82 (1974): 179–89.

Passage Through Gehenna. Baton Rouge: Louisiana State University Press, 1978.

"Variations on a Hawthorne Theme." *Studies in Short Fiction* 15 (1978): 277–83.

"The Impulse to Fiction." *Southern Humanities Review* 14 (1980): 211–20.

Season of the Strangler. New York: Doubleday, 1982.

"A Good Man's Predicament." *Southern Review* 20, No. 4 (1984): 836–41.

"Robert Penn Warren as Novelist," 39–57 in *A Southern Renascence Man: Views of Robert Penn Warren*, ed. Walter B. Edgar. Baton Rouge: Louisiana State University Press, 1984.

"The Writer's Sense of Place." *South Dakota Review* 26, No. 4 (1988): 93–120.

Last Things. Baton Rouge: Louisiana State University Press, 1989.

Interviews

"Madison Jones: An Interview." *Southern Quarterly* 21, No. 3 (1983): 5–26.

"An Interview with Madison Jones." *Southern Humanities Review* 23, No. 1 (1989): 39–51.

Studies of Madison Jones

Bradford, M. E. "Madison Jones," 523–26 in *The History of Southern Literature*, ed. Louis B. Rubin, Jr., et al. Baton Rouge: Louisiana State University Press, 1985.

Cohen, Sandy. "Images of Allegory: Madison Jones's *Passage Through Gehenna*." *South Atlantic Review* 53, No. 1 (1988): 67–81.

Gretlund, Jan Nordby. "The Last Agrarian: Madison Jones's Achievement." *Southern Review* 22, No. 3 (1986): 478–88.

Hiers, John T. "Buried Graveyards: Warren's *Flood* and Jones' *A Buried Land*." *Essays in Literature* (Western Illinois University) 2 (1975): 97–104.

Sullivan, Walter. *Death by Melancholy: Essays on Modern Southern Fiction*. Baton Rouge: Louisiana State University Press, 1972.

Vauthier, Simone. "Gratuitous Hypothesis: A Reading of Madison Jones' *The Innocent*." *Recherches Anglaises et Americaines* 7 (1974): 191–219.

Beverly Lowry
(1938–   )

With her settings selected from places she has lived—Greenville, Mississippi; Houston; New York; rural Texas—Beverly Lowry blends jaunty prose with precise and "typically Southern" details of character, landscape, and community. Each of her five novels is distinctly different, yet each normally includes themes repeated from another work and often inverts previously developed characters or situations. Lowry's hallmarks are her irreverently audacious humor and her resilient imagination. Her fiction is complex, sometimes experimental, and unpredictable. It ranges from the virtuoso portrait of a female high school football hero in *Come Back, Lolly Ray,* to the extravagant verbal fireworks in *Daddy's Girl,* to the psychological tour de force surrounding incest in *The Perfect Sonya,* to the tamped-down depiction of suffering parents who fail lovingly in *Breaking Gentle.*

BIOGRAPHY

Beverly Lowry was born August 10, 1938, in Memphis, Tennessee, to parents from Arkansas. Since the relatives of David Leonard and Dora Smith Fey remained in their home state, no extended family cushioned Memphis blows in "typically Southern" fashion—a lack Lowry considers a liability for a Southern fiction writer. The Fey family eventually included two younger brothers who were born 3 years and 12 years later than Beverly. As do many first-borns, she developed an only-child perspective.

When Beverly was 6 years old, her family moved to Greenville, Mississippi, which closely resembles her fictional Eunola. Eunola is never identified with a particular state, but it sits on a big river that runs, topographically, through delta-like country. Although she later put these Mississippi childhood and adolescent years to work in fiction and journalism, Lowry felt in Greenville both aggressively dominant, like Lolly Ray, and marginalized, like Emma Blue. As a high school student she excelled in academic and extracurricular activities; she was a competitive swimmer and went to majorette camp to improve her baton twirling. Yet when her always economically unstable family moved back to Memphis in 1958, she neither expected nor desired to return to Greenville. Years later, she did go back for an autograph party and discovered hanging across the bookstore facade a banner reading "WELCOME BACK, BEVERLY FEY LOWRY. WE LOVE YOU." It was one of her life's dearest triumphs.

Lowry attended her first two years of college at the University of Mississippi in Oxford and then transferred to Memphis State, from which she graduated in 1960. Though she remembers doing a great deal of writing in high school, she recalls none in college beyond required papers. Her college life was busy, for she completed double majors in speech/drama and English literature. As before, her interests were not solely academic, for she also enjoyed working in the theater. She met her husband-to-be, Glenn Lowry, at the time a sales representative for the National Cotton Council, in a Little Theater group in Memphis. The two married June 3, 1960, immediately after her college graduation.

After their wedding, Beverly and Glenn Lowry moved to New York City, where Glenn eventually worked as public relations manager for the National Cotton Council. In their five New York years, Beverly found the social activism of the 1960s intimidating for a displaced Southern writer. The birth of their first son Colin triggered voluminous journal writing, as well as Beverly's attendance in acting classes and attempts at a theatrical career. She also performed in a water ballet, produced in 1962.

Meanwhile, Glenn Lowry was growing disaffected with New York City. The family moved to Houston in 1965, where Glenn soon became a stockbroker for Paine Webber. Then in 1966, their second son Peter was born, and Beverly began seriously to write fiction. Her breakthrough occurred in 1973, when she met Donald Barthelme in a writer's workshop. Barthelme helped her by reading and editing her work. Her first novel, Come Back, Lolly Ray, was published in 1977, quickly to be followed by Emma Blue in 1978 and Daddy's Girl in 1981.

Since by this time Glenn Lowry could practice his profession via computer, the family fulfilled a long-held dream and moved in 1981 to a home on ten acres with spring-fed river frontage, on Route 80 outside San Marcos, Texas. Beverly wanted proximity to water; Glenn, enough land to pasture one or two quarter horses. Meanwhile, Beverly Lowry was not only writing steadily but also teaching in various creative writing programs from Florida to California. Her marked generosity toward other writers made her a favorite reviewer in the New York Times, Washington Post, Dallas Times Herald, and many other newspapers.

A great deal of Beverly Lowry's energy in these years went into civic, service, and organizational activities. For example, she was president of the Texas Institute of Letters from 1982 to 1984; coorganizer of PEN/Southwest, as well as panelist for the National Endowment for the Arts, 1981–84 and 1988; panelist for the Texas Commission on the Arts, 1981–84; and panelist for the Cultural Arts Council of Houston, 1979–80.

Then came the terrible year of 1984, in which life seemed to fall apart. Her mother had already died when Beverly's diabetic father was required to have both his legs amputated. He metamorphosed from a large man not unlike Big Stovall of *Daddy's Girl* to "pint-sized," not entirely dissimilar to Jack Miller of *The Perfect Sonya* (1987). Far worse, Beverly's troubled 18-year-old second son was killed in a hit-and-run accident. As Lowry said to a *New York Times* interviewer: "While I've practiced saying it, it's no easier now than it was then. It wrecks your life."

Presently Lowry is writing again, working on another Eunola novel, a play, a novella tentatively called "The Indian's Ghost," and a Broadway musical named *Heart's Desire*, which is based on her story "Out of the Blue." She has also recently published the brilliant nonfiction *Crossed Over: A Murder, a Memoir* (1992), her account of a young pickaxe murderess convicted in 1984, who is now rehabilitated on death row in Gatesville, Texas.

MAJOR THEMES

In tone and style, as well as in thematic emphasis, the works of Beverly Lowry fall into two distinct groups. This break is also reflected in her major short stories. The cause of the break is easy to identify: It coincides with the deeply traumatic events of 1984. Its results color the later fiction a somber shade. Although recent work is not devoid of lightness or laughter, it is certainly more darkly ironic and less impudent or frolicsome than her first fiction was.

Lowry's first three novels—*Come Back, Lolly Ray; Emma Blue*; and *Daddy's Girl*—revolve around energetic young women determined to forge identities of public significance. In their very distinctive ways, the three protagonists demand and receive attention while exploring the options they imagine, uncover, or create. The next two novels, however, explore disruptions and disasters. Disheartening setbacks exist in the first three books, but obstacles do not impinge for long on the enterprise, or slow the forward drive of the heroines. Although many of the same symbols and images recur both before and after the break, the import is decidedly more ominous in *The Perfect Sonya* and *Breaking Gentle* (1988). But nothing Lowry has ever written is so strongly shocking and ironic, as well as profoundly hopeful, as *Crossed Over*.

Dreams, for example, serve structural and thematic ends in all five Lowry novels, plus her nonfiction memoir. The dreams of Lolly Ray and Sue Muffaletta, in the first and third novels, respectively, often concern glory. Emma Blue also longs for recognition as strongly as her mother, Lolly, or her fictional successor, Sue. Strategies differ from novel to novel and plots strongly differ, but recognized goals of the protagonists can be linked.

One kind of linkage, of course, is a reversal; in Lowry's work, reversals occur between and also within the novels. Dreams that amuse in *Daddy's Girl*, for example, and amuse partially because they are improperly shared by two or more characters, turn into private nightmares in *The Perfect Sonya*. In the former, "good girls . . . in place of testing, dreamed," especially of "the bear of our dreams, after us." In the latter, fledgling actress Pauline Terry dreams of a huge bear, "a dreamlike presence which did not yield to common measure," but was "dark . . . the shadow of something." Pauline's bear springs from memories of a stuffed bear into whose threatening embrace she refused to step at age 11, thereby triggering the fury of her father. In her dreams, Pauline's world is dangerous because of threatening, pursuing males, and the malevolent males are explicitly related to her father. For Pauline, dread lurks in the night. Her task, and the donnée of the novel, is to find a way to deal with Daddy Bear, who always remains a stranger and a symbol for danger. Yet reversals occur within single novels as well. And it does not simplify a reader's task when the symbol of the bear turns androgynous. Before the fiction is finished, Pauline's mother, too, appears bearlike and walks like a bear. Actress Pauline realizes that "if she ever wanted to use Mavis for a part, she would not think of her mother but the bear." Other symbols in *Daddy's Girl* and *The Perfect Sonya* reverse their first established connotations. The standard phallic snake turns female in *Sonya*, metamorphosed into the Snake Woman central to *The Legend of Snake Creek*, Uncle Will Hand's famous book. Big Stovall, the daddy in the earlier novel, in effect functions frequently as a mothering parent figure in his daughter Sue's family, as Sue in turn serves as Little League father for her son.

Such all-encompassing symbols as bear or snake, or a parent named Big, establish another Lowry theme—the androgynous switches within genital power. It is central to the legal and moral predicament of Karla Faye Tucker, of *Crossover*, who boasted an orgasm for every blow she struck with her pick-axe. This theme may achieve its most arresting form in the tour-de-force descriptions of fellatio within the story "Mama's Turn" (1975).

Food serves as a motif of central importance in Lowry's fiction. Its preparation demonstrates the soundness of a marriage in *Breaking Gentle* and the inadequacy of a trailer home in *Lolly Ray*. Food serves most centrally as a communion substitute in "If You're Not Going to Stay Then Please Don't Bother to Come" (1981). In this story, an incongruous pair share nothing but apartment space, soup, and Sara Lee pies. Finally the woman throws frozen pies at her bathing roommate with such accuracy that she first knocks him out and then watches him drown. Normally, however, food signifies Lowry's key themes of nurturance, comfort, connection, and love. Love, in turn, is defined as "the sense of paying notice to another human being with persistence and selflessness" (*Sonya* 237).

While dream and death are acknowledged intellectually in the events of Lowry's first three novels, they are central themes in the novels and stories published after 1984. In this more recent fiction, "fear exists on the other side of knowing" (*Sonya* 7). Perhaps most graphically illustrating these threatening themes is the story "Out of the Blue." Within this realistically rendered depiction of a nightmare predicament, a young man is abducted by sadistic thugs, who eventually tie him up and deposit him in the middle of a road to nowhere, after which they roar toward his immobilized body in his wife's once-prized automobile. As the story ends, he has no way to save himself, but knows that he must still try. This graphic depiction of helplessness (paralysis before an automobile) more violently repeats and relates to the confusion of Hale and Diana Caldwell, the helpless parents of *Breaking Gentle* who must save vulnerable children, pets, and property without clear knowledge of how to accomplish their task. They merely acknowledge the terrible responsibility to perform it.

The point of view from which Lowry's first four novels are written duplicates that of a grown child who must struggle through parental legacies from the past. In *Breaking Gentle*, as well as in the moving story "So Far from the Road, So Long until Morning" (1986), we discover instead the struggles of a mother to deal with an intractable adolescent. The offspring is a daughter in the novel and a son in the story, but a central theme in both tales is parental helplessness. *Crossed Over* ends with moving simplicity: "You bump up against the final, most unacceptable thing, you see what you can come up with."

Lowry seems to define human life as a mixture of fact and fantasy, reality and fancy. And it is life itself that her fictional parents are unable to protect. Lowry confronts the fact explicitly in "What Love Can Do" (1988), which features a couple who lost their adored baby in a crib death. The child's death, of course, is inexplicable. It symbolizes total loss, which leaves parents with no consolations more concrete than good music. Yet throughout Lowry's fiction, any momentary or permanent departure of a family member, whether parent or child, triggers terror. Lolly Ray and Emma Blue long for their physically or psychologically absent mothers, as Sue Muffaletta and Pauline Terry fear the departure or deaths of their fathers. A central preoccupation of all Lowry heroines is keeping a family, or a bonded unit of some kind, together. Thus family plots provide a recurrent theme, as family networks are a recurrent focus in this fiction.

One can say of all Lowry protagonists that they remain gamely willing to keep trying, however unpromising their prospects. Thus, Lolly Ray Lasswell practices obsessively at baton twirling, "unrepentantly brazen in her pursuit of glory," and determined that she "would not be deposed by time." Emma Blue tries to emulate her idealized and absent mother in order to become "herself only: what she is and has chosen to be, apart altogether, and on her own." Sue Muffaletta, once "all American honor girl," asserts: "I have this fantasy. When I walk in a room, people notice." Sue tries to fulfill her dream through her work as a songwriter, honky-tonk singer, and solid citizen. Pauline Terry, always the daredevil, "had loved the theater, its isolation, the immediacy of its risks and terrors and satisfactions." Lowry's most recent fictional heroine, Diana Caldwell, breaks rules to help her rule-breaking daughter. In the direst predicaments Lowry can contrive, her women trust the moment, put one foot in front of another, keep on keeping on, and, above all, keep trying.

Thus, perhaps the most important theme of Lowry's writing affirms the openness of possibility. The most delightful possibilities here are sexual, and usually Lowry's story lines begin with puberty. Repeated throughout the fiction, however, is the phrase, "But still . . . " The implied view in this resounding echo perhaps explains Lowry's penchant for open endings, for works that always leave room to imagine further action, after the plot is done. As the humorous refrain running throughout *Emma Blue* has it: "You never know, girl, you just never know." The words can be hummed to the tune of hope.

SURVEY OF CRITICISM

Only two scholarly articles have appeared on Beverly Lowry's fiction, both written by Merrill Maguire Skaggs as up-to-date surveys of Lowry's novels, major themes, and general characteristics. Whereas "Deprivation Makes no Desert," the most recent summary, covers all five novels, "Eating the Moment Absolutely Up" focuses in detail on *Daddy's Girl*, exploring among other subjects the novel's innovative structure and experimental style in the context of its predecessors.

More frequently, critical comment on Lowry's work appears in reviews. The novels have been reviewed widely, in flattering places and in some flattering detail. Richard Lingeman, for example, describes *Come Back, Lolly Ray* as "a series of brooding tableaux, acted out against the backdrop of the town's secret soul." The review added: "If Beverly Lowry does not always visualize her characters fully, if her book is a bit static, she has nonetheless succeeded stunningly in drawing a fully shaded portrait of Eunola, placing it with Winesburg, Sauk Center and the others on our literary map." Several reviewers placed Lowry's first novel in a Southern context. Susan Horowitz added: "Lolly's ability to transcend her background . . . is an act of imagination and will, a sign that, like her baton, the South will rise again."

To a large and predictable extent, the Southern motif continued to run through reviews of *Emma Blue*. A review in the *Virginia Quarterly Review* maintained that "while her choice of fictional locale and her origin establish her as a Southern writer, her coy bittersweetness makes her, like her heroine, an outsider. Unlike most Southern fiction writers, Lowry writes fairy tales." In *Publisher's Weekly* a reviewer found in *Emma Blue* "completely convincing characterizations of people of all ages who make of the town of Eunola a Deep South version of 'Our Town' and a place worth visiting." A reviewer in *The New Yorker* also said: "This is an elegant novel, and the narrator moves nimbly to reveal cautious characters taking one another, and themselves, by surprise."

Daddy's Girl, which eventually won the Jesse Jones award for the best work of fiction written in 1981, was recognized by the reviewer from the *West Coast Review of Books* as a four-star book of sufficient quality to make the reviewer conclude: "If you relish life, you'll love this book." Yet qualifications were certainly sounded. Alice Denham remarked: "*Daddy's Girl* is like a honky-tonk.

You adore it, you get high on it. Then you weary of it. The problem is the voice, which is marvelous. Beverly Lowry is dancing as fast as she can, too wildly to slow down and deal with the material.'' Thus Denham finds the novel ''broad rather than deep,'' but ''wide-striding, boot-clicking Cowtown fun.'' Elizabeth Stone also issued qualified praise for the novel she found ''zesty and rambunctious,'' but with events that ''don't accrue.''

There is some sign that the critics were puzzled by the unexpected change in tone between *Daddy's Girl* and *The Perfect Sonya* and especially nonplussed by the change of locale from exclusively Southern settings to New York City. The review in *Publisher's Weekly* concluded: ''This new novel . . . will add to her reputation as an original, talented writer; it is not, however, an entirely successful effort.'' Ann Fisher shrugged it off as ''middling contemporary fiction of the self-discovery variety, not unappealing, not altogether successful.'' Lynn Freed seemed basically noncommittal: ''One wishes that the characters themselves were more compelling and that the transitions in time and place were more smoothly effected. What is memorable in *The Perfect Sonya* is Pauline's isolation, the way she stands outside events, observing.''

Most reviews of *Breaking Gentle* must be classified as qualified. They illustrate the predictable results when a writer whom critics look to for inebriate humor instead hands them sober medicine. As a representative judgment, Eric Larson decreed:

Both Roger and Bethany, of course, are sending out classic cries of help, and one of the most puzzling things about this peculiarly unsatisfying novel is watching these kids' presumably (one might add certifiably) enlightened parents remain blithely deaf to their cries—while the author presents them to us, at the same time, with the seeming assumption that they are listening with all their hearts. For all the detail cascaded upon them (and it's a lot) Hale and Diana Caldwell in the end seem realized only from the exterior and remain illustrated figures.

In a prominently featured review in the *New York Times Book Review*, however, William H. Pritchard asserted that *Breaking Gentle* ''widens the scope and complicates the tone of her fiction. . . . The new book deals with a family of four, each of whose minds Ms. Lowry explores confidently, bringing to the exploration an ironic ease that, page by page, makes sentences and paragraphs fresh and often funny.'' It is an appropriate summary of the fiction.

BIBLIOGRAPHY

Works by Beverly Lowry

''Mama's Turn,'' 238–50 in *Bitches and Sad Ladies: An Anthology of Fiction by and about Women*, ed. Pat Rotter. New York: Dell, 1975.
Come Back, Lolly Ray. New York: Doubleday, 1977.
Emma Blue. New York: Doubleday, 1978.

Daddy's Girl. New York: Viking, 1981.
"If You're Not Going to Stay Then Please Don't Bother to Come." *Mississippi Review* 10 (Spring/Summer 1981): 118–32.
"So Far from the Road, So Long until Morning," 85–101 in *Prize Stories: Texas Institute of Letters*, ed. Marshall Terry. Dallas: Still Point Press, 1986.
The Perfect Sonya. New York: Viking, 1987.
Breaking Gentle. New York: Viking, 1988.
"Out of the Blue." *Southwest Review* 73 (Spring 1988): 255–72.
"What Love Can Do." *Boston Globe Magazine* (October 16, 1988): 30–41.
"The Writing Lesson." *Gettysburg Review* 2 (Autumn 1989): 559–61.
Crossed Over: A Murder, a Memoir. New York: Alfred A. Knopf, 1992.

Studies of Beverly Lowry

Denham, Alice. "Fame and Fiction." *Nation* 234 (January 2, 1982): 25.
Fisher, Ann H. Rev. of *The Perfect Sonya. Library Journal* 112 (June 15, 1987): 84.
Freed, Lynn. "She Didn't Cheat on Chekhov." *New York Times Book Review* 92 (July 26, 1987): 10.
Horowitz, Susan. Rev. of *Come Back, Lolly Ray. Saturday Review* 4 (February 19, 1977): 28.
Larsen, Eric. "Spare the Rod, Spoil the Horse." *Los Angeles Times Book Review* (October 16, 1988): 3, 10.
Lingeman, Richard. "A New Portrait on America's Literary Map." *New York Times* (February 25, 1977): C21.
Pritchard, William H. "The Unpredictable Dailiness of Life." *New York Times Book Review* 93 (August 14, 1988): 9.
Rev. of *Daddy's Girl. West Coast Review of Books* 8 (April 1982): 36.
Rev. of *Emma Blue. Publisher's Weekly* 214 (July 3, 1978): 60.
Rev. of *Emma Blue. New Yorker* 54 (October 2, 1978): 147.
Rev. of *Emma Blue. Virginia Quarterly Review* 55 (Summer 1979): 98.
Rev. of *The Perfect Sonya. Publisher's Weekly* 233 (June 17, 1988): 68.
Skaggs, Merrill M. "Deprivation Makes No Desert: Beverly Lowry's Fiction." *Mississippi Quarterly* 42 (Winter 1988–89): 19–26.
———. "Eating the Moment Absolutely Up: The Fiction of Beverly Lowry." *Southern Quarterly* 21 (Summer 1983): 67–82.
Stone, Elizabeth. "A Tall Tale with a Country Twang." *Ms.* 10 (October 1981): 38.
Wilson, Austin. "What It Means to Be a Southern Writer in the '80's: A Panel Discussion with Beverly Lowry, Reynolds Price, Elizabeth Spencer and James Whitehead." *Southern Quarterly* 26 (Summer 1988): 80–93.

JOSEPH M. FLORA

Bobbie Ann Mason
(1940–   )

On the basis of her first collection of short stories, Bobbie Ann Mason earned recognition as an exemplar of a kind of Southern writing (sometimes called "K-Mart Chic"); she also gained recognition as one of the major short-story writers in America. Including a Mason story in anthologies of American, Southern, and contemporary literature quickly became obligatory. A second collection of stories confirmed her place among America's best short-story writers. *In Country* (1988) her single full-length novel, ranks with the most influential fiction dealing with the Vietnam War.

BIOGRAPHY

Mason was born on May 1, 1940, in Mayfield, Kentucky (the Hopewell of her fiction), daughter of Wilburn A., a dairy farmer, and Christie (Lee) Mason. During her childhood, she performed such farm chores as hoeing and blackberry picking, but she also found outlets for her imagination. She reports herself "not interested" in suntans and pajama parties. She enjoyed reading, and she read a great deal, if not discriminately. In her essay "Reaching the Stars: My Life as a Fifties Groupie" (1986) she recalls some sample titles: *The Search for Bridey Murphy, The Practical Way to a Better Memory, The Report on Unidentified Flying Objects*. She also consumed Nancy Drew mysteries and other series with girl-sleuth heroines. In her maturity, she would reread many of those mysteries and write a study on the significance they might have had for her and for other young girls. Shy in school, she grew up in a loving family. She has a brother and two sisters

From her childhood on, popular music was a passion, and in this activity her parents were her allies. The Masons regularly stayed up late listening to the radio. Mason listened to it constantly. The addiction provided the chief source of glamour to her high school years.

In the 1950s, the Hilltoppers were a popular male quartet, and Mason liked their singing. Because they had begun as students at Western Kentucky State College, their success helped feed Mason's own ambition to find fame, and throughout high school she lived vicariously through them. She started a Hill-toppers fan club—a turning point in her young life—and her loyalty led to her elevation as national president of the Hilltoppers Fan Club. She wrote and mailed a newsletter to 300 fan-club chapters and conducted request campaigns to disc jockeys, urging that Hilltoppers' songs be played on their programs. Encouraged in these activities by her parents, she began her first travels away from Mayfield. With her mother she journeyed first to Cincinnati to hear the group; later trips would take her to such places as Vincennes, Indiana; Centralia, Illinois; Blythe-ville, Arkansas; and Cape Girardeau, Missouri; as well as St. Louis and Detroit. The Hilltoppers were grateful to the president of their club, supported her ac-tivities, and counted her as friend. Through them, she met other stars. Bright, she was also learning about fame and its meaning. Popular culture would become an essential ingredient of her fiction.

Mason was good at her schoolwork, too. When she started her studies at the University of Kentucky, she gave up being president of the Hilltoppers Fan Club. She was ready for the large world she found in college. In addition to reading widely, she studied French, psychology, philosophy, and volleyball. And she listened to rock and roll. Possessed with the writing habit, while a student she worked in 1960 for the *Mayfield Messenger*. After graduating from the University in 1962, she went to New York City to work for Ideal Publishing Co. and for such magazines as *Movie Stars, Movie Life*, and *T.V. Star Parade*. Again, however, she could not be satisfied by popular culture only. She earned an M.A. in English at the State University of New York at Binghamton (1966). On April 12, 1969, she married Roger B. Rawlings, a magazine editor and writer. In 1972 she completed a Ph.D. in English at the University of Connecticut with a dissertation on Vladimir Nabokov's *Ada*. From 1972 through 1979 she was an assistant professor at Mansfield State College in Mansfield, Pennsylvania.

Mason's writing apprenticeship was lengthy, but in it she mastered her craft. She had distanced herself from her native Kentucky, but as her stories began to appear in such magazines as *The New Yorker, The Atlantic*, and *Redbook*, it became clear that her native region fed her imagination and that she was now equipped to share her vision. Her dissertation, published as *Nabokov's Garden: A Guide to Ada* (1974), along with *The Girl Sleuth: A Feminist Guide to the Bobbsey Twins, Nancy Drew, and Their Sisters* (1974) make clear that she could have remained on an academic course, but a different kind of stardom awaited her, one that transcends such fame as the Hilltoppers found. *Shiloh and Other Stories* (1982), her first published book of fiction, was a worthy recipient of the Ernest Hemingway Award for 1983. That same year, Mason received a National Endowment for the Arts fellowship and a Pennsylvania Arts Council grant. In

1984 she received a Guggenheim fellowship. While still residing in rural Pennsylvania, she continues to use her Southern heritage—merging the artistic demands of high culture with the popular culture that helped shape her and still
fascinates her.

Although Mason gives occasional readings at colleges and universities, she
gives her main energies to writing. She has no children, but is devoted to her
many cats and is a keen observer of their ways.

MAJOR THEMES

A writer whose fiction made its mark in the 1980s, Mason takes as a major
theme the profound changes in American culture in the 1960s. Her lens for
viewing these changes is Southern, but her statement is not confined to the
Southern scene. The change that Mason marks came with the Vietnam War, a
war in which the nation lost its innocence. Although Mason viewed the war as
a national tragedy, she saw other consequences: Its aftermath brought changes
that Mason treats as liberating, holding out possibilities for greater freedom and
greater self-realization.

Post-Vietnam culture in America can be wonderfully gaudy. America offers
an abundance of goods in its many shopping malls, and malls are a dominant
symbol in Mason's work. New music, rock and hard rock, crowds the airwaves.
Television (Mason's structures are sometimes described as "televisional") brings
national gaudiness into remote Kentucky homes. Superhighways simplify travel
from small Kentucky towns like Hopewell to Paducah, Lexington, and Nashville.
Rituals and styles dominant in earlier times are fading quickly.

In her fiction, Mason captures the meanings of these outward changes most
poignantly in her many renderings of the relationships between men and women
and in the many challenged or failed marriages she portrays. Even the grandmothers in Mason's stories might be found at the Paducah mall wearing pantsuits.
Mason is clear that many of the daughters and granddaughters of those women
are seeking freedoms and opportunities that the grandmothers had never imagined. The new freedoms do not necessarily bring the younger women happiness,
but Mason skillfully conveys their searchings, longings, and frustrations in pursuing that goal. Intent on presenting the dramatized event, the television scene,
as it were, Mason is not polemical. Her stories depend on scene and symbol.
Typically, the narrator is effaced. Her endings are open-ended—giving the sense
that the characters, not the narrator, will play the next scene. These endings
give, collectively, a sense of hopefulness to Mason's fiction. Although there
may be a good deal wrong in the overconsuming society Mason portrays, the
new questionings and the new searchings provide possibilities for new resolu-
tions.

The title story of Mason's first collection of stories identifies these concerns
and methods: "Shiloh" prepares the reader for numerous forays into various
marriages in crisis or in need of adjustment or new understanding. Leroy and

Norma Jean Moffitt have been married for 15 years—neither blissfully happy nor miserably unhappy years. They have lived largely unexamined lives. "Shiloh" is a positive story precisely because events have transpired to force the characters to reflect on their lives and to change them. Mason's characters are often lower middle-class or middle-class people, usually undereducated if not uneducated. But Mason's democratic impulse is always to show the lives as important, worthy of study, deserving of affection. The Moffitts were 18 when they married, the event hastened by Norma Jean's only pregnancy. Schooling had never awakened them to possibilities for examining the world around them, much less themselves. They survived the sudden death of their infant son and settled into routines that made their lives bearable—Leroy, a truck driver, often on the road; Norma Jean selling cosmetics at the Rexall drugstore. Leroy is, so to speak, "king" of his house; Norma Jean, like Marilyn Monroe (whose real name was Norma Jean), part victim.

Typically, Mason is the chronicler of change. In "Shiloh" life alters for the Moffitts after Leroy is in a serious trucking accident. He becomes housebound, and gender roles begin to shift. Leroy takes up needlepoint as well as craft kits. Norma Jean, having more of Leroy than she is accustomed to, takes more seriously than he the body-building exercises he undertakes; she enrolls in a body-building class. She also takes an English class at Paducah Community College—and begins to grow beyond Leroy. Change is further heightened when Norma Jean's mother finds her daughter smoking. On a trip to Shiloh that the mother had promoted, Norma Jean confesses to Leroy that the discovery set something off in her: "She won't leave me alone—*you* won't leave me alone." At Shiloh, Norma Jean and Leroy talk as they have not talked during all the years of their marriage. Shiloh is the past, and the past must be understood. As the story ends, Leroy is beginning to understand the new woman with whom he lives. Mason leaves open the question of their future—and, by extension, that of the modern South: "Now she turns toward Leroy and waves her arms. Is she beckoning to him? She seems to be doing an exercise for her chest muscles. The sky is unusually pale—the color of the dust ruffle Mabel made for their bed."

Understanding the past is the inciting motivation for the action of *In Country*, Mason's study of the effects of the Vietnam War on the American psyche. Like Margaret Mitchell, who was also shaped by the realities of a lost war in which she was not a participant, Mason realized how profoundly the war had changed her South, her America. Her point of view for the novel belongs to Samantha Hughes, whom we catch in the summer after her high school graduation as she perseveres to find the truth about the Vietnam war, a war that she knows has touched profoundly the lives of most of the people she meets daily. Her highest priority is to understand her father, who was killed in that war before she ever saw him. Seeking to find him, she also begins to understand her mother, from whom she has been distanced in the same cultural cataclysm. By means of Sam's youth and gender, Mason gives an essential optimism to *In Country*. Those facts also define the fictional challenge Mason had accepted: A war novel from the perspective of a young protagonist who is female—a believable Nancy Drew.

Mason's skill in portraying the world of young girls is also evident in several short stories, especially "Detroit Skyline, 1949" and "State Champions." Both are first-person stories; both show the protagonist's growing understanding of her culture, each touching the mystery of life and death that transcends culture.

Skilled as Mason is at portraying the surfaces of popular culture, she is attracted to characters who struggle toward comprehension and articulation. In *In Country*, Sam is about to leave Hopewell for a larger world, but she will increasingly realize that her roots deserve study; they should be explored and even cherished. *In Country* is a novel not just about the young. It reaches across gender and across generations.

The reader speculating about what might lie before Samantha Hughes after she finishes college at the University of Kentucky might appropriately think of Nancy Culpepper and the short story of that name, as well as of "Lying Doggo," which gives us a look at Nancy's marriage to Jack Cleveland and her life in the North. Nancy is one of the "transients" of Mason's fiction, like one of the cats who wanders far from the home farm. (Mason's fiction is filled with a large number of cats—some of whom like to stay close to home; others like to explore.) But in her midlife, Nancy becomes increasingly interested in her distant relative, also Nancy Culpepper, and in the photographs of the past. Prior to the creation of Nancy Culpepper, Mason gave her readers familiar terrain, but not reappearing characters. Nancy, however, seemed to touch Mason's emotional experience in a more direct way. Nancy is special to Mason's imagination, as Miranda was to Katherine Anne Porter and Nick Adams was to Ernest Hemingway.

In *Spence + Lila* (1988) Mason places short-story character Nancy Culpepper into a novel. The novel explores the impact of an event common in modern life, but also one that is a major challenge to families and one that raises crucial gender issues. In writing a brief novel with a mastectomy at its center, Mason is able to portray gender and generational issues from several angles. Nancy has returned to Kentucky as her mother—Lila Culpepper—faces the possibility of a mastectomy. Like any surgery, this one and the artery-scraping that follows are performed with the possibility that death may be a consequence. The Culpeppers are quite ordinary people—hardly material for *People* magazine—but Mason means to celebrate their ordinariness and to suggest the wonderful in a world in which change, uncertainty, disease, and death hold sway. Even in unexceptional people, hospitals raise fundamental questions about human lives. Thus, Mason's deceptively flat prose strikes the concerns of her work in its opening paragraph:

On the way to Paducah, Spence notices the row of signs along the highway: WHERE WILL YOU BE IN ETERNITY? Each word is on a white cross. The message reminds him of the old Burma-Shave signs. His wife, Lila, beside him has been quiet during the trip, which takes forty minutes in his Rabbit. He didn't take her car because it has a hole in the muffler, but she has complained about his car ever since he cut the seat belts off to deactivate the annoying warning buzzer.

Although this paragraph paints a scene that may evoke Flannery O'Connor's South and method, O'Connor would ultimately take her readers in a different direction: O'Connor would take the question about eternity literally. (Although Mason does not share O'Connor's religious vision, she shares O'Connor's reverence for life; she challenges her readers to ponder life's ultimate significance.) Mason's satirization of the fundamentalist South is muted, for the literal goal of Spence and Lila's journey is a hospital. Lila's silence on the forty-minute trip suggests that something is amiss. For the moment, it might be her annoyance with Spence over the car. That the car is a Rabbit with seat belts and buzzer lets us know that the scene is contemporary; the deactivated buzzer signals that this world is not completely comfortable to Spence—the safety features are not pleasing to him. *Rabbit* is also a passé term, almost in need of a footnote along with *Burma-Shave* and its distinctive advertising technique. In the next paragraph, the couple passes a shopping center. As she does so often, Mason has her characters and her readers situated in the contemporary world, a world with rapidly changing styles.

Although the inciting action of the story is Lila's breast cancer and surgery, Mason constantly reminds her readers of the flux in her characters' lives. Lila's trauma intensifies numerous memories of World War II for Spence, who since that war has found his fulfillment in his farm and family and has felt no need to journey farther than Paducah. Spence would like to keep his world steady. Lila, who married while still in her teens, never regretted her choice or her life, though it has been in many ways intensely restricted. While Spence was in the service, she lived with his parents, then in a house next to them, and finally had her aged mother-in-law living with her. Only the past few years have given her the freedom to wander far from her home and family; she has felt a craving to do so and has taken numerous excursions, though Spence usually remains at home. Going or staying, rootedness or uprootedness, are among the themes that fascinate Mason. Always, and especially in *Spence + Lila*, she has been aware of the claims and values of the rooted life. She has been aware also of the difficulties of holding on to such a life, especially in the second half of the twentieth century.

The gathering of Lila's children at her bedside accents the rapidly changing world. Nancy, the oldest and now in her 40s, is a professional woman with a career in computers; her parents do not really understand what she does. Nancy lives in Massachusetts; she is married to a photographer; they have one son, now a teenager. Robert does not see his grandparents often. Nancy's status as expatriate Southerner is an engaging element in Mason's earlier short stories "Nancy Culpepper" and "Lying Doggo." Nancy is Mason's intellectual heroine, her most independent, the one who seems closest to Mason herself. Nancy is and has always been an avid reader. Spence recalls that when she was a child, she read and reread her books, as if she could will the stories into life. Like Nancy Drew (who as girl sleuth personifies a freedom most girls do not find), this Nancy wishes to take a strong hand in how things will work out. Her marriage, by her parents' standards, is highly unconventional. When Lila says that Jack was "good" to let Nancy make the visit, Nancy flinches: "He didn't *let* me! He had nothing to do with it. You're my mom and I came to see you." Nancy's ticket from the farm and her Kentucky environment had, in fact, been books. She went away to college and will likely never return for more than a visit. Nancy's views of almost any subject are very different from her parents' views, and even further from those of her grandparents. In addition to freeing her, Nancy's reading has given her burdens: She worries about environmental protection, cholesterol, politics, the world.

Mason contrasts Nancy sharply with her siblings. They did not go away to college, and their world is not as large as Nancy's. They have remained in the Paducah corner of Kentucky. But though her sister Cat is now divorced, she seems more at ease with herself than Nancy does. Her parents seem to understand Cat better, though they worry about her, especially now that she has begun to date again. Cat's relationship with her brother Lee is marked by a tension that suggests they are trapped in sibling competition. Lee is caught between two worlds. He left the farm for the factory, but must work long hours to meet his family responsibilities. He is edgy, and Nancy now sees that he might be more fulfilled if he had learned farming, though in earlier years she had encouraged him to move to town for his factory job. Now Lee urges Spence and Lila to think about using their land for subdivision development.

Mason's work strikes chords that validate the credo of the Vanderbilt Fugitives, who in *I'll Take My Stand* (1930) had warned about the impact of modern technology on the quality of life. Although Mason is keenly interested in the family dynamics of the Culpepper family, she privileges the views of the parents whose names title the book. Late in the novel, looking over his farm from a rise, Spence meditates: "This is it. This is all there is in the world—it contains everything there is to know or possess, yet everywhere people are knocking their brains out trying to find something different, something better. His kids all scattered, looking for it. Everyone always wants a way out of something like this, but what he has here is the main thing there is—just the way things grow and die, the way the sun comes up and goes down every day. These are the facts of life. They are so simple they are almost impossible to grasp" (132). Lila understands completely Spence's view (Spence himself could not effectively articulate it, but they have communicated its essence to each other in their years together); she is intimately connected to the land, and returning to the farm after her surgery becomes the best possible therapy for her and provides the celebratory note with which Mason ends the book.

In all of her work, Mason studies gender determinations, and the very title of her novella alerts her readers to this concern. *Spence + Lila* provides the bringing together of male and female to a degree that we seldom find in her characters who have left the land. Mason does not, of course, think that we can turn back the clock, but the equation "Spence plus Lila" provides an inspiring vision. They have learned to live with the land and with each other. Their marriage is neither matriarchal nor patriarchal. Having seen and grasped the reality of war, Spence has no macho pretensions; he is farmer, not hunter. With mastectomy as the inciting reality of the book, Mason calls attention to both the maternal and the sexual. Lila's breasts were once her glory, but her femininity does not depend on them, and the final chapter of the work makes clear that Spence finds her as much female as ever. Mason's strength as writer is that she reveals her characters in ordinary situations, feeling their own emotions. The truths of their lives can stand without authorial preachment.

SURVEY OF CRITICISM

Criticism about Mason's work is burgeoning. It is still too soon, probably, for collections about her work or for definitive studies. It is too soon for a biography or a major book, but her views matter, and interviewers have been eager to seek her out. Readers and critics are taking Mason seriously, and those who wish to write about her have many opportunities to see what others have thought.

Reviewers of *Shiloh* were mainly positive. Perhaps no praise about the collection was more satisfying to Mason than that of Anne Tyler, who called Mason "a full-fledged master of the short story" and the book "a treasure," a book to buy in order to cast a vote for "real literature." Robert Towers judged *Shiloh* "among the best of recent good collections that have once again brought the short story to the forefront of literary interest," although he found Mason conforming too closely to the conventions of women writing for *The New Yorker*. Patricia Vigderman was more censorious, finding the stories lacking in "emotional gravity" and judging the open-endedness as "aimlessness." The consensus has been closer to Tyler's view.

The writer making a strong beginning with the short story will feel the pressure to match it with a novel. No one could fault Mason for the ambition of her first novel, *In Country*. Reviewers were not, however, carried along on a tide of enthusiasm. Many found the plot contrived. Jonathan Yardley judged the novel stillborn, and Thomas de Pietro found it "bloated, condescending to its characters, pretentious in its feigned naivete." Joel Conarroe, seeing the book in the tradition of the bildungsroman (traditionally male-centered), came closer to giving Mason her due as he made relevant analogies to James Joyce's *Dubliners* and to the fiction of Mason's Southern compatriots Carson McCullers, Harper Lee, and Flannery O'Connor.

No reviewer thought to accuse Mason of "contrivance" in her structuring of *Spence + Lila*. Frank Conroy wished, rather, that Mason had risked more, tried harder to take readers "under the surface of things instead of lingering there so lovingly and relentlessly." Peter S. Prescott thought the book "gently tedious."

But Mason's previous successes ensured the novel extensive review in the popular press, and the reviews were usually affirmative.

Reviews of *Love Life* indicate that Mason is regarded first as a writer of short stories. Lorrie Moore caught the tone of many reviews as she stamped "wonderful" on the stories. Publication of this second collection affirmed as well Mason's acceptance in the academic world, and it occasioned a review essay by Devon Jersild, who gave strong praise to *Love Life* and to the work that preceded it.

From the academy, scholars, mainly in the South, have explored Mason's themes and techniques. Whereas Linda Adams Barnes considered Mason's characters in the tradition of the Southern grotesque (especially that of O'Connor), Robert H. Brinkmeyer, Jr. set Mason's work in a new generation of Southern writers who portray a world less cohesive than that in the fiction of Eudora Welty and other writers of the Renascence, but concluded that Mason shares the vision of an Allen Tate in insisting that understanding of the past is necessary for individual growth. Brinkmeyer emphasized that Mason sees the South as becoming increasingly like the rest of the country: Understanding "Southernness" becomes much like understanding "Americanness." In a later article, Brinkmeyer explored Mason's use of rock and roll music.

Several scholars have explored Mason's feminism and her attention to gender issues; others her portrayal of the Vietnam War and the Vietnam veteran. Examining three stories—"Shiloh," "Third Monday," and "The Retreat"—Richard Giannone insists on a core of mystery of the heart of Mason's characters, on their transcendent worth. The best evidence of Mason's stature in the academy—and her importance to Southern literature—is Fred Hobson's *The Southern Writer in the Postmodern World*. Hobson memorably contrasts Mason's minimalism with the achievement of the Modernists. In *In Country*, he saw the Vietnam War as counterpointing the Civil War in Southern experience.

Owen Gilman, Jr., explored extensively the Southern dimensions of *In Country*, arguing that Mason's answer to Vietnam "is indeed 'in country'—which is the affinity of the South for making the past live." Clearly in a short time Mason's work has produced an impressive body of significant scholarship.

BIBLIOGRAPHY

Works by Bobbie Ann Mason

The Girl Sleuth: A Feminist Guide to the Bobbsey Twins, Nancy Drew, and Their Sisters. Old Westbury, N.Y.: Feminist Press, 1974.
Nabokov's Garden: A Guide to "Ada." Ann Arbor: Ardis, 1974.
Shiloh and Other Stories. New York: Harper and Row, 1982.
"Reaching the Stars: My Life as a Fifties Groupie." *New Yorker* 62 (May 26, 1986): 30–38. Rpt. in *A World Unsuspected: Portraits of Southern Childhood*, ed. Alex. Harris. Chapel Hill: University of North Carolina Press, 1987.

In Country. New York: Harper and Row, 1988.

Spence + Lila. New York: Harper and Row, 1988.

Love Life. New York: Harper and Row, 1989.

Interviews

Bezner, Kevin. "Into the Darkness and Back Again: An Interview with Bobbie Ann Mason." *Washington Post Book Review* (January 1986): 13–14.

Havens, Lila. "Residents and Transients: An Interview with Bobbie Ann Mason." *Crazyhorse* 29 (Fall 1985): 87–104.

Shomer, Enid. "An Interview with Bobbie Ann Mason." *Midwest Quarterly* 28 (Spring 1986): 87–102.

Smith, Wendy. "*Publishers Weekly* Interviews Bobbie Ann Mason." *Publishers Weekly* 228 (August 30, 1985): 424–25.

Wilhelm, Albert E. "An Interview with Bobbie Ann Mason." *Southern Quarterly* 26 (1988): 27–38.

Studies of Bobbie Ann Mason

Arnold, Edwin T. "Falling Apart and Staying Together: Bobbie Ann Mason and Leon Driskell Explore the State of the Modern Family." *Appalachian Journal* 12 (Winter 1985): 135–41.

Barnes, Linda Adams. "The Freak Endures: The Southern Grotesque from Flannery O'Connor to Bobbie Ann Mason," 133–44 in *Since Flannery O'Connor: Essays on the Contemporary Short Story*, ed. Loren Logsdon and Charles Mayer. Macomb: Western Illinois University, 1987.

Blais, Ellen A. "Gender Issues in Bobbie Ann Mason's *In Country*." *South Atlantic Review* 56 (May 1991): 107–18.

Brinkmeyer, Robert H., Jr. "Finding One's History: Bobbie Ann Mason and Contemporary Literature." *Southern Literary Journal* 19 (Spring 1987): 22–33.

———. "Never Stop Rocking: Bobbie Ann Mason and Rock and Roll." *Mississippi Quarterly* 42 (Winter 1988–89): 5–17.

Conarroe, Joel. "Winning Her Father's War." *New York Times Book Review* 15 (September 1985): 7.

Conroy, Frank. "The Family at Her Bedside." *New York Times Book Review* 112 (March 12, 1989): 7.

Durham, Sandra Bonilla. "Women and War: Bobbie Ann Mason's *In Country*." *Southern Literary Journal* 22 (Spring 1990): 45–52.

Giannone, Richard. "Bobbie Ann Mason and the Recovery of Mystery." *Studies in Short Fiction* 27 (Fall 1990): 553–66.

Gilman, Owen W., Jr. *Vietnam and the Southern Imagination*. Jackson: University Press of Mississippi, 1992.

Hobson, Fred. *The Southern Writer in the Postmodern World*. Athens: University of Georgia Press, 1991.

Jersild, Devon. "The World of Bobbie Ann Mason." *Kenyon Review* 11 (Summer 1989): 163–69.

Kinney, Katherine. " 'Humping in the Boonies': Sex, Combat, and the Female in Bobbie Ann Mason's *In Country*." In *Fourteen Landing Zones*, ed. Philip K. Jackson. Iowa City: University of Iowa Press, 1991: 38–48.

Moore, Lorrie. "What Li'l Abner Said." *New York Times Book Review* 112 (March 12, 1989): 7.

Morphew, G. O. "Downhome Feminists in *Shiloh and Other Stories*." *Southern Literary Journal* 21 (Spring 1989): 41–49.

Myers, Thomas. "Dispatches from Ghost Country: The Vietnam Veteran in Recent American Fiction." *Genre* 21 (Winter 1988): 409–28.

Pietro, Thomas de. "In Quest of the Bloody Truth." *Commonweal* 112 (November 1, 1985): 620–22.

Prescott, Peter S. "Bored and Bred in Kentucky." *Newsweek* 112 (August 1, 1988): 53.

Towers, Robert. "American Graffiti." *New York Times Book Review* 29 (December 16, 1982): 38–40.

Tyler, Anne. "Kentucky Cameos." *New Republic* 187 (November 1, 1982): 36–38.

Vigderman, Patricia. "K-Marts and Failing Farms." *Nation* 236 (March 19, 1983): 345–47.

Wilhem, Albert E. "Making Over or Making Off: The Problem of Identity in Bobbie Ann Mason's Short Fiction." *Southern Literary Journal* 18 (Spring 1986): 76–82.

———. "Private Rituals: Coping with Change in the Fiction of Bobbie Ann Mason." *Midwest Quarterly* 28 (Winter 1987): 271–82.

Yardley, Jonathan. "Bobbie Ann Mason and the Shadow of Vietnam." *Washington Post Book World* (September 8, 1985): 3.

JERRY LEATH MILLS

Cormac Mccarthy
(1933–   )

Cormac McCarthy stands among the finest living craftsmen of the American language, yet he has no single "signature" style. Through six novels he has evolved a chameleonic, endlessly variable prose that shapes and reconfigures itself in accordance with the tone, mood, and pressure of phenomena as occasions require. It is a prose of taxonomical precision and allusive resonance, of inspired neologism and etymological inventiveness, alternately—sometimes simultaneously—photographic and evocative. In its capacity to accommodate and poise against each other the extremes of experience—depravity and innocence, comic vulgarity and great dignity of spirit, unimaginable horror and mind-arresting beauty—it expresses its author as a tragic artist who sees in life the constant presence of loneliness, sorrow, and loss, and whose perception of these conditions makes him more closely attuned to and more capable of rendering intensely life's contrasting moments of beauty, community, and joy.

BIOGRAPHY

This most Southern of writers was born in Providence, Rhode Island, on July 20, 1933, one of six children of Charles Joseph McCarthy, an attorney, and his wife, Gladys McGrail. He was initially named Charles, after his father, but his parents soon rechristened him in honor of the fifteenth-century Irish king who built Blarney Castle. In 1937 the McCarthys moved to Knox County, Tennessee, where Charles served as a high-level counsel to the Tennessee Valley Authority (he later went on to prominence as an attorney in Washington, D.C.). The McCarthy children grew up in a large home on Marlin Mill Pike in terrain that Cormac's former wife, Anne DeLisle, considers especially influential on his first novel. "Cormac ran all these forests and hills," she told Don Williams of the *Knoxville News-Sentinel*; "he used to put his traps out there; he trapped muskrats and things. If you read *The Orchard Keeper* this is exactly where it took place. This is where they ran the whiskey and up on the hill is where the Green Fly Inn used to just hang over the edge like it would fall into the gully at any time.''

Like Flannery O'Connor, whose influence is often evident in his work, McCarthy experienced a Roman Catholic childhood in the Protestant South, graduating from Catholic High School in Knoxville in 1951. Throughout the subsequent academic year he was a liberal arts major at the University of Tennessee, but he left school at the end of the term for a year of wandering and shifting employment. Don Williams has suggested that this move was accompanied by "some sort of falling out with his father." If so, it is interesting to recall the alienation of McCarthy's protagonist Cornelius Suttree from his father and that father's strictures on the undirected life: "If it is life that you feel you are missing I can tell you where to find it. In the law courts, in business, in government. There is nothing occurring in the streets. Nothing but a dumbshow composed of the helpless and the impotent" (*Suttree* 14).

McCarthy joined the United States Air Force in 1953 for a 4-year enlistment, some of it in Alaska, before returning to the University of Tennessee and the city of Knoxville whose seamier precincts he renders so vividly in *Suttree* (1979). Although he left in 1960 without taking a degree, he must have found encouragement at the university for a literary vocation. He won an award for creative writing during his final year of studies and left with work begun on at least two novels, *The Orchard Keeper* and *Suttree* (*Suttree* was eventually to be his fourth published book). After several years of refining and polishing at various addresses in Tennessee, North Carolina, and Illinois, *The Orchard Keeper* was published by Random House on May 5, 1965, and won the William Faulkner Foundation Award for the most distinguished first novel of that year.

A few weeks later McCarthy boarded the ship *Sylvania* for Ireland and Europe on an American Academy of Arts and Letters travel fellowship. Also on board was Anne DeLisle, a young dancer and musician from England. A shipboard romance led to marriage, less than a year later, in an old Norman church in Hamble, England, where the bride's parents lived. With his characteristic ability at practical and mechanical enterprises, McCarthy bought and repaired an old Jaguar in which they traveled over Europe for two years during the composition of *Outer Dark* (1968). In that period they lived in France, Italy, Spain, and the island of Ibiza off the Spanish coast. "That was a time when Ibiza was all writers and musicians," DeLisle told Don Williams, "and it really was a bohemian time and everybody was avant garde, and I think it was like people were trying to recapture a feeling of '20s Paris with Hemingway and all that stuff.''

The McCarthys imported some of that bohemianism to Rockford, Tennessee, in 1967, where they rented a small farm dwelling for a time before settling on another farm near Louisville, Kentucky, for work on *Child of God* (1973) and *Suttree*. DeLisle told Williams that her husband "didn't carry insurance. He was such a rebel that he didn't live the same kind of life anybody else on earth lived. . . . We did everything that there was to do in life. That's the kind of people we were.'' On the Kentucky farm McCarthy renovated the barn that became their house, cutting his own timber and doing his own masonry with rocks from the surrounding fields. DeLisle ran a dance studio until about 1976, when the pair separated, and later a fashionable restaurant (''Annie's Restaurant'') in Knoxville until moving to Florida in 1990.

Cormac McCarthy continues to move and to write. As Vereen Bell notes, ''he is said to work mainly in motels and to live austerely.'' For the past decade he has lived chiefly in El Paso, Texas, where he moved to write *Blood Meridian* (1985), but he travels often and visits Knoxville with some regularity. He does not grant interviews or appear publicly in connection with his books. Those outside his own circle of friends who have been able to talk with him report him a gracious and congenial man, willing to talk candidly about ideas and about writers he admires (e.g., Milan Kundera and Jorge Luis Borges) but seldom about his own work. Although obviously devoted to longer prose fiction—his three periodical publications are all excerpts from the novels—he is interested in film and has written a television play, *The Gardener's Son*, directed by Richard Pearce for public television in 1977. Dramatizing a historical murder—of a mill boss by an offended worker in 1876—the film was made on location in textile villages near Graniteville, South Carolina, and Burlington, North Carolina.

In May 1992, Alfred A. Knopf published *All the Pretty Horses*, the first novel of McCarthy's projected ''border trilogy.'' Novelist Larry Brown's comment in an Oxford, Mississippi, newsletter was typical of the early reviews: ''To my mind it is flawless, a finely polished jewel that reverberates in the memory long after the book has been closed.'' By mid-June McCarthy was represented, for the first time in his career, on the best-seller list. In November 1992, the novel earned its author the National Book Award. McCarthy is currently preparing a play, *The Stonecutter*, for presentation in Washington, D.C.

MAJOR THEMES

McCarthy's novels are thematically uninsistent, seldom resolving conflicts neatly or displaying anything that might be taken as an overtly interpretive attitude toward the experience they depict. Nonetheless, they do as a whole replicate a canon of familiar situations, images, and ideas that imply a consistency of philosophical stance. That standpoint is, first and foremost, tragic—not in any purely formal, Aristotelian terms, but in the general sense that Thomas Wolfe defines when he says in an essay entitled ''God's Lonely Man'' (in *The Hills Beyond* [New York: Sun Dial Press, 1943], pp. 186–97) that the tragic writer understands how the beauty, glory, and joy of life are always pierced ''by the premonitory sense of loss and death'' and that ''the best and worst that the human heart can know are merely different aspects of the same thing, and are interwoven . . . into the tragic web of life.''

In keeping with such a vision, McCarthy's novels hold before us images of loss, displacement, and alienation from a community interspersed with scenes of human warmth, uncritical friendship, and natural beauty. Repeatedly we encounter emblems of a fallen Eden, most concretely in *The Orchard Keeper*, whose action moves in and out of a literal ruined orchard, but also elsewhere—in junkyards littered with man's wreckage (*Child of God*, *Suttree*), in swamps (*Outer Dark*), and in wind-scarred deserts bearing petroglyphs and other evidence of a vanished ancient life (*Blood Meridian*). Floods in *The Orchard Keeper*, *Child of God*, and *Suttree* reinforce the biblical suggestiveness of a world constantly offering hints but never confirmation of meaning and moral order. But, in the dialectical way that McCarthy's exposition typically moves, images of lost perfection are countered with Darwinian scenes suggestive of aboriginal and eternally accessible barbarism in the human heart. Caves and caverns abound—each of the novels except *Outer Dark* contains at least one subterranean scene—and there is much talk of troglodytes and primitive forms, bearing out the implications of one of the epigraphs to *Blood Meridian*, a newspaper item noting that a recently discovered prehistoric skull showed signs of having been scalped.

In McCarthy's writings, as in Flannery O'Connor's, there seems to lie a belief in the objective existence of evil, an existence not amenable to clarification by psychology or correction by social means. Thus, to seek psychological causes for what Lester Ballard does in *Child of God* is to ignore the point of the title, although McCarthy does provide enough details to start us on that reductionistic path if we fall for the temptation. The evil trinity of marauders in *Outer Dark* (whose literary line goes back through O'Connor's "A Good Man Is Hard to Find" to Joseph Conrad's *Victory*) are probably best understood by noticing that one has on shoes whose semi-detached sole gives the appearance of a cloven foot. The comic, literal-minded honesty of Gene Harrogate in *Suttree* seems very much to the point here: When he relates how he burned down an old lady's house as a prank, he remembers his sister "told em I didn't have no daddy was how come I got in trouble. But shit fire I was mean when I did have one. It didn't make no difference" (145).

With McCarthy, as with Wallace Stevens, death is the mother of beauty. Violence in the world is a necessary component of the tension his aesthetic requires. Violence and beauty are seldom separable in nature as he depicts it. One thinks of the western landscapes of *Blood Meridian*, the hunting scenes in *The Orchard Keeper* and *Child of God*, the old railroader's description of a burning train against the mountain night in *Suttree*, and of Lester's dream of a journey in *Child of God*: "Each leaf he passed he'd never pass again. They rode over his face like veils, already some yellow, their veins like slender bones where the sun shone through them. He had resolved himself to ride on for he could not turn back and the world that day was as lovely as any day that ever was and he was riding to his death" (170–71).

The inadequacy of social institutions is everywhere evident in the novels, not as a function of social satire or a plea for reform, but simply as a fact of life put to service as metaphor for the human condition (Cornelius Suttree, we remember, was asleep during the commission of the crime for which he was imprisoned as accessory). Police and legal systems fare especially badly, typically finding representation in characters like the vindictive deputy Gifford and Legwater the dogcatcher in *The Orchard Keeper* and the racist, head-cracking cop Tarzan Quinn in *Suttree*, and in the lynch-law episodes of *Outer Dark* and *Blood Meridian*. Jails, prisons, and cages appear in all six books, along with other forms of legal confinement, such as the mental institution (*Child of God*, *Suttree*) and the county home (*The Orchard Keeper*). Religion's adherents are corrupt (*Outer Dark*) or insane and hopelessly out of touch with the actual world (*Suttree*).

As with the larger social forms, the family order in McCarthy's world has gone to ruin. An intact and functional family unit is hard to find. More often, we discover travesties of traditional family structures, such as Culla Holme's incest with his sister Rinthy in *Outer Dark* and the junkman's with his daughter in *Child of God*, not to mention Lester Ballard's seraglio of violated female corpses. Gene Harrogate, lacking wife or human lover, copulates with watermelons in *Suttree*, where Weird Leonard gives us a twist on filial piety when he cares for his father's ravaged body for several months beyond its death in order to keep the welfare payments coming.

In other instances, the failure of conventional institutions generates substitutes that bring out warmth and humanity in the midst of great distress. The most extended example is *The Orchard Keeper*, in which the fatherless John Wesley Rattner is reared into manhood by a bootlegger, Marion Sylder, and an old recluse called Uncle Ather. The two adults do not know each other and are both ignorant, as is John Wesley, of the fact that a man Sylder once killed and whose burial place has been long tended by Uncle Ather was in fact John Wesley's natural father. The boy grows up honest and strong, but his surrogate fathers are carted off respectively to prison and the county home, and none of the characters ever learns anything close to the whole story. On one hand the plot seems to lend credence to a theory of blind chance as a governing principle, but on another it implies a mysterious, providential order behind events, with its time scheme organized into multiples of seven years and its correlation of the stately progression of the seasons with the seasons of human life.

The several scenes of human communion in *The Orchard Keeper*—Uncle Ather with the young rabbit hunters in the purifying snow, Sylder and John Wesley on the coon hunt, Uncle Ather sharing a humble but gracious last supper with some generous men—have their raucous counterparts in *Suttree*'s "fellowship of the doomed" (23) among the dispossessed members of Knoxville's lowlife, the drunks, brawlers, and sociopaths who stand in for Suttree's own hopelessly fractured family. Such scenes, with those of the people who befriend Rinthy in *Outer Dark* and the episode of the Diegueño Indians in *Blood Meridian*, perhaps establish that if there is indeed no cause for optimism in human affairs there is at least no imperative for despair.

SURVEY OF CRITICISM

Walter Sullivan, who sees in Southern fiction since World War II a history of more or less steady decline, looked to McCarthy in 1972 as a potential rejuvenator, listing him in *Death by Melancholy* with Madison Jones and Elizabeth Spencer as one who ''might write the book that has the same enduring magnificence as a Faulkner novel or a Katherine Anne Porter short story.'' But by 1976 he had written him off, in *Requiem for the Renascence*, as an artist ''not merely bereft of community and myth; he has declared war against these ancient repositories of order and truth.'' Deeply offended by *Child of God*, which he regarded as ''an affront to decency on every level,'' Sullivan ranked McCarthy with Erskine Caldwell, Carson McCullers, and James Dickey as a purveyor of what he opprobiously called ''grotesque local color.'' However, in reviewing *Suttree* for the *Sewannee Review* in 1979, Sullivan found a kind of compromise in praising McCarthy's enormous stylistic resources while continuing to deplore his preoccupation with the grotesque and criticizing what he considered a lack of structure in the novel. By then Sullivan was willing to grant that ''McCarthy's Faulknerian prose achieves a lyricism that touches the heart and a dignity which endows some of the ugliest aspects of creation with a certain beauty.''

Few other critics have been so grudging with their endorsement. Despite his lack of popular acceptance (Vereen Bell records that hardcover sales of the first five novels totaled fewer than 15,000 copies), McCarthy has won the admiration of a formidable array of critics, scholars, and other novelists, the latter group including Larry Brown, Clyde Edgerton, Tim McLaurin, and Lee Smith. Bell begins his book on McCarthy with the premise that he is ''a major writer in all the conventional senses of the word, our best unknown writer by many measures.'' Mark Royden Winchell, though unwilling to grant McCarthy a ''place among the immortals'' except for *Child of God*, nonetheless calls him ''the most highly respected unknown writer in contemporary southern letters.'' Mitchell, like Sullivan, stresses McCarthy's stylistic brilliance, as do Vereen Bell, Anatole Broyard, Guy Davenport, and John Ditsky.

McCarthy's moral vision is of special interest to Robert Coles, William Schafer, and Lewis Simpson. Coles discovers religious feeling in *Child of God*, whose protagonist defies psychological analysis and belongs with those figures in Greek tragedy and medieval literature whose fates evince a combination of self-ignorance and impersonal forces of destruction, reminding us of our essential inadequacies at piercing the ultimate mysteries of life. Schafer explores McCarthy's presentation of reverberative action in his plots, charting the ongoing consequences of the characters' deeds. He finds at the hearts of the novels ''human and natural evil, the perversity of social and individual psychology, the tension between the human mind and the natural world.'' Simpson, who admires the ''chilling precision'' of *Child of God*, sees its main character, Lester Ballard, as a literary descendant of Sut Lovingood, the creation of nineteenth-century Tennessee writer George Washington Harris. Like Sut, Lester carries to terrible extremes the American individualist tendencies toward "emancipation of the self, at any cost, from the community of past and present." (Simpson's comments were written before the publication of *Suttree*, whose hero, also a drop-out of sorts from regular society, is nicknamed "Sut" by several other characters in the book.)

Several critics have discussed McCarthy in the context of influence and traditions in Southern fiction, especially traditions of the gothic and the grotesque. In additional to Harris' Sut Lovingood, Lewis Simpson finds a place for Poe's "The Fall of the House of Usher" in the backgrounds of *Child of God*. Numerous writers point to Faulkner and O'Connor as important models—Bell writes that the influence of both is obvious "because McCarthy without embarrassment lets it be, in fact forces it toward our attention both as an homage and as a means of putting himself in a hypothetical American pantheon." But Ditsky justly observes that "dictionally, tonally, McCarthy simply goes *beyond* Faulkner" in carrying the reader further into the darkness of human experience. Like Joyce, with whose work McCarthy's—especially *Suttree*—has unexplored affinities, McCarthy is a meticulous researcher, having drawn, as John Sepich has discovered, upon upward of 250 separate historical sources for *Blood Meridian*.

Bell's *The Achievement of Cormac McCarthy* is, to date, the only book-length study of McCarthy's art, discussing each of the novels in detail in separate chapters—the longest devoted to *Suttree*, which Bell regards as McCarthy's masterpiece—and providing an introduction to the general principles at work in the fiction as a body. Bell stresses the peculiarly "unmediated" nature of McCarthy's narratives, whereby McCarthy presents experience in raw and apparently uninterpreted form, denying the reader the conventional prop of a central intelligence through whose perceptions a paraphraseable "meaning" is invested in facts and events. Bell further remarks on the absence of "normative" characters and the abundance of characters who are solitary, inarticulate, and lacking in curiosity about the world around them. "When the world is perceived innocent of moral form in this way," Bell writes, "it stands forth in language vividly and, for better or worse, thrives there."

Bell's book has lent impetus to a growing interest in interpretation and evaluation of McCarthy's achievement. The *Southern Quarterly* devoted its Summer 1992 issue (vol. 30, no. 4) to essays on McCarthy's work.

BIBLIOGRAPHY

Works by Cormac McCarthy

"Bounty." *Yale Review* 54 (1964–65): 368–74.
"The Dark Waters." *Sewanee Review* 73 (1965): 210–16.
The Orchard Keeper. New York: Random House, 1965; Ecco Press, 1982.
Outer Dark. New York: Random House, 1968; Ecco Press, 1984.
Child of God. New York: Random House, 1973; Ecco Press, 1984.

Suttree. New York: Random House, 1979; Vintage, 1986.
"The Scalphunters." *TriQuarterly*, 48 (Spring 1980): 15–28.
Blood Meridian; or The Evening Redness in the West. New York: Random House, 1985; Ecco Press, 1986.
All the Pretty Horses. New York: Knopf, 1992.

Studies of Cormac McCarthy

Arnold, Edwin T. Rev. of *Blood Meridian. Appalachian Journal* 13 (1985): 103–4.
———. "Naming, Knowing and Nothingness: McCarthy's Moral Parables." *Southern Quarterly* 30 (1992): 31–50.
Bell, Madison Smartt. Rev. of *All the Pretty Horses. New York Times Book Review* (May 17, 1992): 9, 11.
Bell, Vereen M. *The Achievement of Cormac McCarthy.* Baton Rouge: Louisiana State University Press, 1988.
———. "The Ambiguous Nihilism of Cormac McCarthy." *Southern Literary Journal* 15 (Spring 1983): 31–41.
Brown, Larry. Untitled note, p. 3 in *Dear Reader.* Oxford, Miss.: Square Books, 1992.
Broyard, Anatole. "Daddy Quit, She Said," in *Aroused by Books.* New York: Random House, 1974.
———. "Where All Tales Are Tall." *New York Times* (January 20, 1979): 19.
Cheause, Alan. "A Note on Landscape in *All the Pretty Horses." Southern Quarterly* 30 (1992): 140–42.
Coffey, Michael. "New Grit: The Dawn of the McCarthy Era." *Village Voice* (May 19, 1992): 70.
Coles, Robert. "The Stranger" (Rev. of *Child of God). New Yorker* (August 26, 1974): 87–90.
Cox, Dianne L. "Cormac McCarthy," 224–32 in *American Novelists since World War II*, Second Series, ed. James E. Kibler, Jr., *Dictionary of Literary Biography*, Vol. 6. Detroit: Gale Research, 1980.
Daugherty, Leo. "Gravers False and True: *Blood Meridian* as Gnostic Tragedy." *Southern Quarterly* 30 (1992): 122–33.
Davenport, Guy. "Appalachian Gothic." (Rev. of *Outer Dark). New York Times Book Review* (September 29, 1968): 4.
———. "Silurian Southern" (Rev. of *Suttree). National Review* (March, 16, 1979): 368–69.
Ditsky, John. "Further into Darkness: The Novels of Cormac McCarthy." *Hollins Critic* 18 (April 1981): 1–11.
Draper, Robert. "The Invisible Man." *Texas Monthly* (July 1992): 42–46.
Grammer, John M. "A Thing Against Which Time Will Not Prevail." *Southern Quarterly* 30 (1992): 19–30.
Gray, Michael Toby. "Beyond the Pale: A Search for Themes in the Novels of Cormac McCarthy." Unpub. Honors Essay. Chapel Hill: Department of English, University of North Carolina, 1989.
Longley, John Lewis. "Suttree and the Metaphysics of Death." *Southern Literary Journal* 17 (Spring 1985): 79–90.
Luce, Dianne. "Cormac McCarthy: A Bibliography." *Southern Quarterly* 30 (1992): 143–51.

———. "Cormac McCarthy's First Screenplay: 'The Gardener's Son.' " *Southern Quarterly* 30 (1992): 51–71.

Mills, Jerry Leath. "Cormac McCarthy." *Independent Weekly* (Durham, N.C.) (June 1, 1989): 9–10.

———. "Discovering Cormac McCarthy." Raleigh, N.C. *News and Observer* (July 12, 1992): 46.

Murray, James G. Rev. of *The Orchard Keeper*. *America* 112 (1965): 866.

Pissaro, Vince. "The Best Unknown Writer in America." *Mirabella* (May 1992): 52–53.

Ragan, David Paul. "Values and Structure in *The Orchard Keeper*." *Southern Quarterly* 30 (1992): 10–18.

Salmans, Sandra. "Down and Out in Knoxville" (Rev. of *Suttree*). *Times Literary Supplement* (May 2, 1980): 500.

Schafer, William J. "Cormac McCarthy: The Hard Wages of Original Sin." *Appalachian Journal* 4 (1976–77): 105–19.

Sepich, John Emil. "The Dance of History in Cormac McCarthy's *Blood Meridian*." *Southern Literary Journal* 24 (1991): 16–31.

———. "Notes Toward an Explication of Cormac McCarthy's *Blood Meridian*." Unpub. Master's Thesis. Chapel Hill: University of North Carolina, 1989.

———. " 'What kind of indians was them?': Some Historical Sources in Cormac McCarthy's *Blood Meridian*." *Southern Quarterly* 30 (1992): 93–110.

Shapiro, Steven. " 'The Very Life of the Darkness': A Reading of *Blood Meridian*." *Southern Quarterly* 30 (1992): 110–21.

Simpson, Lewis. "Southern Fiction," 189–90 in *The Harvard Guide to Contemporary American Writing*, ed. Daniel Hoffman. Cambridge, Mass.: Harvard University Belknap Press, 1979.

Sullivan, Walter. *Death by Melancholy: Essays on Modern Southern Fiction*. Baton Rouge: Louisiana State University Press, 1972.

———. "Model Citizens and Marginal Cases: Heroes of the Day" (Rev. of *Suttree*). *Sewanee Review* 87 (1979): 337–44.

———. *A Requiem for the Renascence: The State of Fiction in the Modern South*. Athens: University of Georgia Press, 1976.

Tidmore, Kurt. Rev. of *All the Pretty Horses*. *Washington Post* (May 3, 1992): 1–2.

Trachtenberg, Stanley. Rev. of *The Orchard Keeper*. *Yale Review* 55 (1965–66): 149.

Wallace, Garry. "Meeting McCarthy." *Southern Quarterly* 30 (1992): 134–39.

Williams, Don. "Annie DeLisle: Cormac McCarthy's Ex-wife Prefers to Recall the Romance." *Knoxville News-Sentinel* (June 10, 1990): E1–E2.

———. "Cormac McCarthy: Knoxville's Most Famous Contemporary Writer Prefers His Anonymity." *Knoxville News-Sentinel* (June 10, 1990): E1–E2.

Winchell, Mark Royden. "Inner Dark; or, The Place of Cormac McCarthy." *Southern Review* 26 (April 1990): 293–309.

Woodward, Richard B. "Cormac McCarthy's Venemous Fiction." *New York Times Magazine* (April 19, 1992): 28–31, 36, 40.

Young, Thomas Daniel. *Tennessee Writers*. Knoxville: University of Tennessee Press (1981): 99–107.

Young, Thomas D., Jr. "The Imprisonment of Sensibility: *Suttree*." *Southern Quarterly* 30 (1992): 72–91.

LYNN Z. BLOOM

Jill Mccorkle
(1958–   )

Jill McCorkle is a prolific (four novels and a collection of short stories in 8 years) North Carolina writer whose overarching theme of adolescent growth, development, and maturation, predominantly female, is latently and pleasantly feminist. Her North Carolina small towns and rural areas are reminiscent of Faulkner's vast and varied Yoknapatawpa County, modernized and in a major key.

It's hard to resist an autobiographical reading of the works of Jill Collins McCorkle, who uses her own birthdate, July 7th, as the title of her novel that anatomizes a small town very much like Lumberton, North Carolina, where she grew up. Indeed, as McCorkle explains in an essay on how and why she writes about adolescents, "What to Wear on the First Day at Lumberton High": "When I begin constructing a scene . . . the setting that always comes first to my mind is . . . my hometown as it was when I was an adolescent. I rely heavily on that flat pine wooded landscape, the rise and fall of traffic on I–95, the way the light fell on my bedroom walls on a winter afternoon . . . the cool moldiness of the cemetery where a friend and I rode our bikes and mourned the deaths of people who died before we were born" (10). Lest readers concentrate too closely on the parallels between McCorkle's characters and her life, however, the novelist adds: "When I write, I have the freedom . . . to pick and choose, to disappear and then reappear as any and many different characters." Some of her characters "wear the clothes and say the things that I would never choose to wear or say. I find that there's always an alter ego character for me, someone confident, too confident sometimes."

BIOGRAPHY

Daughter of Melba Collins McCorkle, a medical secretary, and John Wesley McCorkle, Jr., a postal worker, Jill McCorkle was born July 7, 1958, in Lumberton, North Carolina. She grew up steeped in the lore of a family to which she remains "very, very close." Says McCorkle: "I believed all the stories, every word. As a child I was fascinated by my grandmother," who told many of these stories, "and hung out with her all the time. She lived across town in an old house, and going there was like going back in time" (Stead 26)—a restorative journey the "miserably pregnant" Ginny Sue of *Tending to Virginia* (1987) intuitively makes. Like the heroine of *The Cheer Leader* (1984), McCorkle herself, exceptionally attractive, was a cheerleader, but wrote the novel "to bust up the cheerleader stereotype"; Jo Spencer is far closer to Jo March of *Little Women* in her intelligence and literary aspirations than to the effervescent airhead the term connotes.

McCorkle focuses her writing on adolescence because in her own life "it was terrible and wonderful and good and bad; it was heaven and hell and I loved it and I hated it. . . . To forget what it feels like to be adolescent is to forget how it *feels*—period. Along with the hormones, the emotions are working in their purest, simplest forms." Sitting down to write fiction, she says, "is really not much different from making sure the bedroom door is locked after everyone else is asleep and then pulling out the diary, finding the pen with purple ink, and turning to a brand new page." But "I do not plot. When a novel starts taking shape, I write it just straight through, and then re-work individual parts" (conversation with Lynn Z. Bloom, August 17, 1990).

In 1980 McCorkle graduated from the University of North Carolina at Chapel Hill with highest honors in creative writing. The following year she earned an M.A. from Hollins College, where she was awarded the Andrew James Purdy Fiction Prize, and married Steven Alexander. They were divorced in 1984. She began publishing with stories in the literary magazines of both colleges that were later reprinted—"Carson" in the first issue of *Crescent Review* (Fall 1983), a Winston-Salem literary magazine, and "The Spell and the Beautiful Garden" in *Seventeen* (September 1984). For the next 4 years McCorkle worked at various jobs to sustain her writing—as a receptionist, librarian, teacher, and secretary. In 1984 McCorkle made an unusual double debut for a new writer when Algonquin Books of Chapel Hill published her first and second novels simultaneously, *The Cheer Leader* and *July 7th* (1984).

Favorable reviews brought invitations to teach creative writing part-time, at Duke University and her alma mater; and from 1987 to 1989 at Tufts University during the residency of her husband, Daniel Shapiro, M.D., whom she married in 1987. A daughter, Claudia, was born on July 25, 1989. In fall 1989, having returned to Chapel Hill with her husband, McCorkle again taught at the University of North Carolina. She soon published two more novels and a collection of short stories with Algonquin—*Tending to Virginia* (1987), *Ferris Beach* (1990), and *Crash Diet: Stories* (1992). A son, Robert, was born on December 27, 1991, in Chapel Hill. In 1992 the family moved back to Boston, and McCorkle began teaching creative writing at Harvard. She speaks as she writes, in a lyrical Southern accent, and smiles often. "It's frustrating," she says, "when people expect you to be real weird and you aren't. One person asked me, 'Did I ever have a normal life?' I think I do.'' That McCorkle's life currently combines marriage, motherhood, teaching, and a fast-track career as a novelist attests to her unusual energy, talent, and an organizational ability that yield not only success but an inspiring joie de vivre.

MAJOR THEMES

A bildungsroman, like an autobiography of childhood, is a novel of education and maturity and this is a central theme of all four of McCorkle's novels. Although all her novels are set in North Carolina, the characters and themes transcend the region to assume quintessentially American significance. Their major characters move from innocence through experience to understanding— of themselves, their Southern world, and human nature—within the context of one's family and without. That this understanding is incomplete reflects the tentative status of these characters, who are still in the process of growing up when the novels end. But they've made a good start, and, although they learn from an unpredictable combination of the bitter, the sweet, and the horrifying, the novels' prevailing mood is of resolute, sometimes utterly comic, good cheer. The characters' maturation is paralleled by McCorkle's maturation in literary techniques and intellectual complexity.

Another major theme of McCorkle's fiction, including many of the stories in *Crash Diet*, is the opportunity for "a wish [to] come true, a new start, a second chance." Many of her characters attain this through a combination of their own efforts, good fortune, and the benevolent outcome of tragedy and suffering. McCorkle's novels readily admit of a Christian interpretation: Acknowledgment of sin and atonement for it engenders forgiveness, happiness, and peace on earth. The novels' themes are intertwined, for these fruits of reconciliation, too, are in some measure the fruits of maturation, as well. These fruits ripen most readily in the context of a cohesive extended family, or of a community that functions as both a supplement to and surrogate for the family. Thus family, for better and for worse, and the continuity of generations become important motifs in McCorkle's works, gaining in significance as they are integrated with the other major themes.

The Cheer Leader, McCorkle's effervescent first novel, is invariably compared with Sylvia Plath's *The Bell Jar*. It explores the nearly fatal, self-determined loss of innocence of Jo Spencer and in the process anatomizes a host of small-town coming-of-age rituals, mostly female, of the late 1960s and early 1970s. For much of high school, Jo, an aspiring Barbie doll with a brain, enjoys what she has been preparing for since birth. Buttressed by her three best friends, Tricia, Lisa, and Cindy, Jo parlays her cute figure, stylish clothes, summer tan, and superficial social finesse into an enviable status as her senior year begins. She is a cheerleader and May queen, a straight-A student who loves Edna St.

Vincent Millay and Emily Dickinson, popular, and a virgin. She is, as she says, "fit"—in perfect control of her life in the Garden of Eden.

But Edens never last. Jo's crumbles from within, as she courts experience and danger through departure from her safely bourgeois existence. She convinces herself that she's in love with Red Williams, an older construction worker whom she idealizes as the embodiment of the best of the blue-collar virtues—a hard worker with aspirations to "maybe go to school, maybe one day own his own garage and just run things." She also attributes to him her own code of conduct—sparing use of alcohol, avoidance of drugs, and, particularly, monogamy—closing her eyes to the fact that Red practices none of the above, until she can close them no longer. During her freshman year in college, Jo, by this time an aspiring poet, suffers an anorexic breakdown in a futile attempt to regain control of her life through ritualistically adhering to rules she invents to keep at bay the need to confront and resolve the contradictions of her life: "She must eat only once a day at exactly five-thirty . . . one cup of Dannon's yogurt (preferably banana) or one cup of cottage cheese. . . . She must not try to sleep at night because that is when the dream comes, the dream where she is running, running, running, looking for [Red] because something is wrong."

Jo's salvation begins at the end of spring semester, through supportive parents, validation of her talent from her poetry teacher, and a wise psychiatrist, who encourages her to come to terms with the past she "can't change or control" and to face the future with honesty rather than self-deception, engagement rather than forced detachment, acceptance of a world of plurality and possibility. After graduation, 4 years later, and at least a partial reaffirmation of the family values she had rejected as a high school senior, she assesses her status as still tentative but hopeful: "Presently, I have many choices to make. . . . I am smart but I am not Jewish. I am Christian but I am not Catholic and Catholics are Christians. . . . At least right now I know that I am moving, sliding, changing."

July 7th is a fascinating, raucous "technical *tour de force*," as Madison Smartt Bell has called it, encompassing a 24-hour period in the life of Marshboro, North Carolina, not Lumberton, says McCorkle, but "just any town along I–95," "groups of little boxes that blur a passer-by's peripheral vision, a common denominator." Its teenage protagonist, Sam Swett is, like Jo Spencer, as aspiring writer running away from bourgeois privilege, full of, says Bell, "unjustified *angst*" at the process of finding an identity and a calling (in Moss, 368). Swett, hitchhiking from New York, arrives at the Quik Pik convenience store just in time to witness the random murder of night attendant Charlie Husky, the most bizarre occurrence in a superabundance of events that interweave the fantasies and realities of the entire populace.

Swett gropes toward maturity through wondering what it would be like to be each of the people he meets. His own voice intermingles with the delightfully off-key harmony of some twenty early 1980s residents who verge on caricature. Ernie Stubbs, nouveau riche real estate developer, fulfills a fantasy by cheating on his wife, "a little friendly recreation simply because there is too much power

bottled up inside of a successful man to limit his limits.'' His gum-chewing
"protegée," Janie Morris ("Wow, I've never been a protegée before''), is really
in love with Tommy McNair. McNair, a black graduate student, remains the
pride of his mother, Fannie (Stubbs's housemaid, a more cynical version of
William Faulkner's equally powerful Dilsey), even when he is erroneously accused of the murder by Keystone cop Bob Bobbin. Cosmetician Juanita Suggs
Weeks, proprietor of "Hair Today Gone Tomorrow,'' herself having succumbed
to passion in a meat locker at the Winn Dixie, seeks forgiveness from her
husband, Harold (who discovered the corpse during yet another night of drunken
separation), fantasizing their reunion.

July 7th, 1983, is also the 83rd birthday of Granner Weeks, Harold's mother
and mother-in-law of Ernie, who she accurately believes is trying to shove her
into a nursing home so he can profit from her land. Weeks is also the grandmother
of Corky Revels, the sweet, shy Coffee Shop waitress who has survived her
father's bloody suicide to become Sam's salvation. Granner's birthday party, a
loving burlesque of the way the young treat the old and the old treat the young,
brings everyone together, reaffirming that the entire town is interrelated not only
literally but metaphorically. Even a new grandchild (Brantley Rhett Tyner) is
born during that time. In the ensuing atmosphere of forgiveness and reconciliation, everyone gets a second—or third or fourth—chance, to find shelter and
succor, to live right and do well: The weak, the vain, the foolish, the profligate,
the adulterers, even the murderer. Sam Swett, all set to return home, understands
intuitively what he cannot yet articulate: That, although the "familiar service
stations and restaurants that line the highway at every stop . . . all seem the same
at first glance,'' they will on examination prove to be diverse, individual. His
knowing this "makes it count, settling and accepting makes it different . . .
something to look forward to,'' as he writes.

Tending to Virginia, like all of McCorkle's works, focuses on the maturation
of the central character, Virginia Turner (Ginny Sue) Ballard, in the context of
her extended family in a small town. It is an exuberant weave of Southern
women—three generations of widows, wives, mothers, and mothers-to-be—
talking to each other as they attempt to understand the meaning of life and their
multiple roles in an ever-changing world. In major and minor keys, each tells
fragments of her own story: What men have made (and would like to make) of
them and what they have made of themselves, their children, each other. In
learning who they are now, they discover strength and resilience for the women
they will become.

Ginny Sue, about to deliver her first baby at 28, is upset about moving to
Richmond with Mark, her lawyer husband, farther away from her family than
she has ever been: "I feel like I'm going to lose everything, that bit by bit
everything that I love is going to be taken away from me.'' Having confessed
her previous love life to Mark before their marriage, she expected but did not
get reciprocal revelation. Six months into her pregnancy, Mark finally reveals
that his first marriage ended not by mutual agreement, as she had originally

believed, but because his wife had aborted the baby he had desperately wanted her to bear. Interpreting Mark's disclosure not as a sign of trust, which it is, but betrayal, Ginny Sue sulks, scolds, decides to leave him, and seeks solace in Saxapaw, her hometown. Yearning for the "quiet coolness" of her grandmother's old house (torn down and replaced by a Piggly Wiggly), Ginny Sue is stricken with toxemia and confined to bed in the cramped, too-hot duplex where Gram, whose voice and mind waver between past and present, now lives.

There she is tended by her silent, selfless mother, Hannah, a seamstress who gains voice and presence as Ginny's own recuperation progresses, and her own life choices become apparent. For Hannah, marriage to good but unglamorous Ben meant resignation to the inevitable: "I was never going to live in New York and be a fashion designer. . . . I was never going to be a housewife and sip coffee and chat. No, I was going to work; I was going to send my children to school with keys around their necks." Her advice to Ginny Sue, who is finally ready to listen: "What's gone is gone. Mark is a human. He made a mistake and you made a mistake" in leaving him.

Hannah's cousin, drab Madge, joins the chorus, gradually acknowledging the truth of her pathetic marriage to an indifferent husband, Raymond, who had committed suicide 8 years earlier. "I think I gave up so long ago that for awhile I forgot there was anything different," she says. "How I lived was not right." So she never told him that his sexually suggestive behavior toward their daughter, Cindy, and his tending toward Virginia, killed their marriage long before she helped him pull the trigger. Twice-divorced Cindy, brash, buoyant, brand-name conscious (instead of exercising, she "Fondas"), and ever on the alert for a new man, also participates in "True Confessions in the Twilight Zone," and advises: "You can't hold Mark's past against him." To confront the truth of the past is to be able to live with the reality of the present; the truth has set these women free. So Virginia, reinforced by her family community of women strong and brave, can allow herself and her unborn child to be Mark's second chance—and her own.

" 'Gram? Were you ever unhappy?' " asks Ginny Sue, seeking reassurance when she arrives in flight. " 'No,' she says. 'James never caused me to hurt and I knew I had found . . . the best this world could offer out to me.' 'Always? You knew that always?' 'Always.' " By the novel's end Virginia has learned, with the wisdom of new maturity, that salvation lies in a tempered reality rather than in the absolutes of "always" and "never."

Ferris Beach, an "entrancing coming-of-age novel," as noted by Ellen Chase in the *Library Journal* (102), again merges McCorkle's major themes. The novel spans nearly a decade (mid-1970s to mid-1970s) of Kate Burns's childhood and adolescence in Fulton, North Carolina, where houses and places are as important as people. Kate, the only child of Fred (for Alfred Tennyson), an incurable romantic math teacher, and proper Bostonian Cleta Burns, lives in a large, gracious antebellum house from which she can see the dwellings of two people who significantly influence her maturation. Misty Rhodes moves into the new split-level across the street ("The split-levels are coming!" warns Mrs. Poole, the neighborhood do-gooder busybody) when Kate is 9 and quickly becomes her best girlfriend. Merle Hucks has always lived down behind the adjacent graveyard, in the cardboard-thin blue house with the tar-paper roof and tool-strewn yard; he is the straight-arrow scion of the town "powhitetrash," who slowly, ever so slowly, becomes her first boyfriend.

The trio turn out to have family secrets to live down—and live with. These are symbolized by the tension between respectable Fulton and Ferris Beach, which, instead of the Ferris wheel glamour of its namesake, is a tawdry town of "a trailer park and rows of small pastel houses" like the Huckses. Misty's family had lived there before they moved, and her pretty mother, Mo, whose purple wooden earrings swing as she dances to "Heartbreak Hotel," enthralls Kate with her free spirit and casual generosity. Angela, Fred's equally uncon-ventional niece whose mother died in childbirth without revealing the father's name, continues to live there. Her occasional visits to the Burnses, in desperation at holidays or upon the failure of each successive love affair, invariably evoke Kate's desire to be like her glamorous aunt at the same time they provoke the only antagonism that surfaces between Kate's parents.

On the fourth of July when Kate and Misty are 13, Mo Rhodes, having won over most of the town matrons with her good cooking and cheerful spirit, leaves town and her family with patrolman Gene Files, taking 6-month-old Buddy ("for Buddy Holley") with them. Two days later, on the journey to return Buddy, the trio ("cheap and dirty") are killed in a car crash, providing the opportunity for instant rehabilitation: "Mo Rhodes had made a mistake and was on her way home. . . . Now that she was no longer alive . . . no one would say that what she had done was *right* or *wrong*." Mr. Rhodes soon marries Sally Jean, a colorless replacement who grows dramatically in character and attractiveness as she per-severes in the thankless role of stepmother to become "an answer to a prayer, a second chance."

As Kate's own sexuality burgeons, she begins to understand Angela's nature and the source of her parents' tension. Only after Fred dies of a heat stroke when Kate is 16, precipitating another crisis of understanding (" 'To hear him tell it,' says her mother, his sister 'was a virgin and Angela a miracle of the flesh' "), can Kate truly learn to love her mother. A second chance. And her mother loves back, enough to overcome her shock at finding Kate and Merle Hucks in bed together the day before the Huckses, burned out by arson, move thirty miles away. Merle, his bad-seed brother murdered in the fire, has the opportunity to "have a wish come true, a new start, a second chance." In this novel, like the others, there are no unmitigated villains, only varying degrees of goodness. So *Ferris Beach* ends in growth and glory, "a whole world of possibilities spinning around," the Ferris wheel fulfilled at last.

SURVEY OF CRITICISM

McCorkle's work is too recent to have attracted much scholarly critical at-tention. The critical commentary in reviews has been generally laudatory, particularly from other Southern women novelists. From the start, McCorkle has been encouraged by praises from such writers as Elizabeth Spencer and Lee Smith. Among reviewers, comments by Alice McDermott are representative. In *Tending to Virginia*, McCorkle's "exuberant third novel," says McDermott:

> Three generations of Southern women are talking. They are talking to one another and talking to themselves, talking about their pasts as wives and mothers and children and about their lives now, in nursing homes and wheelchairs, in new retirements and young marriages. They are talking about the ties that bind them and the secrets that set them apart; about letting go and getting on. It is this talking—the perfect dialogue, the vivid recollections, the memories and emotions that in the end will not fit neatly into the shape of its plot.

This is the stuff that makes this novel, like McCorkle's other novels and short stories, a memorable revelation—not merely of friendship and family, but of abiding love.

BIBLIOGRAPHY

Works by Jill McCorkle

The Cheer Leader. Chapel Hill, N.C.: Algonquin, 1984.
July 7th. Chapel Hill, N.C.: Algonquin, 1984.
Tending to Virginia. Chapel Hill, N.C.: Algonquin, 1987.
Ferris Beach. Chapel Hill, N.C.: Algonquin, 1990.
Crash Diet: Stories. Chapel Hill, N.C.: Algonquin, 1992.

Studies of Jill McCorkle

Chase, Ellen. *Library Journal* (September 15, 1990): 102.
Gottlieb, Annie. "Manic Jo and Romantic Sam." *New York Times Book Review* (October 11, 1987): 9.
Graham, S. Keith. "Southern Foibles Eloquently Washed Ashore." *Atlanta Journal and Constitution Book Review* (September, 30, 1990): 1.
Hill, Jane. Rev. of *Tending to Virginia*. *Atlanta Journal and Constitution Book Review* (September 13, 1987): 1.
James, Sheryl. "North Carolina Author Pleased to Be Noticed." *Greensboro News and Record* (February 14, 1985): B1.
Lewisohn, Ron. "The World across the Street." *New York Times Book Review* (October 7, 1990): 10.
McDermott, Alice. "Back Home in Carolina: *Tending to Virginia*." *New York Times Book Review* (October 11, 1987): 1, 26.
Moss, Ann DeWitt. "Jill McCorkle," in *Dictionary of Literary Biography Yearbook: 1987*. Detroit: Gale Research, 1988): 366–70.
Stead, Deborah. "Holding On and Moving On." *New York Times Book Review* (October 11, 1987) 26.
Summer, Bob. "Jill McCorkle." *Publishers Weekly* (October 12, 1990): 44–45.

Tim McLaurin
(1953–   )

In 1990, director Gary Hawkins' film on Tim McLaurin appeared as the first of a series of public television documentaries entitled *The Rough South*. Hawkins' placing of McLaurin in company intended subsequently to include Harry Crews and Larry Brown reflects his accurate perception of McLaurin as chronicler of a working-class South of mill, farm, and military people, a South of frequent violence but equally frequent examples of dignity, beauty, and simple grace. The film, like McLaurin's own writings, made clear that his is a perspective both loving and objectively honest, critical of a good many ideas in the mind of the South today, yet firm in his appreciation of the complex and occasionally self-contradictory culture he examines in his books.

BIOGRAPHY

The facts of Tim McLaurin's life are readily accessible in his 1991 autobiography, *Keeper of the Moon*. The eldest son and second of six children of Reese and Darlene McLaurin, he was born in Fayetteville, North Carolina, on December 12, 1953, and grew up in a nearby settlement known as Beard. Beard, then as now, was a community on the margin between suburban and rural settings, where most residents held salaried work such as Reese's job at the Merita Bakery in Fayetteville, yet lived on enough land to be able to raise a few hogs and chickens, vegetables for canning and freezing and perhaps a small tobacco allotment, usually "rented out" to a full-time farmer who tended acreage on several different farms.

McLaurin's childhood was scant on material comforts but abundant, as he is quick to point out, on love and attention within the family circle. He describes his mother as a firm believer in firmness—but as quick with a hug as with a switch—and his father as an essentially kind man given to excesses with alcohol in response to the fatigue of overwork and relentless responsibility. The family was and is a very tightly knit group; McLaurin claims to remember no quarrels or resentments among the siblings that lasted more than half an hour. At present, five of the children live within a few minutes' walk of their mother in Beard, and Tim is a frequent returnee from his home in Chapel Hill.

In childhood McLaurin worked summers in the neighboring tobacco fields while developing two strong interests, snakes and astronomy, that continue to engage his imagination and recur frequently as topics in his writing today. In high school he added team sports to his enthusiasms and performed as varsity forward on the Cape Fear High School basketball squad. Despite such healthy pursuits, and despite a religious background that included exposure to both Southern Baptist and Primitive Baptist teaching, he also developed a fondness and appreciation for the wild side of the distinctly unsedate army town next door, and his novels and nonfiction alike attest to considerable exposure to bar society and its attendant violence—to cockfights, dogfights, fistfights, and fast and reckless driving—and the panoply of dangerous, interesting people associated with those pursuits.

After high school graduation in 1972, McLaurin joined the Marine Corps, spending tours of duty in Cuba and the Canal Zone before returning home in 1975 to a job as Pepsi-Cola route man and marriage to his high school sweetheart. During this brief marriage McLaurin renewed his acquaintance with Fayetteville's seamier precincts with considerable zeal, and the union came to its predictable end one night when his wife came home to discover her bourbon-soaked spouse asleep in bed with an overgrown lion cub, purchased on a credit card for 500 dollars, complementing an already crowded menagerie of snakes, monkeys, and other exotic pets housed here and there about the premises. Thereafter, McLaurin grew long hair and moustache and started a new career, on the road as Wild Man Mack with the Last Great Snake Show, attached to a carnival. As Wild Man Mack he handled a variety of venomous creatures before audiences throughout the South.

Other jobs—laborer, carpenter, newspaper reporter—followed until 1979, when McLaurin went to college, first to North Carolina Central University in Durham and then to the University of North Carolina at Chapel Hill. In 1980 he married Katie Early of Memphis, Tennessee, via Davidson College, and with her decided in 1982 on a 2-year interruption in his degree program for service with the Peace Corps in Tunisia, where their daughter Meghan was born in 1984. (A son, Christopher, followed in 1986. Both children's names, along with his wife's, appear in a tattoo on McLaurin's right arm.)

After returning to North Carolina in July 1984 because of his father's terminal illness, McLaurin resumed studies at Chapel Hill, where he graduated with a B.A. in journalism in 1986. At the university McLaurin attended creative writing classes with Max Steele and Doris Betts and advanced expository writing with Robert Bain, all of whom he credits with helping him discover an ability that enabled him to follow a long-standing interest in writing. By 1988 *The Acorn*

Plan was in print, displaying concrete and imaginative use of the experience of growing up around Fayetteville. *Woodrow's Trumpet*, his second novel, followed the next year, displaying McLaurin's thoughts and feelings on the process of change and cultural stress he perceived in current North Carolina and the South as a region. In early summer 1989, having just completed a draft of a third novel with the working title "A Common Cry," he was diagnosed as having myeloma, a frequently fatal variety of cancer.

Chemotherapy brought McLaurin's disease to the stage of remission optimum for a bone marrow transplant, a lengthy and complex procedure that was to require a year in the Veteran's Administration Hospital in Seattle, Washington. During his successful treatment he began *Keeper of the Moon* and conceived a plan for another volume, pairing a long narrative poem with a prose novella, tentatively entitled "Pieces of Fire." McLaurin currently lives in Chapel Hill with his wife and children. He teaches writing courses at North Carolina State University in Raleigh and at Duke University in Durham while planning his next book, a nonfiction volume about working in tobacco in the North Carolina of his youth.

MAJOR THEMES

In addition to the autobiographical authority it bears, *Keeper of the Moon* records the experiential bases of major themes and issues in McLaurin's writing and provides an archive of the materials that occur, transmuted, in his fiction. Two themes form the intellectual center of his work: the relationship of the individual will with social pressures within its environment, and the drastic alteration of that environment in the present-day South by a number of forces opposed to traditional values and assumptions inherited from a previous generation.

The first of these issues is the mainspring of *The Acorn Plan*, the story of a young man's crisis of choice and commitment. Billy Riley, the protagonist, grew up rough and returned home rougher after a stint in the Marine Corps. The novel opens with a violent scene at a drive-in restaurant in which Billy enters a pointless affray with a soldier and hospitalizes the serviceman with a knife wound in the lung. Upon recovery, the soldier seeks out Billy and cuts him in revenge, and there develops a High Noon situation in which the expectations of East Fayetteville poolroom and saloon culture become a kind of social destiny, a fate that envelops Billy and carries him toward a third, decisive showdown. Such a face-off equates courage with ignoring the virtual certainty of imprisonment (Billy is on probation), serious injury, or death and defines personal honor as embracement of a primitive code of retribution at any cost.

But there are others who value Billy more highly than he values himself. One is Billy's uncle, Bubble Riley, an intelligent and sensitive drunkard who has functioned for years as Billy's mentor and surrogate for a cold, distant father. Bubble plans a monumental and extended bout of drunkenness in which he appears determined to "drink all the wine in the world" (9) in order to educate his nephew by negative example and show Billy the logical consequences of the self-abandoning course Billy seems to have chosen. Bubble is a tragicomic figure, at once heroic and ridiculous, and also self-sacrificial, as it turns out, in the ultimate extreme.

Billy's Aunt Ruby also serves on the side of the angels, loving and nurturing both Billy and his drunken uncle despite tragic circumstances of her own. Like James Joyce's Molly Bloom or William Faulkner's Lena Grove, Aunt Ruby possesses a capacity for endurance that holds the strings of life together and keeps intact her vision of a life for Billy beyond the dead-end existence of his present state. Another woman—Cassie, an "exotic" dancer in one of Fayette-ville's Hay Street strip joints—teaches Billy about ambition and keeping dreams alive, both through her own example and in the relationship that grows between them.

The decisive episode of this artfully constructed story resolves the issue of setting versus self and the conflict between polarized value systems with a strong assertion of the primacy of the individual will—but not, however, without es-tablishing that the difficulty of Billy's position goes beyond what mere logic can solve.

Writing in *Keeper of the Moon* about his life in Chapel Hill, McLaurin laments the changing of the North Carolina he knew in his youth into a homogenized culture not noticeably different from other regions of the United States: "If I walk out my front door and turn in a circle, I cannot see a single house occupied by a family native to North Carolina. I often wonder how I can plug my children into the heritage of this state where they will not see it as a series of interlocking streets and towns, a population of well-educated people who do not speak with my accent" (105). A similar sense of change, loss, and even violation pervades his second novel, *Woodrow's Trumpet*, which investigates, among other issues, the ways in which idealistic impulses can be adapted to the service of self-interest and greed.

The setting of *Woodrow's Trumpet* is Oak Hills, a fictional community in piedmont North Carolina within convenient distance of Durham and Chapel Hill. Formerly an agricultural community abundant with wildlife and rural charm, its population has changed radically as the old established landowners have sold off farmland for residential development. The New not only mixes with the Old but threatens to render the Old extinct. Into Oak Hills comes Ellis McDonald, a teenaged orphan who hires out as farmhand to Woodrow Bunce. Woodrow is a peaceful though large and powerful man whom the local people consider intellectually deficient, a man traumatized in Vietnam and now threatened by opportunistic brothers who hope to manage his holdings in the family land for their own financial ends. Woodrow first befriends and then falls in love with a black woman, Nadean, recently returned home from several years of prostitution and drug addiction in Washington, D.C. The three principal characters move in together to form an unconventional family that answers to the needs of each.

Many of the older Oak Hillians resent having in their midst a relationship both interracial and unblessed by matrimony, but the union is a source of delight and opportunity to Mary and Jeffrey Stewart, newcomers from Connecticut bent on "cultivating" the odd couple and in effect appropriating them as trophies of their own liberalism. But the Stewarts' true measure of tolerance is soon taken, and it proves deficient. Naively seeking to fulfill one of Nadean's childhood fantasies, Woodrow landscapes his inherited property to represent a sandy oasis with swimming pool, palm tree, and—to the horror of the Stewarts and their social set—pink plaster flamingos. The natives, for all their conservatism, none-theless respect Woodrow's right to decorate his land as he pleases. However, the flamingos bring out the worst in the new liberals, for whom social justice is one thing but threats to property values quite another. Among the many ironies of the story is that the interracial couple begin planning to move to Mississippi in order to escape the chaos of the New South as wrought by well-intentioned apostles of social change.

McLaurin finds room for considerable social satire and comedy within what becomes finally a tragic tale, and he avoids posing clear-cut rights against equally clear-cut wrongs to produce an artificial symmetry in what really has no altogether satisfactory solution. His characters are developed realistically rather than as simple embodiments of the ideological positions they take. Both Mary Stewart and Woodrow's brother Benson reveal depths of complexity that help explain their behavior in other than social terms. They remind us that coercion and manipulation of social change frequently reflect someone's inability to separate personal requirements and desires from what it may be convenient to regard as the needs of other people.

SURVEY OF CRITICISM

At this writing, only 5 years after the appearance of McLaurin's first novel, there are no published critical studies apart from the reviews and feature articles that followed publication of the individual books. Lately, however, McLaurin's work has come up frequently as the subject of papers and panel discussions at conferences on Southern literature and culture. For example, the Southern Hu-manities Conference at Chapel Hill in February 1992 included papers on McLaurin by Josef L. Mandel of Pembroke State University and by Donnalee Frega of the University of North Carolina at Wilmington.

Reviews of McLaurin's works have been overwhelmingly favorable, most of them stressing the detail and accuracy in his evocation of Southern scenes and customs. Non-Southerners, as well as writers from McLaurin's home grounds, have expressed admiration: Robb Forman Dew, herself a novelist, reviewing *Keeper of the Moon*, writes: "I find it hard to mourn the loss of the South that Tim McLaurin describes, but I'm enormously grateful to him for giving me this unsparing portrait of a world I never knew." Like many of the more thoughtful reviewers, Dew perceives behind the violent surface of McLaurin's writing "eloquence and an elegance of language that does derive, in his case, from a hardscrabble Southern upbringing."

BIBLIOGRAPHY

Works by Tim McLaurin

The Acorn Plan. New York: Norton, 1988.
Woodrow's Trumpet. New York: Norton, 1989.
Keeper of the Moon. New York: Norton, 1991.
"Below the Last Lock," in *The Rough Road Home: Stories by North Carolina Writers,* ed. by Robert Gingher. Chapel Hill: University of North Carolina Press, 1992.

Studies of Tim McLaurin

Albright, Alex. Rev. of *The Acorn Plan.* Raleigh, N.C. *News and Observer* (August 14, 1988): 4D.
Alderson, Laura. "Southern Writing in Their Bones." Canberra, Australia *Times* (April 29, 1990): 22.
Broili, Susan. "Snakes Alive! Author Tim McLaurin Is up to His Old Tricks." Durham, N.C. *Herald-Sun* (November 24, 1991): E1–E2.
———. "Writing and Writhing: Tim McLaurin Handles Both at Festival for the Eno." Durham, N.C. *Sun* (June 30, 1988): section D.
"Cancer Patient Plans 100-mile Canoe Trip." Charlotte, N.C. *Observer* (January 7, 1991): 4B.
Christian, Nichole. Rev. of *Woodrow's Trumpet. Detroit Free Press* (September 3, 1989): n.p.
DeFrange, Ann. Rev. of *Woodrow's Trumpet. Sunday Oklahomian* (August 27, 1989): n.p.
Dew, Robb Forman. "Silence of the Father" (Rev. of *Keeper of the Moon*). *New York Times Book Review* (January 19, 1992): 8.
Dezern, Craig. Rev. of *Woodrow's Trumpet.* Forth Worth, Tex. *Evening Star-Telegram* (November 10, 1989): n.p.
Eder, Richard. Rev. of *The Acorn Plan. Los Angeles Times* (July 7, 1988): n.p.
Gaughan, Thomas. Rev. of *Woodrow's Trumpet. Booklist* (August 1989): n.p.
Gingher, Bob. Rev. of *The Acorn Plan.* Greensboro, N.C. *News and Record* (July 31, 1988): n.p.
Gingher, Marianne. Rev. of *Woodrow's Trumpet. Washington Times* (August 16, 1989): E2.
Goodrich, Chris. Rev. of *The Acorn Plan. New York Times Book Review* (September 4, 1988): n.p.
Hall, Wade. Rev. of *Woodrow's Trumpet.* Louisville, Ky. *Courier-Journal* (February 17, 1990): n.p.
Hemesath, James B. Rev. of *Woodrow's Trumpet. Library Journal* (August 1989): n.p.
Hill, Dennis, et al. "Tim McLaurin's Noble Adventure." Goldsboro, N.C. *News-Argus* (January 10, 1991): 4A.

Huffman, Eddie. Rev. of *Woodrow's Trumpet*. Durham, N.C. *Herald* (Chapel Hill ed.) (August 1989): 1–2.

Lunsford, Jane Eagle. Rev. of *Woodrow's Trumpet*. Salisbury, N.C. *Post* (August 27, 1989): 6E.

Martin, Gerald. "McLaurin Retraces His Backroads to Manhood." Raleigh, N.C. *News and Observer* (November 17, 1991): 5J.

Merritt, Robert. Rev. of *The Acorn Plan*. Richmond, Va. *Times-Post-Dispatch* (August 14, 1988): n.p.

Mills, Jerry Leath. Rev. of *The Acorn Plan*. Raleigh, N.C. *Spectator* (July 21, 1988): 5.

———. Rev. of *Woodrow's Trumpet*. Durham, N.C. *Independent Weekly* (August 10, 1989): 24.

Moose, Ruth. Rev. of *Woodrow's Trumpet*. Greensboro, N.C. *News and Record* (September 3, 1989): E5.

Morrison, Tommye. "Author Tim McLaurin: His Love for South Runs Deep." High Point, N.C. *Enterprise* (August 27, 1989): section E.

Moser, Bob. Rev. of *Keeper of the Moon*. Durham, N.C. *Independent Weekly* (November 6, 1991): 40.

Nicholson, David. Rev. of *Keeper of the Moon*. *Washington Post* (November 4, 1991): D3.

Obermeyer, Jon. Rev. of *Keeper of the Moon*. Greensboro, N.C. *News and Record* (November 10, 1991): B5.

O'Briant, Don. "An Ailing Tim McLaurin Is Prolific in His Adversity: Three New Works Due." *Atlanta Journal and Constitution* (August 19, 1990): N9.

———. "Former Snake Handler Now Rattling Readers." *Atlanta Journal and Constitution* (November 23, 1989): section U.

Parker, Roy Jr. Rev. of *The Acorn Plan*. Fayetteville, N.C. *Observer-Times* (November 11, 1990): n.p.

———. Rev. of *Woodrow's Trumpet*. Fayetteville, N.C. *Observer-Times* (August 13, 1989): 14E.

Pate, Nancy. Rev. of *The Acorn Plan*. *Orlando Sentinel* (August 11, 1988): E2.

Pattishall, Roy. Rev. of *Woodrow's Trumpet*. *Atlanta Journal and Constitution* (November 23, 1989): U7.

Porter, William. Rev. of *Keeper of the Moon*. Charlotte, N.C. *Observer* (October 20, 1991): 5B.

Rev. of *The Acorn Plan* (unsigned). *Publishers Weekly* (May 27, 1988): 50.

Richards, Jeffrey. Rev. of *Woodrow's Trumpet*. Raleigh, N.C. *News and Observer* (August 13, 1989): 4D.

Rogers, Dennis. "The Mean Streets of Fayetteville Nurture a Tough Writer." Raleigh, N.C. *News and Observer* (August 5, 1988): n.p.

" 'Rough South' on TV Is McLaurin Profile." Southern Pines, N.C. *Pilot* (November 12, 1990): n.p.

See, Carolyn. Rev. of *Woodrow's Trumpet*. *Los Angeles Times* (September 18, 1989): n.p.

Schlosser, Jim. "Writer Weathered Storm of Cancer." Greensboro, N.C. *News and Record* (January 8, 1991): A1, A4.

Schroeder, Joan. Rev. of *Woodrow's Trumpet*. Roanoke, Va. *Times and World News* (August 20, 1988): F4.

Shumaker, Jim. "A Writer Finds His Form." Charlotte, N.C. *Observer* (April 17, 1988): n.p.

Starr, William. Rev. of *The Acorn Plan*. Columbia, S.C. *State* (September 18, 1988): section F.

———. Rev. of *Keeper of the Moon*. Columbia, S.C. *State* (October 6, 1991): section F.

———. "Gifted Writer with Cancer Still Hopeful." Columbia, S.C. *State* (September 9, 1989): section F.

———. Rev. of *Woodrow's Trumpet*. Columbia, S.C. *State* (August 13, 1989): section F.

Steele, Max. "Writer to Writer" (Interview with McLaurin and Lawrence Naumoff). Raleigh, N.C. *Spectator* (August 11, 1988): 5, 8.

Stephenson, Shelby. Rev. of *Woodrow's Trumpet*. Southern Pines, N.C. *Pilot* (August 13, 1989): 3B.

Syme, John. Rev. of *Woodrow's Trumpet*. Winston-Salem, N.C. *Journal* (November 5, 1989): n.p.

Waters, Randy. Rev. of *Woodrow's Trumpet*. Macon, Ga. *Telegraph and News* (September 3, 1989): 10E.

White, Julia. "A 100-mile River Ride for a Cause." Durham, N.C. *Herald* (Chapel Hill ed.) (January 7, 1991): 3.

James Alan McPherson
(1943–   )

James Alan McPherson's short stories explore the neutral ground where white and black, old and young, rich and poor act out the diversity and contradictions that are America. By examining the shared complexities of the human condition and not emphasizing our differences, McPherson's art transcends regional or racial labels. Often compared to Ralph Ellison, McPherson emerges a discerning critic of American culture. Awarded the Pulitzer Prize for *Elbow Room* in 1978, McPherson writes penetrating essays and wonderfully crafted stories that force us to confront our prejudices, challenge our complacencies, and expand our capacities to love our fellow human beings.

BIOGRAPHY

Born on September 16, 1943, James Alan McPherson grew up in what he called "a black lower-class" section of multicultured, historical Savannah, Georgia. His father, James Allen McPherson, was a master electrician, and his mother, Mabel Smalls McPherson, worked as a domestic in a white home. In addition to the example of hard work set by his parents, McPherson was further nurtured by E. J. Smith, the family physician who delivered him and encouraged him throughout his youth. McPherson attended segregated public school (he was 11 when the Supreme Court decided in favor of *Brown v. the Board of Education*) and learned about the indomitability of the human spirit from the disciplined, proud, self-reliant black teachers represented in his fiction by Esther Clay Boswell. He expanded his education in human nature through part-time work at the M&M Supermarket, the probable scene of his narrator's coming of age in the short story "A Matter of Vocabulary."

Despite the burdens of a racist culture, McPherson recalls that the adults he knew during his youth did not impose the harsher realities of their segregated experience on their children, and he grew up sensing an optimism at all levels of his black community. He believes that though his early community "was a limited world, it was one rich in possibilities for the future."

By 1961 McPherson was a student at Morris Brown in Atlanta. During summer breaks he worked as a dining-car waiter on the Great Northern Railway, work that helped ensure the broad perspective of his art. In addition to seeing the spectacular part of the country that lies between Chicago and the Pacific Northwest, McPherson began to appreciate the complexity of American culture represented in the microcosm of life on a train. From the older waiters he also learned the art and joy of storytelling. Impressed by the "magnificently diverse panorama" of the 1962 Seattle World Fair, he returned to his undergraduate studies imbued by the spirit expressed in the fair's theme, Walt Whitman's *Leaves of Grass* epigraph: "Conquering, holding, daring, venturing as we go the unknown ways." McPherson took from the trains an expanded and all-embracing perspective of American culture. He also began to write. He was prompted to write in order to enter a *Reader's Digest* and United Negro College Fund creative-writing contest, but that first story was lost.

After spending 2 years at Morgan State University in Baltimore, McPherson completed his B.A. at Morris Brown in 1965. That fall McPherson enrolled in the Harvard University Law School and successfully met legal and literary challenges. McPherson says he began law school thinking that "a lawyer was a good guy who helped people." The more he studied, the more he felt that Harvard "brought in the sons and daughters of the middle class to perfect their skills to be moved into law firms to help those great fortunes pass from one generation to the next," talents not much in demand in black communities. As a student in a district attorney project in the Boston courts, McPherson's imagination kept taking him beyond the facts of the case. He understood and felt the human dimensions of the legal drama too well to practice criminal law comfortably. Meanwhile, he supported himself as a janitor in an apartment building in Cambridge. There, he said, he "had the solitude, and the encouragement, to begin writing seriously." Edward Weeks and his staff at *The Atlantic* awarded his short story "Gold Coast" first prize in their creative writing contest. After "Gold Coast" was published in *The Atlantic*, a law professor he greatly admired, Paul Freund, casually remarked to McPherson: "Oh, you're the one who writes for *The Atlantic*. You've gone beyond the law." His casual remark led McPherson to decide on a career as a writer.

After receiving his LL.B. in 1968, McPherson spent the summer in Cambridge writing. A year later *The Atlantic*, in conjunction with Little, Brown, would publish those stories in *Hue and Cry*. That September he went on to the Writers Program at the University of Iowa and began his career as an educator by teaching writing in the law school. Meanwhile he continued to write feature articles for *The Atlantic* and accepted a position as contributing editor, a post he still holds.

When *Hue and Cry* was published in 1969, critics praised McPherson for his artistic achievement, mature perspective, and capacity to accept the contradictions and multitudes of American culture. After earning an M.F.A. from Iowa, McPherson continued to write as he served on the faculties of the University of California, Santa Cruz; Morgan State University, Baltimore, Maryland; and the University of Virginia, Charlottesville. A Guggenheim Fellow in 1972–73, he published *Elbow Room* in 1978, for which he received the Pulitzer Prize. In 1981 he earned a MacArthur Fellowship and accepted the position of professor in the University of Iowa's Writers Program where he teaches and writes today. He is currently editing a collection of stories by students he has taught.

MAJOR THEMES

In his short story "Elbow Room," McPherson uses the following excerpt from William Carlos Williams's *In the American Grain* as an epigraph: "Boone's genius was to recognize the difficulty [of settling the new land] as neither material nor political but one purely moral and aesthetic." McPherson's major themes echo and extend Boone's genius. He agrees that the solution to modern American problems does not lie in adjusting our culture's material or political balances, but in raising the country's moral consciousness. Because the difficulty facing Americans today is a lack of compassion, and because we are a country in great need of "spiritual civility," McPherson believes that writing that reveals our common humanity can help change the meaner cultural realities of contemporary American life.

In his stories he finds inroads through the wilderness of our culture's indifference to suffering. By honestly and objectively revealing the tragedies of the human spirit in modern America, McPherson fervently hopes that a recognition of our common humanity will carry us beyond the despair generated by our society's age, sex, race, and class discrimination. His characters cry for a higher level of moral consciousness that recognizes, receives, and imparts grace in a complex and contradictory American culture. Without sentimentality or bitterness, his stories explore and chart the human heart.

In his first collection of short stories, *Hue and Cry*, McPherson raises moral alarms. He quotes Pollock and Maitland's *History of English Law*: "When a felony is committed, the hue and cry (*hutesium et clamor*) should be raised. If, for example, a man comes upon a dead body and omits to raise the hue, he commits an amerciable offense, besides laying himself open to ugly suspicions. Possibly the proper cry is 'Out! Out!' " McPherson's stories raise a hue and cry over our culture's felonies of the spirit: intolerance in all its forms of prejudice and indifference, the absence of grace, the absence of love. In the first story of the collection, "A Matter of Vocabulary," young Thomas Brown comes of age when he sees his church's deacons pocketing the collection. Contemplating the dimensions of his own mortality and witnessing his brother's humiliation, he begins to understand why the Barefoot Lady came in a drunken anguish to moan before the dark and locked doors of the Herbert L. Jones Funeral Parlor, "Mr. Jones! I love you, Mr. Jones!" He begins to "feel what she must feel" and realizes that "she came always in the night to scream because she, like himself, was in misery, and did not know what else to do."

Subsequent stories in the collection continue the cry. In the story "On Trains" an old black pullman porter silently suffers the outrages of racism when an old woman refuses to sleep in the same car where he performs his duty. Another story describes how a folk hero, the archetypal Waiter's Waiter and perhaps McPherson's most memorable character, Doc Craft, is destroyed by the company's bible of bureaucracy. In the prize-winning tale "Gold Coast," the apprentice janitor narrator slowly discovers and then turns his back on the burden of common humanity he shares with the trapped and tormented Irish outcast, James Sullivan. Other stories explore confusing quests for racial and sexual identities in our complex culture.

The protagonist of "Private Domain," a young black named Rodney, struggles with his inability to fit "on either side of the coin" in the black or white world, and, "flipping the coin in his mind," sacrifices his ability to love to his obsession with the dilemmas of racial identity. In the title story of the volume, the despair surrounding Margo Payne's relationship with three troubled men concludes McPherson's hue and cry over failures of humanity in American culture.

In reviews of *Hue and Cry*, some critics complained that McPherson's stories needed sharper articulation. McPherson more than answered those critics with his second collection of short stories, *Elbow Room* (1977). His mature, unsentimental, and complete grasp of the art of storytelling provides powerful revelations of a reality that demands sympathy. He challenges readers to open their minds enough to accept those who suffer as fellow human beings. These finely focused stories of people struggling for identity encourage tolerance. They create elbow room in the consciousness of the reader, moral space enough to accept the weaknesses, the differences, and the needs of all citizens regardless of class or caste.

In an essay on his Southern roots, "A Region Not Home: The View from Exile," McPherson articulates the dominant theme of *Elbow Room* when he challenges his native region and the rest of America to embrace the spiritual essence of Thomas Jefferson's principle, which he recasts as "all souls are created equal and they are endowed by God with certain inalienable rights, among which are immortality, free will and access to grace." He despairs over the plight of the many good-hearted people who struggle to solve complex human problems in a frequently morally bankrupt and politically indifferent culture. He calls for a new level of consciousness, one aware of the spiritual dimensions of our shared humanity. Such new awareness would amend that code of behavior that often excludes the humanly complex person from full and spiritually productive integration in American society. The short stories in *Elbow Room* challenge readers to be more tolerant of human complexity and frailty.

Elbow Room begins with a Southern black narrator explaining why he likes country music and concludes with a black narrator struggling with the form of the story of an interracial married couple trying to adjust to each other and to their place in American society. In between are other tales that explore what it means to be an American and the uses and limits of language in that quest. In "The Story of a Dead Man," McPherson creates a larger than life character named Billy Renfro whose lusty physical life and language embarrass his cousin William who is trying to fit into the middle-class black society of Chicago. As we learn when William unintentionally reveals his own dead soul, they are the two halves of a whole man. In "The Faithful," John Butler, a barber and minister unwilling to accept new ways, suffers the economic and spiritual consequences of intolerance. "The Problems of Art" tells the story of a white lawyer's inability to distinguish logic from truth as his preconceived notions of how things should be get in the way of his seeing things as they are. "The Story of a Scar" also challenges preconceived assumptions. As the woman in the doctor's waiting room explains the story of her scar, the narrator's flip curiosity turns to sympathy, and he remembers too late the most important question he should have asked: "What is your name?" He learns, as McPherson hopes his readers learn, to recognize himself in the deeper human dimension of the story and to feel some responsibility for someone who in the true sense of the word is his "sister."

"I Am an American" emphasizes people as people through the evolving consciousness of an American black who culturally stereotypes Japanese while in London. "Widows and Orphans" examines the human cost of the American success story through the lives of a black mother and daughter. "A Loaf of Bread" examines the dynamics of social protest and presents the conflict between members of the black community and a white grocer who overcharged them. At the end of the story the white grocer and the community organizer, Nelson Reed, have come to an understanding, a meeting of the mind, and a common sympathy and understanding for each other. In "Just Enough for the City," McPherson demonstrates how even religion can distort human decency when it leaves love out. In "A Sense of the Story" Robert L. Charles kills his white boss in cold blood for ignoring his humanity. McPherson sees the human motivation for the crime and calls into question the courtroom meaning of justice.

In his essay "On Becoming an American Writer," McPherson argues for a new model of citizenship based on human sympathy and understanding, one able to synthesize the many contradictions of American culture. He believes "that the United States is complex enough to induce that sort of despair that begets heroic hope," and "if one can experience its [America's] diversity, touch a variety of its people, laugh at its craziness, distill wisdom from its tragedies, and attempt to synthesize all this inside oneself without going crazy, one will have earned the right to call oneself 'citizen of the United States.' . . . One will have begun on that necessary movement from . . . a hopeless person to a desperado," a movement from despair to heroic hope. McPherson's essays and fiction are full of the "heroic, absurd, and mad hope" that comes from heartfelt despair. He writes to raise the consciousness of his readers to a full appreciation of the complexity and commonality of their humanity. He carefully sifts for the "grains of gold" in the heart. He encourages wider spiritual prospecting. McPherson's enduring theme is our own best but too often forgotten selves and the ability of an honest storyteller to help us remember what contemporary society sometimes makes us forget. His fiction and nonfiction are clear and compelling cries for "spiritual civility."

SURVEY OF CRITICISM

Like any gifted artist, McPherson presents problems for critics who want to label him simplistically. The radical segment of our society that persistently attacks the notion that one group can speak for another must confront the honesty of his sweeping analysis of American culture. Defenders of the status quo must take into account the traditions of black literature at work in his art. McPherson's genius defies easy and reductive classification.

Early critics greeted McPherson favorably but struggled to explain how his ability as an artist fit into the expected patterns of contemporary black writing. Some criticized McPherson's aesthetic perspective in terms reminiscent of the famous Irving Howe–Ralph Ellison critical exchange over art and protest. In his review of *Hue and Cry*, Granville Hicks praised McPherson's universal human sympathy and craftsmanship. Hicks quoted Ralph Ellison's jacket cover statement at length and endorsed Ellison's claim that McPherson transcended "those talented but misguided writers of Negro American cultural background who take being black as a privilege for being obscenely second rate." Disagreeing with Howe's thesis that the black voice in literature was by necessity a voice of protest, both Hicks and Ellison praised McPherson's full focus on American society.

Irving Howe did not find "much desire for a nationalist or separatist black literature" among the younger black writers he reviewed. He found them "a decidedly individualistic lot," especially James McPherson. Reviewing *Hue and Cry*, he called McPherson "a born writer—which means a writer who works hard on every sentence, thinks lucidly about his effects, and knows that in art meaning, even salvation, depends on craft." Howe described McPherson's writing as "beautifully poised" and praised him for not having the "psychology" of an inquisitor or victim, "which for a black writer these days [1969] seems exactly right."

In contrast to Howe's praise of McPherson's style, Ronald Christ claimed McPherson's language was "flat, almost clinical." But Christ's foremost complaint was that McPherson ignored his obligation as a black writer to protest. Christ believed he tried too hard to balance "opposites to achieve a fair picture." Christ concluded that "black and Negro will necessarily become literary as well as social terms" and McPherson is sadly one of the "prejudicially pale" Negro writers. In his *Newsweek* review of *Hue and Cry*, Robert Gross was more evenhanded in his comparison of McPherson to his contemporary black writers and saw in all their work "the quest for authentic communication between people, the effort to make sense out of a meaningless world," the themes McPherson writes large.

Although debate over McPherson's "black writer" authenticity perhaps detracted from an appreciation of the full moral and aesthetic authority of his work, it remains a point of departure for many critics. Ruthe T. Sheffey took issue with Robie Macauley's claim in the *New York Times* that McPherson was a writer and black, but not a "black writer," by pointing out the common pattern his stories share with the "wryly comic and serious Afro-American folktales." She writes that theirs is a common theme of "the violent stripping off of the mask, the exposure of cant and hypocrisy, and the illumination of life's paradoxes." Sheffey argued that, contrary to those critics who do not hear in McPherson a distinctive black voice, his greatest powers are drawn from his Southern Afro-American perceptions. William Domnarski argued that the critics who praised the diversity of McPherson's stories and noted conscious attempts to repress the blackness of the characters were wrong. He believes that "a careful working out of the themes of McPherson's fiction reveals his attempt to analyze comprehensively the difficulties blacks face at every turn."

Other critics accepted McPherson's work for what it is—the product of a gifted black American consciousness disciplined by the demands of his art. Edith Blicksilver wrote that "McPherson's stories tend to reflect the dilemma confronting the black intellectual in America: on the one hand attracted by much that the white society has to offer . . . on the other hand embittered by that same society's racist record." She concluded that the black predicament and the predicament of women were for McPherson "too challenging and too complex to be dissected with false simplistic labels. Instead both are part of the larger predicaments faced by human beings of all races, all colors and both sexes in today's complex, impersonal society." Rosemary M. Laughlin pointed out McPherson's contribution to the wealth of American folklore with his creation of Doc Craft, the Waiter's Waiter, a welcome addition to the occupational heroes and work giants of American myth.

More recently, critics have focused on the subtleties of McPherson's literary technique to create the fictional spell found in his stories. Herman Beavers explores McPherson's use of rhetorical screens and the relationship between authorial intention and the narrator's visibility in "The Story of a Dead Man." Jon Wallace discusses how three of McPherson's narrators use language to separate and thus protect themselves from society. In his 1988 criticism of McPherson, Wallace points out the failure of imposed form on the story of the major characters in "Elbow Room" and explains the ways McPherson demonstrates how a story's plausibility depends as much on form as on content. Perhaps this recent focus on McPherson's versatility with language may mark the end of criticism that concerns itself too much with the race of the artist instead of the realities of the art.

BIBLIOGRAPHY

Works by James Alan McPherson

Hue and Cry: Short Stories. Boston: Atlantic–Little, Brown, 1969.
Railroad: Trains and Train People in American Culture. (Ed. with Miller Williams.) New York: Random House, 1976.
Elbow Room. Boston: Atlantic–Little, Brown, 1977.
Foreword to *Breece D'J Pancake, The Stories of Breece D'J Pancake.* Boston: Atlantic–Little, Brown, 1983.
Shacochis, Bob. "Interview with James Alan McPherson." *Iowa Journal of Literary Studies* (1983): 7–33.
"A Region Not Home: The View from Exile," in *The Prevailing South: Life and Politics in a Changing Culture*, ed. Dudley Clendinen. Atlanta: Longstreet, 1988.

Studies of James Alan McPherson

Beavers, Herman. "'I Yam What You Is and You Is What I Yam: Rhetorical Invisibility in James Alan McPherson's 'The Story of a Dead Man.' " *Callaloo* 9, No. 4 (Fall 1986): 565–77.
Blicksilver, Edith. "The Image of Women in Selected Stories by James Alan McPherson." *CLA Journal* 22 (June 1979): 390–401.
———. "Interracial Relationships in Three Short Stories by James Alan McPherson." *CEA Critic*, 50 (Winter–Summer 1987–88): 79–88.
Bone, Robert. "Black Writing in the 1970's." *Nation* 227 (December 16, 1978): 677–79.
Christ, Ronald. Rev. of *Hue and Cry. Commonweal* 19 (September 1969): 570.
Domnarski, William. "The Voices of Misery and Despair in the Fiction of James Alan McPherson." *Arizona Quarterly* 42, No. 1 (Spring 1986): 37–44.
Fikes, Robert. "The Works of an 'American' Writer: A James Alan McPherson Bibliography." *CLA Journal* 22 (June 1979): 415–23.
Fuller, Hoyt. "Some Other Hue and Cry." *Negro Digest* 18 (October 1969: 49, 50, 88.
Gervin, Mary A. "Developing a Sense of Self: The Androgynous Ideal in McPherson's 'Elbow Room.' " *CLA Journal* 26, No. 2 (December 1982): 251–55.
Gross, Robert A. "The Black Novelists: Our Turn." *Newsweek* (June 16, 1969): 94, 96, 98.
Hicks, Granville. "Literary Horizons." *Saturday Review* 52 (May 24, 1969): 47–48.
Howe, Irving. "New Black Writers." *Harper's* 239 (December 1969): 130–146.
"Hum inside the Skull: A Symposium." *New York Times Book Review* (May 13, 1984): 28–29.
Laughlin, Rosemary M. "Attention, American Folklore; Doc Craft Comes Marching In." *Studies in American Fiction* 1 (Autumn 1973): 220–27.
Llorens, David. "Hue and Cry." *Negro Digest* 19 (November 1969): 86–87.
Macauley, Robie. "White and Black and Everything Else." *New York Times Book Review* (September 25, 1977): 31.
Sheffey, Ruthe T. "Antaesus Revisited: James A. McPherson and 'Elbow Room,' "

122–31 in *Amid Visions and Revisions: Poetry and Criticism on Literature and the Arts*, ed. Burney J. Hollis. Baltimore: Morgan State University Press, 1985.

Wallace, Jon. "The Politics of Style in Three Stories by James Alan McPherson." *Modern Fiction Studies* 34, No. 1 (Spring 1988): 17–26.

———. "The Story behind the Story in James Alan McPherson's 'Elbow Room.' " *Studies in Short Fiction* 25, No. 4 (Fall 1988): 447–52.

CHRISTINA ALBERS

Berry Morgan
(1919–   )

The published work of Berry Morgan so far has been small and closely inter-connected. Her novels are distinctive for their immersion in character grounded in an intimate knowledge of their Southern setting. Like William Faulkner before her, Morgan has created her own fictional territory in Mississippi, in her case King County, and her own central families, black and white, from whose per-spectives she examines it. Both of her novels, *Pursuit* (1966) and *The Mystic Adventures of Roxie Stoner* (1974), and all but two of her eleven uncollected short stories are connected to King County or its families.

BIOGRAPHY

Berry Morgan's life has been marked by devotion to writing and to farming, to her family and to her faith. She was born on May 20, 1919, at Hillcrest Plantation near Port Gibson, Mississippi, to a prestigious Roman Catholic family who had lived there since 1798. Her ancestors were farmers and intellectuals. A great-grandfather was "put out of the church for lecturing the congregation on Darwin"; others were early advocates for the abolition of slavery. Her parents, John Marshall and Bess Berry (Taylor) Brumfield, she recalls, were "very interested in Hegel and the economy and so forth, and they didn't pay much attention to the children" (D. S. Onley, *Martinsburg West Virginia Journal*, March 10, 1990). As a result, she and her brother spent most of their time with the family's black workers, gaining a knowledge and appreciation of black culture that would prove invaluable to her work. In 1921 the family sold the plantation and moved to the Berry family's town house; later that decade, discouraged by the decline in Mississippi politics, her invalid mother again moved the family, including 5-year-old Berry, to Colorado Springs. In 1934 Morgan went from there to Lake Charles, Louisiana, where she worked as a secretary at a bank until her marriage. Her next move was to New Orleans, the city her family traditionally visited "to play" or dine. There she attended Loyola University in 1947, and then, from 1948 to 1949, Tulane, where she was told she did not have the "scholastic background" to pursue a degree. Afterwards, she lived with her oil-geologist husband at Albena Plantation in Port Gibson, traveling each month to New Orleans, and spending the summers on a 200-acre family farm in West Virginia. Her time was also taken up by their four children: Scott Ingles, Betty Lee, Aylmer L. (IV), and Frances Berry.

Morgan was fascinated by literature from an early age. By 11 she had finished the library at Colorado Springs. Reading, she says, has shaped both her writing and her life. In addition to the "great English novelists," she cites as favorites the Europeans Leo Tolstoy, Fyodor Dostoyevski, Thomas Mann, Albert Camus, Sigrid Unset, and Isak Dinesen, writers who, for the most part, explore the issues of family and faith that have occupied Morgan's work as well.

"I started telling myself stories when I couldn't have been over three or four years old—just to amuse myself—to get out of reality. That may have been the beginning. Perhaps the little routine of telling myself stories made a very subtle transition into the desire to write something down on paper. I don't remember. It seems to me now I've always wanted to write." Morgan, however, was unable to put her keen interest in writing into practice for several years. Later, she recalled, "there was a time when I wanted to write so much that I actually would lie about having written something." Morgan finally began writing in her 30s. In the early 1950s she finished her first piece, a long mystery story of 50,000 or 60,000 words. She sent it to Hiram Haydn at Atheneum, who told her the writing was of professional quality, and, although he did not accept it, recommended she submit it elsewhere. She did not: "I knew there was something wrong with my work, but I couldn't figure out what it was" (all quotations from Cremeens).

At 43 she began again: "I decided it was now or never. I said, 'Well, girl, you're either going to make it or you're not. You can't start much older than this, so you had better get going.' I *did* start, and I stayed with it. After a time, I was like a person possessed. I wrote *reams*. Perhaps a million words. I just kept writing. I had turned on the tap, and I didn't care what I wrote" (Cremeens). Several short stories were the result, but again, while encouraging her work, no one offered to publish it.

During the 1960s Morgan's life was busy in other ways. Under the influence of Walker Percy's thinking and writing, Morgan, a Catholic by birth, became a Catholic by conviction. In the late 1960s, she was involved in the civil rights movement in Mississippi, working to register black politicians and participating in voting-rights marches with Dorothy Day, who also visited at Albena. Day impressed her, she says, by the way she approached the problem of discrimination not from a social or justice viewpoint, but a Christian one.

Finally, in 1966 at age 47, Morgan became a published author. She had sent Houghton Mifflin a "feeler" saying how much she had written, which eventually led to her being awarded the Houghton Mifflin Literary Fellowship for a projected series of novels, "Certain Shadows." The fellowship meant "five thousand dollars and a whole lot of encouragement," enough to sustain her through four rewritings of her first book, *Pursuit*. In writing it she drew on her local surroundings—the imaginary King's Town is modeled on Port Gibson—and family background—her protagonist, Ned Ingles, comes from an old Roman Catholic, plantation-owning family. When it appeared that year, the book bore an endorsement by Walker Percy, by now her editor and mentor, who heralded it as "the most exciting novel to come out of the South since the death of Flannery O'Connor." The novel shows Percy's influence as it traces Ned's obsession with his dying son and his search for faith.

The same year, Morgan succeeded in placing her first short story, "Andrew," the first of many short stories Morgan wrote using the black woman Roxie Stoner, who lives in a shack on the Ingles plantation, as narrator. It was also the start of her connection with *The New Yorker* where her editor for many years was Rachel Mackenzie, a woman she praises as a friend and great editor capable of taking a story that does not seem "too promising," seeing what the author intended, and "gently" leading her to it. In 1967 "Andrew" was included in *The Best American Short Stories* for that year; between then and 1973, five other stories by Morgan were listed on its "Roll of Honor" and four were noted as "distinctive." In 1974 she published her second novel under the Houghton Mifflin fellowship, *The Mystic Adventures of Roxie Stoner*, dedicated to Rachel Mackenzie and consisting of fifteen of her *New Yorker* stories, revised and rearranged to fit into a tale of Roxie's life and encounters.

Morgan has said that work is her hobby. In 1968 she placed farming next to writing as her favorite work. Four years later, when she accepted a post as writer-in-residence at Northeast Louisiana University, Morgan added teaching to her list of professions. In 1974, after her marriage ended, Morgan moved with her two youngest children to the West Virginia place where they used to spend the summer, a place, she says, no one else seemed interested in. There, about a mile from northern Virginia, Morgan and her family grow vegetables organically for distributors in Washington and Baltimore. Having taught at George Washington University, she now commutes twice a week to Catholic University of America to teach fiction and short-story writing.

Since her two novels appeared, Morgan has published ten short stories, one of which—"Point of Rocks" (1979)—was cited as one of the year's 100 "distinguished" stories by *The Best American Short Stories*. Most focus on Dana Ingles, the grandson of the protagonist of *Pursuit*, taking him from King County to northern Virginia. Dana will also probably be the central character in the third novel of the series she began in 1966. Originally entitled "Fornika Creek," it is now *The Mississippian*, perhaps to emphasize the change in setting. She avoids predictions, however, because where it goes, she says, is up to it.

MAJOR THEMES

Although proud of the South and Mississippi, Berry Morgan does not consider herself a Southern writer. She doesn't "think like that," she says. Instead she simply writes what comes to her, without categorizing, organizing, or thinking ahead. That her writing is marked by themes that have long characterized Southern writing—religious faith, the family, the role of the past and the sense of place, the conflicts of race and of gender—indicates her strong roots in the South, not deliberate policy. She writes just what is, without political or socio-economic intentions, and removes herself further from her work by presenting her stories through the voices of their central characters, allowing them their individual, often distorting, perspective on events. Still, her keen observation of what is makes her work rich in implications, and her accuracy in portrayal reveals her characters for what they are, despite their seeming control of the narration.

In Morgan's first novel, *Pursuit*, the central consciousness is that of Ned Ingles, a university instructor. The novel opens in 1937 as Ned returns from New Orleans to Ingleside, his family plantation in King County, Mississippi. Feeling unsettled in the city, and relying on whiskey to provide relevance, Ned is at first, like Walker Percy's moviegoer, an alienated urban modern. "People who moved away" from the country, he later reflects, "faded from the unique into the general as soon as they reached civilization." It is to counter such a fading away that he returns to the old order on the plantation, to the land's "original and authentic viewpoint," where he is "surrounded by attestations of himself, the land, Laurance [his illegitimate son], the Negroes, the dead, the yard oaks, even the furniture." His egotism is clear, as is its reliance on a sense of privilege and of place.

Ned's search for continuity drives the novel's plot. On his return, Ned rapidly becomes obsessed with Laurance. He wants Laurance to marry and have children to perpetuate the family, but Laurance wants to become a priest. As a member of the county's "only well-to-do Catholic family," Ned honors his Catholicism as a matter of family tradition, a sign of superiority over the county Protestants and their middle-class morality, but considers it absurd for Laurance to be so "enmeshed in religion." To "extricate" him, he enlists the help of the only other Catholic family of note in town, Anna Meredith and her daughter Annabella, hoping that Laurance will want to marry the young Annabella. When Laurance instead begins an affair with the mother, Ned marries the daughter himself, bringing the mother to Ingleside to keep Laurance contented, hoping that Laurance will eventually take his place with Annabella. Ned's plan, however, already unsettled by the birth of his and Annabella's son Dana, is seriously threatened by the revelation that Laurance has Hodgkin's disease. While Ned, who feels he has ruined his life, longs for death and his place in the family cemetery, he is equally determined for Laurance to live.

The novel is also a chronicle of spiritual struggle. Like the speaker of Francis

Thompson's poem "The Hound of Heaven" that provides the novel's title and epigraph, Ned Ingles is a man lost in the "labyrinthine ways" of his mind, seeking to evade God. His life is a web of nerves, despair, and hysteria, his thinking increasingly irrational. Suspicious of facts and in need of reassurance in the face of his son's death, Ned would seem ready for conversion. But his final acceptance of faith seems anticlimactic and technical: "In his mind's eye, he seized his will, like a palpable thing, and threw it, almost as one would throw a wet fish, at God." He feels "no change" and heads off for a drink. Rather than make the leap from facts to faith, Ned settles halfway between in a renewed obsession with family. Even when, after Laurance's death, Ned sets himself the task of passing on his dead son's religion to Dana, he does it more out of devotion to Laurance than to God.

Because of Ned's cultivated, seemingly rational voice, the reader is inclined to take Ned's attitude for the norm, so that the first hints of his disintegration seem mistakes on the author's part rather than the character's. But more and more we see Ned's flaws. His speech occasionally resembles that of Faulkner's Jason Compson, another son of a declining family and champion at hard-hearted, pseudological self-justification. For example, when he learns of Annabella's pregnancy, he goes to his room to sulk, but leaves the door open: "For it stood to reason that a wife who would come in at such a time deserved to be shot like a barn rat and he would set up the test and let her fail if she had to." Morgan has said: "I think most writers are instinctive liars, pathological liars, because all his life, what a writer *thinks* has to be so much more important than what is *true.*" This quality is marked in Ned, who seeks to plot his life much as a writer of Southern Gothic might, convincing himself, and seeking to convince the world, that Dana is Laurance's son, not his own, in order to gain a new generation for the Ingles family.

Ned's behavior is based on a casual, often startling, acceptance of his own privileges. In youth, he was the "inevitable hero," raised by a mother who "often told him that no one who ever lived was as handsome, as brave and considerate as he" and a father who taught him a policy of noblesse oblige he follows only imperfectly. As an adult, he considers himself superior to anyone who does not belong to his own sex, race, religion, or even family. His attitudes, perhaps not unusual for a man of his time and position, are nevertheless repellent.

The "old Cavalier instinct" Ned follows contains a definite double standard. Ned may depart from the code, but not the women. Following the system is no guarantee of his approval, either. He mocks Anna not only for her departures from the code (her agnosticism), but for her conformity to it. Softly subordinate and supportive, she is spoken of "very much as hosts will pass around a superb dish of what nobody seems to like." His conflicting attitudes contain an alarming hostility whose roots are not clear, although they may well lie in a suppressed resentment, fueled by his alcoholism, of the code itself. In one brief passage, Ned reveals he detested the father who taught him to follow it.

To the black community he has been raised to feel kindly but superior. The novel's only direct consideration of race is prompted as Ned passes through "bloody Tangipahoa" and recalls with horror a previous trip when he had been shown a gruesome picture of three lynched black men. Reaching his home state he reflects: "There was the familiar billboard announcing that you were in the State of Mississippi, with a picture of its huge pale flower, the magnolia. Its very sickly whiteness was supposed to imply to the traveler that the dark half of the state wasn't there. Meanwhile the Negroes went their usual way, attending church, eating, begetting, hoping and fearing, officially unadmitted to. It seemed to him, looking back, that it was his father's friendship with Wheeler that had saved Ingleside from the cruel separation of black and white." Such insight comes to Ned only in glimpses. He is unhappy with Laurance's close association with blacks, although his own friendship with Roosevelt Frank, Wheeler's son and successor is second only to his love for Laurance. Ned and Roosevelt played together in childhood as brothers, and Ned wishes their adult relationship to recreate that of his father and Roosevelt's father. But Ned's nostalgia requires the continued subservience of Roosevelt's family. Although he considers Roosevelt his "only intimate friend, the companion of a lifetime," his fondness for Roosevelt does not change his generally condescending view of blacks, and he is capable of referring to him on occasion as "the Negro." When Roosevelt demands some respect, Ned considers it "seditious nonsense" and tells Roosevelt that he doesn't "even know what respect means."

Ned's respect for those who died with "their attitudes still fixed" makes it impossible for him to progress beyond them. He fails equally in living up to the chivalric code of the past and in finding one to replace it. Yet Ned continues to use his devotion to the past to oppress others, and eventually it destroys him. In the end, after he is committed to an asylum following a ludicrously mangled suicide attempt, he escapes home, hoping to live in "a little tent inside the cemetery" near his ancestors and dead son. He believes he is living in the past, talking to Laurance. Safely with people who cannot talk back, he is happy but insane.

In *Pursuit*, the white narrator's point of view makes the black community seem comfortably subordinate, but for her second novel, *The Mystic Adventures of Roxie Stoner*, Morgan chose to delve inside that community, taking as her narrator a black woman the same age as Ned Ingles, living on the same plantation, but minus the privileges of his social position, money, sex, and race.

Roxie is a minor character in *Pursuit*, seen only from Ned's perspective. She seems almost too happy with her position, the perfect black servant, praising the mother Roosevelt considers "vicious and selfish"; flattering the young white heir, Dana; and feeling "so happy" when the "good Lord [has] more housework for her." In *The Mystic Adventures of Roxie Stoner*, where we see the world from her vantage point, Roxie moves from being a stereotype to an individual with a greater awareness than is evident from outside. Still, her character remains the same, although it is clearer that Roxie is somewhat retarded mentally. Through Roxie, however, Morgan depicts a world of unjust discrimination and suffering. Emphasizing the picture, Morgan has changed some of the facts where the plots of the two novels overlap. In *Pursuit*, only after Roxie's ailing mother dies does Anna offer Roxie work. In *Roxie* Anna summons Roxie to work while her mother is ill, making her stay by reminding her of her debt to the family, with the result that Roxie's mother dies while she is away, and Roxie is left at the end still waiting to hear her mother forgive her. The difference heightens the reader's sense of the power of the Ingles family and Roxie's powerlessness.

Consisting primarily of stories originally printed in *The New Yorker*, the novel is episodic, linked by Roxie's narration and the few milestones of her life—her mother's death, her confinement to a mental asylum, her release. Just as Ned Ingles's obsessiveness and egotism fit with a tightly plotted and focused work, so the form here fits Roxie's outward and inclusive gaze. The episodic structure makes room for the life stories Roxie learns from the people she meets, as she unassumingly involves herself in their lives, thinking they "might be like Jesus's lost sheep."

Roxie's world is full of hypocrisy and greed. In "Barrand's Landing," the young couple names their latest child for a sickly and wealthy uncle, while trying to fire their cook for "nerves" in order to avoid paying her back wages. Greed is also a theme in the story of Miss Sweet, who spends her life guarding a gully near the white cemetery for the white people who don't "want to wake up after a big night rain and find their loved ones, slabs and all, down in the Mississippi." After her death, her house is removed for a development: "Some said she died of a heart attack but there was an axe mark on her head." Roxie's commitment to the asylum, too, is motivated by people's desire to get hold of her land. Her case is, as Dana Ingles says, "just one more blot on the State of Mississippi."

The central hypocrisy, of course, is the discrimination the county's whites practice against the blacks while claiming to be both charitable and Christian. "Robert" tells the story of an abandoned black boy adopted by a Presbyterian family. Despite their religion, they never think of letting Robert attend church with them, and they are relieved there is no black church near since it might lead to "risky" associations. They believe they have created "a near perfect Negro." Still, when their son marries, Robert must move to the chicken house and even that doesn't satisfy the in-laws. After the family dies, no one else wants a "near perfect Negro." In fact, his statement to a police officer that he, a black man, is a Presbyterian is the cause of his commitment to the asylum. Tragically, Robert accepts their bigoted judgments, to the point of being frightened by his own image in the mirror, "strange and shocking. Dark."

Roxie, too, is naturally a victim of such discrimination. She begins "The Organ Piece" by saying, "I had lived right here on this plantation on to fifty-odd years and never had had a bit of confusion with white or colored." Her tale, however, is a good example of such confusion. In it, when Laurance sneaks Roxie into a white church to hear him practice the organ, she is found inside by a woman she cleans for, who asks her "broken-hearted, 'don't you know this is God's house?'" Afterward, when Laurance is sorry only for himself without realizing the danger she faced, Roxie recalls: "But I saw he didn't care or understand about that, he wanted me to sorrow for *him* over it, and I did— or anyway I tried to." Roxie knows that as a black woman, she is supposed to sympathize for the white boy, but here she cannot bring herself to do so. Still, in other ways, Roxie accepts her inferior status as a black woman, praying to God that if her mama does not find out about the trouble, she "would never mix again," as if even God disapproves.

Morgan has said that the slave owners taught their slaves Christianity, and that the slaves "took the religion seriously," but the owners didn't. Generations later, as Morgan depicts it, the discrepancy continues. Roxie takes her religion seriously, and at the same time that it provides her with strength, her adherence to its doctrines of self-forgetfulness and devotion to others makes that strength necessary. Throughout, Roxie is overworked and taken advantage of by people who find ways around their religion while relying on her being true to hers. At the hospital, for example, where she is given the duties of a nurse's aide, while she works to collect lost sheep for Christ, the hospital staff is hoping her efforts will improve the mental health of their residents enough that they can move them from private to group rooms and save money.

By having Roxie committed to an insane asylum, Morgan is playing with the idea that in a corrupt world the insane are the ones with the clearest vision. Roxie's "insanity" is different from Ned's in *Pursuit*: Ned's is egotistical and hurtful, Roxie's outgoing and altruistic. Whatever her mental capacity, she is considered insane because she is too good, as even those who disapprove of her judgment recognize. As her doctor explains to her: "I liked to do for people. . . . The trouble was that whoever I got in with I started to celebrate. That was why we were here *in* the nerve hospital. . . . We had tried to force the world to our way and the world had gotten too much now to fool with."

Roxie is, in many ways, the archetypal Mammy, all homely wisdom, love, and forgiveness. She is, however, progressively worn down by all the wrongs she learns of. She calls them "bewilderments," and they cause her life to fade so that she is "just floating around according to His will." If her constant faith can be difficult for a reader who wishes she would show more indignation, Morgan shows its toll. Roxie, too, is capable of recognizing and standing by her view of a wrong, and her recording of the various wrongs, however uncomplaining, serves as testimony against them.

In the concluding chapter Morgan added for the novel, Roxie, growing old and wanting to be sure she is buried next to her mother, writes Dana Ingles, who comes to rescue her from the asylum. The chapter has an uneasy sentimentality, reminiscent of the conclusion to *Uncle Tom's Cabin* when the young George Harris comes, unsuccessfully, to rescue Tom. Morgan, however, undercuts the sentimentality. Dana speaks casually of firing Laura's current nurse in a manner similar to the greedy couple in "Barrand's Landing": "He didn't want me carrying on and trying to make big news out of her. He knew the way Negroes acted when they took each others' jobs." He then teaches her how to pray: "There was just one prayer left I could say from now on, and never change a word. He'd hear it for me in the chapel, but he would tell me now, so I could get used to how I had to pray . . . that would leave me listening out for just one voice." However well meaning, Dana's presumptuous dictatorialness here indicates that, although she is free from the hospital, Roxie is not yet free from people who wish to control her life. Even as she listens for the one voice of God, earthly voices interfere.

The conclusion provides in another way a nice rounding off to the stories. Dana asks Roxie to tell him the story of the day she was fired by his grandfather Ned. Evidently, she is a recognized storyteller: "Dana told me he would like to have me give him one of my stories, but not about my whiteface, or the likes of Mr. Dock." We see then that all the stories we have read are indeed being told, shaped, and selected by Roxie. Her power of narration restores to her control over her own life—or at least the ability to define it afterward. What to others are "shady" episodes or accidents are to her "mystic adventures."

In her later stories, Morgan has continued the study of King County, examining it from ever new points of view. "The Headrag" (1977), for example, is told through the consciousness of Willie Ruth, the nurse Dana Ingles is ready to replace at the end of Roxie. In "Arthuree" (1978), Morgan returned to the story of the Stoners, showing how Roxie's illiterate brother returns to school as an adult to learn to read and write, over the objections both of his mother who disapproves of his refusal to go by the name she gave him, John Henry, and of the banker who disapproves of the school because it is run by the federal government. The final word of the story is her brother's signature "Arthuree," the sign of his victory. In Morgan's most recent story, "Mr. Doll" (1986), she retells the opening events of Pursuit, but this time from the perspective of Anna Meredith, thereby undercutting much of Ned Ingles's reading of his own life. The reader sees the outwardly subservient Anna carefully read and play on Ned's pride—his confidence in his own charm, his desire to be treated as a benefactor—in order to remove her daughter and herself to the luxuries of Ingleside.

Five other stories focus on Dana Ingles. The first story, "The Desertion" (1978), shows life at Ingleside as seen by Dana, "the child they forgot about and left here to nurse a drunkard," the day Anna finally gives up and leaves for New Orleans. Morgan resumes his story in "The Lower Pontalba" (1984), a highly evocative rendering of the impressions of a teenaged Dana as he returns from a sanitarium to his mother's home in New Orleans. Three stories—"Point of Rocks" (1979), "The Tenant" (1981), and "The Auction" (1986)—form a sequence as Morgan moves the adult Dana to northern Virginia, near her own present home in West Virginia. Although now a simple farm worker, his circumstances at this point resemble his father's in many ways: A heavy drinker, he has fled the city, seeking "a sanctuary," and has devoted himself to his child. He seems to have received the religion his father pledged himself to pass on to him, but at the end of the last story, he is still tottering between hope and despair, somewhat as Ned was at the start of Pursuit, and learning like him that you can give a child life but cannot assure the direction that life will take. These stories will most likely make up the basis for her third novel, *The Mississippian*, which she described in 1980 as a "look at the darker, or diabolic side of human nature—the hardest to speak of." It appears likely that in it Morgan will continue to undertake the challenge of presenting a complex reality through a single lens.

SURVEY OF CRITICISM

Most of the critical attention Berry Morgan's work has received has been in the form of reviews. A selection from these appears in the 1976 volume of *Contemporary Literary Criticism*, edited by Carolyn Riley and Phyllis Carmel Mendelson. Ironically, for a writer who disavows the Southern label, most critics approached her first novel, *Pursuit*, as an example of Southern Gothic, with its plantation setting, its obsessively prideful protagonist, its concern with family continuity, and its depiction of unusual family relationships. Both Joyce Carol Oates writing for the *New York Times Book Review* and the anonymous book critic for *Time* found it too Southern, almost to the point of parody (*Time*, October 14, 1966, 132). Oates, who argued that Morgan substituted genre conventions for character motivations, seems to miss the point when she complains that Ned is "indeed mad, but not gloriously and tragically mad like Faulkner's Sutpen." It would be giving in to Ned's deluded sense of himself to translate his madness into heroic dimensions. Morgan's work is not mythic like Faulkner's, but religious. Other reviewers considered its links to "typical" Southern writing more positively. Roderick Cook, for instance, declared that "it is very much of the South, but there isn't a bit of Spanish moss dripping from any part of it. . . . Though the family involves itself in some out-of-the-way relationships, these are never thrust at you in that defiantly decadent way that some Southern novels have a tendency to do."

The critics did not concentrate entirely on the novel as an example of Southern writing. Mary Frances Berry saw Ned as "unconsciously seeking reconciliation with God," a desire apparent in his "preoccupation with timelessness and continuity." According to Berry, Ned "fastens obsessively" on Laurance "unwittingly as a substitute for God." Because of his focus on Laurance, he is closed to God—although, as Berry observed, for Ned even to admit that God exists is a "fairly monumental" achievement. David Hales wrote of the way the narrative provides a "humorous commentary" to the action, although seeing the comedy as "dark indeed." John Updike confined his praise to parts of the book, including the portrayal of Annabella (her "evolution from a frightened poor-white school-girl into a determined and sexually confident young woman is the breath of life that quickens this mournful fable out of remoteness") and Ned's conversion ("so honest and intimate it is comic"). He concluded that "moments such as this do not quite accumulate into the forward momentum of fate," but advised the reader, as did most of the critics, to "look forward to her next installment."

Indeed, Morgan's "next installment," *The Mystic Adventures of Roxie Stoner*, received uniformly favorable reviews, although it, too, was treated in the context of Southern literature. *Choice* called Roxie "perhaps the most memorable black woman in Southern fiction since Faulkner's Dilsey became a 'They' and 'endured.' " Victor Howes noted the way the stories present "a cumulative composite of a vanishing world, its folkways, its folklore, its folk."

Two other critics pointed to the universal qualities of the work. Michael Wood contended that Roxie through her "persistent project to rewrite the world . . . becomes a reflection not so much on the South as on the general moral poverty of what we call the real world." Phoebe Adams saw the book as a "delicate, ironic put-on, for the author's actual purpose is to describe a general, vicious decline in morality and manners." Wood and Adams were right to point to the universal implications of the novel, but in doing so they may have passed somewhat too quickly over its anchoring in a specific time and place.

In most reviews there is a surprising lack of outrage about the specific conditions Roxie describes. This may partly be the effect of Roxie's own forgiving gaze. Adams, for example, wrote: "Seen through Roxie's unworldly eyes, the nasty view becomes comic." Wood located in the novel "the replacement of a community which could tolerate and support Roxie by a community which can only confine her," but Morgan never presents a community that fully "supports" Roxie; rather, the community expects her to support it. Surely, it is missing the lessons of the book to maintain, as Howes did, "yes, the Old South exploited its blacks, paid them far too little for far too much, treated them at times shamelessly. But yes, it also protected them. . . . And if Roxie is 'taken in' (exploited) by her community, she is also 'taken in' (embraced) by it." More accurately, Mary Frances Berry recognized that the book depicts a "hard world, and Roxie doesn't prevail over it."

There is valuable biographical information on Morgan in the 1968 interview by Carlton Cremeens in *Writer's Digest*. Martha Adams's essay in the *Dictionary of Literary Biography* (1980) contains further information and marks the start of fuller critical attention to Morgan's work. Adams locates "the content of her art" in her "acute and accurate perception of the relationships among blacks and whites." She continues by showing the similarities between Morgan's two main protagonists, Ned and Roxie: "Each flourishes in only one small locale and 'feels real' only there; each sees his life as a link in a long, long chain of his own ancestors stretching far into the past; each makes his decisions on the narrow basis of his inherited family code . . . and, finally, each believes that he is exempt from local authority. (Ned's invincibility derives from his money and family background and Roxie's protection comes from God.)" The list shows again the importance of the specific and the individual when one considers the different results Ned and Roxie achieve by their broadly similar world views.

In a 1983 essay Margaret Jones Bolsterli discusses what she calls "the androgynous, bi-racial vision" of Morgan's writing, saying that her achievement is to have come "so close" to understanding the "areas of experience" distinctive to one sex or race. Praising Morgan's ability to get "inside" the head of her diverse characters, Bolsterli recalls how she originally believed Morgan must be a black man in order to have the knowledge her novels reveal. (She is not the only one to be misled by Morgan's fictional impersonations—*The History of Southern Literature* mistakenly includes Morgan in a list of promising black women writers.) Bolsterli demonstrates how this ability heightens the picture of the suffering of black people *Roxie* describes: "For the full impact, such testimony must come from a black person. It is appalling that the things that Roxie tells happen to people, even more appalling that they can be related in such a matter-of-fact way."

When Morgan's third novel *The Mississippian* appears, it will no doubt prompt new critical attention, and it will be interesting to see what direction it takes. There is certainly room for further, closer consideration of the literary, social, and religious implications of Morgan's work.

BIBLIOGRAPHY

Works by Berry Morgan

Pursuit. Boston: Houghton Mifflin, 1966.
Cremeens, Carlton. "Interview with Berry Morgan." *Writer's Digest* 48 (November 1968): 38–41, 97–98.
The Mystic Adventures of Roxie Stoner. Boston: Houghton Mifflin, 1974.

Uncollected Stories

"The Pier Glass." *New Yorker* (August 29, 1970): 73–76.
"The Headrag." *New Yorker* (August 8, 1977): 20–23.
"The Christmas Bush." *New Yorker* (October 17, 1977): 43–45.
"Arthuree." *New Yorker* (March 27, 1978): 36–38.
"The Desertion." *New Yorker* (July 10, 1978): 28–31.
"Point of Rocks." *New Yorker* (January 22, 1979): 37–40.
"Mr. Winston." *New Yorker* (April 2, 1979): 36–37.
"The Tenant." *New Yorker* (June 29, 1981): 33–37.
"The Lower Pontalba." *New Yorker* (March 12, 1984): 46–47.
"The Auction." *New Yorker* (January 27, 1986): 32–38.
"Mr. Doll." *New Yorker* (November 17, 1986): 48–53.

Studies of Berry Morgan

Adams, Martha. "Berry Morgan." *Dictionary of Literary Biography* 6 (1980): 241–43.
Adams, Phoebe. "Short Reviews." *Atlantic Monthly* 234 (September 1974): 103.
Anon. Review. *Choice* 11 (December 1974): 1479.
Berry, Mary Frances. "Holy Folly." *Books: A New Orleans Review*, supplement to the *Courier* (December 12, 1973): 13, 18.
Bolsterli, Margaret Jones. "The Androgynous, Bi-racial Vision of Berry Morgan." *Southern Quarterly* 22 (Fall 1983): 47–60.
Cayton, Robert F. *Library Journal* 99 (August 1974): 1985.

Cook, Roderick. "Books in Brief." *Harper's* 33 (November 1966): 143.

Hales, David. "Return of the Prodigal Father." *Saturday Review* (October 22, 1966): 56.

Howes, Victor. "People Too Good to Miss." *Christian Science Monitor* (September 11, 1974): 11.

Oates, Joyce Carol. "Heritage of Doom." *New York Times Book Review* (October 16, 1966): 66–67.

Riley, Carolyn, and Phyllis Carmel Mendelson, eds. "Berry Morgan." *Contemporary Literary Criticism*, Vol. 6. Detroit: Gale Research, 1976.

Sullivan, Richard. "Just Plain Folks." *Critic* 25 (October–November 1966): 107–8.

Updike, John. "Books." *New Yorker* (October 29, 1966): 241–45.

Wood, Michael. "Fiction in Extremis." *New York Review of Books* (November 28, 1974): 29–31.

SUSAN SNELL

Helen Norris
(1916–   )

For most students of contemporary fiction, Helen Norris appeared *ex nihilo* in 1985—though she was then in her 70th year and had been publishing serious fiction since 1940. The six stories and novella she published in September 1985 as *The Christmas Wife* caught the attention of the *New York Times* and within months secured the admiration of her peers. This collection was nominated for the 1986 PEN/Faulkner Award. Later that autumn, Zondervan Publishing House, a small midwestern press, brought out her novel *More Than Seven Watchmen*, released it, that is, into oblivion so far as the literary East was concerned. This work also garnered an audience (it was a book club selection) and a prize—the 1985 Gold Medallion Award from the Christian Publishers Association. But Norris had published her first book, a novel entitled *Something More Than Earth* in 1940, and she had a second writing career in the late 1950s. Norris' books of the 1980s, commanding more attention than her earlier work, have invited critics to reexamine the whole career.

BIOGRAPHY

Helen Norris was born to Elmer W. and Louise W. Brown Norris in Miami, on June 22, 1916. In her second year the family returned to a five-hundred-acre farm, on Vaughn Road, east of Montgomery, Alabama, where Helen grew up with three sometimes boisterous and unruly brothers. Cotton prices in the "black belt" between the wars fluctuated wildly from boom to bust, although children in what still could be identified as the South's planter class were largely insulated from knowledge of their relative economic instability. The Norris siblings apparently enjoyed a storybook equanimity, undisturbed by the gruesome poverty and illiteracy outside their immediate environs.

Helen Norris learned her love of literature at home. To her parents literature was an intrinsic, "natural part of life"; the classics demanded awe. As bride and groom they had read together *Les Misérables* on their honeymoon, their only daughter was told. "My mother believed that writing a novel with characters that live is the finest thing you can do," Norris said. Her "apprenticeship," however, commenced with a poem, when she was 8 years old and a student at Cloverdale School. At 9 she amused herself parodying the Bobbsey Twins, her initial fictional exercise. Her first novel, a mystery, she started writing in the seventh grade. The plot thickened and thickened and thickened; any of a dozen suspects might have committed the crime: The trouble was their creator herself could not settle on a culprit. So she abandoned the genre in favor of less worrisome literary projects.

Once Norris was enrolled at Lanier High School, the child's indulgence with words on paper gave way before the societal imperatives of gender. One hears nothing else about the writing until Norris' senior year at the University of Alabama. As an undergraduate she pledged Alpha Zi Delta sorority and "was active in all social life of the campus," affirmed a 1940 local review. Receiving her A.B. in 1938, Norris was also initiated into Phi Beta Kappa.

The prospect of the young woman's graduating with no June wedding in sight unsettled even Helen Norris' enlightened parents. She learned that they had determined to make a dean of women out of her, a decorous profession somehow made to order for young maiden ladies of good Southern families. Syracuse University was to be her finishing school. But the Norrises had not anticipated their daughter's counterinsurgency. Norris, as custom decreed, attributes her rescue to a male, her teacher and mentor, Hudson Strode. He arranged a graduate fellowship for her at the University of Alabama in exchange for her commitment to write a novel. In the 1980s when she humorously recounted this crisis, Norris said that if she became a dean of women, "no one would ever know me." The rare uncensored remark can be variously interpreted, but never without a glimpse of her stubborn ambition and resistance.

Still, Norris is unquestionably indebted to Hudson Strode, whose fiction classes at the University of Alabama the *Times* of London would deem "brilliantly effective." At his death in 1976, Strode's students had published fifty-five novels and more than one hundred stories. The author of sixteen books—history and literary travelogues in the main—Strode took an eccentric pleasure in never having written a novel himself. In 1938, at the beginning of Strode's prime, Norris, as she and her teacher had agreed, left off writing short stories to give her imagination the range of the novel. Strode apparently impressed upon students that writing was steady, hard labor, not a moment's passion, and that, in Norris' case, its "inspiration" was neither the heavens opening or the "love" to write. She thought, planned, and wrote "because it was there to do"; enjoyment was hardly the term for results perpetually frustrating: "It never seems as good on paper, not as good as it should be," she reflected upon the acceptance of her graduate school novel, in 1940. When *Something More Than Earth* had been completed, Norris entered the manuscript in *The Atlantic Monthly*'s $10,000 novel contest and took second place. The Atlantic Monthly Press, the first to which it was submitted, bought the book as one of four novels on its annual list. The editor, whom Strode quoted in advance reviews, was well pleased with Norris, particularly her "extraordinary power of suggestion." Two other women under Strode's tutelage, Harriet Hassell (*Rachel's Children*) and Gerrie Thielens (*Awake My Heart*), were the first group to place novels with major publishers (the latter only the month before Norris). "I was the third," Norris somewhat ruefully recalled.

In the summer after she took her M.A., Norris married Thomas Reuben Bell, Jr., LL.B., also Class of 1940, University of Alabama; the couple moved to Birmingham, where the attorney began his practice and the author completed details for her novel's autumn publication. In 1940 interviews, she was already "thinking about" a second novel, but a second book did not appear until 18 years later. She and her husband had two children, a son and a daughter, who died in an accident as a child.

On February 11, 1958, the Macmillan Company's Southern sales representative announced the publication of *For the Glory of God*. The book jacket identified the author, "in private life . . . Mrs. T. R. Bell, housewife and mother of two children," adding that "during the war and shortly thereafter she had occasion to make her home in Louisiana, Massachusetts, and Washington, D.C." (Reuben Bell had been an Army Air Corps lieutenant from 1942 to 1945.) The *New York Times* and the *Boston Transcript*, among others, had reviewed *Something More Than Earth* in 1940; the new short novel or novella (at 63 pages) earned notices in *Catholic World* and the *Springfield Republican*. In retrospect, the overtly religious narrative of 1958 is superior in technique and wisdom to the good but "young" first novel.

As Norris explains the first hiatus of her career, she had "waited" until her daughter and son were in school to begin the 1958 fiction, published both in American and English editions, she adds with pride. The mid-1950s clearly were a time her writing was again flowering. A short story, some poetry, and a play won Birmingham Festival of Arts Awards in three consecutive years, 1955–1957. Norris' "1950s" novel that eventually appeared in 1989 must belong to this period. The 1985 "Christian" novel *More Than Seven Watchmen*, "written about 25 years earlier," is another book from a highly productive interval of some years. During the "second" writing career, only *For the Glory of God* made it into print.

The three novels—all short, all with the motif of a lost son, all on profound, Christian themes—may have been too erudite and too painfully reasoned for Norris' readers. As the Eisenhower years were ending, too, the literary avant garde were agnostic at best (or worst, by the prevailing mores). Books on Christian affirmation and reconciliation could be imported from England for Episcopal or Unitarian study groups: C. S. Lewis, Charles Williams, sometimes William Golding (*The Spire*, for example). Flannery O'Connor, J. F. Powers, and Thomas Merton sufficed for the Roman Catholics. Only O'Connor was seriously read, with reservations, outside the church doors. Around 1960 a fervent Episcopal writer from Alabama discovered there was no audience for what she had to write.

"A dry spell," Norris calls it; but after 1958 the next book was to "wait"— until the 1980s . . . twenty-seven years. In 1965 Norris abruptly resumed graduate work in English, at Duke University. She accumulated thirty credit hours during her year's tenure in Durham. Her move to North Carolina had coincided with her son's enrollment at the University of the South. Meanwhile her marriage, after a quarter century, ended in divorce, and she returned permanently to Montgomery in autumn 1966, accepting a teaching position at Huntingdon College. Without the equivalent of Virginia Woolf's 500 pounds' annuity, Bell had a living to make, apparently her first employment outside the home.

Following her resignation from the English faculty at Huntingdon College in May 1979, Norris turned energetically to her third career as a writer. In 1982 *Sun Dog: The Southeast Review* (II) accepted two stories—"Money Man" and "The Christmas Wife," the latter her most famous story. This story has for its premise a lonely widower's "renting" a companion for the holiday season. Norris presents both stories under the guise of realistic fiction, but each suggests in a beguiling, almost sinister donnée and plot, interests covertly postmodern. In "The Christmas Wife," she reanimates age-old story lines, here the courtship or wooing ritual turned on its head, and traces where living and constructing fictions become indistinguishable. Her penetrating life studies, however, were so absorbing that the deftness and originality with which she shaped and mused over her medium could be largely invisible, at first.

Sewanee Review published in spring 1983 Norris' "Love Child"; with that story, she won the Andrew Lytle Award for fiction for that year. *Doubleday's Prize Stories: 1984* included that story, and it won an O. Henry Award. "The Quarry," an enigmatic redneck fable, appeared in Stories #7 in September 1983 and appeared in the 1985 O. Henry anthology. "The Healing," her first story on the mystical idea of "substitution and exchange," appeared in the summer's *New England Review and Breadloaf Quarterly* in 1983. Another story was published in *Western Humanities Review*.

Norris gathered six stories and an unpublished novella as *The Christmas Wife* (1985). That volume included "The Love Child," "The Quarry," "The Christmas Wife," "The Singing Well," "Money Man," and "The Healing." "Starwood," the unpublished novella or long story (a 38-page narrative), concluded the volume. The University of Illinois Press published this collection in its Illinois Short Fiction series.

In 1986 and 1987, George Core, editor of the *Sewanee Review*, led the competition to acquire Norris' short fiction, often vying with the *Southern Review* to publish her stories. By 1988 a less-committed writer might have quit her regimen to bask in such critical response. In late summer 1987 Norris' New York agent, marketing a fresh batch of stories, apparently had little trouble persuading Illinois to break precedent and devote a second volume in its respected series to Helen Norris. The collection, *Water into Wine* (1988), took its biblical title from the volume's final tale. The story itself seems an analogue to Welty's plot in "Death of a Traveling Salesman" and those O'Connor stories set in motion when wayfaring males intrude upon "woman's space." Originally published in *Sewanee Review* (Summer 1987), "Water into Wine" had already given Norris another Andrew Lytle Award.

By the time the book came out, however, it would not be the strongest of her new stories. Themes she had "exhausted" before, Norris deepened, to dazzling effect. In "Mrs. Moonlight," a daughter out to murder her mother's joy is by revisionist memory willed forgotten, simply effaced. In "The Cormorant," a bird carver (a casualty of war) and a blind child, assailed by losses, find solace together and in the transfiguration of art. Her captivating "givens" continue: a bank's hiring a woman as "The Pearl Sitter" to sustain the luster of depositors' gems; a son's splitting half his estranged parents' Christmas tree, in a middle-aged tantrum against divorce ("The Cloven Tree"). Amateur musicians in "White Hyacinths" and a dabbler in watercolors in "The Light on the Water" indicate *Water into Wine*'s ultimate focus—on artifices that are lies and artifices that are, miraculously, true. The *New York Times Book Review*, with others, took note. Those closely following Norris' progress realized that the artist's command of short fiction, her primary medium, by 1988 had increased exponentially.

Meanwhile, the author or her agent, or both, had proven adept in wresting cold cash out of the television and film industries. The campaign got under way fortuitously. While in residence at Yaddo, in Saratoga Springs, New York, in 1985, Norris met the playwright Katherine Jones (recently a soap opera actress) who no sooner read "The Christmas Wife" than she made an offer to adapt the story for television. Two years elapsed; a second option was negotiated; but the project came to fruition. Jason Robards and Julie Harris starred in the production and Home Box Office introduced Helen Norris to a wider American audience. *The Christmas Wife*, filmed in Vancouver, premiered December 12, 1988, was aired throughout the month, and repeated the next Christmas season. It was also nominated for four Ace Awards.

Perhaps Norris' sojourns at Yaddo and at the MacDowell writers' colony in New Hampshire tuned her marketing expertise as much as or more than her pen. She had tried selling an unpublished 1950s novel to Hollywood in 1986, getting past a first option before the deal faltered. "The Love Child" was also taken up for a possible television movie. Currently, a French producer has a two-year option on the early novel, with plans to film it in Nice.

But *Walk with the Sickle Moon* is no longer unpublished. Birch Lane Press of Carol Publishing shrewdly acquired the short novel for their 1989 list, rescuing an important artifact in Norris' literary evolution; editors there did not miss the financial potential of a plot readily mistaken for the best-seller romance (as Danielle Steele writes them). When Norris started the piece thirty or forty years ago, she confessed, she had had mercenary designs on the *Ladies' Home Journal* and *Reader's Digest Condensed Books*. (Norris frets whether the *New York Times*' snide, curt dismissal of that book will undermine the reception of eighteen new stories just published as her third major collection.) It is rather Deborah Stead, the reviewer, who erred. Helen Norris, or Birch Lane, may be accused only of a mistake by suppressing that *Walk with the Sickle Moon* is not of contemporary composition. For the work finally suffers comparison with the precision, the surety, the passion of *Water into Wine* or *The Christmas Wife* simply because since the 1950s Helen Norris has immeasurably matured.

The recent *Times* review notwithstanding, Norris has never published a ''bad'' book. Before *Walk with the Sickle Moon*, 1980s reviewers had merely fallen into a parochial assumption, a distortion the author herself has tacitly abetted. At Huntingdon College in the late 1960s, Norris told students that anyone reading her two previously published novels would earn an automatic F. To ensure their grade-point averages, Norris had removed both from the campus library. The Helen Norris who took up her No. 1 pencil in 1979 could not have been a novice—unless she were indeed a most belated prodigy. In fact, as she puts it to local journalists, the prolific 1980s were her ''third'' writing career. The long and protracted foreground to *The Christmas Wife*, moreover, was hardly occasion for shame or embarrassment. That she persevered to write at all, much less to write so well, is a matter for celebration. For Helen Norris should be numbered with Tillie Olsen's ''survivors,'' the remnant of women of their generation who did not founder or succumb to silence in consequence of our culture's pernicious, ''unnatural thwarting of what struggles to come into being'' in writers of female gender.

Norris' latest book, *The Burning Glass: Stories*, published by Louisiana State University Press in 1992, has yet to receive the full range of critical responses, but that volume promises to enhance further Norris' reputation as a teller of powerful stories.

MAJOR THEMES

To writers of certain temperaments the candor of their truth-telling and self-revelation seems possible only through elaborate disguises, refractions, and other impregnable defenses. Helen Norris is similarly, necessarily, armed, for her fiction tells the truth out loud in ways that chill and sear. Norris' essential story *and* that of her characters is of how humanity ''invents in desperate situations'' (Jean-Paul Sartre's definition of *genius*).

Other authors may take on the world; Norris' subjects are the Flesh and the Devil. Social, political, racial, even historical themes rarely interest her. When she cares to, she conjures up rich milieu. A family farm, the village cathedral, the bell tower are virtual characters in her first three novels. After 1980, the rock quarry, a mountain lodge, a basement, a bank vault, the ocean and shore are pregnant with meaning. Therein lies the function of Norris' settings, as symbolic overlays and embellishments. Elementally, place does not matter. Her tales are contemporary artifices—parables and miracle and morality plays—from Christian art forms, and fables, romances, and theatre of the absurd (namely Beckett), from secular vehicles. One does not notice these frames and their conventions upon first readings.

Norris' focus illuminates quite ordinary lives in their most personal and precarious relations: parent or grandparent and child; wife and husband; lover and beloved; a soul in colloquy alone or with one's art or God. The characters, no mere ciphers, grieve, remember, yearn, reach for—and create: tenuous bonds, evanescent understandings, at times, communion. Evil has mauled the righteous with the guilty, in ways legion and inexplicable. One pines for "something more than earth"; her first novel details her life's estrangements and a massacre of innocents. "Satan" no longer strides to and fro in the valley beneath the cathedral he built "For the Glory of God"; the amoral killer, adulterer, blasphemer has died of cancer. His victims "live" with splintered faith in God and humanity, but, by the novel's end, do live, together. Insidiously, like the priest's withdrawal in *Seven Watchmen*, attempts to render oneself invulnerable to pain nearly accomplish oblivion instead. To be human requires at minimum one other person. No matter what we risk thereby, individuation, Norris reiterates, is the primal curse. By middle age only the calloused have not been terrified by the inherent chasm between soul and soul. Words seldom span it, nor years of physical intimacy. Creatures stricken in heart, mind, and body (the sure legacy of age), society thrusts further away, exasperated, aghast. For requisite companion and mirror, these characters, if need be, "remember" or "invent" an Other. Half a life is usually time enough to have been betrayed, forsaken, and alone. "To be given the burden of life again. I cannot bear it, she wanted to cry" (*Water into Wine* 59). Beth, as "The Light on the Water" concludes, will live after all, but how? Her husband and dear friend are having an affair; the man is dead who gave her life.

How indeed? The means to continue to live are daunting, and death lies beyond. Norris' woodcarver in "The Cormorant" seems to speak for her other characters: yet "deep in him was a kind of elation that it was so." Against all reason, grieving for both a woman and precious artwork, he is reconciled and at peace:

She was driftwood now. If he waited long she might be washed upon his shore, and he would gather her, swollen, discolored beyond all telling that it was she. Until by the scent of the wood he would know her once more risen out of the sea. Driftwood was only a memory of something once alive and green. And out of the memory you fashioned another, a bird or a woman, whatever was sweet. A bird from a woman, whatever was sweet. (*Water into Wine* 23)

Out of the agony of this transitory life, still we fashion art and create more life, affirming all the while the sweetness that is being alive.

SURVEY OF CRITICISM

A primary cost of the "discontinuity" in Norris' "three" writing careers is each phase's being treated as her debut. Four of her six books have gained *New York Times* appraisals. With *The Christmas Wife*, her most noted volume, began the occasional journal review—in *Kenyon Review*, *Studies in Short Fiction*, *North American Review*, and *New Directions for Women*. All four evaluated *Water into Wine*, too, and at least *Kenyon Review* has assigned a reader to *Walk with the Sickle Moon*. Without sustained, cumulative attention from press and journal reviewers, however, Norris has yet to pass the threshold deemed necessary for critical scrutiny. She has written too little too recently. Only the 1985 and 1988 collections "count"; two religious novels neither Catholic nor Jewish can hardly be taken seriously. Her 1940 and 1958 narratives simply go unread. Carolyn G. Heilbrun tells us to expect major writing from gifted women past age 50. This "new" contemporary writer in her 70s, however, must await scholars proficient to read without prejudice the whole of her fine work.

BIBLIOGRAPHY

Works by Helen Norris

Something More Than Earth. Boston: Little, Brown, 1940.
For the Glory of God. New York: Macmillan, 1958.
The Christmas Wife. Urbana: University of Illinois Press, 1985.
More Than Seven Watchmen. Grand Rapids, Mich.: Zondervan, 1985.
Water into Wine. Urbana: University of Illinois Press, 1988.
Walk with the Sickle Moon. New York: Birch Lane Press, 1989.
The Burning Glass: Stories. Baton Rouge: Louisiana State University Press, 1992.

Studies of Helen Norris

Becker, Alida. "Four Voices in the Making." Rev. of *The Christmas Wife*. *New York Times Book Review* (December 15, 1985): 28.
Olmstead, Robert. "Actors and Miracles." Rev. of *Water into Wine*. *New York Times Book Review* (October 16, 1988): 18.
Rev. of *For the Glory of God*. *Catholic World* (June 1958): 230.
Rev. of *The Christmas Wife*. *Kenyon Review* 8 (1986): 122.
Rev. of *The Christmas Wife*. *Studies in Short Fiction* 23 (1986): 211.
Rev. of *The Christmas Wife*. *North American Review* 27 (March 1986): 73.
Rev. of *The Christmas Wife*. *New Directions for Women* 14 (November 1986): 14.
Rev. of *Water into Wine*. *Studies in Short Fiction* 25 (1988): 498.
Rev. of *Water into Wine*. *North American Review* 274 (June 1989): 69.
Rev. of *Water into Wine*. *New Directions for Women* 18 (January 1989): 18.
Rev. of *Water into Wine*. (Chicago) *Tribune Books* (January 15, 1989): 3.

Stead, Deborah. Rev. of *Walk with the Sickle Moon*. *New York Times Book Review* (December 24, 1989): 24.

W., H. W. Rev. of *Something More Than Earth*. *New York Times* (October 6, 1940): 7.

JOHN N. SOMERVILLE, JR.

T[homas] R[eid] Pearson
(1956–   )

Since 1985 T. R. Pearson has published six novels. The first four of these are set in the fictional community of Neely, a small town in contemporary piedmont North Carolina; the latest take place in Virginia's Blue Ridge Mountains. Pearson is best known for his digressive storytelling technique and talents as a writer of comic novels.

BIOGRAPHY

Thomas Reid Pearson was born in Winston-Salem, North Carolina, on March 27, 1956, and lived there until he left home to attend college at North Carolina State University in fall 1974. After completing both a B.A. (1977) and an M.A. (1980) in English, Pearson spent a year teaching English at Peace College, a women's school in Raleigh. When his contract at Peace expired in spring 1981, Pearson entered the Ph.D. program in English at Pennsylvania State University in fall 1981, but remained only one quarter before returning to North Carolina.

Pearson spent the next several years as a carpenter and housepainter in Raleigh. During this time he began to write seriously, waking in the early morning and writing from 5 to 8:30 before leaving for work. He completed his first novel, *A Short History of a Small Place*, in late 1982. Unable to find a publisher for the book—it was considered too slow, too digressive, and therefore unsalable— Pearson went to work on a second novel. This work, *Off for the Sweet Hereafter*, eventually found a publisher in Linden Press, an imprint of Simon and Schuster, and the two novels were brought out in order of composition—*A Short History* in 1985 and *Off for the Sweet Hereafter* one year later.

In late 1985 Pearson moved to New York City, where he lived for two years. In 1987 Linden Press published *The Last of How It Was*, the third volume in Pearson's Neely "trilogy." Though he continues to spend some of each year in New York, Pearson now spends much of his time at the home he built in Carroll County, southwestern Virginia. A fourth novel, *Call and Response*, appeared in 1989, a fifth, *Gospel Hour* in 1991, and his latest, *Cry Me a River*, in early 1993.

MAJOR THEMES

The related issues of the individual and community are significant concerns in each of Pearson's novels. In *A Short History of a Small Place*, for instance, an important element in the story is the developing relationship of the narrator, young Louis Benfield, to the people and events that comprise the community and history of his hometown, Neely, North Carolina. As a narrator who reports and muses on various happenings in the town, Louis is both a voice for the community and a character who gains knowledge as he observes his neighbors' passions and eccentricities. In the central events of the novel, as well—the romantic sufferings and the suicide of Miss Pettigrew—the dynamics of individual and community are particularly important. As becomes clear, the citizens of Neely are quick to explain Miss Pettigrew's madness, yet few understand and even fewer know the woman. The town is composed of interested observers who literally and figuratively lean against the Pettigrew fence watching the woman or her monkey, Mr. Britches, but cannot decide how to act when they are invited into the house for Miss Pettigrew's Fourth of July "get together." The relationship between community and individual in the novel is, in many ways, the tension between public life—typified by crowds and public pronouncements—and private suffering—seen in the experiences of Miss Pettigrew or in the silent grieving of Louis's mother for her dead daughter.

This concern with individual and community is important in Pearson's other novels as well. In *Off for the Sweet Hereafter* he focuses on the short, passionate relationship of Raeford Benton Lynch and Jane Elizabeth Firesheets and describes their brief career as criminals living outside the bounds of conventional society. In *The Last of How It Was* Pearson spends considerable time telling how young Louis Benfield's grandfather killed a black man, a memory that provokes further recollections of the relations between black and white in a small Southern town in the mid- to late-twentieth century. As a meditation on society, the novel also pays substantial attention to matters of family—particularly to the relationships within families and between generations—especially as it is exhibited among the Benfields and their relations. Attention to individual and society again figures in *Call and Response* and *Cry Me a River*, in which the various threads of plot cluster around the relations between men and women, their distress at isolation and need for companionship, and *Gospel Hour*, where Pearson focuses on religious experience in the rural South.

Whatever the emphasis of a particular novel, Pearson also illustrates his concern with community and individual through the language his characters use as they try to order and explain their world. This effort to explain occurs both in their various ways of speaking and in the storytelling preferred by these characters. In *A Short History*, for instance, this variety of language as a reflection of multiple perspectives on life is illustrated in a series of passages beginning with Mrs. Philip J. King's account of the events that changed Miss Pettigrew's life. Mrs. King's exceedingly romanticized version of what happened makes the night on which Miss Pettigrew loses Mr. Alton a "mournful night of reckoning" (239) and transforms Mr. Alton into "a tragic figure" (242) pursued into the night by Miss Pettigrew's brother, the mayor, Mr. Wallace Amory. In the words of Mrs. Philip J. King: "Miss Myra Angelique [Pettigrew] lay on the porch decking and sobbed while the mayor proceeded on out into the front yard and stood under the lightning rent sky in the sheets and torrents and bucketfuls of rain and waved his great-uncle's naked sabre over his head as he hollered after Mr. Alton who brought his touring car away from the curb and disappeared down the boulevard" (242). The version of the story advanced by Louis's father, however, is strikingly different. To the belief that Mr. Alton is a "tragic figure," Louis, Sr., responds, "Roadapples" (285), announcing that this "tragic" character is a "slimy individual" (242) who is not "freshly divorced," nor "very nearly skewered on [Mr. Wallace Amory's] naked sabre" (286), as Mrs. King suggests.

Mr. Benfield's attempts to explain Mr. Alton's motivations, however, reveal the limits of his own use of language. Taking his son with him on a walk, Mr. Benfield tries to clarify the nature of Mr. Alton's interest in Miss Pettigrew and at the same time tell his son the facts of life. The conversation proceeds as a series of questions from the father, followed by young Louis's uncertain responses. His father asks, "Louis, do you know much about romance?" "No sir" (286). "Louis, a man and a woman have a kind of draw for each other. Do you see what I mean?" "No sir," the boy responds, "not exactly" (287). Then, "there are some men, and some women too I suppose, who want to go direct to intimate without ever dancing. Do you see what I mean?" (288). Suddenly and with unexpected clarity, the boy realizes what his father has been saying; "it hit me like a sledgehammer blow to the forehead," he remarks. "Daddy was talking about plugging" (288). "Do you mean sex?," Louis asks his father. "Well Jesus Christ, Louis," Mr. Benfield answers, "why'd you let me suffer so?" (289).

Illustrated in the preceding series of passages is something of the variety of language that exists in Neely, language that may or may not find an audience that understands, and that always describes the world in a way that reflects a unique, perhaps eccentric perspective. The stories that Pearson's characters tell and the words they use reveal this multiplicity of perspectives and try at the same time to make contact with those who will hear these words. And as events are translated into stories—a practice described in the developing account of Uncle Jack, Aunt Della, and the Indian that appears in *The Last of How It Was*— and are passed from speaker to speaker, these words become communal acts, events that have the potential to produce unity out of disparate voices.

Stories told and retold seem, in Pearson's fiction, to offer a solution to the dilemma Louis faces on the evening walk with his father. To his father's question of "why'd you let me suffer so?," Louis answers, "Daddy, I couldn't make out what you were up to" (289). As each individual in Pearson's fiction looks at the world from a singularly private angle, that perspective is reflected in the language the character adopts for describing that world. Pearson seems to suggest, however, that these individual efforts to order the world can be rescued from disunity by the force of telling, through stories that can link event, speaker, and listener, at least momentarily, in a common reading of experience.

SURVEY OF CRITICISM

Critical response to the novels of T. R. Pearson has been limited to book reviews. These reviews have been generally positive in their assessment of Pearson's work, though certain elements in his writing—particularly his digressive storytelling technique and his prose style—have produced widely variable reactions.

From the start critics have noted Pearson's indebtedness to Mark Twain and William Faulkner. Pearson is likened to Twain for his comic tone and—in *A Short History of a Small Place* and *The Last of How It Was*—for his use of a youthful narrator with similarities to Huck Finn. Pearson and Twain are also similar in their use of the vernacular storytelling tradition, a likeness extended by more than one critic to George Washington Harris and other nineteenth-century Southwestern humorists.

Pearson is also linked to Faulkner in his narrative technique, but is compared to Faulkner most often for his creation of a recurring fictional community (Neely, N.C.) and for his style. Although some reviewers have simply noted the resemblance of Neely to Faulkner's Yoknapatawpha County, others (writing before the appearance of his latest two novels) suggested more, contending that by the close of Pearson's career, Neely should occupy as firm a position in American letters as Yoknapatawpha. Contrary to so optimistic an assessment of Pearson's work, however, Jerry Leath Mills writes in his review of *Call and Response* that Pearson's fictional community limits the writer to a "neo-primitivist fantasy land" where he is unable to delineate the depth of human experience Faulkner managed to portray in his Yoknapatawpha fiction.

Although attention has been paid to Pearson's similarities to Mark Twain and to the resemblances between Neely and Yoknapatawpha, critics have responded much more extensively and variously to Pearson's prose style. Some describe the long, meandering sentences as necessary to the humor of the novels or to reproducing the rhythms of oral communication. Others argue that the style is parody, that Pearson's prose is purposely excessive in order to satirize the verbal effusion of the Southern storytelling tradition. Apart from such views, however, many critics express reservations about Pearson's style. His prose is often described as difficult or as an acquired taste, even by those who appreciate his work. Thus, Christopher Lehmann-Haupt writes that the prose style of Pearson's first novel may charm some readers, but strike others as "the tedium of self-indulgence." Few reviewers have responded so harshly as George McCartney, who, in his assessment of *Off for the Sweet Hereafter*, describes the narrative voice in Pearson's novel as that of "the Southern bore trumpeting his conspiratorial knowingness through endlessly serpentine sentences." Indeed, even so staunch a champion of Pearson's fiction as Jonathan Yardley writes in his review of *The Last of How It Was* that "for the first time in reading Pearson's work, I found myself wishing that he would hold off on all that digression and trim down those endless sentences, and just get to the point."

Like his prose style, Pearson's digressive method of storytelling has provoked a variety of critical responses. Some critics encourage Pearson to greater discipline, urging him to establish a stronger sense of unity among his numerous digressions. Fran Schumer, however, while observing that *A Short History* has an "unconscionable number of plot twists," argues that this "meandering" is necessary, for it "leads us to the book's heart, which is in each of the pixilated Neelyites." On a similar note, Lehmann-Haupt asserts that Miss Pettigrew's suicide in *A Short History* is "almost incidental to the elaborate episodes" in which the narrator and reader are "hopelessly and charmingly entangled." Such a view is repeated by several critics, who argue as Bob Summer does, that Pearson's digressions, like his sentences, allow the reader to "hear everything" about Neely, "about the people who make the place remarkable," and that this knowledge is ultimately the substance of the novels.

A further source of critical attention is Pearson's humor. Associated in certain respects with the lessons he has learned from Mark Twain, Pearson's comic fiction is produced through his use of language, dramatic situations, and humorous characterization. Whatever the source of the humor, however, few reviewers have failed to note that Pearson has a knack for writing that produces laughter. These same critics also observe that the comedy in Pearson's novels often arises from circumstances with substantial tragic possibilities. Although this darker element is generally suppressed by the comic tone of the novels, reviewers have offered special praise when, even briefly, Pearson brings this sense of the tragic into the foreground. Thus, Summer writes that in the closing section of *The Last of How It Was*, an account of the death of Louis Benfield's grandparents, Pearson produces his "most transcendentally moving writing to date." Opposed to such enthusiastic assessments of Pearson's tragic sense, of course, there are less sanguine evaluations. Again, we might note Mills's remarks that Neely cannot be properly compared to Faulkner's Yoknapatawpha County and that Pearson's fictional community is "filled with broad carnal humor but protected by a grubby innocence that keeps all its obvious intimations of mortality at arm's length." Mills agrees that Pearson works in a "comic setting," but asserts that "comedy and seriousness of vision need not be at odds. In Neely," he concludes, "they are."

BIBLIOGRAPHY

Works by T. R. Pearson

A Short History of a Small Place. New York: Linden, 1985.
Off for the Sweet Hereafter. New York: Linden, 1986.
The Last of How It Was. New York: Linden, 1987.
Call and Response. New York: Linden, 1989.
Gospel Hour. New York: William Morrow, 1991.
Cry Me a River. New York: Henry Holt, 1993.

Studies of T. R. Pearson

Lehmann-Haupt, Christopher. Rev. of *A Short History of a Small Place. New York Times* (June 20, 1985): C24.

Levering, Frank. "The Gentle Spiral of a Southern Sentence" (Rev. of *The Last of How It Was*). *Los Angeles Times Book Review* (October 4, 1987): 2ff.

McCartney, George. "Sentenced to Sleep" (Rev. of *Off for the Sweet Hereafter*). *National Review* (December 5, 1986): 56–57.

Mills, Jerry Leath. "Long Afternoons of Tedium and T. R. Pearson" (Rev. of *Call and Response*). *News and Observer* (Raleigh, N.C.) (June 18, 1989): 4D.

Richards, Jeffrey. "Pearson Moves North, but the Gab Is Still Neely" (Rev. of *Gospel Hour*). *News and Observer* (Raleigh, N.C.) (February 24, 1991): 5J.

Schumer, Fran. "Crazy Nights and Days in Neely" (Rev. of *A Short History of a Small Place*). *New York Times Book Review* (July 7, 1985): 4.

Summer, Bob. "A Comic, Bittersweet Portrait of a Small Town" (Rev. of *A Short History of a Small Place*). *Atlanta Constitution* (June 30, 1985): J10.

———. "Pearson Continuing the South's Oral Tradition" (Rev. of *The Last of How It Was*). *Atlanta Constitution* (September 13, 1987): J11.

Yardley, Jonathan. "Further Histories of a Small Place" (Rev. of *Off for the Sweet Hereafter*). *Washington Post Book World* (June 15, 1986): 3.

———. "T. R. Pearson's Down Home Tales of Neely, N.C." (Rev. of *The Last of How It Was*). *Washington Post Book World* (October 4, 1987): 3.

Jayne Anne Phillips
(1952–   )

When Jayne Anne Phillips made her debut in 1979 with a national publisher, overnight she became a literary sensation. She gave voice to the dispossessed and utterance to their stories of the desperation of contemporary American life in an original, intensely erotic, memory-haunted style. It seemed there was nowhere her imagination could not go. Five years later, she followed her successful short-story collection with a novel that fulfilled expectations for her. With lyrical compassion, her family saga detailed the American dream and how two wars destroyed it. No one has labeled Phillips a Southern writer or a woman writer; her relentless intelligence breaks those boundaries. And, although her fiction set in West Virginia is evocative of place, it feels universal.

BIOGRAPHY

Jayne Anne Phillips was born on July 19, 1952, in Buckhannon, West Virginia, to Russell and Martha Jane Thornhill Phillips. Her parents, who divorced in 1972, also had two sons, one older and one younger than their only daughter. Her father was of Welsh origin and her mother Black Irish and English. Phillips says that the influence of growing up in the South was "connected to place . . . the constancy, the fact that I was in one place for twenty years and that my family had been there already for two hundred years" (Hill 61). She observes that "West Virginia is a strange state. It's never belonged to the South or the North. The rural population is larger than the urban one. Family and tradition are what's important there. It's hemmed in by hills and valleys. People don't *leave* West Virginia" (Gilbert 65). Yet, as a child, she dreamed of escaping and found the first means through reading: "Very early I got the idea that language was some kind of private, secretive means of travel, a way of living beyond your own life." Later, she would tell David Edelstein for *Esquire*—listing Eudora

Welty, Tillie Olsen, Katherine Anne Porter, William Faulkner, and James Agee
as examples—that "the great writers have a journeyer's wisdom. They have
been somewhere limitless and come back. That's not necessarily what they are
writing about, but you can feel that in the work" (107).

Phillips first started writing when she was about 9. "I wrote a kind of serial
novel, starring myself and my friends, about a girl who moves to New York
City and falls in love with a kid gang leader. I did that to entertain people. I
would read it to my friends and they would be in it. After she was in New York,
of course, they were no longer in it, so everyone lost interest" (Hill 65). She
has said that writers are formed by age 8; it is a primal development. They learn
that there is a self that is stable, a soul that is stable, so that they are able to
imagine being anyone or no one:

I think this is a kind of unconscious knowledge that art involves incredible psychic risks.
And a lot of people go under because the risks are so tremendous. I don't think writers
are intrinsically crazy, or that that is why a lot of them commit suicide. I think it's
because they are under a kind of stress that would kill anyone else inside of two years.
And I think that they start from a place of tremendous stability to even start attempting
it. (Hill 58)

Her mother, a schoolteacher, encouraged her independent spirit and her writing. "She wanted [her children] to be proud, in the sense that we wouldn't be
ground down by anybody, and she communicated that to me especially because
I was the girl and I'd have to protect myself, not my physical self as much as
my spiritual self" (Gilbert 65). Phillips' mother also imparted to her only daughter "the whole story of how she cared for her mother when her mother was
dying" and telling this story became "sort of a mission" that would be fulfilled
in *Machine Dreams*. "What she really handed down to me was a sense of
mission about these lives that would be completely lost otherwise. Because they
were lives that no one knew of, and a kind of both failure and triumph that no
one knew of. And, if it is not written about, it is completely lost" (Hill 63).
And it was not just her mother's story, but her grandmother's story as well, that
Phillips felt mystically inspired to tell. "It's a privilege to have a passion,"
Phillips told *Newsweek*; "it's like being led by a whisper" (Baker 116). Her
grandmother, who died 5 years before she was born, had nevertheless written
Jayne Anne's name in a copy of *The Prophet* by Kahlil Gibran, just after an
allusion to reincarnation. Noting that it was unusual for a woman of her place
and time even to own, much less pore over, such a book, Phillips says that "it
wasn't that she intuited my name. She and my mother had discussed what a
daughter's name would be. But she had that much consciousness about there
being a possibility that I would be born" (Hill 62–63). Clearly she feels a link
to this woman she never knew. Of this grandmother, Phillips says, "she was
completely uneducated, but she wrote poems" (Hill 62).

It was to poetry that Phillips herself first turned her hand, at age 15, with the encouragement of high school teacher Irene McKinney, a poet in her own right. McKinney's voice joined that of Phillips' mother in teaching her how to protect herself spiritually. Recognizing Phillips' talent, McKinney warned: "I want you to remember that people will try to bury you. You mustn't let them" (Baker 116).

After graduation from high school in 1970, Phillips left Buckhannon to attend West Virginia University in Morgantown, rather than opting for West Virginia Wesleyan in her hometown. Her mother made a trip to Morgantown to see Judith Stitzel, then running a writing laboratory at WVU. After learning that it was a remedial rather than a creative writing laboratory, she still delivered to Stitzel the message she traveled to bring: "I think my daughter has a gift for writing. I don't want her to get lost." She need not have worried, Stitzel told *Esquire* magazine: "What stunned me from the beginning was the wisdom and maturity and knowledge from so young a person. She was very beautiful, and it's hard for a person to be as striking as she was. . . . But she knew how to use it. She was always aware of the pull between intellect and sensuality. Jayne Anne's only control was the ability to shape reality" (Edelstein 109). At the university, Phillips encountered the work of contemporary poets and began publishing her own poetry in small literary magazines. To help pay her way through college, she taught remedial reading and went door to door in mining camps selling home improvements. She traveled every summer and began to explore what she terms "adjacent realities—transcendent states, drugs, Eastern philosophy, Carl Jung, and Carlos Castañeda" (Edelstein 109). Phillips was desperate to observe and get into other people's heads, to recreate their thinking, Stitzel told *Esquire*:

She was always clear about the need not to stay in West Virginia. She undertook a deliberate expansion of geographic space. She hitched a lot of rides, and she met a lot of weird people. She wasn't a self-destructive person. She just wouldn't curb her life out of fear—she's unshockable and very curious. And I think that helped her in writing about home, too: she was much more confident when she knew she wasn't being provincial." (Edelstein 109)

Yet Phillips saw trouble ahead. "It was an apocalyptic time on campuses," she told *Newsweek*. "Everything from the '60s was over, and some people were trying to obliterate themselves—the drug thing. I could see it happening" (Baker 116). Still, in 1972, Phillips and a girlfriend decided to hitchhike to California rather than work on Cape Cod for the summer. Despite an aura of danger and even threats of physical violence—"I learned what it meant to be afraid" (Baker 118)—Phillips again chose the road after finishing a B.A. in 1974, driving to California this time with two friends and her dog:

People I knew in West Virginia and in college were the same kind of people that I ran into later. They were people who were sort of unattached, involved with drugs a bit— they were hippies. And that was what I became. I wanted to live that way, too. It seemed to be a way of living that had some integrity to it. And people were bright. They talked about what happened. They talked about internal feelings in a way that I hadn't experienced growing up. (Hill 66)

Phillips and her traveling companions settled in a black section of Oakland near Berkeley for "a difficult period: there was no work in California, and I was going through a delayed adolescence and childhood, which I find American college graduates tend to have" (Edelstein 109).

By 1975 Phillips had left California and traveled to Colorado, where she audited a poetry course and supported her poetry writing by waitressing. There she met Annabel Levitt, who would later found Vehicle Editions and publish two of Phillips' short books, *Counting* (1978) and *Fast Lanes* (1984). With several other women, they founded a workshop that met in Phillips' apartment. Some of the long narrative poems she wrote during that period would evolve into short stories such as "Lechery." Finally, however, Phillips tired of the drifting life and went back to West Virginia because "I ran out of steam. I didn't have any money, and I had been sick" (Hill 66). She had gathered, by then, the material that later appeared in stories about drug addicts, hustlers, stripteasers, and drifters. It was part of the experience of her generation. Pieces of the return to West Virginia, with all the bittersweetness of going home, turn up in the fine short story "Home."

During six months at home she saved money and applied to the University of Iowa writers' program. She had, by then, become interested in writing prose: "I was interested in Rilke's journals, *Illuminations*, Rimbaud, and Merwin's *The Miner's Pale Children* and I wanted to start using that form." She was challenged by the difficulty of writing fiction and found it incredibly liberating. "Form is very important, and paragraphs work in a more subversive way. In a poem you're always having to confront the identity of the writer. But a paragraph, people are not armored against it. They read a paragraph and feel involved in normal life" (Hill 66–67).

In 1976 Phillips was accepted at Iowa. In the summer of that year, on her twenty-fourth birthday, Truck Press in Carrboro, North Carolina, brought out an edition of twenty-four one-page prose pieces in a collection called *Sweethearts*. Sections of the book won the 1976 Fels Award in Fiction from the Coordinating Council of Literary Magazines, and portions appeared in *Pushcart Prize II: The Best of the Small Presses* in 1977. Iowa provided her with her first experience of a creative writing program and a community of writers. In 1977 she took a workshop with Frank Conroy in which she wrote some of the stories in *Black Tickets*.

In 1978 Levitt's Vehicle Editions published *Counting*, twenty-two short emotional outbursts filtered through the personae of a 26-year-old writer and his lover, a 41-year-old dancer. This collection won the 1978 St. Lawrence Award for Fiction. At the St. Lawrence University writers' conference that year, Phillips met Seymour Lawrence, then an editor at Delacorte. In a now much-celebrated and much-repeated exchange, Phillips asked Lawrence, "Do you publish short stories?'' and he answered, ''Not if I can help it.'' She pressed on him a copy of *Sweethearts* and received a postcard saying, ''You're a real writer. Bring your stories to Boston.'' Phillips, who had finished an M.A. at Iowa that year and accepted an assistant professorship at Humboldt State University in California, sent him the manuscript for what would become *Black Tickets*. In a scene ''much too contrived for anything Phillips would write,'' her mother rushed out of the house in Buckhannon as Phillips was pulling out of the driveway, the car loaded for California, to flag her daughter down and tell her that Lawrence was on the phone and ''he wants to buy your book'' (Edelstein 110). Both the National Endowment for the Arts and the Yaddo Corporation granted Phillips fellowships.

When *Black Tickets* appeared in 1979, it made Phillips the first recipient of the American Academy and Institute of Arts and Letters Sue Kaufman Prize for First Fiction. The book consisted of sixteen very short pieces, many of them reprinted from *Sweethearts*, and eleven longer stories. ''Books of short stories weren't as accepted then,'' Seymour Lawrence said. ''So we sent proofs of *Black Tickets* out to an awful lot of people. The response was unbelievable'' (Edelstein 111). Lawrence used many of the quotations on the book jacket and did a simultaneous paperback and hardcover printing: 25,000 in paperback and 2,500 in hardcover. Sold to twelve countries, the book earned Phillips acclaim as one of America's most promising writers.

Phillips was offered a fellowship at the Provincetown Fine Arts Center but turned it down to take the teaching job at Humboldt. There she put the finishing touches on *Black Tickets* and worked on new stories. But she ''realized pretty quickly that I did not want to be a college teacher, full-time, and not do anything else'' (Hill 68). She wrote Provincetown that she had changed her mind, applied again, and in 1979 left California for Cape Cod. In 1980, Phillips accepted a Bunting Institute fellowship at Radcliffe College and moved to Cambridge. By then she was working on what was to become her first novel.

Phillips is a painstaking writer, working very slowly, ''like a poet, really, one line at a time'' (Gilbert 66). *Machine Dreams* would take her 4 years to complete. She does not have any kind of plan when she writes ''because the whole point is to follow the story to its center, not to impose some point of view. I believe that you are led to discover what things mean and how things relate to each other through the process of doing the work. The real risk is to be strong enough to understand and accept what you're going to find out so that you are not destroyed by what you find'' (Gilbert 66). Phillips says that writing is more painful for her than anything else. ''Real writers serve their material. They allow it to pass through them and have the opportunity to move beyond the daily limitations of being inside themselves'' (Baker 116). Part of what makes her writing difficult is that ''you don't have any exterior guidelines. I had no exterior guidelines in *Machine Dreams*, except for a sort of list of happenings'' (Hill 68). She wrote the book by sections, and the title evolved from the section ''Mitch: Machine Dreams,'' based ''loosely on an imagination of my father in World War II'' (Hill 54).

By the time the book appeared in 1984, Phillips was teaching creative writing at Boston University, had traveled to India, and had married a Boston doctor. Seymour Lawrence had moved from Delacorte to Dutton, the publisher of *Machine Dreams*. The novel was a best-seller in the United States, and foreign rights were sold for record amounts in England and Germany. Pocket Books paid $100,000 for the paperback rights.

Phillips now lives outside Boston with her husband and two young sons. In 1987 Dutton brought out a short-story collection entitled *Fast Lanes*. Many of these stories were written between *Black Tickets* and *Machine Dreams*, and some had won prizes after appearing in the small presses. "Something That Happened" was selected by Joyce Carol Oates for *The Best American Short Stories 1979*, and "How Mickey Made It" was included in *The Pushcart Prizes VII*. Phillips has broken barriers, gone across lines. Readers wait expectantly for what she will deliver next.

MAJOR THEMES

Phillips says that she is writing about the deracination of her generation and the tragedy the traditional male-female roles wreak on people when those roles no longer exist in society: "I'm interested in what home now consists of. Because we move around so much, families are forced to be immediate; they must stand on their relationships, rather than on stereotypes or assumptions of a common history" (Baker 118). The epigraph of *Fast Lanes*, "I have begun my freedom and it hurts" (Alan Dugan, "Stability Before Departure," *Collected Poems*), echoes like the cry of a whole generation.

Lost on the open road or in sordid urban underbellies or in families whose bonds have frayed, Phillips' first-person narrators, both in short and longer prose pieces, are often anguished. "What about your heart?" asks the narrator of "Black Tickets," degenerating in drugs and isolation. The question is a cry of pain in a world increasingly mechanistic and isolating. As Michael Adams writes of the collection *Black Tickets*: "Phillips explores the banality of horror and the horror of the banal through her examination of sex, violence, innocence, loneliness, illness, madness, various forms of love and lovelessness, and numerous failures at communicating and feeling" (297).

The failure to feel and communicate feeling is perhaps her most intense theme. It is most tragically evoked in families where her characters want to feel known and loved, and want to feel the love they think they should, but cannot. Often the failure seems to spring from the deep and tragic separation between the sexes. One group of short stories in *Black Tickets* deals with the violent lives of drug addicts and prostitutes. The flamboyance of style conveys her sense of the desperation of contemporary American life. Another group, dealing with family life in the rural South, explores—in a different but related way—loneliness and the need to love and be loved. These stories suggest that people's weaknesses and prejudices are intensified when they are with their families, but that these difficulties must be struggled through. Her American landscape is riven by the upheaval of the Vietnam era and the breakdown of family structure. Her writing probes the deepest psychic wounds inflicted on both men and women, black and white, in urban or rural settings, by the violent clashes of an age of transition. *Machine Dreams* is about expression and how it operates. Partly, expression is maimed in the novel by a displacement of meaning onto objects, particularly machines. "When suffering seems reasonless," a mother tells her daughter in the novel, "people come together and want to understand." The deepest communion in Phillips' fiction is generally between mother and daughter, although the brother-sister communion in *Machine Dreams* is also intense. The displacement of faith from people onto machines annihilates this necessary human community, and *Machine Dreams* examines the effects of technology on our lives. Of this saga, which evokes the American dream and its shattering through the disintegration of a family, Phillips remarked: "The urgency of this book has to do with warning. I mean this spiritually, as well as politically" (Gilbert 65). Phillips' fiction reflects an America in the grip of deep and painful transition and suggests that only communication and a new sense of connection will save us. The old certainties have slipped away, and rootlessness is the price paid for freedom.

Vietnam emerges in *Machine Dreams* as a war that maimed us all. Both Vietnam and the divorce in that novel are emblematic of a demythologizing process with which an entire society would seem to be struggling. "Politically, the whole experience in Vietnam was not mythologized, like World War II was," Phillips says:

It came down as exactly what it was, without all the romance. Just as the family has come to be more obvious, without the romance of—it's going to last forever. It remains a kind of haunting that is never going to be resolved. That haunting could be really instructive and revolutionary in its effects. It hasn't been because governments—institutions—don't seem to operate that way. (Hill 60)

The failure of large bureaucracies to respond to human need, the human cost of institutionalized loneliness, is pervasive in Phillips' work. Official bulletins are set into *Machine Dreams* in a way that exposes their almost ludicrous inhumanity. Danner hates hearing the deferential tone in her father's voice as he calls government officials—"faraway, successful men"—to try to learn something about his son who is missing in action in Vietnam. When Billy prays at a Christmas Eve dinner with his mother and sister just before he leaves for the army, a memory suddenly flashes across his mind with "startling clarity: watching the snow plow with Danner, both of them small, standing in snow to their knees. The big yellow machine rumbling by, slow, all-powerful. Engine roar, shrill jangling of chains. The powdery snow thrown up in fanned continuous spray as the heavy machine pressed on." Although she does not define herself as a political writer, Phillips says that "writing about so-called ordinary people is a political statement because it's talking about everyday life and why it's precious and why it's worth defending against whatever forces'' (Gilbert 66). The preciousness of everyday life, and the presence of the deepest emotion in the smallest circumstances, is part of what charges her work's search for a sense of a connection ''because, to me, that is what is at stake. It's the whole point of writing—to make it clear to myself that human life is important. That it's not just ants in an anthill. It's not just meaningless and random'' (Hill 60).

Her sense that the writer's mission is to make apparent the connections is part of what infuses her work with urgency. ''If I had lost my faith, the faith that I have that things are connected—that the subconscious is almost an entity that is godlike—and that goes beyond personality and, hopefully, beyond life—I don't think I would write'' (Hill 67). Her explorations into her characters, then, are a search for the secrets of the human heart that are what we call the truth.

In 1980, Phillips addressed the role of writers in a time of national spiritual crisis when she wrote that ''American writers in particular must concern themselves with a history of the spirit in personal and intrinsically national terms, with an exploration of what survives as American, with what continues, with matters of loss and strength.'' At the emergence of a new decade, she invoked Ezra Pound's maxim from the *Cantos*: ''What thou lovest well remains / the rest is dross,'' and concluded that ''Loving well, and with intelligence, seems the task ahead, or what must be saved will not be saved'' (''How Is Fiction Doing?'').

SURVEY OF CRITICISM

The writing of Jayne Anne Phillips has evoked a deep response from critics and fellow writers alike. She has been generally assessed to be a new, quintessentially American voice. John Irving attested to the healing power latent in her prose when he wrote that in her short piece, ''Slave,'' ''she offers men and women a vision of orgasm that is so sympathetic to the differences in our sexes that we should read the book for it alone. It might make us think less of conquering each other and more of caring for each other.'' Her style has evoked as much commentary as her subject matter. Jay McInerney wrote that ''the author's best prose is metaphor-laden and sensual, with a minimum of connective tissue.'' Peter S. Prescott wrote that ''the surest way to start a rush for the exits is to announce the appearance of a young woman writer whose principal theme is love. Nevertheless, a new talent claims our attention most effectively when it treats old themes with fresh energy. I believe Jayne Anne Phillips is indeed a remarkable new talent.'' Both by sheer talent, then, and by the urgency and contemporaneity of her themes, Phillips has been singled out, in the words of *New York Times* critic Michiko Kakutani, as having ''stepped out of the ranks of her generation as one of its most gifted writers.''

The most common complaint from critics has been that sometimes Phillips' style overwhelms her subject matter. Daphne Merkin wrote of *Black Tickets* that "most of the metaphors lack . . . figurative commitment. They simply and baldly call attention to themselves." Kakutani complained that half the stories in *Fast Lanes* "feel like little more than virtuosic exercises meant to show off the author's ventriloquial talents." Kakutani, echoing Irving, concluded that Phillips moves her readers and sheds light on history only when she moves out of the claustrophobic isolated voice into deeper and broader themes. Anne Tyler, too, found Phillips more effective in *Machine Dreams* where "shocks arise from small, ordinary moments, patiently developed, that suddenly burst out with far more meaning than we had expected. And each of these moments owes its impact to an assured and gifted writer."

In general, critics have ultimately forgiven Phillips her exercises because of the depths she dives to elsewhere. Irving wrote of *Black Tickets:* "I hope Miss Phillips is writing a novel because she seems at her deepest and broadest when she sustains a narrative, manipulates a plot, develops characters through more than one phase of their life or behavior. I believe she would shine in a novel." Doris Grumbach similarly reflected:

As I look over this book once more, I have the feeling that there is too much here, too much insight, too much unusual compassion for those who are lonely and cut away from human sympathy, especially those in the same family who are bound by parental ties, to be used up by a first book. I am more than willing to believe that with the publication of *Black Tickets* we have something to celebrate—and a writer to watch closely.

Machine Dreams was generally assessed as a novel that met what Adams described as "the high expectations so many have for her." Robert Phillips wrote: "With her second book Jayne Anne Phillips has earned the acclaim critics were so eager to give her the first time around." Others, however, found the novel less effective than the short stories. Judith Gies expressed the opinion that, in *Machine Dreams*, "the tenderness toward people she knows outweighs objectivity, and as a result, the novel lacks the true, frightening clarity of the stories." Jonathan Yardley, however, while objecting to the scheme of the "heavily programmatic" novel, found its tenderness its strength: "Above all, Phillips manages to convey her love for these people and to persuade the reader to share it. Ordinary people can be extraordinary, she is saying, and what happens to them is terribly important. She is right, and the best parts of *Machine Dreams* do honor to them."

What is striking thus far in the treatment of Phillips' works is the lack of thematic analysis. So original is her writing that attention has been focused on language. Janneken Overland and Roril Moi's "Du et det su ser: Samtale med Jayne Anne Phillips" appeared in *Vinduet* in 1983; Elisabeth Bronfen's "Between Nostalgia and Disenchantment: The Concept 'Home' in *Machine Dreams*" appeared in 1988 in *Arbeiten aus Anglistik und Amerikanistik*. On home soil, Phyllis Lassner's "Jayne Anne Phillips: Women's Narrative and the Recreation of History" was published in 1989 in a collection of essays entitled *American*

Women Writing Fiction: Memory, Identity, Family, Space edited by Mickey Pearlman for the University of Kentucky Press. Among other themes, Lassner analyzes how Phillips' mothers and daughters, particularly in *Machine Dreams*, create connection and continuity. Undoubtedly, the first wave of response to the writing of this gifted young woman will slowly give way to deeper investigation into her restless fiction.

BIBLIOGRAPHY

Works by Jayne Anne Phillips

Sweethearts. Carrboro, N.C.: Truck Press, 1976.
Counting. New York: Vehicle Editions, 1978.
Black Tickets. New York: Delacorte/Seymour Lawrence, 1979.
Machine Dreams. New York: Dutton/Seymour Lawrence, 1984.
Fast Lanes. New York: Vehicle Editions, 1984.

Interviews

Baker, James N. " 'Being Led by a Whisper.' " *Newsweek* 94 (October 22, 1979): 116–18.
Edelstein, David. "The Short Story of Jayne Anne Phillips: She Transforms Isolation and Dark Obsession into Exquisite Prose." *Esquire* 104 (December 1985): 106–12.
Gilbert, Celia. "Interview with Jayne Anne Phillips." *Publisher's Weekly* 225 (June 8, 1984): 65–66.
Hill, Dorothy Combs. "Interview with Jayne Anne Phillips." *South Carolina Review* 24:1 (Fall 1991): 53–73.
"How is Fiction Doing?" *New York Times Book Review* (December 14, 1980): 3.
Simpson, Mona. "An American Beauty." *Vogue* 174 (July 1984): 117–18.
Stanton, David M. "An Interview with Jayne Anne Phillips." *Croton Review* 9 (Spring–Summer 1986): 41–44.

Studies of Jayne Anne Phillips

Adams, Michael J. "Jayne Anne Phillips," 297–300 in *Dictionary of Literary Biography, 1980*. Detroit: Gale Research, 1981.
————. "Phillips, Jayne Anne (1952–   )," 481–83 in *Postmodern Fiction: A Bio-Bibliographical Guide*, ed. Larry McCaffery. Westport, Conn.: Greenwood, 1986.
Benét, Mary Kathleen. "Below the City on the Hill" (Rev. of *Machine Dreams*). *Times Literary Supplement* (November 23, 1984): 1359.
Bronfen, Elisabeth. "Between Nostalgia and Disenchantment: The Concept 'Home' in Jayne Anne Phillips' Novel *Machine Dreams*." *Arbeiten aus Anglistik und Amerikanistik* 13 (1988): 17–28.
Brown, Joseph. Rev. of *Black Tickets*. *America* 141 (December 8, 1979): 376.
Burke, Jeffrey. "Ineffable Pleasures" (Rev. of *Black Tickets*). *Harper's* 259 (September 1979): 99–100.

Carter, Liane Kupferberg. Rev. of *Machine Dreams*. *New Directions for Women* 13 (November/December 1984): 23.

Clemons, Walter. "A Family Wreckage" (Rev. of *Machine Dreams*). *Newsweek* 104 (July 16, 1984): 78.

Cushman, Keith. Rev. of *Black Tickets*. *Studies in Short Fiction* 18 (Winter 1981): 92–94.

Dillard, Annie. "Critics' Christmas Choices." *Commonweal* 106 (1979): 693–94.

Edelstein, David. "The Short Story of Jayne Anne Phillips: She Transforms Isolation and Dark Obsession into Exquisite Prose." *Esquire* 104 (December 1985): 106–12.

Edwards, T. R. Rev. of *Black Tickets*. *New York Review of Books* 27 (March 6, 1980): 43–45.

Greenwood, Gillian. "How It Happens" (Rev. of *Machine Dreams*). *Spectator* 253 (November 3, 1984): 28.

Grumbach, Doris. "Stories Caged in Glass" (Rev. of *Black Tickets*). *Books and Arts* 1 (November 23, 1979): 8–9.

Hulbert, Ann. Rev. of *Machine Dreams*. *New Republic* (December 24, 1984): 36.

———. "Jayne Anne Phillips." *New Republic* (September 2, 1985): 25.

Irving, John. "Stories with Voiceprints" (Rev. of *Black Tickets*). *New York Times Book Review* (September 30, 1979): 13, 28.

"Jayne Anne Phillips." *Harper's Bazaar* (October 1984): 213.

"Jayne Anne Phillips's *Fast Lanes*." *Booklist* (February 1, 1987): 809.

Jenks, Tom. "How Writers Live Today." *Esquire* (August 1985): 123.

Kakutani, Michiko. Rev. of *Fast Lanes*. *New York Times* (April 11, 1987): 11.

———. Rev. of *Machine Dreams*. *New York Times* (June 12, 1984): C17.

Lassner, Phyllis. "A Bibliography of Writings about Jayne Anne Phillips," 207–10 in *American Women Writing Fiction: Memory, Identity, Family, Space*, ed. Mickey Pearlman. Lexington: University of Kentucky Press, 1989.

———. "Jayne Anne Phillips: Women's Narrative and the Recreation of History," 193–206 in *American Women Writing Fiction: Memory, Identity, Family, Space*, ed. Mickey Pearlman. Lexington: University of Kentucky Press, 1989.

Lasdun, James. Rev. of *Machine Dreams*. *Encounter* (February 1985): 42.

Maguire, Gregory. Rev. of *Machine Dreams*. *Horn Book* (November/December 1984): 793.

"Major Authors in Minor Presses." *New York Times Book Review* (December 23, 1984): 4.

"Making It Big at 30." *Harper's Bazaar* (October 1984): 206.

McGowan, William. "*Machine Dreams*: Retooling Fiction." *Washington Monthly* (March 17, 1984): 42.

McInerney, Jay. "Lost on the Open Road" (Rev. of *Fast Lanes*). *New York Times Book Review* (May 3, 1987): 7.

Mellors, John. "American Nightmare" (Rev. of *Machine Dreams*). *Listener* 112 (December 1984): 30.

Merkin, Daphne. "Mastering the Short Story" (Rev. of *Black Tickets*). *New Leader* 62 (December 3, 1979): 18–19.

Moyer, L. L. Rev. of *Machine Dreams*. *Christianity and Crisis* 46 (July 14, 1986): 253–54.

Overland, Janneken, and Toril Moi. "Du et det su ser: Samtale med Jayne Anne Phillips." *Vinduet* 37 (1983): 23–33.

Peterson, Mary. "Earned Praise." *North American Review* 264 (Winter 1979): 77–78.

Phillips, Robert. "Recurring Battle Scars" (Rev. of *Machine Dreams*). *Commonweal* 111 (October 19, 1984): 567–68.

Pooley, E. "Jayne Anne Phillips' American Dream." *New York* (July 23, 1984): 14.

"Portrait of Jayne Anne Phillips." *Harper's Bazaar* (October 1984): 213.

Prescott, Peter S. "A Debut to Celebrate." *Newsweek* (October 22, 1979): 116.

"Publishing's New Starlets" [women writers]. *U.S. News and World Report* 101 (December 1, 1986): 61–63.

Skow, John. Rev. of *Machine Dreams*. *Time* (July 16, 1984): 69.

Tyler, Anne. "The Wounds of War. (Rev. of *Machine Dreams*). *New York Times Book Review* 89 (July 1, 1984): 3.

Walsh, John. "Ordinary Life" (Rev. of *Machine Dreams*). *Books and Bookmen* (December 1984): 25–26.

Yardley, Jonathan. "Jayne Anne Phillips: West Virginia Breakdown" (Rev. of *Machine Dreams*). *Washington Post Book World* (June 24, 1984): 3.

JOHN L. IDOL, JR.

Charles [McColl] Portis
(1933–   )

Such a blockbuster was *True Grit* (1968) that Charles Portis seemed destined to lose his previously established reputation as a fresh talent working in the traditions of comedic fiction and Southwestern humor, a reputation based on the publication of *Norwood* in 1966. *True Grit*, for all its comedy and humor, put more than one good boot in the camp of Western novelists. Subsequent novels showed Portis to be a writer of wide talent, one well versed in the traditions of fiction, whether comedic, satiric, picaresque, sociological, or psychological. His skillfully, carefully crafted work earned him a following among other writers.

In practicing his craft, Portis joins a tradition as old as the art of storytelling, the tradition followed by the poet of the *Epic of Gilgamesh*, by Homer, by the author of the legends of Hercules and Jason, and by Torquato Tasso, Miguel de Cervantes, Edmund Spenser, Thomas Nashe, John Bunyan, Henry Fielding, Mark Twain, and countless other writers—the tradition of putting a character on the road and recording what happens along the way. Portis' approach is thus a time-tested method of seeing how a character develops in his or her confrontation with the world at large. Except for long stretches of *Masters of Atlantis* (1985), all of Portis' novels feature protagonists discovering and measuring themselves in their travels. In that work, Lamar Jimmerson spends much of his time at home, but the larger world intrudes upon his quiet and indolent ways in the person of the restless Popper.

BIOGRAPHY

Charles McColl Portis was born in El Dorado, Arkansas, on December 28, 1933, the son of Samuel and Alice Waddell Portis. His father was a public school superintendent, and both parents were staunch Presbyterians, a fact that would bear fruit in the faith of Mattie Ross in *True Grit*. Portis attended public schools in Hamburg and other south Arkansas towns. Upon graduating from high school, he joined the Marine Corps, serving from 1952 to 1955 and rising to the rank of sergeant. After his discharge, he entered the University of Arkansas, where 3 years later he received a B.S. in journalism. For the next several years, he worked as a reporter, putting in stints at the *Commercial Appeal* in Memphis, the *Arkansas Gazette* in Little Rock, and the *Herald Tribune* in New York. His work in Manhattan enabled him to become better acquainted with many of the new breed of journalists, among them Jimmy Breslin, Dick Schaap, and Tom Wolfe. He continued to build a reputation for himself as a droll Southern wit, a figure he had cut with growing success in his columns for the *Arkansas Gazette*.

When the *Tribune* gave him one of its choicest plums, appointment as its London correspondent with the privilege of doing a personal column, it appeared that Portis was set for a distinguished career in journalism. But as Tom Wolfe put it: ''Portis quit cold one day; just like that, without warning. He returned to the United States and moved into a fishing shack in Arkansas. In six months he wrote a beautiful little novel called *Norwood*. Then he wrote *True Grit*, which was a best seller.'' The first of these appeared in 1966, the second in 1968. Ten years would pass before he published his third, *The Dog of the South* (1979). Six years later his fourth novel, *Masters of Atlantis* (1985), followed. Another 6 years later his fifth novel appeared, *Gringos* (1991); it reflects the time he spent in Mexico following the publication of *True Grit*. Meanwhile, he continues to live in Little Rock, after his extended stay in Mexico and Belize. He is little seen in Little Rock except in some favorite taverns, where he enjoys his life as a bachelor and celebrated raconteur and where he now occasionally does a piece of journalism.

He refuses to play the role of the artist and says little about himself in his correspondence, but he did write a *Newsweek* reviewer about how he came to realize the true value of his work. The discovery came, Portis says, when a friend's car was pillaged by thieves: '' 'They took everything . . . old envelopes, a broken screwdriver. . . . But they didn't touch *The Dog of the South*. They were probably right. If they hadn't heard of it, what were the chances it was any good?' ''

MAJOR THEMES

The tug between being on the road to somewhere and wanting to be at home doing everyday things in normal routines underlies all of Portis' novels and gives rise to his chief themes: Restlessness and the desire to plant roots. His quotation of a passage from Sir Thomas Browne as a preamble to *The Dog of the South* fixes these themes as central to Portis' purpose: ''Even Animals near the Classis of plants seem to have the most restlesse motions. The Summerworm of Ponds and plashes makes a long, waving motion; the hair-worm seldom lies still. He that would behold a very anomalous motion, may observe it in the Tortile and tiring stroaks of Gnatworms.'' Like Browne, Portis sees restlessness everywhere, both as a part of man's nature and as a result of some triggering event that puts homebodies on the road, where some of them may have events swirling to meet them as fast as Huck Finn found them confronting him as he rafted down the Mississippi. Norwood takes to the road to reclaim an unpaid debt; Mattie Ross rides off behind Rooster Cogburn and Texas Ranger LaBoeuf to track down her father's murderer, Tom Chaney; Raymond Midge drives all the way from Little Rock to Belize in search of his Ford Torino, taken by a friend who ran off with Midge's wife and his credit card; Lamar Jimmerson must at last leave his comfortable chair and messy surroundings at the Gnomon Society headquarters and end up in a mobile trailer in a Texas orange grove; and Jimmy Burns, the expatriate American protagonist of *Gringos*, Portis' latest novel, spends most of his time on Yucatan roads and rivers.

Like travelers from the time of Gilgamesh to that of Jack Kerouac and beyond, fortunate and unfortunate things befall Portis' characters. Norwood finds a wife but has his boots stolen; Mattie Ross brings out the best in Rooster Cogburn but loses her left arm; Raymond Midge recovers his wife, for a time, but not his beloved Torino; Lamar Jimmerson has leisure to do recreational research on arcane subjects but ends up being the puppet of a con artist who combines the worst features of Mark Twain's Duke and Dauphin; Jimmy Burns encounters an array of crooks and New Age seekers as he searches for an archaeologist amidst Mayan ruins.

Just as writers from François-Marie Voltaire, Jonathan Swift, Samuel Johnson, and Thomas Wolfe, among others, have been able to do in staging comic and tragic events for their characters, Portis shows that restlessness has its moments of both high humor and profound sadness. He presents this restlessness as a trait of Americans, as well as a universal fact of man's existence. Unlike the characters of the Beatniks or Barry Hannah, Portis' are granted some repose, some quiet moments when they can be at one with their surroundings, with their friends or family. Norwood comes back to Ralph, Texas, to settle down with his new wife and to be with his sister and brother-in-law; Mattie returns to Dardanelle in Yell County, Arkansas; Midge settles once again to his studies and musing in Little Rock; Jimmerson pours contentedly over his books in the decaying Temple of Gnomons in Indiana and, later, looks forward to a life of ease in Texas; and Burns, none too eagerly to be sure, is headed for a quieter life as coowner of a small Mexican hotel. In their travels, Portis' restless characters take a few hard knocks, learn some hard lessons, and encounter both good and despicable people; yet they can, in a sense, go home again, wiser, tougher, of course, but not soured.

Related to the theme of restlessness is spiritual dry rot, something little touched on in *Norwood* and *True Grit*, but a major concern in *The Dog of the South*, *Masters of Atlantis*, and *Gringos*. Although it could be argued that the shyster Grady Fring the Kredit King of *Norwood* and trigger-happy Rooster Cogburn of *True Grit* have poured little or no water on their spiritual roots for years, they live in far less arid spiritual zones than do Reo Symes of *The Dog of the South*,

Austin Popper of *Masters of Atlantis*, and the cluster of expatriate hippies infesting the towns and ruins of Yucatan. If Reo, Austin, and Dan, the leader of the hippies, were to find themselves in Dante's Inferno, they would surely be assigned to a far lower level of hell than the two former, the reason being the latter's greater abuse of the human intellect. All three seem to be intent on changing whatever environment they inhabit into a spiritual wasteland. Moreover, all three would disgust good-hearted and trusting Norwood and evoke a stern lecture from straitlaced Mattie Ross.

If they were to cross Mattie or do her wrong, she would be tireless in her pursuit of revenge, another of the important themes in Portis' works. It's the paramount one in *True Grit*, of course, for Mattie will make Tom Chaney pay for his crime, but it figures prominently in the other novels as well: Norwood gives one of Grady Fring's hot cars to a whore and abandons another when he discovers he has been hired to drive a stolen vehicle and tow a second; Midge wants to settle scores with Guy Dupree for taking his Torino; Pharris White seeks to capture and punish Popper for snubbing him when he tried to enter the Gnomon Society; Burns feels a special delight in killing Dan, in the guise of *El Mago*, at the City of Dawn. An element in most of these attempts for revenge is the sense that the abuser has treated the victim unfairly, that an injustice has been done. The theme of justice flows through every root and branch of Portis' writing.

Fairness is an important theme running throughout Portis's works, showing up first in Norwood's belief that his ex-Marine friend should have repaid him the seventy dollars he borrowed from him at Camp Pendleton. Fairness is one of the pillars of Mattie Ross's faith. The theme is taken up once again in Ray Midge's disgust upon finding that Guy Dupree left behind merely "a rusty little piece of basic transportation" when he fled with Ray's cherished and spotless Torino. But ironically, Ray does make it all the way to the Fair Play Hotel in faraway Belize in his search for Guy. There is much effort made by Lamar Jimmerson's friends to see that his role as one of the masters of Gnomonism isn't overshadowed by the claims and actions of a rival master, Sir Sidney Hen, and Jimmy Burns reveals his sense of fair play whether he is dealing with expatriated countrymen or native Mexicans.

Playing just at or below the surface of Portis' novels is the theme of love. Sometimes seriously but more often comically treated, this theme occurs in every work. To his and her surprise, Norwood and Rita Lee find love in a bus; Mattie Ross, despite her outbursts against Rooster Cogburn for his drunken and uncouth ways, comes to love the man and, following his death, wants his corpse buried near her home; Ray Midge and Norma patch things up in Belize and live contentedly in Little Rock until Norma once again becomes restless; Lamar and Fanny Jimmerson have a bond that never entirely breaks; and Jimmy Burns agrees that his carefree days of bachelorhood are over when Louise decides that they are meant for each other, if only to become the owners of a mom-and-pop hotel.

Central also to Portis' themes is his concern for how his countrymen use and abuse language. He appreciates its range, whether spoken by schoolmarmish Mattie or sloganeering Austin Popper; its color, as revealed by Rooster Cogburn or Edmund B. Ratner, "the world's smallest perfect man"; and its ability to show the quirks of human personality, as in the cases of Ray Midge and Cezar Golescu, the Swiftian-like Hungarian scientist who tries to extract gold from creeping bagweed in *Masters of Atlantis*. Portis takes note of the American tongue as it appears on billboards, placards, and walls; as it spills from the mouths of radio announcers; and as it does the work of advertisers, scribblers of graffiti, journalists, politicians, peddlers of arcane literature, and workaday America. He is more than chagrined by the slovenly speech of hippies and the metaphysical soulbutter spread by New Age advocates. His ear is as good as Mark Twain's or Sinclair Lewis's, his eyes as attentive as those of H. L. Mencken. And his disgust that Americans abuse their tongue is as profound as that of William Safire or Edwin Newman.

Like Twain, Lewis, and Mencken, Portis also explores through language how some Americans practice deceit and hypocrisy and try to conceal their inhumanity to man. Beginning with Grady Fring the Kredit King and continuing on through Colonel Stonehill, the horse trader in *True Grit*, Dr. Reo Symes in *The Dog of the South*, and Austin Popper, Sir Sidney Hen, and others in *Masters of Atlantis*, Portis presents slick, hustling, fast-talking characters capable of everything from spreading soulbutter to cranking out position papers for aspiring politicians. They prey on the innocence, trust, and piety of Portis' good-hearted people when they can, though characters as sharp as the precocious Mattie Ross seem able to spot a liar and hypocrite a mile off. Concern for these themes carries Portis along in ways similar to those of such humorists and satirists as Twain, Lewis, Wolfe, William Faulkner, Eudora Welty, and Flannery O'Connnor. He is thus able to have his say as a social critic without having to take to a soap box.

Perhaps the theme for which Portis will be remembered longest, however, is grit—true grit. We see so much of that trait in Rooster Cogburn, Ranger LaBoeuf, and especially Mattie Ross that we tend to overlook it in Norwood when he stands up to Grady Fring, when Ray Midge presses on single-mindedly through Mexico to retrieve his Torino, when Austin Popper defends Gnomonism in a Texas senate subcommittee hearing, when Jimmy Burns confronts a weird assortment of hippies and New Age seekers at a Mayan ruin. Portis likes to have his characters face odds, to test their mettle, to examine their spirits and wits. In this he inevitably places himself in the tradition of some of the language's greatest novelists—Fielding, Charles Dickens, Herman Melville, Twain, and Faulkner. Amidst all the humor, high jinks, and genial satire, he injects a noble indignation and a thought-provoking seriousness.

On the road, his characters have greater opportunities to face odds, have more occasions to test their mettle, and have more call to show their spirit and use their wit. Nevertheless, Portis no doubt feels more comfortable with characters on the go, for they can be continuously in action, even if some of them long for the quiet and rest of home. That longing creates a tension, adds another dimension to his characters, and reflects Portis' habit of sticking around Little Rock until struck by wanderlust. More than anything else, that time on the road provides windows and doors to the follies and foibles of American life and offers Portis the material he needs to portray the values and vicissitudes of American society, whether it be late Victorian or contemporary. As his characters hit the road, Portis endows them with enough homebred values and memories to make them either dream of, or head for, home (or a reasonable substitute) before his novels end. They light out for new territories as his novels open but try their best to be back on familiar turf before his works close. It is on the road, however, that Portis defines them and adds them to that long list extending from Gilgamesh down to the accidental tourist and beyond.

SURVEY OF CRITICISM

Portions of *Norwood* first appeared under the title ''Traveling Light'' in the June 18 and July 2, 1966, issues of the *Saturday Evening Post*. Upon publication of the novel, reviews began appearing in the popular press, the critics linking his name with Mark Twain and Ring Lardner as they sought to describe the quality and flavor of Portis' talents. Martin Levin, writing for the *New York Times Book Review* (July 24, 1966), was reminded of Vladimir Nabokov's *Lolita*. Levin observed that Norwood's travels covered ''the same territory as Humbert Humbert: the neon desert invested with the totems of midcentury America. But Mr. Portis's simple hero, unlike Mr. Nabokov's, is *with it*. Roller Dromes, bus stations, bowling alleys, chili parlors—these are his habitat and he thrives among them.'' Reviewers for the Worcester *Telegram* and the *Washington Post* also found *Norwood* to be a comment on America: The critic for the *Telegram* said that Norwood ''makes no comments and no observations on America; instead he is America himself'' (as quoted from the back cover of the Ballentine paperback edition). Elaborating on that point, the *Washington Post* reviewer explained that Portis ''populates his exotic landscape with odd but clearly homespun America types, and in his dialogue he has caught to perfection the special intonations of American vocal chords, the motley concerns—ranging from eternal salvation to a quick buck—that occupy the American soul. . . . If it weren't so darned funny, it would be a tragedy'' (August 21, 1966).

Here then was sounded a note that had to be played, and justly so, time and again when Portis' later novels appeared. For all his humor and comic escapades, Portis had something sober and sobering to say about how Americans spun out their lives. Because it was a blend of parody, the American tall tale, a revenge story with an avenger as monomaniacal as Ahab, and an adventure fable joined to an initiation narrative, *True Grit* evoked the greatest outpouring of criticism that any Portis novel would receive. Brian Garfield's review for the *Saturday Review* (June 29, 1968) aptly encapsulated what others were saying:

Charles Portis's new novel, *True Grit*, will lift the standards [of novels on the American West] still higher—and may even take its place as an American classic. This remarkably moving book possesses a universality long lacking in American fiction. As delightful to a twelve-year-old as to a cultivated adult, *True Grit* is a lively, uproarious high adventure. It is also a commentary on the American character, then and now. Although the tale is straightforward, told in an ingenuous nineteenth-century style, its nuances are endless.

Agreeing with Garfield's discovery that the novel appealed to young and old readers alike, Walker Percy said: "It is a delight. Mattie Ross from near Dardanelle, Arkansas, is here to stay, like Huck Finn. This must be true because I read it with complete delight and so did my 13-year-old daughter" (excerpt from dust jacket of the book club edition). The association with Huck Finn appeared again in Charles Elliott's review in *Life* (June 14, 1968): "Charles Portis does a whole lot better in the Huck genre than anybody since Twain has."

Such remarks were prompted in part by the character of Mattie Ross, but mostly by Portis' handling of point of view. As the first-person narrator, the story is Mattie's. Elliott's remark speaks for several critics: "[Portis] has the unusual ability to slide inside a character so neatly you hardly know he's there. Portis may have his name on the title page of *True Grit*, but he doesn't come into it. Only Mattie does." She comes in as a plucky, prim, pious, talkative, determined, Bible-quoting, law-and-order old maid, who in the 1920s is looking back to the 1880s when she left her home near Dardanelle to seek revenge for her father's death. The way in which she told the story and the time when the novel appeared—the era of the movie *Bonnie and Clyde*—brought the label "camp," the best expression of that classification coming from the review in *Newsweek* (July 22, 1968): "[Mattie's] voice is still full of true grit, spunky, perky, taking no bull from anyone. Her story is pure Western, but her voice is a perfectly sustained take-off on Wild West lingo, bluff, brave and, by this point in history, camp."

So impressed were these early reviewers by Mattie's voice and character that they gave but sparse attention to other characters. Rooster Cogburn's rough, rowdy ways and gruff wit are mentioned, but only Elliott seems to have sensed what might lie ahead for the right Hollywood star: "*True Grit* is good enough for me, it is good enough for you, and if it isn't good enough for some movie company, then the free enterprise system really is going to hell." Movie rights were sold for $300,000, and John Wayne, in the role of Rooster Cogburn, won the only Oscar of his career for his portrayal of Portis' camp hero.

Helped along by the success of the screen version, *True Grit* sold well over 1,500,000 paperback copies after having enjoyed sales of over 60,000 hardbound copies in its twenty-one week run on the best-seller list. Nothing else from Portis' hand comes anywhere close to these figures. Impressive as the work was in the marketplace, most critics agree that the quality of its art will keep the novel around and will give it a place as an American classic. What to label it has proved something of a challenge, however. Is it a parody of the old dime novels, Hollywood Westerns, or adventure stories like the *Perils of Pauline*? Is it an initiation story with a Western setting? Is it a camp tragicomedy? Is it a prose mock epic? Not satisfied with any of these terms, R. Baird Shuman argued that the novel might best be called an entwicklungsroman, a development novel.

The decade-long wait for Portis's third novel, *The Dog of the South*, left some readers disappointed, others pleased. Most outspoken in his disappointment was Larry L. King, whose review in the *New York Times Book Review* (July 29, 1979) called this latest odyssey a "lesser book." King found Ray Midge tedious, a piddler. Writing for *Newsweek* (July 9, 1979), Walter Clemons spoke most succinctly for those who found the novel pleasing: "Midge's voice is precise, persnickety and daintily convinced of its own sweet reasonableness. His narrative is a classic piece of American gab, in the line of Lardner's 'The Golden Honeymoon' and Welty's 'Why I Live at the P.O.' Intent and absorbed, Midge is gravely certain we will find every detail of his absurd junket interesting and each of his decisions logical. And so we do. He is a perfectly wonderful creation, and reading 'The Dog of the South' is like being held down and tickled." Once again an association was made between Portis' art and traditional comic modes, this time by the *New Yorker* reviewer: "Given the space of a sentence, one might simply say that the hero is a cross between Buster Keaton and Don Quixote—innocent, generous to a fault, indefatigable, and perfectly deadpan—and that Charles Portis blessed him with a supremely funny adventure."

Although the novel was a selection for the Book of the Month Club, it never made its way to the best-seller list. Though engaging in their own way, Ray Midge, his wife, Norma, Dr. Reo Symes, Jack Wilkie, and a host of other characters obviously lacked the appeal of Mattie Ross and Rooster Cogburn. A few critics were quick to respond to Portis' satiric glimpses at American life as seen on the road in Arkansas and Texas and as witnessed among expatriates in Mexico and British Honduras. Yet Ray Midge, the semiprofessional student and Civil War history buff, as a questing avenger wasn't Mattie Ross. His perils were far more mundane, less camp. In short, this third novel seemed not to be read on its own terms.

But it could be said that Portis was becoming more cerebral, that he wanted to explore the nature and quality of the American mind. At least that was the direction his fourth novel, *Masters of Atlantis*, took. Admitting that the handle applied to Portis had not held, Gene Lyons in his *Newsweek* review (September 30, 1985) wrote: "Just when a critic thinks he has a handle on Southern writing, along comes someone like Charles Portis. Not only does the 51-year-old Little Rock author bear little resemblance to any other writer of the region; none of his previous books—'Norwood,' 'True Grit,' and 'The Dog of the South'—have much in common either. Now comes 'Masters of Atlantis,' by far the oddest of Portis's peculiarly and terribly funny novels." John Anthony West put the case against Portis for trying something different. West's review in the *New York Times Book Review* (October 27, 1985) found Portis' chronicle of the 60-year history of the Gnomon Society dull, a record of a bland group of people, a missed opportunity to do something comic and satiric about America's sects, cults, and secret societies. Christopher Lehmann-Haupt, writing for the *New*

York Times (October 7, 1985), acknowledged that Portis wins his highest marks when he writes about characters on a comic quest and then added: "The only trouble with Lamar Jimmerson as a quester is that he lives a life of the mind." Yet he is prepared to find this intellectual quest "exhilarating." "A purpose infuses the craziness, a sense that the author is after something bigger than jokes. He is giving us a picture of Main Street made silly, of Babbittry gone goofy. Yet for all its ridiculousness, there is a sweet, dopey integrity to Lamar Jimmerson's innocence." Moving the discussion one step further toward the cerebral, Thomas M. Disch in *The Nation* (November 30, 1985) comments on the novel as a kind of American *Candide* with Jimmerson as a Candide-like doughboy caught up in a swirl of "quixotic self-deception" in a world seeking gurus, millenial prophets, new faiths, and fresh politics. Acknowledging that Portis has mingled the comic with the serious, Disch argued:

There is not a chapter of the twenty-four without its bounty of good jokes, all framed on the ageless opposition between quixotic self-deception and public perception. Portis, like Dickens, takes an unashamed delight in grotesquery and freakishness and in the intractableness of stupidity, as though it were a prodigious weed to be marveled at. Indeed, the closest literary cousin to *Masters of Atlantis* I can think of is *The Pickwick Papers*, with which it shares not only a climactic courtroom scene but also a reconciling holiday feast.

It is that feast that disturbs Disch, for here he finds Portis being too charitable to "his crew of numbskull mystagogues." He sees in his acceptance a trend toward an American tolerance of a split between the bright and the dumb, a mandarin and a simple shepherd class. Here we have come a far distance from the good-natured trek of Norwood and the dogged quest of Mattie Ross. To the surprise of some of Portis' readers, serious thought must now be given to his comic characters and adventures.

  Gringos represents a fuller fusion of Portis' early and later art, bringing together his tested pattern of comic adventure and misadventure and his growing concern for ideas and values. His success in combining the best of his material and art is reflected in the dust-jacket tribute from fellow novelist Larry McMurtry: "I've always thought Charles Portis had a wonderful talent—original, quirky, exciting. *Gringos* demonstrates that he's only gotten better. It's an engaging, touching book."

  Academic critics have been slow to explore Portis' life and works, the earliest remarks coming from Shuman in an essay attempting to fit a proper label on *True Grit*, the final decision being to categorize it as an entwicklungsroman. In affixing the label, Shuman examines Mattie Ross's character closely, necessarily because she is seen as the person undergoing development. To define Mattie's character and conduct, Shuman must also explore Rooster Cogburn, the result being the most thorough study of Portis' methods of characterization published in the 1970s. Also concerned with Portis' depiction of Mattie is John Ditsky, who considered the terms "grit" and "true grit" as understood in nineteenth-century fiction and in Portis' novel. He goes beyond Mattie's days in the Oklahoma Territory as avenger and sees her as "a pitiable creature who surrenders her womanhood in order to do a man's work." Indeed, she is a female Huck Finn, he says, but, having surrendered both her innocence and femininity, she lives out the rest of her days a kind of Miss Watson championing a puritanical code of conduct and enjoying her bank shares. Seeking a man with true grit, she found him within herself, thus fulfilling "an American classic myth: the good little girl who turned herself into a self-made man.'"

Combining a brief biographical sketch with criticism of Portis' first three novels, Michael E. Connaughton's essay in *Dictionary of Literary Biography. American Writers since World War II* is the most extensive account of Portis' place in American letters except John L. Idol's in *Beacham's Popular Fiction in America*. Connaughton looks briefly at Portis' career as a journalist, finding it highlighted in an article for *Saturday Evening Post* entitled "The New Sound from Nashville" (February 12, 1966) and displaying his "ear for dialogue and emphasis on striking, almost novelistic detail." He then examines Portis' three published novels, offers a plot summary of each, comments on themes and style, analyzes major characters, and succinctly remarks on the nature of Portis' assessment of the American scene. He considers *True Grit* as Portis' "best work," a bildungsroman with large chunks of regionalism tossed in. For him, Portis is "the whitest of white humorists," a writer carrying the tradition of Southwestern humor and merging it in fresh ways with narrative and descriptive practices taken from new journalism.

Idol's piece follows a reference book format calling for a discussion of Portis' one best-seller, *True Grit*. It covers the novel's publishing history, critical reception, social concerns, themes, characters, techniques, literary precedents, and adaptations. It explores the novel in greater depth and breadth than any previously published essay and links its themes, characters, and techniques to each of Portis' other novels, including *Masters of Atlantis*. Attempting to suggest Portis' literary forebears, Idol finds folkloristic traces of the oral literature as well as similarities to Cervantes, Voltaire, Hugh Henry Brackenridge, Johnson J. Hooper, George Washington Harris, Twain, Welty, Faulkner, and O'Connor. He argues that if Portis leaves no other literary mark behind him, he will have carved a special place for Mattie Ross among the most memorable of our nation's fictional creations. Finally, Idol observes that Portis' lean style borrows much from journalism while at the same time revealing linguistic variety in his use of such widely discrete modes as deadpan narration, domestic sentimentality, advertising jargon, and political sloganeering.

BIBLIOGRAPHY

Works by Charles Portis

"The New Sound from Nashville." *Saturday Evening Post* (February 12, 1966): 30.
"Traveling Light." *Saturday Evening Post* (June 18, 1966): 54; (July 2, 1966): 48.

Norwood. New York: Simon and Schuster, 1966.
True Grit. New York: Simon and Schuster, 1968.
The Dog of the South. New York: Knopf, 1979.
Masters of Atlantis. New York: Knopf, 1985.
Gringos. New York: Simon and Schuster, 1991.

Studies of Charles Portis

Connaughton, Michael E. "Charles Portis," 264–68 in *Dictionary of Literary Biography.*
    American Novelists since World War II. Detroit: Gale Research, 1980.
Ditsky, John. "True 'Grit' and 'True Grit.' " *Ariel* 4, No. 2 (1973): 18–31.
Idol, John L. "Charles Portis." *Beacham's Popular Fiction in America,* Vol. 3. Wash-
    ington, D.C.: Beacham Publishing, 1986.
Shuman, R. Baird. "Portis' *True Grit:* An Adventure or *Entwicklungsroman? English
    Journal* 59 (1970): 367–70.

THOMAS M. CARLSON

Padgett Powell
(1952–)

Few contemporary Southern writers have had a more auspicious literary debut than Padgett Powell. His first novel, *Edisto* (1985), received glowing tributes from Donald Barthelme and Walker Percy, got excellent reviews in the *New York Times*, *Time*, and *Newsweek*, was nominated for an American Book Award, and was purchased by Metro-Goldwyn-Mayer. Two years later, Powell's second novel, *A Woman Named Drown* (1987), received fewer enthusiastic reviews, and many readers who praised the first novel were openly disappointed. Since *Drown*, he has published several literary reviews, a short childhood memoir, and a collection of short fiction entitled *Typical* (1991), but Powell, described by Saul Bellow as "the best American writer of the younger generation," has not yet fulfilled the expectations raised by the publication of *Edisto*.

BIOGRAPHY

Like Taurus and Mary Constance Baker, the "no bio" characters in *Edisto* and *Drown*, Powell has been reluctant to disclose the details of his own life. The young narrator of *Edisto*, Simons Manigault, who is conducting his own inquiry into the facts of life, compares himself to an inquisitive reader: "It's like you've seen the text and now you can consult the critics or the artist." Simons interviews the artist, a promiscuous teenager, and discovers that "artists are somewhat famous . . . for playing around with people who ask them what it all means, which is why one interview spawns more critical essays than the books ever did. So I had to be careful."

Powell was born in Gainesville, Florida, on April 25, 1952, and raised in Tallahassee, Jacksonville, and Florence, South Carolina. In 1975, he graduated from the College of Charleston with a degree in chemistry. In 1982 he received an M.A. in creative writing from the University of Houston. *Edisto* was his graduate project, directed by Donald Barthelme. Powell's literary awards include a Whiting Writers' Award in 1986, a Rome Fellowship from the American Academy of Arts and Letters in 1987, and a Fulbright Award in 1989. He is currently a member of the department of English at the University of Florida in Gainesville. In 1984 he married Sidney Wade, a poet whom he met at the University of Houston, and they have one child, born in 1987. Other particulars of his life, in Powell's own words, may be apocryphal.

Powell says he first contemplated a career in writing at an early age after his maternal grandmother, Rubylea Hall, a popular writer of romance fiction, dedicated one of her novels to him. He was a sports reporter in junior high and high school and also edited an underground newspaper named *Tough Shit* that was banned by school authorities. At the College of Charleston he wrote for the school newspaper and majored in English until poor teaching and poor grades convinced him to change his major to chemistry where the teachers "know something about form and linearity and cleanliness." Powell briefly undertook graduate study in chemistry at the University of Tennessee, but found life outside the lab more educational. Like Al, the narrator of *A Woman Named Drown*, he dropped out of graduate school and traveled around the Southeast. The rest of his life story is documented in interviews that sound as understated and consciously crafted as his fiction: The Houston roofer who enrolled in graduate school to meet girls, wrote *Edisto* as an academic exercise, dreamed up the subject of *A Woman Named Drown* while sleeping in class, and continues to fish and drink beer when he isn't meeting creative writing classes at Kate's Fish Camp outside of Gainesville, Florida.

This laid-back description of a very successful career confirms what Al discovers in *Drown*: that "life is self-directed drama." In his childhood memoir, "Hitting Back," Powell describes his mother as "an accomplished costumer" whose theatricality [is] undiluted." Further descriptions of a "pistoling, noveling," maternal grandmother and an equally independent paternal grandmother "who belted jiggers and shuffled cards" indicate the origins of Mary Constance Baker, the woman named Drown, who is the most lovingly rounded of all characters in Powell's fiction.

MAJOR THEMES

Mary's literary ancestor may be James Joyce's deliquescent Molly Bloom, who also yearns for younger men, but her predecessor in Powell's own fiction is the "Doctor, Duchess, Soldier" who becomes "Penelope" and finally Simons's "Mother" at the end of *Edisto*. Hard drinking, with a "purple heart" from sexual warfare, she also has an affair with a younger man, exhibits androgynous qualities (Simons calls her "the man in charge"), and, like all women in Powell's fiction, is painfully lonely. While *Edisto* presents a picture of the traditional Southern family in trouble, it also parodies sentimental Southern themes. As Simons puts it, the "Southern Barony" has been reduced to a "two-square-mile patch of desert where the greatest natural resource is a toss-up between sand flea and mosquito.'' The ''planter'' (Simons's father) has abandoned the family and the land and lives off other people's troubles (he's a lawyer). The faithful servant flees, leaving the ''planter's wife . . . short on domestics.'' The future generation of the South (Simons) finds itself a little lost and undomesticated. A mentor mysteriously appears for this Telemachus figure, a ''process server'' who enables Simons to survive the process of puberty. He also performs ''paralegal service'' for the Duchess while her lawyer husband is absent: Simons discovers they have been sleeping together. The identity of this mysterious stranger remains ambiguous throughout the novel, but several mythological allusions (especially to *The Iliad* and *The Odyssey*) suggest a sequence of roles moving toward a resolution to the sexual battle at the heart of the book. The stranger may be an ex-marine from Parris Island cohabiting with the Duchess in a Troy-like edifice built on ''Juno Boulevard by a depressed speculator'' (he moves in when the servant, Athenia, leaves). He may be a divine guest—an ''Islander's God''—who inspires Simons's father to return to his Penelope. Simons calls him ''Taurus,'' a sobriquet derived from the symbol on Taurus's favorite drink, Schlitz Malt Liquor. The commercial slogan serves as admonition to the reader throughout the novel: ''Watch out for the Bull.'' At the end of the novel Simons's father takes the warning literally and hauls Penelope and Telemachus off to an ''Arab-financed, model railroader's plot of Paradise'' called Hilton Head.

Taurus comes from Powell's literary past, an alter ego who appeared in sketches Powell wrote while he was a student at the College of Charleston. Powell says that early drafts of *Edisto* used a third-person narrator with Taurus controlling the point of view. Shifting to the 12-year-old first-person narrator provided ''a more human, confused, distorted mediator.''

Simons, like Al, his older counterpart in *A Woman Named Drown*, is searching for the right role in life. Both novels are picaresque narratives in which Adamic characters seek identity in a post-Vietnam America littered with ''veterans.'' The children of Southern gentry, they begin their quests by leaving the future (their parents' expectations) in the past and becoming participants in life's drama. Truancy initiates the process. Al abandons his doctoral studies in chemistry as well as a substantial family inheritance in order to hit the road and experience life as a process rather than a set of predetermined goals. Simons escapes the educational regime established by his mother (''the doctor''). Both become writers who record life's experiences. Simons's ''assignment'' begins when his father leaves; Al starts taking ''lab notes on life'' after his fiancée breaks off the engagement and he flees the lab. Both abandon what Simons calls a ''then-next'' existence: He sadly remembers the past; his mother has planned his future. Each discovers the ''now'' with the help of a companion or guide about 20 years older who replaces an absent parent and introduces him to the serious play of life. *Edisto* describes the end of Simons's ''boy act'' and the beginning of puberty. A fortunate fall from the back of a school bus and eventual weaning from a black bar named the ''Baby Grand'' facilitate the process. Along the way Simons discovers, while overhearing his previously estranged parents make love, that "chemistry never changes." His life, despite its apparent randomness, is assuming some kind of design with "attainable hopes"—a family is about to be reunited—but Simons clearly understands and appreciates the sexual euphemism pertaining to body chemistry. Soon after this scene, Taurus the bull disappears from the novel, leaving Simons a gift that sums up the facts of life for this observant teenager. The gift is "an old wooden stereo-viewer" containing one card with "two separate pictures . . . of chickens in the air." When Simons focuses the picture, the chickens "suddenly . . . fell together" into a "glorious" cockfight witnessed by "wild spectators."

Such language play is unrelenting in both novels. It can be dazzling, but it can also cloy. In rejecting lives that are all work and no play, both narrators become the pawns of stage and sports metaphors. As if fulfilling the desire of Simons's father who wanted his son to play baseball, not just read books, Al leaves graduate school and moves in with an older woman who fits "like a ball glove handed to you in the seventh inning, used by someone else during the critical innings." Obviously they play ball. Like Simons, Al also discovers in the lab of life that chemistry never changes and concludes that his life has been "a tour of titration, admiring the true titraters of life as I found them." Beyond its scientific usage, "titration" is a euphemism for alcoholic consumption that Al learned from members of his chemistry department—in both novels the protagonists "find themselves" in bars where other people are getting lost. Unfortunately, through the transmogrifying process of "new utterance," "titration" becomes "tit rating" at the end of *Drown*, a behavioral pattern reminiscent of the beach scene in *Edisto* where Simons discovers his "first love," a "big wobbly blessing" who provides him with a vision of "tits floating." Clearly, Mary Baker, the soft "trained glove" of *Drown* is the embodiment of Simons's brief "vision of snug harbor."

Both women amply demonstrate what Simons describes as "a smudge of abandon." The phrase aptly describes the theory of language developed in *Drown*. It is not limited to double entendres. It includes literal name-dropping as these precocious Adams try to describe a new world with new names. Al considers "the proper use of new utterance, its true relation . . . to the formulations I have been borne along on." Puns are the most important component of new utterance. Born again, both narrators discover the world through a language as hyperactive as themselves. Tumbling syntax, elliptical constructions, sentences as "back-broke" as the best of Donald Barthelme's constitute a linguistic rebellion against what Simons calls "the alphabet of success" spoken by the "country-club set" on Hilton Head. Simons learns to jive at the Baby Grand where "they go for something larger than words, but no essays . . . like these James Brown guitar riffs of five notes that run twenty minutes, and then one of the five notes goes sharp and a statement is made. A whole evening hums, and then there's a new note—razor out." Powell's style in both novels is a series of "riffs" (short rhythmic phrases) with occasional sharp notes that sometimes make statements with the "razor out." But no one is ever hurt, for this is part of the process of play on a mock-Shakespearean world stage. Both narrators cease being spectators and participate in that drama. Seeking the right role involves finding the right word or phrase. Simons moves from being his mother's protégé to becoming a son. Al moves from his role as supporting actor for a lonely actress to becoming the star of the show after Mary abandons him in Florida, allowing him to choose his own role. He chooses to be a son, a scholar, a businessman, and her lover. At that point a rather tawdry road show that often seems to be little more than dress rehearsal (Al wears the clothes of Mary's dead husband) becomes a standing engagement back home. Or perhaps the play comes to an end. Mary, a "no bio" actress through much of the novel ("Mary is never Mary"), acquires a past in the final pages, and all roles are abandoned as art becomes life.

If the world is a stage, Al discovers that all the actors (not just poets, lunatics, and lovers) are of imagination all compact; however, he also finds within this seemingly random comedy of errors something of great constancy. Her name is Mary *Constance* Baker, an earth angel who turns this novel into a comic quest for the "real" Mary, serene in her garden. She calls herself "Muhv" (my love? mother/lover?). Like Shakespeare's *A Midsummer Night's Dream*, this novel reveals how close the tradition of courtly love can be to romantic farce.

Such unlikely syntheses describe the "hybrid vigor" of both novels. Synthetic characters unite opposing qualities: Mary is mother lover; Taurus may be half black; Minnie, the titrating maid in Al's building, is half white; and Al's most important "function" is to serve as "reagent" or "binding surfactant," attempting to unite the random elements in his life. This process includes finding a common purpose in the seemingly conflicting disciplines of art, religion, and science. Life is "self-directed drama," life is the search for Mary, but only chemistry "never changes." As he leaves his laboratory studies of inorganic chemistry to engage in the pleasures of organic chemistry with Mary, Al attempts to graph life and plot his function—he never escapes the scientist within himself. Neither can Padgett Powell who says he has "a poet's degree in chemistry." Pseudo-science is a game he plays more skillfully than any other recent fiction writer except Walker Percy. Both move casually from science to metaphysics in their fiction. Al's formulation of a "reaction-series theory of life" is a fuzzy amalgam of modern physics and Eastern mysticism that resembles the central argument in Fritz Capra's *Tao of Physics*. Faced with the dilemma of the scientist who can measure position or momentum but not both, Al chooses to measure momentum. Abandoning his role as objective observer and choosing to participate in the experiment of life, Al verifies quantum theory, which destroyed the concept of the world as separated from the scientist. Discovering that all phenomena in this world of change are dynamically interrelated, he confirms the findings of the atomic physicists Heisenberg and Chew, but sounds suspiciously like Blake and Emerson or those Zen masters of the Beat Movement, Ginsberg and Kerouac. From this perspective, "new utterance" is a seemingly random spontaneous description of life as a series of reactions, interractions, collisions, and resonances that transcend explanations but take on a mysterious order of their own.

This kind of theoretical exploration in *Drown* has disenchanted readers who admired the more conventional narrative structures of *Edisto*. Powell believes that *Drown* is a better novel but has described the theoretical basis of his book as "hokey." Such hokum elicits an ironic response, for *Drown* parodies all theoretical approaches to life, and its conclusion suggests that the novel, like life, is simpler than it appears to be. As in *Edisto*, "the old order" yields to "new business," which turns out to be "the family business." In both novels the narrators come to terms with their fathers and mothers. Freed from the constrictions of expectation, they become what their parents want them to be.

Given his inclination to parody all categories of thought, especially recent literary theory, the influences of other writers are difficult to trace in Powell's fiction. In his writing assignments, Simons alludes to Williams, Welty, Warren, and Faulkner; however, *Edisto* is more obviously indebted to Twain, O'Connor, and Percy (Powell dismisses any association between *Edisto* and *Catcher in the Rye*, but several reviewers including Percy have noted similarities). Powell's use of grotesque characters, his reliance on parody, his focus on language as subject, and his playful use of pseudoscience in *A Woman Named Drown* suggest the influences of John Kennedy Toole and Barry Hannah, but especially the fiction of John Barth, Robert Coover, Thomas Pynchon, and Donald Barthelme, "my literary uncle, my coach." The structure of *Drown* resembles Barthelme's "principle of collage" in which "unlike things are stuck together to make, in the best case, a new reality," and both of Powell's novels, like those of Barthelme, use mythic frames within which fragments of life are assembled and vaguely ordered. *Edisto* is a Telemachiad in which the son witnesses the reuniting of his "Penelope and Ulysses." It is also an undivine comedy in which "Vergil" is a one-legged exhibitionist. Reason is not a compelling force in either book, but in its movement toward Mary, serene in her garden, *A Woman Named Drown* is Powell's mock Paradiso.

Al's reaction-series theory of life is the thematic equivalent of Pynchon's "entropy," and Powell may share Pynchon's aversion to biography; however, he seems closer to Barth than to any other contemporary writer or literary theoretician except Barthelme. Like several of Barth's novels, *Edisto* and *Drown* exhibit remarkable symmetry, and in his best fiction Powell rises above the disjunction and irrationalism of typical postmodern writing to achieve what Barth calls "synthesis or transcension of . . . antitheses," creating "a fiction more democratic in its appeal."

Powell's short fiction, much of it written since the publication of *Drown*, constitutes the collection of twenty-three stories called *Typical*. Most of the works of prose clearly indicate the influence of postmodern style and thought. "Flood" is a dream-like fragment about perception, language, and "today's poet" who knows little about either. Like some of Barthelme's "verbal objects," it begins with an elaborately complex parenthetical construction, moves toward increasingly simple and lucid sentences, but refuses to make a statement. The flood itself metaphorically represents the life-as-process theory developed in *Drown*, but sheer momentum allows no time for plot or character to emerge. The reader is likely to agree with the narrator who concludes that "very little in a good flood makes sense."

Pop nihilism is the subject of "Dr. Ordinary" and other brief allegorical sketches such as "Mr. Desultory" and "Miss Resignation" in which Powell assumes the role of an American Becket trying to shake the habit: "Dr. Ordinary found solace in nothing." The title story of the collection, "Typical," a Pushcart Prize selection and included in *Best American Short Stories 1990*, provides a more complex portrait of nothingness. A hostile first-person confession of "trash" by an unemployed boozed-up blue-collar worker who has gone from a then-next to a then-now existence, the story provides unsettling moments of amusement amid sordid surroundings. Another role player, this narrator calls himself "John Payne . . . a common long-term drut." His episodic recital of how you become nobody deconstructs the story he is telling: "Not being worth being listened to is the discovery we make in our life." Describing the seeds of white racism and foreshadowing certain domestic tragedy, the sociological surface of this narrative hides a Cain-Abel plot that briefly appears at the end, but language once again is Powell's primary concern. Instead of forging community ties, language throughout the story is an instrument of destruction. In the final paragraph this "typical" Cain-like narrator acknowledges his guilt, contemplates self-destruction, and abandons language as a weapon: "I don't feel so hot about running at the mouth. . . . What call is it to drill people in their ears?"

Although such stories may reflect Powell's frustration with readers and publishers who prefer more conventional fare, this collection does not indicate that he is contemplating early retirement. He uses sharply honed language to drill beneath the typical and the ordinary to an inside narrative that continues his commentary on biography, language, and art. The results are clever, often amusing, but uninvolving. Too often character is reduced to form, form to language; and the reader is left to contemplate the contours of new utterance, or nothing at all. Al stated the dangers of such linguistic exploration in *Drown*: "The maker of new utterance is taking a chance that he will not close the gap toward meaning, that he may in fact widen it."

The most recent stories included in *Typical* reveal an attempt to close that gap. "Mr. Irony" is an allegorical spoof of postmodern language and themes in which the picaresque quest in *Edisto* and *Drown* becomes a worldwide pursuit of nothingness by noncharacters who only start to develop when they find themselves in the backwoods of Georgia and South Carolina. Following a wickedly funny scene on a logging truck with some backwoods grotesques, the narrator is shocked into real feeling and perception and abandons allegory: He even abandons the story he has concocted, running off to Mexico with his girl to start—we assume—a real life. Described at the beginning of the story as a

"resistant student," the narrator at the end decides "to defect" from the tutelage
of Mr. Irony. In leaving this alter ego for "certain final things, in the nature of
excretions and animal noises and the quality of ardor" (things that Mr. Irony
"chooses not to know") is Powell, like William Butler Yeats, returning to the
rag and bone shop of the heart?

"The Winnowing of Mrs. Schuping" suggests a turn in that direction. Em-
ulating the title character of "Mr. Irony Renounces Irony," Powell kicks irony—
like his old clothes—"into the clothes hamper," and decides instead to be
"surprisy." Mrs. Schuping is a surprisy antitype of Faulkner's Miss Emily
Grierson whose Homer Barron (the 300-pound local sheriff) leaves a living
impression in her bed and on her character. Possessing more real life than any
creature in Powell's fiction since Mary Constance Baker, Mrs. Schuping may
indicate that Powell is moving away from allegory toward comically grotesque
but sympathetically developing characters. As usual in his fiction, the theory is
bluntly stated toward the end of the story: "She felt herself becoming a character
in the gravitational pull of the sheriff despite, she realized, efforts nearly all her
life not to become a character—except for calling herself Mrs. Schuping." This
story may indicate a movement back toward conventional narrative structure,
abandoned since *Edisto*. Its most unique feature is the breezy third-person omniscient narrator who replaces the first-person actor found in most of Powell's
fiction.

SURVEY OF CRITICISM

Although Powell disclaims autobiography in *Edisto*—"I was not anywhere
near as perceptive as [Simons] was"—his childhood memoir, "Hitting Back,"
suggests otherwise. An album of subjective "snapshots" describing his early
acceptance of people out of the mainstream, especially blacks, "Hitting Back"
echoes many of Simons's observations about the regulars at the Baby Grand.
Powell's interest in the underclass may have crystallized while he was working
as a roofer in Houston. In interviews he has described enjoying the manual labor
and, in particular, the people: "I got to rub elbows with people with no expectations." They become the most precisely and affectionately crafted creatures in
his novels, but they usually remain in the background. Although Al contemplates
hiring several of these "better fools" to help him run his future "business,"
we never see him do so. In fact both narrators end up with comfortable middle-
class lives, materially far better off than they began. Al's reward for dropping
out is a Ph.D., a $2 million inheritance, and the favors of Mary. Such romantic
farce prompted T. Coraghessan Boyle to comment in a review: "While the
suggestion is that [Al] has been liberated and humanized by his experience, as
Simons Manigault was by his, I am not convinced. I can't help thinking that
despite his protestations to the contrary, he has merely been slumming." More
negative reviews focus on Al's "anti-actualization quotient" defined as "ambition, times self-centered custodial purpose, divided by one's natural oppor-

tunities for going up in the world.'' It sounds like a parody of humanistic psychology and in particular Maslow's self-actualization theory, but Al appears to take it seriously. On his ''little downside sabbatical,'' he discovers that people with limited opportunities who reduce their ambition in order to live relaxed and uncomplicated lives are usually happier than those who will not adjust to their social situations. Although he outlines his own philanthropic ambitions at the end of the novel, his theory suggests that people of limited means should adjust their ambitions accordingly. Pop psychology, hokey sociology, or a condescending attitude toward working-class blacks? As Al himself says several times in the novel, ''it won't do well to pursue this too far.''

Although he praises Powell's ''terrific hyper-real dialogue'' in *Drown*, Boyle also complains about the random episodic structure, especially toward the end of the novel. Mary Mackey describes Powell as the ''uncrowned king of the new maximalists,'' those protégés of Faulkner who are ''marked by an intoxication with language.'' Paul Gray praises *Drown* as an ''extravagantly comic . . . exercise in word spinning for the sheer uncertainty and pleasure of what might pop up next.'' Most other reviewers of *Drown* are less complimentary. R. D. Pohl dismisses it as a failed novel of ideas. Lee Milazzo describes Powell as ''a stylist of the first order,'' but concludes that ''lyrical prose is not enough to rescue the thin material.''

Edisto fared much better at the hands of literary reviewers whose comments are summarized by Barbara Carlisle in Volume 34 of *Contemporary Literary Criticism*. Although most reviews were favorable, a few reviewers felt that in places language was an end in itself. Richard Eder argues that ''Simons is his language, and he is not a great deal more. His narrative compulsion, and its witty and baroque offshoots, are quite marvelous in themselves but the person behind them is suspect.''

Neither novel has received much attention in academic journals. The only extended study of a novel is Sybil Estess's ''The Eden of 'Edisto': The Fall into the Then-Next,'' in *Southwest Review*. In 1987, Carlisle wrote a short but helpful description of Powell's life and works for *Contemporary Authors*.

Typical, Powell's collection of short fiction, elicited a mixed but generally unenthusiastic response from book reviewers. Amy Hempel praises ''the range and excellence'' of several stories but observes that ''not all of Mr. Powell's more unconventional pieces work. Some are reminiscent of Donald Barthelme stories gone from tellingly absurd to just absurd.'' Michiko Kakutani particularly likes the title story and ''The Winnowing of Mrs. Schuping,'' which she describes as ''Carson McCullers-esque,'' but harshly condemns many of the stories as ''a brittle, self-indulgent lot devoid of subtlety, inventiveness or craft.'' Concluding that such pieces ''don't belong in a collection of published writings, and they don't do justice to a writer as gifted as Mr. Powell,'' she echoes the disappointment of other readers who admire Powell's talent but dislike many of his recent efforts.

Like his fictional narrators, Padgett Powell appears to be playing a number of roles, all part of a process leading toward some unknown end, but one that may be more conventional than expected if the conclusions of his first two novels provide a clue. Powell has not proven to be a prolific writer. Like Al toward the end of *Drown*, he has demonstrated since the publication of that novel a "high propensity to dalliance, the incalculable willingness to step sideways and backward before forward." However, "The Winnowing of Mrs. Schuping" may indicate that Powell, in the words of those talented, hyperactive narrators of *Edisto* and *Drown*, is ready "to step forward" once again and be a "pioneer."

BIBLIOGRAPHY

Works by Padgett Powell

"Edisto." *The New Yorker* (November 14, 1983): 49–106.

Edisto. New York: Holt, 1985.

"Edisto," 211–19 in *New Writers of the South: A Fiction Anthology*, ed. Charles East. Athens: University of Georgia Press, 1987.

"Hitting Back," in *A World Unsuspected: Portraits of Southern Childhood*, ed. Alex Harris. Chapel Hill: University of North Carolina Press, 1987.

"Learning to Hit Back." *Harper's* (August 1987): 23–28.

"Our Southern Words and Pictures." *Southern Living* (January 1990): 92–93.

Rev. of *The Old Forrest and Other Stories*, by Peter Taylor. *Houston Post* (March 23, 1985): E1.

Rev. of *The History of Southern Literature*, ed. Louis D. Rubin, Jr. *Florida Historical Quarterly* (Fall 1986): 241–43.

Rev. of *In the Country of Last Things* by Paul Auster. *New York Times Book Review* (May 17, 1987): 11–12.

Rev. of *A Virtuous Woman* by Kaye Gibbons. *New York Times Book Review* (April 30, 1989): 12–13.

Rev. of *Ganado Red* by Susan Lowell. *Georgia Review* (Fall 1989): 609–10.

Typical. New York: Farrar, Straus, 1991.

"Voice from the Grave." *Esquire*. (January 1987): 100–103.

A Woman Named Drown. New York: Farrar, Straus, 1987.

"A Woman Named Drown," 125–32 in *New Visions: Fiction by Florida Writers*, ed. Omar F. Castanada. Orlando: Arbiter, 1989.

Studies of Padgett Powell

Boyle, T. Coraghessan. Rev. of *A Woman Named Drown, New York Times Book Review* (June 7, 1987): 9.

Carlisle, Barbara. "Padgett Powell," 345–47 in *Contemporary Authors*, Vol. 126. Detroit: Gale Research, 1984.

———. "Padgett Powell," 97–101 in *Contemporary Literary Criticism*, Vol. 34. Detroit: Gale Research, 1984.

Childress, Mark. "A Southern Doctoral Dropout Takes to the Open Road." *Philadelphia Inquirer* (June 14, 1987): 3.

Eder, Richard. "Discoveries on the Frontier of Boyhood." *Los Angeles Times Book Review* (April 22, 1984): 2, 9.

Estess, Sybil. "The Eden of 'Edisto': The Fall into the Then-Next." *Southwest Review* 69, no. 4 (Autumn 1984): 477–81.

Frakes, James R. "Romping through Dark, Hilarious Dixie." *Cleveland* (Ohio) *Plain Dealer* (July 5, 1987): 21.

Gray, Paul. "A Little Downside Sabbatical." *Time* (May 18, 1987): 79.

Hempel, Amy. "A Lesson in Hard-Boil." *New York Times Book Review* (July 21, 1991): 6.

Kakutani, Michiko. "A Potpouri of Characters and Their Stories." *New York Times* (August 16, 1991): C21.

Mackey, Mary. "Southern Discomfort with a Bitter Taste." *San Francisco Examiner and Chronicle* (July 19, 1987): 32.

Milazzo, Lee. "How to Drown in a Stylish Way." *Dallas Morning News* (June 7, 1987): 10.

Pohl, R. D. "Endorsement Isn't Enough to Save Novel." *Buffalo News* (July 26, 1987): 32.

LINDA WELDEN

Ferrol Sams
(1922–   )

Although he is primarily a practicing physician who has turned to writing only recently, Ferrol Sams has produced an impressive collection of literary works and has become an important Southern writer. Through masterful storytelling he captures and preserves in both fiction and nonfiction a time, a place and a culture that have all but vanished from the South.

BIOGRAPHY

When Ferrol Aubrey Sams, Jr., writes about life in the piedmont of Georgia after World War I, it is with the truth and accuracy of one who was there to experience it. He was born September 26, 1922, in a spacious, two-story, white-clapboard farmhouse his great-grandfather Porter built in 1848 to accommodate a large family and generations to come. The house stands on the Brooks-Antioch Road outside Fayetteville in Fayette County, Georgia. It was also the birthplace of Sams' father and paternal grandmother. Now known as the Old Sams Place, it is currently home to a sixth generation of the Sams clan. The house and the more than 800 acres of farmland surrounding it are central to Sams' first novel, *Run with the Horsemen* (1982).

Sams peoples his fiction with characters drawn from life. The father and mother in his novels are strikingly similar to Sams' own parents. Ferrol Sams, Sr., was born in 1892. He graduated from Mercer University and taught English and Latin at a small college in Florida. After serving as captain in the infantry in World War I, he received a law degree from Emory University, returned to the farm, and was elected Fayette County school superintendent. When his sister brought a fellow schoolteacher, Mildred Matthews, home for a visit, Sams met and later married her. His new wife left her Cartersville home in Bartow County, Georgia, and moved to the farm with her husband, his parents, and several other relatives. Ferrol and Mildred added four children to the household: Jimmie Kate, Ferrol, Jr., Janice, and Sara. Ferrol, Sr., gave his only son the nickname "Sambo," an affectionate term that has endured and is now preserved in the novels.

Mildred Sams was a firm but gentle influence who took Ferrol "and anything that wiggled" (unpublished interview with Linda Welden, June 15, 1990, Fayetteville, Georgia) to the Woolsey Baptist Church and read to him each night from the *Story Book Bible*. She also read from Joel Chandler Harris, Charles Dickens, and popular writers of the day, introducing Ferrol to the joys of reading and owning books. His life was changed forever when he entered first grade at the Rest School, a combination Masonic Hall and schoolhouse, and learned to read in the *Baby Ray* reader.

In third grade he began to attend school in Fayetteville as one of the "county children." That year his mother, posing as Santa Claus, gave him his first book: *The Cash Boy*, or *Paddle Your Own Canoe*, by Horatio Alger. Ferrol's fifth-grade teacher, Miss Kathleen Moon, fueled his enthusiasm for reading by offering a prize to the student who would read the most books over the summer. The only student who accepted the challenge, he read forty-five books and won a box of Cracker Jack.

Like other rural children growing up during the Depression, Sams filled his days with farm work. His people were landed gentry; the land he worked had belonged to his family since the Indians were driven out of Georgia, and he developed a strong sense of place and origin. A significant influence on the boy who was to become a writer was the tradition of family storytelling. His grandfather was a gifted storyteller who would sometimes forget the presence of a young child and tell true stories "about people who were murdered and thrown in the river." Jim Sams' penchant for background details and for stories based in fact had a deep influence on his grandson's rich narrative style.

By the time he entered Fayetteville High School, the young Sams already knew that he wanted to be a doctor, and he was an exceptionally gifted student. In addition to regular classwork he took private lessons in expression and entered and won district literary meets. James R. Colvin, his history teacher, fired his love for learning and the liberal arts. Like Porter Osborne, his fictional counterpart, Sams was senior class president, valedictorian, president of Future Farmers of America, and a member of the Beta Club. He was among thirty-eight graduates of the class of 1938.

Ferrol Sams, Sr., hand-delivered his son to his own alma mater, Mercer University. Sams' college experiences provided the factual basis for his second novel, *The Whisper of the River*, (1984). He joined his father's fraternity, Kappa Alpha, and excelled in scholarship, achieving Phi Eta Sigma, Blue Key, and Sigma Mu. He did not join the latter, Mercer's equivalent of Phi Beta Kappa, because the ten-dollar fee was prohibitive during the Depression. He found time for pranks and practical jokes; stories of his exploits were legend before they made their way into his fiction. A pre-med major, Sams credits Dr. Fred Jones, his freshman English professor, with teaching him to write about what he knew. He still feels Jones' presence over his shoulder as he writes, cautioning him about comma faults and style.

During the winter quarter of his senior year at Mercer, the Japanese bombed Pearl Harbor, and Sams knew that he would probably go to war. Faced with the knowledge that many were dying in battle and that he might not see Fayette County again, he took the fifteen class cuts granted to those who had made the dean's list and went home. For three weeks he plowed the land ''as smooth as a featherbed.'' Working the red clay was a religious experience that prepared him for what lay ahead. When the task was done, he returned to Mercer and made three B's for the quarter. Had he needed a sixteenth cut for any reason, he would have failed to graduate.

Because of the war, Emory University School of Medicine started its first quarter in June. Immediately upon graduation in 1942 Sams entered medical school and studied for two quarters. He was quickly disenchanted: The teaching was ''brutal, degrading, and dehumanizing.'' Upon leaving school he joined the United States Army Medical Corps and served as a surgical technician in the operating room of a field hospital in France. His unit landed in Normandy and set up their first hospital in a cow pasture near Isigny. Following General Patton's Third Army, the unit moved to Metz in Lorraine, where Sams achieved the rank of sergeant. His service in World War II solidified his determination to be a doctor as he observed the callous treatment many servicemen had to endure at the hands of army doctors. He risked court martial twice because of his unwillingness to ignore medical decisions he deemed heartless.

In 1946, returning to Emory with new maturity and determination, he met a fellow medical student, Helen Fletcher, ''over a cadaver.'' He and Helen were married in 1948, and in 1951 they went into medical practice together at the Sams Clinic in Fayetteville, Georgia. Both Helen and Ferrol, widely known with reverence as ''Doctor Helen'' and ''Sambo,'' are still full-time practicing physicians. They and two of their sons, Ferrol III and Jim, established the Fayette Medical Clinic, with thirteen full-time partners and another fifteen physicians practicing part time. Dr. Ferrol Sams, Jr., is medical director, and the Sams' daughter, Ellen, is physicians' representative at the clinic. A third son, Fletcher, is district attorney of Fayette County. To date, ten grandchildren have joined the family.

In addition to his medical career, Sams has filled his life with community service. For 12 years he served on the North Central Georgia Health Systems Agency Planning Board. He has taught a freshman course at Emory Medical School and for many years served on the Fayetteville City Council. When one of his grandchildren was born with Down's syndrome, he helped to initiate the Early Years Program in the county to fill a void in the education of challenged children. The honoraria from his frequent speaking engagements go toward scholarships for the program. He also joined the Fayetteville United Methodist Church with Helen and taught Sunday School for 25 years. Both his undergraduate and graduate universities have honored his humanitarianism and his writing. In 1986 Mercer University invited him to deliver the commencement address and awarded him a D. Litt. In 1990 Emory University conferred the D. Lett., and Mercer gave him the Distinguished Alumnus Award.

Ferrol Sams had always known that he was a writer, and at age 58 he began writing his first novel. Having written only "examinations, prescriptions, and an occasional letter since 1939," he wrote laboriously until he learned his craft, and the writing became a compulsion. The founder of Peachtree publishers was enchanted with his manuscript and served as editor of the first book, *Run with the Horsemen*, published in fall 1982. It was an immediate success, rising immediately to the top of the best-seller list in Atlanta and maintaining that position for an unprecedented twenty-two weeks. Chuck Perry at Peachtree became the editor of the second novel, *The Whisper of the River* (1984), and of a collection of short stories, *The Widow's Mite and Other Stories* (1987). After Perry moved to Longstreet Press he brought Jim Harrison, an artist from South Carolina, to meet Sams. Perry's idea was to have Sams write a text based on Harrison's paintings of scenes from the vanishing South. The book became *The Passing: Perspectives of Rural America* (1988). The nonfiction stories from that volume have been reprinted in paperback as *The Passing Stories* (1990). Perry also had the idea for Sams to write a Christmas memoir, which became *Christmas Gift!* (1989). *When All the World Was Young* (1991), the final novel in the Porter Osborne trilogy, fictionalizes Sams' experiences in medical school and World War II. The books have all been best-sellers in the Atlanta market, and some have achieved that status beyond the region.

Sams continues to write, following his established routine of rising at 5 A.M. and writing in longhand for two hours. Then he calls his sister Jimmie Kate, who types the manuscript. Finally, he begins his work at the Fayette Medical Clinic, where he sees fifty patients daily. He says, "My primary function is looking after sick folks." Writing is not an avocation for him, however; it is a passion.

Sams, as surely as any other Southern writer, has a keen sense of place and of self, and the two are intertwined. To know his writing is to know the writer, for he writes about himself and the place and people he knows best. With skill, humor, and sensitive insight he blends fact and fiction to reconstruct a world existing now only in memory.

MAJOR THEMES

Ferrol Sams looks at his world and sees that the way of life that shaped his existence has all but disappeared from Fayette County, Georgia. Like most other rural communities within a half-hour's drive of Atlanta, his hometown of Fayetteville has become a suburb in the decades since World War II. Although Sams finds more evil than good in the change, he does not romanticize the past. Instead, he recognizes the need to capture and preserve the vanishing culture before it is completely absorbed and before all who remember it are gone. A pervasive theme of his writing is an abiding love for the land in Fayette County entrusted to his family. His writing is the fulfillment of the trust. As Sams has said: "When you want to keep something, well, if you write it, then it's there."

Even in the rural areas of his region that survive, the advent of sophisticated equipment has brought major changes in the rituals of farming. The practices of Sams' childhood are no longer employed in planting and harvesting. Although he does not advocate a return to the old ways, believing that to lose knowledge of them would be to lose a part of history, he records the procedures used on the farm in his day. He weaves into his narratives detailed and descriptive explanations of harnessing mules, pulling fodder, milking cows, chopping cotton, killing hogs, making syrup, and other practices that have passed from experience. As he promises in *Run with the Horsemen*: "This was the way it was in the Piedmont of Georgia between World Wars" (2).

Sams is not content to preserve only the sights and activities he remembers from his youth. He realizes that the regional sounds are also destined to vanish, and he is determined to recapture the way people talked. He faithfully records not only their dialects but also their colorful phrases. He remembers many expressions; others he collects in interviews with elderly acquaintances in the county. He has reflected that "some of these old folks could have died and I never would have heard these sayings"; instead, the sources "still come up with things that absolutely refresh me." Able to mimic speech expertly, Sams is also gifted with the ability to write so that a reader can hear the voice created on the page. He has become a master of folk wit and folk idiom.

The titles of Sams' books provide clues to his themes. The name of his first novel, *Run with the Horsemen*, is an allusion to the twelfth chapter of Jeremiah. In the novel Porter's mother quotes the biblical passage and then explains its lesson to her son: "We are not a family of footmen to start with, and you have to run with the horsemen whether you always feel like it or not, but this is still the land where we dwell secure" (294). Her discussion reveals the morality that is a major theme of all Sams' work. The land, the church, and the home undergird the family's honor. His mother's values constitute a behavioral code that Sams labels "Raised Right," and the code pervades his fiction. As Porter Osborne, Jr., struggles toward maturity, these values govern his actions, his pride, and his guilt.

In conflict with his mother's philosophy, however, is the lifestyle of his "Raised Right" father, who is a hero to his son even though he defies every taboo of the code. In addition, the boy's experiences on the farm and his developing body make him aware of his sexuality. Ferrol Sams synthesizes and honors the conflicting influences of his early life in his first published sentence: "In the beginning was the land." The biblical style and content honor his mother; the reference to land honors his father and his heritage.

Sams novels are a celebration of the life force in man and nature, and his protagonist explores the meaning of life. In *The Whisper of the River*, sequel to

Run with the Horsemen, Porter's journey to adulthood continues with his entering college and finding each of his childhood beliefs challenged. The first chapter describes the church of Porter's youth and discusses the bedrock values it symbolizes. After arriving at Willingham University, Porter matures, changes, and loses his innocent faith; but underneath he hears "the whisper of the river" assuring him that his foundation will be constant and continuous. The novel ends on the lowest point of Porter's life. The tragedy of the death of college friends in the advent of World War II leads him to challenge his beliefs, and the conclusion of the novel finds him cursing and smoking in rebellion against his own mortality and his shaken faith. This abrupt ending demands the denouement of another novel to complete the story and the trilogy.

Porter's fans were at last able to witness his arrival at adulthood in 1991 when Longstreet Press published *When All the World Was Young*. Like the two books that preceded it, this book contains episodes of hilarity, but they are incidental to the overpowering seriousness of the novel. The title is taken from a line in G. K. Chesterton's "Lepanto." The poem is printed at the beginning of the book, and lines from it are used as chapter headings. Like the poem's romantic hero, Don John of Austria, Porter heads into battle with the idealistic notion of saving the world. The novel records his quest and the subsequent loss of his innocence. The trilogy ends when the romantic boy becomes the subdued realist who says, with mature conviction, "I have sure as hell discovered America!" In Sams' skilled hands his protagonist, Porter L. Osborne, Jr., has come to symbolize the world that changed forever with World War II.

Although the trilogy seeks to restore a vanished past and to explore the growing to adulthood of a young man, it also develops other themes. The protagonist is a master prankster in the best Southern tradition. Small for his years, like his literary counterpart Brer Rabbit he must survive by wits rather than by brawn. Porter's ribald pranks and practical jokes, reminiscent of frontier humor, provide much of the comedy that enriches the novels.

Porter is keenly sensitive to discrimination, and part of his code of chivalry is to champion the misfit. Although some of Sams' most delightful characters have a physical deformity, they are not the oddities of Southern Gothic but the creations of a medical scientist who can observe them clinically while celebrating their humanity. Sams also champions in his fiction two other targets of discrimination: women and blacks. He avoids stereotypes and develops characters who are strong-willed, independent, intelligent, and capable of overcoming prejudice. The care given to the development of these characters and the depth of communication between them and the protagonist belie any criticism of racism or sexism.

In his third book Sams departs from the ethnohistorical fiction of his novels to experiment with the short story. He continues his use of biblical allusions in the title, *The Widow's Mite*, which refers to one of the parables of Jesus. Most of the stories in the collection are filled with memorable characters and boisterously funny dialogue and events. Through a variety of narrative styles the stories explore a common theme: The weaknesses and triumphs of human nature. The title story is told in the rambling dialect of a lower-class woman who has little education but who proves to be shrewd in business. The widow's mite becomes the widow's might. "Howdy Doody Time" is another first-person narrative. The story develops the friendship of three people who have in common a sense of the ridiculous in life. As in many of the stories, one of the characters is a doctor, but the narrator is a city official motivated by greed and jealousy as well as by platonic love. In "Judgment," Sams creates another multidimensional character who lives by a literal interpretation of the Bible. Her frequently hilarious anecdotes comprise a perceptive satire of the Methodist Church and its clergy and politics. The narrator of the story "Fulfillment" is limited in omniscience to the character of Mamie Kate, a 6-year-old child with spina bifida who gets an education when she sits on a neighbor's porch and makes herself invisible while the ladies rock and talk. The oral tradition of veranda storytelling is the vehicle for a satire on the practice of shielding fragile women.

"Saba (An Affirmation)" departs from the style of the other stories. It is a nonfiction tale in the form of a letter to the children of Dr. Saba, a Lebanese friend of Sams. In willing to the Saba children a gift he received as a blessing from their grandfather, Sams unravels a moving story "of continuity, of love, of the importance of the land" (129).

In "Big Star Woman," a female narrator speaks in a rural dialect of the Georgia piedmont, punctuating her story with question marks to indicate her habit of lifting the pitch of her clause-terminal sounds. Her story satirizes the conflicting values of the natives whom she represents and those of the outsiders who have moved into her community. Through the narrator's experiences with changing legal and medical practices, Sams provides a complex study of the contingencies of morals.

The book's two concluding stories further investigate morality, but they are chilling tales that depart severely from the light-hearted whimsies of the other collected fiction. "FUBAR" is a title synonymous with the military expression "snafu." (The acronym's second syllable is "beyond all recognition.") The narrator is a fatherless boy struggling to survive and to find acceptance. The final story, "Porphyria's Lover," takes its title and its conclusion from Robert Browning's poem. The narrator is a bisexual sociopath who has contracted AIDS and destroyed the lives of those who loved him. The tales in *The Widow's Mite* demonstrate the flexibility of the short story as an art form and add new voices to the retrospective monologues so prevalent in Southern literature.

Sams has written two nonfiction works that illuminate the themes of his fiction. *The Passing: Perspectives of Rural America*, is a compilation of sixteen essays loosely based on Jim Harrison's paintings of rural Americana; Sams reminiscences further preserve the Fayette County of his youth. *Christmas Gift!* takes its name from a custom of beating another person to shouting "Christmas gift!" on Christmas morning and expecting a gift as a prize. The book itself is a gift to succeeding generations. It demonstrates the importance of ritual while it hands down the customs of the past.

SURVEY OF CRITICISM

Although Ferrol Sams' writing career began too recently to have received much critical attention, his books collectively have sold over a half-million copies, attesting to public recognition of his creative ability. Readers and reviewers from across the nation have discovered Sams, and sales have been as brisk in other parts of the country as they have been in the South. His setting is a tiny section of rural Georgia, but his stories transcend regionalism. Reviews of his work are primarily in newspapers and magazines, and to date no detailed literary criticism has appeared. The available reviews, however, occasionally provide insights worthy of discussion.

Early reviews of *Run with the Horsemen* recognized its roots in the oral tradition and frontier humor. Rex Burns applauded the "highly entertaining recreation of the variety of dialects" and called the book "an unsentimental and thoroughly believable memoir." Burns found within the work both characters and stories that "illuminate humanity." He and other reviewers compared the book with those of Harper Lee, Margaret Mitchell, and William Faulkner. Critic Jane Zinman was captured by the "bald, terse . . . bare prose style" and by the universal appeal of the protagonist. She praised the book for penetrating "the hypocrisies and falsehoods" she saw underlying "the entire framework" of the South. Robert Miner noted "a genuine respect that gives everything its due, counterpointed by a highly developed sense of irony." Although some critics were unable to accept that a reminiscence could become a novel or that a physician could become a writer (obviously forgetting Anton Chekhov and Walker Percy), most were charmed by the story and by the writing. The reviewer for *Publishers Weekly* probably reflected the dismay of readers outside the region who found it strange that a white protagonist would be called "Sambo," or that the father never got into serious trouble because of his exploits, facts that would likely go unquestioned in much of the South. Another writer recognized that the final chapter was inconclusive and that a second novel must surely follow.

Mixed criticism greeted the second novel. Critics who understood that the book was not merely a series of college pranks viewed it favorably. The reviewer for *Southern Living* commended *The Whisper of the River* for bravely questioning "the beliefs and customs on which we were raised" and for "allowing us to laugh as we examine traditions." David Cooper claimed that the novel missed the mark its predecessor had established, but he called Sams "a fine novelist who writes with passion, pathos, and humor often lacking in American fiction of recent years." *Book World* called it "a rollicking tale, a regional story of growing up." Other reviewers, however, took issue with the novel. *Publishers Weekly* erroneously identified the setting as Kentucky and accused the author of "avuncular piety" in the narration. Although editor George Core of the *Sewanee Review* found fault with the slow pace in the middle of the book, he recognized *The Whisper of the River* as an "ambitious novel" that included "generational clashes, race relations, the importance of knowledge, and moral conflict." Even though some critics had strong negative reactions to the protagonist, they generally praised the development of other characters; and the realistic creation of Boston Harbor Jones, the black man who befriends Porter Osborne, met with widespread acclaim. Many readers among Sams' local contemporaries had felt that *Run with the Horsemen* was the book they had always wanted to write. The Great Depression, however, prevented them from attending college, and they have found *The Whisper of the River* to be somewhat inaccessible. The book has remained popular among college students and is required reading in a number of college classes throughout the country. Forrest McDonald summarized recent reflections on both novels: "If Ferrol Sams' two autobiographical novels . . . don't grab you by the heart, you don't have a heart to grab."

The Widow's Mite and Other Stories* received national attention and acclaim. From outside the region Shelby Hearon called it "a fine assemblage of tales," and Albert Wilhelm praised "the earthy vernacular, gossipy digressions, and down-home wisdom." He also commented on the grim irony and compared the work with the tales of Ring Lardner. Maylon Rice wrote that it was "one of the best short story collections by a modern writer." John Connelly in the *Atlanta Journal-Constitution*, Sams' local newspaper, gave a mixed review and analysis. He praised the strength of the book's literary sense of place and asserted that in Sams' best writing he "sprinkles the stories with wisdom—after he has packed them to bursting with native phrase." On the other hand, the review held that some of the stories "might be hindered by too much cleverness" and faulted Sams for a certain lack of "resonance" in the writing and "self-doubt" in the characters. Wayne Greenhaw in the *Journal-Constitution* had only praise, however, for *The Passing: Perspectives of Rural America*: "There is poetry in the words and pictures . . . haunted with a nostalgia of what once was." Eleanor Drake Mitchell called it "a book to savor and enjoy."

The review in *Southern Living* predicted that Sams' second work of nonfiction, the memoir, *Christmas Gift!* "is destined to become a traditional read-aloud book" and praised it for leaving the reader with "a sense of the season, the family, and the South." An Atlanta critic faulted the use of dialect, seemingly unaware that, like Mark Twain, William Faulkner, and Eudora Welty, Sams is attempting to preserve the speech of Southerners, black and white, which he sees as a kind of folk art destined for oblivion if not captured in writing. Any scholar looking for a key to the references in the literary works of Sams would be well advised to begin the search in the books of nonfiction.

Reviews of *When All the World Was Young* were favorable. Tyson Blue called Sams "one of the most precious stones in the South's literary treasure trove" and the book "simply another facet of this excellent writer's seemingly inexhaustible talent." Blue praised the "well-drawn and realistic" characters along with Sams' "eye for details, mannerisms, and personality quirks that enables him to sketch those characters in without slowing the flow of his story, which is the finest skill a writer can develop."

Benjamin Griffith praised Sams as "a natural-born storyteller with a puckish wit, an obsession with words" who "continues to widen and deepen his skills." Griffith described *When All the World Was Young* as "a fully realized 610 page comic novel" and Porter as "a Tom Sawyer who yearns to be a Huck Finn."

The novel was awarded the Townsend Prize for Fiction in 1992. Administered by Georgia State University, the prize was established to honor Atlanta magazine editor Jim Townsend by recognizing Georgia's best work of fiction. The book also received national attention through its 1992 performance on American Public Radio on the "Radio Reader" program. The prize gives increased visibility to all of Sams' work. Although that work has yet to receive the critical attention it deserves, his books offer vast research material not only to literary critics but also to sociologists, anthropologists, historians, and linguists. Perhaps scholars will soon discover what thousands of readers have already learned: Ferrol Sams has a gift for teaching and delighting through candid, elucidative, and often very funny stories about his world.

BIBLIOGRAPHY

Works by Ferrol Sams

Run with the Horsemen. Atlanta: Peachtree, 1982.
The Whisper of the River. Atlanta: Peachtree, 1984.
The Widow's Mite and Other Stories. Atlanta: Peachtree, 1987.
The Passing: Perspectives of Rural America. Paintings by Jim Harrison. Marietta, Ga. Longstreet, 1988./Rep. *The Passing Stories*. Marietta, Ga.: Longstreet, 1990.
"Writing with the 'Raised Right' Stuff," ed. Bill Garner. *Kappa Alpha Journal* (Spring 1988): 16–18.
"Recording Small-Town Traditions," ed. Don O'Briant. *Atlanta Weekly* (October 16, 1988): 7–14.
Christmas Gift! Marietta, Georgia: Longstreet, 1989.
When All the World Was Young. Marietta, Ga.: Longstreet, 1991.

Studies of Ferrol Sams

Blue, Tyson. " *The Passing* Showcases Sams' Vast Literary Talents." Macon, Ga., *Telegraph and News* (June 18, 1989): 9E.
———. "Sams' Latest Ends Trilogy: Porter Osborne Return Well Worth the Wait." Macon, Ga., *Telegraph* (December 22, 1991): 6E.
"Books about the South." *Southern Living* 20 (October 1985): 120.
———. *Southern Living* 24 (December 1989): 86.
Burns, Rex. "Regional Novel Harks Back to Neglected Literary Tradition." *Denver Post* (September 12, 1982): Newsbank LIT 30:C9.

Cheuse, Alan. "Education of a Pre-Lunch Georgia." *Los Angeles Times* (December 16, 1982): Newsbank LIT 54:G11.

Connelly, John. "Collection of Short Stories Hits, Misses." *Atlanta Journal-Constitution* (November 29, 1987): Newsbank LIT 11:B2.

Cooper, David. "Seconds for Fans of Ferrol Sams." Akron, Ohio, *Beacon Journal* (November 11, 1984): Newsbank LIT 60:G8.

Core, George. "Procrustes' Bed." *Sewanee Review* 93 (April 1985): 39.

Greenhaw, Wayne. "Imagery, Poetry: Putting Rural America in Perspective." *Atlanta Journal-Constitution* (October 23, 1988): 8K.

Griffith, Benjamin. "A Wit at Loose in a World at War." *Atlanta Journal-Constitution* (October 20, 1991): N9.

Hearon, Shelby. "Selfishness Begins at Home." *New York Times Book Review* (March 5, 1989): 34.

McDonald, Forrest. "Books for Christmas." *American Spectator* (December 1987): 46.

Miner, Robert. "Three Novels." *New York Times Book Review* (November 28, 1982): 27.

Mitchell, Eleanor Drake. "Passing Is Evocative." Nashville *Banner* (January/December 1988): Newsbank LIT 133:C11.

Paschal, Douglas. "Novel a Southern 'Animal House.' " Nashville *Tennessean* (May 26, 1985): Newsbank LIT 123:D9.

Rev. of *Christmas Gift!*. *Bloomsbury Review* 9 (November 1989): 29.

Rev. of *Run with the Horsemen*. *Publishers Weekly* 221 (June 11, 1982): 58.

Rev. of *The Whisper of the River*. *Book World* (February 23, 1986): 12.

Rev. of *The Whisper of the River*. *Publishers Weekly* 226 (September 28, 1984): 97.

Rice, Maylon. "Physician-Author Has Right Prescription." Little Rock *Arkansas Democrat* (April 10, 1988): Newsbank LIT 66:B9.

Weeks, Linton. " 'Christmas Gift!' Is Wrapped in Family Anecdotes." *Atlanta Journal-Constitution* (December 9, 1989): 28.

Wilhelm, Albert. Rev. of *The Widow's Mite and Other Stories*. *Library Journal* (December 1987): 129.

Zinman, Jane. "What They Like about the South." San Diego *Union* (September 26, 1982): Newsbank LIT 30:C8.

Mary Lee Settle
(1918–   )

Like William Faulkner in his generation, Mary Lee Settle in hers is distinguished through her creation of a world both realistic and mythic. Just as Faulkner's Oxford is transformed into Jefferson, Settle's Charleston, West Virginia, has become Canona, appearing in nine of her twelve novels. Unlike Faulkner, however, Settle has traveled beyond her little postage stamp of the world to encompass with palpable realism four centuries and four continents.

Settle's riskiest enterprise and most brilliant achievement is her Beulah Quintet, a series of novels begun in 1954 with the composition of *O Beulah Land* and concluded in 1982 with publication of *The Killing Ground*. This 28-year effort was a precarious one because Settle's explicit purpose throughout was to write serious, artistic, historical fiction. She did so in an era in which readers perceived the genre as only popular potboilers—melodramatic, formulaic, and hastily written. Her success in elevating what has been conventionally understood to be mere entertainment attests to her abilities as a writer, but her insistence on using a form currently unacceptable to the academy and literary circles has probably been costly as far as recognition by these groups is concerned.

Even without the Beulah Quintet, Settle's literary accomplishment is impressive. Her bibliography includes three juvenile books, a memoir of her experiences in World War II, and seven other novels. Besides those books she has written numerous personal articles, travel essays, and occasional book reviews. Each of her novels has been well received by the press, and *Blood Tie*, her 1977 novel set in Turkey, won the National Book Award for 1978. Nevertheless, her work has not yet received the critical attention it deserves.

BIOGRAPHY

Settle was born in Charleston, West Virginia, on July 29, 1918. When she was 1 year old, her parents, Rachel Tompkins and Joseph Edward Settle, took her to Harlan County, Kentucky, where her father owned a coal mine. After living for a time in Pineville, Kentucky, the family moved to Orlando, Florida, where her father worked as a civil engineer. When she was 10 they lived for a year with her grandmother in Cedar Grove, West Virginia; she reports that as she rode the school bus she remembers on winter mornings seeing "the miners going to work in the dark with their carbide headlamps lit" (Garrett, *DLB* 282). Her teenage years were spent in Charleston, where she graduated from high school in 1936. After 2 years at Sweet Briar College she worked for a summer at the Barter Theatre in Abingdon, Virginia, where a scout from Selznick found her and took her back to Hollywood to test for *Gone with the Wind*. She then spent a year in New York modeling for the Powers and Conover agencies. *The Love Eaters* (1954), *The Kiss of Kin* (1955), *The Clam Shell* (1971), and *The Scapegoat* (1980) are partially based on these early experiences.

In 1939 she married an Englishman, Rodney Weathersbee, and moved to Canada, where her son, Christopher, was born. She and her husband separated after he joined the Canadian army, and she took Christopher back to West Virginia to live with her parents. In 1942 she began a 3-year stint in the Women's Auxiliary Air Force, working first in the Signals Corps in rural England and later in the Office of War Information in London. *All the Brave Promises: Memoirs of Aircraft Woman 2nd Class 2146391* (1966) and an article in a 1987 *Virginia Quarterly Review* entitled "London: 1944" deal with her military experiences.

When she returned to New York in 1945 she worked briefly as assistant editor for *Harper's Bazaar*, but soon gave it up, deciding that if she were to write seriously she could not hold a daily job. She moved back to England with Christopher and was divorced. In 1946 she married Douglas Newton and began working as a free-lance journalist. For a year she conducted an etiquette column as Mrs. Charles Palmer in *Woman's Day*. In 1949 she joined the staff of the short-lived *Flair* magazine. During this time she reports that she had manuscripts for six plays and four films, none of which have been published.

Her publishing career began in 1954, when *The Love Eaters* appeared. It was her second novel. Her first, *The Kiss of Kin*, appeared the following year. Both of these works, as well as six other books, have been published in England and the United States. In 1954 she also began work on the first of the Beulah series, finding material for the book in the British Museum.

In 1956 she was divorced from Douglas Newton and returned to West Virginia. For the next dozen years she was supported by two Guggenheim fellowships (1957–58 and 1959–60) and intermittent jobs editing for *American Heritage*, working with the American Place Theatre on the production of her play, *Juana La Loca*, and teaching at Bard College. She also completed what she then termed the Beulah Trilogy: *O Beulah Land* (1956), *Know Nothing* (1960), and *Fight Night on a Sweet Saturday* (1964). George Garrett has called her experience with publishers during this time "an almost classic example of American publishing malpractice," most egregiously demonstrated by Viking's refusal to bring out the Beulah Trilogy as a trilogy and its insistence on so cutting *Fight Night on a Sweet Saturday* that it made no clear connection with the earlier two and was to the author a literary disaster (*DLB* 284). The book later became a substantial portion of *The Killing Ground*, the fifth Beulah book.

Settle left the country in 1968 because, as she writes, "I said that if Nixon was elected president I was going back to Europe. He was and I did" (*CAAS* 319). She published *The Clam Shell*, a fictional account of her college experiences that she calls her only autobiographical novel, in 1971, the same year she began researching material for *Prisons* (1973) at the Bodleian Library in Oxford and the British Museum. *Prisons*, set in seventeenth-century England, was to become part of the Beulah Quintet. In the next year she went to live in Turkey, completing *Prisons* there and beginning work on *Blood Tie*. Because of the Cypriot war in 1974 she returned to Virginia, finding a place to live in Charlottesville. Published in 1977, *Blood Tie* won the National Book Award in 1978, an event she sees as a watershed in her career in that it brought both recognition and respect from the literary community. After that award was discontinued, Settle was instrumental in establishing the PEN/Faulkner Award for Fiction. Of it she says: "I felt I owed it to other writers to see that there would be a prize that would be judged on merit alone" (*CAAS* 321).

In 1978 she married historian and columnist William Littleton Tazewell and moved to Norfolk, Virginia, where she wrote the book that became the fourth of the Beulah Quintet, *The Scapegoat* (1980). The final volume of the quintet, *The Killing Ground*, followed in 1982. George Garrett reports that in 1987 she was confirmed in the Roman Catholic Church (*Understanding Mary Lee Settle* 8). Currently she lives in Charlottesville, Virginia, where she continues an imposingly active professional career, having published five of her sixteen books and uncounted essays in the last decade.

MAJOR THEMES

Settle's prevailing theme is the struggle for freedom, whether it be presented panoramically and historically as it is most often in the Beulah series, or intimately and domestically as it is in her earliest and latest novels. Her topics, characters, and scenarios are so numerous and varied that they do not immediately appear to be so unified, but closer examination reveals that a unifying thread for each volume is attention to the attempt to rectify past abuses of individual, familial, or political liberties. Even in her books that deal most explicitly with wartime politics, Settle explores family relationships and frictions. Prominent as a recurring character in her work is a domineering matriarch, often struggling to maintain a standard of living beyond her means. Ironic commentary on the behavior and attitudes of the upper middle class persists throughout her work, most often set in her mythical city of Canona, her name for Charleston, West Virginia. Reference to classical myth is also evident in her work.

The Love Eaters, a modern version of the Phaedra myth, deals with an amateur theatrical group and the events set into action with the arrival of two newcomers in Canona—a manipulative director and the Hippolytus figure, Martha Dodd's grown stepson. *The Kiss of Kin*, a revision of Settle's unpublished play, "Deed," takes place in a single day when the family clan gathers to hear the reading of Anna Mary Passmore's will. In its tightly knit structure and scenic quality each novel reflects the author's early interest in drama, and each is somewhat flawed by a melodramatic ending. Nevertheless, the two first novels anticipate the more mature craft of the Beulah novels, which quickly followed.

Settle's most stunning accomplishment is unquestionably the Beulah Quintet, published over a 26-year span. As in the case of James Fenimore Cooper's Leatherstocking novels, the chronology of the writing does not correspond with historical time. Earliest historically is *Prisons*, set in mid-seventeenth-century England. Written as a monologue, the book tells of Johnny Church, a volunteer in Oliver Cromwell's army during the British Civil War, relates his changing attitudes, and foretells his death as a traitor after he had opposed Cromwell. Because he had fathered an illegitimate child named Lacy, Church is the progenitor of one of the principal clans of the other novels, all of which take place in America. *O Beulah Land* concentrates on the period at the beginning of the Revolutionary War and continues beyond to the settlement of the western Virginia mountains. The wilderness travail of Hannah, progenitor of the lower-class Catlett tribe, constitutes the unforgettable prologue. Hannah's story contrasts sharply with that of Sally Lacey, who tries vainly to maintain old Virginia mores in the transmontane society. *Know Nothing*, set just before the Civil War, deals with marriage and money as much as it does conflicting attitudes toward slavery, which is seen dramatically through the eyes of two opposing brothers. *The Scapegoat*, covering only one day in 1912 but using both a flashback and flashforward technique, continues to treat the Laceys, owners of the coal mine, in their conflict with the Catletts, leaders of the mine workers. *The Killing Ground*, set in 1978, shows Hannah McKarkle, descendant of Hannah Catlett, in Canona giving a speech about the books she has written, whose titles are those of Settle. Hannah tries to make sense of her brother Johnny's death at the hands of Jake Catlett, and through conversations with her mother and aunt, a character in *The Scapegoat*, she comes to terms with her role in the family.

Settle has said more than once in interviews and magazine articles that her impetus to write the Beulah Quintet was her attempt to answer a question: "I had a picture of one man hitting another in a West Virginia drunk tank one Saturday night, and the idea was to go all the way back to see what lay behind that blow" (Baker 467). As she explains in an essay for the *Southern Review*, childhood memories and research in the British Museum yielded the Beulah Quintet. She also explains that she has used the theme of *Antigone* as well as the American frontier myth, exemplified here by Brother Jonathan rather than Uncle Sam. "Sustaining the patterns and details of the whole *Beulah Quintet*," she writes, "was the most preoccupying and exhausting occupation I have ever demanded of myself" (Rosenberg 23).

One of the early events in *The Killing Ground* is the report of Charley Bland's suicide. Charley Bland also figures prominently but briefly in what she calls her most autobiographical novel, *The Clam Shell*, a fictional memoir of her freshman year at Sweet Briar College. But he is given full attention as the central character of her most recent novel, *Charley Bland* (1989). In it an unnamed narrator recounts her unhappy love affair with him and her difficulties with his mother and other members of the country club set of Canona. Far less complex than any of the Beulah Quintet, these two novels provide another perspective for Settle's Canona saga.

Were it not for the National Book Award, Settle's Quintet and the other four Canona books would entirely overshadow the books written with international settings. These books deserve critical attention as well, articulating the theme of the search for personal freedom in more exotic settings than her other books. *All the Brave Promises*, her memoir of her experiences in England during World War II, emphasizes the disillusion accompanying her actual experience with the military. The title underscores her reaction to being knocked on her back into the mud by other recruits, when she feels the "massed fury against the ignominy of all the brave promises" (51). Her most recent book, *Turkish Reflections: A Biography of Place* (1991), is a travel book that considers sympathetically several cities in Turkey.

The two novels with international settings, *Blood Tie* and *Celebration* (1986), represent, according to Garrett, "the most successful and serious international fiction written by an American in our time" (*Understanding* 129). *Blood Tie*, set in the imagined Ceremos in Turkey, features Ariadne, an American, who serves as a bridge between the elaborately drawn expatriate community and politically beset citizens of the city. Filled with a large number of discretely drawn characters, it proceeds much like an introspective thriller. Similarly, *Celebration* may be categorized on one level as an international thriller and love story whose real business is a spiritual journey. Teresa Cerrutti, recently widowed and recovering from cancer, meets in London both her future husband, Ewen, and a memorable African Jesuit, Father Pius Deng. Although this book has autobiographical elements, Doris Betts says that the author "has steadily moved the boundaries of her region out to encompass the human spirit" (211).

SURVEY OF CRITICISM

In light of the length and scope of her career, Settle's work has until recently received disappointingly little critical attention. Almost all of her seventeen books have attracted positive reviews, and a small number of followers have begun to pay more careful attention to her work as a whole. Settle might well be her own best critic, for an unusually large number of interviews and articles written by her provide insight into the work. In the last few years critical attention has burgeoned, exemplified by the literary festival honoring her and her work that was held in October 1990 at Emory and Henry College. There, in an interview with Brian Rosenberg, Settle took issue with critics who attempt to find autobiographical resonances in her work, insisting that her most autobiographical figure is Johnnie Church, the seventeenth-century protagonist of what she unwaveringly calls her favorite of her books, *Prisons*.

Long-time supporter Garrett has written most prolifically about Settle and her work, including the first book length study, *Understanding Mary Lee Settle*, published in 1988 in the University of South Carolina series *Understanding Contemporary American Literature*. Garrett has also written a biographical piece for the *Dictionary of Literary Biography* and has published several articles on her work.

While attention to her work is increasing, so far the Beulah Quintet has received most of the critical analyses, including Brian Rosenberg's book length study (1991). Those studies have emphasized her craft in plotting, use of language, attention to details, ability to change voices, and astute political commentary. Granville Hicks' introduction to the Ballentine edition of *O Beulah Land* in 1965 and Roger Shattuck's introduction to the uniform edition of the Quintet brought out by Ballentine in 1982 encouraged interest in these books. The other Canona novels and her international books have by and large been neglected by critics.

Reviews have been numerous and of course mixed. Detractors find her intricate plots and large casts too difficult to follow, the ironic tone too dry, or the technical manipulation too unsettling. Those who admire her work find the same elements, but couch them in positive terms.

BIBLIOGRAPHY

Works by Mary Lee Settle

The Love Eaters. New York: Harper, 1954. London: Heinemann, 1954.
The Kiss of Kin. New York: Harper, 1955. London: Heinemann, 1955.
O Beulah Land. New York: Viking, 1956. London: Heinemann, 1956.
Know Nothing. New York: Viking, 1960. London: Heinemann, 1961.
Fight Night on a Sweet Saturday. New York: Viking, 1964. London: Heinemann, 1965.
All the Brave Promises: Memoirs of Aircraft Woman 2nd Class 2146391. New York: Seymour Lawrence/Delacorte, 1966. London: Heinemann, 1966.
The Story of Flight. New York: Random House, 1967. [Juvenile]
The Scopes Trial: The State of Tennessee v. John Thomas Scopes. New York: Watts, 1972. [Juvenile]
The Clam Shell. New York: Seymour Lawrence/Delacorte, 1971. London: Bodley Head, 1972.
Prisons. New York: Putnam, 1973. Published as *The Long Road to Paradise*. London: Constable, 1974.
Blood Tie. Boston: Houghton Mifflin, 1977.
The Scapegoat. New York: Random House, 1980.
The Killing Ground. New York: Farrar, Straus, 1982.
Water World. New York: Dutton, 1984. [Juvenile]

Celebration. New York: Farrar, Straus, 1986.
Charley Bland. New York: Farrar, Straus, 1989.
Turkish Reflections: A Biography of Place. Intra San Morris. Englewood Cliffs, N.J.:
Prentice-Hall, 1991.

Selected Articles

"Mary Lee Settle," 307–23 in *Contemporary Authors Autobiography Series*, Vol. 1, ed.
Dedria Bryfonski. Detroit: Gale Research, 1984.
"Recapturing the Past in Fiction." *New York Times Book Review* (February 12, 1984):
36–37.
"Life Is Really a Dance." *U.S. News and World Report* (December 22, 1986): 64.
"London: 1944." *Virginia Quarterly Review* 63 (1987): 565–87.
"The Search for Beulah Land." *Southern Review* 24 (1988): 13–26.

Selected Interviews

Baker, John F. "Mary Lee Settle," 466–68 in *Contemporary Authors*, Vols. 89–92.
Detroit: Gale Research, 1980.
Brown, Laurie L. "Interviews with Seven Contemporary Writers," 3–22 in *Women
Writers of the Contemporary South*, ed. Peggy Whitman Prenshaw. Jackson:
University of Mississippi Press, 1984.
MacPherson, Myra. "Mary Lee Settle, Forthrightly." *Washington Post* (January 15,
1987: C9.
Neal, G. Dale. "Filling an Empty Room—The Art of Mary Lee Settle." *Student* (Wake
Forest University) (Spring 1980): 18–22.
Rosenberg, Brian C. "The Price of Freedom: An Interview with Mary Lee Settle."
Southern Review 25 (1989): 351–65.
Shattuck, Roger. "A Talk with Mary Lee Settle." *New York Times Book Review* (October
26, 1980): 43–46.
Taormina, C. A. "On Time with Mary Lee Settle." *Blue Ridge Review* 1 (1978): 8–17.

Studies of Mary Lee Settle

Betts, Doris. Rev. of *Celebration*. *America* (October 18, 1986): 211–12.
Dyer, Joyce Coyne. "Embracing the Common: Mary Lee Settle in World War II."
Appalachian Journal 12 (1985): 127–34.
———. "Mary Lee Settle's *Prisons*: Taproots History." *Southern Literary Journal* 17
(1984): 26–39.
Garrett, George. "An Invitation to the Dance: A Few Words on the Art of Mary Lee
Settle." *Blue Ridge Review* 1 (1978): 18–24.
———. "Mary Lee Settle," 281–89 in *Dictionary of Literary Biography: American
Novelists since World War II*, 2nd series, ed. James E. Kibler, Jr. Detroit: Gale
Research/Bruccoli Clark, 1980.
———. *Understanding Mary Lee Settle*. Columbia: University of South Carolina Press,
1989.
Houston, Robert. "Blood Sacrifice" (Rev. of *The Scapegoat*). *Nation* (November 8,
1980): 469–71.
Joyner, Nancy Carol. "The Beulah Quintet: 'The Feral Edge of What Has Made Us.' "
Now and Then 4 (1987): 44.

————. "Mary Lee Settle's Connections: Class and Clothes in the Beulah Quintet," 165–78 in *Women Writers of the Contemporary South*, ed. Peggy Whitmire Prenshaw. Jackson: University of Mississippi Press, 1984.

O'Hara, J. D. "What Rogue Elephants Know." *Nation* 20 (May 1978): 605–6.

Rosenberg, Brian C. "Mary Lee Settle and the Critics." *Virginia Quarterly Review* 65 (1989): 351–65.

————. Mary Lee Settle and the Tradition of Historical Fiction." *South Atlantic Quarterly* 86 (1987): 229–43.

————. *Mary Lee Settle's Beulah Quintet: The Price of Freedom*. Baton Rouge: Louisiana State University Press, 1991.

Tyler, Anne. "Mary Lee Settle: Mining a Rich Vein." *Washington Post, Book World*, (September 28, 1980): 1.

Schafer, William J. "Mary Lee Settle's Beulah Quintet: History Darkly, through a Single Lens Reflex." *Appalachian Journal* 10 (1982): 77–86.

Vance, Jane Gentry. "Historical Voices in Mary Lee Settle's *Prisons*." *Mississippi Quarterly* 38 (1985): 391–413.

————. "Mary Lee Settle: Ambiguity of Steel," in *American Women Writing Fiction: Memory, Identity, Family, Space*, ed. Mickey Pearlman. Lexington: University Press of Kentucky, 1989.

————. "Mary Lee Settle's The Beulah Quintet: History Inherited: History Created." *Southern Literary Journal* 17 (1984): 40–53.

Bob [Robert G.] Shacochis
(1951–   )

The earlier grants, awards, or recognitions coming to Bob Shacochis were effective predictors of the American Book Award for First Fiction, which he received from the Association of American Publishers and which gained him wide national attention in 1985. *Easy in the Islands* (1985) called special attention to itself because of the shared Caribbean setting of its stories, and although the striking differentness of the collection was acknowledged to be more than the result of exotic location, Shacochis obtained, along with the glory, the immediate burden of proving himself to be other, and more, than writer about the Caribbean. Through additional published short stories (including ''Where Pelham Fell,'' a prototype ''Southern'' achievement in the genre), assorted periodical essays and articles, explanation and assertion in personal appearances and printed interviews, and continuing work on a novel, Shacochis is presently addressing that task. Odds are that he will succeed, and with sufficient further publication, critical consideration of his work will, properly, redirect itself to the depth rather than the surface of his achievement.

BIOGRAPHY

Robert G. Shacochis has spent little of his life at or above the 41½° north latitude of his birthplace. The third and last son of the four children of John P. and Helen Levonski Shacochis, he was born September 9, 1951, in West Pittston, Pennsylvania, between Wilkes Barre and Scranton. His family moved from Pennsylvania when he was 2, and all his growing-up years were spent in McLean, Virginia, just outside Washington, D.C., where his father was assistant director of the Bureau of Naval Personnel—a far cry from the Pennsylvania coal fields of his birth.

As a high school student, Shacochis was attracted to writers of the New

Journalism (Tom Wolfe, Gay Talese, Gail Sheehy, Hunter Thompson), and decided, on the basis of the school's reputation, to study journalism at the University of Missouri, from which he received a B.A. in 1973. Disappointed in American journalism education and disillusioned about the United States itself, he set out on his own for South America. He got no farther than the southwest Caribbean, where as treasure hunter, fisherman, and wanderer he quickly developed a passion for the region. Returning to the mainland he joined the Peace Corps and requested assignment to the West Indies, a request that resulted in his appointment as an agricultural journalist with the Ministry of Agriculture on the island of St. Vincent. After his house was broken into and he was knifed by a local criminal, subsequent legal proceedings produced a good bit of tension, and he was reassigned to Barbados and St. Kitts. Discontinuation of the idyll continued. After the death of a close friend and, temporarily, the loss of his money and his health, Shacochis, the idealistic young professional abroad, found it time to take serious personal inventory.

Conclusions of this account-taking were that he wanted to write fiction and that he needed to get into a university creative writing program. It was about this time, too, that Barbara Petersen ("Catfish") came into his life—and has remained an important part of it. His educational options apparently limited to his alma mater, Shacochis went back to Missouri, where he completed requirements for an M.A. in 1979. He spent the next year in West Palm Beach, Florida, working for the *Palm Beach Evening Times* and, when he could, writing fiction. He first published short story, "Hunger," appeared in the *Missouri Review* in 1980. Discovering that financial support for young writers working on a first book was available from the Writers' Workshop at the University of Iowa, but available only to their graduates, Shacochis made application for admission, submitting the story "Celebrations of the New World."

Shacochis was accepted at Iowa, and securing an agent during his first year there, found his fiction being sold to such magazines as *Playboy* and *Esquire*. His thesis for the Iowa M.F.A., which he received in 1982, was a group of short stories with a Caribbean coherence, the core of what finally appeared in 1985 as the nine-story collection *Easy in the Islands*. That his agent wanted to wait until Shacochis also had a novel to offer is one explanation for the delay in its publication, but several publishing houses turned down the collection manuscript before it was accepted at Crown in 1984. With its appearance early the next year, however, and then the nomination and subsequently the winning of the American Book Award, Shacochis quickly found himself in the limelight.

To those who already knew his work, such national recognition was not surprising. He had already received a literary fellowship from the National Endowment for the Arts and support from the Yaddo Corporation, the James Michener Award from the Iowa Writers' Workshop, the best new contributor in fiction award from *Playboy*, and a scholarship from the Bread Loaf Writers' Conference. Other honors and awards—including a Pushcart Prize, selection for the annual best stories from the South, a Bread Loaf fellowship, and the American

Academy/Institute of Arts and Letters' Rome Prize for Literature—have followed. Moreover, his visiting teaching appointments at the University of Missouri in 1984–85 and at the University of Iowa in 1985–86 proved to be prelude to demands for similar service and shorter creative-writing teaching/judging appearances all over the country—from Eastern Washington University to the Hemingway Days Writers' Workshop in Key West, Florida. Since 1982, residence for the peripatetic Shacochis, including an affecting year on the Outer Banks of North Carolina, time in San Francisco, and more recently six months in Rome, has not been lengthy anywhere. Tallahassee, Florida, is now about as firm a home address as he has had for years.

Shacochis' second collection of stories, *The Next New World*, was published in 1989. Although a projected novel, which has carried the working title "Swimming in the Volcano," remains, after some massive restarts, still a work in progress, Shacochis had generated an extensive bibliography of periodical nonfiction by the time *World* appeared, and he has since continued this kind of writing. In essay and article form, his work has repeatedly been in *Harper's*, *Vogue*, and *Gentlemen's Quarterly*. These pieces exhibit both a humor and a seriousness that are both expected and unexpected from his fiction, displaying a wide range of tone and dealing with, at least on the surface, a diversity of subjects. Shacochis has produced extensive international "Reports" for *Harper's*, becoming a contributing editor of that periodical, and in December 1988 he began writing the "Dining In" department for *Gentlemen's Quarterly*. Among topics he has been concerned with in his recent journalism—to cite some "content" categories of standard bibliographic indexes—are government, politics, society, and economics of the Third World; American literary history and criticism (a piece on John Fante); cooking/meat, cooking/vegetables, and "cocktails"; psychological security and insecurity; and dogs.

Shacochis has put some interesting characterizations into print about himself and his life. He was, he says, a "surf-struck, fish-crazed" child; as an adult, he is "a cautious but stubborn member" of the "starry-eyed breed" of idealists. Each day he has a "slow morning grope for identity," Shacochis claims, a time early when he tries to "patch the world together" for himself. "Mine," he has said, "is a desk-bound free-lance existence with a delinquent feel to it, on the one hand, and yet so blissfully mired in domestic ritual as to be outright housewifery."

MAJOR THEMES

His first book, said Shacochis, contained stories "loosely gathered around the theme of expatriate life as [he] had found it in the islands of the West Indies." In *Easy in the Islands*, he felt, some journalists at least saw little connection to contemporary American life, "found little more" than a "rum-spiked swallow of the exotic" being offered to readers. Certainly he had attempted more, and he thought, rightly, that he was offering more. The epigraph of this first collection, two sentences from Joseph Conrad's *Heart of Darkness*, is appropriate for all his work, wherever the setting, whoever his characters, whatever the literary genre: "Watching a coast as it slips by the ship is like thinking about an enigma. There it is before you—smiling, frowning, inviting, grand, mean, insipid, or savage, and always mute with an air of whispering, Come and find out."

The "coast" that Shacochis is interested in is what he calls "the larger world" or "the world at large"—"the forces that sweep across the planet" and "make the world the way it is," forces "of natural and human power" that move "across the surface of the earth and through mankind." Reacting to what is termed realism and neorealism, modernism and postmodernism in twentieth-century American literature, he reacts especially to domestic minimalism and its restrictiveness. He agrees with William Kennedy, he says, that "there's more to the human experience than realism will allow." There is a baroqueness, a magicalness, an exoticness, a "spirituality to it that has to be addressed if your work is going to embody the full spectrum of human experience."

Clearly Shacochis writes, in several respects, directly out of his own experience, and he believes that what he produces is firmly rooted in "reality"—if this term is rightly, inclusively defined. The "cross-cultural element" or "cultural conflict" so evidently and importantly informing his fiction is not something he had to leave the United States to experience. The grandchild, from both sides, of immigrants who came to the United States from Lithuania around the turn of the century, he had one grandfather who never spoke English. From the first, he says, he was an "outsider." He writes as an outsider or about outsiders because he has "lived it," because it has happened that his "lifestyle parallels an esteemed storytelling tradition in literature." The incongruities inherent in the state of being an "outsider" may of course lead to rather dark meditation or may become the source of humor. With Shacochis they do both.

A related, plainly consequential literary tradition or theme in Shacochis' fiction is the "test." "Pressure," Shacochis avers, "always produces the truth," and he uniformly puts his characters under pressure. Here is where and how one's "true nature" is revealed, he believes: The greater the severity of events, the greater the clarity and extent of the evidencing of character. This testing Shacochis frequently provides through great natural phenomena—sea, storm, disease, gender, time, death—but it may also have social or familial or historical or political sources, or seemingly sometimes be fundamentally individual. Whatever else he or she is doing, however, a Shacochis character will be *contending*.

Human life everywhere, not just in the Third World, may be like "swimming in the volcano," to use the working title of Shacochis's novel. As one of his book titles indicates, however, there is also and always prospect of a "next new world." True for characters and readers, this prospect is true also for writers, though it may not initially seem to be. Human beings and human questions "have been the same from the very beginning," Shacochis believes, and all writers are necessarily faced with recombining and updating themes and stories that already "have been done." But this updating is new and it is supremely important. Recording and chronicling their own age is, plainly if not so simply, what writers do. "What would be a higher goal than to leave a record of how it was for us?" Shacochis asks. For the tasks of both living and writing, he testifies, the human and the natural realities of the world include "both good news and bad news."

How a writer deals with and best communicates what he or she finds reality to be—and what Bob Shacochis' own inclinations and literary goals are—Shacochis revealingly comments on in talking about writers he admires. William Kennedy, Barry Hannah, Joseph Conrad, Richard Hughes, several of the figures of the New Journalism, among others, he acknowledges as having provided inspiration or example at one time or another. But his "heroes" are George Orwell and Mark Twain, masters of political, cultural inquiry and deep, informing humor, artists of both fiction and journalistic nonfiction. These two, says Shacochis, are his "models for what a writer should be in the twentieth century."

SURVEY OF CRITICISM

Critical attention to Shacochis' work has to the present understandably been limited mainly to reviews of his two short-story collections. As time passes, this fiction will receive more studied evaluation. And with more time, greater nonfiction production on his part, and the continuation of what seems a new critical interest in the genre of the essay, Shacochis' other work may also draw the direct attention that it deserves.

Reviews of both *Easy in the Islands* and *The Next New World*, while not unmixed, were generally and predominantly positive. One summary of criticism about this first collection describes the book's "heroes" as "usually rough-and-ready men caught in absurd predicaments" and characterizes the book's author as treating these predicaments with "deprecating humor" as he "contrasts the wide-eyed tourist's view of the tropics with a cynical insider's knowledge of the ugliness and frustrations of island life." Reviewers generally, according to this summary, although observing that Shacochis is not successful with every story, "find his vivid evocations of the book's tropical settings a strong point in the collection."

The *Publishers Weekly* reviewer of *Easy* (November 30, 1984, 81–82) believed some of the tales "too contrived and labored"; Mary Ellen Quinn in *Booklist* (December 1, 1984, 484) found some too repetitive; and the *Kirkus Review* writer (December 1, 1984, 1116) thought several of them had "a slightly sophomoric edge" with none being "a moral tale with the weight of prime [Robert] Stone or [V. S.] Naipaul." At the same time these three critics respectively attested "to the author's gift of ear and eye, and his promise as a storyteller"; "good storytelling and vibrant imagery"; and, "even at his weakest," a writing "from fresh angles, with a strong sense of narrative surprise." If one reviewer found the prose of the book sometimes "overripe," another found it "everbright.'' The feminist perspective of Cheri Fein led her to receive only ''temporary gratification'' from the stories. But George Garrett found them ''excellent,'' and Paul Gray praised their creator's ''keen awareness of lush disparities'' and discovered an overall talent that was ''more than a match for the subjects at hand.'' Stephen Goodwin called the collection ''a stunning first book'' (*Washington Post* 108, March 18, 1985, D9).

Paul Stuewe's view of *The Next New World* as ''a disappointing, overhyped volume'' was a minority report. Writing in *Quill and Quire* (May 1989, 23) Stuewe granted Shacochis ''an undeniably creative imagination'' capable of producing ''colorful and shocking'' stories, but found truly significant human elements absent, discovering only the ''raw materials of successful fiction'' present. Gray, on the other hand, found not only a continuation but an advance of Shacochis' impressive abilities: ''The fashion in stories these days runs to attentuated aperçus.'' But ''none of these will be found'' in *The Next New World*—''only pieces that are unstylishly generous and memorable.''

In their judgments of Shachochis' second collection, both Marcia Tager (*Library Journal*, December 1988, 135) and Richard Bausch addressed the restrictedness of setting that was at the same time the blessing and the curse of *Easy in the Islands*. Both react extremely positively to where Shacochis had traveled with his new collection. In *The Next New World* Tager found the presentation of ''a South—both American South and Caribbean—that is less a geographic place than a mystery or metaphor seen through gauze.'' The stories, she says, operate on ''several symbolic levels,'' and although they are demanding, they are insightfully rewarding. Praising Shacochis for ''courageously'' exploring ''the possibilities of variation in the art of story writing,'' and finding the various stories of the new collection ''marvellously controlled,'' Bausch believed each to ''take its own new form in language that is pure, charged with wit and style without ever being merely showy.'' He expresses admiration for the ''sureness'' with which Shacochis ''imbues his people and places with life—the virtuosity with which he moves from theme to theme, subject to subject, character to character.'' This second book, Bausch believes, proves Shacochis ''to be capable of visiting any time, any place, any heart or mind.''

BIBLIOGRAPHY

Works by Bob Shacochis

Easy in the Islands. New York: Crown, 1985.
''Thighs and Whispers.'' *Vogue* 177 (February 1987): 390, 460.
''An Island between Seasons.'' *Harper's* 274 (February 1987): 57–60, 62–64, 66.
''Yesterday's Revolution.'' *Harper's* 275 (October 1987): 41–49.
''Dog Soldiers.'' *Gentlemen's Quarterly* 58 (December 1988): 304–7, 343–44.
The Next New World. New York: Crown, 1989.
''In Deepest Gringolandia.'' *Harper's* 279 (July 1989): 42–50.

[selected columns] "Dining In," *Gentlemen's Quarterly*, 58 (December 1988); 59 (February, March, April, May, June, November, December 1989); 60 (April, June, August 1990); 61 (July, August, October, December 1991); 62 (January, February 1992).

"Written in the Big Wind." *Harper's* 283 (September 1991): 45–53, 55, 57.

"Miss Defy." *Gentlemen's Quarterly* 61 (November 1991): 191–92, 194, 196, 198.

Studies of Bob Shacochis

Bausch, Richard. "Stepping through the Trapdoor" (Rev. of *The Next New World*). *New York Times Book Review* 94 (February 19, 1989): 10.

Fein, Cheri. "Free, White and Hairy-Chested" (Rev. of *Easy in the Islands*). *New York Times Book Review* 90 (February 17, 1985): 13.

Garrett, George. Rev. of *Easy in the Islands. Dictionary of Literary Biography Yearbook: 1985*, 242.

Gray, Paul. "Moving North" (Rev. of *The Next New World*). *Time* 133 (January 16, 1989): 72.

———. "Paradise Lost" (Rev. of *Easy in the Islands*). *Time* 125 (February 18, 1985): 100.

Interviews

Berkley, Miriam. "Uneasy in the Limelight." *Publishers Weekly* 228 (December 20, 1985): 50, 52.

Graham, Matthew. "An Interview with Bob Shacochis." *AWP Newsletter* 20 (May 19, 1988): 1–4.

Plath, James. "An Interview with Bob Shacochis." *Black Warrior Review* 16 (Spring/Summer 1990): 38–51.

Ross, Jean W. "CA Interview." In *Contemporary Authors*, vol. 124, pp. 399–402. Detroit: Gale Research, 1988.

Susan Richards Shreve
(1939–   )

A highly dramatic writer of psychological novels, Susan Richards Shreve has received both criticism for her melodramatic plots and intrusive editorial style and praise for her development of strong, vivid central characters and her sensitive handling of familial relationships.

BIOGRAPHY

Susan Richards Shreve was born on May 2, 1939, in Toledo, Ohio. Her father, Robert Kenneth Richards, whose own father died when Robert was 10 years old, was from a working-class family of Welsh descent. After college, he became a crime reporter for the *Cincinnati Post*. Shreve's mother, Helen Elizabeth Greene, who also suffered an early loss—her mother died when she was 8—was from an upper middle-class family. Harboring thwarted dreams of becoming a New York artist, model, or dancer, Helen followed her father's advice and became a schoolteacher. For years she was engaged to an ex-basketball player. Shortly before the wedding, though, perhaps in compensation for her relinquished dreams, she left her fiancé to marry the crime reporter.

On the way to Cincinnati after their wedding, Robert Richards displayed his crime reporter's sense of the dramatic, which would later fill his daughter's childhood and much later suffuse her fiction. Seeing a paper bag on the darkened road, he convinced himself and his new bride that the bag contained a baby. He stopped the car to examine the bag and found it empty. When he returned to the car with the empty bag, his bride asked him why he thought there was a baby in the bag. He replied: "There could have been a baby." Later he explained that he "couldn't imagine that it was simply an empty paper bag." Having lived in a house full of her father's stories, Shreve notes, "I grew up believing that there could be a baby in an empty paper bag."

In 1943, when Shreve was 3 years old, her parents moved from Toledo to Washington, D.C. There her father pursued a job as war correspondent in Europe but accepted a position as head of radio censorship for the war office. During the war, Shreve and her family lived in a house filled with soldiers and war correspondents who told exciting stories.

Several childhood illnesses—polio, rheumatic fever, and pneumonia—contributed to her sense of drama and later figure prominently in her fiction. During these illnesses, she listened to radio soap operas, which were full of violence, and acted out her own melodramas with paper dolls. These illnesses made her both aware and fearful of how precarious life can be. She confesses that even today she sees imminent danger everywhere; she believes "instinctively" that life demands "energy" and a "readiness to fight." This sensitivity to danger and instinct for survival is exhibited by the characters in her fiction.

After her convalescence, Shreve continued to make up stories in which she was the heroine. Walking home from school, she "engaged in imaginary conversations." She wrote, directed, and acted in dramas that she produced in her family's living room. She wrote moralistic stories and published them in her own newspaper, which she sold door-to-door. "Invention," Shreve explains, "seemed to me as true as the facts of things, truer because it showed the facts for what they were."

Near the end of the war, Shreve moved with her parents and younger brother to a farm in Vienna, Virginia, an experience that forms the core of her seventh novel, A Country of Strangers (1989). Shreve's father, eager to put into practice his democratic ideals, tried to educate the local Southerners in equal treatment of blacks. Despite the blacks' uneasiness, he invited them into his home, visited in their homes, and arranged to have their children play with his children. At one point, his officiousness nearly led to violence.

Later, the family moved back to Washington, which, according to Shreve, was at the time a small Southern town; it was segregated and everyone knew everyone else. She attended Sidwell Friends School, where she was exposed to liberal ideals and to the hypocrisy of those who espoused those ideals. During this time, Shreve explains, she had absolute faith in nothing but her family. In her parents' house, she enjoyed the company of colorful guests, "decent people down on their luck," whom her father took in. Dinnertime was an occasion for good stories and laughter.

Shreve's strong family ties have played a central role in her life and fiction. On the one hand, she has drawn from these ties the energy and resolve to face both real and imagined adversity. At 6 years old, Shreve remained unshaken when Sister Kenny, an expert on polio victims, proclaimed that Shreve would not be able to walk by the time she was 12 years old. Explaining her imperturbability in the face of Sister Kenny's prognosis, Shreve says: "My mother told me I could walk. . . . And I believed her." On the other hand, her family's overprotection fostered romantic fantasies that made Shreve not fully prepared for some of life's challenges. Shortly before she was married, she lost weight and "reassumed the body of a young girl, hoping . . . to ignore" the responsibilities of marriage.

Those romantic fantasies are evident in an early novel Shreve wrote when she was 19. Neither this work nor an even earlier, autobiographical novel was published. For a decade after writing these works, Shreve did not write another novel. Soon after graduating magna cum laude from the University of Pennsylvania, where she studied literature and writing, Shreve gave up her dream of a writing career for marriage and a career as a teacher and, later, a mother. On May 26, 1962, at Washington Cathedral, she married Porter Gaylord Shreve, an ex-football star and "a man of reserve and dignity," whom she first met on a blind date when she was 16 years old. For several years, she taught in various elementary schools in Cheshire, England, Philadelphia, and Washington. In 1966 she had her first child, Porter Gaylord Shreve III. Three more children, Elizabeth, Caleb, and Kate, followed. In 1968, she and her family moved to rural Virginia, where she and her husband received M.A.s from the University of Virginia. At the university, Shreve studied under Peter Taylor, who, she says, paid "attention . . . at a moment when it really made a difference." With his encouragement, she resumed serious writing.

In 1970 Shreve and her family moved back to Philadelphia, where in 1972, she, her husband, and her brother founded an alternative high school. In the same year, she began work on a novel, *A Fortunate Madness*, which was published in 1974. In 1975, as if to recapture their childhoods, Shreve and her husband moved back to Washington, D.C., settled into a large house not far from the house in which Shreve grew up, and sent their children to Friends schools they had attended. Shortly afterward, Shreve's brother and his wife and Shreve's mother and her new husband moved nearby. The house was filled with children, pets, relatives, friends, and boarding students. In 1976, Shreve accepted a professorship at George Mason University, where she has taught ever since.

In 1977 Shreve published a second novel, *A Woman Like That*, as well as *The Nightmares of Geranium Street*, a book for older teens. Since then, in addition to six adult novels, Shreve has published two books for older teens and nine books for younger children. Two new works for children, *Joshua T. Bates Takes Charge* and *The Girl Who Was Like Her Mother*, are expected in spring 1993. Most of Shreve's children's books are novels that draw on her own childhood experiences and those of her children. Author of short stories, essays, and reviews, Shreve usually writes for two hours in the morning before she goes to teach at the university.

Shreve and her husband were divorced in 1987. That same year, she married her literary agent, Timothy Seldes. She continues to live in Washington, D.C., and to write novels. She is currently working on her ninth adult novel, *A Sense of the Heart*, a love story set in the capital.

MAJOR THEMES

Seven of Shreve's eight published adult novels are set in part or entirely in her hometown, Washington, D.C., during the 1940s, 1950s, and 1960s. Although

Shreve points out that Washington at that time was still a small Southern town, Shreve's fiction largely reflects its cosmopolitan aspects. Two other major settings of her novels, New York City and Philadelphia, are obviously cosmopolitan. In fact, many of Shreve's characters have come to Washington to escape the constraints of small Midwestern towns, which have more in common with the small towns of most Southern fiction than does Washington, D.C. Only in treating racial tension in the capital city and in a small community in rural Virginia does Shreve capture a culture that is identifiably Southern. Ironically, the only novel set entirely above the Mason-Dixon line, in a small community in Massachusetts, captures the provincialism evident in much Southern fiction.

Shreve develops her novels in short narrative passages, moving from character to character and from the present to the past and back again. All of her novels are psychological novels. Most of her characters are upper middle-class professionals—doctors, lawyers, senators, Supreme Court justices, bureaucrats, advertising executives, professors, psychologists, architects, journalists, writers, artists, and actors. Nearly all of them are driven, in an almost Dreiser-like fashion, to achieve, to make some large gesture with their lives. Shreve uses a broad stroke in painting the exterior lives of these characters, usually concentrating on dramatic deeds. She gives, however, just enough detail about their day-to-day existence and surroundings to provide a sense of their everyday lives and a sense of place. The intensity and drama of her characters' actions are matched by the intensity of their interior lives. Her characters most often reflect on their own struggles for identity and conflicts with other characters. When her characters are not making grand gestures or being quietly introspective, they are usually talking with each other, most often interpreting and evaluating each others' lives.

Though not uniquely Southern, many of Shreve's major themes are staples of Southern fiction. Her central theme is the search for meaning and identity. This search most often involves Shreve's characters' reconciliation with their own personal and family history. Frequently the reconciliation is to the loss of a loved one. Shreve also develops several other major themes: The acceptance of a nontraditional family, the conflict between family and career, insanity, the cruelty of innocents, the development of the artist, the role of the artist in the community, and interracial relationships.

Shreve's first published novel, *A Fortunate Madness*, describes a woman's search for self-knowledge after the death of her husband. The first half of the novel describes the woman's growing disillusionment with her marriage: Her boredom with the traditional role of housewife, her dissatisfaction with her husband's uncommunicativeness, and her resentment at his failure to provide for his wife and son. The second half of the book describes the woman's breakdown after the death of her husband and her struggle to come to grips with guilt, fear, and her own self-image.

In an important scene of the novel, the woman, Susanna MacPherson, and her husband, Peter, lose their way in the Italian Alps. To help allay her fears, Peter tells Susanna ''a story about a little boy who kept a dragon in a clock box.

The dragon . . . grew and grew until his wings were not soft anymore and then he flew away." As Peter tells the story, Susanna envisions herself "curled beneath the comforter in darkness, falling asleep to her father's voice as he read to her." The fetal images here of the dragon and of Susanna beneath the covers emphasize her childlike dependence on a father figure to protect her. Like the dragon, though, Susanna in the course of the novel—through Peter's death and her subsequent breakdown—grows wings that allow her the courage and faith to stand without the support of a man. Her breakdown is fortunate because it gives her insight not only into her own vulnerability and strength but also into the vulnerability and strength of both her husband and widowed mother. Paradoxically, she also learns the valuable emotional resource of family ties and, thus, can at the end of the novel reestablish relationships with her mother and her son.

In her second novel, *A Woman Like That*, set in Washington, D.C., Philadelphia, and New York City, Shreve again focuses on a woman's search for identity. In this novel the search ends in tragedy. Shreve also develops here a related theme, one's inability to escape the past. Whereas Susanna MacPherson is forced out of the cocoon of a secure childhood, in *A Woman Like That*, Emily Fielding faces the consequences of an insecure childhood. About midway through the novel, Emily, a sculptor and soap opera star, responds to a fan who complains about her television character's choice of men. "Someone else writes the script," Emily explains. This is Emily's problem in real life as well—someone else has written the script. As a child, Emily suffers from parental neglect. Furthermore, as an adolescent, she witnesses her father murder her mother and subsequently perjures herself to protect him.

From childhood on into adulthood, Emily responds to parental neglect and later the tragedy of her mother's death with remarkable spunk and self-possession. Early in her childhood, she reacts by misbehaving in school. As a young adolescent, she turns to religion and then promiscuity and art as a stay against the chaos of her homelife. As an adult, she pours her energy and sense of fulfillment into her art and illegitimate child. The emotional fortress she has maintained since adolescence is penetrated, however, when she falls in love with a psychologist. At first she is happy in the relationship, but when she returns to her grandparents' home—the scene of her early childhood neglect—and, later, when she finds that her daughter has run away, her own childhood insecurity, guilt, and fear resurface and she descends into madness and eventually commits suicide. Unlike most of Shreve's characters, Emily is unable to come to grips with the past.

In her third novel, *Children of Power* (1979), set in Washington, D.C., and Manawa, Wisconsin, Shreve again focuses on the search for identity and the coming to terms with the past. She also develops the theme of the abuses of power and the cruelty of innocents. The novel covers six days in the lives of a host of characters with flashbacks ranging back 60 years. The central character, Natty Taylor, has played for her overprotective father the role of the perfect daughter despite, or because of, her withered leg. As a teenager, though, Natty is seeking some independence from her father, Sam Taylor, chairman of the Federal Communications Commission, in part because he has offered refuge to the fallen and drunken Joseph McCarthy even though he has earlier denounced McCarthy's political witch-hunt. Unfortunately, in establishing independence from her father, Natty takes up with a group of fellow students from Sidwell Friends who, in displaced anger at Natty's involvement with a star athlete from a rival school, plot to remove her father from the FCC, ostensibly because of his association with McCarthy. With some moral qualms and a misguided belief that she is protecting her father, Natty agrees to fake her own kidnapping in order to force her father to resign. The ruse ends disastrously in the death of one of the students.

Both Natty and Sam are reacting to an inordinate sense of responsibility to their fathers. Natty, in rebelling against this self-imposed expectation, learns of her own potential for evil. Sam comes to the realization that his offer of refuge to McCarthy and excessive love for his daughter are compensations for his sense of loss and sense of responsibility in the death of his alcoholic father. Numerous other characters in the book come to similar revelations about what part familial relationships and events, most often the loss of a parent or spouse, play in their motivations to achieve success or to protect their children. As one critic notes, this novel is not only about the politics of politics, but also about the politics of love. As in her earlier two works, Shreve here emphasizes the power and value of love, along with the need for personal boundaries and accountability.

In her fourth novel, *Miracle Play* (1981), set mainly in rural Pennsylvania and New York City, Shreve again focuses on a central character's search for identity. Taking her own family as inspiration, Shreve develops further the theme of familial relationships, this time to the point of making the family a major character of the novel. In addition, Shreve develops the theme of the developing artist. The first part of the book focuses on the marriage of Cally and Nat Howells—specifically, Nat's decision to forego a career to rear his four children in the face of his wife's physical and intermittent emotional paralysis. The remainder of the book focuses on their daughter Julia and her attempts to come to terms with her father's death and to find independence from her overprotective family by pursuing drama, first as an aspiring actress and later as a playwright.

As several reviewers have pointed out, Julia attempts to escape her family through her art only to find herself writing about her family. Unconsciously, Julia is doing what Shreve says she is attempting to do through her art: "What I do know is that we inherit from the lives of our parents a complex of patterns which can give a sense of order to our lives. When I write, I am looking for these patterns."

After Julia's disturbed son, whom Julia has neglected in pursuing her art, burns down a portion of the family home in rural Pennsylvania, Julia comes back from New York City to attend to her children and her crumbling marriage. At the end, we find Julia writing another play, again about her family. This time, however, Julia appreciates her family ties and, in creating her "miracle play," purposefully draws upon her family, which she realizes is in itself a miracle play in its ability to survive misfortune and to find solace in the precious and ephemeral moments of familial intimacy, like those moments described in the closing scene of the novel: "After the festivities . . . the Howells children lay around. . . . There was in the room a wonderful spirit of accord that must come to soldiers in the trenches after a long volley has been survived—a company knowledge that the treasure of living comes in moments and is prized because the moment does not last."

In her fifth novel, *Dreaming of Heroes* (1984), Shreve again focuses on a central character's search for identity. Early in the novel, the central character, Jamie Waters, refers to her mother's story of a woman "who metamorphosed into a moth so that she could get to France to meet her lover." It is obviously such imaginative stories that prompt Jamie to tell her mother that she'd "like to be [a] hero kind of saint." Later, as an adult, Jamie is described as having "an urgent need to touch some larger spirit than her own, to be eaten alive and emerge whole." The novel, a bildungsroman, describes Jamie's pursuit of this goal.

At the beginning of the novel, Jamie and her mother, somewhat like the moth in the story, move from a small town in Ohio to Washington, D.C., to pursue a man whose picture they have seen in the paper. The man has been hailed as a hero for saving the president from an assassin and bears a remarkable resemblance to Jamie's father, who has supposedly died in the war. Though neither Jamie nor her mother ever meets this man, the search for this image of a heroic father figure gives Jamie the opportunity to become the hero she envisions herself becoming.

In Washington, Jamie survives a near-fatal bout with meningitis and the unsuccessful pursuit of a young love. Finally, she turns to religion—first Catholicism and later the Episcopal priesthood—for a sense of meaning and order in her life. Working within the Episcopal Church, the charismatic Jamie inspires others to believe in themselves, establishes a nationwide network of homes for runaway girls, and organizes a national rally against nuclear armament.

When, at the rally, one of the runaway girls, a girl who has become Jamie's almost constant companion, is crushed to death beneath the stage upon which Jamie is delivering the keynote speech, Jamie is devastated by grief, guilt, and doubts about her vision of herself and her service to others. Like other Shreve protagonists, Jamie through tragedy finds not only personal redemption and an appreciation of the ties that bind human beings but also an acceptance of the fragility of those ties. At the end of the novel, Jamie demonstrates her personal growth when her mother dies. To her astonishment, she is bereaved but not devastated. After her mother's death, as if to fulfill her mother's story of the moth, Jamie goes to France to look for her father's grave.

In distinguishing her sixth novel, *Queen of Hearts* (1986), from *Miracle Play*,

Shreve explains that *Queen of Hearts* is "an act of imagination." Drawing less upon her own personal experience than she does in most of her other novels, she relies more on imagery and symbolism. A central symbol of the novel is the Edenic image of the garden and the snake, the snake representing both the temptation to evil and repressed sexual passion. Within this biblical context, Shreve again develops the themes of the search for identity and redemption and the cruelty of innocents. She also explores the role of the artist in the community. Although the main focus of the novel is Francesca Woodbine's search for identity, a number of other characters in the book undertake this quest. Indeed, the entire community achieves by the end of the novel a better understanding of itself.

Francesca Woodbine discovers her vulnerability to and her own capacity for evil. In the opening chapter of the novel, she is raped by a man who alludes— accurately—to her grandmother's profession, prostitution. Later, pregnant and anticipating her upcoming marriage to the mayor's son, Colin Mallory, she walks along the snake-filled river that winds through Bethany, Massachusetts, the small town in which she lives. Finding Colin with another woman, she leaves and returns with her father's gun and shoots the young man, who is to the town a symbol of the invincibility and virility of youth.

In the aftermath of Colin's murder, the town becomes haunted and paranoid by this murder of innocence. Unable to uncover the murderer, the community is only able to restore communal trust when it is brought together by the devastation of a hurricane. Through the years of rebuilding the town, Francesca, like other Shreve protagonists, finds escape from her personal demons and a sense of meaning and order through art. Symbolically adorning her grandmother's clothes and employing the gift of "magical sight" inherited from her grandmother, she becomes a nationally known songwriter and folksinger. Given the sobriquet "Queen of Hearts," she writes songs about the people "of Bethany, discovering in the blighted lives of her own town, crouched just beneath the surface of pretended happiness, mysteries of the human heart."

Her gift of sight, however, does not extend to herself when she becomes romantically involved with Will Weaver, who, because he has grown up motherless and apparently innocent, has been adopted as the "town mascot." Having given up his boyhood fascination with snakes, Will, unknown to Francesca and the rest of the community, has hallucinations in which he sees his mother decapitated. The town is also unaware that he has murdered a young woman with whom he was once romantically involved. In the climactic scene of the novel, Francesca barely escapes death when Will takes her for an automobile ride and then intentionally crashes the car, killing himself in the process.

In the aftermath of the tragedy, Francesca, in an act of personal redemption, confesses Colin's murder to her father but, to spare the community further suffering, does not make her sin public. Instead, she shares the community's grief and newfound knowledge of itself: In Bethany, "a certain joy had gone. An arrogance and promise captured in the brief life of Colin Mallory. There was no faith in an imagined future. And in the place of the old dangerous innocence, a new spirit of calm and humor which comes of knowing the dark side of the soul and surviving with a capacity for hope had settled in the New England town.''

In her seventh novel, *A Country of Strangers* (1989), Shreve once more draws on personal experience as she explores marital and interracial relationships. During World War II, Charley Fletcher, Deputy Director of Newspaper Censorship, and his family move from Minnesota to a farm in Virginia outside Washington, D.C. He has two reasons for the move. Suffering from impotence and strained relations with his wife, Lara, whom he suspects of having an affair, Charley wants to sequester his wife from further temptation. Also, he has a grand design: He wants to live as friends and equals with the Bellowses, the black tenant family on the farm. In the course of the novel, we learn the underlying motivations for his desire. Charley is driven by his mother's belief that her son has a ''great gift'' to give the world and is haunted by his father's disdain for his mother's expectation of Charley. Though he has excelled in school and in his career, Charley is now suffering a sense of failure, not only because of his strained marriage but also because he has been rejected by the army because of his flat feet.

As would be expected of the time and place, the Bellowses—two couples, Moses and Miracle and Guy and Aida, and their pregnant 13-year-old niece, Prudential—are uncomfortable with Charley's overtures to friendship. At one point, though, the two families come together in the spirit of friendship and familial closeness when, during a blizzard, Charley and his family assist in the birth of Prudential's baby. The newfound closeness between the families is later shattered, though, when the baby dies. In the climactic scene of the novel, Charley is shot protecting Aida from her husband's violent rage. In surviving his near-fatal wound, Charley learns of his own capacity for surviving failure and comes to see that his great gift was ''not for the world as his mother had imagined. But for himself.''

Other characters in the novel also come to better understandings of themselves. Miracle, who mourns the sense of self she found in her affair with the previous landlord, gives up her hallucinations of her former lover when Moses reaches out to help her overcome her madness. Similarly, Lara gives up her fantasies of other men when she realizes that the fantasies are merely a compensation for the loss of Charley. Moses comes to a recognition that his advances toward Lara represent a breach of the ''invisible boundaries between people that ran in the blood and . . . had to be considered.'' In the end of the novel, the Fletchers move back to the farm. This time, they establish a more circumscribed friendship with the Bellowses and share with them a knowledge of those human boundaries that cannot be breached.

Set in Wisconsin and Washington, D.C., Shreve's eighth novel, *Daughters of the New World* (1992), traces five generations of women from the 1890s to the 1990s. With major events of the twentieth century as a backdrop, the novel describes six women forging their identities in the face of personal hardship and tragedy. As in earlier novels, Shreve focuses on familial relationships, particularly that of mother and daughter. She emphasizes her characters' reconciliation with the past and their establishment of a balance between close familial ties and proper personal boundaries.

In her twelve books of juvenile fiction—*The Nightmares of Geranium Street* (1977), *Loveletters* (1978), *Family Secrets* (1979), *The Masquerade* (1980), *The Bad Dreams of a Good Girl* (1982), *The Revolution of Mary Leary* (1982), *The Flunking of Joshua T. Bates* (1984), *How I Saved the World on Purpose* (1985), *Lily and the Runaway Baby* (1987), *Lucy Forever and Miss Rosetree, Shrinks* (1987), *The Gift of the Girl Who Couldn't Hear* (1991), and *Wait for Me* (1992)— Shreve develops themes and characters similar to those of her adult fiction. Nearly all of them are highly dramatic and involve a youthful protagonist's search for meaning and identity in an often confusing world of familial relationships and peer pressure.

SURVEY OF CRITICISM

Criticism of Shreve has been largely limited to reviews, only a few of which eschew plot summary for in-depth criticism. Taken as a whole, the reviews reveal the overall strengths and weaknesses of Shreve's fiction, both adult and juvenile. On the one hand, reviewers almost universally praise Shreve's ability to hold the reader's interest with her compelling and suspenseful storytelling, variously attributed to her novels' foreboding tones, dramatic tensions (often sexual), and skillful unfolding of character. Critics laud her development of strong, vivid central characters and her convincing interaction between characters, developed through close introspective scenes and sharp, realistic, and, sometimes, humorous dialogue. They find her handling of familial relationships both sensitive and profound. Several reviewers applaud her fine sense of place and time and her narrative skill in weaving together different points of view and story lines. Doris Grumbach compares Shreve's use of short narrative scenes to Sherwood Anderson's narrative method in *Winesburg, Ohio*.

On the other hand, some reviewers fault Shreve for being melodramatic. These critics variously describe her plots as unfocused, unrestrained, unbelievable, and contrived (especially her happy endings), and her characterizations as heavy-handed. Specifically, they find the motives and relationships of Shreve's characters overly explained and inadequately realized through action, speech, and thought. Even some of the reviewers who affirm the depth of Shreve's central characters find her supporting characters too sketchily drawn and sometimes stereotypical. Tom Edwards is disturbed by the author's emphasis on giving her characters celebrity status and on anchoring them in actual events, as if personal experience, indeed life itself, only achieves significance in the context of public events and in the company of famous people. Several reviewers feel an emotional distance from Shreve's characters.

Apart from reviews, criticism of Shreve has been scant. James M. Hughes briefly notes how Shreve uses Ohio as a place of origin, sojourn, and, in rare instances, "significant return." In an interview with Shreve, Elizabeth Gleick gives a brief treatment of Shreve's major themes. In Gleick's interview and elsewhere, Shreve's own reflections on her life and work provide insight into her fiction. Susan Wood's interview sheds some light on Shreve's intentions in *Children of Power*. Shreve's essay "Writing for Children vs. Writing for Adults" reveals her general aims as a writer and her assessment of the structure and style of her fiction, both adult and juvenile.

BIBLIOGRAPHY

Works by Susan Richards Shreve

Adult Fiction

A Fortunate Madness. New York: Houghton Mifflin, 1974.
A Woman Like That. New York: Atheneum, 1977.
Children of Power. New York: Macmillan, 1979.
Miracle Play. New York: Morrow, 1981.
Dreaming of Heroes. New York: Morrow, 1984.
Queen of Hearts. New York: Simon and Schuster, 1986.
A Country of Strangers. New York: Simon and Schuster, 1989.
Daughters of the New World. New York: Nan A. Talese/Doubleday, 1992.

Juvenile Fiction

The Nightmares of Geranium Street. New York: Knopf, 1977.
Loveletters. New York: Knopf, 1978.
Family Secrets. New York: Knopf, 1979.
The Masquerade. New York: Knopf, 1980.
The Bad Dreams of a Good Girl. New York: Knopf, 1982.
The Revolution of Mary Leary. New York: Knopf, 1982.
The Flunking of Joshua T. Bates. New York: Knopf, 1984.
How I Saved the World on Purpose. New York: Holt, 1985.
Lily and the Runaway Baby. New York: Random House, 1987.
Lucy Forever and Miss Rosetree, Shrinks. New York: Holt, 1987.
The Gift of the Girl Who Couldn't Hear. New York: Tambourline/Morrow, 1991.
Wait for Me. New York: Tambourline/Morrow, 1992.

Other Works

"Writing for Children vs. Writing for Adults." *Publishers Weekly* 222 (July 23, 1982): 78–79.
"Shreve, Susan Richards," 197–200 in *Something About the Author*, Vol. 46, ed. Anne Commire. Detroit: Gale Research, 1987.
"Susan Richards Shreve," 225–41 in *Contemporary Authors Autobiography Series*, Vol. 5, ed. Adele Sarkissian. Detroit: Gale Research, 1987.
"Memory in Black and White." *Washington Post Magazine* (March 26, 1989): 24–26.

Studies of Susan Richards Shreve

Collins, Anne. "The Politics of Politics, the Politics of Love" (Rev. of *Children of Power*). *Maclean's* 92 (July 30, 1979): 45.

Commire, Anne, ed. "Shreve, Susan Richards," 209–10 in *Something About the Author*, Vol. 41. Detroit: Gale Research, 1985.

Digilio, Alice. Rev. of *The Revolution of Mary Leary*. *Washington Post Book World* (October 10, 1982): 7.

Edwards, Tom. "Just a Woman Rock Star Priest" (Rev. of *Dreaming of Heroes*). *New York Times Book Review* (April 1, 1984): 8.

Evans, Katherine. "A Washington Novel with a Difference" (Rev. of *A Woman Like That*). *Washington Post Book World* (March 23, 1977): B2.

Evory, Ann, ed. "Shreve, Susan Richards," 488–89 in *Contemporary Authors: New Revision Series*, Vol. 5. Detroit: Gale Research, 1982.

Freeman, Suzanne. "Family on the Edge of Fame" (Rev. of *Miracle Play*). *Washington Post Book World* (July 26, 1981): 5, 7.

Gleick, Elizabeth. "Susan Richards Shreve." *Publishers Weekly* 230 (December 19, 1986): 35–36.

Grumbach, Doris. "Four Compelling Novels about the Lives of the Young" (Rev. of *Children of Power*). *Chronicle of Higher Education* 18 (April 16, 1979): R12–13.

Gunton, Sharon R., and Jean C. Stine, ed. "Susan Richards Shreve," 402–405 in *Contemporary Literary Criticism*, Vol. 23. Detroit: Gale Research, 1983.

Holtze, Sally Holmes, ed. "Susan Shreve," 277–78 in *Sixth Book of Junior Authors and Illustrators*. New York: H. W. Wilson, 1989.

Hughes, James M. "Susan Richards Shreve: Ohio Author?" *Ohionana Quarterly* 28 (Spring 1985): 8–9.

Kennedy, Eileen. Rev. of *A Fortunate Madness*. *Best Sellers* 34 (August 1, 1974): 212.

King, Florence. "A Yankee in Virginia" (Rev. of *A Country of Strangers*). *Los Angeles Times Book Review* (March 15, 1989): 7.

Moynahan, Julian. "Slide Show" (Rev. of *Miracle Play*). *New York Times Book Review* (August 16, 1981): 8, 23.

Parini, Jay. Rev. of *Queen of Hearts*. *Los Angeles Times Book Review* (February 8, 1987): 1, 7.

Penner, Jonathan. "School Yard McCarthyism" (Rev. of *Children of Power*). *Washington Post Book World* (April 1, 1979): E3.

Pollitt, Katha. "A Doomful Daughter" (Rev. of *A Woman Like That*). *New York Times Book Review* (July 10, 1977): 28.

Smith, David Lionel. Rev. of *A Country of Strangers*. *America* 161 (August 5, 1989): 68–69.

Urbanska, Wanda. Rev. of *A Country of Strangers*. *Chicago Tribune Books* (January 8, 1989): 6.

Van Strum, Carol. "A Saint Grows up in Cleveland Park" (Rev. of *Dreaming of Heroes*). *Washington Post Book World* (March 25, 1984): 11.

Wood, Susan. "Tell-Tale Trio: John Coyne, Barbara Raskin, Susan Shreve." *Washington Post Magazine* (December 31, 1978): 5.

Yardley, Jonathan. "The Secret Lives of Ordinary People" (Rev. of *Queen of Hearts*). *Washington Post Book World* (December 14, 1986): 3.

ELIZABETH PELL BROADWELL

Lee Smith
(1944–   )

Although she is a gifted writer of short stories that probe domestic crises of identity in contemporary suburbia, Lee Smith is best known for her novels set in the mountains of Appalachia. In these highly acclaimed works, she evokes an unmistakable sense of place and captures the voices of the past. Experimenting with narrative technique, Smith weaves together history, folklore, and legend to explore changes in family, community, class, and culture.

BIOGRAPHY

Lee Smith, the only child of Ernest Lee Smith and Virginia Marshall Smith, was born on November 1, 1944, in Grundy, a small town in the heart of the coal-mining region of southwest Virginia. Her father's family were "real mountain people" who had lived in the area for generations. Her father had the attractive, rough appeal of a mountain man and the business acumen of a successful entrepreneur. A staunch Roosevelt democrat who ran the campaigns for other family members involved in state and local politics, he borrowed money to start a dime store, which remains a successful business in the center of Grundy today. Her mother, a college graduate and a schoolteacher by training, was from the aristocratic east coast of Virginia, far enough removed geographically and culturally from the insular mountain community to cause her to be viewed as a "foreigner" and to make her feel like an outsider. As a child growing up in Buchanan County, the poorest county in the state, Smith remembers her father, who was subject to bouts of depression, as a hard worker and proud of his accomplishments and her somewhat anxious mother as the family organizer with "many notions" about being a lady.

From a very early age, Smith was a voracious reader and a constant writer. She always knew she wanted to be a writer when she grew up. As a child, she published many pieces in the children's magazine *Jack and Jill*. When she was only 9 or 10, she paid other children a nickel each to copy the little handwritten newsletter she wrote monthly and to distribute it to the neighbors. Each issue, which resembled a " 'This Is Your Life' Sketch," would feature a particular neighbor, whom the young writer had interviewed.

Encouraged by both parents to attend a boarding school because it would offer better preparation than the local school for her future career, Smith spent the last 2 years of high school at St. Catherine's in Richmond, Virginia. From St. Catherine's, she went to Hollins College in Roanoke, Virginia, because it had a good writing program and it was "close to home." At Hollins, she studied under Richard W. Dillard and Louis D. Rubin, Jr., took a creative writing class every semester, and met with other writing students every Wednesday night for 4 years in Rubin's home. Although her professors encouraged her to "write what you know," it was only when she encountered the short stories of Eudora Welty in Rubin's Southern literature course that she began to write from her own experiences. As a freshman, she was active in starting an alternative literary magazine so that freshmen would have a format for their writing. As an upper-classman, she and a number of other classmates, motivated by their study of American literature, reenacted Huck Finn's journey down the Mississippi by building their own raft and lighting out from Paducah, Kentucky, for the territory ahead. When Hollins asked Smith to take a hiatus for a year for not adhering to the regulations during the school's program abroad, Rubin arranged for her to work under James J. Kilpatrick at the *Richmond News Leader*. While rooming in a boardinghouse in Richmond and working as an assistant to Kilpatrick, she got to know the journalist's wife, the sculptor Marie Pietri, who, Smith says, was the first woman artist she had ever known personally and who became an important role model.

After returning to Hollins as a senior, Smith won one of twelve fellowships given nationally by the Book of the Month Club for her early version of *The Last Day the Dogbushes Bloomed*, a novel describing an eventful summer in 9-year-old Susan Tobey's life when her parents' divorce and her encounter with a disturbed little boy from the city bring her knowledge of sex and death. When the novel was published by Harper and Row the following year (1968), Kilpatrick wrote an appreciative review in his nationally syndicated column, predicting Smith was "headed for the bright circle of shining stars" that included such writers as Ellen Glasgow, Harper Lee, and Eudora Welty.

Following her graduation from Hollins in 1967, Smith turned down a writing fellowship to Columbia to marry poet James E. Seay after a whirlwind courtship, conducted under "the antiseptic conditions of a girl's school." Supportive of Seay's career, Smith moved every time her husband's work took him to a different university, finding jobs for herself in journalism or teaching at each location and staying home for 3 years when the couple's two children, 1½ years apart in age, were small. Unable to find time to write when she was home with the children, she would make up stories in her head, some of which emerged later as short stories in her volume *Cakewalk* (1981). In Tuscaloosa, Alabama, where sons Josh (December 23, 1969) and Page (May 22, 1971) were born, Smith wrote her second novel, *Something in the Wind* (1971), and worked as a feature writer, film critic, and editor of the *Sun* magazine for the *Tuscaloosa News* (1968–69). Although her second novel was reviewed favorably, it did not receive much critical attention. Like her first novel, *Something in the Wind* is the story of a girl's initiation, but it lacks the intensity of the earlier novel. Smith herself observes it has all the flaws of a second novel, noting specifically that she failed to integrate the two short stories on which the book was based. It was in her capacity as a reporter covering the Tuscaloosa sequicentennial that Smith found her main subject for her third novel, which was written after she and her family had moved to Nashville, where they remained for 3 years. *Fancy Strut* (1973) was hailed by critics as a comic masterpiece and praised for its re-creation of life in a small Southern town.

By 1975, Smith had written her fourth novel, *Black Mountain Breakdown*, but did not immediately find a publisher for this book, which illustrated the dangers of passivity, a characteristic Smith recognized in women who grew up in the South. In 1974 she had moved with her family to Chapel Hill, North Carolina, where Seay had taken a teaching position at the university, and in 1978 she joined him and her former mentor, Louis Rubin, on the creative writing staff. That year Smith won an O. Henry award for her short story "Mrs. Darcy Meets the Blue-Eyed Stranger at the Beach" and two years later, in 1980, she won her second O. Henry for "Between the Lines." Five years after *Black Mountain Breakdown* had been completed, and then taken through numerous revisions, it was published by Putnam's, upon the advice of Faith Sale, who served as Smith's editor for this book and for every book she has published since. Smith marks the beginning of her "second writing career" with having her books edited, and, most especially, with her editor, Faith Sale, whose suggestions for revision, Smith says, she always considers. Her first novel to be set in the mountains of Appalachia and to use what Smith calls an "intrusive, down-home narrative voice," which freed her to write about her characters "without writing down to them," *Black Mountain Breakdown* was Smith's first book to be widely reviewed. Shortly after the publication of *Black Mountain Breakdown*, Smith published *Cakewalk* (1981), a collection of fourteen short stories written over 11 years.

In 1981, around the time of the breakup of her marriage with Seay, Smith accepted a professorship at North Carolina State University in Raleigh, where she remains today. With the publication of her fifth novel in 1983, Lee Smith became a nationally acclaimed author. Smith herself maintains that she really did not know how to write a novel before she wrote this one. Her only novel up to that time whose origin could not be traced back to a short story, *Oral History* was the first novel whose design she fully framed before she began writing. In her desire to preserve a sense of Appalachian people and language of previous generations, Smith immersed herself in histories of the region, biographies, and books on folklore.

Whereas her research for *Oral History* engaged her academically, Smith's preparation for writing her sixth novel, *Family Linen*, involved her in a more active way. Because one of the central characters in this book was to be a hairdresser, Smith began her research at a local beauty shop, where she shampooed customers' hair and took notes on everything from the price of salon chairs to the different types of permanents. Dedicated to her second husband, Hal Crowther—an established journalist formerly with *Newsweek* and *Time* magazines and now with the *Independent*—*Family Linen* was published in 1985, the year Smith and Crowther married. Of all the novels Smith has written, *Family Linen* has the most positive ending. Brought together initially to attend their dying mother and, finally, to celebrate a wedding, family members, whose lives have been conditioned by a past previously unexamined, learn to use the past creatively and to make significant changes during their middle-age years.

Smith's vision darkens considerably in her next novel, *Fair and Tender Ladies* (1988). The tone of this novel reflects the personal difficulties Smith was experiencing at the time. With several family members ill and her mother dying, she wrote an epistolary novel that spans the life of a mountain woman, a character whose strength and voice sustained the author through her own hardships. For years, Smith said, she had been taping her relatives, documenting their lives, their stories, and their language. As she had when writing *Oral History*, she researched Appalachian legends, history, songs, and tales to create a novel that offers both a compelling character, who uses colloquial speech and phonetic spelling, and an appealing history of the Appalachian region. Published in 1988, the year Smith was awarded the John Dos Passos Prize for Literature, it is generally recognized as the author's most fully realized and successful novel. For *Fair and Tender Ladies*, Smith received the Appalachian Writers Award and the W. D. Weatherford Award for Appalachian Literature, both in 1989.

Me and My Baby View the Eclipse, Smith's second collection of short stories, was published in 1990. Most of these stories were written after the collapse of her first marriage and are about the "eclipses" in life—divorce, illness, death, and the loss of dreams. For the story "Mom" from this collection, Smith received the PEN/Faulkner Award in 1991. Recently awarded a Lyndhurst Foundation Grant, she has been appointed a Fellow of Duke University's Center for Documentary Studies in the South. On leave from North Carolina State University, she completed *The Devil's Dream* (1992), her eighth novel, which is a history of a singing family in country music, as they moved from the mountain valleys of Virginia, where they lived generations ago, to Nashville, where they live today.

In advance of writing a novel, Lee Smith spends a long time, perhaps 1½ years, completing research, outlining the design, and making detailed notes about the characters. She writes everything out in longhand on yellow legal pads. She may use twenty sheets of paper planning one character, and if it's a male, as much as a whole legal pad. She works best in her Chapel Hill home, which is surrounded by woods and wildflowers. Appalachian quilts, colorful reminders of her mountain heritage, decorate the walls of her house. Speaking in the lilting rhythms of her native mountain homeland, greeting friends and strangers alike with an irresistible smile and wide blue eyes, Smith immediately conveys a refreshing acceptance of others and of herself.

MAJOR THEMES

Like many Southern writers before and during her time, Lee Smith writes about woman's search for identity, the growth of an artist, the relationship of language to the quest for meaning, and the function of the past in the present. Smith herself has said that Southern writers ''don't have any new material'' and so they must ''make'' their subject ''new through language—through point of view, through tone, through style,'' Although she demonstrates in her earliest works a thematic interest in language, Smith has increasingly realized this goal of recasting her subject in her later works, especially in those that center on the region and people of Appalachia.

Central to Smith's earliest novels is a young girl's or woman's search for identity, a quest that is conducted in the context of the Southern family and Southern society. In *The Last Day the Dogbushes Bloomed*, *Something in the Wind*, and *Black Mountain Breakdown*, the protagonist is impeded rather than aided by her parents. With their separate bedrooms (in *The Last Day the Dogbushes Bloomed*, separate floors as well), the parents in all three books represent the opposing values of the public and private spheres. The mother's domain is social; the father's is often artistic. (Brooke's father, whose pragmatism marks him as much a part of the public sphere as does his wife's social facility, is the exception; in *Something in the Wind*, the artistic, private realm is best represented by crazy Aunt Bet.) In each book, the daughter is torn between the opposing values embodied in her parents, who are themselves extreme examples of human fragmentation in Southern society.

Even the traditions and heritage of Southern society, which embrace a reality that is principally social, offer only formula and ritual instead of meaning and integration. In each novel, the protagonist tries but fails to find meaning in inherited religion or in the past. In these three novels, which focus on a loss of innocence and an initiation to sex and death, Smith creates protagonists who are progressively older and whose initiation becomes increasingly experiential and more devastating. Finding in their Southern environment only circumscribed social images and codes of behavior rather than encouragement toward self-definition, the protagonists develop defenses that prevent them from acknowledging and examining the fragmented condition of their world and from achieving an integrated sense of self. Susan Tobey constructs a fairy-tale illusion to prevent knowledge of her parents' impending separation; Brooke Kincaid consciously splits her "mind" into "two brookes"; and Crystal Spangler vascillates between the social world of beauty contests and political functions and the private world of a suicidal lover and, finally, catatonia. Despite these psychological defenses that facilitate their movement in the social world but hinder their progress toward self-discovery, these main characters, all developing artists, use language to order and shape their world and to create a sense of self.

In the first-person narratives of *The Last Day the Dogbushes Bloomed* and *Something in the Wind*, language functions as the main character's response to and re-creation of the world. In *Black Mountain Breakdown*, the use of omniscience results in both a greater emphasis on place, which becomes more integral to character, and a greater indictment of society, which seems more volitional in its oppressiveness of the individual. Smith's shift in point of view, from a single first-person narrator to omniscience and multiple perspectives, causes language to be less a preoccupation of character and more a concern of the text itself. In her later books, in which the focus shifts from the individual as such to the individual in the context of her environment, Smith's use of omniscience or of multiple perspectives yields a closer and a more complex examination of the Southern community.

The evolution of Smith's use of multiple perspectives, a technique most fully realized in *Oral History* and *Family Linen*, began with her third novel, *Fancy Strut*. Here Smith creates a range of characters and employs the limited omniscient point of view to emphasize the network of social and family relationships in which the individual moves. Like the later novel *Family Linen*, this book examines a central event from the perspectives of different characters. In *Fancy Strut*, the focus is a small town's week-long preparation for its sesquicentennial; in *Family Linen*, family members gather to attend to their mother, whose sudden illness and death uncover family secrets long buried. The multiple points of view in both books suggest the subjectivity of knowledge and the inaccessibility of the past. In *Fancy Strut*, where Smith's purpose is satire, characters' efforts to re-create the past are defeated by their own ambivalence and by Smith's comic vision. In *Family Linen*, characters literally dig up the remains of their father, unearthing the mystery of his murder and gaining access to their own subconscious drives.

In Smith's Appalachian novels the theme of the presence of the past is most pervasive, and language becomes the subject of the text. In *Oral History* and *Fair and Tender Ladies*, a traditional, rural mountain culture is set against an increasingly industrialized and homogenized modern society. For all of its limitations, the past holds characters of nearly mythic stature with voices that resound in the next holler and reverberate into future generations. With strong passions and stronger convictions, Smith's mountain people live in harmony with their landscapes, whose power and beauty provide an appropriate setting for their grand passions and simple rituals, such as storytelling and hog killings, which mark the passing of time. In contrast to such a vital past, Smith juxtaposes the modern day, where the effects of industrialization are seen on the land and in the people. The land has been stripped of its coal and its lumber, and characters are distracted by the effects of materialism and the passage of time. Talk is often substituted for action. Although it clearly holds some of the substance of times past, the present is associated with a tragic sense of loss.

The search for meaning informs the point of view and the structure of both *Oral History* and *Fair and Tender Ladies*. In *Oral History*, which follows the Cantrell family over four generations and uses multiple perspectives, characters' desire for something beyond the familiar and ordinary leads them to attempt to find meaning in otherness rather than in self. In contrast, Ivy Rowe's collection of letters, which forms *Fair and Tender Ladies*, reveals her own inner-directed search for meaning. The use of interior monologues in *Oral History* and letters to a dead sister in *Fair and Tender Ladies* reinforces Smith's emphasis on perception and language. Both novels are about storytelling, mythmaking, and the use of language for self-definition. In *Oral History*, Granny recounts in minute detail events at which she was not present, and a rumor beginning in one generation (Red Emmy's curse) exists as fact by the next generation. In *Fair and Tender Ladies*, the sense of audience is vital to the storytelling process: Just as the Cline sisters need each other to tell their stories, Ivy needs Silvaney for her audience. Here and in many of her other works as well, Smith embraces the process of life and art. In both novels, the text is, finally, subversive. Although Smith has said that the first-person narratives in *Oral History* are what Jennifer's tape recorder picks up, Granny's reveries into pure fiction, the novel's written journal entries, the occasional lapses into omniscience during the first-person narratives, and Sally's own subversive narrative all point to a text that calls attention to itself and to its narrative techniques. In *Fair and Tender Ladies*, Ivy's last two letters underscore Smith's concern with the techniques of fiction and the associated epistemological theme. When Ivy recalls how she burned all the letters she had written, which constitute the text of Smith's novel, and then creates in her dying moments a stream-of-consciousness prose poem, the text deconstructs so that language and perception become the subjects.

Like her novels, Lee Smith's short stories often portray a character caught in a dualistic world, struggling for some kind of integration or resisting all but temporary moves toward such change. In both short-story collections, *Cakewalk* and *Me and My Baby View the Eclipse*, Smith captures moments in women's lives where small choices involving relationship mirror larger issues related to self-definition and self-fulfillment. Many of her short stories use an ironically limited first-person point of view to underscore the discrepancies in the characters' own view of reality as well as those in the world itself.

SURVEY OF CRITICISM

Since publication of her first volume in 1968, reviews of Smith's work have been increasingly appreciative. While praising her first books for their clear narratives and honest characterizations, reviewers predicted that in her later works Smith would find material that would match her skill. The prediction proved accurate when *Black Mountain Breakdown* appeared. After publication of her fifth novel, *Oral History*, Smith was compared to William Faulkner and lauded for her integration of place, time, and character.

Of the seventeen analyses of Smith's work, seven are overviews of her entire canon, seven discuss the single work *Oral History*, and the remaining three are devoted separately to *Black Mountain Breakdown*, *Family Linen*, and *Fair and Tender Ladies*. The disproportionately large number of essays on *Oral History* reflects the enthusiasm it generated, both for its treatment of regional material and for its narrative techniques.

Each of the comprehensive analyses provides a detailed thematic study of Smith's books. In "Artists and Beauticians: Balance in Lee Smith's Fiction," Lucinda H. MacKethan observes that "the value of balance"—of texture and tone, of satire and sympathy, of the ordinary and the mysterious—is central to all of Smith's work. Ann Goodwyn Jones in "The World of Lee Smith" traces the development of the author's technical achievements with point of view and of Smith's major themes—language and its relationship to authenticity in the struggle between the desire for selfhood and the demands of the Southern world of ritual and denial. Katherine Kearns's entry in the *Dictionary of Literary Biography Yearbook: 1983* includes an extensive biography and an examination, both of Smith's major themes—identity, language, and art—and of the thematic parallels among her books. In "From Shadow to Substance," Kearns examines the conflict between the artist and mother figures in Smith's fiction, arguing that "there is a steady progression in the novels from the female characters as self-perceived artistic product to the female character as artist" and that only as the author herself began to accept her identity as artist did her characters begin to resolve this conflict.

Dorothy Combs Hill's *Lee Smith*, the first full-length study of Smith's fiction, takes a feminist approach to the author's work, tracing the process of female development through the novels and examining the mythic qualities and parallels of Smith's characters. For Hill, Smith's fiction depicts the contradictions of Southern womanhood; only in the later novels do female characters discover any freedom from the structures that circumscribe women. Harriette C. Buchanan, who presents a detailed plot summary of each of the novels through *Family Linen*, shows how Smith's artistry has developed, with increasingly complex plots and intricate character interrelationships in the later novels.

On October 11, 1985, Emory and Henry College, a small school located in the mountains of Virginia, not far from Smith's own hometown and from the fictionalized setting for *Oral History*, sponsored a Lee Smith Literary Festival, an indication of the author's growing popularity as a regionalist and of her acceptance by the academic community. The three essays presented at the festival, which focused primarily on *Oral History*, were then collected and published in "the Lee Smith issue" of the *Iron Mountain Review* 3 (Winter 1986).

In her essay in this collection, Ann Goodwyn Jones extends and narrows the argument of her earlier article, which identifies Smith as a postmodernist for her experimentation with point of view and her testing of the empirical limits of fiction. Jones argues here that orality is "inscribed" in *Oral History* and takes preference over literacy. Her essay explores the relatedness in the book of speech, sexuality, and prophecy, which are connected etymologically, to explain why the relationships in the novel based on romantic sexuality, as opposed to non-romantic sexuality, end in loss and tragedy.

The remaining two essays published in this collection show how the dialects and the many voices in the book reflect the Appalachian culture and people. Ben Jennings examines generational changes in the nuances of regional speech in *Oral History*, which reflect changes in the culture and character and economy of the Appalachian people from the late nineteenth century to the present. Frank Soos shows how in *Oral History* characters' response to the presence of mystery in the insular Appalachian community depends on their position in the community—insiders react with understanding; outsiders react with occasional moments of such knowledge and feeling; and more recent natives, who try to escape their identity, have only rare insight.

In her discussion of *Oral History*, Suzanne W. Jones contrasts the attitudes of the novel's "outsiders," whose preconceptions prevent them from real "self-discovery or true communion with the Appalachians," with the more complex and corrective vision created by the entire novel, which cannot be delineated by simple categories of "insider" and "outsider" or "rural" and "city." Rosalind B. Reilly argues that in *Oral History* there is a relationship between generations of dreamers who yearn for self-actualization and their storytellers, whose narratives provide meaningful myths and the power to revitalize impoverished imaginations.

Corrine Dale's is the first analysis of Smith's work that is based on feminist theory. Like Ann Jones, Dale reads *Oral History* as a postmodernist text, finding similar contrasts between the older and younger generations and giving a similarly positive emphasis to the character Sally. Dale argues that in *Oral History* Smith explores the relationship of linguistic expression, sexual anxiety, and alienation. Although Smith's mountain women are silenced by the symbolic language of patriarchy, whether the "academic father speech" of Richard and Jennifer or the vernacular language of manhood of the mountain songs and stories, Dale finds that they do express themselves in "the genuine and primal voices of semiotic discourse"—the prelogical voice that does not construct a linguistic barrier between authentic experience and passionate expression. For Dale, Sally's subversive narrative, which reconciles the language of the body with the language of the mind, parallels Smith's own in the novel *Oral History*. In contrast to Dale and Ann Jones, Fred Hobson argues that Smith is essentially not a postmodernist inventing her world, questioning the nature of fiction or the assumed relationship between the narrator and the narrative; like other contemporary Southern writers,

Smith "accepts" her world. Hobson says that in *Oral History* Smith portrays the reliability of oral history and the invasion of the world of folk culture by the world of mass commercial culture.

In the only essay to date devoted exclusively to *Black Mountain Breakdown*, John D. Kalb claims that by denying her ability to be happy without a man, Roger's verbal onslaught, which is structurally parallel to the literal rape by Devere, undermines the incipient sense of self-worth that Crystal had gained through her success as a teacher and constitutes her "second" rape.

For years reviewers have noted a comparison between Smith's fiction and works by Faulkner and other Southern writers. Susie Paul Johnson's essay, the first analysis to examine the resemblances of single novels by Smith and Faulkner, illustrates the similarities in character, structure, and theme of *Family Linen* and *As I Lay Dying*. Although both novels have as their central theme the presence of the past, Faulkner's novel suggests we can never free ourselves from the past, whereas Smith's suggests we can be liberated by the past to find greater meaning in the present.

In the final chapter of *Daughters of Time: Creating Woman's Voice in Southern Story*, MacKethan compares *Fair and Tender Ladies* to Alice Walker's *The Color Purple*, finding in both epistolary novels a woman's alienation from and search for self, her discovery of sisterhood, her reunion through language with her lost self, and her restoration to wholeness. With its epistolary format that reflects different levels of self-consciousness and the letter writer's awareness of different readers, *Fair and Tender Ladies* should continue to draw attention, particularly by postmodernist and feminist critics. Increasingly, scholars are recognizing Smith for her accuracy in portraying an older, regional South along with a contemporary, suburban South; for her skillful mastery of narrative techniques; for her vivid characterization; and for the depth and range of her vision. Hers is a major voice in contemporary Southern fiction.

BIBLIOGRAPHY

Works by Lee Smith

The Last Day the Dogbushes Bloomed. New York: Harper and Rowe, 1968.
Something in the Wind. New York: Harper and Row, 1971.
Fancy Strut. New York: Harper and Row, 1973.
"Staying in Touch with the Real World," with Mark Scandling. *Carolina Quarterly* 32 (Winter 1980): 51–57.
Black Mountain Breakdown. New York: Putnam's, 1980.
Cakewalk. New York: Putnam's, 1981.
Oral History. New York: Putnam's, 1983.
"An Interview with Lee Smith," with Edwin T. Arnold. *Appalachian Journal* 11 (1984): 240–54.
Family Linen. New York: Putnam's, 1985.
"The Voice behind the Story," 93–100 in *Voicelust: Eight Contemporary Fiction Writers*

on Style, ed. Allen Wier and Don Hendrie, Jr. Lincoln: University of Nebraska Press, 1985.

"Every Kind of Ritual," with Dorothy Combs Hill. Appendix II in "The Female Imagination in an Age of Transition: The Fiction of Lee Smith" by Dorothy Combs Hill, 296–322. Ph.D. diss., University of North Carolina Chapel Hill, 1988. Portions of this interview repr. in *Iron Mountain Review* 3 (Winter 1986): 25–27, and *Southern Quarterly* 23 (Winter 1990): 5–17.

"The Storyteller's Story." Appendix II in "The Female Imagination in an Age of Transition: The Fiction of Lee Smith" by Dorothy Combs Hill, 323–25. Ph.D. diss., University of North Carolina, Chapel Hill, 1988. Repr. in *Southern Quarterly* 23 (Winter 1990): 18–19.

Fair and Tender Ladies. New York: Putnam's 1988.

Me and My Baby View the Eclipse. New York: Putnam's, 1990.

"On Regionalism, Women's Writing, and Writing as a Woman: A Conversation with Lee Smith" with Virginia A. Smith." *Southern Review* 23 (1990): 784–95.

The Devil's Dream. New York: Putnam's 1992.

Studies of Lee Smith

Buchanan, Harriette C. "Lee Smith: The Storyteller's Voice," 324–45 in *Southern Women Writers: The New Generation*, ed. Tonette Bond Inge. Tuscaloosa: University of Alabama Press, 1990.

Dale, Corinne. "The Power of Language in Lee Smith's *Oral History*." *Southern Quarterly* 23 (Winter 1990): 21–34.

Hill, Dorothy Combs. "The Female Imagination in an Age of Transition: The Fiction of Lee Smith." Ph.D. diss., University of North Carolina, Chapel Hill, 1988.

———. *Lee Smith*. New York: Twayne Publishers, 1992.

Hobson, Fred. "A Question of Culture—and History: Bobbie Ann Mason, Lee Smith, and Barry Hannah," in *The Southern Writer in the Postmodern World*. Athens: University of Georgia Press, 1991.

Jennings, Ben. "Language and Reality in Lee Smith's *Oral History*." *Iron Mountain Review* 3 (Winter 1986): 10–14.

Johnson, Susie Paul. "Lee Smith's Smoking Pistol: *Family Linen* and William Faulkner's *As I Lay Dying*." *POSTSCRIPT* (Journal of the Philological Association of the Carolinas) 7 (1989): 45–51.

Jones, Anne Goodwyn. "The Orality of *Oral History*." *Iron Mountain Review* 3 (Winter 1986): 15–19.

———. "The World of Lee Smith." *Southern Quarterly* 22 (Fall 1983): 115–39. Repr. 249–72 in *Women Writers of the Contemporary South*, ed. Peggy Whitman Prenshaw. Jackson: University Press of Mississippi, 1984.

Jones, Suzanne W. "City Folks in Hoot Owl Holler: Narrative Strategy in Lee Smith's *Oral History*." *Southern Literary Journal* 20 (Fall 1987): 101–12.

Kalb, John D. "The Second 'Rape' of Crystal Spangler." *Southern Literary Journal* 21 (Fall 1988): 23–30.

Kearns, Katherine. "From Shadow to Substance: The Empowerment of the Artist Figure in Lee Smith's Fiction," 175–95 in *Writing the Woman Artist*, ed. Suzanne W. Jones. Philadelphia: University of Pennsylvania Press, 1991.

————. "Lee Smith," 314–24 in *Dictionary of Literary Biography Yearbook: 1983*. Detroit: Gale Research, 1984.

MacKethan, Lucinda H. "Artists and Beauticians: Balance in Lee Smith's Fiction." *Southern Literary Journal* 15 (Fall 1982): 3–14.

————. "Postscript: Writing Letters Home," in *Daughters of Time: Creating Woman's Voice in Southern Story*. Athens: University of Georgia Press, 1990.

Reilly, Rosalind B. "*Oral History*: The Enchanted Circle of Narrative and Dream." *Southern Literary Journal* 23 (Fall 1990): 79–92.

Soos, Frank. "Insiders and Outsiders: Point of View in Lee Smith's *Oral History*." *Iron Mountain Review* 3 (Winter 1986): 20–24.

BEVERLY JARRETT

John Kennedy Toole
(1937–1969)

In 1981, the Pulitzer Prize for fiction was awarded to John Kennedy Toole's *A Confederacy of Dunces*, a novel published in 1980 by Louisiana State University Press. Toole had committed suicide in 1969, but the posthumous publication and critical acclaim awarded this novel have assured him a place among major Southern writers of the twentieth century. His only other work, *The Neon Bible*, a novella written when he was only 16 years old, was finally published in 1989. Although this less mature and far less accomplished piece of fiction merited publication, Toole's reputation and claim to stature rest squarely on his achievement in *A Confederacy of Dunces*.

BIOGRAPHY

The fullest account we have of John Kennedy Toole's relatively brief life was by his mother, Thelma Ducoing Toole, in a memoir she provided for inclusion in the 1981 Flora Levy Lecture in the Humanities that was given by Robert Coles in commemoration of Toole. According to this "Mother's Remembrance," John Kennedy Toole was born in New Orleans, Louisiana, on December 7, 1937. He completed elementary school at 12 and high school at 16. Tulane University, where he began his college work at 16, was the first school to provide any challenge for him, his mother avers. He was, upon graduation from Tulane, awarded a Phi Beta Kappa key, a Woodrow Wilson Fellowship to Columbia University, and honors in the English Department's large graduating class.

After earning an M.A. in English from Columbia, Toole taught for a while at Hunter College. He also taught at Southwestern Louisiana State University in Lafayette and at St. Mary's Dominican College in New Orleans. In 1962 and 1963 he served in the U.S. Army and was stationed at Fort Buchanan in Puerto

Rico. During these two years, says Mrs. Toole, he wrote *A Confederacy of Dunces*.

The novel was finished in 1963 and submitted for publication to Simon and Schuster; Toole entered into "a lengthy and still mysterious correspondence with [editor] Robert Gottlieb." After Toole completed several revisions, the novel was finally rejected by Simon and Schuster in 1965 or 1966; the author made no further efforts to publish it.

In January 1969, Toole left New Orleans, saying he was going to visit a friend with whom he had taught at Lafayette. In March, his body was found near Biloxi, Mississippi; he had asphyxiated himself in his antiquated Chevrolet. According to Pat Carr, Toole left a suicide note beside him on the seat of the car, but this note was read and then destroyed by Thelma Toole. The 31-year-old novelist died without publishing any of his work.

After Toole's death his mother directed her energy and attention toward finding a publisher for *A Confederacy of Dunces*. The single copy she had became more and more battered looking as it was returned from one publisher after another. Eight houses had rejected the novel before Thelma Toole had the good fortune to make connection with novelist Walker Percy in 1976 and persuaded him to read her son's work. Percy, as is well known by now, recognized the value of the novel and sent it along to Louisiana State University Press, which had very recently begun to publish full-length fiction. The Press's director, L. E. Phillabaum, and its fiction editor, Martha Lacy Hall, both responded to the novel with enthusiasm, and a contract for its publication was signed with Thelma Toole.

Before all of the publicity associated with *Confederacy*'s winning the Pulitzer Prize for fiction, LSU Press enjoyed considerable pleasure in working with Thelma Toole toward readying the book for publication. Martha Hall recalls that her own copyediting of the manuscript was exceedingly restrained. A fiction writer herself, Hall was determined that no changes should be made in the deceased author's text unless they were clearly the correction of typographical errors or similar clean-up changes. Virtually the entire staff of the press got acquainted with the author's determined mother during the months of readying the book for publication and preparing to market its newest novel. There was much excitement about the book and much energy devoted to it long before the award (which was announced in 1981). By the time the book appeared, in May 1980, it had already received some rave reviews. Sales began to escalate, Book of the Month Club bought the book, paperback rights were licensed to Grove Press, and a movie option was being negotiated.

After the overwhelming success of *A Confederacy of Dunces*—after the sale of many thousands of hard- and softcover copies and nearly a dozen foreign language editions—a predictably Byzantine exchange among relatives and friends surrounded efforts to publish John Kennedy Toole's earlier novel, *The Neon Bible*. That brief book, almost a novella actually, had been written by Toole at the age of 16 for submission in a high school fiction competition. It hadn't won the competition, and LSU press declined the opportunity to publish it after *Confederacy*'s success. But some of Toole's relatives—who had signed over to Thelma all their rights to the award winner before it was published—pursued their claims to *The Neon Bible*. Virtually no reference is made to John Kennedy Toole's father in the ''Mother's Remembrance'' Thelma Toole published; nor did Mrs. Toole ever speak of him in her dealings with the LSU Press editors who handled *Confederacy*. He died before its publication, but Louisiana's Napoleonic inheritance laws left half of both *Confederacy* and *The Neon Bible* (in manuscript) to five relatives of the father. Although Mrs. Toole had purchased their rights to *Confederacy* before it won the Pulitzer, the in-laws were unwilling to part with their claim in *The Neon Bible*. After Mrs. Toole's death and a couple of lawsuits, the in-laws succeeded in forcing its release for publication in 1987 by Kenneth Holdich, heir to the manuscript and protector of Thelma Toole's wish to keep the novel from being published to the profit of these in-laws, who had, in her opinion, slighted her son.

The public will never know the whole truth about John Kennedy Toole's brief life. His mother maintained, privately and publicly, that the depression that led to his suicide resulted directly and singly from the rejection of his novel. Those who knew, or claimed to have known, either the author or both the author and his mother have suggested that there was surely more than this one cause for the depression that led to Toole's untimely death. After even a brief acquaintance with Thelma Toole and her New Orleans, it is tempting to read *Confederacy* as at least partially autobiographical—and to draw the perhaps facile conclusion that Ignatius J. Reilly's mother (who resembles Thelma) contributed significantly to her son's failure to lead a normal life. But precisely what role the author's family or other personal relationships may have played in his decision to end his life at 31 can never be known. All we can and do know is that he left behind a remarkable novel that evokes the New Orleans of the 1960s—its idiosyncratic, special, ordinary society—as no other fiction has done so well. Whether Toole's masterful satire of Ignatius' world and family in any degree contradicts Thelma Toole's myth about her son's devotion to her and hers to him must remain pure speculation.

MAJOR THEMES

Flannery O'Connor wrote, in a 1956 letter included in Sally Fitzgerald's *Habit of Being* (147–48): ''It is popular to believe that in order to see clearly one must believe nothing. This may work well enough if you are observing cells under a microscope. It will not work if you are writing fiction. For the fiction writer, to believe nothing is to see nothing. . . . Everything I believe is thoroughly moral, thoroughly Catholic.'' Unlike O'Connor who, according to Martha Stephens, ''was never in doubt as to what her purposes were,'' John Kennedy Toole was a Southern Catholic writer for whom the loss of faith was critical. Even as early as 16, when he wrote *The Neon Bible*, Toole already believed that the church had failed him. The failure of religion for contemporary man is a central theme throughout both his novels.

In that first book, religion is the undisguised villain. It is the local minister's determination to save young David's ailing mother by removing her from the only place she called home, and it had earlier been the minister and the local churchgoers who judged the boy's Aunt Mae, and ultimately the boy himself, unacceptable. The novel opens with David riding the train away from his home, leaving his dead mother and the preacher he had killed out of fear. The train ride makes him recall his childhood, when he'd had a toy train and when his father had had work and the family had had friends because his parents "were paying church members then, with their names on the rolls" (4). That soon into the novel the reader is introduced to its central theme: The failure of religion. As we follow the story of the family's hard times—the father's lost job; the family's move to the wrong side of town and thus its inability to enjoy the church community since there was no longer any money to contribute; the father's death in the war and the mother's resultant insanity—we watch a lonely little boy grow up knowing he's not quite good enough. We enjoy Aunt Mae, who is also unacceptable because she chooses to be herself; when she has to take charge of David for the first time, she asks him to come kneel with her by the bedroom window, to pray "that you and I won't be hurt too bad tomorrow or ever again" (38). That's when the neon bible is first seen; it halts the little boy's prayer at first, but when he looks up from the distortion to the stars above, he is able to pray.

Throughout the narrative, all that seems genuine is judged unworthy by the town. All of the local power resides with the false goodness of the church, a church symbolized by a big neon bible that equates money and power with goodness. Poverty and impotence like that suffered by David and his family are judged harshly throughout. As the novel ends, with young David riding off alone, carrying the knowledge of death and murder in his heart, we have no more idea where he's headed than he does. It's a sad ending; there's no reason to hope for a better life for David. He's not been given much more than a neon bible in place of Christian charity.

In the 15 intervening years, Toole seems to have found little more ground for faith, little else to believe in or follow. But he's becoming far more sophisticated in his handling of religion's failure. *A Confederacy of Dunces* faults not just the church, but the state, the academy, and most of society. This novel—a satire that some have called double-edged, or reverse, satire—is far funnier (*The Neon Bible* isn't funny at all) and far sadder than the earlier work. "Seeing twentieth-century America as the culminating horror of an abominable degeneration that began with the Renaissance," writes David McNeil, "Ignatius J. Reilly—the novel's comic hero—is a brilliant embodiment of reverse satire because he epitomizes the very perversions against which he rages."

Unlike the young David who directly expresses the repulsion he feels for a neon bible, Ignatius passes judgment on the church in wittier fashion—but it's the same harsh judgment. His mother tells her friend Irene how much the nuns had loved her son, how he had always won "little holy pictures for knowing his catechism." Examples of a dead church, now a collection of gaudy trinkets—the little holy pictures or the rosary raffles or the huge cross Ignatius was building for his Levy Pants office that was to have gold leaf letters spelling *GOD* and *COMMERCE* on it—abound in the book. Ignatius' actual leaving of the church, related by one of the nosey neighbors to Mr. Levy when he came to the Reilly home, is told hilariously—but it remains nonetheless a sad story of a little boy for whom religion (and the religious) offers no comfort. In Miss Annie's words:

That Idnatius [intentional misspelling] was okay until that big dog of his died. He had this big dog usta bark right under my window. That's when my nerves first started to go. Then the dog dies. Well, I think, now maybe I'll get me some peace and quiet. But no. Idnatius is got the dog laid out in his momma's front parlor with some flowers stuck in its paw. That's when him and his momma first started all the fighting. To tell you the truth, I think that's when she started drinking. So Idnatius goes over to the priest and ax him to come say something over the dog. Idnatius was planning on some kinda funeral. You know? The priest says no, of course, and I think that's when Idnatius left the Church. So big Idnatius puts on his own funeral. A big fat high school boy oughta know better. You see that cross? . . . That where it all happened. . . . And Idnatius had on a big cape like Superman and they was candles burning all over. The whole time his momma was screaming out the front door for him to throw the dog in the garbage can and get in the house.

If there is one central theme in Toole's work, it is the loss of faith and the failure of the church to meet contemporary man's needs. In both novels the hero is a little boy, but in *Confederacy* the little boy is 30 years old; as one critic has said, he has a master's degree and a Mickey Mouse watch. But for both the young and the older little boy, the deepest human needs and feelings are discredited.

Toole's condemnation of the consumerism that pervades twentieth-century society is, likewise, a theme presented directly in *The Neon Bible* but with more subtlety in *A Confederacy of Dunces*. Whereas David simply acknowledges his lack of worth because of his lack of wealth, Ignatius Reilly repudiates the need to earn a living—all the while choosing to ride to work at Levy Pants in a cab (after his mother forces him to find a job), or to eat more hot dogs than he sells during his tenure as a hot dog vendor. His contempt for a society he finds so lacking in culture is expressed in hysterical tirades as he watches bad movies or television programs—but he watches them with avid attention.

More pervasive in *Confederacy* than in the earlier novel is a contempt for humankind that almost totally defines the novel's main character. Ignatius seems to have no understanding or sympathy for the mother who supports him after sending him off to college where he "learnt everything except how to be a human being." His contempt for the "workers" he organizes at Levy Pants prompts him to generate a riot that will jeopardize their security for no purpose or gain.

Ignatius refers to the police officer and his aunt who befriend Mrs. Reilly as "depraved specimens of mankind who regularly bowl their way to oblivion." There is almost no character in the book whom Ignatius does not condemn for one failing or another. And all of his histrionic pronouncements against others serve repeatedly to call the reader's attention to Ignatius' own selfish and self-centered view of the world. By the novel's end, the reader feels pity for this antihero who despises himself so much that he must live and speak and think in disguise, playacting instead of taking part in the real world.

Unlike young David of *The Neon Bible*, who tried to believe in something—family, community, church—until he was abandoned by family and betrayed by the church, Ignatius tries throughout *Confederacy* to create a fantasy world in which reality need not be encountered. The grown-up little boy believes in nothing, lives in the past instead of the present, without hope for or vision of the future. In both novels, a constant theme is man's inhumanity to man; in the later novel, Toole has mastered the techniques for realizing that thematic stance.

It is perhaps doubly ironic that John Kennedy Toole had supposedly set out to visit the place where Flannery O'Connor lived and worked in January 1969. Whether he reached that destination before he took his life will probably never be known. What we do know from his fiction—and may speculate about because of his suicide—is that he seems to have longed for but never found the faith that so empowered O'Connor.

SURVEY OF CRITICISM

Although the 1980 publication of *A Confederacy of Dunces* was received almost immediately with rave notices in *Time*, *Newsweek*, the *New York Times*, the *Washington Post*, and many other daily or weekly publications, there have been relatively few serious reviews or review essays on the book. No full-length study of Toole's work has appeared to date.

Among the review essays that have been published, one of the best is William Bedford Clark's "All Toole's Children: A Reading of *A Confederacy of Dunces*." Clark looks beneath and beyond the hilarity of the novel and focuses on the "moral abuse of children and the young" as a thematic constant. Not only does Clark call attention to such instances of child abuse as Santa Battaglia's being banged about by her mother and her own banging about of her grandchildren, he argues that "the entire plot of Toole's novel finally revolves around a pornography ring aimed at corrupting minors." Even more significant, perhaps, is Clark's suggestion that Ignatius himself, "a monstrously overgrown child," bears a decidedly close resemblance to what little we know of Toole: "The world as reflected in *A Confederacy of Dunces* is full of threats for a child, even from within the family circle, and Toole's delineation of that world clearly mirrors certain autobiographical pressures. We know enough of Mrs. Toole's obsession with her boy-genius to infer that theirs was less than an ideally nurturing relationship."

Another thought-provoking essay is Richard F. Patteson and Thomas Sauret's "The Consolation of Illusion." Whereas most critics have assumed that the novel's antihero is the genius against whom the "confederacy of dunces" conspires, Patteson and Sauret present a more poignant view of Ignatius as an unhappy, frightened misfit who has little contact with reality: "This Ignatius J. Reilly is neither a crusader for Taste, Decency, Theology and Geometry (as he sees himself) nor wholly an obese and selfish buffoon (as others tend to see him). He is, instead, a lonely outsider who finds what consolation he can, not so much in philosophy as in fiction. The 'worldview' he constructs . . . is in fact a screen that shields him from the vicissitudes of life."

Several critics have compared Toole's comic irony with Mark Twain's. But to my knowledge, none has called attention to the similarity between Twain's Nigger Jim and Toole's Burma Jones. Both of these fictional blacks are considerably smarter than the whites among whom they move, chiefly because society has made it necessary for them to develop survival skills that their white compatriots could manage without. In fact, there are scenes in *A Confederacy of Dunces* that suggest Toole's real genius figure may well be Jones. Coles compares Jones to Faulkner's Dilsey, whose "dignity" he compares to Jones' "attentiveness"; but whereas Dilsey's dignity grows out of her unquestioned and unquestionable superiority to the Comptons she tends, Jones' attentiveness springs from his fear of the white society's unquestioned power over him and his destiny.

Almost all of the serious essayists, though, do focus on the childishness of Ignatius. Like Clark, who reminds us that Ignatius remains his mother's 30-year-old baby, Lloyd M. Daigrepont, in "Ignatius Reilly and the *Confederacy of Dunces*," notes Ignatius' surrounding himself with "the paraphernalia of childhood: Big Chief writing tablets, Blue Horse notebook paper, a Mickey Mouse watch, a yoyo, and Batman comics." Daigrepont also makes reference to Ignatius Loyola, founder of the Jesuits and the novel's hero's namesake, as does McNeil in his "*A Confederacy of Dunces* as Reverse Satire." McNeil defines Toole's comic hero as "a debased caricature" of Saint Ignatius: "Meant to be a moment of intensified Jesuit-like prayer," McNeil writes, "Ignatius' spiritual ecstasy is nothing more than masturbation perversely inspired by a vision of his long-dead pet collie, Rex."

Several Critics have noted the conservative political stance of Toole's work. Keith D. Miller's "The Conservative Vision of John Kennedy Toole" highlights the novel's repudiation of such 1960s social reform as that espoused by Myrna Minkoff, the professional protester who bled money from her father for her various reform projects and made periodic inspection tours of the South, where all people were "illiterate cowboys or—even worse—white Protestants." In one of his looseleaf notebook entries, Ignatius had described Myrna's politics with acumen:

When I failed to agree with her braying and babbling, she told me I was obviously anti-Semitic. Her logic was a combination of half-truths and clichés. . . . She assaulted me (almost literally) with greasy copies of *Men and Masses* and *Now!* and *Broken Barricades* and *Surge* and *Revulsion* and various manifestos and pamphlets pertaining to organizations of which she was a most active member: Students for Liberty, Youth for Sex, The Black Muslims, Friends of Latvia, Children for Miscegenation, The White Citizens' Councils. . . . She was only happy when a police dog was sinking its fangs into her black leotards.

Myrna's rather stereotypical full-time student crusades are no less harshly depicted than are those of the older, bored, rich housewife, Mrs. Levy. McNeil suggests that Mrs. Levy is "a satiric portrait of the business behaviorist who simplistically applies psychological theory to management situations" in her handling of Miss Trixie. Mrs. Levy's determination to make Miss Trixie feel needed if it kills her can only now call critical attention to the preacher in *The Neon Bible*, whose caring concern for David's mother did actually kill her. In the boy-narrator's struggle to understand the preacher's kindness, he says: "I was getting tired about what the preacher called Christian. Anything he did was Christian. . . . If he stole some book he didn't like from the library . . . or took somebody off to the state poor home, he called it Christian."

There has, as yet, been little critical response to *The Neon Bible*. Kenneth Holditch's foreword offers a summary of the book's travails on the route to publication, and provides a generally sympathetic response to the admittedly juvenile craftsmanship. Pat Carr has written another interesting note on the convoluted publishing history of this earlier work. But Toole's claim to recognition and respect as a novelist will surely continue to reside in his achievement with *A Confederacy of Dunces*.

BIBLIOGRAPHY

Works by John Kennedy Toole

A Confederacy of Dunces. Baton Rouge: Louisiana State University Press, 1980.
The Neon Bible. New York: Grove Press, 1989.

Studies of John Kennedy Toole

Bell, Elizabeth S. "The Clash of World Views in John Kennedy Toole's *A Confederacy of Dunces*." *Southern Literary Journal* 21 (Fall 1988): 15–22.
Carr, Pat. "John Kennedy Toole, *The Neon Bible*, and a Confederacy of Friends and Relatives." *Modern Fiction Studies* 35 (Winter 1989): 716–18.
Childress, Mark. "Happy Birthday, Ignatius." *Southern Living* (December 1982): 130, 132.
Clark, William Bedford. "All Toole's Children: A Reading of *A Confederacy of Dunces*." *Essays in Literature* 14 (Fall 1987): 269–80.
Coles, Robert. "Gravity and Grace in the Novel *A Confederacy of Dunces*." The Flora Levy Lecture in the Humanities, No. 2. Delivered as a lecture, September 18, 1981, at the University of Southwestern Louisiana, Lafayette, and published as

a booklet by Savoy-Sicie Press, Lafayette, in 1983. Includes "A Mother's Remembrance: I Walk in the World for My Son," by Thelma Ducoing Toole (pp. 10–13).

Daigrepont, Lloyd M. "Ignatius Reilly and the *Confederacy of Dunces*." *New Orleans Review* 9 (Winter 1982): 74–80.

Holditch, Kenneth W. "Jordi Kennedy Toole: El Triunfo de Mamá." *Quimera: Revista de Literatura* 92 (September 1989): 12–17.

McNeil, David. "*A Confederacy of Dunces* as Reverse Satire: The American Subgenre." *Mississippi Quarterly* 38 (Winter 1984–85): 33–47.

Miller, Keith D. "The Conservative Vision of John Kennedy Toole." *Proceedings, Conference of College Teachers of English of Texas* 48 (1983): 30–34.

Nelson, William. "The Comic Grotesque in Recent Fiction." *Thalia: Studies in Literary Humor* 5 (Fall–Winter 1982–83): 36–40.

———. "Unlikely Heroes: The Central Figures in *The World According to Garp, Even Cowgirls Get the Blues*, and *A Confederacy of Dunces*," 163–70 in *The Hero in Transition*, ed. Ray B. Browne and Marshall W. Fishwick. Bowling Green, Ohio: Popular Press, 1983.

Patteson, Richard F., and Thomas Sauret. "The Consolation of Illusions: John Kennedy Toole's *A Confederacy of Dunces*." *Texas Review* 4 (Spring–Summer 1983): 77–87.

Reilly, Edward C. "Batman and Ignatius J. Reilly in *A Confederacy of Dunces*." *Notes on Contemporary Literature* 12 (January 1982): 10–11.

Roberts, David. "Genius among Dunces." *Horizon* (September 1980): 4, 6, 8

Wilson, Katharina M. "Hrotsvit and the Tube: John Kennedy Toole and the Problem of Bad TV Programming." *Germanic Notes* 15 (1984): 4–5.

Zaenker, Karl A. "Hrotsvit and the Moderns: Her Impact on John Kennedy Toole and Peter Hacks," 275–85 in *Hrotsvit of Gandersheim: Rara Avis in Saxonia?*, ed. Katharina M. Wilson. Ann Arbor, Michigan: Marc Publishing, 1987.

ANNE R. ZAHLAN

Anne Tyler
(1941–   )

Over the course of a career that now spans several decades, Anne Tyler has demonstrated ever-surer mastery of fictional form, as well as an unerring eye for the surfaces of the American environment and an unerring ear for the rhythms of American speech. Her twelve novels and numerous short stories have won her the devotion of readers, as well as public recognition and critical acclaim. With the accolade of the Pulitzer Prize—awarded for *Breathing Lessons* (1988)—Tyler's reputation as an important writer was secured. The particular value of her contribution lies in a sanely comedic world-view and in the compassion inherent in the truth that she tells about American life.

BIOGRAPHY

"Vestigial Quakerism and engagement in a peculiarly Southern debate conjoin to provide the central dynamic of Tyler's fiction." This assessment, from Joseph C. Voelker's *Art and the Accidental in Anne Tyler's Fiction*, applies also to a life shaped by a heritage of Quaker idealism and the experiences of a North Carolina childhood. Born in Minneapolis, Minnesota, on October 25, 1941, Tyler is the only daughter among the four children of Phyllis Mahon and Lloyd Parry Tyler. Tyler recalls her social worker mother (later a journalist) and her chemist father as parents who "supported and encouraged anything their children did that was creative." From the time of Anne's birth, the family moved from one "commune-like arrangement" to another seeking to live life by some "Emersonian ideal." During Anne's sixth year, the family settled in Celo, North Carolina, at what the author has described as "an experimental Quaker community in the wilderness." When 5 years later they moved to Raleigh to take up a relatively ordinary middle-class existence, Anne was 11; she had never used a telephone and could "strike a match on the soles of [her] bare feet."

In Raleigh, Tyler attended Broughton High School, where she came under the influence of a gifted English teacher, Phyllis Peacock, who a few years earlier had taught and encouraged Reynolds Price. In the Broughton library, she discovered Eudora Welty and learned from Welty's stories that "literature could be made out of the ordinary things encountered in life." By the time she graduated from high school in 1958, Tyler's desire to be an artist had turned into an ambition to be a writer. Although she had hoped to go to college farther from home, Tyler accepted a full scholarship to Duke University in Durham and enrolled before she turned 17. At Duke, Reynolds Price taught her English; he "turned out to be," Tyler has said, "the only person I knew who could actually teach writing." During her university years, Tyler was on the staff of the literary magazine, the *Archive*, where her first published fiction appeared. Two of her stories were included in an anthology of student writing entitled *Under Twenty-Five*, and Tyler twice won the Anne Flexner Award for creative writing. An honor student, Tyler was elected to Phi Beta Kappa before her September 1961 graduation from Duke. Subsequently, she attended Columbia University in New York, where she completed coursework for an M.A. in Russian.

By fall 1962, Tyler was back in North Carolina where she worked for nine months as Russian bibliographer at the Duke University library. The following spring she married Taghi Mohammad Modaressi, a young doctor from Iran who was at Duke as a resident in psychiatry. The wedding took place on May 3, 1963, and in July the Modaressis left North Carolina for Canada. After six months in Montreal, Tyler accepted a job at the McGill University law library, where she worked until September 1965. During that initial period of what she later described as "unemployment," Tyler wrote what was to be her first published novel. Three of the young author's short stories had already appeared in national periodicals when, in 1964, Alfred Knopf issued *If Morning Ever Comes*. *The Tin Can Tree* was published in 1965. On October 24 of that year, the Modaressis' first daughter was born; a day after Tezh's birth, Tyler celebrated her own birthday. At the age of 24, she was a wife, a mother, and a published author.

In 1967 the Modaressis moved to Baltimore, where their second daughter, Mitra, was born that same year. As Tyler cared for first one and then two children, she wrote mainly at night, and most of the published work of this period is short fiction. She did manage to produce two "nocturnally composed" books, one of which, *Winter Birds, Winter Apples* has never been published; the other was *A Slipping-Down Life* (1970). Through the 1970s and into the 1980s, Tyler wrote, as she has told us, "between 8:05 and 3:30" during those periods not taken up with visiting relatives or school holidays.

In addition to novels issued at impressively regular intervals, Tyler has also written articles, short stories, and book reviews. Over the years, Tyler has contributed reviews to such publications as the *National Observer* and the *Washington Post*; she continues to write for the *New York Times Book Review* and regularly for the *New Republic*. Tyler's short fiction has appeared in a range of periodicals, both popular (*Seventeen, Mademoiselle*, and *McCall's*) and sophisticated (*Harper's, Southern Review*, and *The New Yorker*). Tyler stories have won inclusion in several anthologies, including the O. Henry Awards *Prize Stories* volumes for 1969 and 1972 and *The Best American Short Stories for 1977*. With Shannon Ravenel, Tyler edited the 1983 collection of *Best American Short Stories*; her introduction to that volume pledged continued allegiance to the genre and "its special place," as "an art form all its own."

The action of Tyler's fourth novel, *The Clock Winder* (1972), moves back and forth between North Carolina and Baltimore. The book thus marks a geographical transition, as well as the beginning of a second fictional "period" that, according to Voelker, includes *Celestial Navigation* (1974) and *Searching for Caleb* (1976). During the 1970s, Tyler's novelistic power continued to grow, and she gradually won the respect of critics as well as the allegiance of readers. Although she had received a *Mademoiselle* award for writing as early as 1966, it was 1977—the year that *Earthly Possessions* was issued—that the American Academy and Institute of Arts and Letters honored her with an Award for Literature. The 1980 publication of *Morgan's Passing* brought wider recognition and honors such as a Janet Heidinger Kafka Prize and nomination for an American Book Award. *Dinner at the Homesick Restaurant* (1982) won Tyler a P.E.N./ Faulkner Award for Fiction and more nominations, including one for a Pulitzer Prize. *The Accidental Tourist* (1985) was greeted with both critical and popular acclaim; it was awarded the National Book Critics Circle award as the most distinguished work of American fiction published in 1985.

The success of *Dinner at the Homesick Restaurant* and *The Accidental Tourist* confirmed Tyler's claim to be regarded as an important contemporary writer. Her audience was further expanded when a film based on *The Accidental Tourist* was greeted with critical respect and a respectable showing at the box office. At this juncture the determinedly private Tyler had to resist more firmly than ever the clamorous demands of the celebrity culture. (She attended the movie's premiere, we are told, but viewed the proceedings from a separate "reserved" section of the theatre.) Over the years, Tyler has made it consistently clear that her family and her writing are the only endeavors she cares to pursue: "Anything else," she has declared, "just fritters me away." When *Breathing Lessons* (nominated for a National Book Award in 1988) earned Tyler a Pulitzer Prize, it was reported in Baltimore that she told the journalists who besieged her door that she didn't have time to comment: She had a sentence to finish. At midcareer, Anne Tyler shows every sign of continuing creativity, a promise fulfilled with the 1991 publication of *Saint Maybe*

MAJOR THEMES

Continuing a career-long exploration of ties that bind and barriers that divide, Anne Tyler's *Saint Maybe* suggests a deepening moral and spiritual concern. Preceding the tonal and thematic modulations that characterize the 1991 work,

Breathing Lessons recapitulates and reflects on motifs that had occupied the author for nearly a quarter of a century.

Within the passing hours of one "warm, sunny day in September," *Breathing Lessons* enfolds the conversation, thoughts, and memories of Ira and Maggie Moran whose lives are thus caught in an early autumn moment. Like Virginia Woolf's *Mrs. Dalloway, Breathing Lessons* is a meditation on growing older and on the tensions between the mutable and the immutable in the relations of parent and child, friend and friend, man and woman, husband and wife. More precisely than the label "families" might indicate, a major Tyler theme is connectedness and separateness, the tensions between them, and the myriad forms they can assume.

As counterpoise to the weighted-down lives and accumulated households she evokes so well, Tyler has often explored the urge to cast off encumbrances and travel. From Ben Joe Hawkes to Macon Leary, Tyler characters find themselves on the move—in trains, in planes, or on the road. In *Breathing Lessons*, the one-day-in-the-life of Maggie and Ira Moran is a day of travel. Thus, in addition to its exploration of connectedness, Tyler's prize-winning eleventh novel recapitulates a second theme prominent in her fiction: The journey as figural representation of the experience of human life.

Beginning with a funeral that imitates a wedding, *Breathing Lessons* acknowledges all the milestones: birth and death; marriage and divorce; childhood and old age. Time is distilled into the hours of a particular Saturday and space into Baltimore and its Maryland and Pennsylvania environs. The book's journeying takes place along a Tylerland route dotted with highway convenience stores and gas stations with old-fashioned pumps. Tyler renders the demotic minutiae of her landscape with the same loving particularity that Virginia Woolf lavishes on Mrs. Dalloway's London. Meditating on those universal matters of life and death that also occupied the elegant Clarissa, Tyler translates into the particular idiom of characters whose memories replay the innocent pop culture of the American 1950s.

Whereas *Breathing Lessons* represents a mid-life pause to consider the unplanned trek of human experience, Tyler's earliest novels depict young characters attempting to set themselves on a life course. In so doing, they often confront the need to move away from the relationships they were born into and construct new families of their own. Ben Joe Hawkes of *If Morning Ever Comes* feels so painfully responsible for his mother, grandmother, and five sisters that he goes AWOL from Columbia law school and takes the train south to North Carolina. Having faced the ironic fact that the women of his family are self-sufficient and that it is he who cannot let go, Ben Joe returns to New York only after acquiring a wife-to-be who from then on would wait for him "like his own little piece of Sandhill transplanted."

The Tin Can Tree traces the effects of a child's death on her bereaved family and the other occupants of a ramshackle three-family house perched on the edge of a tobacco field. Continuing the exploration of separateness and togetherness begun in the first novel, Tyler here introduces another theme central to much of her work: The dilemma of the artist whose creativity demands a solitude that humanity rejects. James Green, photographer and the first of Tyler's artists, is torn between obligations to his petulant "invalid" brother and the girl he presumably loves. Failing to resolve his private confusions, James succeeds in using the power of his lens to fix the disparate inhabitants of the "ark" into an immutable image of unity.

In a July 1972 *National Observer* interview, Tyler admitted abiding affection for *A Slipping-Down Life* as the one of her early books in which characters change. Although the teenage protagonist has no real home with either father or husband, by novel's end she has changed enough to be capable of making a home for her child. Evie Decker, "a plump drab girl" whose chief companion is her radio, is possessed by infatuation for a would-be rock singer called Drumstrings Casey. When she emerges from the ladies' room at the Unicorn Club with the letters of his last name carved raggedly on her forehead, Drum is moved to take a wary interest, and eventually the two elope. Pregnancy and the death of her father shock Evie into a hitherto uncharacteristic "taking hold," and she moves back into her inherited house, focused now on the baby who is to be born.

The Clock Winder opens a period marked, according to Voelker, by advances in both "realist technique" and "psychological accuracy." Certainly Elizabeth Abbot, the "clock winder," is a more defined character than any in Tyler's first three books. A misfit in her own family, Elizabeth finds an unexpected niche among the Emersons of posh suburban Baltimore. She cleans and fixes, tends and prunes, and around the nucleus of her "irritating" presence, a new family forms. The novel closes in paradox: The Emersons, who by now have absorbed Elizabeth, are barricaded in the family home fending off a plague of invading locusts, but the youngest son, realizing that he cannot survive within his birth family, has escaped to establish a new family with the Georgia waitress he has married. "Bye," Peter's young nephew tells the fleeing couple, "as if every day of his life he saw people arriving and leaving and getting side-tracked from their travels."

Celestial Navigation depicts older and still more formed characters in a narrowed and intensely focused setting. In Tyler's most overt treatment of the dilemma of the artist, an agoraphobic Jeremy Pauling spends his time in an upstairs studio creating first collages and later intricate three-dimensional paper sculptures. When his mother dies, Jeremy is cut adrift, and when Mary Tell, also adrift, takes a room in the house and with her child becomes part of the household, it is not long before the unlikely pair get together. The apparently sexless Jeremy not only lives in harmony with the beautiful young woman but also fathers children, all the while going on with his art. The union gives way, however, when Mary, absorbed by maternity, unwittingly absolves and so deprives Jeremy of the responsibility necessary to love. When Jeremy finally bestirs himself to claim his family, it is too late: Having opted, however passively, for the work, he is left with a husk of the life.

Searching for Caleb, the story of a quest for a lost brother, is built around the metaphor of travel so important throughout Tyler's works. Sixty-one years before the book's opening, Caleb Peck fled the restrictions of family for the freedom of art. Caleb's escape is opposed by his brother Daniel, who determines to find the defector and prevail on him to rejoin the family and accept the Peck values of property and stability. In recounting the struggle, Tyler does not cheat. She convincingly conveys the happy vagabond life of Duncan and Justine— cousins as well as man and wife, the younger-generation Pecks who get away. She also establishes the strong bond that connects Justine to Daniel, the grand-father who joins her bohemian household without relinquishing one whit of his quintessential Peckness. The impulses fuse as Justine and Daniel journey together in search of Caleb.

In *Earthly Possessions*, the contrary impulses are laid out with symmetry. Here Tyler presents experience from the perspective of the protagonist: Charlotte's first-person narrative alternates neatly between present events and the memories they provoke. Movement in space parallels movement in time, and Charlotte, taken half-heartedly hostage by a bumbling bank robber, travels south-ward away from her Maryland home. Thus she is compelled to make the journey she had longed to take in order to escape the demands of family and the clutter of a lifetime spent in one house. By the time she reaches Florida, Charlotte's reveries have brought her up to the morning that abduction interrupted her own preparations for flight. The novel concludes with her realization that the journey that is life renders actual travel unnecessary: "I can't see the need. . . . We have been traveling for years, traveled all our lives, we are traveling still. We couldn't stay in one place if we tried."

Morgan's Passing recounts its protagonist's struggle to live not one but many lives. In one of a number of masquerades, Morgan poses as a doctor and delivers a baby. In this way, he comes into the lives of Emily Meredith, a creator of puppets, and her would-be actor husband, Leon. When he later moves in with Emily and her children, the daughter he had delivered and the son he has fathered (Leon having conveniently agreed to go "home" to the bourgeois life he had once renounced), Morgan brings along the clutter of the old life he had yearned to escape. Whereas Morgan is perplexed by the albatross of accumulation, Emily understands that vitality can be drawn from objects, from the "souvenirs of dozens of lives raced through at full throttle." Assuming the puppet-master role that Emily's husband abdicates, Morgan becomes known as Leon Meredith, thus doing away with "Morgan Gower." Momentarily shaken on reading his own obituary, Morgan quickly recovers from the shock of "passing," and indeed, comes to find in it an ultimate emancipation: "Everything he looked at seemed luminous and beautiful and rich with possibilities."

A dark vision informs *Dinner at the Homesick Restaurant*, Tyler's novel about the Tulls of Baltimore, abandoned by the father and cut off from community by circumstance and the mother's character. As in most of Tyler's books, the material dwelling is inseparable from those who live in it, leave it, or return to it: In the narrow row-house where mother and children accidentally alight, Pearl Tull struggles incessantly to tighten, repair, and fortify. But the fortress Pearl creates is devoid of warmth, and her daughter and two sons live out the consequences of affective deprivation. Jenny, the daughter, endures two unhappy marriages before finding Joe St. Ambrose, left alone to raise six children, with whom she creates a "large" and "noisy" family. Handsome and superficially successful, Cody is frozen in childhood jealousy and hatred of his gentle brother Ezra. Cody steals the girl his brother loves, but Ezra remains undeterred from the pursuit of the dream with which he counters emotional deprivation, the dream of the Homesick Restaurant. "Ezra's going to have him a place where people come just like to a family dinner," explains a friend: "He'll cook them one thing special each day and dish it out on their plates and everything will be solid and wholesome, really homelike. . . . Really just like home." In Tyler's world as in the real world, home is not always what it should be. Gathering around the table can test as well as affirm the unity of family, and it is only after Pearl's death that the Tulls get through a meal together. But the Homesick Restaurant is the site not only of wish-fulfillment dreams of happy families, but also of the creative impulse. Like Jeremy Pauling's collages, Elizabeth Abbot's carvings, Emily Meredith's puppets, and Charlotte Emory's photographs, the steaming platters that emerge from the kitchen at the Homesick Restaurant are works of art. In the kitchen as nowhere else, Ezra Tull "came into his own, like someone crippled on dry land but effortlessly graceful once he takes to water."

In *The Accidental Tourist*, Tyler returns to travel as organizing motif to explore in psychic terms the tension between the impulse to roam and the urge to stay put. The protagonist is a traveler who hates to travel, and the novel recounts his reluctant journey out of despair. Born (like the Pecks and Pearl Tull) into the "cautious half" of humanity, Macon Leary must deal with the inner conflict between demanding id and legislating superego. Both the conflict and its eventual resolution find a figure in the logo that replaces signature on the guidebooks Macon writes for travelers whose "concern was how to pretend they had never left home." The work of a man who insulates himself from others with carefully constructed barricades of luggage and a thousand-page novel, the guides manipulate the experience of travel to project a self in thrall to the superego. Reluctant to create a self capable of negotiating life, Macon hides behind the evasions of "the accidental tourist," works marked with the sign of the winged armchair. "While armchair travelers dream of going places," his publisher explains, "traveling armchairs dream of staying put."

The Accidental Tourist is a psychological novel that traces the stages of Leary's painful movement from unfeeling stasis to affective rebirth. As his dreams and memories of his dead son move back in remembered time from the summer the boy was killed to the days of his infancy, as the dialogues he engages in develop from reluctant or desperate telephone calls to intense personal encounters, the image he presents to himself and others changes. In his initial isolation and throughout his cure, Macon is not actually alone; his constant companion is an irrepressible Welsh Corgi named Edward. Acting out the rage and confusion that Macon so carefully represses, Edward is the id in canine form. Muriel Pritchett, trainer and therapist, restores not only dog but man. She who has been nowhere offers to travel with Macon and to show him "the good parts." She manages to dispell his deep-seated distrust in anything that strikes him as alien. Through her, he is reconciled to foreignness and so to otherness, to travel and so to the adventure of life. At the moment Macon determines to make a life with Muriel, "he felt a kind of inner rush, a racing forward": "The real adventure, he thought, is the flow of time; it's as much adventure as anyone could wish."

In *Breathing Lessons*, Maggie Moran confronts time as medium of loss as well as gain: She has "her first inkling that her generation was part of the stream of time." When, near the novel's end, she wonders "what are we two going to live for, all the rest of our lives?" her husband comforts her with a tenderness born of habit. Resting "her head against his chest," Maggie watches Ira play out his hand of solitaire until he reaches what was after all "the interesting part of the game": "He had passed that early, superficial stage when any number of moves seemed possible, and now his choices were narrower and he had to show real skill and judgment." With an "inner buoyancy" reminiscent of the "inner rush" experienced by Macon Leary at the epiphanic moment that concludes *The Accidental Tourist*, Maggie goes to sleep happy, knowing that tomorrow she and Ira have another trip to make. There is still adventure in the flow of time.

A comic work that reflects its author's characteristically benign world view, *Saint Maybe* also marks significant shifts in emphasis and focus. Cameo appearances of Ezra Tull and his Homesick Restaurant, and of the private detective who locates the missing Peck in *Searching for Caleb*, provide humorous confirmation of the links between Anne Tyler's twelfth novel and the works produced during the previous two and a half decades. Cluttered houses, accumulated families, neighborhood eccentrics, holiday gatherings: These by-now beloved elements are all here. Thematically, *Saint Maybe* takes its place among Tyler's explorations of the painful ambivalences of family relationships; structurally, it follows familiar patterns—from sickness to health, from emprisonment to liberation, from fragmentation to wholeness. The tragic happenings that precipitate the plot do not, however, as in *The Accidental Tourist*, function primarily to facilitate the comic resolution. Rather, loss, pain, and guilt exist in their own right, and readers of *Saint Maybe* are not spared the suffering that precedes healing. Most important, the therapeutic process recounted transcends the psychological. For the first time, Tyler's vision admits evil and concerns itself with the health not just of the psyche but of the soul.

Whatever the mitigations of youth and understandable frustration, Ian Bedloe commits a sin. When he tells his brother that his wife is unfaithful and his child is not his own, he looses evil that must play itself out. Forgiveness is possible, but, as Reverend Emmett makes clear, atonement is required: "You can't just say, 'I'm sorry God.' Why, anyone could do that much! You have to offer reparation—concrete, practical reparation, according to the rules of our church." When Ian, at 18, drops out of college to raise the three children orphaned by the deaths of his brother and his sister-in-law, he takes up a penitential burden that ultimately gives his life meaning. As humorous as is Tyler's rendering of the Sisters and Brothers, the Good Works and the Amending, of the Church of the Second Chance, the principles of faith, discipline, and community are never mocked. Whereas she has been both blamed and praised for a philosophical deference to the "accidental," in *Saint Maybe* Tyler does not shrink from insistence on moral responsibility.

The "flow of time" cannot in itself account for the "adventure" of *Saint Maybe*, and the journeying this book recounts covers no earthly territory. Unlike those "accidental tourists" who pretend not to travel, Ian Bedloe, over the long years of his atonement, never does leave Baltimore and home. Making his slow progress from sin to salvation, the protagonist of Anne Tyler's twelfth novel is a pilgrim who accomplishes an arduous and purposeful spiritual odyssey: "Each footstep, Ian felt, led him closer to something important. He was acutely conscious all at once of motion, of flux and possibility. He felt he was an arrow—not an arrow shot by God but an arrow heading toward God, and if it took every bit of this only life he had, he believed that he would get there in the end."

SURVEY OF CRITICISM

By the time Anne Tyler won the Pulitzer Prize, her accomplishments were at last being recognized by critics and scholars, as well as readers and reviewers. The academic world had been slow to take heed: The 1979 *Harvard Guide to Contemporary American Writing*, for instance, had relegated Tyler's short stories to a single sentence and omitted any reference whatsoever to her novels. But 1979 was also the year that Stella Ann Nesanovich's Louisiana State dissertation presaged the end of scholarly indifference, and by the close of the following decade, a number of critical articles had appeared and dissertations were beginning to proliferate. In April 1989, Tyler scholars and Tyler fans gathered in Baltimore to share appreciation of and insights into Tyler's fiction. The success of the Baltimore symposium and the publication of Joseph Voelker's book, *Art and the Accidental in Anne Tyler*, made clear that the academic neglect of Tyler's work was a thing of the past.

Reviewers had not been so slow to appreciate Tyler's talent. Well before *Dinner at the Homesick Restaurant*, Tyler's work was widely and respectfully reviewed. Writer-critics such as Gail Godwin, Joyce Carol Oates, and John Updike had proved influential as well as discerning in their support. Updike's continued praise reflects a realist's admiration for a painstaking rendering of the surfaces of American life. Tyler's concern with the concrete links her not only to the realist tradition but also to the literary culture of her region. Voelker identifies "Southernness" as, second to the Quaker heritage, the "most visible element" in Tyler's fiction, and much of the critical interest in Tyler has come from Southern writers and critics, Southern periodicals, Southern universities, and Southern presses. Having grown up in North Carolina and graduated from Duke, claiming Reynolds Price as teacher and Eudora Welty as primary influence, Tyler has unimpeachable Southern credentials. By now the majority of her writing life has been spent in Baltimore, a city on the periphery of Southern culture, and Tyler has stated that whatever remained "undeniably Southern" in her helped forge her allegiance to Baltimore, a city she has pronounced "wonderful territory for a writer."

The loving and leisurely examinations of "what happens and who it happens to" that Tyler finds in Welty mark her own approach to storytelling, and critics have not hesitated to cite affinities between the two writers. Frank W. Shelton cites a significant use of the "seemingly insignificant" and a "necessary balance" between "a sense of distance . . . and a gift of sympathy." Carol S. Manning identifies "irony, humor, and keen observation of human nature" as shared qualities; in "Welty, Tyler, and Traveling Salesmen: The Wandering Hero Unhorsed," she discusses "intriguing parallels" between *The Golden Apples* and *Dinner at the Homesick Restaurant*, concluding that Welty and Tyler are "not as traditional as we may have thought," that "they share a subtle but incisive feminist spirit."

Links between Tyler's fiction and the works of William Faulkner are less obvious. Voelker cites Faulknerian echoes in *If Morning Ever Comes*, *Celestial Navigation*, and *Earthly Possessions*. At least twice, a case has been made for significant connections between *Dinner at the Homesick Restaurant* and *As I Lay Dying*. Identifying parallels between Tyler's Tulls and Faulkner's Bundrens, Mary J. Elkins' article, "*Dinner at the Homesick Restaurant*: Anne Tyler and the Faulkner Connection," focuses on narrative technique; Elkins demonstrates that both Tyler and Faulkner juxtapose conflicting versions of common experience. Adrienne Bond's essay, "From Addie Bundren to Pearl Tull: The Secularization of the South," emphasizes thematic parallels; examining *Dinner at the Homesick Restaurant* in the context of Southern fiction, Bond suggests that Tyler can indulge in such inter-textuality without being overcome by anxiety of influence because her "urban, secular south is so very different from William Faulkner's rural, Calvinist one."

A preoccupation with family that is characteristically if not exclusively Southern is a salient feature of Tyler's fiction. Many critics have taken part in the discussion initiated by Nesanovich's 1979 dissertation positing as major theme the isolation of "the individual in the family." In a groundbreaking essay first published in the *Southern Quarterly* in 1983, Doris Betts recognizes Tyler's universalizing treatment of the "family as microcosm" and notes the thematic tension between stay-at-home and runaway. Mary Ellis Gibson's article, "Family as Fate: The Novels of Anne Tyler,'' quotes Updike in Tyler's fictional evocation of ''familial limitations that work upon us like Greek fates'' and defines Tyler's conception as lying between ''the classical Greek fats, or *moira*'' and ''the more oppressive . . . *heimarmene* of the gnostic dualists and their anti-metaphysical descendants, the existentialists.'' She observes that ''in Tyler's fiction tragedy and comedy, or the mix of them, grow not from the conjunction of a hero's *hybris* and his fate but from the contest between human caring and nihilism.''

In ''Anne Tyler's Accidental Ulysses,'' William K. Freiert takes up the ''polarity'' between home and wandering, as well as the idea of family as fate. Thus Tyler's characters engage in a constant struggle ''to free themselves from their 'fated' families.'' Comparing Macon Leary to Odysseus ''struggling to get home,'' Freiert analyzes the ''inversions'' Tyler works on the Ulysses theme: New York skyscraper as ''Cyclopean cave,'' a son prevented by untimely death from playing Telemachus, and the haven of home found not with Penelope (Sarah) but with the Circe figure of Muriel. Concluding that the Ulysses inversions serve to ''probe the meaning of family,'' Freiert quotes Mary F. Robertson's assessment of Tyler's use of family in earlier novels as ''a sign of order or disorder in personality and society.'' In ''Medusa Points and Contact Points,'' Robertson argues that Tyler's emphasis on missed connections, at which neither severance nor reconciliation quite happens, and her transgressions of the boundaries between insiders and outsiders serve to undercut the traditional family as touchstone of order.

Although Tyler has claimed to see ''no essential difference between the sexes when it comes to writing,'' her fictional focus on home and family raises issues of particular concern to women. Sue Ann Johnson discusses the relationships of mothers and daughters as they figure in novels by Margaret Atwood, Margaret Drabble, and Tyler. In ''The Daughter as Escape Artist,'' Johnson speculates that, whereas men, expected to strike out on their own, ''sometimes before they are ready,'' may long for home, women, ''traditionally encouraged to stay at home,'' may be impelled toward ''freedom.'' The female urge to freedom, in fiction as in life, may prompt rebellion against the mother ''and the constricting life she represents''; Johnson thus interprets Charlotte Emory's journey in *Earthly Possessions* as a ''flight from the mother'' that is also a ''search for her'' and so ''for the self.'' Concerned also with the importance of mother-daughter bonds, in a paper entitled ''Mentors and Maternal Role Models,'' Theresa Kanoza examines the liberation offered in Tyler's fiction by the establishment of less restrictive ties between mothers-in-law and daughters-in-law in *The Clock-Winder*, *Celestial Navigation*, and *Earthly Possessions*.

Of all familial bonds, Tyler surely examines marriage the most closely, and she has established something of a claim on the conjugal ''ever after.'' As Betts observes, Tyler's interest lies in ''how her people survive and persist *beyond* crisis during their long, steady, three-meal-a-day aftermaths.'' Betts sees marriage—''Tyler's Marriage of Opposites''—as an image that fittingly encompasses all the compromises and reconciliations effected in Tyler novels over the years.

Susan Gilbert, however, is less comfortable with Tyler's compromises and with her eschewing of public concerns in favor of those that are private and traditionally female; she observes that on the "private lives" of Tyler characters, "the great world impinges little." Whereas Gilbert remains suspicious of a fictional domain lacking "historical dimension," Robertson contends that Tyler's stress on the private poses no threat to feminist conceptions of the properly public role of women. Manning credits Tyler with a "feminist spirit" that is "subtle but incisive," and Betts warmly defends Tyler's less than "dramatic" feminism against would-be attackers.

Tyler's feminism appears to have been too subtle for the ideologically orthodox who have largely ignored her, and Robertson and Manning perceive more opposition to patriarchy than meets the eye of most critics. Shelton, for instance, in "Anne Tyler's Houses," contrasts her approach to the question of woman's place with that of Sandra Gilbert and Susan Gubar who, in *The Madwoman in the Attic*, emphasize the confining character of "houses and domestic space" in the works of nineteenth-century women writers. Tyler's houses, Shelton argues, function as "the setting of life as it must be lived," and her novels—particularly *Earthly Possessions*—provide a "revisionist" "version of the female tradition." In "Private Lives and Public Issues: Anne Tyler's Prize-Winning Novels," Susan Gilbert takes Tyler to task for just such acceptance as Shelton finds in *Earthly Possessions* and energetically challenges Tyler's alleged willingness to ascribe crime, poverty, and injustice to some principle of the "accidental."

Margaret Morganroth Gullette takes a new tack in discussing the treatment of families and relationships in Tyler's fiction. For Gullette, Tyler is a chronicler of adulthood whose novels offer guidance through the relatively unexplored mazes of mature development. That tension between wandering and stability that underlies Tyler's plots Gullette ascribes to the author's ongoing exploration of life-course alternatives. Aware that "the old male . . . pattern of wandering followed by stability" does not apply to a female experience more likely to move from early "maternal plenitude" to "later restlessness," Tyler has produced a series of texts that, in Gullette's view, constitute an "interargumentative" "discourse about true and false desire." Whereas Gullette relates Tyler's fiction to practical study of the human life-cycle, Virginia Schaefer Carroll grounds her analysis in anthropology, arguing that in Tyler's fiction, "the rituals, the defining of family and clan, the coded language and gestures all suggest a modern, fictive reworking of a fundamental human situation, the ways in which people are drawn to and limited by the need to feel at home." Citing research on the nature of kinship, Carroll concludes that "Tyler preserves and celebrates what is distinct about kinship—the rituals, codes, language, and myths."

Two critical overviews published in 1986, one by Anne G. Jones in the *Hollins Critic* and the other by Anne R. Zahlan in *Fifty Southern Writers after 1900*, suggest increasing awareness of Tyler's psychological sophistication. Focusing on travel and connectedness as major themes, Zahlan identifies *The Accidental Tourist* in particular as a "psychological novel" that makes use of Freudian concepts in tracing the stages of Macon Leary's reluctant guest for psychic wholeness. Noting the centrality of the issue of "personal psychic growth," Jones relates the questions posed by Tyler's narratives to the theoretical perceptions of Jacques Lacan and Nancy Chodorow. In an essay entitled "Beck Tull: 'The Absent Presence' in *Dinner at the Homesick Restaurant.*'" Joseph B. Wagner cites Freud and later theorists in arguing that Tyler casts Beck and Cody, "father and the oldest son," as "primary players in the central oedipal struggle that shapes all the other relationships in the book." In "Traveling towards the Self: The Psychic Drama of Anne Tyler's *The Accidental Tourist*," Zahlan uses Freudian and Lacanian notions to elucidate Tyler's dramatization of the struggle for control of Leary's embattled psyche, a struggle pitting law-obsessed and language-bound superego against unruly id.

Heightened sensitivity to Tyler's intellectual sophistication is a hallmark of Voelker's book-length study published in 1989 by the University of Missouri Press. Relating psychological and psychiatric theory to a number of Tyler texts, Voelker finds varieties of the agoraphobia that afflicts Jeremy Pauling and Macon Leary in all the early novels; he also traces from the early novels the "paternal abdication" that provides many Tyler works with an apt psychological setting for the unfolding of Freudian scenarios. He relates the family-swapping that goes on in Tyler novels to the concept of *primitive idealization*, the syndrome in which children, whose ideas of the self are still not completely differentiated, yearn to belong to a family other than their own. The Tull siblings of *Dinner at the Homesick Restaurant*, for example, are "parables of primitive idealization": They spend their lives trying "to get free of the selves their family formed for them." Voelker reads *The Accidental Tourist* as "a funny and profound meditation on the text of *Beyond the Pleasure Principle*"; its plot, he observes, represents an "extended process of *anamnesis*, a therapeutic movement." The "narrative structure of *Earthly Possessions*," on the other hand, grows "like a crystal from the idea of primitive idealization, forming . . . a sort of narrative chiasm." All Tyler characters, Voelker concludes, are engaged in constructing autobiographical narratives. And he observes that Tyler, "in her sense of the self," shares one conviction "with Lacanian theory—that at center the self is unstable and constituted by linguistic patterns."

Art and the Accidental is the title Voelker has given his book, and art is a key Tyler theme. From *The Tin Can Tree* on, Tyler has explored in her fiction the possibilities of balance between the life and the work. Two articles in Ralph C. Stephens' collection, *The Fiction of Anne Tyler*, discuss the "tension between creativity and life" as Tyler dramatizes it, particularly in *Celestial Navigation*. In "Art's Internal Necessity," Barbara Harrell Carson concludes that Tyler's work may contain a "reminder . . . that often human connectedness . . . is achieved at the sacrifice of the possibility of high levels of creativity." Sue Lile Inman ends her essay "The Effects of the Artistic Process" on a more optimistic note: "While Tyler shows that the artistic process may exact a dear price from the artist and those surrounding the artist and that art is limited in its power to change people's lives, or their ability to love, she also allows us to see that art done with love can be a way to survive, to endure.'' In a discussion that links Tyler's fictional concerns with art and with psychology, Gordon O. Taylor notes that not only Morgan Gower but many other Tyler characters deal in "improvisations of self." Tyler finds in *Morgan's Passing* a "seismic energy" that "flows through the shifting fault planes of identity and behavior into *recompositions* of experience, in Morgan's mind but in the 'real or invented' world as well." Thus Morgan is not only "an expression of the world's inexhaustible self-artistry," but also a "consummate artist-of-the-self."

Taylor's brief essay on *Morgan's Passing* includes observations on the treatment of time that suggest a philosophical dimension not often attributed to Tyler's fiction. Voelker makes a more substantial case for Tyler's work as expressive of a philosophical position. Considering the first eleven novels in which the "best" philosophical characters oppose an "incomprehensible" world with the "silence, passivity, and compassion" that they share with their creator, Voelker views Tyler as opposing determinism and the notion of "inexorability": "From the accidental death of little Janie Rose in *The Tin Can Tree*, to the 'suicide' of Timothy Emerson in *The Clock Winder*, to the random murder of Ethan Leary in *Accidental Tourist*, Tyler has written about people who occupy an accidental world, in which the fault for life's cataclysmic events is finally unascribable, and the duty of human beings is not to act but to endure, to define the degree of freedom possible within their confinement.''

BIBLIOGRAPHY*

Works by Anne Tyler

If Morning Ever Comes. New York: Knopf, 1964.
The Tin Can Tree. New York: Knopf, 1965.
A Slipping-Down Life. New York: Knopf, 1970.
The Clock Winder. New York: Knopf, 1972.
Celestial Navigation. New York: Knopf, 1974.
Searching for Caleb. New York: Knopf, 1976.
Earthly Possessions. New York: Knopf, 1977.
Morgan's Passing. New York: Knopf, 1980.
"Still Just Writing," in *The Writer on Her Work*, ed. Janet Sternberg. New York: Norton, 1980.
Dinner at the Homesick Restaurant. New York: Knopf, 1982.
The Accidental Tourist. New York: Knopf, 1985.
Breathing Lessons. New York: Knopf, 1988.
Saint Maybe. New York: Knopf, 1991.

*Compiled with the assistance of Walt Wisnewski.

Studies of Anne Tyler

Books

Petry, Alice Hall. *Understanding Anne Tyler*. Columbia: University of South Carolina Press. 1991.

Stephens, C. Ralph, ed. *The Fiction of Anne Tyler*. Jackson: University Press of Mississippi, 1990.

Voelker, Joseph C. *Art and the Accidental in Anne Tyler*. (Literary Frontiers, 34). Columbia: University of Missouri Press, 1989.

Articles and Reviews

Baum, Rosalie Murphy. "Boredom and the Land of Impossibilities in Dickey and Tyler." *James Dickey Newsletter* 6 (Fall 1989): 12–20.

Betts, Doris. "The Fiction of Anne Tyler." *Southern Quarterly* 21 (Summer 1983): 23–37. Rpt. in *Women Writers of the Contemporary South*, ed. Peggy Whitman Prenshaw. Jackson: University Press of Mississippi, 1984.

———. "Tyler's Marriage of Opposites," 1–15 in Stephens, ed., *The Fiction of Anne Tyler*.

Bond, Adrienne. "From Addie Bundren to Pearl Tull: The Secularization of the South." *Southern Quarterly* 24 (1986): 64–73.

Bowers, Bradley R. "Anne Tyler's Insiders." *Mississippi Quarterly* 42, No. 1 (Winter 1988–89): 47–56.

Carroll, Virginia Schaefer. "The Nature of Kinship in the Novels of Anne Tyler," 16–27 in Stephens, ed., *The Fiction of Anne Tyler*.

Carson, Barbara Harrell. "Art's Internal Necessity: Anne Tyler's *Celestial Navigation*," 47–54 in Stephens, ed., *The Fiction of Anne Tyler*.

Cook, Bruce. "New Faces in Faulkner Country." *Saturday Review* 3 (September 4, 1976): 40–41.

Elkins, Mary J. "*Dinner at the Homesick Restaurant*: Anne Tyler and the Faulkner Connection." *Atlantis: A Women's Studies Journal* 10 (Spring 1985): 93–105. Rpt. 119–35 in Stephens, ed., *The Fiction of Anne Tyler*.

Freiert, William K. "Anne Tyler's Accidental Ulysses." *Classical and Modern Literature* 10 (Fall 1989): 71–79.

Gibson, Mary Ellis. "Family as Fate: The Novels of Anne Tyler." *Southern Literary Journal* 15 (Fall 1983): 47–53.

Gilbert, Susan. "Anne Tyler," in *Southern Women Writers: The New Generation*, ed. Tonette Bond Inge. Tuscaloosa: University of Alabama Press, 1990.

———. "Private Lives and Public Issues: Anne Tyler's Prize-winning Novels," 136–45 in Stephens, ed., *The Fiction of Anne Tyler*.

Gullette, Margaret Morganroth. "Anne Tyler: The Tears (and Joys) Are in the Things: Adulthood in Anne Tyler's Novels." *New England Review and Bread Loaf Quarterly* 7 (Spring 1985): 323–34. Rev. as Chapter 5 of *Safe at Last in the Middle Years: The Invention of the Midlife Progress Novel: Saul Bellow, Margaret Drabble, Anne Tyler, and John Updike*. Rpt, 97–109 in Stephens, ed., *The Fiction of Anne Tyler*.

Inman, Sue Lile. "The Effects of the Artistic Process: A Study of Three Artist Figures in Anne Tyler's Fiction," 55–63 in Stephens, ed., *The Fiction of Anne Tyler*.

Johnson, Sue Ann. "The Daughter as Escape Artist." *Atlantis: A Women's Studies Journal* 9 (Spring 1984): 10–22.

Jones, Anne G. "Home at Last and Homesick Again: The Ten Novels of Anne Tyler." *Hollins Critic* 23 (April 1986): 1–13.

Kanoza, Theresa. "Mentors and Maternal Role Models: The Healthy Mean Between Extremes in Anne Tyler's Fiction," 27–39 in Stephens, ed., *The Fiction of Anne Tyler*.

Lamb, Wendy. "An Interview with Anne Tyler." *Iowa Journal of Literary Studies* 3 (1981): 59–64.

Manning, Carol S. "Welty, Tyler, and Traveling Salesmen: The Wandering Hero Unhorsed," 110–18 in Stephens, ed., *The Fiction of Anne Tyler*.

McMurtry, Larry. "Life Is a Foreign Country" (Rev. of *The Accidental Tourist*). *New York Times Book Review* (September 8, 1985): 1, 36.

McPhilips, Robert. "The Baltimore Chop" (Rev. of *Breathing Lessons*). *Nation* (November 7, 1988): 464–66.

Nesanovich, Stella Ann. "The Individual in the Family: Anne Tyler's *Searching for Caleb* and *Earthly Possessions.*" *Southern Review* 14 (Winter 1978): 170–76. (See also "The Individual in the Family: A Critical Introduction to the Novels of Anne Tyler." Ph.D. Diss., Baton Rouge: Louisiana State University, 1979.)

Robertson, Mary F. "Anne Tyler: Medusa Points and Contact Points," 119–41 in *Contemporary American Women Writers: Narrative Strategies*, ed. Catherine Rainwater and William J. Scheick. Lexington: University Press of Kentucky, 1985.

Shelton, Frank W. "Anne Tyler's House," 40–46 in Stephens, ed., *The Fiction of Anne Tyler*.

———. "The Necessary Balance: Distance and Sympathy in the Novels of Anne Tyler." *Southern Review* 20 (Fall 1984): 851–60.

Taylor, Gordon O. "Morgan's Passion," 64–72 in Stephens, ed., *The Fiction of Anne Tyler*.

Towers, Robert. "Roughing It" (Rev. of *Breathing Lessons* and Louise Erdrich's *Tracks*). *New York Review of Books* (November 10, 1988): 40–41.

Updike, John. "Family Ways." *New Yorker* (March 29, 1976): 110–12. Rpt. in *Hugging the Shore*. New York: Random House, 1983.

———. "Imagining Things." *New Yorker* (June 23, 1980): 94–101. Rpt. in *Hugging the Shore*.

———. "Leaving Home." *New Yorker* (October 28, 1985): 106–12.

———. "Loosened Roots." *New Yorker* (June 6, 1977): 130–34. Rpt. in *Hugging the Shore*.

———. "On Such a Beautiful Green Little Planet." *New Yorker* (April 5, 1982): 193–97. Rpt. in *Hugging the Shore*.

Wagner, Joseph B. "Beck Tull: 'The Absent Presence' in *Dinner at the Homesick Restaurant*," 73–83 in Stephens, ed., *The Fiction of Anne Tyler*.

Zahlan, Anne R. "Anne Tyler," in *Fifty Southern Writers after 1900*, ed. Joseph M. Flora and Robert Bain. Westport, Conn.: Greenwood, 1987.

———. "Traveling towards the Self: The Psychic Drama of Anne Tyler's *The Accidental Tourist*," 84–96 in Stephens, ed., *The Fiction of Anne Tyler*.

Alice [Malsenior] Walker
(1944–   )

Even though Alice Walker had been publishing for fourteen years before *The Color Purple* appeared, it was that novel, which stayed on the best-seller's list of the *New York Times* for over twenty-five weeks, and the subsequent film that made her a celebrity. The literary community recognized the quality of the novel by awarding it the American Book Award and the Pulitzer Prize. The general public came to know of Alice Walker through the efforts of film director Stephen Spielberg and jazz artist Quincy Jones, who provided the soundtrack for the film version of *The Color Purple*. Walker is particularly noted for giving voices to and promoting African-American women's experiences and perspectives.

BIOGRAPHY

Alice Walker was born February 9, 1944, in Eatonton, Georgia, the eighth and last child of Willie Lee and Minnie Tallulah Grant Walker. Her parents were sharecroppers, who only made about $300 a year in the cotton fields. Eatonton had also been the birthplace of Joel Chandler Harris, about whom Walker writes: "He stole a good part of my heritage. How did he steal it? By making me feel ashamed of it. In creating Uncle Remus, he placed an effective barrier between me and the stories that meant so much to me, the stories that could have meant so much to all of our children, the stories that they could have heard from their own people" (*Living by the Word*).

Walker also reports that her early education had been "misery"; she attended "a shabby segregated school that was once the state prison and that had, on the second floor, the large circular print of the electric chair that had stood there" (*In Search of Our Mothers' Gardens*). This area of Georgia and the poverty she experienced provided the background for her first novel, *The Third Life of Grange Copeland* (1970), with its black poverty and white economic oppression. In *The*

Temple of My Familiar (1989), Fanny and Tanya, a black child and a white child, grow up together in Georgia, but are made aware of their differences by the adults around them. Fanny recalls: "In high school I watched the integration of the University of Georgia on television. . . . And I was watching the night the whole campus seemed to go up in flames, and white people raged against the enrollment of two of the palest-skinned black people anywhere." Walker credits her parents and others like them with giving her a larger world view: "In large measure, black Southern writers owe their clarity of vision to parents who refused to diminish themselves as human beings by succumbing to racism. Our parents seemed to know that an extreme negative emotion held against other human beings for reasons they do not control can be blinding. Blindness about other human beings, especially for a writer, is equivalent to death" (*In Search of Our Mothers' Gardens*).

Walker's youth also had its private scars, including literal blindness. When Walker was 8, she lost her sight in one eye after a BB gun accident; the scar tissue was not removed until 6 years later. The accident forced Walker into herself and left its psychological scars; but out of that experience she developed acute observational skills, which led her to begin writing poetry. Walker was valedictorian of her senior class and awarded a rehabilitation scholarship, based on her injury, which enabled her to attend college. Her neighbors contributed $75 toward her expenses.

When Walker left Eatonton in 1961 to attend college, her mother, the person who seems to have been the most influential person in her life, gave her three presents: a typewriter, a suitcase, and a sewing machine. These gifts gave her independence. The sewing machine in particular, representing a connection with Southern black women's cultural heritage, surfaces later in the form of the quilts in her story "Everyday Use," also in *The Color Purple*, and, of course, as the source of Celie's economic freedom in that novel, the pants she creates. For two years Walker attended Spelman College, an elite school for black women in Atlanta, Georgia. Spelman at that time was dedicated to training black women for their futures as fine black ladies. Spelman was also affected by the civil rights movement, where Walker's awareness of the issues and its leaders grew. The archives at Spelman provided documents for the characterization of Nettie in *The Color Purple*.

Walker transferred to Sarah Lawrence College in New York, where she received her degree in 1965. Walker had experienced suicidal feelings for a large part of her life and again when she found herself pregnant; she wrote: "'I took out my razor blade and pressed it deep into my arm. I practiced a slicing motion. . . . On the last day for miracles," she wrote, one of her friends called to say she had the telephone number of a doctor who would perform an abortion (*In Search of Our Mothers' Gardens*). Walker had the abortion, an act that led her to write poetry and to share that work with poet and writer-in-residence Muriel Rukeyser. Rukeyser encouraged Walker and introduced her to an editor at Harcourt. Walker also spent a summer in Africa. Her understanding of herself, her heritage, being a black female, her world, and the roles she could take had personal and public manifestations as a result of these accumulated experiences.

After graduation Walker worked for the welfare department in the lower east side of New York City. She left that job for voter registration projects in Georgia, then for Mississippi and civil rights programs. Walker continued to write, and she began to gain recognition. Her first publication, "The Civil Rights Movement: How Good Was It?," won the American Scholar essay contest. In 1966 she was a Breadloaf Writer's Conference Scholar, and in 1967 she received a Merrill Writing Fellowship and a McDowell Colony Fellowship, the latter to begin writing her first novel, *The Third Life of Grange Copeland*. That same year she married Melvyn Roseman Leventhal, a white civil rights lawyer and conscientious objector to the Vietnam War. Their daughter Rebecca Grant was born in 1969, three days after her novel was completed.

Walker's first book of poems, *Once*, including references to her experiences in Africa, was published in 1968. Walker worked with Head Start programs and taught at two Southern colleges, Jackson State in Mississippi, and then a year later at Tougalou College. Her first novel was published in 1970. While on a Radcliffe Institute Fellowship (1971–73), Walker taught at Wellesley College and the University of Massachusetts. In 1973 she received a National Book Award nomination for her third book of poems, *Revolutionary Petunias*. In 1974 *In Love and Trouble*, her first collection of short stories was published, as well as the first of her children's books, a biography of Langston Hughes. The collection of short stories won the Rosenthal Award of the National Institute of Arts and Letters in 1974.

Walker became a contributing editor to *Ms.* magazine in 1975. A year later she and Levanthal divorced. *Meridian*, Walker's second novel, based on her experiences in the civil rights movement and on her experiences at Spelman, was published in 1976. Walker continued to receive recognition for her work, including a Guggenheim Fellowship in 1977 and a teaching appointment at Yale. One of the most significant literary influences on Walker has been Zora Neale Hurston, whose work Walker edited for an anthology. She also published her fourth book of poems, *Good Night, Willie Lee. I'll See You in the Morning*, and a second collection of short stories, *You Can't Keep a Good Woman Down*.

Alice Walker moved to a rural area outside of San Francisco to write *The Color Purple*, which won the American Book Award and the Pulitzer Prize in 1983. She was the first black woman to receive the Pulitzer. This novel was inspired by Walker's great-grandmother, who had been raped at the age of 12. Walker has said that the characters in this novel would not emerge while she was living in the city. When she moved to the country, an environment much like rural Georgia, the characters' stories came to her, or through her, as a medium. Although much of Walker's work has been her writing, she has spoken for causes as well. In 1981 she was the keynote speaker for the dinner honoring Rosa Parks on the twenty-fifth anniversary of the civil rights movement. A year later she appeared with Tillie Olsen at a benefit for the Women's Party for

Survival, which opposes nuclear weapons. She read her poetry at an antiapartheid demonstration and encampment on the University of California, Berkeley, campus.

Walker has lectured and taught at Berkeley and at Brandeis. She published *In Search of Our Mothers' Gardens*, a collection of womanist prose. A fifth book of poetry, *Horses Make the Landscape More Beautiful*, was published in 1984; *Living by the Word*, a volume of essays, in 1988. Walker continues to live in Northern California with her daughter and with Robert Allen, former editor of *Black Scholar*.

Subsequently, Walker published two more children's books in addition to the Hughes biography, *To Hell with Dying*, based on her own first published short story, and *Finding the Green Stone*, both illustrated by Catherine Deeter. In *Green Stone*, Walker emphasizes that comfort and peace only come from within: There may be good company for the journey, but the discovery is all our own. Walker's fourth novel, *The Temple of My Familiar*, which has Celie and Shug from *The Color Purple* as part of its framework, was published in 1989. Following publication of her collected poetry, *Her Blue Body Everything We Know: Earthling Poems 1965–1990 Complete*, Walker said:

Examining the poems offered a chance to see whether I had been true to myself, and to see my life as almost that of an expatriate, even though I'm an expatriate in my own country. Northern California, where I live now, is so different from where I grew up in Georgia. I could grieve over this displacement and admit how much I miss my native land. But I cannot go back to Georgia to live. I need mountains and the ocean. And my memories of the South are really difficult. I was living in Mississippi when Martin Luther King was assassinated. Through it all, I was writing poetry. That was what was given me to make emotional sense of it, to survive.

MAJOR THEMES

"The idea is to be Sojourner Truth and take our books on the road. It is my belief and my faith that whenever you are trying to convey a sense of common reality to people, they will want to read and hear about it" (Walker "The Eighties and Me"). In this 1990 *Publishers Weekly*, article, writers were asked to reflect on how their books had helped shape the 1980s or were shaped by that decade. Walker responded initially from what has become her main theme in her writing, her womanist position, which she had defined earlier: "A black feminist. . . . Committed to survival and wholeness of entire people, male *and* female. Not a separatist, except periodically, for health. . . . Traditionally capable, as in: 'Mama, I'm walking to Canada and I'm taking you and a bunch of other slaves with me.' Reply: 'It wouldn't be the first time' " (*In Search of Our Mothers' Gardens* xi). Walker ends her reply to *Publishers Weekly* with another of her significant themes: hope for the reformation of and for the survival of the whole human race.

In between those two large themes there are many points of conjunction in her works. Among the most prominent themes are those having to do with oppressed black women—the violence, injustice, and brutality of that oppression; the need for creative outlets; discovering personal potential and transforming oneself; sources for spiritual growth; the need for and desire for family and community; and survival through affirmation and change. For Walker, art has a moral purpose. In *"Horses Make a Landscape Look More Beautiful,"* the poet presents herself as a woman offering two flowers whose twin roots are Justice and Hope. She urges, "Let us begin."

Her beginning involves analysis of the oppression of black women. A black woman, Walker writes, is " 'the *mule* of the world' because we have been handed the burdens that everyone else—*everyone* else—refused to carry" (*In Search of Our Mothers' Gardens*). One of those burdens is violence, especially that perpetrated by black men. Male brutality can be seen in Celie's being raped by the man she believes to be her father, in having her children taken from her, and in her treatment by Mr., who beats her. She responds: "It all I can do not to cry. I make myself wood. I say to myself, Celie, you a tree" (*The Color Purple*). For Walker, violence is a product of sexism and racism. That theme is portrayed in the first two of Grange Copeland's three lives. It is seen again in the stories from *You Can't Keep a Good Woman Down*.

Part of the discovery of oneself and one's potential and therefore one's freedom comes in finding creative outlets for outrage. Celie and Sophia create a quilt using a pattern called Sister's Choice. In *The Temple of My Familiar*, Zede' creates headdresses and capes from exotic bird feathers. Mem, in *The Third Life of Grange Copeland*, plants flowers and greens. In the title essay from *In Search of Our Mother's Gardens*, Walker writes that "these grandmothers and mothers of ours were not Saints, but Artists; driven to a numb and bleeding madness by the springs of creativity in them for which there was no release." Walker's mother "made all the clothes we wore . . . made all the towels and sheets . . . spent the summers canning vegetables and fruits . . . spent the winter evenings making quilts." In part of her conclusion to this essay, Walker writes: "I notice that it is only when my mother is working in her flowers that she is radiant, almost to the point of being invisible—except as Creator: hand and eye."

The Creator undergoes several revisions in Walker's works. For Celie, the Creator is freed from a white patriarchal authority figure. In *The Temple of My Familiar*, Shug has founded her own religion. Fanny reports:

My grandmothers [Celie and Shug] formed their own church; a tradition long standing among black women. Only, they didn't call it a "church." They called it a "band." Sometimes a prayer band. Sometimes a band of angels, sometimes a band of devils. "Band" was what renegade black women's churches were called traditionally; it means a group of people who share a common bond and purpose and whose notion of spiritual reality is radically at odds with mainstream or prevailing ones.

Spirituality is linked to family and community in Walker's works. Grange Copeland, although unable to reconcile with his son, does raise his granddaughter. In *The Color Purple*, there is a reunion of Celie's family wrought after years of separation. Walker says *Temple* is "about the last five hundred thousand years." While several of its characters, male and female, find the spiritual strength to re-create their lives, it is the female characters, forging themselves out of their maternal progenitors, who lead the way. Walker's male characters are not beyond redemption. Mr. in *The Color Purple* is now Albert. He has found his own creative outlet: sewing shirts to go with Celie's pants. He now knows how to wonder and to love and to be friends. And he is in the final family portrait.

It is through affirmation of oneself and others that change occurs. For Walker change means possibility for survival of individuals, communities, and the universe. Johnny, in Walker's children's story, *Finding the Green Stone*, has lost touch with his inner spirituality. He suffers; he is mean and sad and fearful, until he finds his source of wholeness once again. In her Afterword to *Grange Copeland*, Walker writes: "I believe wholeheartedly in the necessity of keeping inviolate the one interior space that is given to all. I believe in the soul." Walker also lauds the healing power of love. Copeland comes halfway when he admits to his granddaughter, Ruth: "I don't know that loves works on everybody. A little love, a little buckshot, that's how I'd say handle yourself." For Walker, violence does not stop anything but life. In *The Color Purple*, Celie writes: "The only way to stop making somebody the serpent is for everybody to accept everybody else as a child of God." The result is transformation.

Walker's literary forms have been as various as her books and her individual stories. But the form that seems to draw the most critical attention has been the epistolary format of *The Color Purple*, with its two voices, Celie and Nettie. First Celie creates herself and tells her story in her own voice. The reader is invited to identify with this first-person narrator, who has only God, and a silent one at that, to listen. Her letters are short. The white space between each letter invites us to leap ahead. Her readers are eager for the next installment of her life, seemingly being shaped in front of us. Nettie's letters, those of an educated woman whose experiences are far removed from Celie's, provide another voice. *The Temple of My Familiar* is full of voices, too. Characters tell each other their stories, share their life philosophies. This novel is neither character-driven, nor plot-driven but voice-driven. *Possessing the Secret of Joy* (1992), Walker's most recent novel, will focus even more attention on her as a critic of female exploitation: the novel depicts the horror of female circumcision, a rite much more widely practiced than modern readers realize. The principal characters are Tashi, Olivia, and Adam (all known to readers of *The Color Purple* and *The Temple of My Familiar*). The story traces the destructive physical and psychological damage inflicted upon Tashi as a result of circumcision; neither love nor therapy can alleviate her suffering. It is only when she returns to Africa to confront the woman who performed the operation upon her that she is able to transcend the dehumanization of African definitions of womanhood. Walker therefore continues her focus on American and African experiences, and, once again, she highlights the complexity of her story by using multiple points of view.

SURVEY OF CRITICISM

There are two useful book-length annotated bibliographies of Alice Walker's works covering the years 1967–1988. Erma Banks and Keith Byerman's bibliography has the additional advantage of having a lengthy critical introduction, including biographical sketch, plot summaries, and major themes in her works through *Horses Make a Landscape Look More Beautiful*. The third section of the introduction is an overview of the literary criticism of Walker's work, which has focused on influences, religion, race, women, the letter format of *The Color Purple*, folk elements in her works, motherhood, and the family. The controversial nature of Walker's treatment of black men and her equally controversial treatment of black women have their own section of this overview.

Trudier Harris is cited for her analysis of black men in *Grange Copeland* "as victims and victimizers." In one essay, Harris places Walker's men "in the tradition of emasculated black men"; in another essay, Harris "shows how they turn their frustration and anger against other blacks."

Walker's womanist thought, as an ideological point of view and as a force in Walker's writing, also has its own section in this review of criticism. W. Lawrence Hogue is cited for asserting "that Walker sacrifices character development when necessary to prove her point." Harris is particularly critical of *The Color Purple*, which has been virtually canonized and therefore put beyond the reach of evaluation. Harris sees the novel as "a distorted picture of black life," with Walker *the* spokesperson for the experience of black women rather than one voice among many."

Banks and Byerman also published a selected bibliography of Walker's works and critical studies on those works through 1988 in a special section of *Callaloo: An Afro-American and African Journal of Arts and Letters*, in 1989. This special section devoted to Walker also includes four essays, one each on the first two novels, one on the film version of *The Color Purple*, and one on the short-story collection *You Can't Keep a Good Woman Down*. In this latter essay, Byerman examines Jacques Lacan, Robert Con Davis, contemporary feminist critics on the deconstruction of patriarchal order, and finally "womanism [which] manifests itself in what [Barbara] Christian calls 'process narratives,' those stories which do not seek closure, but rather reveal an ongoing creativity." After examining Walker's stories from this perspective, Byerman concludes: "Walker paradoxically reinstates patriarchy in the process of deconstructing it."

There is one book-length collection of essays on Alice Walker, edited by Harold Bloom for his Chelsea House series. This book contains central essays by several important Walker critics. The final essay, "Writing the Subject: Reading *The Color Purple*," by Bell Hooks, was published in this volume for the first time. Hooks sees the novel as "a narrative of 'sexual confession.' "

Celie's desires for other women, particularly her sexual relationship with Shug, are presented forthrightly; yet when Shug leaves Celie, a heterosexual bond is reestablished with Albert. Celie's confession of incest is trivialized when her rapist turns out not to have been her father. Hooks concludes that "radical didactic messages add depth and complexity to *The Color Purple* without resolving the contradictions between radicalism—the vision of revolutionary transformation, and the conservatism—the perpetuation of bourgeois ideology."

Generally, criticism of Walker's works in the past few years has followed the trends of the first two decades. Her fiction is written about more than her poetry; *The Color Purple* is pursued in critical articles more often than the other novels; her first collection of short stories, *In Love and Trouble*, seems to be valued more than the didactic *You Can't Keep a Good Woman Down*; and Walker's womanist thought seems to be defined and redefined to suit critics' needs. Of particular interest in this latter area is "Roundtable Discussion: Christian Ethics and Theology in Womanist Perspective," published in the *Journal of Feminist Studies in Religion* in 1989. These thoughts and responses are unique in terms of the discussion mode of presenting divergent views.

The preponderance of criticism in the past few years focuses significantly on the influences of Zora Neale Hurston, on further examinations of the epistolary format in *The Color Purple*, and on exploring Walker's challenges to patriarchal constructions of female lives. Henry Louis Gates, Jr., sees Hurston's influence on Celie's voice, with his essay centered on "intertextual strategies of narration in *Their Eyes Were Watching God* and *The Color Purple*." Gates also links Walker's epistolary technique with slave narratives.

Molly Hite, in "Romance, Marginality, and Matrilineage: *The Color Purple*," asserts that "the romance paradigm . . . encodes a system of hierarchical relations that have ideological repercussions," notably that the "recognizably conventional system of hierarchical relations is also the ideology of racism and patriarchy." Walker uses the letter format in *The Color Purple* in order "to de-center patriarchal authority, giving speech to hitherto muted women."

Nancy Porter examines novels by several black women writers and writes about the characters in *Meridian*. Their "relationships serve also to 'deconstruct' the civil rights movement by exposing discrepancies between its ideology and practice."

Linda Abbandonato writes on subversive sexuality in *The Color Purple*, maintaining that this novel "is a conscious rewriting of canonical male texts," with an invitation to "trace its [epistolary] ancestry all the way to *Clarissa*." Abbandonato cites Luce Irigaray, who urges women to "come out of [men's] language," and concludes that "the apparently impoverished and inarticulate language of the illiterati [in *The Color Purple*] turns out to be deceptively resonant and dazzlingly rich." In addition to the linguistic success of the novel, Abbandonato finds that the novel "succeeds partly because Celie's sexual orientation provides an alternative to the heterosexual paradigm of the conventional marriage plot."

There continue to be some critics who echo Harris' evaluation that Celie is "a bale of cotton with a vagina" who "gives in to her environment with a kind of passivity that comes near to provoking screams in readers." And there are those who abhor the happy ending of *The Color Purple*. Book reviews of *Temple of My Familiar* critique the lack of narrative power and the presence of long polemical speeches. In general, however, criticism of Alice Walker's work has been quite laudatory and exploratory of its broadest implications.

BIBLIOGRAPHY

Works by Alice Walker

Once: Poems. New York: Harcourt Brace and World, 1968. London: Woman's Press, 1988.

The Third Life of Grange Copeland. New York: Harcourt Brace Jovanovich, 1970.

Five Poems. Detroit: Broadside Press, 1972.

In Love and Trouble: Stories of Black Women. New York: Harcourt Brace Jovanovich, 1973.

Langston Hughes: American Poet, New York: Crowell, 1973.

Revolutionary Petunias and Other Poems. New York: Harcourt Brace Jovanovich, 1973.

Meridian. New York: Harcourt Brace Jovanovich, 1976.

Goodnight, Willie Lee. I'll See You in the Morning. New York: Dial, 1979.

I Love Myself When I'm Laughing . . . and Then Again When I Am Looking Mean and Impressive: A Zora Neale Hurston Reader, editor. Introduction by Mary Helen Washington. New York: Feminist Press, 1979.

You Can't Keep a Good Woman Down. New York: Harcourt Brace Jovanovich, 1981. London: Women's Press, 1982.

The Color Purple. New York: Harcourt Brace Jovanovich, 1982. London: Women's Press, 1983.

In Search of Our Mothers' Gardens: Womanist Prose. New York: Harcourt Brace Jovanovich, 1983.

Horses Make a Landscape Look More Beautiful. New York: Harcourt Brace Jovanovich, 1984.

Living by the Word: Selected Writings, 1973–1987. New York: Harcourt Brace Jovanovich, 1988.

To Hell with Dying, illustrations by Catherine Deeter. New York: Harcourt Brace Jovanovich, 1988.

The Temple of My Familiar. New York: Harcourt Brace Jovanovich, 1989.

Finding the Green Stone, illustrations by Catherine Deeter. New York: Harcourt Brace Jovanovich, 1991.

Her Blue Body Everything We Know: Earthling Poems, 1965–1990 Complete. New York: Harcourt Brace Jovanovich, 1991.

Possessing the Secret of Joy. New York: Harcourt Brace Jovanovich, 1992.

Selected Interviews

Interview with C. Dreifus, *The Progressive* 53 (August 1989): 29–31.

Interview with Jean W. Ross, 471–74 in *Contemporary Authors*. New Revision Series, Vol. 27.

"The Craft of Survival." Interview with A. P. Sanoff. *U.S. News and World Report* 110 (June 3, 1991): 51.

Studies of Alice Walker

Abbandonato, Linda. "A View from 'Elsewhere': Subversive Sexuality and the Rewriting of the Heroine's Story in *The Color Purple*." *PMLA* 106 (1991): 1106–15.

Awkward, Michael. "*The Color Purple* and the Achievement of (Comm)unity," in *Inspiriting Influences: Tradition, Revision, and Afro-American Women's Novels*. New York: Columbia University Press, 1991.

Banks, Erma, and Keith Byerman. *Alice Walker: An Annotated Bibliography, 1967–1986*. New York: Garland, 1989.

———. "Alice Walker: A Selected Bibliography, 1968–1988." *Callaloo* 12 (1989): 343–45.

Bloom, Harold, ed. *Alice Walker*. New York: Chelsea House, 1989.

Bobo, Jacqueline. "Sifting through the Controversy: Reading *The Color Purple*." *Callaloo* 12 (1989): 332–42.

Brown, Joseph A., S.J. " 'All Saints Should Walk away': The Mystical Pilgrimage of *Meridian*." *Callaloo* 12 (1989): 310–20.

Butler-Evans, Elliott. *Race, Gender, and Desire: Narrative Strategies in the Fiction of Toni Cade Bambara, Toni Morrison, and Alice Walker*. Philadelphia: Temple University Press, 1989.

Byerman, Keith. "Desire and Alice Walker: The Quest for a Womanist Narrative." *Callaloo* 12 (1989): 321–31.

Clark, Suzanne. "The Sentimental and the Critical: Maternal Irony, Alice Walker, and a Feminist Conclusion," in *Sentimental Modernism: Women Writers and the Revolution of the Word*. Bloomington: Indiana University Press, 1991.

Collins, Gina Michelle. "*The Color Purple*: What Feminism Can Learn from a Southern Tradition," in *Southern Literature and Literary Theory*, ed. Jefferson Humphries. Athens: University of Georgia Press, 1990.

Gates, Henry Louis, Jr., "Color Me Zora: Alice Walker's [Re]Writing of the Speakerly Text," in *Intertextuality and Contemporary American Fiction*, ed. Patrick O'Donnell and Robert Con Davis. Baltimore: Johns Hopkins University Press, 1989.

Harris, Trudier. "Folklore in the Fiction of Alice Walker—A Perpetuation of Historical and Literary Traditions." *Black American Literature Forum* 11 (Spring 1977): 3–8.

———. "On *The Color Purple*, Stereotypes and Silence." *Black American Literature Forum* 18 (Winter 1984): 155–61.

———. "From Victimization to Free Enterprise: Alice Walker's *The Color Purple*." *Studies in American Fiction* 14 (Spring 1986): 1–17.

Hedges, Elaine. "The Needle or the Pen: The Literary Rediscovery of Women's Textile Work," in *Tradition and the Talents of Women*, ed. Florence Howe. Urbana: University of Illinois Press, 1991.

Hite, Molly. "Romance, Marginality, Matrilineage: *The Color Purple*." In *The Other Side of the Story: Structures and Strategies of Contemporary Feminist Narratives*. Ithaca: Cornell University Press, 1989.

Hogue, W. Lawrence. *Discourse and the Other: The Production of the Afro-American Text*. Durham: Duke University Press, 1986.

Mason, Theodore O. "Alice Walker's *The Third Life of Grange Copeland*: The Dynamics of Enclosure." *Callaloo* 12 (1989): 297–309.

McKay, Nellie V. "Alice Walker's 'Advancing Luna—and Ida B. Wells': A Struggle toward Sisterhood." In *Rape and Representation*, ed. Lynn A. Higgins and Brenda R. Silver. New York: Columbia University Press, 1991.

Porter, Nancy. "Women's Interracial Friendships and Visions of Community in *Meridian, The Salt-Eaters, Civil Wars, and Dessa Rose*," in *Tradition and the Talents of Women*, ed. Florence Howe. Urbana: University of Illinois Press, 1991.

Pratt, Louis H., and Darnell D. Pratt. *Alice Malsenior Walker, Annotated Bibliography: 1968–1986*. Westport, Conn.: Meckler, 1988.

Proudfit, Charles L. "Celie's Search for Identity: A Psychoanalytic Developmental Reading on Alice Walker's *The Color Purple*." *Contemporary Literature* 32 (Spring 1991): 12–37.

Sanders, Cheryl, et al. "Roundtable Discussion: Christian Ethics and Theology in Womanist Perspective." *Journal of Feminist Studies in Religion* 5 (Fall 1989): 83–112.

Strout, Cushing. " 'I, Too, Sing America': Alice Walker's Visible Woman, Meridian," in *Making American Tradition: Visions and Revisions from Ben Franklin to Alice Walker*. New Brunswick: Rutgers University Press, 1990.

Stuart, Andrea. "*The Color Purple*: In Defence of Happy Endings," in *The Female Gaze: Women as Viewers of Popular Culture*, ed. Lorraine Gamman and Margaret Marshment. London: Women's Press, 1988.

Tucker, Lindsey. "Walking the Red Road: Mobility, Maternity, and Native American Myth in Alice Walker's *Meridian*." *Women's Studies* 19 (1991): 1–17.

Wade-Gayles, Gloria. "Black Southern Womanist: The Genius of Alice Walker," in *Southern Women Writers*, ed. Tonette Bond Inge. Tuscaloosa: University of Alabama Press, 1990.

Williams, Carolyn. " 'Trying to Do without God': The Revision of Epistolary Address in *The Color Purple*," in *Writing the Female Voice: Essays on Epistolary Literature*, ed. Elizabeth Goldsmith. Boston: Northeastern University Press, 1989.

Wilt, Judith. "Black Maternity: 'A Need for Someone to Want the Black Baby to Live,' " in *Abortion, Choice, and Contemporary Fiction*. Chicago: University of Chicago Press, 1990.

JOHN M. ALLISON, JR.

James Wilcox
(1949–   )

James Wilcox is known primarily for his novels that chronicle the misadventures of the inhabitants of Tula Springs, a fictional town in Louisiana. His major strength as a novelist derives from his attention to detail in creating characters and situations. An accomplished musician, Wilcox has an ear for nuances of voice. He orchestrates a multitude of remarkable characters and seemingly random events into complex, highly structured plots whose patterns are revealed only as his novels reach their conclusion.

BIOGRAPHY

James Peter Wilcox was born April 4, 1949, in Hammond, Louisiana, the third of five children born to James H. and Marie Wiza Wilcox. When Wilcox was 5, his family moved to Tallahassee, Florida, where they lived for 2 years while his father completed a doctorate in music. In 1955 the family returned to Hammond when his father accepted a position in the music department at Southeastern Louisiana University, where he became chair of the department and eventually dean of humanities.

Although he attended first grade in Tallahassee, Wilcox spent his remaining school years in the public school system in Hammond. Wilcox calls Hammond the site of his formative years and most vivid memories. Thus, the Florida parishes of Louisiana were a natural setting for his short stories and novels.

Music, religion, and literature were constant influences in the Wilcox household. All members of the Wilcox family played musical instruments. In addition to his father's academic pursuit of music, his mother played the oboe, and each of the children studied either piano or violin. Wilcox studied two instruments, piano and cello. During 4 years of high school, he commuted regularly to Baton Rouge to play cello as a member of the Baton Rouge Symphony Orchestra.

Wilcox credits his discipline as a writer to the years of dedicated practice as a musician. He also notes that his work with music gave him a sense of form and structure. For Wilcox, the structure of literature is similar to the structure of music. Both involve the statement of themes, elaboration, building toward a climax, and a sense of an ending.

Wilcox's religious heritage is rife with tensions that find play in his novels. In the public schools, Wilcox was surrounded by Baptists. Marie Wilcox, a devout Catholic, raised her children in the Roman Catholic Church; as a child, he attended catechism classes during the summer. His father attended the Methodist Church. Wilcox recalls being exhorted by the nuns to pray for his father's conversion to the one true church. The religious tensions were compounded when, as a high school student, he accepted a job as organist in the Methodist Church. Though still a practicing Catholic, youthful experiences led Wilcox to a healthy skepticism of the outward trappings and arbitrary rules of organized religions in any form.

Wilcox attributes his love for literature to his mother, an avid reader who encouraged her children to explore books. He remembers his mother attending a reading by Flannery O'Connor at Southeastern Louisiana University and encouraging him to read her short stories. Wilcox identifies O'Connor's short stories as an influence on his writing, noting that they gave him the courage to write novels. Yet, he professes apathy for the heavily doctrinaire novels. Although he does not mind being called a Southern writer, Wilcox is not an ardent reader of other Southern writers. He prefers British novelists, citing E. M. Forster, Anthony Trollope, Charles Dickens, and the early novels of George Orwell, H. G. Wells, and Muriel Spark as influential on his writing. Among American novelists, he professes a waivering interest in the novels of Barbara Pym.

In 1967 Wilcox entered Yale University to pursue a degree in English. In his early years at Yale, Wilcox studied writing with John Palmer, dean of Silliman College and editor of the *Yale Review*. Under the tutelage of Robert Penn Warren, in his junior year Wilcox studied the short story. Warren subsequently tutored Wilcox's senior honors project, a novel he chose not to publish. Wilcox graduated from Yale in 1971 with a B.A. in English.

Through his association with Palmer and Warren, Wilcox met Albert Erskine, a senior editor at Random House, who served as editor for Warren, William Faulkner, and Eudora Welty. Shortly after his graduation, Wilcox moved to New York to accept a job as editorial assistant to Erskine at Random House. Wilcox served in various capacities at Random House for 6 years. In 1978 he accepted a position as associate editor at Doubleday. After a year at Doubleday, at 30, Wilcox decided to leave his job to pursue a full-time writing career.

In January 1981 Wilcox published his first short story, "Mr. Ray," in *The New Yorker*. The story is important in that it introduces Tula Springs, Louisiana, the setting for four of his five novels. The story also introduces Donna Lee Kelley, who figures prominently in two of his later novels. In December of the same year, *The New Yorker* published his second short story, "Camping Out."

Although Wilcox has published three other short stories in *The New Yorker*, *Avenue*, and *Louisiana Literature*, he expresses a preference for the longer novel form. According to Wilcox, the novel allows him the opportunity to be "fugal." Wilcox professes a fascination for the musical aspect of voices. The novel's expansive form allows him freedom to weave together the different voices of his characters. The juxtaposition of the competing voices and perspectives of his self-absorbed characters is the source of Wilcox's comic spirit.

The year 1983 brought the publication of Wilcox's first novel, *Modern Baptists*, which was widely praised. In a review that appeared on the front page of the *New York Times Book Review*, Anne Tyler referred to Wilcox as a writer of "comic genius." Wilcox credits Tyler's review for four additional printings of his first novel. When *Modern Baptists* was in galleys, Dial Press was absorbed by a conglomerate and eventually disbanded. Tyler's review ensured the novel a wider audience. The novel focuses on the misfortunes of middle-aged Bobby Pickens, who over the course of the novel loses his job as assistant manager at the Sonny Boy Bargain Store and sets out in a failed attempt to become a preacher, modernizing church doctrine for a new breed of Baptists.

Wilcox's Catholic upbringing and musical heritage are most evident in his second novel, *North Gladiola* (1985). Ethel Mae Coco leads the Pro Arts, a classical musical ensemble that alternately changes from quartet to quintet to trio. Mrs. Coco, a Baptist turned Catholic, struggles with her loss of faith in the church's teachings and the ensuing upheavals with her husband and six children.

In 1986 Wilcox received a Guggenheim Fellowship to complete his third novel, *Miss Undine's Living Room* (1987). When Olive Mackie, the novel's unlikely protagonist, is fired from her job as secretary to the Superintendent of Streets, Parks, and Garbage, she decides to run against the current superintendent. In order to achieve her goal, Olive must exonerate a senile, bed-ridden uncle (a mnemonic expert) who cannot remember whether he murdered his obnoxious home attendant.

Sort of Rich (1989) portrays a middle-aged, Manhattan socialite now transplanted in Tula Springs. Gretchen Peabody Aiken-Lewes struggles to come to terms with a South that is not quite as Faulknerian as she imagined. At the same time, she is trying to fit in with her husband's household staff. She feels threatened by everyone from the philosophical handyman to the new therapist who tries to help her adjust to her new environment.

Set in New York City, Wilcox's fifth novel, *Polite Sex* (1991), escapes the geography of Tula Springs, but not characters who hail from there. Two women from Tula Springs, who find their way, separately, to New York City, serve as the emotional center of the novel. Emily Brix, a Smith educated, aspiring actress, arrives first and is forced to settle for a position as a script reader at a second-rate production company. Clara Tilman, Emily's younger sister's best friend, moves to New York to escape her abusive fiance, F. X. Pickens, and to seek a career in modeling. Clara receives all the breaks that Emily dreamed of when she moved to the city. The tension between the two women heightens as the novel charts their progress through a series of bizarre and interlocking relationships.

MAJOR THEMES

As one recent reviewer astutely points out, James Wilcox writes novels of manners. Each of Wilcox's five novels owes more to the tradition of Austen and Pym than it does to the writers of the Southern Renascence. Yet, the novels are deeply Southern in their flavor. The New South, which still feels the tug (if not the burden) of history and correct social and religious forms, provides an ideal setting for modern-day novels of manners. Wilcox's characters find themselves constrained by a knowledge of what is "right" and "wrong" according to religious and societal rules, yet motivated by personal desire. The ideas of the twentieth century that tend to erode such constraints have reached Tula Springs through malls and television. Its residents long for upward mobility and are dutiful consumers of messages and products that strain religious and social forms to the breaking point. Yet, they retain enough cultural memory of tradition to provide a fertile ground for comedy that features characters in conflict with their own desires.

One can hardly discuss themes in Wilcox's novels without sounding like a local historian. Although each of his novels focuses on a different set of characters, four of them are set in the same small town. As a result, the town itself becomes an important character. Furthermore, major characters from one novel usually have appeared as a minor character in a previous novel; and, once they have appeared as major characters in one novel, they often make a cameo appearance in subsequent novels.

The inhabitants of James Wilcox's Tula Springs, Louisiana, are cut off from their past and lurching toward an uncertain future. Tula Springs, a small town that lacks the sense of place traditionally portrayed in Southern fiction, might best be described as someplace near a place. Residents long for places other than Tula Springs. Religion and family, the institutions that serve as mortar for a community, are crumbling. Families are either scattered or sharing a troubled coexistence, and mutant religions crop up as residents try to cope with their haphazard existence. Tula Springs is a world where intellectuals and common people find it equally difficult to navigate life's absurdities.

Early in the first novel, Tula Springs is described as part of the Florida parishes, a section of land not originally belonging to the Louisiana Purchase. The settlers there, immigrants from other parts of the young country, rebelled against Spanish rule and "pledged allegiance to no one, not to the U.S., or Spain, or even England." Once the region was incorporated into the nation, "the Illinois Central Railroad began colonizing these parishes with northerners, the shiftless kind that didn't have sense enough to stay where they belonged." Modern-day Tula Springs reflects this lack of a sense of history. In addition to the County Courthouse,

Tula Springs proper contains an assortment of struggling businesses, including the Sonny Boy Bargin Store, which figures prominently in two of the novels. Scattered among these businesses are a number of buildings vacated by failed businesses; one contains a 2-year-old sign announcing the imminent arrival of a new business. Residents of Tula Springs patronize these businesses only when they are constrained by time. When time permits or the errand is sufficiently important, they drive to Ozone or to the mall just across the state line in Eutaw, Mississippi, to conduct their business.

The Keelys, the Cocos, the Mackies, Bobby Pickens, and Frank Dambar are all lifelong members of the community. Yet these people are not privileged by virtue of their history. Bobby Pickens, for example, who was born and raised in Tula Springs, is as insecure as any of the transient characters in Wilcox's fictional town. Although he has a physical history in the town, his fractured family leaves him without a sense of place. Shortly after Bobby was born, his father divorced his mother and moved to nearby Ozone. There he remarried and fathered another son, F. X. When F. X. was convicted of selling cocaine, the elder Mr. Pickens moved to Tucson and refused to have anything to do with either of his sons. Mrs. Pickens, who has been confined to a nursing home in a neighboring parish, pretends that Bobby is a suitor rather than her son when he visits. If anything, hailing from Tula Springs is an obstacle that life residents struggle to overcome.

Outsiders abound in Tula Springs: Duk Soo, a Korean atheist who is working on his Ph.D. in tourism at nearby Saint Jude College; Dr. Murrow, who came from "somewhere out West" to be principal of a private Christian academy; Mrs. Howard, Frank Dambar's German housekeeper; Father Fua, a Samoan Catholic priest; and Dr. Martin Bates, an inept dentist-in-training who arrived in Tula Springs via England and New Jersey. These residents are no more at home in Tula Springs than are the life residents. Often their very presence calls community conventions and individual standards into question. Their own traditions also are called into question in their interaction with residents.

A list of Tula Springs expatriots is equally long: Kay Undine, a psychologist educated at NYU and practicing in New Orleans; Bobby Pickens' father; and the six Coco children, who have left Tula Springs for Baton Rouge, Lake Charles, New York, Canada, and Australia. Although some of the expatriots occasionally visit Tula Springs, it is usually an emergency or a sense of duty that draws them back. Even in *Polite Sex*, the only novel set outside of Tula Springs, Emily Brix ignores repeated pleas from her family to return, or at least visit home, until word of a catastrophic illness reaches her. None of them feel a sense of connection with their hometown or see themselves as belonging to any tradition.

No action better symbolizes the lack of regard for the past than Miss Undine's insistence on expunging the past from her living room. Miss Undine donates a portrait of her daughter that has hung over her mantle for 20 years to the auction at the Baptist Church and makes plans to thin out the numerous pieces of furniture with which her husband had cluttered the house. In spite of a lack of reverence for the past, the citizens of Tula Springs and the expatriots who grudgingly visit manage to form a sense of community. They are bound by virtue of the fact that, for the time being, they do not belong to any other place. Their differences and their collective search for the uncertain future create a sense of community.

Wilcox's province is the domestic arena. His characters have little time to be concerned with anything other than their own problems, which multiply as they try to manipulate others in an attempt to carry out their own hidden agendas. Each character in Wilcox's novels seems to have discovered the Truth and is hell-bent on setting everyone else free. Donna Lee Keely's attitude with regard to her parents is typical of the attitudes of most Tula Springs residents: "If there was one thing Donna Lee Keely tried to impress upon her family, it was the importance of reality. Her parents had a way of forgetting what the world was really like, and Donna Lee, because she loved them, felt it her duty to remind them." In their misguided attempts to help those poor souls who do not have the benefit of their superior insight, characters create more problems than they solve. Donna Lee, for example, manages to move a 37-year-old woman out of the house of her domineering mother only to relocate her on the site of a toxic waste dump. Domestic turmoil abounds as characters work to extricate themselves from tense situations without revealing their role in the creation of the situations. The delicate yet treacherous relationships between family members, lovers, and coworkers are the primary sites of conflict in Wilcox's novels.

Families figure prominently in Wilcox's novels, assuming a variety of increasingly complex incarnations in each successive novel. The fractured Pickens family in *Modern Baptists* gives way in the second novel to more normally strained relationships between Mrs. Coco and her children. *Miss Undine's Living Room* features an extended family not related by blood but more emotionally connected than most blood families Wilcox writes about. *Polite Sex* explores the physical, emotional, and psychological factors that both connect and distance Emily from her parents as well as from the child she may never know.

Family tensions often are grounded in the differing perspectives of parents and their children. As a result of these tensions, most children who have reached their majority have left home, left town, left the state, or left the country. Their parents, however, ever vigilant, offer advice at every opportunity. Mrs. Coco, for example, offers her grown children the benefit of her wisdom on topics ranging from poetry to underwear. The children, who have seen parts of the world outside of Tula Springs, fire salvos of their own, seeking to educate their less sophisticated parents on topics ranging from ecology to cholesterol. No one on either side is ever converted, though most are forgiven their shortsightedness.

Parent-child roles are reversed in *Miss Undine's Living Room*. Olive and Duane Mackie are both having affairs. Their surprisingly mature son, Felix, assumes the parental role in his relationship with his parents. After discovering that her husband is having an affair with her best friend, Olive frantically searches for a bag of marijuana in a desk drawer. Felix appears and lectures Olive on the consequences of her actions: "I guess you don't realize what you're doing every time you take a puff. Every puff means you're saying yes to drug pushers who sell this stuff to children. Every puff means you're casting your vote for child pornography, gun running, heroin addiction, armed robbery, murder, wife-beating, child abuse. . . . Enjoy."

Family assumes a totally unique form in *Sort of Rich*. Although Frank Dambar has grown children from a first marriage, his "family" consists of a German housekeeper, a philosophical handyman, and the handyman's nice, Shaerl, who is working as a maid until she can enter graduate school at LSU. In the previous novels most tension arises from within the family; in this one Dambar's family is besieged by an outsider seeking admittance. Dambar's new wife, Gretchen, finds herself excluded from the family by each of its members in various ways. Mrs. Howard, the housekeeper, dutifully maintains the first Mrs. Dambar's furniture and insists on sprinkling the sheets with the first Mrs. Dambar's perfume. Leo, the handyman, will not speak to Gretchen directly, but airs his grievances about her with her husband. Gretchen, in turn, alienates the household staff by trying to make her new husband understand her point of view and act accordingly. When she perceives an emotional distance opening between herself and her husband, Gretchen resorts to participating in Frank Dambar's unusual sexual fantasies. An unexpected death in the family causes all of the characters to reevaluate their lives and become more self-reliant.

Religion is another site of domestic tension in Tula Springs. Wilcox's mistrust of organized religions is a recurring theme in the first three novels. His handling of the issue, however, is never heavy-handed. His comic assault seems geared toward blind faith in ritual without understanding. In *North Gladiola*, Wilcox provides a comic critique of organized religion by parodying a religious ritual. Mr. Coco begins to say grace over the evening meal when he is interrupted by Lucy, his daughter: "Please, not that again. . . . Let me. Dear father who felt it necessary to have your own son rubbed out just because some poor defenseless woman wounded your precious ego by eating an apple, I thank you that for once we are finally having meatloaf without oatmeal in it. Amen."

At other times, Wilcox achieves comic effect by juxtaposing competing perspectives. In *Modern Baptists* Donna Lee Keely torments the Baptist men's Bible-study class with her literal interpretation of a passage from Nehemiah. After coaxing them into vacillating on their own interpretation of the passage, she draws them into an argument on the inerrancy of the Bible, laces their apple juice with vodka, and leaves them to work out the problem. Wilcox also utilizes competing religious perspectives as a site of tension in *North Gladiola*. Ray, Jr., a 19-year-old schizophrenic, is caught in the middle of a tug of war between Duk Soo, the atheist with whom he lives, and Mrs. Coco, a recently lapsed Catholic. Mrs. Coco tries to tutor Ray, Jr., in Christianity and morality even though she has decided that the concepts have only marginal relevance for her own life. As her faith wanes, Mrs. Coco seeks the advice of her priest, Father Fua. In advising his parishioner, Father Fua delivers a simpler, more serious religious message that has little to do with outward trappings of religion. Fua's advice appears to reflect Wilcox's thinking on the subject:

God commands you to love. . . . It is very dangerous to stop loving, just because you don't happen to feel like it, you're not in the mood. Always there will be reasons not to love and people who will try and make you stop loving. . . . You must fight to love, fight every day, every minute. Use all your muscles, both fists, 'cause most people are against it. Most people don't want love to work, understand. Dey are afraid of it.

Religion survives as a theme but becomes less central in *Miss Undine's Living Room*. Although religion still vexes the residents of Tula Springs in Wilcox's third novel, it all but disappears in *Sort of Rich*. The theme is revived once again in *Polite Sex*, through Hugh Vanderbilt, an atheist who becomes a Roman Catholic priest after divorcing Emily.

Sexual intrigue figures prominently in each of Wilcox's novels. In *Modern Baptists* F. X. plots his own rape by 19-year-old Toinette in order to provide him with the notoriety that will propel him back to Hollywood. The complicated plot of *North Gladiola* hinges on a past sexual indiscretion between Mrs. Coco's eldest daughter and the mayor of Tula Springs. After his divorce from Miss Undine's daughter Kay, Dr. Martin finds himself involved not only with Olive Mackie, but with her best friend as well.

Sexual tension in *Sort of Rich* is multivariate and more subtly handled than in Wilcox's other novels. Mr. Dambar fantasizes about sex with maids and forces Gretchen, his new wife, to assume the role of maid in their sexual play. The novel's most ironic moment occurs in the juxtaposition of two scenes involving characters pressing their legs against one another. Mr. Dambar takes his handyman's niece, Shaerl, to LSU where she is planning to enroll in courses. While having coffee on the portico of the LSU union, Mr. Dambar realizes that he is sitting across from an *actual* maid. When he thinks that Shearl is pressing her leg against his under the table, he responds by returning the pressure. Later, he discovers that it is the concrete leg of the table. In a subsequent scene, Mr. Dambar takes Leo, his handyman, to the movie theatre. He is troubled to discover Leo's leg being pressed against his own. Dambar rationalizes the handyman's action, in spite of the increasing, insistent pressure, failing to realize that Leo has long been attracted to him.

As one would expect, *Polite Sex* includes an ample number of sexual tensions. Whereas at the beginning of the novel Emily is determined to save herself for marriage, a feat that she accomplishes, she manages to become pregnant after a one night stand in which she attempts to help a young man who is unsure of his sexuality. Her husband, by way of contrast, becomes addicted to lesbian pornography and wonders if it is an indication that he is gay. The sexual liaisons in the novel, though complex and intertwined, are less comedic than in previous novels. As in previous novels, however, the events leading up to the liaisons and their aftermath fuel the plot.

Although Wilcox recognizes the humor in his novels, he does not consciously attempt to write comedy. Instead, he focuses on creating fully realized characters who are absorbed in the details of their lives. Although the details of their lives are mundane, Wilcox never trivializes their experiences. Readers share a superior vantage point with his narrator, anticipating conflicts and watching them deftly unfold in masterfully constructed plots.

Even the smallest of details is accounted for by the end of each of his novels. In *Polite Sex*, Emily is embarrassed by the white loafers her father wears on a visit to New York. Only toward the end of the novel does the reader discover why he continues to wear them:

He knew that Emily found it a strain to be alone with him. . . . The looks she sometimes gave him, as if she were ashamed of him, or worse angry—what a stern child she was. From the very beginning she had been strict with him. . . . [W]hen she was a teenager, how worried he used to be when he bought a new tie for himself. He was sure she would make him take it back. . . . Mr. Brix had never cared for white shoes, but when Emily was in the eighth grade, he simply had to wear them. All the other fathers wore them.

Fifteen years later, he still wears shoes he dislikes out of love for his oldest daughter.

Ultimately, Wilcox's characters understand only a portion of the complex events that have seemingly worked themselves out. In the manner of traditional Southerners, they accept the mystery as part of the meaning. Readers, along with the narrator, share the pleasure that comes from understanding how series of seemingly unrelated events fit neatly together. Wilcox has the uncanny ability to reveal the foibles of characters who are often less educated, less sophisticated, and less fortunate, without condescension. Furthermore, with each successive novel, his technique becomes more subtle and more complex.

SURVEY OF CRITICISM

When *Modern Baptists* was published in 1983, it was met with almost univocal critical praise. Following Tyler's lead, most critics agreed that the novel was the work of a promising young writer. Reviews of *North Gladiola* remained largely favorable, praising the increased subtlety of the humor in the second novel. Margaret Walters noted a patronizing attitude toward the major characters in the novel, a flaw sometimes mentioned in reviews of later novels. *Miss Undine's Living Room* brought a number of longer reviews, though few do more than highlight parts of the book's complicated plot. Favorable reviews cited Wilcox's style as his major strength; detractors found the characters and their motivations unconvincing. Reviewers of *Miss Undine's Living Room* began to note similarities between Wilcox's work and that of Barbara Pym, aligning the novel with a tradition other than Southern. Reviews of *Sort of Rich* have been mixed; they tend to be strongly favorable or strongly unfavorable, more than with any of the other novels.

Reviewers of *Polite Sex* return to the almost univocal critical praise that met Wilcox's first novel. The subject matter and the situations in which his characters find themselves in this novel are more serious than in previous novels; consequently, Wilcox does not draw as heavily on his comedic talents. A number of reviewers note the complexity of the dual time line and the re-presentation of scenes from the point of view of a different character later in the novel. Jonathan Prober argues that in spite of the complexity of the novel, the characters are so well drawn that readers will be willing to reread earlier sections of the novel to make sure they understand the significance of the differing points of view.

To date, no book-length studies or monographs have been written about Wilcox or his work. The best biographical source available on Wilcox is a recent interview with William Parrill in *Louisiana Literature*, a literary journal published by the English department at Southeastern Louisiana University. In the interview, Wilcox discusses personal background and major influences on his work. One longer review article of *Sort of Rich* provides greater insight into his work as a whole by attempting to locate Wilcox's novels within a larger tradition. Avoiding comparisons between Wilcox and other Southern writers, Francine Prose heralds Wilcox's novels as a return of the comic novel of manners and places Wilcox squarely in the tradition of Austen and Pym. To overlook Wilcox's connection with the Southern tradition would be a mistake. Among the scant information available on Wilcox, Parrill's interview and Prose's review essay are solid places to begin one's research.

BIBLIOGRAPHY

Works by James Wilcox

Modern Baptists. New York: Dial, 1983.
North Gladiola. New York: Harper and Row, 1985.
Miss Undine's Living Room. New York: Harper and Row, 1987.
Sort of Rich. New York: Harper and Row, 1989.
Polite Sex. New York: Harper Collins, 1991.

Studies of James Wilcox

Daniell, Rosemary. "New at Adultery" (Rev. of *Miss Undine's Living Room*). *New York Times Book Review* 92 (October 18, 1987): 53.
Gingher, Marrianne. "A Comedy of Bad Manners" (Rev. of *Miss Undine's Living Room*). *Washington Post Book World* 17 (August 16, 1987): 11, 13.
Gurlanick, Peter. "Small Town Talk: James Wilcox's Louisiana Quartet." *LA Weekly* (July 7–13, 1989): 41–42.
Jones, Shailah McEvilley. Rev. of *North Gladiola*. *Southern Humanities Review* 20 (Fall 1986): 396–98.
Kakutani, Michiko. "Marooned in the New South" (Rev. of *Sort of Rich*). *New York Times*, late ed. (January 13, 1989): C19.

Kendrick, Walter. "Tula Springs Eternal" (Rev. of *Miss Undine's Living Room*). *Village Voice* 32 (August 25, 1987): 50.

Lipman, Elinor. "Neither Married Nor an Actress." *New York Times Book Review* 96 (July 7, 1991): 10.

McCorkle, Jill. "A Wal-Mart Kind of Life" (Rev. of *Sort of Rich*). *New York Times Book Review* 94 (May 28, 1989): 25.

Parrill, William. "The Art of the Novel: An Interview with James Wilcox." *Louisiana Literature* 5 (Fall 1989): 9–26.

Prober, Jonathan. "Chatting Up the South." *Washington Post Book World* 21 (June 16, 1991): 12.

Prose, Francine. "Mysteries of Tula Springs." *7 Days* (May 12, 1989): 71–72.

Tate, J. O. "The Root of All Good" (Rev. of *North Gladiola*). *National Review* 37 (August 23, 1985): 47–48.

Tyler, Anne. Rev. of *Modern Baptists*. *New York Times Book Review* 88 (July 31, 1983): 1, 22.

Walters, Margaret. Rev. of *North Gladiola*. *London Observer* (September 1, 1985): 18.

Zeidner, Lisa. "Mozart Comes to the Burger Mat" (Rev. of *North Gladiola*). *New York Times Book Review* 90 (June 30, 1985): 12.

Sylvia Wilkinson
(1940–   )

In addition to five novels, Sylvia Wilkinson has written one book on education and two nonfiction works on automobile racing for adult audiences as well as sixteen juvenile books: Four automobile racing mysteries (pseudonymously in the Eric Speed series), and twelve nonfiction books on racing. A regular participant as an automobile race timer/scorer on the national and international race circuits, Wilkinson's uniquely qualified literary attention is naturally drawn to this arena; she writes frequently for automobile race periodicals and has been motorsports correspondent for *Autoweek*. Critics generally agree that Wilkinson's five novels ensure her literary reputation as a Southern writer who portrays vividly rural North Carolina settings and presents female entrapment in Southern patriarchal society. Her sixth novel, *Pole Cat* (1993, Algonquin Books) concerns two brothers whose loving competitiveness leads one to stock car racetracks and the other to Vietnam where he suffers physical and emotional wounds.

BIOGRAPHY

Sylvia Jean Wilkinson was born April 3, 1940, in Durham, North Carolina, to Peggy George and Thomas Noel Wilkinson. The second of three children, she has an older brother, Thomas, and a younger sister, Margot Wilkinson, with whom she owns a home in Chapel Hill, North Carolina, although she spends most of her time in her El Segundo, California, home which she shares with race driver John Morton. From adolescence, Wilkinson's talents and interests indicated her predilection for diversity. She was a competitive tennis player on the local level (she was 1959 Eastern North Carolina Women's champion as well as Durham Girls champion in 1955 and Junior Girls champion from 1956 to 1958), a horseback rider, a painter, and a writer (she won her first writing prize at age 6 with a Santa Claus poem). Wilkinson's first novel, *Moss on the*

North Side (1966), is based on work she began at age 12 in a Blue Horse notebook; pages from this notebook are used in *Bone of My Bones* (1982) as illustrations and to relate to Ella Ruth's "Starrie" stories. When Wilkinson showed her seventh-grade teacher a scene describing her country grandmother picking ticks off her dog, the teacher told Wilkinson, "You write what I tell you to write." Wilkinson addressed this teacher/student relationship in "Three Teachers," in *An Apple for My Teacher: Twelve Teachers Who Made a Difference.* She did not show her work again until she was 20 years old and studying with Randall Jarrell, whose pronouncement, "Miss Wilkinson, you have a gift," provided an impetus to continue writing.

A great motivation in Wilkinson's life was her maternal grandmother, "Mama George," a farm woman whose natural gift for storytelling far exceeded limitations that might have been imposed by her third-grade education and rural background, and who, Wilkinson says, "was worth a thousand teachers." Her grandmother's penchant for storytelling and natural sense of drama and form are evident in Wilkinson's description of Mama George rocking in an iron porch chair, telling stories that were never repeated and never dull, and engaging her young granddaughter's intense interest as she rocked, talked, and scratched her dog's back simultaneously. The inspiration for Miss Liz in *A Killing Frost* (1967), according to Wilkinson, Mama George is a presence throughout the writer's work. Raised on these family stories, along with cowboy movies, Wilkinson's development as a writer thus stems from the front porch, storytelling, oral traditions of the North Carolina Piedmont.

Wilkinson studied with Jarrell at the University of North Carolina at Greensboro, where she received a B.A. in English and art in 1962. In 1963, she received an M.A. in English and writing at Hollins College, where she studied under Louis Rubin (who continues as a strong mentoring influence) completing a near-final draft of her first novel. She was a Wallace Stegner Fellow at Stanford University in 1965–66, where she drafted her second novel, *A Killing Frost.* Wilkinson's awards include the Hollins College Creative Writing Fellowship (1963), the Eugene Saxton Memorial Trust Grant (1964), the Wallace Stegner Creative Writing Fellowship at Stanford University (1965), a *Mademoiselle* Merit Award for Literature presented to "four young women on the threshold of achievement" (1966), two Sir Walter Raleigh Awards for fiction (1968 and 1977), a Creative Writing Fellowship from the National Endowment for the Arts (1973–74), a Guggenheim Fellowship (1977), and the University of North Carolina at Greensboro Alumnae Service Award (1978).

Wilkinson has been instructor in English, art, and drama at the University of North Carolina at Asheville (1963–65); instructor in English and writing at William and Mary College (1966–67); lecturer and visiting writer, creative writing, at the University of North Carolina at Chapel Hill (1967–70); visiting professor of writing, M.F.A. program, Washington University, St. Louis (1984); and associate professor of English in the M.F.A. program at the University of Wisconsin, Milwaukee (1985). She has been writer-in-residence at Hollins College (1969, 1975), and at Sweet Briar College (1973, 1974, 1975, and 1977). Wilkinson has been involved in diverse other activities including writers-in-the schools programs in Kentucky, North Carolina, and Virginia; she was project change consultant for the Learning Institute of North Carolina in North Carolina public schools (1968–69). Special projects in which Wilkinson has been involved include a Ford Foundation workshop for Appalachian teachers in modern literature at King College, Bristol, Tennessee in 1968; a fiction writing workshop at the Hollins College Writers Conference in 1970; and visiting writer for the Kansas City Regional Council on Higher Education in 1974. She has been a member of the National Humanities Faculty since 1975.

Wilkinson's automobile race career includes stints as timer/scorer for Paul Newman's Can-Am Team from 1977 to 1982, timing Teo Fabi, Al Unser, Sr., and World Champion Keke Rosberg; as timer/scorer for Bobby Rahal's team, winner of the Indianapolis 500 in 1986; and as timer/scorer for the Nissan GTP & GTO team in the International Motor Sports Association. Occasionally she times special race events such as Le Mans.

Wilkinson has described the basis of her fiction as ''seeds'' sown in her own life that grow away from reality until they are sufficiently objective to work well in her fiction. Her major theme—losses suffered by females whose normal psychic growth is stunted by societal expectations of women—addresses the need for freedom felt by the pre- and postmenarchael girl who refuses the choice of wife and mother. In the surround of North Carolina rural nature, she depicts her young heroes, the boy Cale as well as the girls, from childhood to young adulthood in what seems a mean, impoverished existence that restricts female experience. Besides her timer/scorer career and working on her sixth novel, Wilkinson studies her investments (a hobby that led to her survival, she says), gardens, and works out aerobically.

MAJOR THEMES

Wilkinson's fiction includes five novels that thematically develop the choices present to young women, and in *Cale* (1970) a young man, who seek to claim a language and literature of their own. Her emphasis on gender and its restrictions and freedoms foregrounds the marking and identifying of individuals as they seek physical and artistic freedom. More than heredity, environment, education, experience, or even love, gender is fundamental to identity, a fact each novel delineates, providing a paradigmatic, complex persona at once an emerging personality and an artist in search of form. Wilkinson's novels are peopled with rural small-town grandparents and parents of limited consciousnesses and grotesqueness. Escape from the resultant enclosure becomes possible only for the young who redefine themselves and the feminine archetype. Wilkinson posits a post-lapsarian Garden of Eden in a community that offers little support or sense of solidarity to the young who do choose new patterns of life. Fred Chappell, in ''Unpeaceable Kingdoms: The Novels of Sylvia Wilkinson,'' describes Wilkinson's towns as "merely square islands of pavement and facade, sterile, lonely, as hostile as the novelist's rural nature. . . . [Her] farm is located at the edge of the wilderness, dark, swamp or dark forest." Although her characters are not physically imprisoned, they are enclosed psychically and artistically. The first two novels—*Moss on the North Side* and *A Killing Frost*—and the most recent— *Bone of My Bones*—form a paradigmatic trilogy, a künstlerroman with a female hero who finally escapes the petty, trapped life of the conventional, rural, ignorant woman, whose role is assigned by the lower-class, Southern patriarchy; failing to find personal definition within the context of community, the girl protagonists seek identity in their art. *Cale*, with a male protagonist, and *Shadow of the Mountain* (1977), the story of Jean Fitzgerald, a young woman whose search for selfhood leads her to imminent danger on a mountainside, are outside the paradigm although thematically related.

In *Moss on the North Side* and *A Killing Frost*, Wilkinson's setting is rural, small-town North Carolina, and her young protagonists metaphors for culturally induced gender differences. Each attempts to order existence through re-creation of her interior world and her view of the feminine archetype. The premenarchael heroes approach but do not reach freedom from the traditional silence of women in the Southern, Christian patriarchy. *Moss on the North Side* reflects the dark view of Cary, the illegitimate child of a prostitute mother and an Indian father, whose intrinsic need for artistic order results from the psychic disorder of her life and her periodic abandonment by Elnora, her mother, whose gender patterning the young girl rejects. An ignorant woman, Elnora supplements a meager income by utilizing her only available resource, her body, to, as she says, "get a little ahead, to buy up a little land, maybe let [Cary] go to school." Cary is confined at a young age to an orphanage where, lacking self-esteem, she endures a half-life as she considers herself a bastard while being rejected by the other children in the orphanage because she has parents. Her creative gifts stifled by poverty-stricken surroundings, she arranges beauty around her with leaves of various shapes and colors and coins she places on the railroad tracks where they are flattened to be made into decorative objects. When she is rescued from the orphanage by Elnora and Claude, the father, who pretend to the authorities they are married, Cary rejects her mother's sensuality and sexuality and the power sex has over Claude. Voiceless, outside of language spoken or written, Cary suffers silently from matrophobia. In her quest for identity beyond the green-world of adolescence, Cary, jealous and fearful, rejects the possibility of becoming "her mother in the bulbous hat with her big breasts creasing in the front opening of her dress where the heavy glass pin only seemed to lower it and expose them more." Her own growing breasts remind Cary of her gender and place in society.

After her father's death in a tenant shack Cary shares with him on the Strawbright Farm, she moves back into town with her mother and sees her mother's prostitution in its harshest light: Her mother caters to dark men, and Cary realizes that her half-Indian heritage is mere chance; she might just as easily have been half-black in a South where such a heritage creates even more obstacles for females than does Cary's Indian/white, lower-class, illegitimate status. Returning as a paid employee to the Strawbright farm, metaphorically to the green-world of preadolescence as she works in the fields and with the horses, Cary seems capable of forming a positive adolescent love for Johnny Strawbright and new esteem for herself. As Wilkinson develops the psychological tension of Cary's retreat from Elnora to another flawed nurturing figure in Mrs. Strawbright, from the awakening sexuality of the two Strawbright sons to her fear of rape by a black farm hand, permanent stunting of Cary's psyche suggests she will seek a different life path.

Finding no creative voice or identity beyond the artistery of the woods lore taught her by her Indian father and grandmother, her only escape from womanhood is back into the green-world of nature. Retreating into her Indian heritage, she recovers her grandmother's books of Indian lore. Such an overstepping of the mother figure for the grandmother figure typifies the rejection of sexuality as lust symbolized by Elnora. Able to accept women only as aged and sexless, Cary experiences the outward emotions of adolescent passion for the Strawbright boy. Inwardly, the threat of sexual identity without a creative role model encloses her in an insular world, leaving her resentful of womanhood, repulsed by her body, afraid of rape and molestation, and totally silent in the Southern patriarchy.

In *A Killing Frost*, second in the künstlerroman trilogy, Ramie, edging closer to exercise of her creative imagination, struggles to escape the confines of typical gender patterning. Ramie is the daughter of Maylean, a woman whose mother, Miss Liz, says "didn't have a smart bone in her body. She never said one word that made good sense." Maylean, through her sensual, sexual woman's role, tries and fails to escape the enclosure of the hardscrabble farm with a soldier-lover killed in World War II. Widowed, Maylean drowns herself in the farm pond, leaving her daughter to be adopted by her Aunt Cecie.

Ramie's attempts to develop artistic freedom are met with limitations imposed by Cecie's interpretation of young girls' roles in society. Attempting to feminize Ramie according to the Southern rural dictates of patriarchal society, Cecie buys her pretty dresses, gives her a room of her own in the in-town home, and sends her to a private school. Miss Liz, the rural farm woman who is sexless because of her status and age, subverts Cecie's efforts by offering the escape into the preadolescent green-world of nature. Ramie, opposed to the restrictions of Cecie's stereotypical life where women wear dresses and keep the house clean, compromises, accepting a need to fit her paints, her attempts at sculpture, her specimen leaves and snails and frogs, into Cecie's immaculate home, the housewife's raison d'être and Ramie's bête noire. In this second quest for a usable pattern for selfhood, Ramie leaves the green-world of adolescence when Miss Liz does. Unable to escape to the rural Eden lost at her grandmother's death, Ramie must begin growing up female in the enclosure dictated by small-town society. In this narrative of the imprisoned self are intimations that Ramie, like Cary, may escape social conformity and identify herself outside the patriarchal dictates. Her artistry finds outlets as Cecie finally abets Ramie's avoidance of the stereotypical Southern girlhood—as long as Ramie keeps her "clutter," her creative projects, in its proper closet—and offers unknowingly the thread that will eventually lead out of the enclosure. Cecie tells Ramie: "I can remember my own grandmother, trying to tell me everything she could remember as if she didn't want to steal a thing from me. . . . She acted as if I would gather up all she said and give it to the next children in the family, and never seemed to realize that all she knew about farming and dressing and making quilts wasn't going to be worth a feather to the next generation." Cecie fails to see the creative thread reaching from grandmother to daughter to granddaughter, the possibility of a pattern that extends from the past to the present and empowers each generation of women to continue similarities while developing very different identities. Cecie, unable to utilize the pattern of the descending maternal role except to emulate it in its less creative, male-driven Ariadne form, provides no role model for Ramie. Cecie's is the patriarchally assigned role: housekeeper, clothes shopper, carpooler to private schools designed to implement stereotypical roles, to feminize young ladies. What Cary longs for and Ramie comes close to, Ella Ruth in *Bone of My Bone* finds—the pattern of the matrilinear past that holds promise for the future outside the voiceless enclosure.

In *Cale*, the lower middle-class, white, Southern patriarchal system encloses and trains young men as it encloses and limits young women. The novel details the life of Cale Jenkins from birth to one month before his eighteenth birthday and provides a shadow figure in the life of Floyd, a black baby born to sharecroppers on the Jenkins farm two months after Cale's birth. Wilkinson has said about *Cale* and its major symbol of the enclosure, the killing of a blue heron, that she began the novel because she was

hurt and angry when a cousin had killed a great blue heron that came to our farm every year. The bird came alone and fed around our pond, thinking it was not threatened. . . . I wrote about it over and over in my journal. . . . I couldn't separate my own anger to fictionalize until I changed the characters. They were no longer my cousin and myself, but Cale, a white boy, and Floyd, a black boy. I had to see the incident from the killer's viewpoint, too. My cousin had killed the bird out of anger at his father who whipped him. . . . Floyd killed the bird in anger over Cale's humiliation of him. It was Floyd saying that I could have aimed the gun from the same woods, moving the barrel a few feet and killed you, Cale.

The death of the blue heron, symbol of elegance and swift flight, analogizes the loss of beauty and freedom in the patriarchal enclosure. Cale, held prisoner as much by his anticipated inheritance of the land as by his obsessive mother and punishing father, cannot develop a nascent interest in architecture, whereas Floyd, whose life is constricted in every sense by poverty and racism, must escape before his violent rebellion shifts from bird killing to murder.

The small farm outside of Summit, North Carolina, a former milltown with two smokestacks as monuments to its desertion by Solomon's Hosiery, descends from Dutch immigrants through Lonza Lemirt, Cale's maternal grandfather. When their only child, Falissa, marries Jerome Jenkins, the Lemirts consider him socially unacceptable; however, Pap Lonza lives into an old-age dependency on Falissa and Jerome who take over his farm where they raise Cale, born to Falissa after 10 years of marriage, and Pearlie Sue, born 4 years later. Three generations of the patriarchy—Papa Lonza, Jerome, and Cale—dominate the enclosure.

The narrative voice shifts from the words of Cale's mother, his father, his grandfather, his uncle, to Cale's own; however, the major presence is that of Falissa. The voice of Falissa is greatly reduced in a revised edition of the novel, published by Algonquin Books in 1986, because, as Louis Rubin quotes Wilkinson in the preface: "A lot of it is dull as hell, . . . mostly because of the monologues by Falissa Jenkins." Editor Rubin himself comments: "It was Cale's book, more than anyone else's, yet Sylvia had become so caught up in Falissa's voice that she had indulged herself, allowing Falissa to meditate, speculate, remember, moralize, and otherwise express herself interminably." These changes seem, however, to redirect Wilkinson's continuing thematic thread of the enclosed Southern female present in Falissa and, by extension, Pearlie Sue, her daughter.

That essence of identity—gender—lies at the heart of the enclosure Cale's mother reveals as she prepares for the birth of her first and long-hoped-for baby. In her childlike, female role—afraid of everyone, her domineering mother as well as her husband—Falissa fears especially the birth process following too closely the loss of girlhood freedom of choice: "When I was a little girl," she thinks, "I built what I pleased. . . . Now when there is something I am supposed to build, I do it just as they say. I just copy down a recipe and when I get it just like Mama's then it's right. Even Jerome throws that up to me." Her greatest fear, however, is bearing a girl baby. When she rings the farm bell, she imagines, everyone will "run to see my baby boy. . . . I'd hold him up and stop them dead in their tracks. A little naked boy and they'd both smile and point at his little tallywack. . . . Women were not made right. Mama says that denies God but I declare it doesn't, God. You know there are some things out of kilter in this world and that people messed up and if Eve hadn't misbehaved you might have made it easier for us." Her first child a male, Falissa lapses into life as an earnest but shallow Christian, a trembling wife, and a loving but overprotective mother. Wilkinson foregrounds Cale's growth against the backdrop of the 1940s and 1950s, the violence of war and racial turmoil of these decades. Cale's rite of passage becomes directed by his Uncle Roe, his father's wild younger brother whose return from World War II introduces the boy to sex with black prostitutes and to alcohol with white, locally made liquor. The shadowy presence of racist Southern attitudes is vignetted in the sharecroppers' lives in the cabin of Floyd's mother, called Aunt Bynum, a victim of abject entrapment in the male-dominated enclosure.

The accretion of family attitudes and habits—Falissa's shallow Christianity,

Pearlie Sue's abandonment of the trappings of adolescent girlhood to embrace a wider awareness of social issues, Jerome's continued drinking and viciousness, and Roe's meaningless, sordid death in a ditch—fuels Cale's desire to escape. When 17-year-old Cale and Floyd share a voyeuristic experience at a carnival strip show, the continued resentment of interracial sex surfaces. Finally, facing each other when Floyd admits killing the blue heron and that he could have, if he wished, killed Cale as well, Cale asks him: "What would you think if I told you I was going to the army? Just go off and leave this farm that's supposed to be mine someday?" Cale's statements do not, however, indicate that he can free himself; his entrapment is almost as secure as that of Wilkinson's female heroes. His Uncle Roe's return from the army as a drinker and womanizer foreshadow just such a failure to escape as does Cale's attachment to the land. Cale thinks, "*If* [emphasis mine] I go off and learn something maybe I'll come back and take those smokestacks down in right fashion for Papa."

Cale might be termed an anti-bildungsroman, for the young protagonist fails to indicate that he will be able to leave home, to become educated, or to accept change. The ending implies that Cale's future lies in farming the land he inherits, rebuilding old cars, and drinking moonshine liquor, much as Papa Lonza, Uncle Roe, and his father, Jerome, have done. Although attracted by a book on architecture and the apparent inheritor of Falissa's talent for building things (he has "Mama's features and Papa's fixtures"), Cale's creative urge must grow stronger if he is to escape the enclosure.

Shadow of the Mountain, Wilkinson's fourth novel, suggests with its wall of mountains enclosing Rocky Gap, North Carolina, that Jean Fitzgerald, a young woman in the process of valuing her self-image, is on the threshold of an already developed but unaccepted selfhood. A writer of journal entries she deposits in a hidden box, foreshadowing Ella Ruth's story box in *Bone of My Bones*, and letters, mainly to Clara, a former school friend, Jean records a larger bitterness toward woman's role than Wilkinson addresses in her other novels. A fortunate daughter of generous parents, Jean nevertheless searches for her selfhood as well as for what is outside her self in the language and traditions of the New Society of the 1960s. When she obtains, partially through the influence of her grandfather's name, a job with the Appalachian Corp., she gathers "material" for her writing, storing it in a "box of notes" that exists as a semiotic item, a link to other signs of the constrictions of women's lives. No psychologically sound people live in the school Jean attends or in the Appalachian mining town she visits. Grotesque characters include college roommates who take her to Ku Klux Klan meetings or tell her their intimate stories of sexual encounters and desertion, a snake-handling preacher fatally bitten during a sermon, a sexually deviate and vicious town drunk, and a 19-year-old woman who chooses suicide over her role as a deserted wife and mother. The failure of these solitaries to achieve spiritual or physical communion with themselves or each other reveals their lack of wholeness.

In the novel's opening pages, Jean discovers the body of 19-year-old Jane

Boey, whose two children had resulted from careless sexual ignorance; she has chosen suicide through the means of sitting on the enclosing mountainside during a freezing night. Jane Boey (opposite in freedom, perhaps, to James Bowie, an echo of Wilkinson's cowboy movie childhood) becomes the metaphoric touchstone for failure to escape the female enclosure; she and Jean are, Wilkinson implies, sisters in their enclosure as are all women. Jean thinks, "the girl with the blue hand [the frozen Boey] took a long walk alone. Like me. She went up to the top of LeConte. Like me." Growing up in the changing attitudes of the 1960s, Jean believes that through usefulness, in this case helping the poverty-stricken inhabitants of Appalachia, she can achieve salvation through community, apparently holding in her mind Jane Boey's solution if her own search for values fails: "Maybe I already am what I am now and can't change it or figure out why by going backwards," she records in her journal.

Rural nature in *Shadow of the Mountain* fails to cultivate growth either for the homegirls and homeboys or for the interloping Jean Fitzgerald. Jean writes of Jane Boey: "America takes care of little children. It just doesn't take care of Jane Boey. Only if she cooks and washes and gets a welfare check and goes to a lawyer for child support." If women accept their childlike roles, they are protected; otherwise, they may be left on the mountainside and, unlike Oedipus, not be rescued. What happens when women are not rescued finds a metaphor in Mollie Burcham, an outcast mountain woman who typifies Wilkinson's aged and sexless female survivor; she has lived through her female years when her baby, Sarah Mae, died as an infant and has become a tough, androgynous mountaineer. Christie, one of Jean's former schoolmates, epitomizes the unrescued, antifeminine stance younger women themselves sometimes find inevitable. Woman as paradox, Christie has hips wide to deliver babies easily but too wide to compete in the beauty market and ensure her husband's fidelity. As Christie notes: "My husband, ex-husband, that is, said it [the width of her hips] was because I sat on my ass all the time, but he would never do anything with me." In her role as interloper, especially in her atypical feminine attire of slacks rather than dresses, Jean has no defense against the animosity of the mountain people; the wall of mountains enclosing the Appalachian mining town recalls her recurring childhood nightmare of mountains falling on her. Also wishing to re-form the archetypal mother role—her own mother a shallow though well-meaning society woman—Jean has no threads to the past, no way to an identity based on matrilineal inheritance. Selfhood threatened from within and without, her last notebook entry reveals a spiritual as well as physical crisis in her need to accept herself rather than "float away." Alone in the midst of hostile mountain people, she endures the threat of death rather than confront the outside world and the biological and social potential for a childbearing role.

In the same small-town geography of Summit, North Carolina, Ella Ruth advances the struggle to break from the confines of family and ambivalent self. In *Bone of My Bone*, last novel in her trilogy, Wilkinson's epigraph identifies her theme of gender identification in the Southern Christian patriarchy: "And the man said, 'This is now bone of my bones, and flesh of my flesh: she shall be called Woman, because she was taken out of Man' '' (Genesis 2:23). Like Cary and Ramie, Ella Ruth must learn to accept the history of the mother archetype while shaping her own personal experience. Entrapped in poverty and voicelessness, Ella Ruth is raised by an obese, simple-minded mother whose youthful prettiness results in unwed pregnancy and a rushed marriage to a drunken husband. The natural science and artistry of Cary and Ramie merge in Ella Ruth into a creative imagination as a writer. The green-world of nature where Cary and Ramie take refuge becomes for Ella Ruth her "time-capsule" or "story-box," in which she keeps her imaginative self. Finally, she rejects her mother's often repeated hints that early marriage and babies encompass her life's role and frees herself and her writing from the semiotic box.

Ella Ruth receives typical gender-patterning for a girl of her low socioeconomic level. From age 5 until her mother dies, the little girl helps with baking fancy candies and cakes to sell to the town's affluent citizens. She grows through the tragic comedy of her high school years that include both a gang rape by the neighborhood boys who have watched her grow up and her high school graduation as valedictorian—ego-boundary events that define her feminine dilemma. Postponing her scholarship award, she accepts a menial job at the local hospital, remaining at home to care for her drunken, widowed father.

Although she can see her mother's goodness, Ella Ruth, too, suffers from matrophobia. Much like Cary's parents, Ella Ruth's parents, Maynard and Maxine Higgins, are Southern grotesques who are ignorantly cruel to each other. As the mean little drunk Maynard abuses the helpless, obese Maxine, Ella Ruth sees both the independent vitality and the weakness of each parent. When Maynard is particularly abusive, Ella Ruth rejects her mother's acceptance of her assigned role as victim: "Her blue eyes were rimmed in red and stared as though someone held a mirror in front of her face and forced her to look. . . . She didn't move. I closed all the doors [Daddy] left open. I never said my feelings but I knew I was madder at Mama than I was at him" (68). Given the helplessness of her mother whose prettiness is lost to thyroid-bulging eyes and layers of fat, whose life is cooking, cleaning, and nagging a drunken husband, and the cruelty of her father's abuse, Ella Ruth finds repugnant the image of submissive housewife, innocent child-woman guarded from adulthood's realities. After Maxine's death, Ella Ruth validates her escape from her daughter role by becoming a writer: "I can go in and out of my worlds now much easier," she thinks, "those I make up and those I find in my memory."

Ella Ruth creates a play in which she divides her self into two personalities: Katella and Elisa Ruth. Entitled "The Family Reunion," the two halves of Ella Ruth's psyche, based on patients in the hospital where Ella Ruth works, examine the collective imagination of women both as innocents guarded from reality and as vital, independent persons engaged in passionate, sensual life. Elisa Ruth, based on Elisa Simpson, a still-feminine older woman hospitalized to have her genetically inherited breast lumps removed, evokes Maxine, dependent on her husband for her identity. Katella, based on Katherine Hinshaw, ex-barmaid at the Rebel Bar where Maynard has spent his drinking hours, is dying of old age; nevertheless, her life represents the independently chosen fullness possible for a woman. Her husbands, her lovers, her children are not the only life Katella has, but they are freely chosen facets of it that fit a pattern of her own selection. "I don't like to change my pattern," she says. By maintaining her pattern, she can maintain life: "There won't be a time in the day set aside for [her] heart to use up its last beat." Remaining in control of her life, Katella shows Ella Ruth how a woman can weave the pattern of her choice rather than accept society's enforced pattern. Ella Ruth's pattern is in a language and literature of her own, not in marriage and childbearing: "That's the way things come to me," she says. "They go into words so I can deal with them." Rejecting a typical female role for one as an artist, she thinks: "Any girl can have a baby, Mama. I have all the things inside me to make one and they probably would work if I used them. . . . But I have to make my life into something that it wasn't going to be naturally. It's important for me to fool people. When I pull the curtain, and they see Katella and Elisa Ruth, not a person in the audience will think they're not real." Through a new knowledge that the feminine model may be redescribed, Ella Ruth frees herself from the mother archetype.

In *Bone of My Bones* Wilkinson resolves the conflict of gender patterning introduced in *Moss on the North Side* and *A Killing Frost* and addressed throughout her works: the difficulty a female encounters in choosing an apatriarchal career of the creative imagination. Ella Ruth also resolves the silence of maternal voices: She sees the vital connection between her chosen pattern and their patterns. She recognizes that images in needlework and quilts as well as gardens are as important as images in writing; all, taken together, form the changing feminine archetype. The play that she writes becomes a metaphor for her mother's quilt-making, a "re-union" of the matrilineal consciousness: "I've put things together that were in a thousand pieces," Ella Ruth thinks. "I have made something that won't go away, something as real as Mama's bed quilts. I just had to find the pattern." Making a connection with mothers' and grandmothers' gardens and quilts, the forms of voice for women without the time and rooms of their own needed for writing in the traditional genres, Ella Ruth achieves matriarchal communion. The ability and courage to imagine beyond the roles society provides for Cary, Ramie, and Ella Ruth create the misery the female hero encounters as she tries to escape the enclosure of the green-world, the adolescent stage from which she must emerge ready to engage patriarchal society. Such imagination permits Wilkinson's female hero to learn to be, to find a voice, to locate a pattern in the interconnectedness she senses between the past and the present, metaphorically enlarging the story-box into a room of her own.

Wilkinson's characters in their loneliness delve into the individual psyche and into the psyche of the family and community, providing absorbing and stimulating portraits of agrarian-rooted Southerners. The women who seek creative freedom from the male-dominated enclosure through a language and voice of their own reveal a disjunction between society's dictates and their own desires. Seeking self-esteem not found within the traditional marriage role for women, they reflect the need to grow outward into a new perception of self. As her female protagonists continue to develop conscious and unconscious ways of experiencing and functioning, Wilkinson unburdens the feminine archetype from restriction to the mother role and releases its structure through changing manifestations of the self.

SURVEY OF CRITICISM

Wilkinson's critical reputation has suffered only from lack of attention. Her first novel was highly acclaimed. Wilma Dykeman called *Moss on the North Side* a work of "high quality," finding Wilkinson's portrait of Cary an achievement of "a memorable character: a girl wonderfully tough and tender who meets life as it comes, brutal or beneficent, and by her own will-power and imagination makes it bearable—yes, enjoyable." *Time*'s reviewer called the novel "a lyric evocation of childhood by one of the most talented Southern bellettrists to appear since Carson McCullers." Dayton Rommel pronounced it "a superior first novel." Marilyn Gardner commented that *A Killing Frost*, "richly detailing a warm grandmother-granddaughter relationship, is credible but not contrived, sensitive but never sentimental. . . . [Wilkinson is] gifted with an uncommon eye and ear for the customs and dialects of everyday Southern life," although C. D. Pipes found the "weighted . . . symbolism" difficult for a non-Southerner. Jane Clapperton commented that, in the story of Ramie, Wilkinson "has built, or rebuilt, a whole inhabited world and opened the gates for us to go in."

Cale was read by most critics as a bildungsroman of a Southern male, with James W. Clark viewing the Jenkins family as stereotypical Southerners. Although *Shadow of the Mountain* evoked the *Choice* reviewer's comment that its time shifts "from past to present, from consciousness to consciousness" were arbitrary, *Publishers Weekly* found that Jean Fitzgerald "makes tenacious entry into the lives of quintessential southern women" and that Wilkinson's "forceful characterizations, her insights into a small, frightening world, illuminate a quietly compelling novel." In *Bone of My Bones*, David Quammen found Ella Ruth's "an effective voice, graced at points with humor, richly raucous language, and illuminations on the travail of female adolescence," although he would prefer more "shape."

Fred Chappell, in "Unpeaceable Kingdoms: The Novels of Sylvia Wilkinson," examines the first three novels and Wilkinson's overall theme. Commenting on the "cartography of the psyche" Wilkinson employs, Chappell says that "if Miss Wilkinson's subject matter, the human personality in the conflicts of change, isn't relevant, nothing is." Chappell recognizes in the first two novels the dual call upon the girl protagonists of the past and the equally insistent future, "often in the form of unpleasant responsibility and sexual fear." Observing the differences in the educations of Cary and Ramie and that of Cale in the third novel, he sees Cale's movement as outward while the females' growth will be inward, or artistic, evoking Carl Jung's anima/animus label. The vibrant, living detail of Wilkinson's novels, Chappell says, prevents an easy picking out of the "pattern" in the works.

A 1982 interview by Jane Vance forms an early perspective of Wilkinson's mother-daughter relationship, as well as insight into the writer's career. Vance elicits important background in the patterning of women's lives that Wilkinson addresses; thus, she gives the critical reader an insight into the individual and community psyche of the works. Also in 1982, Vance's "Fat Like Mama, Mean Like Daddy: The Fiction of Sylvia Wilkinson" appeared, providing a feminist appreciation of Wilkinson's thematic interest: "Her dominate theme," Vance notes, "is the development of the female psyche in the mid-twentieth South. She explores the process of gender identification and probes the limits that this places on the young woman's continuing development of self." According to Vance, with each successive novel "Wilkinson grapples more directly with the basic issue of sexual identity and the possibility of becoming a creative, growing, productive woman in the milieu of twentieth-century southern society."

Katherine Kearn's article in the *Dictionary of Literary Biography Yearbook* for 1986 examines the Wilkinson canon and biography to date. Kearns recognizes Wilkinson's overall feminist view without applying it to each novel. Citing Wilkinson's remark that she left her teaching position at the University of North Carolina at Chapel Hill feeling "that my being a woman had a great deal to do with [her dissatisfaction]," Kearns says that "it would be an oversimplification to see Wilkinson's abandoning teaching in merely feminist terms. . . . The question of her position as a feminist is inevitable, nonetheless, particularly given her many strong, matriarchal characters." Vance's entry in the *Critical Survey of Long Fiction* for 1987 links Wilkinson's work to such Southern women writers as Flannery O'Connor, Carson McCullers, Katherine Anne Porter, and Eudora Welty. Vance furthers her previously published comments on Wilkinson's theme of development of the female psyche in the South.

Joyce M. Pair's "Growing Up Female: The Creative Pattern of Sylvia Wilkinson" discusses the gender patterning of Wilkinson's protagonists who attempt to identify the perspective of women and the need for escape from the enclosure of Southern patriarchal roles. Specifically looking at what she sees as a trilogy in Wilkinson's *Moss on the North Side*, *A Killing Frost*, and *Bone of My Bones*, Pair examines the social awareness of possibilities of recuperating the female archetypal psyche by finding common threads of identity from women's past to their present.

Ann M. Woodlief's "Sylvia Wilkinson: Passages through a Tarheel Childhood" is more descriptive than evaluative; however, the study brings Wilkinson criticism into a valuable collection bound to be noticed by feminist scholars who will provide further study. Woodlief recognizes *Bone of My Bones* for its value as a "kind of culmination, bringing together the strongest aspects of style and theme of each book, highlighting the tenuous dynamics of life as related to art."

BIBLIOGRAPHY

Works by Sylvia Wilkinson

Fiction

Moss on the North Side. Boston, Toronto: Houghton Mifflin, 1966. London: Rupert Hart-
   Davis, 1967. Wiesbaden: Limes Verlag, 1969 (German title: *Wie der Regen im
   Wald*). New York: Avon, 1972 (paperback rpt.). New York: Pocket Books, 1978
   (paperback rpt.).

A Killing Frost. Boston, Toronto: Houghton Mifflin, 1967. Wiesbaden: Limes Verlag,
   1970 (German title: *Wie spates Licht auf Vogelfedern*). Wiesbaden: Deutscher
   Taschenbuch Verlag, 1973 (paperback rpt.). New York: Avon, 1973 (paperback
   rpt.). New York: Pocket Books, 1978 (paperback rpt.).

Cale. Boston, Toronto: Houghton Mifflin, 1970. New York: Avon, 1972 (paperback
   rpt.). Chapel Hill, N.C.: Algonquin, 1986 (rev. ed.)

Shadow of the Mountain. Boston, Toronto: Houghton Mifflin, 1977. New York: Pocket
   Books, 1978 (paperback rpt.).

Bone of My Bones. New York: Putnam, 1982.

Nonfiction

*Change: A Handbook for the Teaching of English and Social Studies in the Secondary
   Schools*. Ed. Sylvia Wilkinson and E. Campbell. Durham, N.C.: LINC Press,
   1971.

The Stainless Steel Carrot, An Auto Racing Odyssey. Boston, Toronto: Houghton Mifflin,
   1973.

Dirt Tracks to Glory: The Early Days of Stock Car Racing as Told by the Participants.
   Chapel Hill, N.C.: Algonquin, 1983.

Juvenile

Can-AM. Chicago: Childrens Press, 1981.
Endurance Racing. Chicago: Childrens Press, 1981.
Formula Atlantic. Chicago: Childrens Press, 1981.
Formula One. Chicago: Childrens Press, 1981.
Sprint Cars. Chicago: Childrens Press, 1981.
Stock Cars. Chicago: Childrens Press, 1981.
Super Vee. Chicago: Childrens Press, 1981.
Champ Cars. Chicago: Childrens Press, 1982.
The True Book of Automobiles. Chicago: Childrens Press, 1982.
Trans-Am. Chicago: Childrens Press, 1983.
Karts. Chicago: Childrens Press, 1985.
I Can Be a Race Car Driver. Chicago: Childrens Press, 1986.

Interviews

Graham, John. An Interview, 70–80 in *Craft So Hard to Learn*. New York: William
   Morrow, 1972.

Graham, John. An Interview, 200–13 in *The Writer's Voice*, ed. George Garrett. New
   York: Morrow, 1973.

"Women and Women Writers." *Washington College Review* (January 1975).
Vance, Jane. "An Interview with Sylvia Wilkinson." *Kentucky Review* 2 (1981): 75–88.
Morrow, Mark, ed. 90–91 in *Images of the Southern Writer*. Athens: University of Georgia Press, 1985.

Studies of Sylvia Wilkinson

Chappell, Fred. "Unpeaceable Kingdoms: The Novels of Sylvia Wilkinson." *Hollins Critic* 8, No. 2 (April 1971): 1–10.
Clapperton, Jane. "An Uncanny Feel for Childhood" (Rev. of *A Killing Frost*). *Life* (October 13, 1967): Book Rev. Sec.
Clark, James W. Rev. of *Cale*. *Carolina Quarterly* 23 (Winter 1971): 73.
Dykeman, Wilma. Rev. of *Moss on the North Side*. *New York Times Book Review* (August 4, 1966): 26.
Gardner, Marilyn. Rev. of *A Killing Frost*. *Christian Science Monitor* (September 14, 1967): 13.
Kearns, Katherine. "Sylvia Wilkinson," 356–66 in *Dictionary of Literary Biography*, ed. Richard Ziegfield. Columbia, S.C.: Bruccoli-Clark, 1986.
Kersh, Gerald. Rev. of *A Killing Frost*. *Saturday Review* (October 7, 1967): 44.
Lennon, Lila. "A Superior Talent in This Tale" (Rev. of *A Killing Frost*). *Chicago Daily News* (September 9, 1967).
Mitchell, Lisa. Rev. of *Bone of My Bones*. *Los Angeles Times* (March 19, 1982): V26.
Mondale, Leon. *Fast Lane Summer: North American Road Racing*. Mill Valley, Calif.: Square Books, 1981.
Pair, Joyce M. "Growing up Female: The Creative Pattern of Sylvia Wilkinson." *Southern Literary Journal* 19, No. 2 (Spring 1987): 47–53.
Pipes, C. D. Rev. of *A Killing Frost*. *Library Journal* 92 (August 13, 1967): 2813.
Quammen, David. Rev. of *Bone of My Bones*. *New York Times Book Review* (February 21, 1982: 13.
Rommel, Dayton. "A Sense of Place." *Chicago Daily News* (July 3, 1966).
Vance, Jane Gentry. "Fat Like Mama, Mean Like Daddy: The Fiction of Sylvia Wilkinson." *Southern Literary Journal* 15, No. 1 (Fall 1982): 22–36.
———. "Sylvia Wilkinson," 2889–96 in *Critical Survey of Long Fiction*, ed. Frank N. Magill. Englewood Cliffs, N.J.: Salem Press, 1983.
Woodlief, Ann M. "Sylvia Wilkinson: Passages through a Tarheel Childhood," 236–50 in *Southern Women Writers: The New Generation*, ed. Tonette Bond Inge. Tuscaloosa: University of Alabama Press, 1990.
Rev. of *Bone of My Bones*. *New York Times Book Review* 87 (February 21, 1982): 13.
Rev. of *Cale*. *Booklist* 67 (January 1, 1971): 355.
Rev. of *Cale*. *Virginia Quarterly Review* 47 (Winter 1971): 47.
Rev. of *Dirt Tracks to Glory*. *USA Today*. (February 20, 1984): 2C.
Rev. of *Moss on the North Side*. *Time* (August 12, 1966): 76 ff.
Rev. of *Shadow of the Mountain*. *Publishers Weekly* (January 24, 1977): 328.

DONALD R. NOBLE

Calder [Baynard] Willingham, Jr.
(1922–   )

At the start of his career, with publication of *End as a Man* (1947), it appeared that Calder Willingham, Jr., was to take his place after Theodore Dreiser and James T. Farrell as America's leading naturalist. He refused to continue to work in this hyperrealistic vein, however, and instead chose to write a series of novels in several experimental modes, exploring many varieties of human sexual experience. He has a gift for Southern setting and speech and has chosen instead to spoof, not join, the second wave of the Southern Renascence. Although his novels were published, and some sold well, Willingham found it necessary and pleasant enough to spend long periods in Hollywood, writing for the screen, and established for himself a considerable reputation there. If he is to enjoy a new wave of popularity or critical consideration, it will surely come from a new appreciation of his first novel *End as a Man*, or, more likely, his powerful and perverse novel, *Eternal Fire* (1963).

BIOGRAPHY

Willingham was born in Atlanta, Georgia, on December 23, 1922. His mother was Eleanor Churchill; his father, Calder, Sr., was a hotel manager and hotels have always figured large in Willingham's writings. He was raised in Atlanta and in Rome, Georgia, and then from 1940 to 1941 attended The Citadel, the Charleston, South Carolina, military academy and the setting for his first novel, *End as a Man*. Willingham left The Citadel after only 1 year and attended the University of Virginia from 1941 to 1943. He then moved to New York City and began a career in fiction. Willingham married Helene Rothenberg in 1945; they had one child, Paul. After a 1951 divorce from Helene, Willingham married Jane Marie Bennett in 1953, and they have five children, three sons and two daughters, and live in New Hampshire.

Willingham, like several others of his generation, Norman Mailer and William Styron for example, achieved early success. *End as a Man*, the story of a group of cadets in a Southern military academy, caused an enormous stir. Farrell, author of the Studs Lonigan trilogy, reviewed the novel and gave it extraordinary praise. He called it "the work of an artist, written with power, honesty and courage; it carries its own conviction on every page. . . . I consider it a permanent contribution to American literature." Most other reviewers agreed, and in fact Willingham was considered to be the heir to Farrell as king of the gritty realists. It was that grittiness—that is to say, the rough language, sexual obsessions, and sadistic cruelty of the young cadets—that caused the novel to become controversial and so thrust Willingham into the public spotlight for the first and only time in his long writing career. The New York Society for the Suppression of Vice obtained a summons against the novel's publisher, charging Vanguard with "intent to sell an obscene, lewd, lascivious, filthy, indecent and disgusting book." The novel was thus attacked twice in the courts, but it was finally cleared of all charges on May 25, 1947. The book sold more than 35,000 copies, and Willingham was, at that time, somewhat infamous. Since then, he has led an extraordinarily private private life.

He followed this book with *Geraldine Bradshaw* (1950) and *Reach to the Stars* (1951)—the first set in a hotel in Chicago, the second in a hotel in Southern California. Both have as protagonist Richard Davenport, a young adventurer and would-be writer. There was to have been another novel in this projected trilogy, but Willingham abandoned the effort. Also in 1951, there was a volume of stories, "essays," and what must be called fragments, *The Gates of Hell*. *Natural Child* (1952) is set in Manhattan among some pseudointellectual Bohemians, while his next novel, *To Eat a Peach* (1955), is set in the Smoky Mountains of North Carolina at a boys' summer camp.

In 1957 Willingham went to Hollywood to adapt *End as a Man* for the screen. The result, *The Strange One* (1975), starring Ben Gazzara, began his second career as screenwriter, a career he said he needed to support his large family. Willingham had previously adapted his novel into a stage play in 1953, and both the play and the film were successful. Stanley Kubrick noticed Willingham's work and hired him to work on adapting Stefan Sweig's story "The Burning Secret" for the screen. That film was not made, but Willingham stayed in Hollywood to cowrite the First World War film *Paths of Glory* with Kubrick and Jim Thompson, adapted from a novel by Humphrey Cobb. Next he did the screenplay for *The Vikings* (1958), from a Dale Wasserman adaptation of the novel by Edison Marshall. This was followed by a western, *One-Eyed Jacks* (1961), adapted from a novel by Charles Neider, *The Authentic Death of Hendry Jones*. Willingham's early career as screenwriter was as remarkable as his debut as novelist. *Paths of Glory* (starring Kirk Douglas) is considered a classic film; *One-Eyed Jacks* was directed by and starred Marlon Brando.

Despite and perhaps one might also say because of his great success in Hollywood from 1957 until 1961, Willingham was able to leave screenwriting, return East, and resume writing fiction full-time. Willingham has, in interviews, been candid about his feelings concerning screenwriting. He has said he "cannot take with any genuine seriousness any of the films on which I have worked," and his "real work has been as a novelist." Willingham, a literary maverick, found the communal, collaborative world of moviemaking not to his liking. He has said that only if he could write, produce, and direct would the movie be truly his own. He finds the stage "an amusement rather than a major form." Writing for the stage seems to him too restrictive. He is a novelist, not a poet, and favors the freedom of narrative, "the inter-play of characters in time and space."

This time away from Hollywood, back East, resulted in what is probably his best work. *Eternal Fire* may be the novel that finally attracts real critical attention and restores Willingham's reputation. It has as its protagonist the mulatto Harry Diadem, as evil a human character as ever was created. And while the novel is a send-up of the Southern Gothic, with Diadem as a kind of "Popeye" figure, the novel is also chilling in its exploration of human cruelty and cold-blooded manipulation.

In 1967 Willingham collaborated with Buck Henry to adapt Charles Webb's novel *The Graduate* to the screen. This film, starring Dustin Hoffman, Katherine Ross, and Anne Bancroft, became the touchstone of 1960s films. Willingham was nominated for an Academy Award; in 1968 he received the Writer's Guild of America West award and in 1969 the British Film Academy award.

Although not as strong as *Eternal Fire*, Willingham's next novel, *Providence Island* (1969), is one of his better efforts. Set on a deserted Caribbean island, this novel is the story of an unlikely ménage-à-trois, and although slow in developing, has more form and conventional plotting than most of his novels.

He returned to Hollywood in 1970 to adapt the Thomas Berger novel *Little Big Man* for the screen. Arthur Penn directed, Dustin Hoffman again starred, and the film was a critical and commercial success. The film is in part a revisionist treatment of the heroism of the American cavalry on the great plains, debunks Gen. George Armstrong Custer, and is in its own way a statement opposing the American involvement in Vietnam.

Calder was to write only one more screenplay. In 1974 *Thieves Like Us* was released, cowritten by Willingham, Robert Altman, and Joan Tewkesbury. Robert Altman directed; Keith Carradine starred. There have been since then three novels. *Rambling Rose* (1972) is a nostalgic novel, set presumably in Rome, Georgia, during his childhood and has as the protagonist a beautiful young woman who has an extraordinarily strong sex drive. *The Big Nickel* (1975) is set in New York City and relates the difficulties of Richard Davenport again, this time as a successful first-time novelist who is having problems with his second novel. *The Building of Venus Four* (1977) is his latest effort and is a blend of science fiction and psychodrama as its protagonist loses touch with reality because of his wife's frigidity and her conversion, perhaps temporarily, to lesbianism. Willingham shared writing credit with Del Reisman in 1978 for a teleplay entitled

Thou Shalt Not Commit Adultery. He had not published a book or had a screen credit between 1978 and 1991 when the movie *Rambling Rose* with Robert Duval and Laura Dern was hailed as a comic masterpiece.

MAJOR THEMES

As is true with any novelist perhaps, a reading of the Willingham oeuvre makes the writer's concerns, even preoccupations, seem clearer (or perhaps more obvious) in toto than they are when the novels are read, as intended, one at a time. In Willingham's case, this seems especially true. He returns often to what might be reduced to four main areas of concern. First and without doubt the most important is the entire question of human sexuality. In book after book, Willingham writes of the relentless seeking for sex of men, young and not so young, the question of whether women have a sex drive or not, the whole complex matter of seduction, especially where it blends into, or in some cases turns into, rape, male and female homosexuality, interracial sex, and incest. There are some sexual variations not to be found in his novels, but not many.

Second, Willingham has an abiding concern with the life and trials of the writer in America. His heroes are often would-be writers, aspiring writers, writers now suffering a block, or writers writing the book and telling the reader of their progress as they write along. As a corollary to this, one might say, is the question of innovation in writing. Although technique is not theme per se, in Willingham the two often blend. He is self-consciously trying to tell stories in new ways, often ignoring plot structure, climax, and satisfying endings, and is sometimes spoofing the old ways of telling stories. His devices are not always successful, and as in the case of *Eternal Fire*, his satire of the overwrought Southern Gothic novel is almost certainly taken by most readers to be an outstanding example of that genre, best exemplified in Willingham's mind, probably, by Faulkner's *Sanctuary*. In interviews, he has expressed his contempt for the typical "best-seller," which he says merely panders to readers' fantasies and prejudices. He also has rejected what he calls the "literary" novel that conforms, in his opinion, to "the aesthetic dicta and passing fashions of an intellectual elite." He then declares himself to have fallen between two stools, although some of his novels have received critical praise and others have been commercially successful.

The third issue often taken up in Willingham's work is the question of "the South." He often deals with the question of the Southerner in the North and the cultural dissonance that results. More often the novel is set in the South and explores what he sees as the peculiarities of Southern culture. In these novels the question of race often arises, as do fundamentalist religion, food, and folkways and even, sometimes, father-daughter incest, although, as F. Scott Fitzgerald's *Tender Is the Night* attests, this is clearly not a question reserved for novels of the American South.

The fourth major concern in Willingham's books might be termed "maturation," or coming of age. The novels are often about boys at the point of initiation into adult life or young men not yet fixed on the direction they will take, professionally or romantically. This last is the major concern of *End as a Man*, and as it is Willingham's best-known novel, it deserves more extended discussion.

The protagonist of this novel is first-year cadet Robert Marquales. He is frightened, impressionable, eager to fit in, and altogether rather typical. He and many of the other cadets fall under the influence of Jocko de Paris, an upperclassman who is not only a drunk, a cheat, and a rogue but also something of a Rasputin and a sadist. De Paris is a forerunner, in a way, of the Satanic protagonist of *Eternal Fire*, but de Paris is still an undergraduate in an institution of privilege. What Willingham is suggesting here is not sociology, but innate depravity, a look at the evil that is to be found in young men's souls when they are given power to torment the weak and the new. In addition, some of these cadets are hopeless incompetents, some are young homosexuals, and some are drunks and seducers. In the end, order is restored when the general expels the worst offenders, purging the institution somewhat, so that the graduates/survivors might possibly end their 4 years there as, indeed, men.

Willingham never repeated this material or set another novel among undergraduates, but several other novels are concerned with maturation and initiation, or the lack of it. Buddy Hillyer, the autobiographical protagonist of *Rambling Rose*, is redheaded and 12 years old; he lives in Rome, Georgia, and is writing this novel as an adult professional novelist many years later. He reports how his parents took in a beautiful oversexed country girl, Rose, 19, who had been the victim of incest by her father and, while essentially an innocent person, was so highly sexed that she initiates even young Buddy into the mysteries of the female body. This is a far gentler novel than a short description might suggest. All the characters are good people; Willingham obviously has a great fondness for them (they are surely based on his own family), and Buddy does profit from the experience of knowing Rose. In *Geraldine Bradshaw* and *Reach to the Stars* the protagonist, Richard Davenport, is 21, but his attitude concerning his work, his future, and especially the opposite sex, is positively adolescent. He is a relentless seducer or would-be seducer, and at the end of each novel he seems to be no wiser or more mature than at the start.

Sex, in seemingly infinite variations, is Willingham's major concern in both his two other most successful novels, *Eternal Fire* and *Providence Island*, and in all the other novels as well. *Eternal Fire*, his best work, is a long and truly engrossing novel. A demonic protagonist, Harry Diadem, comes to the town of Glenville, Georgia (again, perhaps, Rome, Georgia). He is physically attractive, cunning, ruthless, relentless, cold-hearted, contemptuous, and deceitful. Harry hates women really and wishes to excite them, cause them to lose control, then humiliate them, utterly. He discovers in Glenville an innocent love affair between the virgin Laurie Mae and her virgin fiancé Randy. Randy's inheritance is being administered by Judge Ball, who has, of course, embezzled most of it. The unscrupulous judge lives with his wicked sister and their black maid, Melindy, who serves as a kind of conscience and chorus. If Randy marries, he received his inheritance and the judge is caught. In a plot that then becomes truly convoluted, Harry is set by the judge upon Laurie Mae, who is being silently worshipped and guarded by Hawley, a mentally retarded dwarf with gorilla-like strength. Hawley is surely a literary descendent of Boo Radley in *To Kill a Mockingbird* as Harry is a literary son of William Faulkner's Popeye. In this 637-page novel, most of the kinds of interaction between men and women are examined. Randy is timid and believes anyway that Laurie Mae, like all women, wouldn't like sex. Laurie Mae is innocent, but has a strong sex drive she would like to exercise with Randy. This makes her vulnerable to Harry's devious and tireless "blandishments."

As might be obvious, this novel is a kind of satire of the Southern Gothic novel as Willingham feels it was practiced by Erskine Caldwell, Faulkner, and others. The names are meant to be ludicrous. Harry Diadem's life centers on his "family jewels." Randy is really randy, but dense and inexperienced. Laurie Mae has the innocent name but is actually in a state of high readiness to begin her life as a sexually active woman.

What elevates this novel above mock-Gothic or sustained satire is, mainly, the character of Harry. Although he may be intended to be unbelievable and exaggerated, he is not. Harry is a masterful, if inadvert, creation. His evil is chilling, not humorous. The novel is amusing to the reader only at the level of highly conscious literary awareness; at the emotional level it is erotic, frightening, and exceedingly disturbing.

Providence Island is lighter fare. The protagonist James Kittering, 42 and vice president and program director of American International Television and Radio, Inc., is separated from his wife. They have been mutually unfaithful, and his philandering, especially, has destroyed their marriage. He is soon shipwrecked on Providence Island with two women: the sexually frustrated wife of a missionary and a virgin who is, to all appearances, a latent lesbian. Jim begins by trying to seduce Melody Carolucy Dubbs, but in time falls in love with both of them, "marries" both of them, and ends up with Florence Carr, who is not to become a lesbian after all.

This is a male fantasy novel, surely, but it is also erotic and good-natured. Willingham creates something of the same sense of frustration in the reader as he creates in Jim Kittering. Melody agrees to have sex with Jim on page 146, but they consummate their affair on page 287. Jim and Florence finally mate on page 369. This is a 559-page dream, and when they are at last rescued, the true name of their island turns out to be Isla Encantada. Enchanted indeed.

The attempted seduction of sexy women is also the major activity of *Geraldine Bradshaw* and *To Eat a Peach*. In each case, young men devote their full energies to the chase, one in Chicago, one in a boys' summer camp, Camp Walden, in the Tennessee mountains. In these, as in most cases in Willingham's work, the chase may be worth the trouble for the character, but certainly not for the reader.

To Eat a Peach and *Eternal Fire* are set in the American South and are to some degree in the tradition of the Southern novel, while maintaining an ironic distance from the very material being used. At Camp Walden, there are a visiting evangelist, the regular obsession with sport, and a cast of fairly stereotypical Southern characters. *Eternal Fire* is a send-up, a spoof, of the whole genre, while, at the same time, it takes its place among the others. Willingham has such a good ear for Southern speech that, in a sense, he can't help himself. The black and white characters, even the minor players such as the alcoholic policeman and the idiot dwarf, are quite vivid. Had Willingham been inclined to be a Southern novelist instead of the self-appointed scourge of the Southern novel, there might have been some first-class results. Perhaps his exaggerations are simply not grotesque enough to burlesque the subject.

Another related, if minor, kind of Southern concern of Willingham's is the business of the Southerner out of the South. In *Natural Child*, for instance, the "heroine" is a girl from North Carolina who has fallen among Manhattan pseudointellectuals, would-be writers, and Bohemians. Her Southernness, especially her accent, is a constant subject of ridicule among these self-styled cosmopolites, although she surely has as much intelligence as any of them and is the putative author of the novel.

In *The Building of Venus Four* some of the beautiful girls being mentally hijacked into space are Southerners, some black; the sexual stereotypes abound, although the racial ones do not. The Southerner out of the South has been a leitmotif in Southern letters at least since Thomas Wolfe and is found throughout Willingham's books.

Although Willingham is without many critics or readers at the present time, this was not always so. He was regarded not only as a racy novelist, mildly obscene or at least excessively realistic, but for a while also as a radically experimental fiction writer. Many pieces in his volume of short stories and essay fragments are surrealistic, even absurd. They are not considered to be very successful, but they are certainly unconventional, defying the notion of the well-crafted short story. Perhaps they appear too long after the fragments of *In Our Time* to be considered revolutionary.

Writing and writers are on Willingham's mind. The protagonists of *Reach to the Stars* and *Geraldine Bradshaw* are aspiring writers who talk with friends about writing and even exchange manuscripts with friends. Richard Davenport's sister is a New York magazine editor. Jimmy McClain, the protagonist of *To Eat a Peach*, is editor of the Camp Walden newspaper, *Walden Ways*. He has bigger career plans, however. *Natural Child* is told in a kind of pseudostory form. The protagonist, Sue, is in a crowd of writers manqué and so writes this book telling about how the young men in her crowd want to be writers but are "blocked." She, obviously, is not and the book is laced with mildly humorous, because ingenuous, remarks about writing. Sue tells us, yes, writing is hard; it took her a whole hour to write only nine pages of this manuscript. Of course, she admits, her main problem was remembering what everybody at the party last night had said. Here, obviously, Willingham is poking fun at the unimagined novel, the novel of experience remembered.

The "author" of *Rambling Rose*, on the other hand, is a professional novelist, presumably Willingham himself, or close to it, recalling his childhood experiences with Rose. If *Rambling Rose* is in fact not highly autobiographical, Willingham has managed to turn on himself, for surely most readers will think so, unless that is to be, finally, the joke on the reader.

A slightly different technique is used in *The Big Nickel*. Here the main narrative chapters, concerning a successful first-time novelist, are alternated with a wild, unlikely tale of a giant Negro serial killer rapist and a kind of idiot savant whore. It occurs to the reader only slowly that the violent, melodramatic tale is the fantasy of the writer protagonist, a fantasy in which he is indulging because he is unable to begin writing his second novel. Almost all of *The Building of Venus Four*, it develops, is taking place in the mind of a crazed, cuckolded husband, fantasizing about kidnapping a spaceship full of beauty queens with himself as the only potent male on board. In his fantasy, he will be able to satisfy them all. In novel after novel, the subject is, finally, writing itself, and while Willingham may not have pushed out the boundaries of narrative prose fiction in the way that writers like Faulkner have, he must be credited with trying to tell his stories in inventive ways, in novel after novel.

SURVEY OF CRITICISM

Despite his authorship of ten novels, a volume of shorter pieces, fiction and nonfiction and innumerable short stories and magazine articles, not to mention his seven movie credits, television credit, and a Broadway play, Calder Willingham is the subject of only one entry in the *PMLA Bibliography* from 1947 to the present, and that entry is titled, ironically, as it turns out, "Calder Willingham: The Forgotten Novelist" (Parr).

Although he has never been taken up by the academic and critical establishment, Willingham has been written about, even argued over, very extensively, in the form of reviews and articles in newspapers and magazines. His first novel was reviewed enthusiastically by Farrell, who called it "the work of an artist" and "a permanent contribution to American literature." Orville Prescott, on the other hand, called it "one of the most shocking, unpleasant, and offensive books in a long time," but then went on to praise it anyway. This is fairly typical of Willingham's critics over the years. Nearly every commentator has declared the book or books under consideration to be sordid or unpleasant, but then grudgingly admitted that there is a kind of power in these books, a power they do not understand, yet cannot in good conscience deny.

Only R.H.W. Dillard has had unqualified praise for Willingham. Dillard, writing in the entry he prepared for *Contemporary Novelists*, insists that Willingham has been completely misunderstood and is in fact a master ironist in novel after novel and his readers have simply not been up to the job. Without question a reassessment of Willingham's work will take place in the near future, and Dillard's essay will serve as the starting point.

BIBLIOGRAPHY

Works by Calder Willingham, Jr.

End as a Man. New York: Vanguard, 1947.
Geraldine Bradshaw. New York: Vanguard, 1950.
The Gates of Hell. New York: Vanguard, 1951.
Reach to the Stars. New York: Vanguard, 1951.
Natural Child. New York: Dial, 1952.
To Eat a Peach. New York: Dial, 1955.
Eternal Fire. New York: Vanguard, 1963.
Providence Island. New York: Vanguard, 1969.
Rambling Rose. New York: Delacorte, 1972.
The Big Nickel. New York: Dial, 1975.
The Building of Venus Four. New York: Woodhill, 1977.

Studies of Calder Willingham, Jr.

Algren, Nelson. Rev. of *Geraldine Bradshaw. Saturday Review of Literature* 23, No. 11 (March 18, 1950): 29–30.
Barkham, John. "Bellhop's Biography: Part Two" (Rev. of *Reach to the Stars*). *New York Times Book Review* (December 16, 1951): 16.
Dillard, R.H.W. "Calder Willingham," 885–87 in *Contemporary Novelists*, fourth ed., ed. D. L. Kirkpatrick, St. James Press, London and Chicago, 1986.
Farrell, James T. "Sadists in Uniform." *New York Times Book Review* (February 16, 1947): 3.
Feld, Rose. "New York's Quasi-Bohemia" (Rev. of *Natural Child*). *New York Herald Tribune Book Review* (November 30, 1952); 15.
Frakes, James R. "Don Juan in the Caribbean" (Rev. of *Providence Island*). *New York Times Book Review* (March 30, 1969): 40.
Frank, Jeffrey A. "Song of the Southern Gothic." *Washington Post Book World* (May 24, 1987): 10.
Millichap, Joseph. *American Screenwriters*, second series, vol. 44 (1986): 416–19.
Moore, Harry T. "Love in a Summer Camp" (Rev. of *To Eat a Peach*). *New York Times Book Review* (February 27, 1955): 30.
Parr, J. L. "Calder Willingham: The Forgotten Novelist." *Critique II* iii (1969): 57–65.
Stepanchev, Stephen. "In a Military Academy" (Rev. of *End as a Man*). *New York Herald Tribune Weekly Book Review* (February 16, 1947): 14.
Woodburn, John. "Military Man-Factory" (Rev. of *End as a Man*). *Saturday Review of Literature* 30, No. 14 (April 5, 1947): 18.

John Yount
(1935–   )

John Yount has fashioned in five novels a gallery of memorable characters from the hardscrabble South. Focusing mainly on characters from Appalachia, Yount's novels explore with insight, humor, and compassion the lives of mountain and rural folk. An Appalachian native living most of his adult life in the North, Yount draws his characters as an insider who unmasks stereotypes about the region's people and who reveals their struggles as both local and universal. Ivan Doig observed on the book jacket of *Thief of Dreams* (1991) that Yount is also "a writer who can peg a sentence into place as if there could be no other way of saying it." Though Yount has not been prolific, he has earned a reputation as a careful stylist and a creator of characters who linger in readers' memories after they have closed his books.

BIOGRAPHY

John Alonzo Yount was born on July 3, 1935, in Boone, North Carolina, the only child of John Luther and Vera Sherwood Yount. On both sides of his family, Yount's people had lived in Appalachia for several generations. His grandfather Yount, a Lutheran minister, had pastorates in Boone, Conover, Newton, and Deep Gap, North Carolina. The Sherwoods were Baptists and had lived in the region "quite a while." Yount's father was the only son in his family who did not follow his father's Lutheran faith.

Yount's father, who worked in construction and who offended his and his wife's family's religious beliefs with his drinking, moved his own family frequently to follow where the work was. John attended many schools and claims these frequent relocations taught him much about people and the world. Yount spent most of his high school years in Pittsburgh, Pennsylvania, but graduated from high school in Columbia, Tennessee. He spent much time as a child with his mother's parents in the North Carolina mountains. At his grandfather Sherwood's, he heard mountain people telling stories around a potbellied stove; he credits his sense of style to hearing the mountain rhythms of tales about stubborn mules and the cow that jumped over the fence.

After completing high school, he planned to attend Appalachian State University to take courses that would prepare him for school in veterinary medicine. Instead, he entered the U.S. Army in 1954 to serve 2 years in the medical corps. Mustered out of the Army in 1956, Yount decided to prepare himself for medical school. Admitted to both the University of North Carolina at Chapel Hill and Wake Forest University, he chose to study at Wake Forest because a friend had said that the girls at Salem Academy in Winston-Salem were all beautiful. "That tipped the scales," Yount said.

Yount spent the 1956–57 academic year at Wake Forest University where he met James Whitehead and Miller Williams, both later to become poets, and began talking about writing. Deciding that he was interested in writing (which "was and was not true"), he transferred in 1957 to Vanderbilt University, where he received his B.A. in 1960. At Vanderbilt Yount became involved in the civil rights movement and began writing seriously. When he applied for graduate study at Vanderbilt, one of his teachers agreed to write a letter of recommendation for schools only north of the Mason-Dixon line. Despite that caveat, Yount was admitted to Vanderbilt's graduate program and to the creative writing program at the University of Iowa. From 1960 to 1962, he studied in Iowa.

After earning his M.F.A. from Iowa in 1962, Yount taught at the University of New Hampshire in Durham as instructor in English (1962–64). He was assistant professor of English at Clemson University in 1964–65 before returning to the University of New Hampshire, where he taught from 1965 until 1989. He received a Rockefeller Grant for literature in 1967–68, a Guggenheim Fellowship in 1974, and a National Endowment for the Arts Grant for fiction in 1976. Yount was visiting professor at the University of Arkansas in spring 1973.

In 1989 Yount took a tenured professorship in the writing program at the University of Arkansas at Fayetteville. He bought a house there and taught during the 1989–90 academic year, but returned to teach at the University of New Hampshire in the following year. He now directs the graduate writing program at New Hampshire, but has "no title."

Yount married Susan Childs of Kingsport, Tennessee, on September 7, 1957; they have two daughters, Jennifer Sherwood and Sarah Childs, to whom he dedicated *Toots in Solitude* (1984). Yount and his wife were divorced in 1986.

Yount published his first novel, *Wolf at the Door*, in 1967. The story of Thomas Alonzo Rapidan, a 22-year-old college student "from the hills of West Virginia" (27), *Wolf at the Door* traces the protagonist's struggle to find meaning in a bleak, meaningless world. Though critics recognized a talented writer at work, most faulted Yount for not providing sufficient motives for Rapidan's existential dilemma. Yount has called his first novel his "least favorite" and an "angry young man's novel." *The Trapper's Last Shot* (1973) received enthusiastic notices and was a Book of the Month Club selection. That novel presents a complex study of character, the South, and America's grappling with racial issues by tracing the lives of brothers, Beau Jim and Dan Early. Set in the 1960s in Sheraw in Cocke County, Georgia, the novel recounts vividly the tragedy of the two brothers—Beau Jim, who returns from military service with hope for a new life, and Dan, an illiterate dirt farmer who struggles to make a living for his family and who murders seven black neighbors. This novel, while realistic in its rich detail, is also a symbolic exploration of racial issues in the South.

Hardcastle (1980), Yount's favorite book, tells the story of Bill Music's life during the Great Depression in the Kentucky mining town of Elkin. Framed by chapters about Music's life in 1979, the novel focuses on Music's attempts to survive during the Kentucky mine troubles of 1931. *Hardcastle* appeared to enthusiastic reviews. Yount calls his next novel, *Toots in Solitude*, his potboiler, a book in which "he broke every rule I ever lived by." But he sells short his biting commentary on America and his protagonist Macon "Toots" Hensley, a Thoreau-like character, who trashes middle-class respectability for a tree house along a river, who gets involved with a would-be country singer, and who outsmarts two Nashville drug dealers.

Thief of Dreams, perhaps Yount's most autobiographical novel, recounts powerfully the traumatic times of the Tally family—Edward and Madeline and their son James. Yount alternates chapters about the three characters during the time when Edward and Madeline separate and contemplate divorce. Thirteen-year-old James Tally comes of age during this novel set in the country near Cedar Hill, North Carolina, in 1948.

Though Yount says that he did not come from a bookish family, he did come from a family of storytellers. He credits those boyhood hours around the pot-bellied stove with his sense of language, timing, and style. He says that he writes for people who can't read, " which is a silly enterprise." But he wants those non-readers from the mountains to recognize the truth of his work should they chance upon one of his books.

He lists a half-dozen writers who have influenced him, though he believes "none of us is smart enough to isolate influences." Yount admires William Faulkner for his "absolute daring," singling out "Red Leaves" as a story demonstrating "great authority." Among his favorite books are James Agee's *Let Us Now Praise Famous Men* and *A Death in the Family*. He esteems the fiction of Joseph Conrad, F. Scott Fitzgerald, and Ernest Hemingway; in the novels of Fyodor Dostoyevski he finds "great bravery." He believes he is indebted to Robert Frost's poetry for its treatment of "country things, country places."

As a writing teacher, Yount confesses that he has "an old man's crabby response" to contemporary students' shabby grammar, syntax, and inattention to the little things that make prose work. He finds these students "more interested in architecture rather than brick masonry." When John Irving, one of Yount's former students, gave a visiting lecture about the importance of the semicolon, his students were disappointed because they did not want to hear "a schoolmaster.'' Calling himself an ''inveterate reviser,'' Yount claims his students' inattention to brick masonry has made his temper ''grow short over the years.''

Though Yount believes his Appalachian heritage has left ''deep tracks in the brain,'' he never thinks of himself as a Southern and Appalachian writer. He believes that location seems irrelevant if the writer knows that location well. He would be writing, he says, about the same things if he had been born an Eskimo, though he would have ''a lot more to say about snow.'' A man who writes slowly and attends to the details of his prose, Yount has in his computer two chapters of a novel that is not about the South.

MAJOR THEMES

John Yount says that his major theme is ''survival with dignity.'' But as reviewers have pointed out, that territory includes a host of other themes: The importance of place, the need for love, the necessity of forgiveness, the violence that lingers at the edge of consciousness and civility, the problems of race, the idiocy of American tinsel and silliness, and the question of how people should act. Each novel does not deal with all these themes, but they appear in most of his books.

Thomas Rapidan, the central character of *Wolf at the Door*, has ''lost the thread of his life, and he couldn't pretend that he hadn't'' (5–6). Drunk on the darkness in his soul, Rapidan sees in his ''ghostly reflection'' the face ''of a comic hero in the movies who has just had a bottle broken over his head and is sinking slowly to the floor, hearing birds sing''; he vows, ''I'll kill you, you son of a bitch'' (6). Alienated from himself and the rest of humanity and suffering depression about his father's death, Rapidan mistreats his wife, Maggie, looks for solace in drink, and contemplates ways to kill himself.

Believing that he does not ''know how to be a human being'' (65), Rapidan sends Maggie away and buys a stuffed wolf at an antique store. Yount uses the wolf as a symbol for Rapidan's violence, anger, and sickness. Rapidan recognizes himself in the wolf's cruel countenance: ''The wolf *had* scared him. The wolf's eyes had shot him through with fear, as if he'd been brought face to face with some horrible truth about himself he'd never known before. He felt himself change under the impact of it'' (115). Unable to find meaning in love, friendship, God, or community, Rapidan seeks solace with Dixie, a waitress at Mac's Café.

After a bloody fight that follows their lovemaking, Rapidan recognizes his ''insanity'' and ''was somehow relieved and content to accept it, as if now he could forgive himself'' (168–69). The two patch each other up, and, as Dixie carries Rapidan to a doctor, he tries to explain his madness to her:

''And there's a famous psychologist named Carl Jung who talks about the exact same myth [''the Greek myth that tells about how a long, long time ago a man and a woman were the same creature''],'' he told her as she slipped under the wheel. ''He says every man has a dream girl who is his exact female counterpart, you know, like she'd been sliced right off his back, and hell, even Adam and Eve is the same old story, and Jung calls his dream girl an 'anima.' He says a man looks for her all his life. And you know what else?'' Tom said, and his voice grew soft and dreamy. '' 'Anima' in Latin, means 'soul.' I swear it does, no kiddin,'' he said. (182–83)

Though Dixie replies that ''it sounds like a buncha shit to me,'' John Yount in *Wolf at the Door* retells that old story in a modern version.

At the novel's end, Rapidan has exorcised his wolfish desire to destroy; he washes himself clean with a shower and wonders: ''When she [Dixie] stepped out [of her shower], wet and barefooted, would she find him dead, mouth gaped, the volume of air in it stale and still and smelling already of the sweet rot of flesh? Hell no, he thought, she'd find him sitting on the couch, full of lies and evasions, his misery wrapped around him like a fist. He didn't want to die. He didn't want to kill himself'' (195–96). With that realization, Tom Rapidan volunteers to tell Dixie the story of his wolfish nature and his search for selfhood. He asks that ''every time I pause to take a breath, I want you to say, 'You're forgiven.' All right?'' Dixie agrees to forgive.

Yount opens *The Trapper's Last Shot* with a chilling scene of boys swimming in the south fork of the Harpath River; the oldest boy jumps into a pool of cottonmouth moccasins and dies, bitten ''close to two hundred times'' (4). Yount's novel deals with serpents in the Southern Garden of Eden—mainly in the forms of blighted dreams and racism. He centers his story on the lives of Beau Jim and Dan Early, and Dan's wife Charlene and daughter Sheila.

Beau Jim returns home from military service determined ''to amount to something, for he had grown tired of being nobody'' (13). He attends college for a while, but at the novel's end, he is working in construction in an inferno-like atmosphere at Redstone Arsenal in Huntsville, Alabama. Beau Jim carries with him his brother's guilt for murdering seven black neighbors. His brother Dan, who dreams of making a living from farming, confronts frustration at every turn—worn-out land, poverty, and limited understanding. An illiterate man who loves the land and his retarded daughter Sheila, Dan transfers his anger over his barn's burning to Negroes and kills seven of them in cold blood.

Yount conveys vividly his sense of the land and place; he has created in Dan and his wife Charlene powerful and sympathetic portraits of people trapped in poverty and by social and racial attitudes. A frustrated wife sick of poverty and country living, Charlene longs for town life and pretty things. She envies the prosperity of Cass Willard, owner of a service station and a ''fancy white and Pepto Bismol colored DeSoto'' (107). In a scene reminiscent of Pap Finn's speech about blacks in the *Adventures of Huckleberry Finn*, Yount gives Willard a racist redneck harangue about how Negroes have ''ruint the economy and moral fiber of the white people in the country'' (108–9).

The novel's holocaust comes when Charlene burns Dan's barn, hoping that this disaster will cause him to move to town. She blames the fire on her black neighbors. Dan, who is a good but limited man and whom Beau Jim characterizes as his "good brother" (230), becomes the instrument of his society and takes his shotgun on a murderous rampage.

With a clear eye for character and cultural milieu, Yount recounts in scene after scene the social, racial, and human implications of time and place. The scene in which Dan Early visits his daughter's school captures sympathetically the illiterate father's love for his child and his frustration with a situation he cannot understand. When Cass Willard visits the Early house, Yount brings vividly to life Charlene's frustration and anger with her life. As reviewers noted, Yount draws his characters, scenes, and conflicts razor sharp.

Love, loyalty, and friendship provide central themes for *Hardcastle*, and again Yount evokes character and place in prose that resuscitates the Kentucky mine wars of the 1930s. Bill Music goes to Chicago to learn to be an electrician, but discovers no work. He rides the rails during the Great Depression before landing in Kentucky coal mining country. Broke and tired, he befriends Regus Bone and his mother, Ella, who take him in. Regus helps Music secure a job as a mine guard, and the two become the best of friends.

Yount frames his novel about the mine wars with opening and closing chapters set in Switch County, Kentucky, in summer 1979. As Bill Music walks his 4-year-old granddaughter to town for a Popsicle, he remembers those hard times of 1931–32. His grandchild's questions "about a shooting he was mixed up in" (9) set Music to remembering. In twenty-five chapters, Yount tells a story that rivals John Steinbeck's *The Grapes of Wrath* for its power and authority.

Bill Music and Regus Bone side with the miners in the war to form a union at Kenton Hardcastle's mine. Besides Music and Bone, Yount creates a cast of other memorable characters: Ella Bone, Regus' mother; Merlee Taylor, a young widow whom Music marries; Grady and Cawood Burnside, whom Music kills during a shootout; Arturo Zigerelli, a Communist union organizer; Bydee Flann, a lay preacher; Gay Dickerson and Worth Enloe, men who recollect mining before the use of machinery; and many others.

With this cast of characters, Yount recreates events and places from days gone by. In one chapter, he recounts a coon hunt; everywhere he describes the landscape, the now-gone houses, and the complicated conflicts emerging from having to choose sides. Kenton Hardcastle evicts the striking miners, who seek shelter on Bone's property in a squatterville. The strikers fight back, but lose. And the Burnsides ambush and kill Regus Bone; Music kills the Burnsides returning fire. At Music's trial Ella Bone, Bydee Flann, and Charles Tucker give testimony that gets at the truth and exonerates Music. Remembering those hard times, Music thinks: "It is not the [life] he had in mind when he started out, or the one he would have chosen, but merely the one that claimed him. And, all things considered, it has been good enough" (285).

With an impeccable ear for his characters' speech, Yount spins his yarn, capturing the humor of mountain folk who weather bad times. And though his characters are defeated, they survive with dignity. Yount wrote "This book for my father / John Luther Yount / who lived part of it and inspired it all.'' In *Hardcastle*, John Yount created a classic novel for those who want to know about important characters in an important time and place.

Toots in Solitude, a rollickingly comic novel, recounts Macon ''Toots'' Hensley's dropping out of society to return to nature. The novel also satirizes America's preoccupation with success and the material. A Korean war veteran who has lost an eye in combat, Toots Hensley (so named for going on drinking toots) leaves his wife, respectability, and a quarter of a million dollars for peace, solitude, and a tree house along a river. But Sally Ann Shaw, who dreams of being a country singer named May Morning, breaks his solitude.

The mistress of a Nashville country music store owner and drug dealer named Billy Wayne Roland, Sally Ann flees after he beats her up, but not before she knocks Billy Wayne unconscious, shoves a thermometer up his penis, smashes his member with a lamp, and unknowingly steals a briefcase with $200,000 in it. Toots falls for Sally Ann, cuts his beard, and buys new clothes, and they escape from two thugs named Jerry and Esco, Billy Wayne's minions searching for the money. Toots and Sally Ann flee to St. Louis and Minneapolis to avoid discovery, but the romance dies. Toots returns to his river tree house filled with the pain of loss:

[But] a little at a time, sweet solitude began to visit him again. Oh but she was jealous, was solitude, and wouldn't come near if any thought of Sally was in his head, and would withdraw if one of her aspects caused him to think, however fleetingly, of her rival. But by the time the first chilling winter had passed and there were silver sprays of catkins in the March willows, she kept his company. After all, she demanded only that he be faithful and not one thing more. (185–86)

Yount creates in Jerry and Esco two characters similar to the thugs in Ernest Hemingway's ''The Killers.'' He also takes the measure of American materialism in the scenes where Toots shops for new clothes. He satirizes New Age attitudes and American university life when Toots and Sally Ann host a party in Minneapolis. The country music scene gets its knocks, too, as do gangster stories and romance novels.

The tone of *Thief of Dreams* shifts to the elegaic. Friendships, loves lost and refound, and James Tally's coming of age occupy Yount's talents in this novel. Yount presents all three characters—Edward and Madeline Tally and their son James—in depth by focusing chapters upon each as centers of consciousness. Edward and Madeline separate, plan to divorce, and take lovers in this story about a family's falling apart. Thirteen-year-old James Tally forms a friendship with Lester Buck, a mountain boy who hates school, loves nature, and is loyal to James.

When James runs away and gets caught in a mountain ice and snow storm, his parents reaffirm their love. All three characters have had their dreams, but none works out as the three had planned. James loses three toes, his parents reunite, and all three learn that they must lower or at least shift their conceit of attainable felicity in order to survive. In this tightly told tale, Yount spins a remembrance of times past in North Carolina's mountains.

Though Yount has lived most of his adult life outside the South, his themes and characters sit firmly in the traditions of Southern fiction. What the future holds, only those chapters in his computer will tell.

SURVEY OF CRITICISM

Commentary on John Yount's novels appears in short reviews. Except for reviews of *Wolf at the Door*, commentators have praised Yount for his craftsmanship, style, memorable characters, his sense of time and place, and his perceptions of "the human condition" (Carver 10).

Critics of *Wolf at the Door* faulted Yount for not providing sufficient motive for Thomas Rapidan's thinking of suicide (Hicks) and for "a rather forced use of symbolism" (Granat). Robert Granat did not believe Yount's characterization of Rapidan bore convincingly the novel's Freudian freight. But even some harsh reviews of this first novel recognized a writer who "handled [scenes] with mastery" (Mitchell) and who had "the novelist's gift of accurate and keen observation" (Granat). Granville Hicks concluded: "But Yount has managed to convey a sense of Tom's final desperation, and to do that is something."

Reviewers praised *The Trapper's Last Shot* for its insights into Southern rural life and for its characters and language. S. K. Oberbeck wrote that Yount "brilliantly describes the churning violence in a hardscrabble north Georgia township blistering at the first stirrings of true racial integration." Not since Erskine Caldwell, said Frederic A. Moritz, had Southern poor whites been presented with "both realism and insight" and honesty and sympathy. Characters in the novel impressed all the critics: "Yount's characters, especially Dan and his frantic wife, Charlene, are sharp as rifle sights, and his ear for rural speech has perfect pitch. Like Faulkner or Flannery O'Connor, Yount transforms a cruel clarity of vision into warm sympathy" (Oberbeck). Another reviewer said of Dan Early: "He is one of the most memorable fictional characters I've run across in some time and represents the most fully drawn and effective portrait of a Southern redneck that I've seen. He is both vile and sensitive, evil and touching; most important, Yount is able to make one feel sympathy for him, even near the culmination of the novel at the moment of his most crazed act—this is no mean task" (Watkins). Alan Cheuse singled out the language for particular praise: "Yount's language . . . and images . . . give us an earth which is an aspect of the particular vision of the characters who people it. The diction, rather than appearing as ostentatious art speech stooping to describe these 'pure products' of America, offers the impression of natural idiom raised to the level of art" (761).

Hardcastle won Yount even greater accolades. Elaine Kendall and Raymond Carver wrote the two most noteworthy reviews. Kendall compared *Hardcastle* to Steinbeck's *The Grapes of Wrath* as "a classic" about the Great Depression: "The hill counties of Kentucky were a terrible landscape in the early 30s, familiar enough to be recognizable but barren and desolate in their grinding poverty. Yount's people are drawn with such fine shadings that the reader not only sympathizes but identifies." She maintained that the novel "is a story of trust, of conscience and eventually love. It's direct and deceptively simple on the surface, with ramifications both wider and deeper than the plot can suggest." Of the novel's style, she said: "Yount's prose style is so economical and highly concentrated that it has the emotional impact of poetry. Few contemporary novels have conveyed a sense of place so thoroughly and effectively." Kendall concluded that "this is an extraordinary novel, filled with deep affection for a small corner of America, illuminated by total understanding of the qualities that make a time, a place and its people truly memorable."

Carver was equally laudatory. Commenting on the spate of books in which nothing matters, Carver wrote of Yount's novel: "It should be said at once that this is a book about something—and something that matters. It has to do with the nature and meaning of friendship, love, obligation, responsibility, and behavior. Big concerns. But this is a big book, and one that throws light on—I'll say it once and without embarrassment—the human condition." A book about how "should a man act," *Hardcastle* demonstrates "that John Yount has the intelligence and insight and very great literary skill to show us the lives of people who inhabit this fine book revealed in all their glory and imperfection." Carver ended his review with five crisp sentences to delight any writer: "Lionel Trilling has said that a great book reads us. Somewhere in my 20s, I read this and pondered its meaning. What exactly was the man saying? When I finished reading *Hardcastle*, this remarkably generous but unsparing novel, I was reminded of Trillings's words, and I thought, So this is what he was talking about. This is what he meant" (9–10).

Yount's other novels—*Toots in Solitude* and *Thief of Dreams*—have received sparing notices. But Fred Chappell, in a review of *Thief of Dreams*, placed *Hardcastle* in the company of Denise Giardina's *Storming Heaven* and James Still's *River of Earth* as "one of the very best novels about American coal mining." Chappell characterized *Thief of Dreams* as a "bright and pungent new novel of our Western [North Carolina] mountains" and a "tight and rather modest narrative." Chappell continued: "The book's merit—and it is considerable— lies in [Yount's] treatment" of his material.

Though John Yount has not been a prolific writer, future commentators on his work might well reexamine *The Trapper's Last Shot* and *Hardcastle* for their rendering of character and for Yount's remarkable insights about the hardscrabble South and its culture. The returns are not yet in on *Toots in Solitude* and *Thief of Dreams*. Yount's humor, everywhere in his last four novels, needs scrutiny. And someone needs to look carefully at the clear, precise style of all the books to see what makes it tick. That sounds like sufficient work for a while.

BIBLIOGRAPHY

Works by John Yount

Wolf at the Door. New York: Random House, 1967.
The Trapper's Last Shot. New York: Random House, 1973.
Hardcastle. New York: Marek, 1980.
Toots in Solitude. New York: St. Martin's/Marek, 1984.
Thief of Dreams. New York: Viking, 1991.

Studies of John Yount

Allen, Bruce. "Trouble in Coal Country during the Depression" (Rev. of *Hardcastle*). *Christian Science Monitor* (August 11, 1980): B4.
Carver, Raymond. "Fiction that Throws Light on Blackness" (Rev. of *Hardcastle*). *Chicago Tribune Book World* (May 18, 1980): 9–10.
Chappell, Fred. "Rediscovering John Yount" (Rev. of *Thief of Dreams*). (Raleigh, North Carolina) *News and Observer* (April 28, 1991): 5J.
Cheuse, Alan. "Real Coffee, Ideal Coffee" (Rev. of *The Trapper's Last Shot*). *Nation* (June 15, 1974): 760–61.
Gottis, Denise. "John (Alonzo) Yount," 573–74 in *Contemporary Authors*. New Revision Series, Vol. 5. Detroit: Gale Research, 1982.
Granat, Robert. "A Classic Hang-up" (Rev. of *Wolf at the Door*). *Washington Post Book World* (September 10, 1967): 12.
Hicks, Granville. "Nine Bright Beginnings" (Rev. of *Wolf at the Door*). *Saturday Review* (August 19, 1967): 24.
Kendall, Elaine. "Triumph of Spirit over Adversity" (Rev. of *Hardcastle*). *Los Angeles Times Book Review* (January 1, 1980): 19.
Lehman-Haupt, Christopher. "Books of the Times" (Rev. of *Hardcastle*). *New York Times* (May 23, 1980): C29.
Michaud, Charles. Rev. of *Hardcastle*. *Library Journal* 105 (1980): 1664.
Mitchell, Henry. "Tom and Dixie" (Rev. of *Wolf at the Door*). *New York Times Book Review* (July 2, 1967): 19.
Moritz, Frederic A. Rev. of *The Trapper's Last Shot*. *Christian Science Monitor* (September 26, 1973): 11.
Oberbeck, S. K. "Snakes under the Surface" (Rev. of *The Trapper's Last Shot*). *Newsweek* (October 8, 1973): 114.
Rev. of *Hardcastle*. *New Yorker* (June 23, 1980): 101.
Telephone interview with John Yount, December 1991.
Watkins, Mel. Rev. of *The Trapper's Last Shot*. *New York Times Book Review* (February 17, 1974): 31.
Young, B. A. "First Novels" (Rev. of *Wolf at the Door*). *Punch* (May 15, 1968): 725.

Supplementary Material on Nine Contemporary Novelists Included in *Fifty Southern Writers after 1900*

Appendix A updates the selected bibliographies of nine authors who are subjects of essays in *Fifty Southern Writers after 1900*, edited by Joseph M. Flora and Robert Bain and published by Greenwood Press in 1987. Bibliographies in the *Mississippi Quarterly* remain the primary bibliography for Southern literary studies; those wishing full and current bibliographies of Southern writers should continue to consult this indispensable work.

JOHN BARTH (1930–   )

Works by John Barth

The Tidewater Tales: A Novel. New York: Putnam, 1987.
The Last Voyage of Somebody the Sailor. Boston: Little, Brown, 1991.

Studies of John Barth

Birkerts, Sven. *American Energies: Essays on Fiction.* New York: Morrow, 1992. [Includes Barth].
Bradbury, Richard. "Postmodernism and Barth and the Present State of Fiction." *Critical Quarterly* 32 (Spring 1990): 60 ff.
Carmichael, Thomas. "Buffalo/Baltimore, Athens/Dallas: John Barth, Don DeLillo and the Cities of Postmodernism." *Canadian Review of American Studies* 22 (Fall 1991): 241 ff.
Delta (October 1985). Essays on Barth by several contributors.
Dyer, Joyce. "Barth's Use of the Bust of Laocoon in *The End of the Road.*" *Southern Literary Journal* 19 (Spring 1985): 54–60.
Fogel, Stanley. *Understanding John Barth.* Columbia: University of South Carolina Press, 1990.
Fokkema, Douwe and Haas Bertens, eds. *Approaching Modernism: Papers Presented at*

a Workshop in Postmodernism. Amsterdam/Philadelphia: John Benjamins, 1986. Essays by several contributors.

Gladsky, Thomas S. "Good Neighbors: History and Fiction in John Barth's *The Sot-Weed Factor*." *Clio* 14 (Spring 1985): 259–68.

Gorak, Jan. *God and the Artist: American Novelists in a Post-Realist Age*. Urbana: University of Illinois Press, 1987.

Hipkiss, Robert A. *Pynchon, Vonnegut, and Barth*. Port Washington, NY: Associated Faculty Press, 1984.

Kurk, Katherine C. "Narration as Salvation: Textual Ethics of Michel Tournier and John Barth." *Comparative Literature Studies* 24 (1988): 251 ff.

Lampkin, Loretta M. "An Interview with John Barth." *Contemporary Literature* 29 (Winter 1988): 485 ff.

Lemon, Lee. "John Barth and the Common Reader." *Review of Contemporary Fiction* 42 (Summer 1990): 42 ff.

Payne, Johnny. "Epistolary Fiction and Intellectual Life in a Shattered Culture: Ricardo Piglia and John Barth." *Tri-Quarterly* (Winter 1988): 171 ff.

Plimpton, George. "The Art of Fiction LXXXVI: John Barth." *Paris Review* 95 (1985): 144–59. Interview.

Roy, Louis. "A Note on Barth and Aquinas." *American Catholic Philosophical Quarterly* 66 (Winter 1992): 89 ff.

Safer, Elaine B. *The Contemporary American Comic Epic: The Novels of Barth, Pynchon, Gaddis, and Kesey*. Detroit: Wayne State University Press, 1988.

Schulz, Max F. *The Muses of John Barth: Tradition and Metafiction from 'Lost in the Funhouse' to 'The Tidewater Tales.'* Baltimore: Johns Hopkins University Press, 1990.

Sontag, Frederick. "Barth, Romans, and Feminist Theology: The Problem of God's Freedom."*Encounter* 52 (Fall 1991): 389 ff.

Tobin, Patricia Drechsel. *John Barth and the Anxiety of Continuance*. Philadelphia: University of Pennsylvania Press, 1992.

Vickery, John B. *Myths and Texts: Strategies of Incorporation and Displacement*. Baton Rouge: Louisiana State University Press, 1983.

Walkiewicz, Edward P. *John Barth*. Boston: Twayne, 1987.

Weisenburger, Steven. "Barth and Black Humor." *Review of Contemporary Fiction* 10 (Summer 1990): 50 ff.

Ziegler, Heide. *John Barth*. New York: Methuen, 1987.

DORIS BETTS (1932–   )

Works by Doris Betts

Halfway Home and a Long Way to Go: The Report of the 1986 Commission on the Future of the South. Research Triangle Park, NC: Southern Growth Policies Board, 1986.

Report of the Ad Hoc Committee on Athletics and the University. Chapel Hill, NC: The Committee, 1989.

Souls Raised from the Dead. New York: Putnam, 1993.

Studies of Doris Betts

Alderson, Laura. "An Interview with Doris Betts." *Poets & Writers* 20 (January 1992): 36 ff.
The *"Home Truths" of Doris Betts: With a Bibliography*. Proceedings of the Eighth Annual Southern Writers' Symposium, Methodist College, March 17–18, 1989. Ed. Sue Laslie Kimball. Fayetteville, NC: Methodist College Press, 1992.
Walsh, William. "An Interview with Doris Betts." *High Plains Literary Review* 4 (Winter 1989): 83 ff.

HARRY CREWS (1935–   )

Works by Harry Crews

All We Need of Hell. New York: Harper & Row, 1987.
The Knockout Artist. New York: Harper & Row, 1988.
Body. New York: Poseidon Press, 1990.

Studies of Harry Crews

Elrod, Rodney. "The Freedom to Act: An Interview with Harry Crews." *New Letters* 55 (Spring 1989): 51 ff.
Jeffrey, David K. "Murder and Mayhem in Crews's *A Feast of Snakes*." *Critics* 28 (Fall 1986): 45–54.
Nuwer, Hank. "The Writer Who Plays with Pain: Harry Crews." *South Carolina Review* 28 (Fall 1985): 63–73. Interview.
Papovich, J. Frank. "Place and Imagination in Harry Crews's *A Childhood: The biography of a place*." *Southern Literary Journal* 19 (Fall 1985): 26–35.
Randisi, Jennifer L. "The Scene of the Crime: The Automobile in the Fiction of Harry Crews." *Southern Studies* (Fall 1986): 231–19.
Shelton, Frank. "Harry Crews After a Childhood." *Southern Literary Journal* 25 (Spring 1992): 3 ff.

ERNEST J. GAINES (1933–   )

Works by Ernest J. Gaines

The Sky Is Gray [videocassette]. Monterey Home Video: International Video Entertainment, Distributor [1986], c. 1980.
Porch Talk with Ernest Gaines: Conversations on the Writer's Craft. Ed. Marcia G. Gaudet and Carl Wooten. Baton Rouge: Louisiana State University Press, 1990.

Studies of Ernest J. Gaines

Babb, Valerie M. *Ernest Gaines*. Boston: Twayne, 1991.
Doyle, Mary Ellen. "Ernest J. Gaines: An Annotated Bibliography, 1986–1988." *Black American Literature Forum* 24 (Spring 1990): 125 ff.

Meyer, William E. H., Jr. "Ernest J. Gaines and the Black Child's Sensory Dilemma."
    CLA Journal 34 (June 1991): 414 ff.
Rowell, Charles H. "The Quarters: Ernest Gaines and the Sense of Place." *Southern
    Review* 21 (Summer 1985): 733–50.
Simpson, Anne K. *A Gathering of Gaines: The Man and the Writer*. Lafayette, LA:
    Center for Louisiana Studies, University of Southwestern Louisiana, 1991.

ANDREW LYTLE (1902–   )

Works by Andrew Lytle

New Editions of the following books have appeared: *Bedford Forrest and His Critter
    Company* (1984), *The Long Night* (1988), and *At the Moon's End* (1990).
Reflections of a Ghost: An Agrarian View After Fifty Years. Dallas, TX; New London
    Press, 1980.
Stories, Alchemy and Others. Sewanee, TN: The University of the South, 1984.
The Lytle-Tate Letters: The Correspondence of Andrew Lytle and Allen Tate. Ed. Thomas
    Daniel Young and Elizabeth Sarcone. Jackson: University Press of Mississippi,
    1987.
Southerners and Europeans: Essays in a Time of Disorder. Baton Rouge: Louisiana State
    University Press, 1988.
From Eden to Babylon: The Social and Political Essays of Andrew Nelson Lytle. Wash-
    ington, D.C.: Regnery Gateway; Lanham, MD. Distributed to the trade by National
    Book Network, 1990.
Kristen: A Reading. Columbia, MO: University of Missouri Press, 1992.

Studies of Andrew Lytle

Lucas, Mark. *The Southern Vision of Andrew Lytle*. Baton Rouge: Louisiana State Uni-
    versity Press, 1986.

REYNOLDS PRICE (1933–   )

Works by Reynolds Price

The Chapel, Duke University. Durham, NC: Duke University Stores, 1986.
The Laws of Ice. New York: Atheneum, 1986.
A Common Room: Essays: 1954–1987. New York: Atheneum, 1987.
Good Hearts. New York: Atheneum, 1988.
Real Copies: Will Price, Chrichton Davis, Phyllis Peacock and More. Rocky Mount,
    NC: North Carolina Wesleyan College Press, 1988.
Back Before Day. Rocky Mount, NC: North Carolina Wesleyan College Press, 1989.
Clear Pictures: First Loves, First Guides. New York: Atheneum, 1989.
Spring Takes the Homeplace. Rocky Mount, NC: North Carolina Wesleyan College Press,
    1989.
Home Made [short stories]. Rocky Mount, NC: North Carolina Wesleyan College Press,
    1990.

Lost Homes: A Cleared Ring in the Blue Ridge Mountains: A Boy Age Twelve, Now a Middle-aged Man. Chapel Hills, NC: Mad Puppy Press, 1990.
Music: A Trilogy. New York: Theatre Communications Group, 1990.
The Tongues of Angels. New York: Atheneum, 1990.
The Use of Fire. New York: Atheneum, 1990.
The Foreseeable Future. New York: Atheneum, 1991.
Blue Calhoun. New York: Atheneum, 1992.

Studies of Reynolds Price

Crowder, Ashby Bland. ''Reynolds Price on Writing.'' *Southern Review* 22 (Spring 1986): 329–41. Interview.
———. ''Waiting at Duchar: An Interview with Reynolds Price.'' *Southern Quarterly* 26 (Winter 1988): 12 ff.
Hartin, Edith T. ''Reading as a Woman: Reynolds Price and Creative Androgyny in '*Kate Vaiden.*' '' *Southern Quarterly* 29 (Spring 1991): 37 ff.
Humphries, Jefferson. ''Taking Things Seriously: Reynolds Price as Teacher and Writer.'' *Southwest Review* 74 (Winter 1989): 10 ff.
———, ed. *Conversations with Reynolds Price.* Jackson: University Press of Mississippi, 1991.
Reynolds Price: From 'A Long and Happy Life' to 'Good Hearts': With a Bibliography. Proceedings of the Seventh Annual Southern Writers' Symposium, Methodist College, April 15–16, 1988. Eds. Sue Laslie Kimball and Lynn Veach Sadler. Fayetteville, NC: Methodist College Press, 1989.
''Reynolds Price: The Art of Fiction LXXVII.'' Interview with Frederick Busch. *Paris Review* 121 (Winter 1991): 150–79.
''Reynolds Price Interview with Lynn Ballard.'' Columbia, MO: American Audio Library, 1982.
Sadler, Lynn Veach. ''Reynolds Price and Religion: The 'Almost Blindingly Lucid' Palpable World.'' *Southern Quarterly* 26 (Winter 1988): 1 ff.

ELIZABETH SPENCER (1921–   )

Works by Elizabeth Spencer

The Stories of Elizabeth Spencer. New York: Penguin, 1983.
Jack of Diamonds: and Other Stories. New York: Viking, 1988.
The Legacy. Chapel Hill, NC: Mud Puppy Press, 1988.
The Night Travellers. New York: Viking, 1991.
On the Gulf. Jackson: University Press of Mississippi, 1991.

Studies of Elizabeth Spencer

Prenshaw, Peggy Whitman, ed. *Conversations with Elizabeth Spencer.* Jackson: University Press of Mississippi, 1991.

Roberts, Terry. *Ties That Bind: The Fiction of Elizabeth Spencer*. Baton Rouge: Louisiana State University Press, 1993.

WILLIAM STYRON (1925–   )

Works by William Styron

Darkness Visible: A Memoir of Madness. New York: Random House, 1990.

Studies of William Styron

Arms, Valarie Meliotes. "A French View of William Styron." *Southern Quarterly* 29 (Fall 1990): 47 ff.

Cash, Jean W. "Styron's Use of the Bible in *The Confessions of Nat Turner*." *Resources for American Literary Study* 12 (Autumn 1982): 134–42.

Coale, Samuel. "Styron's Disguises: A Provisional Rebel in Christian Masquerade." *Critic* 26 (Winter 1985): 57–66.

———. *William Styron Revisited*. Boston: Twayne, 1991.

Crane, John Kenny. "Laughing Backward: Comedy and Morality in Styron's Fiction." *College Literature* 14 (Winter 1987): 1–16.

Delta 23 (October 1986). Essays by several contributors.

Krome, Sabine. *Das Vaterbild in ausgewahlten Romanen William Styrons*. Frankfurt am Main: P. Lang, 1989.

Laxmana, Murthy S. *Violence and Compassion in the Novels of William Styron*. New Delhi: Prestige Books, 1988.

Papers on Language and Literature 23 (Fall 1987). Essays by several contributors.

Richardson, Thomas J. "Art and the Angry Times: Apocalypse and Redemption in William Styron's *The Confessions of Nat Turner*." *Mississippi Folklore Review* 19 (Fall 1985): 147–56.

Ruderman, Judith. *William Styron*. New York: Ungar, 1987.

Schultz, Lucille M. "*Lie Down in Darkness*: A Story of Two Processions." *Southern Literary Journal* 18 (Spring 1986): 62–75.

Sellery, J'nan Morse. " 'Chronicler of the Human Spirit': William Styron." *Psychological Perspectives* 24 (Spring 1991): 74 ff.

Sirlin, Rhoda. *William Styron's 'Sophie's Choice': Crime and Self-punishment*. Ann Arbor: UMI Press, 1990.

Strandberg, Victor and Balkrishna Buwa. "An Interview with William Styron." *Sewanee Review* 99 (Summer 1991): 463 ff.

West, James L. W. III, ed. *Conversations with William Styron*. Jackson: University Press of Mississippi, 1985.

PETER TAYLOR (1917–   )

Works by Peter Taylor

A Stand in the Mountains. New York: Frederic C. Beil, 1985. [drama]

Studies of Peter Taylor

Griffith, Albert J. *Peter Taylor*. Rev. Ed. Boston: Twayne, 1990.

McAlexander, Hubert H., ed. *Conversations with Peter Taylor*. Jackson: University Press of Mississippi, 1987.

Powell, Dannye Romine. "Peter and Eleanor Ross Taylor." *Mississippi Review* 20 (1991): 41 ff.

Robinson, Clayton. "Peter Taylor." *The Literature of Tennessee*, ed. Ray Willbanks. Macon, GA: Mercer University Press, 1984. Pp. 149–61.

Robinson, David. "Summons from the Past." *Southern Review* 23 (Summer 1987): 754–59.

Robison, James Curry. *Peter Taylor: A Study of the Short Fiction*. Boston: Twayne, 1988.

Sullivan, Walter. "The Last Agrarian: Peter Taylor Early and Late." *Sewanee Review* 95 (Spring 1987): 308–17.

Wright, Stuart. *Peter Taylor: A Descriptive Bibliography, 1933–1987*. University Press of Virginia, 1988.

APPENDIX B

Contents of *Contemporary Poets, Dramatists, Essayists, and Novelists of the South: A Bio-Bibliographical Sourcebook*

Preface

Introduction

Maya Angelou (1928–) *Lucinda H. MacKethan*

James Applewhite (1935–) *George S. Lensing*

Daphne Athas (1923–) *Harriette Cuttino Buchanan*

Gerald William Barrax (1933–) *Lucy K. Hayden*

Wendell Berry (1934–) *Edward B. Smith*

Roy (Alton) Blount, Jr. (1941–) *Merritt W. Moseley, Jr.*

David Bottoms (1949–) *Peter Stitt*

Fred Chappell (1936–) *David Paul Ragan*

Alice Childress (1920–) *La Vinia Delois Jennings*

James Duff (1955–) *Susan Gilbert*

Wilma Dykeman (1920–) *Patricia M. Gantt and Chip Jones*

Charles Edward Eaton (1916–) *Glenn Blalock*

Lonne Elder III (1931–) *John Sekora*

Peter Steinam Feibleman (1930–) *Randal Woodland*

Julia Fields (1938–) *Sara Andrews Johnston*

George Garrett (1929–) *R.H.W. Dillard*

Nikki Giovanni (1943–) *Patsy B. Perry*

Elizabeth Hardwick (1916–) *Susan V. Donaldson*

William Harmon (1938–) *Marlene Youmans*

Beth Henley (1952–) *Hilary Holladay*

Preston Jones (1936–1979) *Kimball King*

Index

*Compiled by Judith K. Logan; page numbers in **bold** refer to main entries.*

Contributors

CHRISTINA ALBERS teaches at Tulane University. She has presented papers on Edith Wharton and Willa Cather. Currently she is working on *A Reader's Guide to the Short Stories of Henry James* and a book on the guardian figure in the works of Henry James and other nineteenth-century American writers.

JOHN M. ALLISON, JR., is assistant professor and director of the program in performance studies at the University of North Texas. His research interests include narrative theory and contemporary Southern fiction.

ROBERT BAIN teaches American literature and composition at the University of North Carolina at Chapel Hill. With Joseph M. Flora, he coedited *Fifty Southern Writers before 1900* (1987) and *Fifty Southern Writers after 1900* (1987). With Beverly Taylor, he coedited *The Cast of Consciousness: Concepts of the Mind in British and American Romanticism* (1987). With Flora and Louis D. Rubin, Jr., he edited *Southern Writers: A Biographical Dictionary* (1979). He has written about Herman Melville, William Byrd, H. L. Davis, and others. He won a Tanner Award for Excellence in Undergraduate Teaching (1976) and from 1987 to 1990 held a Bowman and Gordon Gray professorship of undergraduate teaching.

LESLIE BANNER is special assistant for university affairs in the office of the president at Duke University. She is the author of *A Passionate Preference: The Story of the North Carolina School of the Arts* (1987), a case history of the political and grass-roots strategies that won controversial support for the performing arts in a conservative state legislature.

LYNN Z. BLOOM, professor of English and Aetna chair of writing at the University of Connecticut, for 10 years lived and taught in Virginia, at the College of William and Mary and at Virginia Commonwealth University.

LAURA J. BLOXHAM is professor of English at Whitworth College in Spokane, Washington. She has participated in NEH summer seminars at the University of Washington and at the University of California at Berkeley; participated in a Mellon summer seminar at Stanford University; and has done postdoctoral work at the Graduate Theological Union in Berkeley. She was cited in 1988 as the State of Washington professor of the year by the Council for the Advancement and Support of Higher Education. During 1991–92 she was a visiting lecturer at the University of Georgia.

ELIZABETH PELL BROADWELL is associate professor at Christian Brothers University in Memphis, Tennessee. She has published in the *Mississippi Quarterly*, *Georgia Review*, and *Southern Review*. She is currently completing a book on Lee Smith.

THOMAS M. CARLSON is professor of English and chairman of the department of American studies at the University of the South in Sewanee, Tennessee. His articles on Southern writers have appeared in the *Sewanee Review*, *Southern Review*, and *Encyclopedia of Southern Culture*.

STEPHEN COOPER teaches English at Troy State University in Alabama. He is review editor of the *Alabama Literary Review* and author of *The Politics of Ernest Hemingway* (1987), as well as articles and reviews on modern fiction.

JOSEPH T. COX is associate professor of English at the U.S. Military Academy at West Point, New York, where he directs the freshman composition program and teaches literature. A career army officer who has commanded from platoon to battalion level, Colonel Cox edited the poetry of Robert W. Weir (1976) and is working on an anthology of American war prose.

MARY KEMP DAVIS taught at the University of Houston–Downtown and returned to the University of North Carolina at Chapel Hill as a postdoctoral fellow, then joined the faculty there, where she teaches American and African-American literature. She has published numerous articles on black authors and is completing a study of fictional treatments of the Nat Turner revolt.

MARY ANNE FERGUSON taught briefly at the University of North Carolina at Chapel Hill. After World War II, she lived in Ohio and Massachusetts; she is now professor emerita at the University of Massachusetts, Boston, and lives in Pittsburgh, Pennsylvania. She is editor of *Images of Women in Literature*, now in its fifth edition.

JOSEPH M. FLORA is professor of English at the University of North Carolina at Chapel Hill. He is author of *Vardis Fisher* (1965), *William Ernest Henley* (1970), *Frederick Manfred* (1974), *Hemingway's Nick Adams* (1982), and *Ernest Hemingway: The Art of the Short Fiction* (1989). He edited *The English Short Story 1880–1945* (1985). With Robert Bain, he edited *Fifty Southern Writers before 1900* (1987) and *Fifty Southern Writers after 1900* (1987). With Bain and Louis D. Rubin, Jr., he edited *Southern Writers: A Biographical Dictionary* (1979).

OWEN W. GILMAN, JR., is associate professor of English at Saint Joseph's University in Philadelphia. With Lorrie Smith, he edited *America Rediscovered: Critical Essays on Literature and Film of the Vietnam War* (1990). His most recent publications are "Vietnam, Chaos, and the Dark Art of Improvisation" in *Inventing Vietnam* (1991), edited by Michael Anderegg, and *Vietnam and the Southern Imagination* (1992).

NANCY D. HARGROVE is William L. Giles distinguished professor of English at Mississippi State University, where she teaches twentieth-century American literature. She has held Fulbright lectureships in France (1976–77) and Belgium (1984–85) and has won numerous teaching awards. She has published a book on T. S. Eliot, as well as essays on other modern writers such as William Butler Yeats, Eudora Welty, Sylvia Plath, and Toni Cade Bambara; currently she is completing a book on Plath's poetry.

R. STERLING HENNIS, JR., professor of English Education at the University of North Carolina at Chapel Hill, directs the program for the teaching of English. His research centers on the use of visual language in the classroom.

BARBARA A. HERMAN is professor of English and chair of the department of English at Lenoir-Rhyne College in Hickory, North Carolina. Her area of special interest is the American novel, especially the novels of Edith Wharton.

DOROTHY COMBS HILL has published widely on Southern women writers—Jane Anne Phillips, Lee Smith, and others. Her *Lee Smith*, a Twayne United States Authors Series volume, appeared in 1992.

BERT HITCHCOCK is professor of English and former department head at Auburn University. He is the author of *Richard Malcolm Johnston* (1978) and coeditor, with Eugene Current-Garcia, of the fifth edition of *American Short Stories* (1990). His present work includes coeditorship of a reference book on the literature of Alabama.

KATHERINE C. HODGIN is a free-lance writer and editor.

JOHN L. IDOL, JR., teaches Southern and American literature at Clemson University and has written numerous articles and essays on Southern literature. In addition to his work on Charles Portis, he has written a book on Thomas Wolfe. He also edits the *Hawthorne Review* and has published essays on that author.

BEVERLY JARRETT is director and editor-in-chief of the University of Missouri Press in Columbia, Missouri. Prior to assuming that post in March 1989, she was associate director and executive editor of Louisiana State University Press, where she worked in various editorial capacities for some 17 years. She has edited for several other university presses, and she has taught in the English departments of such schools as North Carolina Central University in Durham, Millsaps College in Jackson, Mississippi, and the University of New Orleans.

DAVID K. JEFFREY is professor and head of the English department at James Madison University in Harrisonburg, Virginia. He has edited a book on the works of Harry Crews, written two books on police procedurals and detective fiction, and written articles about the works of Tobias Smollett, Alexander Pope, Edgar Poe, Herman Melville, and Virginia Woolf, among others. He has taught at Auburn University (where he coedited the *Southern Humanities Review*) and was head of the department at Northeast Louisiana University for several years.

NANCY CAROL JOYNER is professor of English at Western Carolina University in Cullowhee. She has published *E. A. Robinson: A Reference Guide* and several essays on twentieth-century literature, including an article on postmodern Appalachian writers in *Appalachian Heritage* (Fall 1988). Currently she is preparing a study of Appalachian women writers.

BARBARA LADD is assistant professor of English at Emory University, where she is working on a book on race in the work of George W. Cable. She has published on Cable, William Faulkner, and Eudora Welty.

JUDITH K. LOGAN (B.A. Whitworth College and M.A. Eastern Washington University) is a doctoral student at the University of North Carolina at Chapel Hill.

LUCINDA H. MACKETHAN is a professor of English at North Carolina State University in Raleigh, where she directed the freshman composition program and currently teaches Southern and American literature. She is author of *The Dream of Arcady: Place and Time in Southern Literature* (1980) and numerous essays on Southern writing, and is the editor of John Pendelton Kennedy's *Swallow Barn* (1986).

CAROL S. MANNING is associate professor of English at Mary Washington College. She has published *With Ears Opening Like Morning Glories: Eudora*

Welty and the Love of Storytelling (1985) and has edited *The Female Tradition in Southern Literature: Essays on Southern Women Writers* (1992).

JULIAN MASON is professor of English at the University of North Carolina at Charlotte, where he was chair of the English department from 1977 to 1984. His publications include over 50 book or journal articles, including entries for the *Dictionary of Literary Biography*; *American Writers before 1800*; *Southern Writers: A Biographical Dictionary*; *A Bibliographical Guide to the Study of Southern Literature*; and *Fifty Southern Writers after 1900*. He is the editor of *The Poems of Phillis Wheatley*.

JOSEPH MILLICHAP is professor of English and head of the English department at Western Kentucky University, as well as director of its Center for the Study of Robert Penn Warren. His publications include three books, a monograph, and over 50 articles on American literature and film, particularly the fiction of the Southern Renascence.

JERRY LEATH MILLS is professor of English at the University of North Carolina at Chapel Hill and editor of *Studies in Philology*. With O. B. Hardison, Jr., he edited an introduction to literature. He regularly reviews contemporary Southern fiction for the *Independent* and the Raleigh *News and Observer*.

CHARMAINE ALLMON MOSBY teaches Southern and American literature at Western Kentucky University in Bowling Green. She has published articles on Southern writing.

DONALD R. NOBLE teaches Southern and American literature at the University of Alabama. With Joab L. Thomas he edited *The Rising South* (1976); he has also edited George Tucker's *A Century Hence* (1977) and *Hemingway: A Revaluation* (1983), and has published essays in the *Southern Literary Journal*, *Mississippi Quarterly*, *Southern Quarterly*, *Southern Humanities Review*, and *Humanities in the South*.

JEANNE R. NOSTRANDT, professor of English at James Madison University in Harrisonburg, Virginia, has been head, department of foreign languages and literatures, and director of the honors program. She has written on Eudora Welty, Mary Johnston, Max Steele, and William Hoffman; she is currently working on a biography of Mary Johnston.

JOYCE M. PAIR is professor of English at DeKalb College. Founder and editor of the *James Dickey Newsletter*, she also has research interests in the works of F. Scott Fitzgerald, Sylvia Wilkinson, and Toni Morrison.

BARBARA PATRICK teaches American literature at Glassboro State University in New Jersey. She is at work on a book about the ghostly stories of American women writers after the Civil War.

THOMAS J. RICHARDSON is professor of English and coordinator of senior honors in the Honors College at the University of Southern Mississippi. In addition to contributing to *The Grandissimes: Centennial Essays*, he has written a number of essays on Southern literature and culture.

TERRY ROBERTS is assistant director of the principals' executive program of the Institute of Government at the University of North Carolina at Chapel Hill. He has published articles on Herman Melville, Thomas Wolfe, and Elizabeth Spencer, and his book about her was published in 1993.

ANNE E. ROWE is professor of English at Florida State University, where she teaches Southern and American literature. She is author of *The Enchanted Country: Northern Writers in the South, 1865–1910* and *The Idea of Florida in the American Literary Imagination*.

R. REED SANDERLIN, professor of English at the University of Tennessee at Chattanooga, has served as executive director of the Southern Humanities Conference. He coedited *Politics, Society, and the Humanities* and has published a volume of poems.

FRANK W. SHELTON is academic dean and associate professor of English at the University of South Carolina–Salkehatchie University Campus. He has published numerous articles on modern Southern fiction. In addition to entries on Harry Crews and Ernest Gaines in *Fifty Southern Writers after 1900*, he has written about Ellen Glasgow, Cormac McCarthy, Reynolds Price, Anne Tyler, Alice Walker, and Thomas Wolfe.

MERRILL MAGUIRE SKAGGS is presently dean of the graduate school at Drew University. She has written extensively on women writers, Southern writers, and Willa Cather. Her books include *The Folk of Southern Fiction* (1972) and *After the World Broke in Two: The Later Novels of Willa Cather* (1990).

SUSAN SNELL was a student of Helen Norris at Huntingdon College. Now associate professor of English at Mississippi State University, she is secretary-treasurer of the Society for the Study of Southern Literature and author of a biography of Phil Stone, William Faulkner's friend, mentor, and character study.

JOHN N. SOMERVILLE, JR., is assistant professor of English at Hillsdale College in Hillsdale, Michigan.

LINDA WELDEN is professor of theatre at Appalachian State University, where she teaches and directs the performance of literature. Her research interest is in the performance of texts, particularly of Southern writers. She is currently at work on a dramatic adaptation of stories by Ferrol Sams.

MARY ANN WIMSATT is McClintock professor of Southern letters at the University of South Carolina. She is author of *The Major Fiction of William Gilmore Simms* (1989), associate editor of *The History of Southern Literature* (1985), and author of many articles on Southern literature. She is past president of the Society for the Study of Southern Literature and has served on the executive committees of the Southern Literature Discussion Group (MLA), SAMLA, and SCMLA.

LAMAR YORK, associate professor of English at DeKalb College, is editor of the *Chattahoochee Review*. He has published critical essays on contemporary Southern fiction.

ANNE R. ZAHLAN is professor of English at Eastern Illinois University in Charleston. In addition to the fiction of Anne Tyler, she is interested in twentieth-century British fiction and the postcolonial novel in English. She has published essays on Lawrence Durrell, Anthony Burgess, V. S. Naipaul, and Wallace Stegner.